D1295022

Dictionary of Literary Biography

1 *The American Renaissance in New England,* edited by Joel Myerson (1978)

2 *American Novelists Since World War II,* edited by Jeffrey Helterman and Richard Layman (1978)

3 *Antebellum Writers in New York and the South,* edited by Joel Myerson (1979)

4 *American Writers in Paris, 1920-1939,* edited by Karen Lane Rood (1980)

5 *American Poets Since World War II,* 2 parts, edited by Donald J. Greiner (1980)

6 *American Novelists Since World War II, Second Series,* edited by James E. Kibler Jr. (1980)

7 *Twentieth-Century American Dramatists,* 2 parts, edited by John MacNicholas (1981)

8 *Twentieth-Century American Science-Fiction Writers,* 2 parts, edited by David Cowart and Thomas L. Wymer (1981)

9 *American Novelists, 1910-1945,* 3 parts, edited by James J. Martine (1981)

10 *Modern British Dramatists, 1900-1945,* 2 parts, edited by Stanley Weintraub (1982)

11 *American Humorists, 1800-1950,* 2 parts, edited by Stanley Trachtenberg (1982)

12 *American Realists and Naturalists,* edited by Donald Pizer and Earl N. Harbert (1982)

13 *British Dramatists Since World War II,* 2 parts, edited by Stanley Weintraub (1982)

14 *British Novelists Since 1960,* 2 parts, edited by Jay L. Halio (1983)

15 *British Novelists, 1930-1959,* 2 parts, edited by Bernard Oldsey (1983)

16 *The Beats: Literary Bohemians in Postwar America,* 2 parts, edited by Ann Charters (1983)

17 *Twentieth-Century American Historians,* edited by Clyde N. Wilson (1983)

18 *Victorian Novelists After 1885,* edited by Ira B. Nadel and William E. Fredeman (1983)

19 *British Poets, 1880-1914,* edited by Donald E. Stanford (1983)

20 *British Poets, 1914-1945,* edited by Donald E. Stanford (1983)

21 *Victorian Novelists Before 1885,* edited by Ira B. Nadel and William E. Fredeman (1983)

22 *American Writers for Children, 1900-1960,* edited by John Cech (1983)

23 *American Newspaper Journalists, 1873-1900,* edited by Perry J. Ashley (1983)

24 *American Colonial Writers, 1606-1734,* edited by Emory Elliott (1984)

25 *American Newspaper Journalists, 1901-1925,* edited by Perry J. Ashley (1984)

26 *American Screenwriters,* edited by Robert E. Morsberger, Stephen O. Lesser, and Randall Clark (1984)

27 *Poets of Great Britain and Ireland, 1945-1960,* edited by Vincent B. Sherry Jr. (1984)

28 *Twentieth-Century American-Jewish Fiction Writers,* edited by Daniel Walden (1984)

29 *American Newspaper Journalists, 1926-1950,* edited by Perry J. Ashley (1984)

30 *American Historians, 1607-1865,* edited by Clyde N. Wilson (1984)

31 *American Colonial Writers, 1735-1781,* edited by Emory Elliott (1984)

32 *Victorian Poets Before 1850,* edited by William E. Fredeman and Ira B. Nadel (1984)

33 *Afro-American Fiction Writers After 1955,* edited by Thadious M. Davis and Trudier Harris (1984)

34 *British Novelists, 1890-1929: Traditionalists,* edited by Thomas F. Staley (1985)

35 *Victorian Poets After 1850,* edited by William E. Fredeman and Ira B. Nadel (1985)

36 *British Novelists, 1890-1929: Modernists,* edited by Thomas F. Staley (1985)

37 *American Writers of the Early Republic,* edited by Emory Elliott (1985)

38 *Afro-American Writers After 1955: Dramatists and Prose Writers,* edited by Thadious M. Davis and Trudier Harris (1985)

39 *British Novelists, 1660-1800,* 2 parts, edited by Martin C. Battestin (1985)

40 *Poets of Great Britain and Ireland Since 1960,* 2 parts, edited by Vincent B. Sherry Jr. (1985)

41 *Afro-American Poets Since 1955,* edited by Trudier Harris and Thadious M. Davis (1985)

42 *American Writers for Children Before 1900,* edited by Glenn E. Estes (1985)

43 *American Newspaper Journalists, 1690-1872,* edited by Perry J. Ashley (1986)

44 *American Screenwriters, Second Series,* edited by Randall Clark, Robert E. Morsberger, and Stephen O. Lesser (1986)

45 *American Poets, 1880-1945, First Series,* edited by Peter Quartermain (1986)

46 *American Literary Publishing Houses, 1900-1980: Trade and Paperback,* edited by Peter Dzwonkoski (1986)

47 *American Historians, 1866-1912,* edited by Clyde N. Wilson (1986)

48 *American Poets, 1880-1945, Second Series,* edited by Peter Quartermain (1986)

49 *American Literary Publishing Houses, 1638-1899,* 2 parts, edited by Peter Dzwonkoski (1986)

50 *Afro-American Writers Before the Harlem Renaissance,* edited by Trudier Harris (1986)

51 *Afro-American Writers from the Harlem Renaissance to 1940,* edited by Trudier Harris (1987)

52 *American Writers for Children Since 1960: Fiction,* edited by Glenn E. Estes (1986)

53 *Canadian Writers Since 1960, First Series,* edited by W. H. New (1986)

54 *American Poets, 1880-1945, Third Series,* 2 parts, edited by Peter Quartermain (1987)

55 *Victorian Prose Writers Before 1867,* edited by William B. Thesing (1987)

56 *German Fiction Writers, 1914-1945,* edited by James Hardin (1987)

57 *Victorian Prose Writers After 1867,* edited by William B. Thesing (1987)

58 *Jacobean and Caroline Dramatists,* edited by Fredson Bowers (1987)

59 *American Literary Critics and Scholars, 1800-1850,* edited by John W. Rathbun and Monica M. Grecu (1987)

60 *Canadian Writers Since 1960, Second Series,* edited by W. H. New (1987)

61 *American Writers for Children Since 1960: Poets, Illustrators, and Nonfiction Authors,* edited by Glenn E. Estes (1987)

62 *Elizabethan Dramatists,* edited by Fredson Bowers (1987)

63 *Modern American Critics, 1920-1955,* edited by Gregory S. Jay (1988)

64 *American Literary Critics and Scholars, 1850-1880,* edited by John W.

Rathbun and Monica M. Grecu (1988)

65 *French Novelists, 1900-1930,* edited by Catharine Savage Brosman (1988)

66 *German Fiction Writers, 1885-1913,* 2 parts, edited by James Hardin (1988)

67 *Modern American Critics Since 1955,* edited by Gregory S. Jay (1988)

68 *Canadian Writers, 1920-1959, First Series,* edited by W. H. New (1988)

69 *Contemporary German Fiction Writers, First Series,* edited by Wolfgang D. Elfe and James Hardin (1988)

70 *British Mystery Writers, 1860-1919,* edited by Bernard Benstock and Thomas F. Staley (1988)

71 *American Literary Critics and Scholars, 1880-1900,* edited by John W. Rathbun and Monica M. Grecu (1988)

72 *French Novelists, 1930-1960,* edited by Catharine Savage Brosman (1988)

73 *American Magazine Journalists, 1741-1850,* edited by Sam G. Riley (1988)

74 *American Short-Story Writers Before 1880,* edited by Bobby Ellen Kimbel, with the assistance of William E. Grant (1988)

75 *Contemporary German Fiction Writers, Second Series,* edited by Wolfgang D. Elfe and James Hardin (1988)

76 *Afro-American Writers, 1940-1955,* edited by Trudier Harris (1988)

77 *British Mystery Writers, 1920-1939,* edited by Bernard Benstock and Thomas F. Staley (1988)

78 *American Short-Story Writers, 1880-1910,* edited by Bobby Ellen Kimbel, with the assistance of William E. Grant (1988)

79 *American Magazine Journalists, 1850-1900,* edited by Sam G. Riley (1988)

80 *Restoration and Eighteenth-Century Dramatists, First Series,* edited by Paula R. Backscheider (1989)

81 *Austrian Fiction Writers, 1875-1913,* edited by James Hardin and Donald G. Daviau (1989)

82 *Chicano Writers, First Series,* edited by Francisco A. Lomelí and Carl R. Shirley (1989)

83 *French Novelists Since 1960,* edited by Catharine Savage Brosman (1989)

84 *Restoration and Eighteenth-Century Dramatists, Second Series,* edited by Paula R. Backscheider (1989)

85 *Austrian Fiction Writers After 1914,* edited by James Hardin and Donald G. Daviau (1989)

86 *American Short-Story Writers, 1910-1945, First Series,* edited by Bobby Ellen Kimbel (1989)

87 *British Mystery and Thriller Writers Since 1940, First Series,* edited by Bernard Benstock and Thomas F. Staley (1989)

88 *Canadian Writers, 1920-1959, Second Series,* edited by W. H. New (1989)

89 *Restoration and Eighteenth-Century Dramatists, Third Series,* edited by Paula R. Backscheider (1989)

90 *German Writers in the Age of Goethe, 1789-1832,* edited by James Hardin and Christoph E. Schweitzer (1989)

91 *American Magazine Journalists, 1900-1960, First Series,* edited by Sam G. Riley (1990)

92 *Canadian Writers, 1890-1920,* edited by W. H. New (1990)

93 *British Romantic Poets, 1789-1832, First Series,* edited by John R. Greenfield (1990)

94 *German Writers in the Age of Goethe: Sturm und Drang to Classicism,* edited by James Hardin and Christoph E. Schweitzer (1990)

95 *Eighteenth-Century British Poets, First Series,* edited by John Sitter (1990)

96 *British Romantic Poets, 1789-1832, Second Series,* edited by John R. Greenfield (1990)

97 *German Writers from the Enlightenment to Sturm und Drang, 1720-1764,* edited by James Hardin and Christoph E. Schweitzer (1990)

98 *Modern British Essayists, First Series,* edited by Robert Beum (1990)

99 *Canadian Writers Before 1890,* edited by W. H. New (1990)

100 *Modern British Essayists, Second Series,* edited by Robert Beum (1990)

101 *British Prose Writers, 1660-1800, First Series,* edited by Donald T. Siebert (1991)

102 *American Short-Story Writers, 1910-1945, Second Series,* edited by Bobby Ellen Kimbel (1991)

103 *American Literary Biographers, First Series,* edited by Steven Serafin (1991)

104 *British Prose Writers, 1660-1800, Second Series,* edited by Donald T. Siebert (1991)

105 *American Poets Since World War II, Second Series,* edited by R. S. Gwynn (1991)

106 *British Literary Publishing Houses, 1820-1880,* edited by Patricia J. Anderson and Jonathan Rose (1991)

107 *British Romantic Prose Writers, 1789-1832, First Series,* edited by John R. Greenfield (1991)

108 *Twentieth-Century Spanish Poets, First Series,* edited by Michael L. Perna (1991)

109 *Eighteenth-Century British Poets, Second Series,* edited by John Sitter (1991)

110 *British Romantic Prose Writers, 1789-1832, Second Series,* edited by John R. Greenfield (1991)

111 *American Literary Biographers, Second Series,* edited by Steven Serafin (1991)

112 *British Literary Publishing Houses, 1881-1965,* edited by Jonathan Rose and Patricia J. Anderson (1991)

113 *Modern Latin-American Fiction Writers, First Series,* edited by William Luis (1992)

114 *Twentieth-Century Italian Poets, First Series,* edited by Giovanna Wedel De Stasio, Glauco Cambon, and Antonio Illiano (1992)

115 *Medieval Philosophers,* edited by Jeremiah Hackett (1992)

116 *British Romantic Novelists, 1789-1832,* edited by Bradford K. Mudge (1992)

117 *Twentieth-Century Caribbean and Black African Writers, First Series,* edited by Bernth Lindfors and Reinhard Sander (1992)

118 *Twentieth-Century German Dramatists, 1889-1918,* edited by Wolfgang D. Elfe and James Hardin (1992)

119 *Nineteenth-Century French Fiction Writers: Romanticism and Realism, 1800-1860,* edited by Catharine Savage Brosman (1992)

120 *American Poets Since World War II, Third Series,* edited by R. S. Gwynn (1992)

121 *Seventeenth-Century British Nondramatic Poets, First Series,* edited by M. Thomas Hester (1992)

122 *Chicano Writers, Second Series,* edited by Francisco A. Lomelí and Carl R. Shirley (1992)

123 *Nineteenth-Century French Fiction Writers: Naturalism and Beyond, 1860-1900,* edited by Catharine Savage Brosman (1992)

124 *Twentieth-Century German Dramatists, 1919-1992,* edited by Wolfgang D. Elfe and James Hardin (1992)

125 *Twentieth-Century Caribbean and Black African Writers, Second Series,* edited by Bernth Lindfors and Reinhard Sander (1993)

126 *Seventeenth-Century British Nondramatic Poets, Second Series,* edited by M. Thomas Hester (1993)

127 *American Newspaper Publishers, 1950-1990,* edited by Perry J. Ashley (1993)

128 *Twentieth-Century Italian Poets, Second Series,* edited by Giovanna Wedel De Stasio, Glauco Cambon, and Antonio Illiano (1993)

129 *Nineteenth-Century German Writers, 1841-1900,* edited by James Hardin and Siegfried Mews (1993)

130 *American Short-Story Writers Since World War II,* edited by Patrick Meanor (1993)

131 *Seventeenth-Century British Nondramatic Poets, Third Series*, edited by M. Thomas Hester (1993)

132 *Sixteenth-Century British Nondramatic Writers, First Series*, edited by David A. Richardson (1993)

133 *Nineteenth-Century German Writers to 1840*, edited by James Hardin and Siegfried Mews (1993)

134 *Twentieth-Century Spanish Poets, Second Series*, edited by Jerry Phillips Winfield (1994)

135 *British Short-Fiction Writers, 1880–1914: The Realist Tradition*, edited by William B. Thesing (1994)

136 *Sixteenth-Century British Nondramatic Writers, Second Series*, edited by David A. Richardson (1994)

137 *American Magazine Journalists, 1900–1960, Second Series*, edited by Sam G. Riley (1994)

138 *German Writers and Works of the High Middle Ages: 1170–1280*, edited by James Hardin and Will Hasty (1994)

139 *British Short-Fiction Writers, 1945–1980*, edited by Dean Baldwin (1994)

140 *American Book-Collectors and Bibliographers, First Series*, edited by Joseph Rosenblum (1994)

141 *British Children's Writers, 1880–1914*, edited by Laura M. Zaidman (1994)

142 *Eighteenth-Century British Literary Biographers*, edited by Steven Serafin (1994)

143 *American Novelists Since World War II, Third Series*, edited by James R. Giles and Wanda H. Giles (1994)

144 *Nineteenth-Century British Literary Biographers*, edited by Steven Serafin (1994)

145 *Modern Latin-American Fiction Writers, Second Series*, edited by William Luis and Ann González (1994)

146 *Old and Middle English Literature*, edited by Jeffrey Helterman and Jerome Mitchell (1994)

147 *South Slavic Writers Before World War II*, edited by Vasa D. Mihailovich (1994)

148 *German Writers and Works of the Early Middle Ages: 800–1170*, edited by Will Hasty and James Hardin (1994)

149 *Late Nineteenth- and Early Twentieth-Century British Literary Biographers*, edited by Steven Serafin (1995)

150 *Early Modern Russian Writers, Late Seventeenth and Eighteenth Centuries*, edited by Marcus C. Levitt (1995)

151 *British Prose Writers of the Early Seventeenth Century*, edited by Clayton D. Lein (1995)

152 *American Novelists Since World War II, Fourth Series*, edited by James and Wanda Giles (1995)

153 *Late-Victorian and Edwardian British Novelists, First Series*, edited by George M. Johnson (1995)

154 *The British Literary Book Trade, 1700–1820*, edited by James K. Bracken and Joel Silver (1995)

155 *Twentieth-Century British Literary Biographers*, edited by Steven Serafin (1995)

156 *British Short-Fiction Writers, 1880–1914: The Romantic Tradition*, edited by William F. Naufftus (1995)

157 *Twentieth-Century Caribbean and Black African Writers, Third Series*, edited by Bernth Lindfors and Reinhard Sander (1995)

158 *British Reform Writers, 1789–1832*, edited by Gary Kelly and Edd Applegate (1995)

159 *British Short-Fiction Writers, 1800–1880*, edited by John R. Greenfield (1996)

160 *British Children's Writers, 1914–1960*, edited by Donald R. Hettinga and Gary D. Schmidt (1996)

161 *British Children's Writers Since 1960, First Series*, edited by Caroline Hunt (1996)

162 *British Short-Fiction Writers, 1915–1945*, edited by John H. Rogers (1996)

163 *British Children's Writers, 1800–1880*, edited by Meena Khorana (1996)

164 *German Baroque Writers, 1580–1660*, edited by James Hardin (1996)

165 *American Poets Since World War II, Fourth Series*, edited by Joseph Conte (1996)

166 *British Travel Writers, 1837–1875*, edited by Barbara Brothers and Julia Gergits (1996)

167 *Sixteenth-Century British Nondramatic Writers, Third Series*, edited by David A. Richardson (1996)

168 *German Baroque Writers, 1661–1730*, edited by James Hardin (1996)

169 *American Poets Since World War II, Fifth Series*, edited by Joseph Conte (1996)

170 *The British Literary Book Trade, 1475–1700*, edited by James K. Bracken and Joel Silver (1996)

171 *Twentieth-Century American Sportswriters*, edited by Richard Orodenker (1996)

172 *Sixteenth-Century British Nondramatic Writers, Fourth Series*, edited by David A. Richardson (1996)

173 *American Novelists Since World War II, Fifth Series*, edited by James R. Giles and Wanda H. Giles (1996)

174 *British Travel Writers, 1876–1909*, edited by Barbara Brothers and Julia Gergits (1997)

175 *Native American Writers of the United States*, edited by Kenneth M. Roemer (1997)

176 *Ancient Greek Authors*, edited by Ward W. Briggs (1997)

177 *Italian Novelists Since World War II, 1945–1965* edited by Augustus Pallotta (1997)

178 *British Fantasy and Science-Fiction Writers Before World War I*, edited by Darren Harris-Fain (1997)

179 *German Writers of the Renaissance and Reformation, 1280–1580*, edited by James Hardin and Max Reinhart (1997)

180 *Japanese Fiction Writers, 1868–1945*, edited by Van C. Gessel (1997)

181 *South Slavic Writers Since World War II*, edited by Vasa D. Mihailovich (1997)

182 *Japanese Fiction Writers Since World War II*, edited by Van C. Gessel (1997)

183 *American Travel Writers, 1776–1864*, edited by James J. Schramer and Donald Ross (1997)

Documentary Series

1 *Sherwood Anderson, Willa Cather, John Dos Passos, Theodore Dreiser, F. Scott Fitzgerald, Ernest Hemingway, Sinclair Lewis*, edited by Margaret A. Van Antwerp (1982)

2 *James Gould Cozzens, James T. Farrell, William Faulkner, John O'Hara, John Steinbeck, Thomas Wolfe, Richard Wright*, edited by Margaret A. Van Antwerp (1982)

3 *Saul Bellow, Jack Kerouac, Norman Mailer, Vladimir Nabokov, John Updike, Kurt Vonnegut*, edited by Mary Bruccoli (1983)

4 *Tennessee Williams*, edited by Margaret A. Van Antwerp and Sally Johns (1984)

5 *American Transcendentalists*, edited by Joel Myerson (1988)

6 *Hardboiled Mystery Writers: Raymond Chandler, Dashiell Hammett, Ross Macdonald*, edited by Matthew J. Bruccoli and Richard Layman (1989)

7 *Modern American Poets: James Dickey, Robert Frost, Marianne Moore*, edited by Karen L. Rood (1989)

8 *The Black Aesthetic Movement*, edited by Jeffrey Louis Decker (1991)

9 *American Writers of the Vietnam War: W. D. Ehrhart, Larry Heinemann, Tim O'Brien, Walter McDonald, John M. Del Vecchio,* edited by Ronald Baughman (1991)

10 *The Bloomsbury Group,* edited by Edward L. Bishop (1992)

11 *American Proletarian Culture: The Twenties and The Thirties,* edited by Jon Christian Suggs (1993)

12 *Southern Women Writers: Flannery O'Connor, Katherine Anne Porter, Eudora Welty,* edited by Mary Ann Wimsatt and Karen L. Rood (1994)

13 *The House of Scribner, 1846–1904,* edited by John Delaney (1996)

14 *Four Women Writers for Children, 1868–1918,* edited by Caroline C. Hunt (1996)

15 *American Expatriate Writers: Paris in the Twenties,* edited by Matthew J. Bruccoli and Robert W. Trogdon (1997)

16 *The House of Scribner, 1905–1930,* edited by John Delaney (1997)

Yearbooks

1980 edited by Karen L. Rood, Jean W. Ross, and Richard Ziegfeld (1981)

1981 edited by Karen L. Rood, Jean W. Ross, and Richard Ziegfeld (1982)

1982 edited by Richard Ziegfeld; associate editors: Jean W. Ross and Lynne C. Zeigler (1983)

1983 edited by Mary Bruccoli and Jean W. Ross; associate editor: Richard Ziegfeld (1984)

1984 edited by Jean W. Ross (1985)

1985 edited by Jean W. Ross (1986)

1986 edited by J. M. Brook (1987)

1987 edited by J. M. Brook (1988)

1988 edited by J. M. Brook (1989)

1989 edited by J. M. Brook (1990)

1990 edited by James W. Hipp (1991)

1991 edited by James W. Hipp (1992)

1992 edited by James W. Hipp (1993)

1993 edited by James W. Hipp, contributing editor George Garrett (1994)

1994 edited by James W. Hipp, contributing editor George Garrett (1995)

1995 edited by James W. Hipp, contributing editor George Garrett (1996)

1996 edited by Samuel W. Bruce and L. Kay Webster, contributing editor George Garrett (1997)

Concise Series

Concise Dictionary of American Literary Biography, 6 volumes (1988-1989): *The New Consciousness, 1941-1968; Colonization to the American Renaissance, 1640-1865; Realism, Naturalism, and Local Color, 1865-1917; The Twenties, 1917-1929; The Age of Maturity, 1929-1941; Broadening Views, 1968-1988.*

Concise Dictionary of British Literary Biography, 8 volumes (1991-1992): *Writers of the Middle Ages and Renaissance Before 1660; Writers of the Restoration and Eighteenth Century, 1660-1789; Writers of the Romantic Period, 1789-1832; Victorian Writers, 1832-1890; Late Victorian and Edwardian Writers, 1890-1914; Modern Writers, 1914-1945; Writers After World War II, 1945-1960; Contemporary Writers, 1960 to Present.*

Dictionary of Literary Biography®

DOCUMENTARY SERIES

VOLUME SIXTEEN

Dictionary of Literary Biography®

DOCUMENTARY SERIES
Volume 16

The House of Scribner, 1905–1930

Edited by
John Delaney

A Bruccoli Clark Layman Book
Gale Research
Detroit, Washington, D.C., London

Printed in the United States of America

Published simultaneously in the United Kingdom
by Gale Research International Limited
(An affiliated company of Gale Research)

The paper used in this publication meets the minimum requirements
of American National Standard for Information Sciences—Permanence
Paper for Printed Library Materials, ANSI Z39.48-1984.⊚ ™

Library of Congress Catalog Card Number 95-081422

ISBN 0-7876-1931-0

10 9 8 7 6 5 4 3 2 1

Contents

Preface xiii

Acknowledgments...xiv

Permissions xv

Introduction 3

Charles Scribner's Sons:
    Charles and Arthur.......................................10

Illustrated Chronology 47

Scribner Authors
    N. C. Wyeth (1882–1945) 105

    Arthur Train (1875–1945) 117

    John Galsworthy (1867–1933) 128

    Maxwell Struthers Burt (1882–1954) 141

    F. Scott Fitzgerald (1896–1940) 152

Edward W. Bok (1863–1930) 177

Stark Young (1881–1963) 189

Winston Churchill (1874–1965) 200

Thomas Boyd (1898–1935) 213

Ring Lardner (1885–1933) 223

Will James (1892–1942) 233

James Boyd (1888–1944) 249

Ernest Hemingway (1899–1961) 260

Willard Huntington Wright
    ("S. S. Van Dine") (1888–1939) 296

Thomas Wolfe (1900–1938) 305

Cumulative Index 335

To future authors, may their imprints be as illustrious

Preface

The saga of Charles Scribner's Sons continues in this volume but is not completed as originally planned. The firm's wider scope and influence, supported by a richer and fuller archival docmentation, allowed for—and demanded—extended treatment. Hence, a third and final volume, covering the years 1931–1984, will follow.

I have limited the scope of the present volume to the important twenty-five-year period (1905–1930) after the firm's incorporation, which roughly corresponds to the second half of the long presidency of CS II, the founder's son, concluding with his death in 1930. As in volume one, this range of years applies strictly to the illustrated chronology section; for the authors in the authors section, it depicts the period during which they began their careers with Scribners. As both a bridge between volumes one and two and a backdrop to some of the personal and company events of the years covered by them, I have included a selection of letters written between the two brothers, Charles (CS II) and Arthur, who ran the family business together for fifty years.

To represent Scribners' literary output for the period, I have chosen fifteen authors. Many of the names are synonymous with American literature, but all have been significant additions to Scribners' list and illustrate the range and distinction of the company's books for the time. It must be remembered that authors documented in volume one (1846–1904)—such as Henry Van Dyke, George Santayana, Edith Wharton, and Henry James—continued to find success with new Scribner publications after 1904, but those have been covered in the earlier volume. The authors in this volume appear in the order of the date of their first Scribner book, beginning with 1905. While N. C. Wyeth's first illustrated book was published in the fall of 1904, his association with the Scribner Illustrated Classics series argued for his inclusion in this volume; hence, he appears first, before Arthur Train.

As before, the Scribner Archives at Princeton University Library has been the major source of documents in this volume. These have been supplemented with transcriptions of articles and photographs of books drawn from the Library's Rare Books Division (and a few elsewhere). *All sources of non-Princeton items have been identified,* as well as the few other Princeton manuscript collections which have supplied items.

All transcribed documents are presented as accurately as possible; words (and question marks) in brackets indicate places in the text where I guessed at (or questioned) the handwriting.

The shorthand conventions adopted in the earlier volume are maintained here:

CS I = Charles Scribner, 1821–1871
CS II = Charles Scribner, 1854–1930
CS III = Charles Scribner, 1890–1952
CS IV = Charles Scribner, 1921–1995 (who used the form "Charles Scribner, Jr.")
CS V = Charles Scribner, 1951–   (who uses the form "Charles Scribner III")

In all references to the publishing firm of Charles Scribner's Sons I use the word *Scribners* (possessive form = *Scribners'*). As a proper adjective (as in "Maxwell Perkins, the legendary Scribner editor"), the word appears in its singular form.

Acknowledgments

This book was produced by Bruccoli Clark Layman, Inc. Karen L. Rood is senior editor for the *Dictionary of Literary Biography* series. Matthew J. Bruccoli was the in-house editor. He was assisted by associate editor L. Kay Webster.

Administrative support was provided by Ann M. Cheschi and Brenda A. Gillie.

Bookkeeper is Joyce Fowler.

Copyediting supervisor is Jeff Miller. The copyediting staff includes Phyllis A. Avant, Patricia Coate, Christine Copeland, Thom Harman, and William L. Thomas Jr.

Layout and graphics staff includes Marie L. Parker and Janet E. Hill.

Office manager is Kathy Lawler Merlette.

Photography editors are Julie E. Frick and Margaret Meriwether. Photographic copy work was performed by Joseph M. Bruccoli.

Production manager is Samuel W. Bruce.

Software specialist is Marie L. Parker.

Systems manager is Chris Elmore.

Typesetting supervisor is Kathleen M. Flanagan. The typesetting staff includes Pamela D. Norton, Patricia Flanagan Salisbury, and Judith E. McCray. Freelance typesetters include Melody W. Clegg and Delores Plastow.

Walter W. Ross, Steven Gross, and Mark McEwan did library research. They were assisted by the following librarians at the Thomas Cooper Library of the University of South Carolina: Linda Holderfield and the interlibrary-loan staff; reference-department head Virginia Weathers; reference librarians Marilee Birchfield, Stefanie Buck, Stefanie DuBose, Rebecca Feind, Karen Joseph, Donna Lehman, Charlene Loope, Anthony McKissick, Jean Rhyne, and Kwamine Simpson; circulation-department head Caroline Taylor; and acquisitions-searching supervisor David Haggard.

Credit for the photographs in this volume goes to John Blazejewski, the photographer *par excellence* of Princeton University's Index of Christian Art office. The editor wishes to commend him <u>again</u> for a job well done—for the care and efficiency with which he undertook and completed this large enterprise—and to thank Alice Clark and Jennifer Lindabury, of Princeton's Department of Rare Books and Special Collections, for their help in organizing and facilitating the shooting sessions.

Charles Scribner III continued to be very supportive throughout the project and provided useful answers to questions about the Scribner family and Scribner publishing history.

The Department of Rare Books and Special Collections of Princeton University Library made all of its resources available to the editor—many after its normal hours—and the Library's Interlibrary Services office conscientiously located the few Scribner volumes needed for this work that Princeton does not already own.

The editor is indebted to the Library for its extension of a six-month half-time research leave in support of this volume.

To Evelyn and Andrew, again, the editor expresses a grateful appreciation for their acceptance and understanding of the time taken from them for this work.

PERMISSIONS

The Manuscripts Division of the Department of Rare Books and Special Collections, Princeton University Library, granted permission for the use of materials from the Archives of Charles Scribner's Sons and the F. Scott Fitzgerald Papers.

Letters by Maxwell Perkins, Charles Scribner II, Arthur H. Scribner, Charles Scribner Jr., and Charles Scribner III published by permission of Charles Scribner III and Princeton University Library.

Letters by N. C. Wyeth published by permission of Mr. and Mrs. Andrew Wyeth.

Letters by Arthur Train published courtesy of the Estate of Arthur Train.

Letters by John Galsworthy © Trustees of the Estate of John Galsworthy. Reproduced by kind permission of the Trustees.

Letters by Struthers Burt published courtesy of Nathaniel Burt.

Letters by F. Scott Fitzgerald reprinted with permission of Scribner, a Division of Simon & Schuster, from *F. Scott Fitzgerald: A Life in Letters,* edited by Matthew J. Bruccoli. Copyright © 1994 by the Trustees under Agreement Dated July 3, 1975, Created by Frances Scott Fitzgerald Smith.

Letters by F. Scott Fitzgerald reprinted with permission of Scribner, a Division of Simon & Schuster, from T*he Letters of F. Scott Fitzgerald,* edited by Andrew Turnbull. Copyright © 1963 by Frances Scott Fitzgerald Lanahan. Copyright renewed © 1991 by Joanne J. Turnbull, Joanne T. Turnbull, Frances L. Turnbull, and Eleanor Lanahan, Matthew J. Bruccoli, Samuel J. Lanahan, Sr., Trustees under Agreement Dated July 3, 1975, Created by Frances Scott Fitzgerald Smith.

Letters by Edward W. Bok published courtesy of Curtis Bok and the Estate of Edward W. Bok.

Letters by Stark Young published courtesy of the Estate of Stark Young.

Letters by Sir Winston Churchill reproduced with permission of Curtis Brown Ltd., London on behalf of the Estate of Sir Winston S. Churchill. Copyright © Winston S. Churchill.

Letters by Ring Lardner published by permission of Ring Lardner Jr.

Letters by Will James published courtesy of Robert Dufault and the Estate of Will James.

Letters by James Boyd published courtesy of the Estate of Daniel L. Boyd.

Letters by Ernest Hemingway published by permission of the Ernest Hemingway Foundation and John, Patrick, and Gregory Hemingway.

Letters by Willard Huntington Wright published courtesy of the Estate of Willard Huntington Wright.

Letters by Thomas Wolfe published by permission of the Estate of Thomas Wolfe, Paul Gitlin executor.

Maxwell Perkins, "Scribner's and Tom Wolfe," *The Carolina Magazine,* LXVIII (October 1938), pp. 15–17, published courtesy of Bertha Perkins Frothingham and the Office of the Provost, University of North Carolina at Chapel Hill.

Letter by Janet M. Reback published courtesy of Marcus Reback and the Estate of Janet M. Reback.

Letters by Majorie Kinnan Rawlings published by permission of Charles Schlessiger, Brandt & Brandt Literary Agents Inc. Copyright © 1997 by The Norton S. Baskin Revocable Trust.

Dictionary of Literary Biography®

DOCUMENTARY SERIES

VOLUME SIXTEEN

Introduction

A snapshot from the past:

As the tide of migration rolled on toward the Murray Hill district, considered to be roughly between Twenty-third and Fortieth streets, on the East Side, the concentration of publishers created a certain ambiance that was characteristic of this small, almost ingrown society. In the early years of the new century, for example, those in the business could recognize the Scribner contingent—Charles and Arthur, representing the family; W. C. Brownell, their "literary adviser," or editor-in-chief; Edward L. Burlingame, the editor of *Scribner's Magazine,* and perhaps an author like Robert Bridges in tow—on the way to luncheon at the Century Club. They would be seen returning to work exactly an hour later.

[John Tebbel, *A History of Book Publishing in the United States,* volume two, p. 19]

* * * * *

During the "reign" (1879–1930) of Charles Scribner (CS II), Scribners achieved imperial status—whether one measures by its scale of operations, financial success, or literary reputation. Under his watch, the firm launched *Scribner's Magazine;* built successively two Fifth Avenue, New York City, headquarters buildings; established its own press (and press building); and undertook its most significant multivolume publication, the *Dictionary of American Biography.* CS II also personally hired (1910) Maxwell Perkins, upon whose editorial shoulders Scribners would climb to unprecedented literary heights during the 1920s and 1930s.

The 1880s–1930s was also the period during which the firm's Subscription Department was most prominent, publishing specially-named, multivolume editions of the works of international authors. Scribners established a tradition of issuing standard, complete editions of many of its own authors, such as Robert Louis Stevenson, J. M. Barrie, F. Hopkinson Smith, John Galsworthy, Eugene Field, Richard Harding Davis, Theodore Roosevelt, George Santayana, and Henry Van Dyke, but this was a small portion of its subscription efforts. Often sharing production costs with an English publisher, the firm published large editions of the works of Dickens, Dumas, Ibsen, Kipling, O'Neill, Poe, Shakespeare, Shelley, Thackeray, Tolstoy, Turgenev, Wells, and Yeats, among others. A good example of the literary importance of this business is the "New York Edition" of *The Novels and Tales of Henry James,* which was issued in twenty-four volumes between 1907 and 1909; two unfinished novels, published posthumously, were added for subscribers in 1917. Desiring this to be the definitive edition of his work, James revised all of his texts for it. Another unique feature of this edition is the prefaces he prepared in which he narrates the gestation of the book from conception through execution and critically examines the finished work. Taken together, the prefaces constitute a personal philosophy of the art of the novelist by one of the century's most esteemed writers.

The firm's subscription accomplishments were not limited to literature, however. In fact, the largest and best-selling subscription publications were nonfiction, religious, and reference works. The twenty-one-volume *Dictionary of American Biography* (1928–1937) was a monumental publishing achievement and permanent contribution to the entire English-speaking world. Many smaller, important subscription sets appeared, such as James Hastings's *A Dictionary of the Bible* (five volumes, 1898–1904) and Mark Sullivan's *Our Times* (six volumes, 1926–1935).

Under the leadership of Edward Lord, whom CS II had hired in 1893 to resurrect the firm's Educational Department, school and college textbooks, educational series, and academic publications flourished. Several branch offices were eventually established around the country (Chicago, Boston, San Francisco, Atlanta), and the firm was successful in getting states to adopt textbooks for their public school systems. The popular Modern Student's Library, begun in 1917, provided the college and university markets with well-made, inexpensive books, "adequately but not pedantically edited" by leading American authorities. The first three titles, *The Ordeal of*

CS II's private salary notebook, open to a page showing his total payroll for 1894. Grouped by department—"Miscellaneous" (bookstore and editorial departments), "Subscription," and "Magazine"—the figures show a total of two hundred employees dividing a payroll of about $200,000.

Richard Feverel by George Meredith, *Pendennis* by William Makepeace Thackeray, and *The Return of the Native* by Thomas Hardy, suggest an initial preference for English classics, but American works, such as *Selected Essays of Emerson* and Nathaniel Hawthorne's *The Scarlet Letter*, were soon added. By 1930 over fifty titles were included, and both French and Philosophy subseries had been established. Among other educational series were the Scribner English Classics, the Scribner Series of Modern Poets, and the Scribner Series of School Reading.

* * * * *

4

On the inside of an old address book—in worn, brown alligator hide—one reads in CS II's hand:

Charles Scribner
745 Broadway
(Private)

Salaries
Feb. 1ˢᵗ 1889

Most of his entries for employees, roughly arranged alphabetically under the first letter of their surnames, predate 1900, but there are some changes and additions that date to 1923. Regarding Maxwell Perkins, the future legendary editor, one learns, for example, that he joined Scribners in February 1910 at an annual salary of $2,000. Thereafter follow dates of raises, the final one showing an increase in February 1923 to $10,000. Not all employees fared as well, as quickly. W. C. Brownell, hired as the firm's literary adviser in 1888 at a weekly salary of $65 (= $3,380/year), was earning only $5,000 ten years later. But CS II was often generous to the employees on whom he depended. In the section for Edward L. Burlingame, editor of *Scribner's Magazine*, CS II wrote a lengthy explanatory note:

Dec 22ⁿᵈ '91   His condition was as follows:
Down Stairs $3549 against of $2500
Up Stairs $4662 leaving $338 of $5000

I said we would give him $700 cash (which was given by check on 23) with which he was to pay his debt to his brother of $600 & this with the $338 due on Maga. salary he assured me would bring him thru' the year free of debt except $1000 he owed his sister and the fact that he is one month behind on all his bills. I also said I would charge off the $1049 overdrawn on Down Stairs acc't and that for 1892 his salary would be

Down   2500   The $700 was charged
Up   6000   off Down stairs.
    $8500
Nov 3ʳᵈ '92 made credit to E. L. B. downstairs of 1049.51 as above. Lent him personally $350.

Apparently, Burlingame earned two separate salaries: one for his magazine work ("Up Stairs") and one for his general book editing ("Down Stairs"). The last entry, dated "March 1897," shows how his responsibilites had shifted: his salary was increased to $10,000—"$9000 upstairs & $1000 down."

On a loose piece of paper filed under "L" in the address book, next to the Edward Lord en-

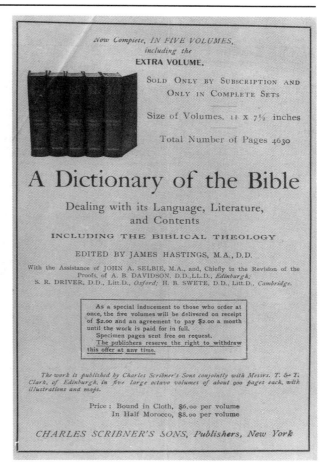

Now Complete, IN FIVE VOLUMES, including the EXTRA VOLUME.

SOLD ONLY BY SUBSCRIPTION AND ONLY IN COMPLETE SETS

Size of Volumes, 11 x 7½ inches

Total Number of Pages 4630

A Dictionary of the Bible

Dealing with its Language, Literature, and Contents

INCLUDING THE BIBLICAL THEOLOGY

EDITED BY JAMES HASTINGS, M.A., D.D.

With the Assistance of JOHN A. SELBIE, M.A., and, Chiefly in the Revision of the Proofs, of A. B. DAVIDSON, D.D.,LL.D., *Edinburgh;* S. R. DRIVER, D.D., Litt.D., *Oxford;* H. B. SWETE, D.D., Litt.D., *Cambridge.*

As a special inducement to those who order at once, the five volumes will be delivered on receipt of $2.00 and an agreement to pay $2.00 a month until the work is paid for in full.
Specimen pages sent free on request.
The publishers reserve the right to withdraw this offer at any time.

The work is published by Charles Scribner's Sons conjointly with Messrs. T. & T. Clark, of Edinburgh, in five large octavo volumes of about 900 pages each, with illustrations and maps.

Price : Bound in Cloth, $6.00 per volume
In Half Morocco, $8.00 per volume

CHARLES SCRIBNER'S SONS, Publishers, New York

Cover of the Subscription Department circular (1904) for James Hastings's A Dictionary of the Bible

tries, are financial tables showing sales, costs, and net profits of the Educational Department for the ten years from 1909–1910 through 1918–1919 (Scribners' fiscal year ended on 31 January). Each year was profitable, the average amount being $51,530. The average annual profit for the Book Trade Department, which included educational but excluded subscription sales, was $133,987 for the same period; hence, educational sales were contributing over one-third of the firm's profits from nonsubscription books.

* * * * *

Over 100 ledgers, bearing such titles as Inventory, Accounts Receivable, Plate Record, Retail Ledger, and Cash Book, occupy twenty shelves in the Archives. Ranging from the 1860s to the 1930s, they convey a Dickensian view of recordkeeping. Nonetheless, they preserve the "business" history of Scribners, and one rum-

Year	Total Sales	Advertising	Salaries	Net Profits
1903–1904	1,457,887.48	83,611.14	70,757.89	170,817.77
1904–1905	1,378,356.64	78,895.43	[n.a.]	130,067.16
1905–1906	1,428,247.44	71,981.29	[n.a.]	156,379.19
1906–1907	1,353,057.62	63,937.24	[n.a.]	163,004.77
1907–1908	1,483,296.17	[n.a.]	[n.a.]	139,406.42
1908–1909	1,518,898.67	69,861.08	146,854.91	85,267.56
1909–1910	1,604,837.27	66,971.62	156,318.27	154,647.92
1910–1911	1,451,338.08	78,465.55	159,785.48	52,203.67
1911–1912	1,548,635.33	60,382.28	155,434.64	148,927.14
1912–1913	1,608,296.21	59,269.42	163,289.85	178,293.01
1913–1914	1,738,236.52	61,844.07	176,492.17	188,709.13
1914–1915	1,465,153.11	45,525.36	181,045.40	110,946.68
1915–1916	1,548,351.75	43,532.23	181,768.28	166,183.64
1916–1917	1,761,102.53	44,133.61	193,382.89	180,752.72
1917–1918	1,701,275.97	45,085.81	198,146.60	104,225.03
1918–1919	1,608,804.41	44,459.76	208,285.55	54,983.03
1919–1920	2,390,945.60	51,880.59	242,257.65	106,253.28
1920–1921	2,630,584.20	55,760.61	284,895.85	201,437.28
1921–1922	2,503,678.93	58,143.97	303,415.56	174,015.03
1922–1923	2,877,083.39	84,713.34	340,979.02	283,696.41
1923–1924	3,056,830.80	127,065.76	365,474.61	291,571,00
1924–1925	3,154,176.14	93,950.11	391,381.51	267,585.27
1925–1926	3,752,894.10	105,947.45	458,090.65	498,060.08
1926–1927	3,783,969.27	110,456.92	464,663.71	486,965.37
1927–1928	3,634,776.01	117,446.14	474,874.81	341,063.31
1928–1929	3,719,170.47	131,459.94	485,447.50	353,588.87
1929–1930	3,749,815.43	142,996.82	518,153.30	342,729.61
1930–1931	3,170,580.40	114,705.31	504,600.46	207,443.26

mages through them and boxes of handwritten accounts reckoning the firm's past health. Profit/loss account sheets provide a capsule financial look of the firm's growth from its incorporation in 1904. Above are the figures for the Book Trade Department through the year of CS II's death. Excluded are figures from the London agency, the printing press, *Scribner's Magazine,* and the Subscription Department.

Several generalizations, applicable to the publishing industry at large, are obvious from the table: 1) salaries outpaced sales growth; 2) advertising/promotion/publicity became and remained a significant budgetary expense; 3) the Twenties were remarkably profitable. In fact, the financial heights reached by Scribners' Book Trade Department during the year of 1925–1926 would only be surpassed once (according to annual reports through 1976–1977): during the war year of 1943–1944.

In sharp contrast, during this halcyon period, *Scribner's Magazine* was accumulating substantial deficits, averaging about $64,000 per year. The magazine earned a small profit of $8,956 in fiscal year 1920–1921 but bled red ink the rest of its life. Even three attempts to revamp its format and editorial policies—in 1928, 1932, and 1936—could not revive the monthly. The audience that had given the magazine the widest circulation ever of the "quality group" in 1909, following the African exploits of former president Theodore Roosevelt, had switched by the Twenties to general market magazines like *The Saturday Evening Post, Ladies' Home Journal, Cosmopolitan, Red Book,* and *Woman's Home Companion; The New Yorker,* founded (1925) and edited by Harold Ross, soon became a favorite of the literati. The financial problems of *Scribner's Magazine* only intensified during the Depression, logically leading to its sale in 1938 and demise in 1939.

* * * * *

In 1928 Asa Don Dickinson, librarian of the University of Pennsylvania, published a volume

6

View of the front of the Scribner building at 597–599 Fifth Avenue, New York City, in May 1917. The flag decorations honoring the visits of the British and French War Commissions include the firm's own patriotic flag, sharing the pole with the Stars and Stripes; presumably, the twenty-one stars represent the number of employees serving in the war effort (photo by Wurts Bros.).

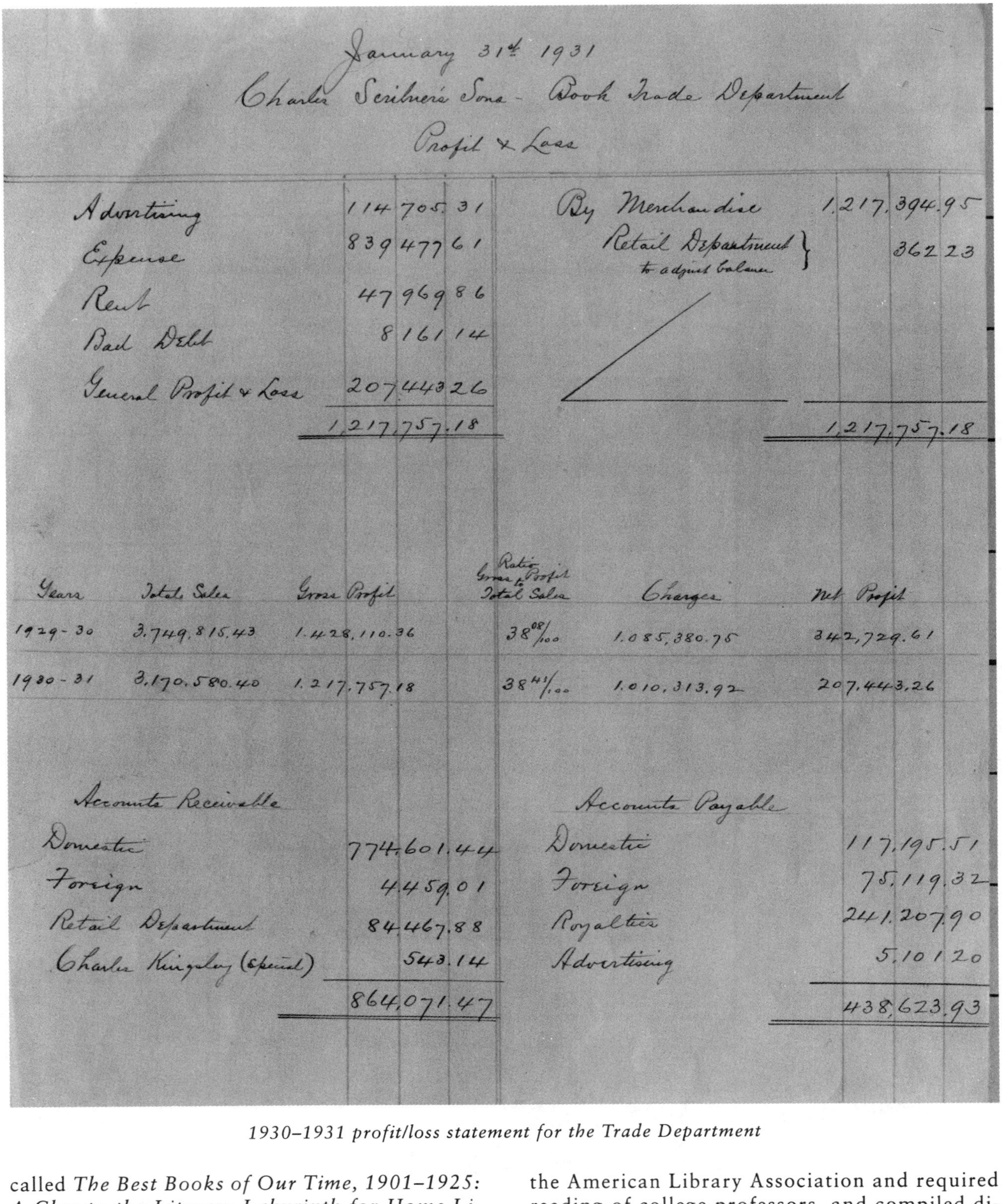

January 31st 1931

Charles Scribner's Sons — Book Trade Department

Profit & Loss

Advertising	114,705.31	By Merchandise	1,217,394.95
Expense	839,477.61	Retail Department to adjust balance	362.23
Rent	47,969.86		
Bad Debt	8,161.14		
General Profit & Loss	207,443.26		
	1,217,757.18		1,217,757.18

Years	Total Sales	Gross Profit	Ratio Gross Profit to Total Sales	Charges	Net Profit
1929-30	3,749,815.43	1,428,110.36	38 08/100 %	1,085,380.75	342,729.61
1930-31	3,170,580.40	1,217,757.18	38 41/100	1,010,313.92	207,443.26

Accounts Receivable		Accounts Payable	
Domestic	774,601.44	Domestic	117,195.51
Foreign	4,459.01	Foreign	75,119.32
Retail Department	84,467.88	Royalties	241,207.90
Charles Kingsley (special)	543.14	Advertising	5,101.20
	864,071.47		438,623.93

1930–1931 profit/loss statement for the Trade Department

called *The Best Books of Our Time, 1901–1925: A Clue to the Literary Labyrinth for Home Library Builders, Booksellers and Librarians, Consisting of a List of One Thousand Best Books, Selected by the Best Authorities.* He studied sixty-two published lists, including annual selections of the American Library Association and required reading of college professors, and compiled diverse opinions to create a composite picture of contemporary, educated preferences. Of the "top" ten authors, Scribners published two—John Galsworthy, who was #1, and Edith Wharton (#5)—and of the ten favorite titles, three were Scribner publications: Wharton's *The House of Mirth* (1905, #5) and *Ethan Frome* (1911, #10) and Galsworthy's *The Forsyte Saga* (1922, #2). This reputation of publishing quality fiction would continue during the editorial reign (1914–1947) of Maxwell Perkins.

Perkins's genius was discovering and/or nurturing new American literary talent. Before the Depression arrived, he had encouraged, found, and/or supported a wide range of writers: essayist-novelist Struthers Burt, autobiographer Edward Bok, story-writer Ring Lardner, historical fiction writers James and Thomas Boyd, and detective author Willard Huntington Wright ("S. S. Van Dine"). And, of course, there were the big three: F. Scott Fitzgerald (first published in 1920), Ernest Hemingway (1926), and Thomas Wolfe (1929), whose successes often overshadowed the achievements of other Scribner writers, such as the courtroom exploits of Arthur Train's Ephraim Tutt, the home-on-the-range stories of cowboy Will James, and the erudite sleuthing of S. S. Van Dine's Philo Vance.

The Twenties witnessed a subtle changing of the Scribner guard—reflective of the changing times and literary sensibilities—from the Englishman John Galsworthy to the American Ernest Hemingway. As Galsworthy was the most prominent Scribner author of the early decades of the twentieth century, Hemingway would become the firm's torchbearer through the 1950s. Both writers became Nobel Prize winners.

* * * * *

What emerges from these documentary pages is the central figure of CS II—the ubiquity of editor Maxwell Perkins—and, ultimately, a realization of the astonishing Scribner contribution to this period in American literature. Of the firm's many voices reverberating all these years, foremost, like a literary mantra, have sounded those of Fitzgerald, Hemingway, and Wolfe.

John Delaney
June 29, 1997
Princeton, N.J.

Charles Scribner's Sons: Charles and Arthur

Charles Scribner (1854–1930) and Arthur Hawley Scribner (1859–1932)

When publisher Charles Scribner (CS I), founder of the company, died unexpectedly in 1871, he left behind three sons: John Blair (age 21), Charles (16), and Arthur (12). Blair, who had already been working in the firm's Broadway (New York City) bookstore, soon entered into new agreements with his father's business partners—Andrew C. Armstrong, Edward Seymour, and Charles Welford—that renamed the publishing company Scribner, Armstrong & Co. and the importing company Scribner, Welford & Armstrong. Graduating from Princeton in 1875, Charles (CS II) joined his brother that summer. In 1878, with the financial assistance of his grandfather and

namesake, railroad capitalist John Insley Blair, Blair bought out Armstrong and Seymour, forming Charles Scribner's Sons—but he died suddenly in January of the following year, leaving Charles alone as head of the publishing company at the age of twenty-four. Arthur, following what had become family tradition, graduated from Princeton in 1881 and immediately went to work in the firm. Thereafter, for nearly fifty years—Scribners' golden period—the two brothers ran the business together. When Charles "retired" from the presidency in 1928 to assume the position of chairman of the board, Arthur finally took official charge.

Roger Burlingame, son of Scribner's Magazine editor Edward L. Burlingame, started with Scribners in 1913 after graduating from Harvard. He began on the editorial staff, became publicity manager (1914–1917), and later became a book editor (1919–1926). Thereafter, he devoted himself full time to writing. In his centennial volume on the firm, Of Making Many Books: A Hundred Years of Reading, Writing and Publishing *(New York: Charles Scribner's Sons, 1946), he provides these character sketches of the two Scribner brothers:*

• Charles (pp. 24–28)

C.S. did not press buttons. Secretaries did not rush in and out of his office. He did not entrust precious, immediate papers to the filing and finding of clerks. His desk was cluttered with old books which had some special trick of beauty for comparison, with catalogs of type and cloth, with complex authors' letters, with contracts containing special clauses; with a dozen things which would be needed at some instant of the day's work and C.S. knew where to put his hand when each was needed. Outside his office eternally hovered a little group of men. They had not made appointments. They could not, for in the normal course of their day, problems arose one hour, which must be solved in the next. They were proud and sensitive men, specialists, and each held in his hand some delicate curiosity different from all others and the only thing that could coordinate them was the long, detailed experience in every specialty of C.S. himself.

It was true that some of these experts—editors, art directors, typographers, pressmen and salesmen, each a kind of artist in his way—often squirmed under C.S.'s insistence on knowing the whole score at any given moment. They called him a dictator—the "Czar"; they called him unreasonable and finicky, capricious and captious. And outsiders, unable to reconcile the fact that a "bad businessman" had successfully conducted a good business for fifty-two years—and held all the strings in his hand—called him, at last, a "genius." . . .

Charles Scribner, with his eye on all these things at once, appeared unreasonable. Some of his workers, facing him in his old-world office were terrified. The benign expression of his bearded father looking down from the wall behind the desk, did not balance C.S.'s challenging face and forbidding eyes. The creaking of his ancient chair, the faded and slightly torn shade at the window, the beam of old-book-dusty sunlight filtering through the tear and the rows of dark old leather volumes against the wall did little to soften the vivid presence of the Chief. So, sometimes, a younger or newer man, hovering by the threshold, would lose his nerve and slink back to his desk reporting along the way that the boss was in no mood. . . .

But those who had lived in this upside-down world, understood the temper of the man who ran it. They knew that C.S. loved and demanded fight. He could not tolerate yes-men because they did not give him the information his restless, probing mind was forever seeking. If you agreed with him, he employed devices to make you disagree. In the midst of a discussion he would reverse his position. And for a man whose peculiar genius was predicated on an infallible memory he had a capacity for "forgetting" which bewildered people. . . .

There were those, to be sure, who never reconciled these devices with the way they thought a boss should behave. Other men, they said, got results through a gentler, kindlier, less bedeviling process. Other men left their employees alone, gave them authority, kept hands off a job which only a specialist could do. They said these things, forgetting that even a specialist's job must be coordinated with the job of another specialist—that a book's cover, for instance, must satisfy author, salesman, bookseller, treasurer, public and the House's tradition all at once.

Yet men rarely left Scribners. On the very threshold of departure a curious charm drew them back to C.S. His smile, unexpectedly following his frown, reduced men to sweat and almost to tears of relief. Sometimes his smile was induced by a humorous sidelight which had flashed upon his mind. Often it came from the sense that he had gone too far or that his worries were small fish in the world's sea of miseries. For C.S. was hounded by a relentless personal conscience. His conscience loathed injustice and, if he believed that he had hurt someone unjustly, he stopped at nothing until he had put his hand on the man's shoulder with a friendliness that was more eloquent than an apology.

• Arthur (pp. 89–91)

Somewhere near the office of C.S. on the editorial floor, there was always, in the firm's middle years, another office slightly smaller, perhaps, but with a similar group of waiting men outside it. In it sat "A.H.," a kind and much beloved man. . . .

A.H. had neither the iron will nor the finality of decision of his elder brother, and his experience in the business was more specialized. At any rate, he acted as a cushion or shock-absorber between Charles and the staff. You did not take a question to C.S. if you thought there was a chance that A.H. might answer it. On the other hand, if it was a question of major importance, you could be sure of a more conclusive, if balder, reply from C.S., because the procedure on large questions was that, if you put it up to A.H., he would evade you with a smile and, after you had left him, walk softly across the hall with it, to his brother's desk. One thing you could be sure of was the smile. That and his cordial welcome, whatever the press of mood or business and the quickness of his humor were the things for which he was loved. A.H. never scolded and rarely frowned. He tried, sometimes, and broke down, was laughing before he finished and though occasionally men left his office uncertain as to immediate action, none ever left hurt.

If you wanted a raise, or time off, or had trouble at home you told A.H. He did not give you the raise, perhaps, but you knew, if you had reason, that he would be your advocate; that you would get it later. His courtesy was infallible and very old-world; to the end of their lives, for instance, he addressed his elders as "Mr. Brownell" or "Mr. Burlingame" and even referred to them so in his private letters to his brother. He was sometimes accused of pinching pennies because he was so meticulous and tireless about figures and it was true he would not use a new pencil till the last half inch of usefulness had been got out of the old one. But he did not pinch dollars. . . .

A.H.'s mastery was in the art of manufacture. He knew all about paper, binding, type-faces, gilt, stamps, cut and uncut leaves. He knew the cost of these things to the last mill; he knew their durability, their fitness and their tradition. He was expert, too, in word estimates and could tell just the number of pages a manuscript, when printed, would fill; he had a fine grasp of the balance of plant and royalty and even the imponderable of "overhead." He had an affection for all the physical properties of books; he would handle a finished job with tender, tactile appreciation.

Arthur Scribner comes into the story here because, once a book was accepted, its terms arranged and its manuscript edited, it was put "in hand," and from that point until it reached the ultimate consumer it was largely his concern.

The most revealing evidence of the brothers' management abilities and business and personal relationship is their correspondence, which was regularly maintained while either one was away from New York on a trip. And these annual trips, hybrids of business and pleasure, often lasted for two, three, even four months at a time—typical of men of their wealth and social class. The nature of the publishing profession, organized around two "seasons" (spring and fall), allowed for much of the business to be conducted by letter; and, thus, a great deal could be—and was—accomplished during these trips. In addition, personal contacts with foreign publishers and authors were established and developed. Absences were coordinated so that one brother was always available at the office; in reality, however, both spent the majority of their time working in New York together, "hands-on."

The letters thus constitute a remarkable record of the two brothers' lives, of the temper of the times, and of publishing as it used to be. The following are a small selection.

• 1884

Summoned to London by an urgent telegram from the daughter of Charles Welford regarding her father's failing health, CS II left New York City by steamer on 6 August. Welford, who with CS I in 1857 had established Scribners' importing company, Scribner and Welford, was the last remaining "outside" (nonfamily) partner of the firm. This is Arthur's earliest letter to his brother in the Scribner Archives.

Aug 22^d 1884

Dear Charles,

Since I wrote to you last I have taken a couple of days' vacation, leaving the City last Friday afternoon, and staying at Whitehead's (West Hampton, Long Island) till Tuesday morning.

I enjoyed every moment of the time which was divided among sailing, tennis, bathing, driving etc., and as a result of the sailing I am quite sunburnt, fully as much so as when I returned from New Castle. Since then I have been quite giddy, taking part in a fancy dress entertainment at the Cranes.

Louise [wife of CS II], who went in a Kate Greenaway [English children's author] costume, looked very pretty, and was much complimented. Altogether the affair was a decided success, especially after the people warmed up to it, which they did very soon as the thermometer was well up in the eighties. We are all well, and Louise is expecting early next week her first letter from you.

The Sheridan [Civil War general Philip Henry Sheridan] matter about which Mr. Burlingame [Edward L. Burlingame, literary adviser and later editor of *Scribner's Magazine*] has already written you, is practically decided, as we have a letter from the General saying that he is very much pleased with our offer. We are now preparing a more formal contract, which he wishes to be ready about the first of next month.

I had some fear in regard to the title, lest he should be unwilling to assume the entire responsibility for the work as we desired, but the form prepared by us proved to be very satisfactory.

This has been rather an important matter to be decided while you were away, especially as it involves the Subscription Dep't. in a new, and we hope larger enterprise.

You know that the acceptance of the Appleton's offer was merely held in abeyance for a week, until we could make our proposition, so that we were obliged to act quickly or lose the chance. We have since learned that their offer was also 15%, but their proposed retail price being less would not have netted Gen. Sheridan so much. Mr. Thomas has great faith in the book, and has no doubt about our exceeding the fifteen thousand copies inside of three years.

I have received a letter from Dunham, Ernest's protege, and have written to him to come early in Sept. having told Frank Potter that he will not be needed for more than two weeks longer. Dunham will, I think, be able to do Potter's work, and also assist Doubleday [Frank Nelson Doubleday, editor of Scribners' periodical *The Book Buyer* and future founder of his own publishing firm] very considerably.

I enclose a letter from Eugene Schuyler about which I scarcely know what to do. On looking up the copyright in Peter [*Peter the Great*, 2 vols.], which was scarcely due (Pub'd Mch 22/84) I found that the account was already so heavily burdened with advances etc., that it stood just about even. I finally decided to send him a statement clearing up everything to date, and also to advance about $250, as I thought that this was safe and yet I scarcely felt like doing more than this.

Things are moving along very slowly now, and everyone is complaining so there is really very little to tell. Fred has been away all this week. Our first publication is fixed for Sept 10th, and includes the four books proposed—Stories Vol. 6, Socialism, Hibbert and Queer Stories. By the way, all of Eggelston's [Edward Eggleston] books seem to be doing quite well, including Hoosier School Boy, which I was afraid had rather come to a stand still.

We have not yet received any word about Mr. Welford, so presume that there can not have been any material change.

Yours
Arthur

Scribners' signed contract (1884) with Sheridan and his co-author, George E. Pond, called for a two-volume work titled The Military Life and Campaigns of Lieutenant General Sheridan, *to be sold by its Subscription Department for $10; but the contract was never fulfilled due to Sheridan's declining health. Pond canceled it on 6 August 1888, the day after Sheridan's death. The publications scheduled for 10 September were* Stories by American Authors *(volume 6 of a series),* Contemporary Socialism *by John Rae,* The Native Religions of Mexico and Peru *by Albert Réville (Hibbert Lectures on the Origin and Growth of Religion, 1884), and Eggleston's* Queer Stories for Boys and Girls. *Welford died the following year, enabling CS II to buy his share of Scribner and Welford from his estate.*

• 1887

CS II left the business in Arthur's hands for the entire summer (late May till early September) while he, his wife, and their young daughter were traveling in Europe: London, Paris, Switzerland, Germany, Holland, London, Scotland, Queenstown (Ireland).

May 20th 1887
Dear Charles:
Your departure was certainly unsatisfactory in so far as saying good-bye was concerned. When the steamer went out I balanced myself on a rickety old barrel and waved frantically, but could not see you and doubt whether you could make me out in the crowd. I shall be looking now in a day or two for the arrival of the steamer, and hope that you have had a pleasant voyage. Very little of importance has happened since you left so I shall send you only a short letter this time.

I found on my return from the steamer the sheets of the Second Series, Obiter Dicta; which I put in hand at once and shall have ready to publish next week. There was some question about a short preface to the American Edition, which fi-

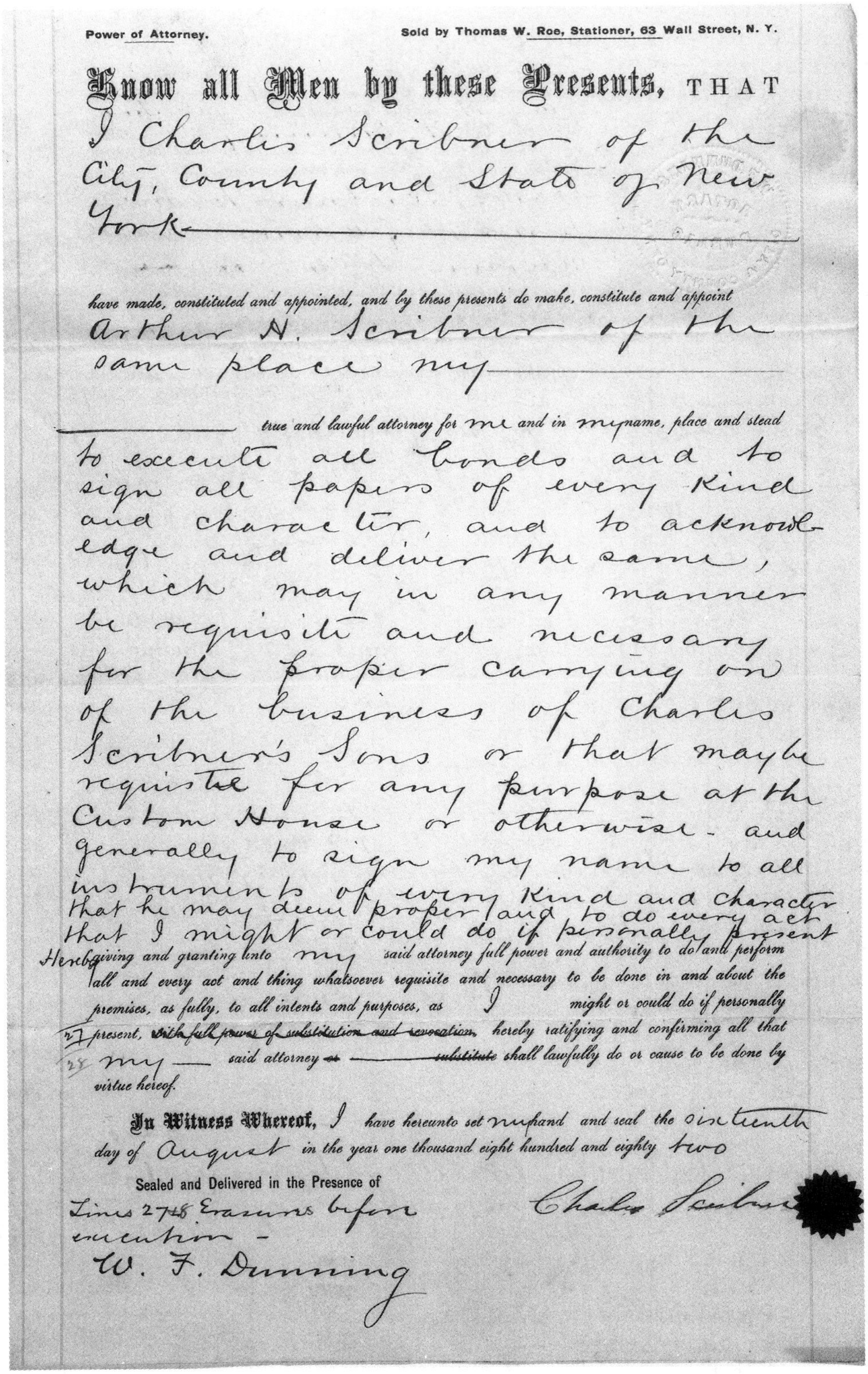

Power of Attorney.   Sold by Thomas W. Roe, Stationer, 63 Wall Street, N. Y.

Know all Men by these Presents, THAT

I Charles Scribner of the City, County and State of New York————,

have made, constituted and appointed, and by these presents do make, constitute and appoint

Arthur H. Scribner of the same place my————

———— true and lawful attorney for me and in my name, place and stead

to execute all bonds and to sign all papers of every kind and character, and to acknowledge and deliver the same, which may in any manner be requisite and necessary for the proper carrying on of the business of Charles Scribner's Sons or that maybe requisite for any purpose at the Custom House or otherwise. and generally to sign my name to all instruments of every kind and character that he may deem proper and to do every act that I might or could do if personally present

Hereby giving and granting unto my said attorney full power and authority to do and perform all and every act and thing whatsoever requisite and necessary to be done in and about the premises, as fully, to all intents and purposes, as I might or could do if personally present, with full power of substitution and revocation, hereby ratifying and confirming all that my ——— said attorney or ——— substitute shall lawfully do or cause to be done by virtue hereof.

In Witness Whereof, I have hereunto set my hand and seal the sixteenth day of August in the year one thousand eight hundred and eighty two

Sealed and Delivered in the Presence of

Lines 27 & 8 Erasures before execution –

W. F. Dunning

Charles Scribner

Power of attorney granted to AHS by his brother

nally after consulting with Mr. Burlingame I decided to omit, for though I have no doubt that it was intended all right its reference to an English author's having no rights in America might easily be misunderstood.

In accordance with Mr. Bang's [Lemuel W. Bangs, successor to Welford as head of Scribners' importing company, Scribner & Welford] letter I am holding the publication of Stevens till we hear from the other side, but it did not seem well to delay Page, so we publish that tomorrow, as before arranged, with Face-to-Face, Paper. I hope to publish Stevens and Obiter Dicta together next week. You will be glad to know that Page seems to start off with some little snap.

Guatemala is going to be larger than was estimated, it having run up from 384 to about 450 pages. You may be interested in knowing this with reference to the English sale, otherwise the books are all going along fully as well as was expected.

I have had something to do nearly every evening since you left, so I have not had any chance to be lonely. One evening there was a very large fire in West 34th Street, and another morning, about 2³⁰, being awakened by a violent ringing at the door-bell, I had the pleasure of going through the house with a police-man in search for a burglar. The cover to the coal slide had been removed, and he thought that someone might have entered. Fortunately there was no one to be found. You see I have not lacked for amusement. Please give my love to all

Yours
Arthur

The books mentioned by Arthur are Augustine Birrell's Obiter Dicta *(second series);* Around the World on a Bicycle *by Thomas Stevens; Thomas Nelson Page's first book,* In Ole Virginia; *Robert Grant's* Face to Face *(paperback edition); and* Quatemala: The Land of the Quetzal *by William Tufts Brigham.*

In the business generally 1st when you know you are right don't mind what anyone says against it & 2nd when you don't feel sure of your ground there is not one case in ten when the question can not be postponed until you *can* see how to act.

— CS II in a letter to AHS, 24 May 1887

• 1889

CS II left New York City on 23 February and arrived back on 23 June, after four months of travel abroad with his family: Le Havre, Paris, Lyons, Marseilles, Monte Carlo, Italy (all over), Versailles, London, Canterbury, Paris, and back to Le Havre. Here he describes unexpectedly meeting Mr. and Mrs. Humphry Ward in Rome. Thomas Humphry Ward was on the staff of The Times *in London; author Mary Augusta Ward (Mrs. Humphry Ward) had recently published* Robert Elsmere *(1888), a novel that had created much interest and debate—and had drawn much attention from American publishers. In fact, CS II thought he had already reached an agreement with her English publisher for her next book and had hoped to visit her in London, for which he had prepared himself with a letter of introduction.*

Rome April 13th [April 14, 1889]
My dear Arthur:

Since my last letter yours of the 26th has arrived. As you have not mentioned the receipt of mine of March 8th from Paris but only the one from Lyons I fear that a letter of either yours or mine is missing but it would not be a serious matter for everything is evidently all right at home. I wrote to you also from Genoa on the 30th, from here on the 6th & to Burlingame from Pisa on the 2nd.

It was a week yesterday since we arrived and although we have had bad weather, most of the time rain, we have seen most of the great sights and we have another week to see more carefully what we most enjoy and to take one or two drives outside the city walls.

We are all well and Wee Wee [daughter, Louise] seems frightfully happy here. Every morning I send her with Mary to the Pincio and in the afternoon she goes out "sightseeing & shopping". That word reminds me that we have made a few small purchases and among them two Etruscan vases, antique; I have had them sent to you and enclosed you will find the original bill which might be required at the custom house. It will probably be six weeks before they arrive: I hope it will not prove a troublesome matter.

This is Palm Sunday and with her usual energy Louise has gone to St. Peter's for morning service (9:30) to be present at the "blessing of the palms." I thought it was a good chance to get off my letters, so have had coffee in my room and am at work.

We have given up Naples and go from here to Florence on the 19th and I now expect to go to London after all.

I have just read your letter once and can find nothing that requires my answer but you will be interested in hearing of my good fortune here; and please let Mr. Burlingame read the letter so that it will answer for both of you.

The day after my arrival I was looking at the registry book (the only time it has occurred to me to do so) and I saw that Mr. & Mrs. Humphry Ward were stopping at this very hotel. I soon sent up my card with the letter of introduction by Whittridge [Frederick W. Whitridge, Ward's American cousin, a New York City lawyer] and had my first sight of them. As the book was secured there was really no business to attend to but of course it was very pleasant to meet them. They were very cordial and Mrs. Ward expressed herself as much pleased that we were to have the book. She looks very much like her photographs and when at her best is very handsome. I was delighted to find Mr. Ward such an agreeable man. He impressed me as a very superior man and I think could do some capital work for our magazine sometime. We naturally saw them frequently and we all dined together once but they were only here five days, had never been here before and had many invitations, so we were not so much together as it might otherwise have happened. As for the new book it is only just begun and it certainly will not be out before next year. It will be about the length of the other (perhaps not so long) and in reply to my question as to whether it would be a philosophical novel Mrs. Ward said it would "certainly deal with the history of ideas." The title is chosen but she did not impart it to me, saying that it was "my copyright" and I did not press for it. There are many little glimpses of what it might be but I could not mention them all. One of the first questions she asked me was about McClure [S. S. McClure, founder of the McClure Syndicate and, later, *McClure's Magazine*] who made a dead set for her in London. He got nothing but a child's story which had been published before and in connection with which she had sent a letter to the editor of the paper which may publish it. McClure proposed that her next book should have St. Paul [as] one of its principal characters and in response to some exclamation from her, said: "but really you know he was a very great man."

I inquired for Burlingame about the end article. She intends to furnish it but finds it difficult to hit upon a suitable subject. She tried very hard to get out of it but I told her we really could not let her off and tried to make it seem less formidable to her. She says that she writes with great difficulty and that even such an article is a great labor for her. I think she is oppressed with the idea of the criticism her new book must meet. She is not without some consciousness of her importance but for the most part is free from all affectations and very charming. She was thinking on making her article one showing a relation between St. Francis of Assisi and Buddha but found it would require considerable study. I told her we should be perfectly satisfied with a simple subject.

As for Mr. Ward there are two items of interest 1st He may prepare the authorised biography of John Bright (this must not be spoken of to anyone). In such a case Cassell [English publisher] would publish and would very likely want America but he said if the way was open for us he would remember my interest in it. 2nd He inquired casually how we should like for the Magazine an article on Christie's (I think I have not spelt it correctly and you will know what I mean—the great London auction place for art objects etc) with illustrations by "his friend" Harry Furness [Harry Furniss]. It was suggested to him by Theodore Child's article on the Hotel Drouet. I replied favorably but nothing would very likely come of it, unless Burlingame should think it worth while to write him about it or let me know that he wants it, in which case I should speak of it again to him when in London. I suppose he would take it up historically and in a descriptive way and it seemed to me attractive, particularly with illustrations by Furness. But more than anything I was impressed that Mr. Ward would make a good thing out of anything he undertook.

I am now expecting the May number. The April "Book Buyer" reached me last week. Tell Morse [Edwin W. Morse, editor of *The Book Buyer*, Scribners' book trade journal] I thought it a particularly good one and that I gave it to Mrs. Ward to read the letter from Arlo Bates [about authors selling out]. It was rather strong medicine but I thought it could do no harm, as it was signed and in the main was perfectly true.

This letter is only four pages but please count the words and you will give me a long credit mark.

My very best regards to Burlingame (How are you getting on Mr. B.?), Brownell, John, Fred, Doubleday and all at home.

Yours ever
Charles

Coded telegram sent by CS II from Cairo, Egypt, to AHS at Scribners ("Halcanero"). Arthur has penciled his deciphering above the words.

Letters from Lemuel Bangs, the firm's English representative, written to the New York City office after CS II had sailed, elaborated on the complexities that had developed in the contract negotiations for Ward's next novel. No agreement could be reached, and Scribners never published any of her fiction in book form. Humphry Ward's illustrated article on Christie's appeared in the December 1890 issue of Scribner's Magazine. Of the men mentioned at the end, W. C. Brownell was book editor and literary adviser, and Frank Nelson Doubleday had become business manager of Scribner's Magazine.

• 1896

This year CS II and his wife left their children home when they went abroad—22 January through 17 May: Gibraltar, Italy, Egypt, Corfu, Greece, Constantinople, Vienna (via the Orient Express), Germany, Paris, and Le Havre.

M'ch 17th [1896]

Dear Charles:

Since I last wrote I have received your cable of the 4th and your letter of Feb'y 22d both from Cairo and also your letter to Doubleday. I am de-lighted that your first impressions of Cairo were so favorable and hope that you enjoyed your stay there. In your route you seem to stick closely to your original plans though I thought that you might conclude to stay longer in Egypt. This morning I cabled you at Athens that we were all well and trust that this reached you. I returned Sunday from my run down South and found the children in fine shape. I dined with Louise [CS II's daughter] and they gave me a great reception, each having a present for me—it happening to be my birthday—Charlie [CS II's son] a fine photograph of himself framed and Louise a pencil. They keep remarkably well and contented. By the way the photographs taken before you left are very good. The ones of you the best that you ever had.

I had a delightful week South with Doubleday, we bicycled, swam in the ocean etc and now and then talked about business. On my return I was greatly impressed with the hard and good work that most of our men are doing. I think that we must be doing well in the miscellaneous business, and it is evident that that is the opinion of others. We have an unusually popular lot of Spring books, and have been able by getting up early announcements & early samples to place them well in advance. The Hope, Burnett, Field & Davis are all successes, and we are putting all the force we can into the Commentary & Library, with I hope good results. I think that I anticipated your request by sending the slips of our publication slips so far.

Brewer after a good deal of hesitation and a ten day's sickness with his eyes finally told me today that he had decided to leave us. I have come to the conclusion that this will be as well in the end as it gives us a chance to develop the other men & Brewer's vacilation rather tired me. I think that we should use Randolph more, possibly in Philadelphia and other near places, though I have nothing definite yet to suggest. Dingman is of course our great weakness in this time.

Dillingham [Charles T. Dillingham, a New York City book-jobbing company] is in trouble again and yesterday I attended a meeting of a dozen of his largest creditors to consider what had best be done. He owes us $4000. Two weeks ago he owed us twice that but I was a good deal worried and sent Gantert down, who bought about $4000 worth of stock, all such as we can use and at favorable prices. I think that his business will be wound up in some way and we should get at least 25¢, possibly 50¢ on the dollar. It is bad, but for the last six weeks we have been trying to squeeze all the money we could out of him and two or three others are in deeper still. I fear we must also shut down on Merriam soon and this leaves the jobbing business in New York in bad shape.

We are having one [of] our periodic hard times in keeping our work at Trow's [Trow Printing and Bookbinding Co.] up to the standard of quality, especially in the printing. This is aggravating when one takes such pains with the paper and binding and I have insisted in several instances in making reductions in their charges hoping that this will have a good effect in making them brace.

There have been a number of applications for the dramatizing of "Lady of Quality" [by Frances Hodgson Burnett] but I have not attempted to step in here in any way, though possibly something could be done if it were not for the trouble.

North [Ernest Dressel North, Scribner rare books employee] went to Washington for a week with some fine books (I stopped there for an hour or two to see him on my way through—at the Shoreham) and sold a little over $4000. The only weakness was that it was nearly all to one party—Mrs. Senator Hurst—showing what a gam-

ble it is. In a couple of weeks he is going to Philadelphia. I firmly believe in our pushing out in these directions. Mr. Smith [Henry L. Smith, head of Scribners' rare books business] last Saturday sold a bill of nearly $8000 to Mr. Borden of Fall River including the MS. of Catriona [alternative title of Robert Louis Stevenson's *David Balfour*] at $1300. A week or two before he sold him the first editions of Ainsworth & Cooper which you will doubtless remember. There is nothing important in the Bangs correspondence though a number of smaller matters come up now and then. Doubleday I think keeps you informed about what is doing with him, and the only unfortunate item there is the loss of Harold Ives, whom we could not hold. We have our eyes on another man, but it will be difficult to fill his place. Altogether, I hope that you will conclude that we are getting along in fairly good shape and personally I keep very well. "The Tragic Idyll" is the Bourget which we have and Brownell is just reading it.

Carter [Carter FitzHugh, brother-in-law] left this afternoon after being here a few days and he reports Isabelle [younger sister of CS II and AHS] very much stronger and better. You have been fortunate in missing the last month or six weeks of bad weather here which has been unusually severe and I hope that you and Louise are both keeping well. It is a great pleasure to hear from you, and I fear that some of my letters to you have been delayed by reaching places after you had left. I have tried to write you every other [week?] and I think that I have with possibly one exception done so. With much love

Yours
Arthur

The "Hope, Burnett, Field & Davis" successes were Anthony Hope's Comedies of Courtship, *Frances Hodgson Burnett's* A Lady of Quality, *Eugene Field's* The House *and* The Love Affairs of a Bibliomaniac *(or perhaps the Sabine Edition of* The Writings in Prose and Verse of Eugene Field)*, and* Cinderella and Other Stories *by Richard Harding Davis. Burnett's book became the #2 best-seller of 1896.*

March 24th [1896]

Dear Charles:

Since writing you a week ago I have your letter of March 1st & 5th and your cable from Corfu to which I replied that we were all well etc. After today I shall address letters to you at Paris. I am so delighted that you enjoyed Cairo for you will remember that I could not enthuse you and Louise

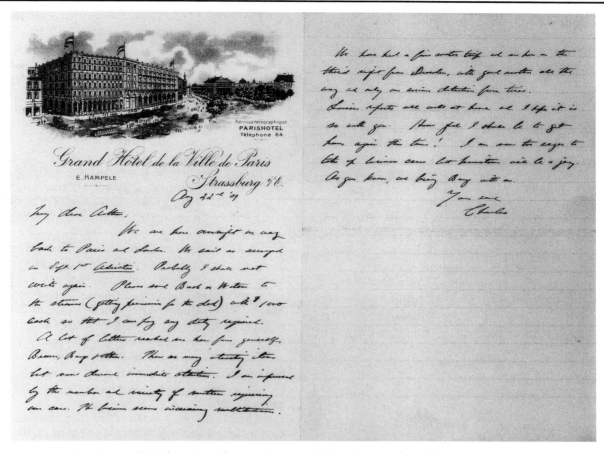

Writing to AHS from Strasbourg, France, CS II observes that "The business seems increasing multitudinous."

over the place before you left home though I felt sure that you would enjoy it when you reached there. The quarantine was unfortunate, and I infer from your letters and cable that you have been able to reach Athens by your round about route. I wonder whether you found the Austrian-Lloyd boat as uncomfortable as I did. At Athens you will have received my cable sent there a few days before the one sent to you at Corfu.

The children are still in as fine shape as possible, and I am sure you need not feel worried about them. I enjoy stopping in to see them and reading the letters from you and Louise. We have also heard of you several times indirectly—from Mrs. Donald S. Mitchell who was at the office a day or two since, from Mr. Brownell through the Hales and from George Parsons Lathrop through his brother. Of course innumerable friends enquire after you but I have not undertaken to report these.

Doubleday and Burlingame have I believe both written you by this or the last mail so I fear you will have your fill of business news, but there

is one matter I want to report even though there is nothing definite yet. From several sources we learned that Stone & Kimball [Chicago publisher] were hard up, the elder Mr. Stone is tired putting up the money, perhaps is a little short himself, and there were indications that they might be willing to part with their Stevenson [Robert Louis Stevenson] rights. We ascertained first that they had made the following arrangements

Vailima Letters $2500 advance on a 20% royalty
Weir of Hermiston $3500 for all Am. Book rights
St. Ives $6000 " " " " "

and today I had a talk with Kimball at their branch office which they have taken a couple of blocks below us. Of course he claimed that he had been offered big bonuses etc and was willing to possibly sell only for the sake of going into other new enterprises. Finally I proposed that we would be willing to assume all their contracts (provided they proved on examination to be in satisfactory shape) including Ebb Tide which they own, Amateur Emigrant on which they pay a royalty of 10 or 15% and the one play which of course does not amount to much and give them a bonus of $1000. This would include taking plates and stock at cost and paying them such of the advance on the V. Letters as the royalty on their copies sold did not meet. The prices for the Weir & St. Ives seem very high at this time now that the Stevenson boom has a little subsided, but it does seem to me that the whole plant received for all time would be most valuable to us. No one else is likely to pay as much (MacMillans have declined) so I think that we can afford to stand awhile on the above, though it might be desirable to close at a slight advance should we be able to do so. I wish that you were here to manage it, but shall do the best I can. Advice I find conflicting and unsatisfactory. It is even possible that nothing may come of this but it is an interesting lead.

We shall get out of the Dillingham matter much better than I expected, receiving probably 75¢. Baker & Taylor have purchased his stock and he is going out of business. Merriam I think is going to pay all right.

Smith has made another fine sale to Borden, over $17,000., between $3000 & $4000 of this being our own stock and balance, stock (a $10000 1st of Dickens, a $4000 Thackeray and a Burns $800) borrowed from Dodd, Mead on which we make a commission of 15%. There is a possibility of still further sales here where we can secure the stock.

—

Nothing further has been heard from E. E. Hale [Edward Everett Hale] after his having written that Roberts claimed rights which would prevent such an arrangement as we proposed and which he would look into.

—

Van Dyke [Henry Van Dyke] is going to take his Yale Lectures to an English house, presumably MacMillans, which I think shows a small and vain streak in him. I am very keenly disappointed and kicked hard, but he had made up his mind though he promised the book to us a little while before.

I am glad you wrote to Allston [W. Allston Flagg, brother-in-law] about the will. He telephoned me and I sent him down all the matter I had on the subject. Of course you have heard of his boy—the greatest in the U.S.

There is one other payment we were obliged to make, a $1000 for your ten shares in the Golf Club.

Jurgensen [?] is here and wants to sell the Tissot [James Jacques Joseph Tissot] illustrations, but there does not seem to be anything in them for me. Business is very good with us though generally reported as poor. With love to Louise

Yours
Arthur

[Vienna] April 8th 1896

Dear Arthur:

Here we are at last! Having arrived very early this morning in a snow storm. The first thing we did was to send for our letters and I am quite excited and confused by their number and interest.

Your telegram of the 2nd was here and I at once replied. So far as I can discover all letters on both sides have been received but of course we were without letters since the receipt of yours of March 3rd whereas here we have those of the 17th & 24th. It is delightful to hear that the children keep so well; they are being so well treated by you all that we fear they will be quite spoiled by the time we return. A telegram from Allston & a letter were also here and we have cabled our congratulations.

My last letter was just before leaving Athens. The sail to Constantinople takes two nights and a day and was made very comfortably though not in the best of weather. We were a little early for Constantinople but I enjoyed it very much more than I expected. It was all so interesting and made more so by the feeling that it could not continue much longer. It seems so uncivilized. We saw the Sultan, Prince Ferdinand of Bulgaria, and many mosques, markets, walls, bazaars, etc. It was rather a long ride here two nights and a day but a very excellent train for Europe & through an interesting and in many places beautiful country. We did not stop at Buda-Pesth [Budapest] for it would have involved getting off in the middle of the night and we arrived here not unfatigued. I hope we shall have better weather here. We plan to remain five or six days and then to Paris by way of Munich, Nuremburg & perhaps one or two other places. I am ready to go straight home but Louise thinks it best not to hurry and as she wants to do some dress-making in Paris we shall probably not get off until the steamer of the 9th. I will cable on our arrival in Paris before the last of the month and let you know the boat. Tell Burlingame (for I may not reply to his interesting letters today) that we shall be delighted to bring his daughter home. We shall write to her at once and arrange it all right—to give himself no uneasiness about it for it will only be a pleasure to us.

As for business I hardly know what to write. There have been so many publications since my departure and so many important transactions that I feel quite out of the running. I only wonder how you have stood it all. For goodness sake be careful and don't worry, for nothing really serious can happen in any event and a little more or less success cannot greatly matter. There are so many details that I hardly know which to touch upon. The Stone and Kimball matter was very curious; it will be very funny if the books came to us and all their fuss has accomplished nothing but worry both firms. There is not a word of advice to add to what you write. Your offer was reasonable and their promises to Stevenson were so large that it should suffice. It is enough; I should not object to your going higher if necessary. I cannot think any other good firm would bid high for this tail end of Stevenson's works but the mean part of it is that one cannot be sure. Whatever the outcome is I shall be satisfied and certain that you have done for the best. I know I should be anxious about the decision if I had to make it and it is just those infernal doubtful things that worry the life out of a fellow.

I suppose the Dillingham failure was to be expected and we got off cheap for the total amount. If we get 50% or 60% it will be large. I am very sorry for Dillingham who was a good fellow and I hardly know what he can do but hope he knows of some position in which he can earn a good living.

Brewer's years of vacilation seem at last to have come to an end. I confess I thought he would come down on the other side [of] the fence but we did well in keeping him so long. He served us well and I hope he will be thoroughly successful in his new business. He leaves with the best of feeling on both sides and I hope we shall be of mutual assistance in the future. Some one else must be found. It is not easy but a way can be found to cover the territory. Walter is a thoroughly good man. That was clever of you to buy so much from Dillingham at the last moment. Dingman and his salary are a terrible drain; it is funny he cannot see the situation in the least. I hope it will be placed to our credit somewhere for I have not the courage to get rid of him though I have the courage to cut his salary in two if it was really necessary.

—

I shall think application for dramatic rights of Mrs. Burnett's book might be sent to her by Brownell if I am right in supposing or rather in my recollection that we did not buy all rights but pay a royalty on copies sold. If she wants us to assist her perhaps we can but most of such applications never pan out. If there should by chance be a genuine one with money behind it the affair would be much simpler—if the man really wanted the rights.

—

What a lot of publications I shall have to read? The Spring list is most popular and I am glad to hear the important books are not disappointing and that the sales keep well up. Between all we are doing downstairs in manufacturing and the elements of the Magazine and Subscription Departments I fear the amount of cash required will be very great but I hope the most painful squeeze will not come until after my return.

Letters from Burlingame (largely about Kipling still in doubt) and from Doubleday about Subscription statement shall be answered separately as soon as possible.

—

There is nothing in that Tissot for us. I looked it up a little before I left. It has been hawked all over London.

—

I hope I may see Bangs in Paris. Sometimes it seems that I should go to London for there is always good business to be done there but it is so fatiguing that I have given up the idea.

I see no American newspaper news of any importance but the items you enclose were of special interest to me.

Give my best regards to all the friends at 153—Brownell, Marvin, Smith & Fred.

Yours ever
Charles Scribner

Scribners had moved into its own, new Beaux Arts building at 153-155 Fifth Avenue, designed by architect Ernest Flagg, in May 1894.

[Nuremberg] April 17th '96

Dear Arthur:

Last night was a most exciting time for us when we arrived here where letters up to April 3rd had been forwarded. There was a fine lot and all good news—letters from you and the children, Burlingame, Doubleday, Jaccaci [August F. Jaccaci, art director of *Scribner's Magazine*] & others.

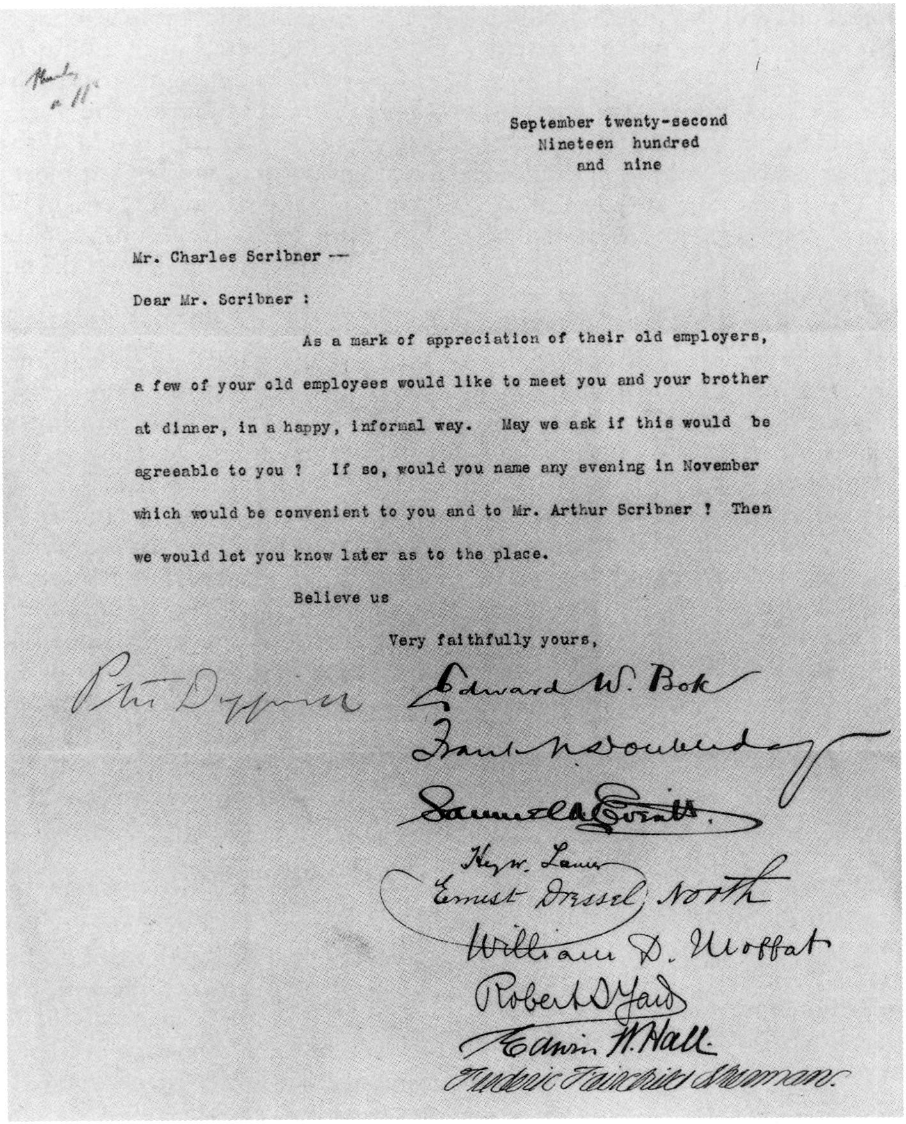

September twenty-second
Nineteen hundred
and nine

Mr. Charles Scribner ––

Dear Mr. Scribner :

As a mark of appreciation of their old employers, a few of your old employees would like to meet you and your brother at dinner, in a happy, informal way. May we ask if this would be agreeable to you ? If so, would you name any evening in November which would be convenient to you and to Mr. Arthur Scribner ? Then we would let you know later as to the place.

Believe us

Very faithfully yours,

Pitts Duffield
Edward W. Bok
Frank N Doubleday
Samuel A. Everitt
Hy. W. Lanier
Ernest Dressel North
William D. Moffat
Robert S. Yard
Edwin W. Hall
Frederic Fairchild Sherman

Letter from former Scribner employees inviting CS II and AHS to an informal dinner. Most of these employees became further distinguished in publishing and literary careers:

Edward W. Bok (1863–1930), best-selling author, editor in chief (1889–1919) of the Ladies' Home Journal

Frank Nelson Doubleday (1862–1934), founder of the publishing firm bearing his name

Samuel Alexander Everitt (1871?–1953), junior partner in Doubleday's firm (1900–1930), becoming treasurer and executive vice president

Henry Wysham Lanier (1873–1958), author, editor

Ernest Dressel North (born 1858), antiquarian and bookseller, author, and literary editor of The Christian Advocate *for twenty years*

William D. Moffat (1866–1946), cofounder and president (1905–1922) of Moffat, Yard & Co., publishers

Robert Sterling Yard (1861–1945), cofounder and editor in chief (1905–1911) of Moffat, Yard & Co., publishers; organizer and general secretary (1919–1934) of the National Parks Association

Frederic Fairchild Sherman (1874–1940), editor and publisher (1913–1940) of Art in America

Pitts Duffield (1869–1938), president (1905–1918) of Duffield & Co., publishers

I'm particularly delighted by the successful termination of the Stevenson purchase; we have now all the works of a great classic and many of them protected—they alone should for many years be no inconsiderable nucleus for a publishing firm. This is the kind of stock which in the care of the N.E. [New England] poets made H.M.&Co. [Houghton, Mifflin & Co., Boston publisher] such an important house. It is certainly better to hold back "Vailima Table Talk" until we see just how matters stand with respect to the wishes of all concerned. Colvin [Sir Sidney Colvin, British Museum curator friend of Stevenson, editor of his *Vailima Letters*] has been a good friend and I should go very far to satisfy him.

The amount of business you are doing seems quite unprecedented with us; it is most encouraging. The Burnett success is very gratifying; I have not read the story and feared it might not catch hold of the public and our advance prove too large. The management of travellers is most judicious and well arranged and I believe we are really better off than ever before.

"Sentimental Tommy" [by J. M. Barrie] will prove another great leader and a good novel will come from Stockton [Frank R. Stockton] in the Fall.

Don't hurry about the stock book; you are attending to what is more important and the statement will come along in time.

The Canadian question is a troublesome one for our rights always seem indefinite but there should be no great hurry until we see just where we stand. I can't see why our regular edition will not satisfy them. I wonder what Harpers did with "Trilby"?

That was great news about the will. Louise goes to sleep with the words "abundant and exhaustless" upon her lips. It was costly but we shall get lots of comfort for our money.

There is nothing much to write about our trip. Munich is a beautiful city and we enjoyed it greatly in spite of rain every day. This is our first clear day in two weeks.

I saw an item in the "Herald" that Williams was in Paris and have a telegram from him in reply to a letter of inquiry. It is possible I may catch him there but it is doubtful.

I remember now that "Bride from the Bush" [by E. W. Hornung] only made one volume. (In the book case in the basement I think with the key in the left hand drawer of the library desk.) But it is doubtful if the new story made enough of a hit to follow it with the old one. If you happen to see Stockton he may have a novelette among his

newspaper publications somewhere. I suppose we could get a collection from Octave Thanet.

The letters from the store are all so kind that I feel quite humble. I really don't see why you should all value my help so much for it seems very feeble to me. But is delightful to work with you all and I appreciate it.

We arrive in Paris next week and you will probably have a cable before this letter.

> Yours affectionately
> Charles

P.S.

I will write to Doubleday about Sub. matters.

• 1898

CS II and his wife went abroad on 15 March and arrived back on 14 May, after two months in England.

April 1ˢᵗ 1898

My dear Charles:

I was very glad to receive your letter and all were interested to know that you were well and had had a comfortable voyage. I dined at No 12 [12 East Thirty-eighth Street, CS II's home] last night and the children are in good shape, both looking forward to going to see Buffalo Bill [William Frederick Cody, the frontiersman turned showman and his famed Wild West show] tomorrow, and Louise planning to do a lot of riding during her vacation. Charlie seems to spend a large part of his time writing to you and Louise.

Emma [older sister of the brothers] is here now staying at Uncle Clinton's. Yesterday she went to Doll's Ferry to see the school to which she expects to send Fay and today she has gone to Princeton and Lawrenceville where Cranston is to be next Fall.

Business continues about the same, nothing very great but every day pretty well filled.

A representative of Roberts Bros. [Boston publisher] called the other day saying that they wanted to sell their business and asking whether we cared to make an offer. Of course we do not, but if any one or two items occur to you as desirable it might be possible to secure them alone. I do not think of anything special. . . .

I also enclose a lot of Marsac [*The Sprightly Romance of Marsac* by Molly Eliot Seawell] matter which I thought perhaps should be forwarded to you, and without causing much delay.

The Frothingham contract [Arthur L. Frothingham, editor of the *Albums to Illustrate the History of Art* series] has come to hand signed without any other word, and also the Richard Mansfield contract [for his dramatization of Robert Louis Stevenson's *St. Ives*].

Nichols is just starting back from San Francisco where he found matters better than we anticipated. Prof Clark who used to be with us is desirous of coming back, but I have not offered him any encouragement.

What would you think of Aesop's Fables as a book for Maxfield Parrish [popular American illustrator] to illustrate? Burlingame suggests it, and I think that it would be the best subject suggested so far for him, but I am not prepared to back very strongly our going into it.

Mrs. Stevenson [Fanny Van de Grift, wife of Robert Louis Stevenson] is here, and I have called on them, and expect to meet them at dinner at Burlingame's tonight. She seems to be content with everything, and Burlingame will no doubt write you fully.

A letter from Quiller Couch [Sir Arthur Quiller-Couch] says that the terms for his serial & book [*The Ship of Stars*] later are satisfactory and that he can send it very shortly.

Proofs of Mrs. Henry Norman's novel [Ménie Muriel Dowie's *The Crook of the Bough*] have just come. The terms I believe are understood in case we accept it, and we shall send a cable in a day or two. Brownell has read only a part but thinks rather well of it so far.

You see these are all details and none of them very important in themselves but as you know they are what fill up the time.

With love to you and Louise I am

Yours
Arthur

[London] April 13th '98

My dear Arthur:

We arrived here safely last evening and found your letter of the first awaiting us. As it was our latest word from home it was especially welcome. The children have been so good about writing and seem happy. There is a steamer in today and probably we shall have a letter in the morning.

We found Clarence & Mildred [Mitchell, cousins] here and are arranging to see something of one another. Clarence is better but not yet altogether well. And it seems that Mildred has had a very severe cold here and confined to the room for a week but is well now.

I fear I did not write you from Ventner [Ventnor, Isle of Wight], but I sent a line to Burlingame. We had particularly good weather there and Louise quite outdid me in coaching. We kept at it nearly every day for a week and I could tell you about every church and almost every tree on the island. It is really a beautiful restful place and (before) we had perfect weather—a thing difficult to get over here.

Today I called at Warnes [Frederick Warne, English publisher] about "Marsac". They have been careless and admit it but Miss Seawell need not be overexcited. I delivered her letter and they will write to her at once, directly. There seemed nothing for us to gain by attempting to regulate her affairs. Poor Stephen Townsend [Stephen Townesend, Frances Hodgson Burnett's secretary-agent] of Burnett fame is having an appalling time with her. I quoted terms for plates with illustrations at £35 and if they publish at all they will probably buy from us.

I also called upon Watt [A. P. Watt, English publisher]—the father was away but the son, whom I always liked, was there. We had a pleasant chat and I secured some information of value and sowed some seed which may ripen—about which I will tell you at leisure. There is no confusion about the payment of Kipling account and I merely told them that if anything was wrong in our letter or statement they might rely on receiving the account according to the agreement: so please actually refer to that document and let the money go accordingly. They are most appreciative of our success with the Kipling [Scribners' Outward Bound Edition of Rudyard Kipling's works] and very anxious to do more business with us.

—

I don't enthuse over "Aesop" for Parrish. It would have to be something more novel. Something will come along.

—

The Roberts announcement is important though there have been rumors before. I don't remember their list very thoroughly but know there are some good books among them. We do not want "Hammerton" [Philip Gilbert Hamerton] which may suggest itself. Some years ago I should have taken "H.H." [Helen Hunt Jackson] but not now except at a bargain. "Balzac" is the best I can think of but they would probably want a high price and there are other translations. It is a valuable "plant" but has already been well worked.

There is lots that could be done here by an energetic man. Coming two years in succession makes it very easy for I can take up everything where I left off last year. I had not realized the value of this.

I will write again in a few days.

Yours sincerely

Charles Scribner

Roberts Brothers was acquired by Little, Brown in June. The works of Louisa May Alcott alone were probably worth the investment, reputed to have been about $250,000. Maxfield Parrish's first illustrated book for Scribners did not appear until 1904: Eugene Field's Poems of Childhood.

• 1900

Arthur and his wife sailed from New York for Europe on 1 June and arrived back on 28 August.

July 29th 1900

Dear Arthur:

I was in town overnight and found your rooms [at the Century Association] very comfortable. Before going to business I write this short letter.

There are some matters of importance that have come up which I will briefly mention. The most important is the question of discount & prices to which I alluded before. Publishers & booksellers seem to think we should now take the initiative. There have been several conferences between Brett, Dodd, Appleton & myself and I have seen Houghton, Century, Putnam & Lippincott (Rideings). We are calling a general meeting for July 25th. What can be done is uncertain but the present plan is the most daring one yet suggested. It is to form an Association & bind ourselves only to sell to those who maintain the retail price of copyrighted books for 18 months. I will send you a rough scheme of what is proposed. I am sorry to get in so deep during your absence but there could be no holding back, and if the action was general I have felt sure it would be satisfactory to you even if you did not thoroughly approve the plan. I should be glad of your views. . . .

Yours ever

Charles Scribner

At the 25 July meeting the publishers agreed to form their own organization, the American Publishers' Association. Bylaws were soon drawn up, and CS II was elected president. Their purpose was to stop the steep discounting of copyrighted books by department stores, such as R. H. Macy in New York City, which was injurious to both publishers and booksellers. Several lawsuits against Macy's were filed on behalf of the new association; thirteen years of litigation ensued. On 1 December 1913 the Supreme Court ruled that copyright was not exempt from the Sherman Anti-Trust Law against monopoly. Though stores could continue to charge any price they wanted for books they sold, the "Macy cases" (as they were called) helped further book trade solidarity and did accomplish, by publicizing the problem and its associated ill will, an end to "rampant" price cutting.

• 1902

CS II and his wife spent April and most of May in England and France.

Apl 15th [1902]

My dear Charles:

I hope that you have had a pleasant voyage and by next mail we are expecting to hear something of it.

I intended to write to you last Friday, but the day was so crowded that I did not have the opportunity. I have naturally been very busy but matters have been moving along pretty well. Offord is out of the office a large part of the day investigating various presses and buildings, and though there is nothing definite to report yet he is, I feel sure, making decided progress. This has brought me face to face with the necessity of securing someone to take up his work here. Marvin as you know is not an easy man to arrange such a matter with, but I have succeeded in pleasing him and in securing, I think, a capital man—Albert S. Davis. He is a Yale graduate of about '96, has been with Macmillan, the Winthrop Press, the American Lithographic Co. and recently in a printing experiment of his own. I have agreed to pay him $40 (Offord has been receiving $43) more than I like, but I believe that he will prove to be a decided acquisition, and we cannot afford to have that Department weakened. You may remember having seen him before you secured Emory.

—

Pinker [James B. Pinker, literary agent of Henry James] is over here with James and other material. I have arranged for two future (the next) James novels on the same terms as the present one [*The Sacred Fount*]—£200 advance on 20%—and a volume of stories for £100 advance on 20%. He wanted a much larger advance but I declined to increase what we were doing. Brownell endorsed strongly a Barry Pain [English humorist] book, and we have also made an offer for that, £50 advance on a 15% royalty with £25 for electros of illustrations. This is less than he wanted and he has cabled the offer to the English publisher Grant Richards.

A book by Wells [H. G. Wells] we did not make any offer for.

—

I enclose copy of an interesting note from Grant [Robert Grant], to whom I have written explaining your absence, but cordially offering to do anything possible if he wishes any action before your return. I think that he will doubtless let the matter rest for the present.

I am trying to make some progress each day or two with the Fall books, and am also pushing the sets for the Subscription & Mag. Subscription Depts.

—

There have been two meetings of the Publishers' Association, but as there has been nothing vital and as I understand that Emory keeps you posted I will not go into this. Wanamaker is still in line.

—

They have doubtless written you from home about the unfortunate and it seems most unprovoked arrest of your coachman, and the consequences. I telephoned Col. Crane [lawyer] and sent the coachman down to see him, and as I expect to go down town tomorrow on another errand I will stop in and see if he thinks that anything can be done.

—

I saw Louise and Charlie yesterday [CS II's children] and they were both very well. With much love to Louise and yourself

Yours
Arthur

Apl 22^d [1902]

My dear Charles:

I was glad to hear that you had a pleasant voyage, and you are settled all right in London. Matters keep moving along here and I enclose copies of a couple of letters. The one shows the Grant matter can safely wait, and the other as you will see is from London and I thought that perhaps you would prefer to attend to it either yourself or through Bangs on the spot. If you wish, I can answer it from here, and the delay will not be vital. It does not look to me very promising, at least for more than the inspection [importation?] of a small quantity.

You will doubtless of heard of the death of Mr. Stockton [Frank R. Stockton, popular Scribner author], which was very sudden, some of us having known of his illness. I at once telegraphed to Mrs. Stockton and expect to go to the funeral on Thursday. In my telegram I stated that you were in London, so that the absence of any word from you would be explained.

—

In the most important business matter, that of printing the Magazine, we have taken definite steps having rented quarters. Offord is writing you himself explaining the advantages of the building and the necessity of decision. At first I was not satisfied with the location, but all up town districts were pretty thoroughly canvassed without success. I went to two buildings before I saw this one, which I believe to be an exceptional opportunity. I was favorably impressed with Mr. Hallenbeck, who is all right financially and does a very successful business. He will be in a position to help us at any time we may be overcrowded with work. We shall also have to decide within a few days concerning one or two of the larger presses. Offord is working carefully and keeping his head.

—

I asked Watson [Robert S. Watson] to forward to you a letter about Quiller Couch's [Sir Arthur Quiller-Couch] book of stories and I have done nothing about this.

—

Col Crane is looking up the matter, whether any damages can be secured for the loss of your horse, but there is nothing definite to report.

—

Helen and I went to Tuxedo [Tuxedo Park, New York] for the day Sunday, to have a look at the house, which we had rented, and were very much pleased with it. We expect to go out there early in May. With love to Louise

Yours
Arthur

The Scribner Press, as it was called, began operation in July on Pearl Street in New York City. Primarily created to take over the printing of Scribner's Magazine, the press soon began printing the firm's books as well, the first title being F. Hopkinson Smith's The Fortunes of Oliver Horn *(29 August). Ultimately, the brothers decided to build their own book manufacturing plant: the Scribner Press Building at 311–319 West Forty-third Street, which opened in 1907.*

• 1906

CS II and his wife sailed from New York on 11 April for a two-month trip to Europe (London, Paris, and a motor trip through France). On the morning of 18 April a violent earthquake, followed by a widespread three-day fire, virtually destroyed San Francisco, where Scribners maintained a West Coast office.

April 27th 1906

Dear Charles:

I am glad to hear through George that Louise received a letter saying that you had had pleasant weather and that your voyage had been agreeable. We are all well here except Mr. Brownell who has not been to the office for a week.

We have had several sample pages for the James [the multi-volume New York Edition of *The Novels and Tales of Henry James*] and have finally worked out one which I think will be satisfactory, so in Mr. Brownell's absence I have written to James fully, sending him a sample and covering the manufacturing situation.

The disaster in San Francisco has been in every one's thoughts and, as you have seen, the responses in the way of subscriptions have been remarkable. A number of publishers have contributed $500. each through the Publishers' Association and we have accordingly done the same. Our own business loss will not be as great, I think, as might at first appear. Our manager Paul lives outside the city at Alameda and his house apparently has not been injured. We have received one telegram from him saying that he was trying to get into the city to ascertain the state of our office. I think there is not doubt that it was destroyed. According to the February statement we had out on the Pacific Coast in the subscription department about $100,000. but the great bulk of this is in the South or North, or the suburbs, and Mr. Dillingham [Edwin L. Dillingham] is sanguine (perhaps too sanguine) that we will lose very little in collections. As most of our orders are taken by regular men who can and will work in other places, there should not be any great loss in new business. In the wholesale department we have owed us less than $3000., the bulk of this being owed by The Emporium and Payot & Upham who should be good. The business last year from the 1st of May to the 1st

of January in San Francisco amounted to about $18,000. and of course we must expect a decided shrinkage here.

> There is no business message. You know all that I do. All we have to do is to make good sales <u>at a good profit</u> and keep our expenses from eating us up. Meanwhile we must work to perfect our business system of management.
>
> —CS II in a letter to AHS, 4 August 1904

The subscription department is still doing well in cash and Mr. Mix [J. Rowland Mix] reports conditions favorable with the Magazine; he says that the advertising in May is a little ahead both in pages and money. Yesterday we received an order for 2500 additional May Magazines from Oregon due presumably to the Curtis article [E. S. Curtis, "Vanishing Indian Tribes"]. The general business seems rather quiet.

We received an order from Bangs for 500 Wilson's JEFFERSON and I sent him early copies of the Kent and Hanks with quotations.

I enclose a letter from Methuen & Co, with a memorandum from Mr. Burlingame. I should not think that, in its present state at least, this interested us, but perhaps you would like to have Bangs attend to it.

I also enclose some pages from the PUBLISHERS' WEEKLY showing the satisfactory decision on the Merriam suit, and also an item regarding Bernard Shaw's suit with the Stones.

Doubleday telephoned yesterday saying that Reynolds had offered him Wells's new book with the statement that he already had an offer giving him $1000. advance. I told Doubleday that he was free to arrange for the book in so far as we are concerned and he evidently expects to publish it.

Davis [Richard Harding Davis] also telephoned saying that he had been approached by another house about the publication of one of his recent plays and suggesting that we make a volume of his two new plays together with MISS CIVILIZATION. I responded cordially and expect to see him within the next few days.

I hope that you found Bangs well and that you and Louise are having an enjoyable time in London. Mr. Brownell is in the worst shape that he has been in yet, and I do not see how he can pull up short of a complete change.

Yours

Arthur

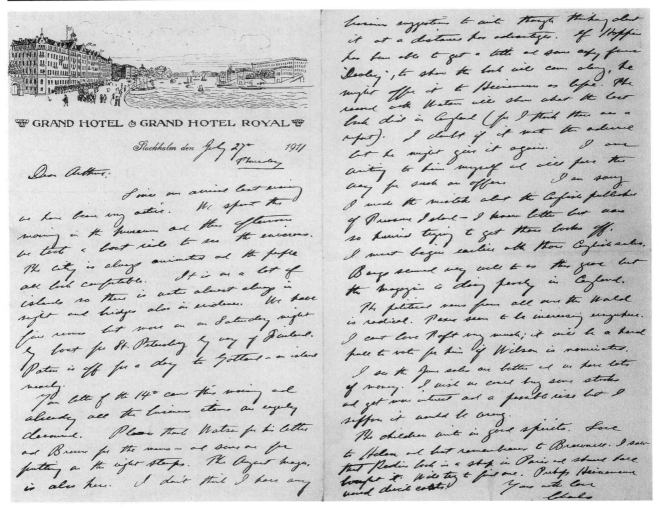

Letter to AHS from CS II, written from Stockholm, Sweden. After dealing with business matters, he notes that "The political news from all over the World is radical."

• 1911

Through July and August CS II and his wife traveled in Europe: Queenstown (Ireland), London, Paris, Hamburg, Copenhagen, Stockholm, Finland, Moscow, Vienna, Paris, London, Queenstown.

[Paris] July 21st 1911

Dear Arthur:

All our arrangements are made as we leave at noon for Hamburg, Copenhagen, Stockholm, Finland & so on. We had trouble about the maid's passport but Henri fixed it up. The Courier seems a good one. We have had hot weather but I like it.

I did not do much in London. I had one good night with Barrie [J. M. Barrie]. The book is only about 50,000 and is called "Peter Pan, the boy who would not grow up." But H&S [Hodder & Stoughton, English publisher] are going to hold back all particular announcements as they think the book will advertise itself. I arranged for duplicates of the twelve illustrations with title & cover design. The ms. is finished.

I was sorry to send the troublesome telegram about the Gibson [Charles Dana Gibson] but Lane [English publisher] would not buy with the present title and neither of us ever liked it. Chapin [Joseph Hawley Chapin, Scribner art editor] should be able to get another suggestion. Anything simply descriptive would be better.

I hope things go well with you. Burlingame dined with us in Paris and seemed in better condition. Love to all.

Yours ever
Charles

July 28, 1911

Dear Charles:

Since I wrote you I have the cable in regard to the title of Gibson's book and after corresponding with him we have arranged that the title should be changed to "OTHER PEOPLE" (with no date on the cover), which title I have cabled to Mr. Bangs. I also have a cable for 2000 Wharton's [Edith Wharton] "Ethan Frome" for Macmillan. Mrs. Wharton is now at Lenox and we are sending her today complete proof of the book, so that there should be no difficulty in having it printed in sufficient time for us to forward sheets well in advance of publication. Brownell has a letter from her to-day in which she says that the copy for "The Custom of the Country" will be ready in the early Winter and that she will sail at latest on September 7th. She hopes to see you before she sails, but will evidently just miss you.

I enclose copies of my letter to the Custom House Inspector and of a letter from Ordway. Nothing else transpired until to-day when the Inspector called with the current invoice and asked whether there was anything in it on which we paid royalty. There was not and I am of course watching each invoice as it comes in. He claimed that for the present, in the case of any item subject to royalty, we should make a note of it on the invoice, and I will do so, subject of course to objection if duty is levied on the royalty. He was pleasant and said that the other publishers were much worked up over this and were talking the matter up with the Secretary of the Treasury, though, according to him, the ultimate decision would rest with the Appraiser and perhaps the Customs Court. I have heard nothing from the other publishers, except the enclosed line from Putnam to which I have replied. The Inspector was surprised that these two were the only cases which we had. He could not be affected by argument, as he had made up his mind, and it must rest with those above him; and I think it will be some time before anthing is decided. I do not want to trouble you with all these papers but thought perhaps you would prefer to see them.

I also enclose a note from Fox [John Fox Jr.], in accordance with which I felt obliged to send him the $3000 additional.

Just after you left a long letter came from Mr. Beebe [William Beebe] in regard to the Monograph on Pheasants. I don't know what your attitude is toward this and it does not seem to me to require early decision. It is evidently a fine thing and I should favor arranging for it on a commission basis, though I realize that our system at present of keeping track of such items is very imperfect.

In your letter to Unwin [T. Fisher Unwin, English publisher] offering him Upper Yukon you directed him to turn over the material to Bangs in case he did not accept our offer. Instead of this he came back with an alternative offer 6d lower, so I asked him to turn the material over to Bangs and sent Bangs all the information necessary so that he would be in a position to offer it elsewhere in case Unwin did not yield.

I enclose some clippings from to-day's Sun in regard to the Tobacco 4s [bonds], but evidently there is no haste about this.

Judge Harlan writes that he was used by the heat and has not yet come to any decisions as to whether he will undertake his book, but we appear to be in the position to secure it if he does.

The wire partition [for Scribner cashier office] for Mann [Joseph McElroy Mann] has been completed and I enlarged it considerably from what Brown proposed, so I hope you will think it right as it now is. Mann is fairly content with it, though a little touchy.

I have worried some over the congestion in the composing room, but a number of items are clearing up now and I do not anticipate much further difficulty. Offord returned Monday in good spirits and will help all he can.

I have sent over a few items to Bangs and will send others as quickly as they materialise. The Fall list generally is making progress and on the whole is, I think, coming out very well.

Last Sunday we spent with Clarence, motoring over from Mount Kisco on Saturday, and had a delightful time. This change and the one down on Long Island quite rested me. I hope that you and Louise are both well and enjoying the trip. More copy as you doubtless know has been received from Mason [A. E. W. Mason], and I am looking forward to some word from you about the Barrie. The orders seem good and there are a good many Educational manufacturing items.

Yours
Arthur

Mann invented (some claim) the curveball while a student at Princeton (Class of 1876) and, after coming to Scribners, helped Arthur organize the firm's baseball teams.

[Vienna] Aug 14th 1911

My dear Arthur:

On arrival here the 12th I found your letter of July 28th awaiting me and I seem to have missed no letters. All the items of news are interesting and the various small matters seem to have come out satisfactorily. The change in title of the Gibson should enable Bangs to complete the order. I have letters here from Heinemann [William Heinemann, English publisher], who expresses interest in another "Dooley" and also in the Rodin book, and from Meredith. It now seems necessary to me to return to London; so I can attend to some of these questions, also the Barrie book. I don't like to return home without seeing Gertrude Abbey [wife of artist Edwin Abbey, who had just died]. Under all the circumstances it seems inconsiderate to do so.

I never gave any special encouragement about that Pheasant book further than expressing a willingness to consider it when the plan could be definitely presented. It seemed to be a worthy book with lots of money behind it but I could not see much market for it and our inability to manage accounts on manufacturing for such an enterprise as now organized must be considered; and I don't know that we could help them much or make anything without robbing them. I think it can wait.

The Tobacco 4s seem likely to cause some trouble but I don't see why we should lose anything.

The question of royalties on imports is one which I have thought much about. Ordway seems to state the law correctly and to interpret it exactly as the Custom House does and under his letter we should apparently pay duty on royalties in both our cases, for we do not claim to have them as a "gratuity or as compliment"—even in the Stevenson case; though our definite obligation in this last case is not so clear we do feel bound to pay the royalty. On the other hand the royalties are not paid "as the result" of "any understanding with the publishers" abroad. We have independent contracts with the authors and of course the English publisher knows this and that he sell to no one else. These legal questions all differ in particular cases. In my opinion now I should give all the information wanted by the Customs and make any payments demanded, simply making such a protest as would entitle us to recover if any decision went our way. I would not go to much further expense and would not join any others to contest the point. Ordway states the case against us and though he seems to me to overlook certain points, I would not pay money to try to convince anyone to a different opinion. What he states is perfectly true but he does not state our cases.

Don't bother to try to understand what I have written, for it has been more to relieve my own mind. The gist of it will be clear.

Tomorrow I go down the Danube with Paton [David Paton, old friend] to Buda-Pesth and return by rail the next afternoon—4 hours. Louise will stay here.

Then we motor to the French frontier; and then for Paris, London & home.

Burlingame seems to be in good shape again. I shall be glad to get home but not to take up all the business details.

Yours with love
Charles

Heinemann's request for "another 'Dooley'" was for another book by the Chicago journalist and humorist Finley Peter Dunne featuring his popular character Mr. Dooley, an Irish saloon keeper who in a thick brogue and with native humor criticizes and comments on current political and social events. Scribners had recently published Mr. Dooley Says . . . *(1910), the seventh in the series.*

• 1915

CS II and his wife vacationed during the month of March in White Sulphur Springs, West Virginia.

March 7th 1915

Dear Arthur:

This is a great place and was about right for the first four days since which time it has been snowing and the prospects for golf are not immediately promising. However, I am willing to loaf for a time and there is a very large covered way for walking and the baths seem worth while.

I have kept up with my letters or nearly so and have the business much in mind. Probably you read the surprising letter from Palmer. He seems thoroughly jealous and consequently wrongheaded.

Davis [Richard Harding Davis] has written saying that he must have some money and I have telegraphed that you would help him out—"do the needful". I don't know what he wants but think it nearer 2000 than 1000. He has always made good and can be trusted to do so again.

I replied to Robert Grant's letter that next Autumn was the time for his novel but that we should have now an outline of it for our advance announcements for which we were gathering information.

I have written Whigham of the Metropolitan about Reed's book [John Reed's *The War in East-*

ern Europe, illustrated by Boardman Robinson].
He wanted 25% after 5000 or suggested that such
a royalty would be fair as it had been offered by
others. I replied that we could not increase the
rate beyond 20 but would modify our first requirement that we have the right to use the illustrations without any payment—that we were willing to make moderate payment for such as we
used. I think it will come out all right. [Scribners
published it in 1916.]

The Forman [Justus Miles Forman] novel
came safely but I have not yet finished it. I notice
there is no novel by him among the 50 best-sellers
of last year, as published by the Publishers'
Weekly and I wonder whether he issued any last year. The
same inquiry is on my mind regarding Herrick
[Robert Herrick] who is absent from the list. We
need more good sellers. I thought Morris [Gouver-
neur Morris] should be on it but we have only Galsworthy & Mason [A. E. W. Mason]. Our second
flight does not seem yet to make good.

Mix has written me a good letter and I shall
keep on writing to him. We should do better with
the magazine next year, unless advt. collapses,
but it will require constant attention. Mix is better but a little slow yet. I think the two year Subscription proposition most desirable.

The sales for Feb. and the estimate of profit
are neither very encouraging. Under present volume of business and for efficient work done our
salary list of over $14,000 is very high. If you can
suggest any reduction, please do so. Marvin & Mead
are of course unnecessary and the Burlingame-
Brownell combination expensive.

If Watson is there, please hand the enclosed
to him. If not, it will not cause you much trouble.

Our cash keeps strong—almost too much
so—but can hardly pay dividends out of surplus
alone.

That was a great piece of work done by Lord
[Edward Lord, head of Scribners' Educational
Department] in Va. and I hope you will express
personal appreciation of it. I think we must do
more for him—that it is about the only case
where an increase is demanded—not by him
but by the conditions. I think we pay him
$8000. What would you say to $10,000? He
has a 20,000 block of stock but it yielded almost nothing to him last year. I don't see how
we could fill his place.

Give Charlie my love and remember me to
"all inquiring friends".

Yours affectionately
Charles Scribner

*The Scribner best-sellers for 1914 mentioned by
CS II were John Galsworthy's* The Dark Flower
(#26 on the Publishers' Weekly *list) and A. E. W.
Mason's* The Witness for the Defence *(#34).*

March 13, 1915

Dear Charles:

I enclose two copies of the lease for portion
of the rear of the seventh floor with the people
who put the heating apparatus in this building.
We shall get the cheque for the first month's rent
as soon as we return one copy signed. You will remember this is the floor on which the German
Publication Society is, and if the balance of the
rear is rented at the same rate as this present lease
it would make the rental for the entire floor
$6,000; so that even with a considerable conces-
sion in rent on the balance of space the total will
not be so bad. The lease, you will see, runs for an
odd period so that it may expire at the same time
with the German Publication Society's lease.

I had yesterday afternoon your note of the
11th, and forwarded the inquiry to Fred Burlingame [lawyer].

I am here for only an hour or so this morning, as I am running out to the country for part of
the day. . . .

March 17, 1915

Dear Charles:

I forwarded the sheets of Cook's "Kaiser,
Krupp and Kultur" as I thought you might have a
personal interest in this and also that it might require early decision. Mr. Marling has, however, just
shown me a bill in the present invoice for 520/500,
so apparently Mr. Bangs made the purchase.

I enclose a letter from Murray about another
small item which I should think could be disposed
of here but shall wait to hear from you before doing anything.

I also enclose a letter from Mrs. Terhune
[Mary Virginia Terhune, a successful Scribner
author who wrote under the pen name "Marion
Harland," mother of Albert Payson Terhune,
well-known author of dog stories], and in response
to a telephone from her I called to see her. She has,
completed I understand, the manuscript of a new
novel, the scene of which is located in northern
New Jersey, and the story treats of the characters
there somewhat in the same manner as Mrs. Deland does her neighborhood in "Old Chester
Tales" and Mrs. Wilkins in her New England stories. It seemed to me a case where we would not
wish to request to see the manuscript unless, on
our knowledge of the circumstances, we should

MEMORANDUM, in duplicate, made this *sixth* day of April, 1912, between CHARLES SCRIBNER and ARTHUR H. SCRIBNER, WITNESSETH:

WHEREAS by deed dated March 15, 1912, Emma Flower Taylor conveyed to Charles Scribner and Arthur H. Scribner the premises known as Nos. 597 and 599 Fifth Avenue, Borough of Manhattan, City of New York, in consideration of the sum of Seven hundred and fifty thousand Dollars ($750,000) of which Four hundred thousand Dollars ($400,000) was paid by the execution and delivery to said Emma Flower Taylor of the joint and several bond of said Charles and Arthur H. Scribner in the sum of Four hundred thousand Dollars ($400,000); and

WHEREAS three-fifths of the purchase price for said premises was advanced by Charles Scribner and two-fifths by said Arthur H. Scribner,

NOW, THEREFORE, in consideration of the premises IT IS HEREBY UNDERSTOOD AND AGREED between the parties hereto, who hereby severally declare the facts so to be, that said property belongs to and is held by them in the following proportions: Three (3) equal undivided one-fifth parts thereof by Charles Scribner and two (2) equal undivided one-fifth parts thereof by Arthur H. Scribner, and that their liability under their bond aforesaid as between themselves is in the same proportion as their ownership in the said premises.

IN WITNESS WHEREOF the parties hereto have hereunto set their hands and seals the day and year first above written.

Agreement between CS II and AHS to a three-fifths and two-fifths division in ownership of their new property, 597–599 Fifth Avenue, future site of Charles Scribner's Sons

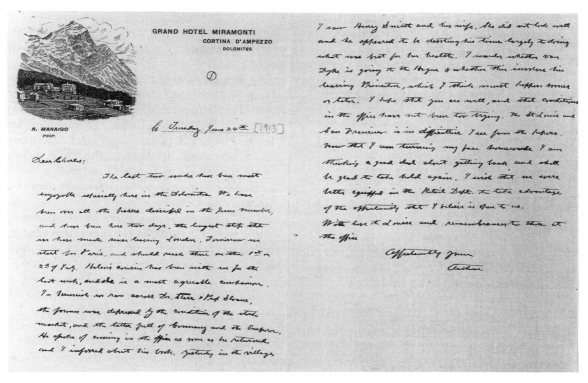

Writing to CS II from Cortina d'Ampezzo, Italy, AHS mentions Scribner author and friend Henry Van Dyke, who had recently been appointed U.S. ambassador to the Netherlands and Luxembourg. He wishes that "we were better equipped in the Retail Dept. to take advantage of the opportunity that I believe is open to us."

think it likely that we would want to publish it; so I avoided a direct statement, taking a little time for consideration with an opportunity to consult you. Will you let me know what you think it desirable to do? She of course talks very entertainingly, but I fear a characteristic novel by her in our hands now would seem old-fashioned—like going back some years—as at her age [84] she is not likely certainly to do anything better than she has already done. At the same time, some of her novels in the past have of course been popular and have had a considerable sale.

Mr. Brownell's report of Foreman's novel—with which I understand Perkins [Maxwell Perkins] substantially agrees—is not encouraging and I should think it better not to undertake it, writing him in the vein that we feared that under present conditions the probable sale in our hands was not likely to justify the exploitation which he would expect and that we feared the result would be disappointing to him. If you would telegraph me your advice on this I would be obliged, for from something Davis said yesterday afternoon I think an early letter would be desirable.

Mr. Fullerton [W. Morton Fullerton] called just before sailing and said that he had signed a contract with Little, Brown & Company for a book to follow the one [new, revised edition of *The Problems of Power*] he is now preparing for us. He made light of it—being simply some magazine articles collected together—but he stated definitely, and it seemed to me he took pains to do so, that he had signed a contract; so I made no comment but I fear you may be disappointed.

With reference to the Sub. Dept. it seems to me something definite was accomplished last year. Though the final estimated profit was less than the monthly figures indicated that is not the whole story. The alarming element of unexpected shrinkage in accounts which particularly worried me and to which I gave special attention was practically eliminated, the difference being due almost entirely to a definite error which could be located. This should have been detected at once, as you write, by the account being proved as indeed I supposed was being done, and which I did arrange unless I am misinformed as soon as the error was finally discovered. In a bad year with about $100,000 less business the downward tendency was checked and the profit increased from $4000 to $18,000. I will look further into some of the other questions.

Yours
Arthur

WHITE SULPHUR SPRINGS W VA MARCH 19 1915
ARTHUR H SCRIBNER
   597 FIFTH AVE NYC
ADVISE DECLINE FORMAN AND TERHUNE.
       CHAS SCRIBNER
          853 PM

A note is penciled on the telegram: "Both declined on receipt of telegram AHS."

Though Scribners turned down Terhune's novel, A Long Lane, *it did publish her next and last work,* The Carringtons of High Hill *(1919).*

March 29th [1915]

Dear Arthur:

We are having fine weather and greatly enjoying it.

I write particularly to say that there is a special train from here now on Sunday night and I have arranged for accommodation. You may therefore look for me some time next Monday.

Nothing new seems to have happened. One or two more boats have been torpedoed but I doubt whether we are any nearer war.

Yours affectionately
Charles

P.S.

Please tell Watson not to send any mail after Friday night

•1918

CS II and his wife vacationed for about six weeks during the summer in Asheville, North Carolina. The couple hoped to have an opportunity to see their son, who was stationed with his regiment in Jacksonville, Florida.

June 23rd 1918

Dear Arthur:

We arrived very comfortably yesterday in time for luncheon. This is a fine hotel and wonderfully well run. The food is particularly good. The situation grand and the air very bracing—almost too much so thus far. It is far from warm and I wore an overcoat this morning riding to church in a trolley. That seems to be the trouble this year: it is constantly chilly.

It must be that both Louise and I will pick up here. I eat well, digest well and sleep well but am infernally weak and nervously run down with this cold and cough.

Louise [daughter] telephoned us last night from Spartanburg and will be here tomorrow for two days and perhaps again next Saturday with George [George Schieffelin, her husband] and Col. Forster who talk of motoring over for Sunday. She has taken a small house as the hotel would have been impossible in Summer and will establish herself there with some Morristown servants, and George and a tutor.

We are really not much nearer Charlie and in one sense farther off, for I cannot now see his letters to Vera [CS III's wife] which kept me in touch with him. This war really changes all the family plans.

No ideas have come that are worth writing about. If I sometimes send detailed directions to Watson or Perkins or another is only to save you trouble in doing unimportant things.

This is not a fashionable place and I am not likely to meet friends but last night I came [?] against David Lawrence [Washington correspondent for *New York Evening Post*] and had an interesting talk. He was very friendly and has interesting information. He surprised me by saying that he had not spoken to the President for over a year and seems to have some sympathy with the notions that the President is rather exclusive and carefully guarded. He certainly does take good care of himself and I suppose that is what he should do—save himself for the most important business.

The golf links are directly in front of the hotel and are fine. I have my clubs and hope I may be up to it later. It is not yet tempting. The movies are about my size now. Yesterday afternoon I saw Mary Pickford for the first time and they give a show in the hotel every night. Oh! things are fine and you are told every few minutes how much they cost. "Don't drop ink." The rugs cost thousands, etc, etc. But the price is not prohibitive—$175 for a double and single room and bath with meals included for three of us—per week, of course.

Take good care of yourself and don't worry. I feel very badly about Helen's [Arthur's wife] loss.

Yours with love
Charles

July 3rd 1918

Dear Arthur:

Your letter was most welcome and disposes of some details.

I return the Putnam & Appleton [American publishers] letters and quite agree that it would be better to leave things as they are. All we wanted was war relief because of the embargo on sheets and the delay and uncertainty of the mails. This will give the English a permanent advantage out of all proportion and make us belated publishers of all English books. It would be used by them to secure Canada & other parts of the World now competitive markets.

I can't find that Putnam specifies even what relief <u>we</u> are to have. Whether it is a month or two's time or provision that publication in Canada would be sufficient for English copyright. And yet he suggests Olin [Stephen H. Olin, lawyer] prepare a bill and we go to Congress which [with?] the chances of all kinds of wild amendments. The difficulty with Barrie [J. M. Barrie] is to the point. We have cabled & written Hodder [English publisher] and they have intentionally held back "copy" from us, meanwhile selling the plays in Canada. I should think this matter had better be let drop (rather than dispute with Putnam) unless the temper of the other publishers is against us.

The Patriotic League seems suitably organized and anything which gives the free an increased interest is desirable.

A few days ago I called upon the bookseller here and found our salesman (Retic?) was in town. He spoke to me over the telephone, as he will tell you. He also gave me the latest news of Charlie, which was very satisfactory.

There is nothing very new. Louise was here on Sunday and Georgie leaves for Spartanburg on Friday which will leave us all alone. Perhaps some of the de Peysters may come for a few days. We have no acquaintances in the Hotel now except the Seeleys who run it and are very polite.

The news about the robbery is most exciting and we shall eagerly await developments. It is a ticklish situation. I suppose you are sure that the maid who is leaving is not in the plot.

In some haste as Louise is calling
Yours ever
Charles

● **1923–1924**

From late November 1923 until early April 1924 CS II and his wife wintered in Pasadena, California. Though Charles was slowly disengaging himself from the daily concerns of the business, he was still effectively directing it from wherever he was.

December 4, 1923
Dear Charles:

We were delighted to be assured by your telegram that you had had a satisfactory journey to the Coast and that Louise has stood it without becoming overfatigued, and since then Charlie has had his first letter. He is keeping you so well posted that I fear I cannot report much that will be new to you.

We had something of a flurry over Jesse Lynch Williams's story, which certainly created unusual interest when published in the Saturday Evening Post, and we rushed through the book [*Not Wanted*] in a few days. Darrow welcomed the excitement. It was fortunate we took it up with Jesse at once, for he had already had applications from two publishers and though it may not be a great success it is not a large venture and I think it should certainly justify itself, with a possibility of a considerable success. The copy of the book mailed last Saturday will probably reach you before this letter.

Perkins has just received a letter from Mrs. Gerould [Katharine Fullerton Gerould] in which she says that she has finally decided to give her time to her novel, to be called "Outrageous Fortune", and will require some payments to enable her to give up other work, so we sent her a cheque for $1500 which she now wishes, on account of a $5000 advance as proposed by us some time ago. Helen is chairman of the Entertainment Committee at the Woman's Cosmopolitan Club and introduced Swinnerton [?] at the meeting last week, Mr. and Mrs. Gerould being there as our guests. They seemed to enjoy it very much and were as nice as they could be.

James Boyd has just been in to see Perkins, to report that he has finished the manuscript of his novel [*Drums*, his first book] and it will be sent us as soon as it is typewritten.

Mr. Howe asked for the thousand dollars which was to be given him for his special work on the Sullivan matter [Mark Sullivan's *Our Times: The United States, 1900–1925*], and I gave him a cheque, charging it, at least for the time being, to the Subscription Department as it seemed as though the main venture would be there and any division can be made later.

The Roosevelt orders [for the Memorial edition of Theodore Roosevelt's works] come in steadily, now totaling 723, and the total of the Galsworthy [for the Manaton Edition of John Galsworthy's works] is 477, three orders having been received last week and three the week before. The amount of weekly business continues distinctly larger than last year.

Letter to CS II from AHS [1921?], he and his wife having just embarked on a three-month trip to Japan and China. In addition to keeping costs down, Arthur agrees with his brother that "we must be more cautious in accepting Mss."

Charlie has undoubtedly told you that Brentano is coming up to Fifth Avenue and 47th Street in a big building going up there, mainly west of the Avenue but with an ell coming around the corner of thirty odd feet on Fifth Avenue. It seems to me that on the whole their being in our neighborhood may work for our good if we can keep up the class of our establishment. The Brentanos are good merchants, but two or three times lately I have been told by friends that they could find in our place the class of books which Brentano does not seem to carry.

There have been no specially difficult problems so far and our fall books seem to be pretty generally having a fair sale, though with no great outstanding success.

Breasted's <u>Egypt</u> [James Henry Breasted, *A History of Egypt*] the big book is running low, a thousand copies having been printed in March, 250 of these going to England and only about 150 now left. As I understand he is now in Egypt and proposes revising that book and as there already has been trouble about his other book, I am in doubt as to what should be done.

We are sending a copy of the Roosevelt to Arthur Page [editor of *The World's Work*] and are receiving acknowledgments—in all cases most appreciative—from those which have been sent.

I hope that as you get settled you will find congenial society and that Pasadena will agree with Louise.

Gerould was not able to progress much further with "Outrageous Fortune"; she later fulfilled her contract by substituting a new work, The Light That Never Was, *which Scribners published in 1931.*

Feb'y 16th [1924]

Dear Charles:

Thank you for your letter, but please dismiss from your mind any idea of the possibility of resigning from the Presidency [of Scribners]. I have never for an instant wished this, and would use all the influence I have to prevent it. You are necessary and though I realize you must be away more than formaly your work while here and your di-

Great beck—

Dear Mr. Scribner:

It'll be a great pleasure for me to be there. Thanks for the opportunity. Enclosed is my check for $5.00. If I can be of any help let me know. I think its a great idea — and I'll keep it dark

Sincerely

F Scott Fitzgerald

Dictated   **H.v.D.**   October 6, 1923.
Avalon,
Princeton, N.J.

My dear Arthur:-

Your second note of October 5th in regard to the birthday dinner to be given to Charles on the 18th is at hand.

I am very much gratified, indeed I may say flattered, by the suggestion that I should preside at the dinner. It is an honour which I have done nothing to deserve. But if you and the other men of the House think that I should do it, it goes without saying that I will accept. It will be a chance for me to express my gratitude to you and your brother for all that you have done, not only for me, but for the cause of literature in these United States.

Your suggestions in regard to speakers seem to me excellent. Bok "has a way with him". Bridges is one of the pillars of the House. It would be a good thing if one of the public favorites, like Mrs. Wharton, or Galsworthy, or FitzGerald, were within reach and could be added to the list of speakers. I hope that Brother Paul is coming to the dinner, and Cousin John also. John has certainly "taken the bull by the horns" in his Rembrandt book, which I have not yet read, but from which I hope to derive much enjoyment in the future, both because he writes well on every subject that he touches, and because his latest production is certain to arouse almost as much contrarious enthusiasm as a bull fight.
Ever faithfully yours,

Henry van Dyke

Acceptances by Scribner authors F. Scott Fitzgerald and Henry Van Dyke to invitations to attend AHS's birthday dinner for his brother. Van Dyke was host.

THOSE PRESENT

JOSEPH BUCKLIN BISHOP	MEREDITH NICHOLSON
EDWARD W. BOK	ALEXANDER D. NOYES
ROBERT BRIDGES	HENRY FAIRFIELD OSBORN
W. C. BROWNELL	LLOYD OSBOURNE
FREDERIC A. BURLINGAME	LEIGHTON PARKS
STRUTHERS BURT	DAVID PATON
NICHOLAS MURRAY BUTLER	MAXWELL E. PERKINS
JOSEPH HAWLEY CHAPIN	WILLIAM LYON PHELPS
ROYAL CORTISSOZ	J. O. H. PITNEY
C. WHITNEY DARROW	MICHAEL PUPIN
FRANK N. DOUBLEDAY	R. J. SAFFORD
JOHN FINLEY	GEORGE R. D. SCHIEFFELIN
F. SCOTT FITZGERALD	ARTHUR H. SCRIBNER
ERNEST FLAGG	CHARLES SCRIBNER, JR.
ROBERT GRANT	HENRY A. SHERMAN
JOHN GRIER HIBBEN	WILLIAM M. SLOANE
W. D. HOWE	FREDERIC J. STIMSON
CHARLES H. KEYES	PAUL G. TOMLINSON
H. H. KOHLSAAT	HENRY VAN DYKE
EDWARD T. S. LORD	JOHN C. VAN DYKE
BRANDER MATTHEWS	PAUL VAN DYKE
CARROLL B. MERRITT	ANDREW F. WEST
CLARENCE B. MITCHELL	JESSE LYNCH WILLIAMS

University Club
October 18, 1923

List of attendees—Scribner authors and staff—at AHS's surprise dinner party given for CS II on the occasion of his sixty-ninth birthday, 18 October 1923, at the University Club in New York City (from the dinner keepsake)

rection while away are essential. I will do all I can to help you.

I fear I have been too free in writing of difficulties here, but it does not mean that I am rattled and while I was crowded a bit last month I have caught up now and am in good condition.

Now I am looking over the royalty reports and in a few days shall begin valuing the sheets & bound stock. While these involve some work, it is work I enjoy for I feel that I can do it fairly well and it puts me in touch with conditions.

There is not the slightest need of my going away, any worries I may have would be the greater for not being on the ground. If Helen [wife] goes to Atlantic City for two or three days I may go with her, but that would be to keep her company.

So far everyone is pleased with the move to 43rd St. [of third-floor offices of 597 Fifth Avenue] & I think that it will be a great success.

You no doubt saw notice of the death of Mr. Appleton [publisher William Worthen Appleton]

and I fear that Charlie Munn [publisher Charles Allen Munn] is losing ground.

With love to you & Louise
Yours
Arthur

At the end of the 1923 fiscal year (31 January 1924) the assets of Charles Scribner's Sons exceeded by over $1.3 million the capital stock of $2.0 million which had been authorized and distributed at its incorporation in 1904. As a result CS II proposed that the firm double its capital stock by issuing an additional two thousand shares of no par value, to be called Class B stock, which would participate in future profits but have no voting rights. (The original two thousand shares with a par value of $1,000 each, of which he and his brother initially owned 99 percent, would be designated as Class A stock.) He felt it would be in the interests of the company to distribute the new stock to employees so that they would more directly be involved in its financial performance.

March 20th 1924

Dear Charles:

I have never replied to your suggestion that I put down any thought I may have about the distribution of B. Stock. I will make the effort but you must not take it too seriously. Darrow & Perkins come first & should be treated liberally. Darrow is the more ambitious financially, but this is not a bad trait for his ambition is linked up with the success of the business.

—

No one could be finer in every way than Perkins during your absence.

—

Suppose each were given 150 shares.

—

Howe I think very valuable, for his wide acquaintance and his faculty for keeping in touch with matters outside the office. He seems to give authors great satisfaction. He is of course over sanguine requiring some steadying. I do not think he is so ambitious financially, but he wants to live on a scale which necessitates a large income. What would you think of 100 shares for him?

—

All look forward to the greater success of the business within the next few years & there is of course the value of the stock when taken up by the company.

—

At present I think that the others can be taken care of in the success of the individual department with which each is connected—even Merritt in some way. This may seem too conservative and I am willing to go as far as you think desirable, but I have in mind reserving some B stock for future developments. I should add that I think it might be well to give Lord 50 shares. He has a large increase as it is, but this might remove any friction between departments, & make it easier to effect some minor adjustments of expenses between the trade & educational depts. I am a little embarrassed by the uncertainty of the division between us. Our ownership was on the basis of 60 to 40, but your giving stock to your family has thrown this out. Should these shares be distributed on the basis of the original ownership? This would seem logical, but I can appreciate that this would leave your individual ownership of B. stock all out of proportion to our relative value to the business.

—

It is too bad that the magazine is not doing better and I think that Merritt has been on the wrong track in not making more use of the Subscription Dept, and in sending out such quantities of inferior circular material. He is a wonder at securing advertising which in addition to its financial value gives an air of success to the Magazine in the eyes of the public.

—

It seems as though Bridges should do better & I do not quite understand why he does not. In some ways he seems out of touch with the modern spirit. I should think that he would like going after the sort of articles we need.

I may not write you again, so I hope that you will have a comfortable trip & good weather after you are home

Yours
Arthur

Special meetings of the board of directors were held in April and May, and resolutions amending the company's articles of incorporation and approving the new class of stock were passed. At its regular monthly meeting in September 1924 the board agreed to distribute 1,100 shares of Class B stock as follows:

50 shares to Robert Bridges (editor of Scribner's Magazine)

200 "   " Whitney Darrow (business manager)

200 "   " Will D. Howe (editor)

200 "   " Edward T. S. Lord (head of Educational Department)

100 "   " Carroll B. Merritt (head of Subscription Department)

200 "   " Maxwell E. Perkins (editor)

50 "   " R. J. Safford (head of Retail Department?)

100 "   " Charles Scribner Jr. (CS III, secretary of firm)

The remainder were kept for contingencies.

> Don't let anything worry you and be sure that I shall accept all decisions by you with confidence.
>
> — CS II in a letter to AHS, 16 February 1925

•1928

From the end of January to the end of March CS II and his wife wintered in Augusta, Georgia. Soon after his arrival, business called his attention to Benito Mussolini, the Italian fascist dictator who was making international news.

JAN 31 1928

CHARLES SCRIBNER
HOTEL BON AIR VANDERBILT HOTEL
REYNOLDS OFFERS MUSSOLINI AUTOBIOGRAPHY TRANSLATED AND SUPERVISED BY EXAMBASSADOR RICHARD WASHBURN CHILD FORTY THOUSAND DOLLARS ADVANCE ON FIFTEEN PERCENT ROYALTY AFTER SERIALIZATION IN POST DATE OF PUBLICATION INDEFINITE PROBABLY NEXT FALL MINIMUM LENGTH EIGHTY THOUSAND WORDS PRESUMABLE LENGTH HUNDRED AND TEN THOUSAND IS RECEIVING OFFERS BUT IS CONSIDERING NONE UNTIL WE DECIDE NO COPY AVAILABLE TEMPTING FOR WE REALIZE INTEREST IN PERSONALITY BUT DISINCLINED TO TAKE RISK ESPECIALLY IN VIEW OF POST SERIALIZATION

ARTHUR H SCRIBNER

1928 FEB 1

ARTHUR H SCRIBNER
597 FIFTH AVE
MUSSOLINI VERY IMPORTANT PRICE HIGH IF POST MEANS SATURDAY EVENING POST WISH WE HAD MORE ASSURANCE OF CONTENTS WHY NOT TRY THIRTY THOUSAND

PAYMENT SHOULD BE CONDITIONAL ON BOOK APPEARANCE SIMULTANEOUS WITH LAST INSTALLMENT AND ENGLAND OPINION OF ASSOCIATES WOULD INFLUENCE ME

SCRIBNER

FEB 1 1928

CHARLES SCRIBNER
    BON AIR VANDERBILT HOTEL
REYNOLDS CABLING CHILD IN ITALY THIRTY THOUSAND DOLLARS OFFER WILL REPORT TO US LORD AND OTHERS SANGUINE AND PREPARED TO GO TO FORTY THOUSAND IF NECESSARY CONDITIONS MENTIONED ACCEPTED PERIODICAL IS SATURDAY EVENING POST
    ARTHUR SCRIBNER

Feb. 14, 1928

Dear Charles:

The Mussolini matter has been rather a drawn-out affair but we have finally secured it, advancing forty-two thousand dollars on a fifteen per cent royalty, simultaneous publication with the last issue of the Saturday Evening Post and book publication in England being assured and Canada included. Our first offer was thirty thousand dollars, with which Reynolds [Paul R. Reynolds, literary agent] seemed satisfied, and it was arranged that he should at once send a cable, but on inquiring two or three days later we learned that he had not cabled but had written instead. This was very annoying and a cable was then sent. On inquiring over the telephone whether there was any answer to this he said that Child had answered that decision would be reached at a meeting the following Monday, Perkins replying that this looked favorable. A few minutes later Reynolds rang up and said that he had cabled another offer. I had him down here and was very much annoyed at the way he had handled the matter, in not having cabled instead of writing and in having been indisposed to tell us there was another offer in the field. I assume, whether rightly or wrongly, that the offer was in the neighborhood of forty thousand dollars, and I revised our offer under these conditions to forty-two thousand dollars, provided he would not advise the other publisher that we had made another offer. He squirmed at this but finally sent the cable and to-day reports the answer: "Scribner offer accepted. Will get family signatures." Of course this is a bit of a gamble but we all agree here that the prospects

are favorable and that the risk is fully justified, and I should hate to have lost it. . . .

My Autobiography *by Benito Mussolini was published on 26 October 1928. Presumably because of the work's prior serialization in* The Saturday Evening Post, *sales of the book were disappointing—only about twenty-two thousand copies: the brothers lost their gamble.*

•1929

Again, CS II and his wife spent February at the Bon Air Vanderbilt Hotel in Augusta, Georgia.

Feb. 9, 1929

Dear Charles:

Perkins has just returned [from Key West], looking very much refreshed, and he reports that he landed a tarpon. He has brought with him the manuscript of Hemingway's novel [A Farewell to Arms], about 120,000 words, and says that it is remarkably fine, though there are a few passages the realism of which will have to be modified. He is giving it to Bridges to be put into type at once [for serialization in Scribner's Magazine] and no doubt will write you himself.

I have been busy with various details but nothing of special importance has come up since you left. You may be interested in seeing the enclosed bunch of orders, and we have now placed just over 50,000 of the "Bishop Murder Case" [by S. S. Van Dine], with a prospect of further orders at the time of publication. The first printing, scheduled to be 75,000 copies, will run up to about 80,000, and we have ordered paper for another printing if needed.

I expect a representative of the American Writing Paper Company here next Wednesday, with some new samples of paper, and I hope we can come to some conclusion, for, as you know, this has worried me very much.

There are various inquiries for 3 East 48th Street, none of them as yet satisfactory, but these show decided interest in the building, and sooner or later we should be able to make an advantageous lease.

We had a telegram from Charlie [CS III] asking for some additional material, which we replied to, forwarding at once the letters desired.

In a general way the manufacturing of books is progressing with no special complications, and Cadmus was back at the press last Monday morning. Young Carter has been laid up with the "flu" but he will soon be about again.

Enclosed is a letter from Frank Dodd, and Stokes [Frederick A. Stokes, publisher], whom I saw at the Lunch Club on Wednesday, says he understands that the matter has been held up for the present.

Helen and I are going to Blair's [nephew, John Insley Blair Larned] consecration Monday morning. Although I am not specially keen about it, I think we should show this interest in his becoming Bishop.

All the above seems rather fragmentary, but there is nothing else, I think, of importance to write of, and I hope that you are having a satisfactory rest. . . .

The Bishop Murder Case became the #4 best-seller of 1929. The brothers' Scribner Realty Company owned several properties for rental purposes, including 3 East Forty-eighth Street, which was around the corner from the firm's headquarters building at 597–599 Fifth Avenue.

•**1930**

In the spring Arthur and his wife left for a six-week trip abroad, planning to spend most of their time in Italy. In this letter, the last he would write to his brother, Arthur mentions meeting Benito Mussolini and talks of the value of maintaining personal author/publisher relations with the firm's most important English authors, J. M. Barrie and John Galsworthy.

Florence Friday April 18th [1930]

Dear Charles:

On landing at Naples we went at once to Rome, staying there two weeks and arriving here last Monday. We leave next Monday, the day after Easter.

Mr. Garrett our Ambassador to Italy was very cordial having us to luncheon and arranging a meeting for me with Mussolini which was very interesting but brief. His face lit up at once at any praise of Italy and of Italian ships, but he did not respond to mention of his book, and as he does not understand English very well I am not sure that what I said was clear to him. Helen attended an audience with the Pope and was much interested.

Though we had both been to Rome a couple of times there was so much to do that our stay was not very restful, but here we have taken it more easily and in both we took a couple of day trips out of the city by motor which were most enjoyable.

From here we go to Paris with a detour of a couple of days to see Helen's cousins at Freiberg, then to London and so home on the Mauritania May 10th due the 16th.

I shall of course hope to see Barrie and Galsworthy, and it seems desirable for some one of us to see the latter from time to time to explain better than can be done in correspondence the continued efforts we are making to promote the sale of his books.

I am not sure that I told you that when we printed the second ten thousand of the "Compact Edition" he wrote a very appreciative letter saying that our judgment had been fully justified.

I fear that you think I have acted too hastily in the matter of the lease of No 3. [3 East Forty-eighth Street] and this worries me. I would not have gone so far had I not at the time felt sure of its having your approval.

It was the only definite offer at all acceptable which we had received in nearly a year's time and the outlook was not promising, but I should have left it for consideration by you. Coming as it did just as I was leaving I was thrown a bit off my balance. I am sorry.

I have just received two good letters from Darrow and please tell him how much I appreciate them, every item being of interest and particularly to know that you are stronger.

With love to you and Charlie and remembrances to all at the office

Yours

Arthur

The following day Arthur received a telegram that CS II had died from a heart attack. He caught the first steamship home, reaching New York in seven days. Condolence letters from all over poured in—from friends, fellow publishers, and Scribner authors.

April 26, 1930

Dear Mr. Scribner:

I have just returned home after an absence of some days and desire at once to express to you and to the other members of the family my sympathy, joined with my deep regret, at the death of your brother. In my contacts with him, extending over a series of years, I had every occasion to learn and to admire and esteem his fine personal qualities. And I wish also, as a representative of the Council of Learned Societies, to voice our sense of loss to liberal studies in this country. In our dealings with Charles Scribner's Sons in connection with the publication of the Dictionary of

American Biography, we have felt—and with ample ground for this opinion—that your house was not treating it as exclusively or even primarily a commercial undertaking, but was influenced constantly by its desire to be associated with and to aid a work of such fundamental importance for American letters and American life. The firm has constantly evidenced that you are not simply book manufacturers, but publishers in the large and noble connotation of the word.

Very sincerely yours,
Edward C. Armstrong

[chairman of the American Council of Learned Societies, under whose auspices Scribners published the *Dictionary of American Biography* and, later, the *Dictionary of Scientific Biography*]

Paris. May 22, 1930.

My Dear Arthur,

I first knew your brother Blair, & was a pallbearer at his funeral [1879].

Charles I have known for many years & I have always had the greatest respect for his judgment. He was so cordial whenever I had the luck to meet him, & he ever struck me as a fully equipped publisher & a sincere friend. I am old now, in my eightieth year, & have had a long experience in the publishing business, & I can say with all honesty, I have never met a man in our craft who appealed to me more closely as the ideal American publisher. He was so modest but essentially capable, & with-all a courtly gentleman ready to weigh conflicting opinions with a conciliatory mind.

To you, & his immediate family, I beg leave to offer my profoundest sympathy, with the hope that Scribner & Sons may always retain their proud position as one of the leading publishing houses of our country.

Faithfully yours,
J. Henry Harper [publisher]

June 30, 1930

Dear Mr. Harper:

It is good to have such a fine letter of sympathy from one who has been a friend of both my brothers. It is now fifty years since Blair died, and you may be interested to know that Skidmore College for Girls founded by his widow, and named for her parents, has grown from small beginnings to be larger than Princeton was when Charles and I graduated. Charles was one of the trustees, and in this, as in all his

Condolence letter to AHS from Frederick A. Stokes (1857–1939), founder of the publishing house bearing his name, on the occasion of CS II's death

activities, his rare personality was manifest, and his efforts contributed to the success of the college. The book publishing world is constantly changing, and no one in the future is likely to occupy quite the position that he did. But it will be our effort to keep alive in our own business the spirit which animated him. It is rare for two brothers to be so close to one another for so many years as he and I have been, and his loss will be deeply felt by us all.

Because of the long time association, I was tempted to address you in kind by your first name, but being the younger, hesitated to do so. Though not so much the younger, for I am now in my seventieth year, and find myself, with an exception or two, the oldest in the business. Charles often expressed his high regard for you, and it is a pleasure to see your son from time to time, and I hope that he will continue to do well.

Faithfully yours,

[Arthur H. Scribner]

June 30, 1930

Dear Mrs. Wharton [Edith Wharton]:

I trust you will pardon me for not having acknowledged sooner your kind and sympathetic letter, but unfortunately I was abroad at the time of Charles's death, and though I came home immediately, there have been numerous matters pressing for attention. His friendship with you was one of those he valued most, and characteristic of the time when the relations of authors and publishers were much closer than today. But notwithstanding the changes which have and are taking place, it will be the constant endeavor of us all to keep alive the spirit which animated him,—the spirit which makes publishing worthwhile and something more than commercial business.

Thanking you again for your kind letter which we much appreciated, I am,

Sincerely yours

[Arthur H. Scribner]

ILLUSTRATED CHRONOLOGY

Significant Scribner Dates

This chronology provides a list of important dates and events in the history of the firm and its personnel, noting staff changes and organizational developments. In addition, significant publications and publishing series—selected for the importance of the authors, from a literary standpoint and/or from their commercial benefit to the firm, for the subject, or for the publishing achievement itself, such as the number of volumes involved and the quantity of illustrations—are identified for each year. Many of the authors noted by their "first Scribner book" are covered at greater length in the "Selected Authors" section and are not mentioned further here.

1905–1909

1905

January	Scribners brings a lawsuit against R. H. Macy and Company, the New York City department store, charging infringement of copyright for cutting prices on books copyrighted by Scribners—one of similar cases, all involving the American Publishers' Association's attempt to end discounting of members' books.
5 June	CS II and Arthur Hawley Scribner purchase property at 311–319 West Forty-third Street for future printing plant; the closing takes place on 5 September.
14 October	Publication date of Edith Wharton's *The House of Mirth*, the #8 best-seller of 1905 and #9 of 1906

1906

May	Publication of Charles Dana Gibson's *The Gibson Book: A Collection of the Published Works of Charles Dana Gibson* (two volumes)
June	Publication of the first twenty-three volumes (of twenty-eight) in the Elkhorn edition of *The Works of Theodore Roosevelt*, which is completed in 1920
October	Princeton University Press incorporates with CS II as president. Located in Princeton, N.J., the company reorganizes as a nonprofit corporation in 1910.
27 October	Publication date of the first volume (of thirteen) in the Viking edition of *The Collected Works of Henrik Ibsen*, revised and edited by William Archer, which is completed in 1911
8 December	Publication date of J. M. Barrie's *Peter Pan in Kensington Gardens*, illustrated by Arthur Rackham

1907

April	The Scribner Press Building at 311–319 West Forty-third Street is ready for occupancy.
14 December	Publication date of the first two volumes (of twenty-six) in the New York edition of *The Novels and Tales of Henry James*, which is completed in 1917

1908

1 June	The Supreme Court, in the Scribner/Macy suit, rules against the right of the publisher "to restrain the selling at retail of books copyrighted under the laws of the United States, at prices less than those fixed by complainants, and the buying of such copyrighted books

except under the rules and regulations of the American Publishers' Association." Other legal aspects of the "Macy cases" are argued until the Court's ruling of 1 December 1913: copyright is not exempt from the provision of the Sherman Anti-Trust Law against monopoly.

29 July	An early morning fire heavily damages the third- and fourth-floor offices (home of *Scribner's Magazine* and the Subscription Department) in the firm's headquarters building at 153–157 Fifth Avenue.
29 August	Publication date of F. Hopkinson Smith's *Peter: A Novel of Which He Is Not the Hero,* the #6 best-seller of 1908 and #9 of 1909
8 October	Publication date of Kenneth Grahame's *The Wind in the Willows,* the first American edition of this children's classic
17 October	Publication date of John Fox Jr.'s *The Trail of the Lonesome Pine,* the #3 best-seller of 1908 and #5 of 1909

1909

January	Publication of the one-volume edition of *Dictionary of the Bible,* edited by James Hastings, one of the firm's most popular religious reference works
17 April	Publication date of Edith Wharton's *Artemis to Actæon, and Other Verse,* her first volume of poetry
October	This month's issue of *Scribner's Magazine,* containing the first of Theodore Roosevelt's African hunting articles, reaches a circulation of 215,000 copies, the largest to date for a high-priced magazine.

> CS II DIARY ENTRIES:
> Monday 5 June 1905
>
> Pay $5000 and close purchase for 43rd St property
>
> Friday 30 June 1905
>
> Call on Ernest who estimates new Press Bld. @ 475,000
>
> *Ernest Flagg, architect and brother-in-law of CS II, was hired to design the Scribner Press Building at 311–319 West Forty-third St.*

NOTE:
"Charles Scribner's Sons to Run a Printing Plant," *Publishers' Weekly,* 10 June 1905, p. 1598.

CHARLES SCRIBNER'S SONS have purchased the block of land, No. 311 to 319 West Forty-third Street, on the north side, between Eighth and Ninth Avenues, occupying an area of 125 x 100.5 feet. It is the intention of Messrs. Scribner's Sons to erect a building on this site for the accommodation of an up-to-date printing office, including a bindery and stereotyping plant for the manufacture of their own and, possibly, outside work. The firm has for some time controlled a printing plant largely for magazine purposes, which is now to be developed in the new quarters for all their work.

ARTICLE:
"John H. Dingman's Golden Anniversary," *Publishers' Weekly,* 16 September 1905, pp. 573–574.

At the time of his death in 1912, Dingman had spent more than sixty years with Charles Scribner's Sons—more than any other employee before or since.

Upwards of fifty years ago there came to New York City a youth from up State—Rensselaer County—eager to learn, impatient to become of some use in the world. . . . He was naturally attracted to an advertisement of "A boy wanted in a book store." His credentials proving satisfactory John H. Dingman became office boy for Charles Scribner, Sr., at 36 Park Row in the building formerly occupied by the Brick

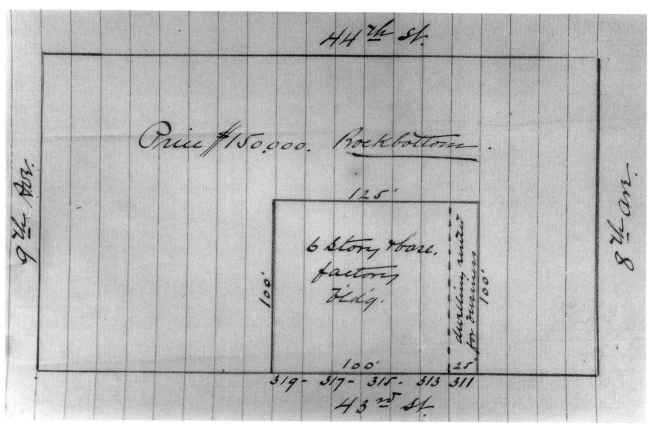

Diagram (1905) by George Milne of the property on West Forty-third Street that the Scribner brothers wanted as the site for their future printing plant. As their real-estate agent, Milne was able to negotiate the price down to $140,000.

Church, afterward the site of the New York Times building. It was on a Monday morning, September 10, 1855—nine years after the Scribner business had been started—that young Dingman joined the Scribner staff; and it was therefore that his associates met on the evening of the 11th inst. at the rooms of the Aldine Association, to greet him, and to do him honor on the eve of his entry upon the sixth decade's service in the ranks of the house which it was always his aim to honor and by hard work and enterprise to help place in the very front rank of the trade.

The anniversary celebration took place in the gaily decorated dining room of the Aldine Association, and was noteworthy for its sustained interest during the entire evening. Samuel W. Marvin acted as toastmaster, and . . . . presented Mr. Dingman a handsome silver loving cup, suitably inscribed.

In response, and at the request of his associates, Mr. Dingman made a lengthy address recalling to their memories some of the most striking events in the history of the house, and traced in a careful manner items of value concerning its earliest life. . . .

Other addresses were made by Mr. Mix, H. L. Smith, E. T. S. Lord, Mr. Stolle, and Mr. Offerd. Mr. Charles Scribner then arose and made the most marked address of the evening. Referring to the many important achievements of the house—which had been secured, he said, by the most strenuous efforts—he insisted that success could not have come but for the strong individual help of the many competent men who had occupied positions of responsibility and trust with his father, his brothers and himself. He urged this point of view with force and spoke with cordiality and intensity of his appreciation of it. He then turned to Mr. Dingman and in a very impressive manner thanked him for all the efforts he had made during these fifty years, and then, with a charm which is indescribable, added: "I speak in the name of those who are not here, and in the name of my brother Arthur and myself as well." . . . .

Shortly after this, those present dispersed . . . .

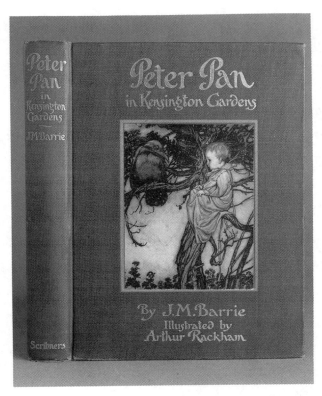

A first-edition copy of J. M. Barrie's Peter Pan in Kensington Gardens

Mr. Dingman's services to the trade at large consisted in the preparation of a "Directory of Booksellers and Stationers in the United States and Canada," the first of its kind published in this country, which met a real need and became so popular and profitable that he issued it for four years, from 1870 to 1873 [actually, 1867 to 1870]. He was obliged to discontinue it because it took too much of his time from other important business engagements. . . .

RELATED LETTERS AND DIARY ENTRY:
Letter from Joseph Hawley Chapin, art editor at Scribners, to CS II, 20 May 1906; letter (excerpt) from Arthur H. Scribner to CS II, 21 May 1906.

Chapin had been hired by Scribners in 1897 on the recommendation of CS II's brother-in-law, the artist Charles Noel Flagg, founder of the Connecticut League of Art Students in Hartford where Chapin had studied. His primary responsibility was directing the art department of Scribner's Magazine. "Mr. Pyle" is Howard Pyle, the well-known artist, and author and illustrator of many Scribner books.

Dear Mr. Scribner

You have undoubtedly heard of the changes in the S. S. McClure Co.: reorganization is now under way and I have been offered a position with a salary of seven thousand eight hundred a year with promises of either stock or a percentage of the profits of the business. Their new magazine has been postponed but I am assured that when it materializes it would further add to my opportunities.

Mr. Pyle who is drawing three hundred and fifty dollars a week (three days only in the office) intends to stay on for a period but with the idea that I will succeed him.

Mr. McClure, Mr. Pyle and Mr. Beady are all most cordial in their desire to have me join them and while I appreciate the compliment fully I do not want to leave you.

This offer of Mr. McClure's with what he predicts for the future seems at first glance like a great opportunity but on the other hand have I not a real opportunity with Charles Scribner's Sons?

For some time it has seemed to me that C. S. Sons were entering upon a new era. We are expanding in some directions and there is the possibility of a new publication, changes are sure to follow such growth and sooner or later you and your brother will find it necessary to get rid of some details which you are now close to. If this proves to be the case, then are not some of the younger men to become more important factors in the business as time goes on?

I have some reason to believe that my efforts are appreciated and that I can hope for increased responsibilities in the future. In other words I feel that my real opportunity is with Charles Scribner's Sons.

If my analysis of this situation is correct and I am not asked to make too great a sacrifice in the matter of salary should I let the McClure offer go, cable me the one word "stay" and I will turn down the McClure proposition and trust to you for the rest. I feel sure that my interests are safe in your hands if you but say the word.

I am sorry to have to write for at first I was told that they would wait for my answer until your return but now they are anxious for it as soon as possible and I am forced to lay the matter before you in this way.

I have given Mr. Arthur Scribner a full account of the affair and he agreed that it was best for me to write you at once.

With kind regards, believe me
Yours sincerely
J. H. Chapin

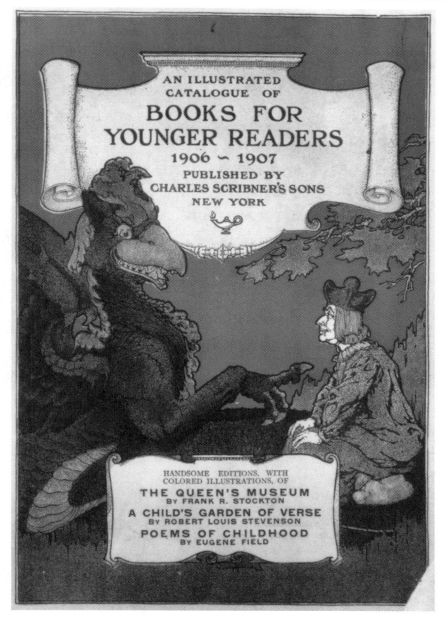

The Scribner children's catalogue for 1906–1907

Dear Charles:

 . . . Chapin has talked to me about his being approached by McClure. It seems that Pyle in connecting himself there was particularly interested in the opportunity offered by the starting of a new magazine, a 5¢ one, of which McClure has talked. Phillips [McClure partner] & others were always opposed to this, or whether in any event it would have materialised is uncertain, but now it is naturally postponed. Partly for this reason and partly no doubt because Pyle found the work more irksome than he anticipated he wants to get out as soon as possible, and it is by his advice that they came after Chapin. Chapin, of course, prefers remaining here, but their offer, $150[00] week, with additional though indefinite promises for the future, and their undoubted financial success unsettle him. It is not merely a question of salary as he is ambitious to do something beyond the present magazine work. The book work so far has been an element in keeping him satisfied, and I believe it would be well if sometime all this could be under him, the responsibility perhaps of the regular routine work being put upon our own manufacturing. I don't think he will be unreasonable and I hope that we can do what is necessary to keep him, as he is undoubtedly one of the best men we have, really contributing something to the progress of the house; and he seems to me in the book work in which I have come in closest touch with him to study expense much more carefully than a year or more ago.

    With love to Louise
           Affectionately yours
           Arthur

CS II was traveling in Europe with his wife, Louise, at the time but managed to convince Chapin to remain with Scribners when he returned in June, shown by his diary entry for 21 June 1906:

    Lunch with Chapin & agree to give him $1000 more beginning with June 1st

Chapin continued as Art Editor until 1936 and was working with N. C. Wyeth on the Pulitzer Prize Edition of Marjorie Kinnan Rawlings's The Yearling *when he died in 1939.*

COURT DECISION:
"Decision in Book Case. United States Court of Appeals Says Dealer May Fix Price," *New-York Tribune,* 21 June 1906, p. 14, col. 1.

A landmark decision, upheld by the Supreme Court in 1908, that opened the door for steep discounting of books by retailers. The American Publishers' Association, which sought to uphold the publisher's right to enforce its "net" prices, fell victim to the decision and dissolved in 1914.

    A decision was handed down in the United States Circuit Court of Appeals yesterday in the case of Charles Scribner's Sons against R. H. Macy & Co., in which the contention of Macy & Co. that they have a right to sell copyright books at whatever prices they see fit is sustained. The decision is on an appeal from that of Judge Ray.
    The litigation between Macy & Co. and the American Publishers' Association and its individual members has been in the courts for four years. The last decision reverses the ruling of Alton R. Parker while he was Chief Judge of the Court of Appeals. In the action brought by Macy & Co. to declare the American Publishers' Association an illegal combination Judge Parker ruled that so far as copyright books were concerned, a combination might not be considered

The Scribner Press Building at 311–319 West Forty-third Street

illegal although it was illegal as to uncopyrighted books. The effect of the last decision will be to place copyrighted books, so far as regulation of price is concerned, on precisely the same basis as uncopyrighted books.

ARTICLE:
"Scribner's New Printing Office," *Publishers' Weekly,* 9 March 1907, p. 907.

    The fourteen-story building put up by Charles Scribner's Sons for their manufacturing plant at No. 311 to 319 West Forty-third Street, just west of Eighth Avenue, in New York City, will be ready for occupancy by the end of next month. The building, which is within a block of the Times Square subway station, four-and-a-half blocks from the Grand Central Station and ten blocks from the new Pennsylvania R. R. station, has been designed by Ernest Flagg, the well-known architect, who is now also engaged on the new Singer Building and the Naval Academy buildings at Annapolis. No pains and expense have been spared to combine in its contruction perfect adaptability to business requirements, with artistic effect.

It is built of steel and brick, fireproof throughout, and has been constructed for the carrying of heavy machinery. It is absolutely fireproof, with metal doors and window frames, and is provided with the Sprinkler system throughout.

Seven of the fourteen floors will be occupied by the Scribners themselves for manufacturing purposes, and of the remaining space two floors have been taken by the Redfield Brothers, printers, and the fourteenth floor, together with a roof house specially constructed for its needs, has been leased by the Color Plate Company.

The headquarters of Charles Scribner's Sons will remain at 153–157 Fifth Avenue.

NOTE:
Under "Journalistic Notes," *Publishers' Weekly,* 18 May 1907, p. 1548.

CHARLES SCRIBNER'S SONS are establishing a house of their own in London, and hereafter *Scribner's Magazine* will be published from there under the management of W. Irving Hamilton, now of the New York Office, who will go abroad the end of this month.

As before, the magazine would continue to be edited and printed in New York, but now the English edition would bear Scribners' name instead of Heinemann's, the current English "publisher"; Hamilton was sent to handle the business details.

RELATED LETTERS:
Letter from Curtis Brown, English agent for Kenneth Grahame, to Scribners, 18 February 1908; letter from CS II, 3 March 1908, in reply.

Initially, Scribners was not interested in a new book by English author Kenneth Grahame. When shown two of its stories by American literary agent Paul R. Reynolds in early December 1907, CS II responded: "There have been so many of these animal stories lately that I think the public is too tired of them and the outlook for a new book is not particularly promising" (16 December 1907). However, he changed his mind.

CS II DIARY ENTRY:
Wednesday 29 January 1908

Call on President in morning and then take luncheon at White House, including himself and Mrs. Roosevelt, her sister Miss Carow, Bridges, &c. Most interesting & friendly. Will not go to Senate & travel in civilized countries at expiration of term.

As the president's major publisher, CS II was a welcome visitor at the White House and at Roosevelt's home in Oyster Bay, N.Y.

Dear Sirs:

I have just been having a long talk with Mr. Kenneth Grahame about his new book, and perhaps it will clear the situation if I write to you about it. Mr. Grahame says he would much prefer to have the book published by the house of Scribner than by any other firm. He has received two offers for the American rights at $2000 advance on 20%, but would rather take one of $1500 advance on 20% from you, if you really care about the book. As I understand it, your first offer of $3000 advance on 20%, provided the book should be along the lines of "The Golden Age," was withdrawn on the ground that you thought "Mr. Toad" (as the new book probably will be called) was not likely to have a similar sale. We did not gather, however, that you do not really care for this new book. If that is the case, of course nothing more is to be said. But as Mr. Grahame would so much rather you have the book than anyone else, it seems best to lay this offer before you—especially as the later chapters contain more and more of human interest and humour and aimiable satire on modern social conditions. I suppose EVERYBODY'S MAGAZINE will print some 40,000 words of it, but the book will have at least 60,000 words, and it is hoped that it can be published next autumn. It is a little difficult to make out from the correspondence exactly what your attitude toward the book is, but I hope it will be perfectly clear that Mr. Grahame has no wish to press it upon you, and also that there is no wish to be over-exacting in the matter of advance royalty, for I am supposing that you will take my word for it that the offers of $2000 advance are genuine and remain open to acceptance. Presumably this letter will reach you by Thursday February 27th, and it would be a courtesy greatly appreciated by Mr. Grahame if, in case you care for the book, you would on receipt of this letter cable me to BROWNCURT: LONDON the word "GRAHAME", signifying that you will accept his offer of $1500 advance on 20%; or the word "KENNETH", signifying that you would rather not undertake the book. I am sending a copy of this letter to Mr. Reynolds, as, after he had kindly approached you on the subject, it would be hardly fair to him to write to you direct about it without letting him know what I had said.

Yours sincerely,
Curtis Brown

Dear Sir:

In response to your letter about Kenneth Grahame's new book we cabled yesterday the word "Grahame" indicating that we would accept it on the terms now offered—$1500 advance on 20% royalty. We are very appreciative of your own and Mr. Grahame's wish that we should become the publishers for the book and shall do our best to make an entire success of it. Please let us know when the book publication is to be and please send complete copy in time for simultaneous publication. Unless we hear to the contrary, we shall assume that we are to expect copy from you and not reprint from the magazine.

Yours very truly,
[Charles Scribner II]

CS II DIARY ENTRY:
Sunday 28 June 1908

Bridges up for day
Telegraph Roosevelt
25,000 for articles & $10,000 advance on
    20% for book

On the basis of the tremendous interest shown by publishers in his proposed African hunting book, Roosevelt convinced Scribners to raise their offer to $50,000 for a minimum of eight (but no more than twelve) articles about his trip—to appear in Scribner's Magazine—*and accepted their royalty rate of 20 percent for the book.*

Referred to in subsequent correspondence under various titles—"The Mole and the Water Rat," "Mr. Toad," "The Wind in the Reeds"—*the book was published on 8 October 1908 under the title by which it has become famous,* The Wind in the Willows.

ARTICLE:

"Scribners to Print the Roosevelt Hunt. Big Prize of the Book World Goes to the President's Former Publishers. And On a Royalty Basis. Mr. Roosevelt Will Get Large Percentage of the Profits from Sale of His African Adventures," *New York Times*, 9 July 1908, p. 1.

During his presidency Theodore Roosevelt made plans to lead—after his term had ended—a Smithsonian-sponsored expedition to Africa to collect specimens for its national museum in Washington, D.C. Rights to the future story was a keenly sought prize for American publishers. From the beginning Roosevelt preferred Scribners—because of his already-established relationship with the firm, its high reputation, and the exposure he had enjoyed (and would continue to benefit from) in its magazine. But he was able to use the heightened publicity around it to secure a very generous contract. With the title African Game Trails: An Account of the African Wanderings of an American Hunter-Naturalist, *the book was published on 24 August 1910, and it included over two hundred illustrations from photographs by Roosevelt's son Kermit and other members of the expedition.*

The prize so eagerly sought by the publishers of the United States, a contract with Theodore Roosevelt for a chronicle of his big game hunt in the wilds of Africa, has gone to the firm of Charles Scribner's Sons of this city.

The contract was made following the second visit of Robert Bridges, business manager of the publishing house, to Mr. Roosevelt at Oyster Bay. Last Tuesday Mr. Bridges dined with the President and put the case of his house before him for the second time, and won.

S. S. McClure, representing the McClure publications; Caspar Whitney, representing Outing, and the representatives of many other large publishing concerns vainly visited President Roosevelt and used all their wiles to get this contract, which is considered among publishers to be the most promising in the money-making line that has been open for competition since the days when Kipling asked and got a flat rate of 25 cents a word.

*Scenes in the aftermath of the 1908 fire: "At about five o'clock on the morning of July 29, fire broke out in the third floor of the building occupied by Charles Scribner's Sons, 153 Fifth Avenue, New York City, which shortly spread to the fourth floor. These floors were occupied by the magazine and subscription departments of the firm, and contained the records of these branches and a number of original paintings and drawings for the magazine. Fortunately, the records were uninjured, but the paintings and drawings were considerably damaged, if not entirely destroyed. The work · of these departments has been promptly distributed and taken care of in different parts of the building and will not be interrupted. The fire was restricted to the two floors mentioned, the wholesale and retail departments escaping with but slight damage, so that the entire business will continue without delay or inconvenience to the patrons of the firm" (*Publishers' Weekly, *1 August 1908, p. 278). The one-line note about it in* The New York Times *estimated the loss at $5,000.*

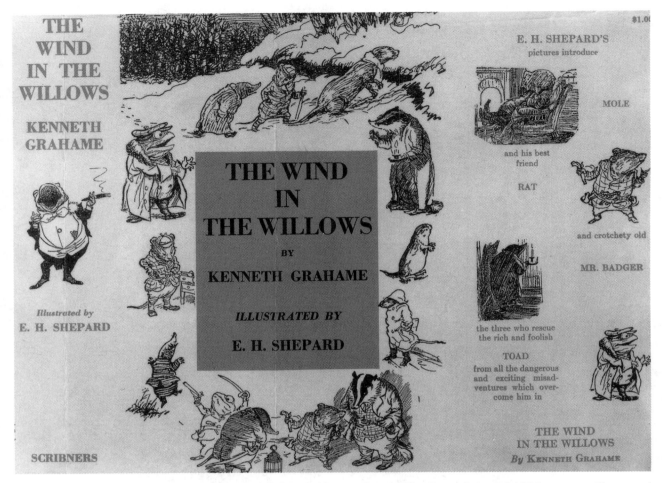

Dust jacket of the 1933 illustrated edition of this children's classic. The first edition of 1908 was not illustrated.

There has been talk of an offer of $1 a word for the big game story of Mr. Roosevelt. One offer of $60,000 was made to him and declined. The average novel runs from 60,000 to 75,000 words, and writers of "best sellers" seldom, if ever, reach that amount of pay for their work on the percentage basis.

But with all of the popularity which Mr. Roosevelt has achieved and with the suspense that will follow his plunge into Africa with his son, Kermit, it is believed that the story of the big hunt and the long trek through the jungle will sell as never a "best seller" has sold before.

So the contract with Mr. Roosevelt has been made on the royalty plan. He will get a very large percentage of the money which the sale of his book brings to the Scribners—perhaps the largest royalty ever paid to an author. The exact figures, however, are not revealed.

At the offices of Charles Scribner's Sons, 153 Fifth Avenue, yesterday Mr. Bridges was asked by a TIMES reporter for some further details as to the contract between the firm and the President.

"Where did you get that information?" asked Mr. Bridges.

"From a reliable source," he was told.

"You will have to get any announcement there may be through Mr. Loeb," Mr. Bridges replied, after pausing for a moment.

"Will Mr. Roosevelt be paid by the word, or on royalty?" was asked.

"I cannot discuss the matter of such a contract," said Mr. Bridges. "You will have to get a statement from Mr. Loeb. When you have that we may give a statement to the press from the firm."

Mr. Bridges would not deny that a contract had been closed through his efforts, but reiterated that it would not be proper for any statement to come through Scribners until a statement had been issued by the President or his secretary.

List of writing supplies provided by Scribner to Theodore Roosevelt for his use in the hot, moist climate of Africa during his hunting expedition. In his letter (17 February 1909) accompanying the portfolios, Robert Bridges, editor of Scribner's Magazine, *explained to Roosevelt some of the weatherproof properties of the material: "The carbon sheets are wrapped in tin foil to keep them from dampness. . . . The outer case may seem superfluous but I am told that it is very necessary to keep heavy rains out of the inner case. A friend of mine who has been to Africa also tells me that there is a species of white ant that devours everything."*

He was asked again if Mr. Roosevelt would be paid by the word.

"Our firm does not do much in handling work that is paid by the word," he said. "Successful writers are paid on royalty, and the amount of royalty depends on the sale of their works."

The Scribners published Mr. Roosevelt's "The Rough Riders," running it first serially in six numbers of Scribner's Magazine in 1899. Mr. Roosevelt had then just returned from the Spanish war. He wrote "The Rough Riders" when he was running for Governor of New York. The story was published later in book form.

The next work of importance Mr. Roosevelt turned out was "Oliver Cromwell." This was written in 1900 and ran through six numbers of

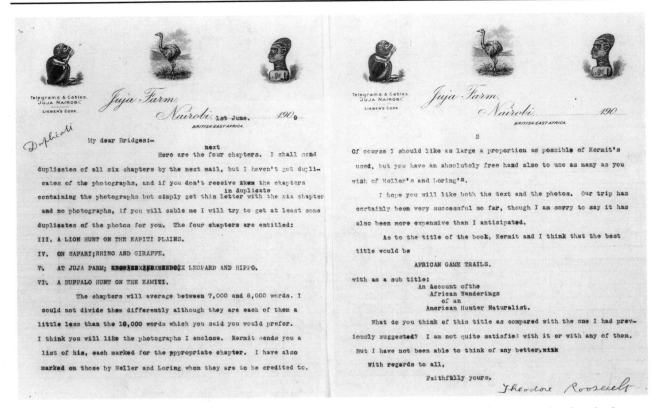

Letter by Roosevelt to Robert Bridges accompanying several chapters of his African hunting book, which were to be used as magazine articles

Scribner's. It was published later in book form, attracting wide attention.

In 1905 Mr. Roosevelt's pen once more gave profitable matter to the Scribners. As President of the United States he found time to do some hunting in the cane brakes of Louisiana and elsewhere, and after the hunts to write of them. "Outdoor Pastimes of an American Hunter" resulted and sold well. A new edition of this work, with added tales of the hunt, was got out this year.

Mr. Bridges said yesterday that Mr. Roosevelt's works had been very successful from the point of view of the publisher.

The Scribners also gathered all of the writings of Mr. Roosevelt and published them in a uniform edition called the "Elkhorn Edition." This edition, handsomely printed and bound, was limited and sold by subscription.

The news that the Scribners had landed the big prize in the Roosevelt contract trickled from publishing house to publishing house late yesterday afternoon, creating in many of the keenest of the bidders no end of excitement and some envy.

MEMO:
"Mem. of visit to President Roosevelt July 15th 1908" by CS II.

Having secured the rights to President Theodore Roosevelt's African articles, CS II went to his home in Oyster Bay, N.Y., to discuss details. These notes of the visit were apparently made for Scribner's own use after he returned, for at the bottom of the last page he has written: "(This is a very rough & hurried account but I have thought it might be worth writing as I wish I had done before with other interviews with Roosevelt, & with Stevenson, Kipling, Meredith, Grant, Harrison & others.)" "Collier" is Robert Joseph Collier of Collier's, a national weekly magazine, and one of the main contenders in the battle for serial rights to Roosevelt's articles.

Having been invited to luncheon I took the 10:30 train for Oyster Bay. Mr. Frank Millet [American artist] came into the car and sat down by me and I soon learned that he also was to lunch with the President. He has been appointed one of the Commissioners for the Japan Exposition and is also arranging for the medal, for Panama service, with a medalion of Roosevelt. On arriving at the station there were two autos in waiting with a list of those expected.

At the house we were taken into the newer and larger library room at the back of the house and soon the president appeared dressed all in white (duck) and was most cordial. Besides Millet & myself there were Prof. Henry Osborn, Dr. Lambert, Dr. Kerns (?) [Edgar A. Mearns] the army surgeon who is to accompany the President on the African expedition, Mr. Moore & his son who had been to Africa hunting, Mr. Modaira [?], Mr. Whitehouse, two or three others.

Almost at once on entering the President asked me to come with him and we sat on the side piazza. He said that he had another letter from Collier, since the acceptance of our $50,000 offer for the articles, increasing his offer from $75 to $100,000 and that Collier said he was writing to me. He was in no way disturbed with his contract with us but seemed very anxious that we should be entirely pleased. I assured him of this. He said he thought it was quite possible for him to accept too much for the articles and be made anxious about them - be compelled to write, to meet such a high price, something different from what he might wish to write, and he could not complain if the exploitation of the articles was sometimes made objectionable in order to make them pay. He would not feel comfortable if anyone was paying too much, and that Secretary Root agreed with him in all this.

I told him that it had occurred to me that he might think it strange that we had doubled our price from 25,000 to 50,000, that it suggested we might have been willing to buy them for less than they were worth but that their importance had increased with us as we knew more about them and saw the great attention of the public and the interest of the publishers. He said his own mind had been affected in the same way—that he would have accepted 25,000 if definitely made at first by Bridges and he called my attention to the fact that the contract was really offered by him. He said he always wanted us to have the articles, that he liked our ideals and the way we realized them— that he might almost be a little "snobbish" about the matter. I spoke highly of Collier as having facilities for making the best of such material but told him that I thought McClures might have been plunging a little. He said that was exactly the word "they are plunging."

Cover of the Scribner's Magazine *issue beginning the Roosevelt series of African hunting articles. Roosevelt provided material for ten articles, which ran consecutively in the magazine through July 1910; all were announced on the cover.*

He then said that he thought highly of the "Outlook" and had arranged with them to give them for a year after his return the exclusive right to any "sociological or political articles," that they were to pay him $12,000. They would take anything he might write from 500 to 5000 words. I suggested that he reserve book rights—that I thought they would so understand it but it might be well to make it clear. He said it was a good thing to do, that he was glad I had suggested it, and he would do it.

We talked for some time about the trip, the times the articles might be looked for (there may be one or two sent out but 1910 will be the year), the way he would go to Africa. He wanted to avoid England [English?] and any entertaining but I told him there would be a pavilion wherever he landed.

We particularly spoke of possible fever. He said he was certain to have it but he hoped not badly, that he had been laid up in camp two or three days on his last Western trip as I knew. I spoke of Baron Ismay [English general] being taken ill after he got back to London. He said he did not care what happened if he could only accomplish what he wanted—that he was always willing to take the consequences or pay for his pain. I thought of his refusal to pardon a man, when he was Gov, who had killed his unfaithful sweetheart & saying he did not blame the man, that he would probably have done the same himself but that he would have "taken his medicine." But I said I quite understood—"one step enough for me." He said "exactly; one step enough for me."

He spoke of the surgeon who was going with him and who had been suggested by Osborne; also about the photos which Kermit would take.

When we went to luncheon I sat on Mrs. Roosevelt's left. She was entirely free from affectation and cordial and simple—as always. I only mentioned the trip once when I asked her how she felt about having her husband go. She said she had been anxious for him to take a doctor but that he said it could not be and that she had not spoken about it again. She was delighted now that Dr. Kerns [i.e., Mearns] was going and that it showed that if you were patient things often came out better than you expected—that "the President" could not have afforded to take anyone but a very young and inexperienced doctor. (The surgeon goes as a taxidermist—one of the two furnished by the government—he is well qualified I am told.)

The sons Theodore & Kermit were at table. Kermit has just entered Harvard but is going to give it up for the trip. "Anyone would give up college for such a trip as that." He was very keen for all information and seems to have studied up about Africa.

After luncheon we returned to the library. Roosevelt was frankly pleased by a story told by Moore about his visit to Arabia with Homer Davenport the cartoonist. D. drew pictures for the Arabs of Roosevelt as a rough rider. They were tremendously interested and seemed to know of only two men, Solomon & Roosevelt, and no one between them.

There was a general talk over the map about where and what game could be had and I left early with Millet to catch the 2:40 for N.Y. & Morristown.

NOTE:
"A Testimonial to the Scribners," *Publishers' Weekly,* 20 November 1909, p. 1416.

Fifteen former employees of the firm of Charles Scribner's Sons gave a dinner on the evening of November 18 at Sherry's, New York, as a mark of appreciation to their former employers—Charles Scribner and Arthur H. Scribner. The singular fact was revealed that although some of the men at the table had left the employ of the publishing house more than twenty years ago every man had remained in the publishing business. There were no speeches. A feature of the dinner was the presentation to the Messrs. Scribner of a handsomely bound souvenir volume of the occasion. Those at the table were Edward Bok, of *The Ladies' Home Journal;* Frank N. Doubleday, Henry W. Lanier, Samuel A. Everitt, all of Doubleday, Page & Co.; Owen W. Brewer, of Chicago; Ernest Dressel North; W. D. Moffat, Robert S. Yard and Edwin W. Hall, all of Moffat, Yard & Co.; A. F. Jaccaci, William Agnew Paton, Winfield Scott Moody, Pitts Duffield, Robert Gilbert Welch, Fredrick F. Sherman and George G. Bell.

LETTER:
Letter from Maxwell Perkins to CS II, 18 December 1909, on *New York Times* stationery.

Perkins had graduated from Harvard in June 1907 and was currently a reporter for The New York Times. *His strongest reason for wanting a "regular and unexciting life" was a desire to marry Louise Saunders. He had to wait a few months for CS II to decide, but shortly after Perkins was hired as advertising manager in the spring of 1910 the couple got engaged; they were married on New Year's Eve. Perkins was promoted to book editor in 1914, and his subsequent thirty plus years at Scribners proved legendary.*

Dear Mr. Scribner:
From my talk with you last month I learned that you and Professor Wendell were friends. For that reason, and because his knowledge of me, though more general, is more recent than Mr. Coit's, I thought a letter from him would give you better material on which to form an opinion of me. I spoke to my brother about this, and his mention of it to Professor Wendell resulted in the letter herewith enclosed. I might have sent you letters from people of Harvard who knew me better, but from none, I thought, whom you knew better.

Of course, those who could most competently recommend me are my superiors on the Times, and

Letter of introduction for Maxwell Perkins written by his English professor at Harvard, Barrett Wendell (1855–1921), who was also a Scribner author and a close friend of CS II: "He has in him the right stuff. He is really the sort one can depend on" without their recommendation I could hardly hope for the position of which you spoke to me. Yet I cannot afford to set my bridge afire while I am crossing it. So far, I have said nothing here of my intention to leave the newspaper business. But if things so work out that the want of recommendation from my editors alone stands in my way with regard to this position, I shall instantly ask for it.

I know that people generally, and with considerable reason, suspect a newspaper man of wanting the quality of steadiness. They do not think him capable of settling down to a regular and unexciting life. In case you share that idea, I want to tell you that aside from my natural interest in books and all connected with them, I am anxious to make this change because of my desire for a regular life; and I have the strongest reasons a young man can have for desiring such a life, and for liking it once I have it.

This letter from Mr. Wendell came to me in a roundabout way, and that is why it was somewhat delayed in reaching you. If you do come to feel that a letter from my City Editor or from any others in authority here would be satisfactory, I will get such a letter, or such letters, on a word from you.

Very truly yours,
Maxwell Evarts Perkins

1910–1919

1910

February	Maxwell Perkins starts his career with the firm as Scribner advertising manager.
26 February	Publication date of *The Stoic and Epicurean* by R. D. Hicks, the first title in the Epochs of Philosophy series
24 August	Publication date of Theodore Roosevelt's *African Game Trails*

1911

1911	John Hall Wheelock, a promising poet, begins work at Scribners as a bookstore employee. He becomes an editor in 1926 and retires in 1957 as editor in chief.
30 September	Publication date of Edith Wharton's *Ethan Frome*
30 September	Publication date of the N. C. Wyeth–illustrated edition of Robert Louis Stevenson's *Treasure Island,* the first work in the Scribner Illustrated Classics series
October	Princeton University Press moves into its new $125,000 building at 41 William Street in Princeton, N.J., erected and equipped with funds provided by CS II.
21 October	Publication date of J. M. Barrie's *Peter Pan and Wendy* (the version with Neverland and Captain Hook), illustrated by F. D. Bedford

1912

17 February	CS II signs contract to purchase 597–599 Fifth Avenue for new building site; he closes the purchase on 15 March.
29 June	Publication date of James Weber Linn's *The Essentials of English Composition,* which would prove to be one of the most popular college publications of the Educational Department through World War II

1913

10 March	Publication date of John Fox Jr.'s *Heart of the Hills,* the #5 best-seller of 1913
11 March	At a special meeting, stockholders of Charles Scribner's Sons, Inc., approve the proposal by its board of directors to drop the term *Incorporated* from the firm's name.
May	Charles Scribner's Sons moves to 597–599 Fifth Avenue into another building designed by Ernest Flagg, CS II's brother-in-law.

24 May	Publication date of Price Collier's *Germany and the Germans,* the #2 nonfiction best-seller of 1913
14 July	Charles Scribner (CS III), having graduated from Princeton in June, joins his father and uncle in the family publishing firm

1914 Maxwell Perkins becomes an editor.

11 April	Publication date of *London: Critical Notes on the National Gallery and the Wallace Collection* by John C. Van Dyke, the first volume (of twelve) in his New Guides to Old Masters series, which he completes in 1927
25 April	Publication date of Frederick Palmer's *The Last Shot,* a novel that predicted much of World War I, the only book about war to sell appreciably during the war's first two years
May	Edward L. Burlingame retires; Robert Bridges takes over the editorship of *Scribner's Magazine.*
17 July	CS II pays $140,000 to settle Macy lawsuit over the store's right to sell copyrighted books at any price it chooses.

1915

18 September	Publication date of F. Hopkinson Smith's *Felix O'Day,* the #7 best-seller of 1915

1916

22 January	Publication date of *The Book of the Homeless,* edited by Edith Wharton. Scribners' profits from this volume of original and unpublished poetry, prose, and artwork, donated by well-known authors and artists, went to support Wharton's World War I refugee work in France.
8 April	Publication date of Frank H. Spearman's *Nan of Music Mountain,* the #8 best-seller of 1916
20 May	Publication date of J. J. Jusserand's *With America of Past and Present Days,* winner of the 1917 Pulitzer Prize for history
9 December	Publication date of Alan Seeger's *Poems,* the #4 general nonfiction best-seller of 1917 and #10 of 1918

1917

14 April	Publication date of the first three titles in the Modern Student's Library: *The Ordeal of Richard Feverel* by George Meredith, *Pendennis* by William Makepeace Thackeray, and *The Return of the Native* by Thomas Hardy
6 June	Scribners purchases Forbes and Company, the publisher of *Architecture* magazine; the August issue is the first bearing the Scribner imprint.
(end) June	Whitney Darrow, manager of the Princeton University Press, becomes the book advertising manager at Scribners.
16 November	Publication date of Richard Harding Davis's *Adventures and Letters of Richard Harding Davis,* the #7 general nonfiction best-seller of 1918

1918

29 April	Publication date of Jesse Lynch Williams's *Why Marry?,* the winner of the 1918 Pulitzer Prize for draía
7 June	Publication date of *War Letters of Edmond Genet, The First American Aviator Killed Flying the Stars and Stripes,* edited, with an introduction, by Grace Ellery Channing

1919

| September | Charles Kingsley arrives in London to become Scribner English representative, succeeding Lemuel W. Bangs. |
| 12 September | Publication date of Theodore Roosevelt's *Roosevelt's Letters to His Children,* edited by Joseph B. Bishop, the #3 nonfiction best-seller of 1920 |

Maxwell Perkins, legendary Scribner book editor. Perkins began in the spring of 1910 in the advertising department, became an editor in 1914, and was editor in chief and the firm's vice president at the time of his death in 1947.

ARTICLE:
"New Scribner Building," *Publishers' Weekly,* 22 June 1912, pp. 1974–1975.

The plans for the new Scribner building, at Nos. 597 and 599 Fifth Avenue, New York, just above 48th Street, with a frontage of 53.5 feet, have been filed, and the construction is well under way, the excavation and foundations being nearly completed. The building will be larger and higher than the present building, but in general character similar to it. The elevation shows a ten-story building of granite, limestone and ornamental iron work, and the architect, Ernest Flagg, who recently completed the Singer Building, has designed a facade that will compare favorably artistically with anything on the avenue.

The Scribners are reserving the lower stories for their retail business and publication offices, and a number of applications from prospective tenants have been received for the upper stories. The retail store, with the entrance in the middle, will be 30 feet high, and an unusual feature will be an exhibition gallery, in the rear, with broad galleries on each side.

The entrance to the rest of the building will be on the south, with large elevators and stairways, and the upper stories will have light on all four sides, being above the roofs of the buildings on the north, south and rear—all these being low buildings, just rebuilt on twenty-one-year leases. The top floor will be specially designed for art purposes, with north light and skylights, and janitors' quarters will be provided on the roof.

The building will be absolutely fireproof, and will be completed next May, when the Scribners will move from their present building on Fifth Avenue, which it is expected will be leased by one of the wholesale houses looking for quarters in that locality. This is also a modern fireproof building, and, built only a few years ago, is to-day one of the most attractive buildings in the neighborhood.

ARTICLE:
"The New Scribner Building," *Publishers' Weekly,* 17 May 1913, pp. 1804–1805.

The publishing house of Charles Scribner's Sons is now established in its new home on Fifth Avenue and 48th street. It is a ten-story building of steel, brick and concrete, without any woodwork whatever, except in the furnishings and fittings. Utility as much as beauty was the aim of the architect, Ernest Flagg, who is also the designer of the former Scribner Building at 153 Fifth avenue. Windows, therefore, form practically the entire

Future site of the Scribner building at 597–599 Fifth Avenue, on Tuesday, 21 May 1912, after demolition work had been completed

CS II DIARY ENTRIES:
Saturday 17 February 1912

Sign contract for purchase of new building site for business on Fifth Ave.

Friday 15 March 1912

Close purchase of Nos. [blank] Fifth Ave.
Cost 750,000—mtg 400
Pay 315,00 & 2,000 for tax on mtg
Borrow 60,000 from Park
(35,000 pd on agreement to purchase)

These notes refer to the purchase of 597–599 Fifth Avenue in New York City.

front and back of every floor, so that the rooms in which the various departments of the house are placed, are flooded with daylight, whose effect is still further heightened by the white plaster ceilings and walls, and the concrete floors.

The first five stories of this building are occupied entirely by the firm. The retail department occupies the entire ground floor; the wholesale, educational, and religious literature departments, the second floor; the subscription book department, the third floor; *Scribner's Magazine*, the art department, the manufacturing department, and the advertising department, the fourth floor; and the financial, executive, and book publication offices, the fifth floor.

In point of beauty there is little doubt that the Scribner Book Store stands first in this country, and possibly in the whole world. It is a large slightly oblong room, lighted from both the front and the rear. Its arched ceiling of a whitish stone is supported by pillars of the same substance. Its walls, broken by a gallery, are completely covered by a stock of handsomely bound books upon glass shelves. The entire front of the building—that is, the first story of the building—is in reality one great window, set in a metal frame-work of a graceful design, and faced with brass. Over the glass door, which forms a section of this great window, is the name CHARLES SCRIBNER'S SONS, in gold letters, and lower down the familiar emblem of the house—the lighted lamp and the open book, surrounded by a wreath.

As you enter the store, and look directly through it beyond the counters and tables of quartered oak, you face a low handsome stairway, which leads up to a wide gallery, slightly below the level of the narrow gallery that runs around the store. This is a new feature in a book store,—an exhibition gallery for the display of groups of books to which some particular event

*Early interior views of the building's first floor—and stairway
and mezzanine—site of the New York City "landmark"
Scribner Bookstore*

*The 597–599 Fifth Avenue building occupied by Charles Scribner's Sons from 1913
until 1984, designed by Ernest Flagg, CS II's brother-in-law, who had also
designed the firm's previous headquarters at 153–157 Fifth Avenue*

or occasion may give an especial interest, and also
for the display of original photographs, drawings,
and paintings used in book and magazine illustrations in the course of the year. This gallery is so
arranged, that its corners, extended beyond the
line of the building, and, roofed with glass, admit
a flood of daylight which helps to illuminate the
store, but makes perfect the situation of the gallery for the examination of pictures, books, or
manuscripts. The floor directly below this gallery
is on a lower level than the main floor of the store,
and here the various retail offices are located.

Bookbuyers frequently compared the old Scribner
Book Store, on lower Fifth avenue, to a private library, and the effect of the new store gives this
impression still more strongly; or perhaps the
comparison to an extremely handsome small public library would be more apt.

The wholesale offices of the house are on the
second floor but the sample room is a sort of
closed gallery, not noticeable from the book store
itself, but lighted by arched windows from which
you look down directly into the store. This gives a
greater advantage for the display of a line of

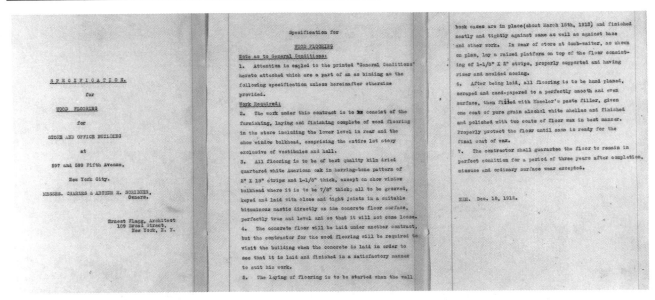

Architect's specifications for flooring on the building's first floor and display windows

books than was offered in the old quarters of the house.

This splendid new building is the seventh home of Charles Scribner's Sons, Publishers and Importers. When the house was founded in 1846 by Charles Scribner, Sr., its offices were a part of the Chapel of the old brick church on the point of Nassau street and Park Row at City Hall Park. In 1856 Mr. Scribner moved the firm to 377–379 Broadway; in 1858 to 124 Grand street, and later to 654 Broadway. Charles Scribner, Sr., died in 1871, and three years later the house moved to 743 Broadway, where it remained until 19 years ago, when it moved to 153–157 Fifth avenue. That was the first building erected by the house, and was looked upon as a bold move, for Madison Square was then considered far up-town for purposes of commerce, and practically all of Fifth avenue below 23d street was given over to private houses.

ARTICLE:
"The New Scribner Building," *Book Buyer*, 38, no. 4 (May 1913): 81–82.

The article quickly becomes an advertisement for the ground floor bookstore—emphasizing "the old tradition of the book trade" under which customers can still find sympathetic clerks and where old, beautiful, and specialized books are displayed and sold in company with the latest domestic and foreign publications. The author argues that, while regular bookselling has become just another merchandising aspect of the "great department stores" (like Macy's), the location, convenience, service, and stock of the Scribner bookstore sets it apart.

Charles Scribner's Sons are now established in their new ten-story building on the east side of Fifth Avenue at 48th Street. The work of manufacturing books and Magazine is conducted as hitherto in the Scribner Press Building on West 43d Street, but the editorial and business offices of these departments are in the new building, which is represented on the cover of this number of the BOOK BUYER. That picture gives an idea of its beautiful proportions—its architect was Ernest Flagg, designer of several of New York's finest structures—and the interior corresponds to the exterior in a certain harmonious simplicity which is one of the rarest qualities produced by any art. It has been said that beauty and fitness are largely the same thing—the beautiful yacht is the swiftest, and the handsomest horse is the strongest, and indeed, what is grace in motion—one expression of beauty—but the doing of a thing in the easiest and quickest manner. Certainly, if there is this close relation between the two qualities, the new Scribner Building is perfectly adapted to its purpose. It is fitted for carrying on the same work with a greater skill than formerly. And this is especially true of its retail department.

In its new setting—as indeed to a high degree it did in the old—the Scribner Book-Store suggests a very large and handsome private library in which elegance combines with convenience. A great oblong room, flooded at the front and rear with daylight; lofty, arched ceiling, supported by gray stone-like pillars; walls, broken by two galleries, aglow with the rich deep blues, greens and reds of leather bindings; woodwork tables and partitions of quartered oak:—to step directly into such an atmosphere from the clatter of Fifth Avenue traffic will always be a pleasant sensation. In fact, the general appearance and arrangement of the store give many interesting points for observation, and visitors, whether purchasers or not, will always be welcome.

The most obvious advantage that comes to the store by its change of quarters is that of location. It is now at the centre of the uptown retail district; could hardly be more conveniently situated for people that live in almost all residential sections of the city. The next great advantage is that of size. Its more commodious quarters enable it to carry a larger stock of current books, American and foreign; of rare books, and of first editions as well. The stationery department shares in this: its stock will be larger and more attractively displayed. Then, too, the larger space has allowed of the introduction of a novel feature—an exhibition gallery for the display of groups of books to which some particular event or occasion may give an especial interest, and this gallery is so arranged at the rear of the store, as to light and shape, that photographs, drawings, and paintings used in illustrations are there perfectly shown;—no insignificant thing, since in the course of the year there are many pictures used in this way, both for holiday books, ordinary books, and for the Magazine, which have a great intrinsic beauty, now often not recognized, because their character, as pictures simply, is lost by connection with the text in their character as illustrations.

The store has always been conducted in recognition of a certain principle, to which it will now be able to give further exercise—that the patrons, and the public generally, have a right to expect of a bookstore, as distinguished from any other kind of store—quick understanding of individual tastes and desires and an accurate attention to them. Now that bookselling has so largely passed, with the sale of everything else, into the hands of the great department stores, so that books have come, in a certain measure, to be looked upon as only one of a thousand forms of merchandise, this sort of understanding and at-

tention is almost forgotten. But while Scribner's is a store where all the latest literature of any kind may be had immediately—where promptness is put among the first objects—yet the old tradition of the book trade, under which visitors could feel as if they were not shopping and would find clerks who could enter into some measure of sympathy with their wants, is maintained. From this, it is evident that the resemblance to a library is not merely superficial. It is like one also in that the books are grouped on their glass shelves according to their topics, and so representative is each collection, that the desired volume can be easily found.

In fact, the Scribner Book-Store long ago became a place never to be neglected by such as sought some special book that derived its rarity from age, beauty, or the specialized nature of its contents. Several of its heads were Phi Beta Kappa men, all college graduates; a wide scholarship was needed in dealing in so wide a range of subjects exactly; intimacy with literature was essential in the purchase and sale of rare editions and manuscripts.

In that latter branch of bookselling the retail department has long excelled. Among the innumerable precious volumes that have passed through their hands are the first four folios of Shakespeare. They now have a new Shakespeare folio, the first edition of Gulliver's Travels, Dickens's and Scott's works as first issued, early editions of Milton, valuable Napoleonic manuscripts in French and English, the first edition of Goldsmith's Vicar of Wakefield; many volumes of value, beauty, and curious interest bound with the elaborate art of the old-time binder.

But this does not mean that the popular taste is neglected. A representative bookstore must carry full stock of current publications, including, of course, the latest novels; and that love for the permanent in form and content which inspired the creation of such a store with its personal connections among collectors—its attention to the best in foreign production—its various handsomely bound editions of the world's great writers—its original manuscripts—its early editions of the great books—has not precluded that enterprise which must enliven the bookseller to the general public.

CONGRATULATIONS:
Best wishes to CS II from two best-selling Scribner authors on the occasion of the firm's move to its new building on Fifth Avenue.

•Richard Harding Davis (1864–1916), 11 April 1913, author of *The Soldiers of Fortune* (1897):

Dear Mr Scribner

I passed the new building yesterday when motoring in from the farm [in Mount Kisco, where Arthur H. Scribner also lived] and before I knew what building it was, I was busily and gratefully admiring it. It is <u>fine</u>!!! I have always admitted that I built the one at 22nd Street with Soldiers of Fortune and Arthur's house out here with "Gallegher", but, I had nothing to do with this new palace. I will <u>never</u> get the courage to enter it; so, in the end, it may save you a lot of <u>money</u>!!!

Again, let me tell you what a splendid, and graceful and good piece of work it all is, and let me congratulate you both, heartily.

Faithfully yours
Richard Harding Davis

•Edith Wharton (1862–1937), 19 May 1913, author of *The House of Mirth* (1905):

Dear Mr. Scribner,

. . . Till I opened the May Scribner I had no idea that you were moving into new quarters. It breaks up a long series of pleasant associations to write another address under your name; but I hope the chain will be taken up, & new links added to it, & that the next chapter in the career of the firm will be as prosperous as those preceding it.

Yours very sincerely
<u>Edith Wharton</u>

NOTE:
Under "Literary and Trade Notes," *Publishers' Weekly*, 25 October 1913, p. 1381.

A FRENCH BOOK DEPARTMENT has been opened in the new Scribner building at 5th Avenue at 48th Street, New York City. This department is in a position to supply from its stock any and every French book. New books as well as standard works of fiction, classics, memoirs, art, social questions, music, philosophy, works by French lecturers in America, educational, fine books and gift books are always in stock. A stock of bound books and sets is kept and exceptional facilities for special bindings are offered. French papers, stationery, cards, etc., are also in stock. A special wholesale division of the French Book Department is equipped to insure to the trade a satisfactory delivery, a liberal discount, and a prompt and accurate answer to all inquiries. The discount

Scribner catalogue for 1911–1912 holiday books, bearing the endpaper illustration by N. C. Wyeth for Robert Louis Stevenson's Treasure Island *(1911)*

sheet, and a special proposition for French book advertising will be sent on request.

NOTE:
Under "Literary and Trade Notes," *Publishers' Weekly*, 6 December 1913, p. 1954.

MOST PEOPLE cannot make presents of original pictures at Christmas-time because the prices of pictures of real merit are so very high. But this is not the case with pictures that were painted to illustrate books. The mere fact that such was the primary purpose of the artist, though it frequently does not detract in the least from their excellence simply as pictures, results in a far lower price. Original illustrations are now exhibited and put on sale in the exhibition gallery of the Scribner book store. Such pictures as "On the Island of Earraid," by N. C. Wyeth, one of the illustrations for the holiday edition of "Kidnapped," the pictures by Mr. Peixotto for his "Pacific Shores from Panama," and Paul

Bransom's illustrations for "The Wind in the Willows," are offered.

NOTE:
Under "Literary and Trade Notes," *Publishers' Weekly,* 10 January 1914, pp. 157–158.

AFTER THE EXHIBITION illustrating the processes by which a book is manufactured, now on view in the gallery of the Scribner Bookstore, is closed, it will be sent, upon payment of transportation charges, to various booksellers about the country. Any bookseller who wishes to display this exhibition in his store, for the interests of his customers, may make arrangements by applying to Charles Scribner's Sons. Of course, it will only be possible to lend the exhibition to a limited number of booksellers, but every effort will be made to so adjust conflicts in dates, etc., as to satisfy as many as possible. The exhibition consists of 55 pictures and pieces, all framed, the largest measuring about 3x2½ feet, and the smallest very much less. Copies of the little illustrated pamphlet accompanying the exhibition, called "The Story of the Making of a Book," will be supplied to the bookseller on request. But besides this pamphlet, which is complete in itself, a brief printed explanation is fixed upon the frame of every picture and object, explaining it.

CS II DIARY ENTRY:
Tuesday 5 May 1914

Bridges & Arthur dine with me
& tell B—of his taking editorship

Robert Bridges assumes editorship of Scribner's Magazine on retirement of Edward L. Burlingame.

NOTE:
"Charles Scribner's Sons Using Attractive Ads. in Vacation Campaign," *Publishers' Weekly,* 26 June 1915, p. 1867.

CHARLES SCRIBNER'S SONS are launching a three-times-a-week newspaper campaign in some of the big cities throughout the country. The advertisements themselves, each playing up but a single book, are dignified examples of book advertising which stand out from the ruck of advertising.

The Scribner Book Store, also, is running at the present time in New York papers a number of

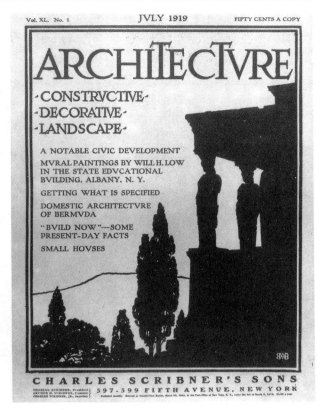

The July 1919 cover of Architecture *magazine, which Scribners purchased in 1917 and published until 1936*

retail advertisements, similar to the above in appearance, but aimed not at exploiting single books, but at securing general vacation orders. The whole spirit of these advertisements is to make bookbuying easy for the man on vacation. "It doesn't matter," says one of these, "who publishes the book—it may be an English, French or American publisher. It doesn't matter what the book is—it will appear as soon as the United States mail can get it to you." We reproduce below another of these advertisements: [text only]

"Too Much Trouble to pack a dozen books in your trunk. It is an old fashioned idea, a relic from stagecoach days, this business of taking everything you will need with you.

Here is a scheme. Write a list of the books you will need during the summer. Put a date opposite each book. Send the list to the Scribner Book Store, Fifth Avenue at 48th Street. Then when you have finished one book, the next will arrive automatically. This is what we mean when we talk about 'out-of-town service'."

NOTE:
Under "Periodical Notes," *Publishers' Weekly,* 29 September 1917, p. 1095.

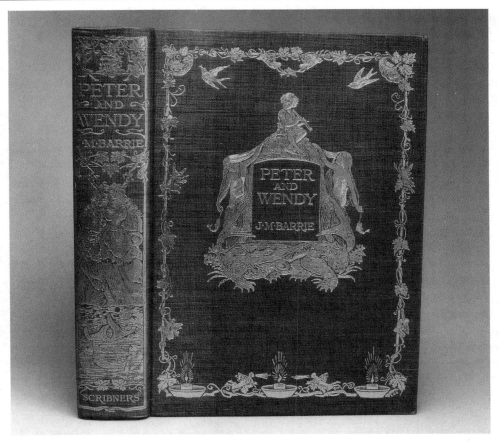

First American edition copy (1911) of this children's classic, the version of the story with Captain Hook and Neverland, illustrated by F. D. Bedford

CS II Diary Entries:
Tuesday 29 May 1917

Lunch with Mr. Forbes & offer 60,000 for "Architecture"

He offered to sell for 68,000

Wednesday, 6 June 1917

Buy Architecture for $60,000

Scribners published Architecture *magazine through May 1936.*

WITH THE NOVEMBER ISSUE, the price of *Scribner's Magazine* will be raised to $4 a year, 35 cents a copy.

ARTICLE:
"Oppose German Language. Advertising Club Urges Suppression of Papers Using It," *The New York Times*, 11 May 1918, p. 18.

. . . Copies of the resolution of the Women's Organization petitioning the President to forbid the publication of German language newspapers have been circulated in this city and are being sent to clubs throughout the country. These petitions are to be sent to the office of the American Defense Society, from where they will be forwarded to President Wilson. Mrs. Oliver Cromwell Field, President of the American Relief Legion, induced Scribner & Sons to abstain from publishing books printed in German during the war.

NOTE:
"Energetic Book Advertising," *Publishers' Weekly,* 26 April 1919, p. 1158.

The increasing confidence of the trade publishers in the state of the book market is again illustrated by the full page spread that the Scribners are giving to their leading spring titles on the back page of the New York *Times's* regular issue for Saturday, April 26th.

The page is well worth studying for its typographical effectiveness, its method of playing up the books' characteristics before giving titles, the careful balance of interest in the kind of books emphasized and the lack of stress on the Scribner name which, in so large a display in what is not only a New York but a national medium, should have a decided effect on distribution.

LETTER:
Letter from Charles Kingsley to Arthur H. Scribner, 1 July 1919.

Since 1878 Scribners had maintained an office in London, begun by Charles Welford, who had been CS I's partner in "Scribner & Welford," the early importing branch of the firm. Lemuel W. Bangs succeeded Welford on his death in 1885. When health problems began to plague Bangs in 1918, CS II began to look for a replacement. His choice, Charles Kingsley, was a graduate of Yale and a previous Scribner employee.

My dear Mr. Scribner:

As I indicated in my conversation with you yesterday afternoon, I am not only willing but anxious to resume my relations with the firm of Charles Scribner's Sons, and to accept the offer made by Mr. Charles Scribner last week.

When Mr. Safford first spoke to me, and again at the interview with you and your brother, I referred to the question of income tax. I had heard something about the high rates prevailing in England, and expected there would be a tax of several hundred dollars at least. I have investigated this question and find that my fears are more than realized. Inquiry at the British Consulate develops the fact that incomes of all residents of Great Britain whether British subjects or not are taxable. The rate on incomes ranging from £1000 to £1500 is 3/9 on earned income and 4/6 on unearned income. This would bring my British income tax to £224 approximately, or slightly over $1000. Moreover, my lawyer informs me that as long as I retain my American Citizenship I am taxable in this country no matter where I reside, here or abroad, and that there is no loophole for escape. Under the English law there are no abatements, as they call them, on incomes over £700, and no allowances for wife, children or dependents on incomes over £1000, so I face an income tax of approximately $1200.

Much as I should like to, I hardly feel as though I would be justified, under the present uncertain conditions, and with the cost of living in England so greatly advanced over pre-war figures, in attempting to live on the salary you mention, reduced as it would be by over 20%. Undoubtedly, even at the present time, certain commodities are cheaper in England than in this country. I have talked with a number of people who have recently come from England, and while their reports are somewhat contradictory, the consensus of opinion is that at the present time the difference in the cost of living between the countries is very small.

One thing is certain, and that is that the cost of educating my children will be considerably increased. The English Parish and District Schools are quite impossible, which means of course that I should have to send them to private schools. I am sure that you will understand my position and that you will see the reasonableness of it.

In case you should decide in favor of making allowance for the above mentioned conditions and appoint me your representative, I understand that you would be willing to pay the expense of moving my family and my lares and penetes. There is also a question of disposing of the lease of my house in White Plains which expires May 1, next, and which is at the rate of $60 a month. I think it quite possible and even probable that it might be sublet for the balance of the term. I should hesitate to mention this under normal circumstances, but my recent illness has so far depleted the usual reserve that the payment of double rent for the next six or eight months would seriously embarrass me.

For the same reason, having resigned my present position, and thereby cutting off my salary from that source, I should be glad to have my

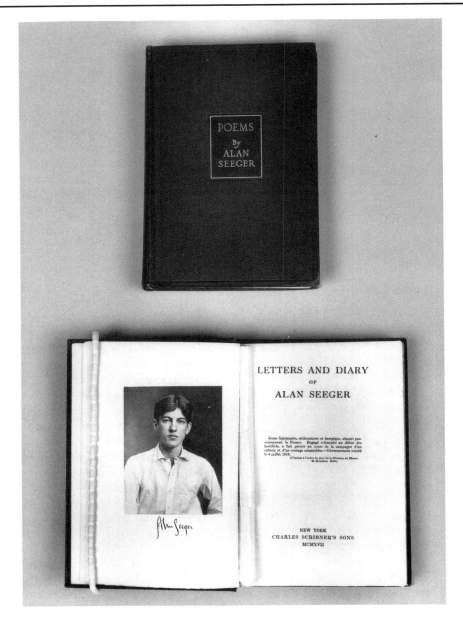

First editions of Alan Seeger's two posthumous works. Probably nothing Scribners published during World War I captured the country's heart like Seeger's Poems, which was the #4 nonfiction best-seller of 1917 and #10 of 1918. Born in New York City and a graduate of Harvard (1910), Seeger was living in Europe when the war began—traveling, writing poems, settling on a literary life. He quickly joined the French Foreign Legion, for he had become devoted to France and, especially, Paris. On 28 June 1916, knowing his unit was soon to participate in a difficult battle, he wrote to a friend: "We go to the attack tomorrow. This will probably be the biggest thing yet. We are to have the honor of marching in the first wave. No sacks, but two musettes, toile de tent slung over shoulder, plenty of cartridges, grenades, and baïonnette au canon. I will write soon if I get through all right. If not, my only earthly care is for my poems. Add the ode ["Ode in Memory of the American Volunteers Fallen for France"] I sent you and the three sonnets to my last volume and you will have opera omnia quæ existant. I am glad to be going in the first wave. If you are in this thing at all it is best to be in to the limit. And this is the supreme experience" (Letters and Diary, p. 211). Several days later, on the evening of 4 July, Seeger fell to German machine-gun fire in the first wave of attack at Belloy-en-Santerre, a death which he had anticipated in his poem "I Have a Rendezvous with Death."

salary begin with July 1, although it is hardly likely that I will be able to take up active work before the early part of August. Such matters as these, however, I feel confident may be left for your decision.

My doctor seems to think that I can get away on or about the 10th of the month, so that I can be reached at this address up to the latter part of next week. If you write or 'phone me, I can come to New York at short notice.

You know that I lived for a number of years in England and am consequently fairly well acquainted with English customs and ways of thought; and feeling confident, as I do, that I could make a good record in London, I trust that we will be able to come to a satisfactory arrangement.

In the meantime, I beg to remain
Yours very sincerely,
Charles Kingsley

The Scribner brothers thought Kingsley's terms were satisfactory: they assumed the English income tax on his salary and used 1 July as his starting date. By 11 September Kingsley was in London, where he remained as Scribners' English representative until the beginning of World War II. Urged by CS III to come back to the States in the late spring of 1940, Kingsley turned over the responsibilties of running Scribners' English office to John Carter, who had joined the London branch in 1927 as buyer of rare books for the New York bookstore.

1920–1930

1920

26 March	Publication of F. Scott Fitzgerald's first book, *This Side of Paradise*
24 September	Publication date of Edward Bok's first book, *The Americanization of Edward Bok,* winner of the 1921 Pulitzer Prize for biography, and the #3 nonfiction best-seller of 1922, the #8 of 1923, and #10 of 1924

1921

12 May	Publication of *What Really Happened at Paris: The Story of the Peace Conference, 1918–1919, by American Delegates,* edited by Edward M. House and Charles Seymour
October	Publication of the first two volumes (of twenty-six) of the Vailima Edition of *The Works of Robert Louis Stevenson,* which is completed in 1923
15 December	Death of Lemuel W. Bangs, head of Scribners' London office from 1884 to 1919

1922

24 March	Publication date of John Galsworthy's *The Forsyte Saga*
22 September	Publication date of F. Scott Fitzgerald's *Tales of the Jazz Age*
15 November	Death of Edward L. Burlingame, first editor (1887–1914) of *Scribner's Magazine*

1923

16 February	Publication date of Arthur Train's *His Children's Children,* the #2 best-seller of 1923
23 February	Publication date of Stark Young's first Scribner book, *The Flower in Drama: A Book of Papers on the Theatre*
6 April	Publication date of Edward Bok's *A Man from Maine,* the #10 nonfiction best-seller of 1923
6 April	Publication date of the first two volumes (of five) of Winston Churchill's first Scribner book, *The World Crisis*

23 September	Publication date of Michael Idvorsky Pupin's *From Immigrant to Inventor,* winner of the 1924 Pulitzer Prize for biography

1924

9 May	Publication date of Ring Lardner's first Scribner book, *How to Write Short Stories (With Samples)*
19 September	Publication date of Will James's first book, *Cowboys North and South*
15 October	Publication date of the first two volumes (of twenty-eight) in the Atlantic Edition of *The Works of H. G. Wells,* which is completed in 1927

1925

10 January	Publication date of Edward Bok's *Twice Thirty,* the #7 nonfiction best-seller of 1925
February	1st issue of *The Scribner Bookstore* [News], a periodical (pamphlet) offering a selected list of current books from all publishers
27 March	Publication date of James Boyd's first book, *Drums*
10 April	Publication date of F. Scott Fitzgerald's *The Great Gatsby*

1926

12 March	Publication date of Volume I of Mark Sullivan's *Our Times,* the #4 nonfiction best-seller of 1926
28 May	Publication date of Ernest Hemingway's first Scribner book, *The Torrents of Spring*
9 July	Publication date of John Galsworthy's *The Silver Spoon,* the #6 best-seller of 1926
September	Publication of the first volume (of ten) in the Julian Edition of *The Complete Works of Percy Bysshe Shelley,* which is completed in 1930
10 September	Publication date of Will James's *Smoky, the Cowhorse,* winner of the 1927 Newbery Medal for best children's book
8 October	Publication date of Willard Huntington Wright's first Scribner book, *The Benson Murder Case,* published under the pseudonym S. S. Van Dine
22 October	Publication date of Ernest Hemingway's *The Sun Also Rises*

1927

3 June	Scribners signs contract with the American Council of Learned Societies to publish the multivolume *Dictionary of American Biography.*
22 July	Publication date of Conrad Aiken's first Scribner book, *Blue Voyage,* the first novel by this American poet
September	John Carter assumes responsibility for Scribners' London rare-book business.

1928

	George McKay Schieffelin, eldest grandson of CS II, becomes assistant treasurer, moving to the firm from the Scribner Press, where he had been assistant to the manager. Over the next fifty-four years—the longest tenure of any Scribner family member—he will assume greater management responsibilities: 1936, treasurer; 1953, senior vice president; 1963, executive vice president; 1970, chairman of the board; 1978, director of Scribner Book Companies.
	Arthur Hawley Scribner assumes presidency of Scribners when CS II "retires" to become chairman of the board.
January	First issue of *Scribner's Magazine* in its new format, with a cover designed by Rockwell Kent

24 March	Publication date of Willard Huntington Wright's *The Greene Murder Case* (under the pseudonym S. S. Van Dine), the #4 best-seller of 1928
10 July	Publication date of John Galsworthy's *Swan Song,* the #3 best-seller of 1928
22 July	Death of W. C. Brownell, Scribner editor and literary adviser, who started with the firm in 1888
26 October	Publication date of Benito Mussolini's *My Autobiography*
8 November	Publication date of the first volume (of twenty-one) of the *Dictionary of American Biography,* which is completed in 1937 with the index volume, though later supplements are published

1929

20 February	Publication date of Willard Huntington Wright's *The Bishop Murder Case* (under the pseudonym S. S. Van Dine), the #4 best-seller of 1929
June	Boston bans this month's issue of *Scribner's Magazine,* which begins the serialization of Ernest Hemingway's novel *A Farewell to Arms,* on complaints that his fiction is "salacious." July's issue is treated similarly.
27 September	Publication date of Ernest Hemingway's *A Farewell to Arms*
October	Publication of the first two volumes (of eighteen) in the Peter Pan Edition of *The Works of J. M. Barrie,* which is completed in 1941
18 October	Publication date of Thomas Wolfe's first book, *Look Homeward, Angel*
15 November	Publication date of Conrad Aiken's *Selected Poems,* winner of the 1930 Pulitzer Prize for poetry

1930

February	Robert Bridges retires as editor of *Scribner's Magazine* to become a literary adviser to the firm. Associate editor Alfred S. Dashiell becomes "managing editor" (new title) of the magazine.
April	*Scribner's Magazine* announces in this issue the offer of a prize of $5,000 for the best "long" short story (between 15,000 and 35,000 words) submitted by an American author by 30 September—won by John Peale Bishop's "Many Thousands Gone."
18 April	Publication date of Leon Trotsky's *My Life: An Attempt at an Autobiography*
19 April	Death of Charles Scribner (CS II)
1 August	Publication date of Will James's *Lone Cowboy,* the #5 nonfiction best-seller of 1930
September	Scribners' London office, having outgrown its quarters in Regent Street, moves to 23 Bedford Square, the new publishing center of the city, near the British Museum.
12 September	Publication date of Bernadotte E. Schmitt's *The Coming of War, 1914* (two volumes), winner of the 1931 Pulitzer Prize for history

View of Scribners on Fifth Avenue in the early 1920s

CS II DIARY ENTRY:
Saturday 18 Novemnber 1922

Obliged to attend Burlingames funeral @ 3—Act as pallbearer.

Edward L. Burlingame was the first editor (1887–1914) of Scribner's Magazine.

ARTICLE:
"A Half Century of Publishing, Charles Scribner Honored by His University and Friends," *Publishers' Weekly,* 20 June 1925, p. 1996.

Fifty years ago, Charles Scribner graduated from Princeton University, as his father had done thirty-five years before, and entered the publishing business. Four years later, on the death of his older brother, John Blair Scribner, he became the head of the business, which he has since directed with very great distinction and cumulating success. During these years he has found time to give such continuous and valuable service to his university and also to the general interests of the publishing profession that both have many reasons to do him honor.

At the commencement exercises at Princeton University this week, President Hibben, in happily worded phrases, bestowed on Mr. Scribner the degree of Doctor of Letters in recognition of his service to the field of letters and to the university.

DOCTOR OF LETTERS—*Charles Scribner of the Class of 1875. The house of Scribner, founded by Charles Scribner of the Class of 1840 and just entering its eightieth year, has been directed for now half a century by the second of his name until its expanding influence has spread wherever our language is read. Including in its purpose true literature, from the graver books of thought to enchanted tales, histories, poems and adventure, it has discovered young authors and given them readers, advanced the fame of older authors and not infrequently has acquired and issued writings of rare timeliness and power. It stands today as a symbol for whatever is most courteous, honorable and fruitful of good in American endeavor. In his half century since graduation the head of the house has given every year to labor and love for Princeton. Intimate in her counsels, alert in stimulating her literary life, old in wisdom and young in spirit, constant in helping her needs, his unobtrusive, bright and kindly influence is part of all the best we have.*

Mr. Scribner's contributions to his university have been many, and not the least of these was the establishment of the Princeton University Press which has fully justified the hopes of its founder by the scholarly distinction of its publications and the typographical excellence of its product.

The story of the fifty years' growth of the publishing organization of the House of Scribner is of outstanding significance and deserves to be recorded in detail; it provides one of the best possible examples of a fully developed general publishing business with successful educational and subscription departments, special departments for children's books, religious books, music books, a retail store, two magazines and a printing plant. And [that] all this has been accomplished while still finding time for friendly and cooperative contacts with his fellow publishers is indicated by comment which this occasion has brought out.

MEMORANDUM:
Maxwell Perkins, "The New Writers" [early 1926?].

In this memorandum, intended for circulation within the firm for comment and discussion, Perkins proposes starting a new magazine devoted to previously unpublished, talented writers. He would not get his wish directly—but, as Scribners' chief book editor, he would accomplish for new writers, such as Ernest Hemingway, Thomas Wolfe, and Marjorie Kinnan Rawlings, much of what he envisaged in this "credo." And, no doubt, his views influenced the editors of Scribner's Magazine, *which would revamp its format and herald "new writers" in 1928.*

The position of a publisher reputed to have a sincere and lively interest in assisting young writers; to be sympathetic to new ideas and eager to encourage them; to be anxious to provide an easily opened gateway into the literary field, would be an enviable one: He would have obviated that sentiment toward himself, sometimes amounting almost to hostility, that writers, especially the young, entertain toward a publisher because of the weight he must give to commercial considerations: he would be regarded by writers in general with an uncommon and sympathetic respect.

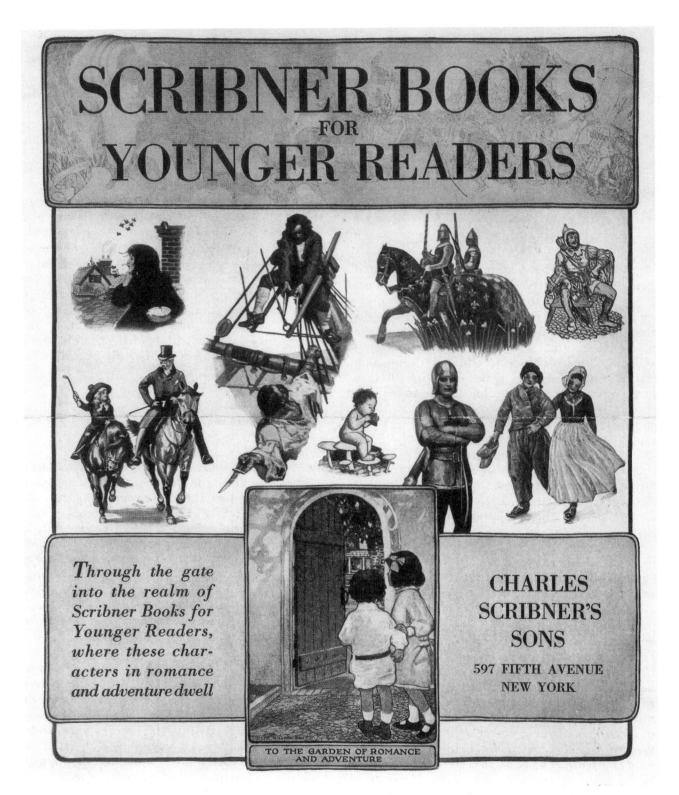

1923 brochure listing children's books, including all the titles in the Scribner Illustrated Classics series and the Scribner Series for Young People

Should he actually furnish such a gateway he might expect it to be the means by which brilliant talents were realized, and he would associate himself with these talents at the start;- a situation by which he should not only immensely profit, but, as one who visibly encouraged and definitely advanced the developments of letters, he should be rightly proud.

This memorandum is to suggest how Charles Scribner's Sons might come into such a siuation by publishing a monthly magazine entitled "The New Writers" which should limit its contributors to such as fell within the meaning of the phrase as interpreted by the publisher's purpose.

According to his purpose, the writers excluded would be those already recognized and placed by previous publication; and it might be thought that this would be the case with those who had published a book. No other limitation would be needed; for the magazine should be miscellaneous, its pages open to poetry, essays, articles, stories, even serials.

The instant you consider the proposal certain objections occur. For instance, the restriction of contributors to those who had not yet gained reputation might result in immature, crude, perhaps "vealy" collections of writing. But we are not confined to beginners in life, only to beginners in writing for signed publication; and the earliest writings of the leading writers have been more often than not, among their best. Perhaps not within the last seven or eight years, the years when talents were too soon rendered productive in the forcing-house of war; but this phase is passing if it has not passed: we shall return to a more nearly normal development, like that represented by Davis, Fox, James, Burt, O. Henry, etc. We should, of course, be the target for the first shots of the young aspirants, but might we not hope to find a sufficient number who had the natural faculty chastened by study, and by newspaper and magazine experience to shoot true? At all events, we should have a particular class to draw from without a competition from the regular magazines as close as that which Scribner's Magazine must now meet.

Another objection would rise from the danger that we should be thought to be throwing out a dragnet from which we might select and secure what individuals we thought valuable in the catch, and throw back the worthless. But if the magazine were conducted with convincing sincerity and enthusiasm-qualities without which it could never succeed anyway-would not this suspicion instantly evaporate? Particularly as we are

plainly not in a position to be <u>forced</u> to any such device: what with Fitzgerald, Turner, Marquand, Burt, Woodward Boyd, Eastman, and shortly Biggs, Gilkyson and Price, if they turn out well, we can now stand with any publisher as producers of literature admired by liberal opinion. Our point would be that the new writers are not at a great disadvantage: those already established are preferred, and rightly, other things equal, because their names are in themselves of great and obvious value. The beginner cannot compete with them on equal terms. He finds it extremely difficult because he <u>is</u> new to get a foothold. But in this magazine he would know that a judgment on the basis of intrinsic quality would be rendered.

The difficulty of finding for editor one who combined a taste for discovery with a due regard for the true and permanent standards of literature would raise a third objection:- the temptation to play upon the momentary taste for the sensational; to yield to the seemingly popular view that vulgarity has in itself a value, that restraint is cowardice, that cheap cynicism is fearless veracity, would certainly be strong,- especially in the case of one with a sense for publicity and a desire for striking announcements. And no greater folly could be perpetrated by a house of the tradition of this one than to issue a "jazzy" publication. The Editor should have standards to measure by, he should be one whose nature would enable him to appreciate this danger; but if he possessed these qualitites and yet was not shackled and conventionalized by them the magazine might become something of a directing and controlling power upon the tendencies of American literature. Surely we might reasonably hope to find such a man to act in conjuction with a committee of two or three in our Editorial department which could be counted upon for sympathetic and appreciative counsel, and yet would insure a propriety of taste and the application of a sense of permanent value in instances where decision was difficult.

The interest of "The New Writers" to those concerned with the development of literature and all it stands for is obvious; but the number of these is small, and it is a question whether such a magazine could be profitable,- a question which a few years ago would probably have met a final 'no'. But the number who now take a lively interest in literature is far greater,- a fact that is one of numerous strong evidences that we are on the edge of a period of great literary activity.

Moreover, a magazine of this sort would produce a greater volume of publicity than the usual publication, -Newspaper and Review Edi-

TO
CHARLES SCRIBNER, ESQ.
ON
HIS SIXTY-NINTH BIRTHDAY
—

"CAESAR MIHI HOC DONAVIT",
SUCH THE CLASSIC AFFIDAVIT
THAT WAS GRAVEN BY A SCHOLAR
ON A CERTAIN CERVINE COLLAR,
MEANING, AS IS CLEARLY STATED:
CAESAR HAD THIS (HOC) DONATED
TO THE STAG WHICH, HUNTED, HARRIED,
THIS BRONZE ROYAL NECKLACE CARRIED
AS A TROPHY TALISMANIC,
KEEPING ITS DEER HEART FROM PANIC,
THROUGH THE CENTURIES SEQUENTIAL
TILL ANOTHER KING POTENTIAL,
CHARLES THE SIXTH, BEHELD HIM WANLY
WAND'RING IN THE WOODS OF SENLIS*
—

SO I FIND MY WISH LACONIC:
THAT YOUR COLLAR COLOPHONIC

MAY BE FOUND IN FUTURE AGES
CIRCLING MANY PRECIOUS PAGES
WITH ITS LETTER-PRESS CARESSES
(SUCH E.G. AS R.L.S's) —
BOOKS THAT STILL HAVE CIRCULATION
'MID THE PULP-WOOD'S FORESTRATION
GROWING IN THE STACKS SECLUDED
WHILE THE MOUNTAINS ARE DENUDED —
EACH ONE — BOOK OF PROSE OR SONNET —
WITH THE NAME OF "SCRIBNER" ON IT
AS A CROWNING AFFIDAVIT:
"SCRIBNER MIHI HOC DONAVIT."

JOHN QUILL

OCTOBER 18, 1925

* Stevenson in Forest Notes tells of the capture of a stag in the forest of Senlis by Charles the Sixth, bearing a collar with the inscription "Caesar mihi hoc donavit."

Birthday poem by John Huston Finley (1863–1940), associate editor (1921–1937) and future editor in chief (1937–1938) of The New York Times. *Also a Scribner author, Finley had been president of City College of New York (1903–1913) and the New York State commissioner of education (1913–1921).*

tors, Columnists, etc., would wish for one thing, to encourage it; and the novelty of its material and design would give it a 'newsy' quality.

Is it fantastic to think, in view of these conditions and of the fact that payments to contributors, as beginners, would be low, that a monthly, unillustrated, printed simply, and compact in format, would at least break even on the average?- Not if this could be managed on a circulation of 20,000 to 30,000.

Such a circulation would depend to a greater degree upon the skill of the editor than is the case with existing magazines whose standards are fixed by conventions and whose contributors are mostly established writers. The Editor of "The New Writers" should have more latitude; he should not be rigidly bounded in his choice, for he would be dealing with a class which produces innovators and should be sympathetic with experiment.

But almost as important as his sense for selection should be that for display: he should know how to set out in appropriate but conspicuous parts of the magazine, the points of his contributions and his contributors. He should establish a personal relationship with the subscribers. He should "sell" the contents of each number to those who turned his pages on a news stand.

When all is said, these two questions still stand: could a magazine of sufficient substance and merit come from a restricted source; and if so, could it be made to pay;- questions that can only be answered with certainty if the thing is attempted. But what a splendid thing it would be to do. What an inspiring influence upon our organization. What vital and refreshing influence it might have in forming American literature and taste.

LETTER:

Letter from Arthur H. Scribner to author Henry Van Dyke, 27 April 1926.

Brother of CS II, Arthur Scribner had responsibility for much of the day-to-day affairs of the firm. During the 1920s he organized an "author meets salesmen" dinner as part of the send-off for the new spring books.

Dear Dr. van Dyke:

We have recently given each year a very informal dinner to our salesmen before they start out on their fall trips, and this year the dinner is to be next Friday, May 7, at the Princeton Club, at seven o'clock. This is the climax of a week's intensive work with them on our new books and serves to start them off in good spirits, particularly when we can have an author or two present, as they then feel that they have been let in behind the scenes, which gives them an added importance with their customers. Last year Struthers Burt, Will James and [Captain John W.] Thomason were present, and we have just asked Kermit Roosevelt if he can come this year, and I wonder if it is possible for you to join us, which may be convenient as you sometimes spend the week-end in New York. They would particularly appreciate meeting you and would receive directly from you a much clearer idea of the purpose of your new book [*The Golden Key: Stories of Deliverance*] than can be conveyed to them in any written paragraphs — indeed, you could quite inspire them. They are a fine set of young men, about twelve in number, of whom we are proud, and it is an encouragement to our authors to know the class of men who represent them.

As I have said, the dinner is very informal and they come in their day clothes, though a dinner coat may be worn if more convenient. If this does fit in with your plans, I hope that you will be able to come.

Faithfully yours,
[Arthur H. Scribner]

LETTER:

Letter from CS II to the Committee of Management of the *Dictionary of American Biography*, 19 October 1926.

The newly organized American Council of Learned Societies appointed a committee in 1922,

Volume I, Number 1 (February 1925) of The Scribner Bookstore [News]. *Begun as an occasional pamphlet offering a selected list of current books from all publishers, this house publication went through various formats.*

chaired by Dr. J. Franklin Jameson, to consider the preparation of an authoritative national biography comparable to the scope and scholarship of the British Dictionary of National Biography. *Plans were formulated, contingent upon the raising of adequate funds; the committee estimated $500,000 would be required. Solicited by the committee, Adolph S. Ochs, owner and publisher of* The New York Times, *agreed to fund the project at $50,000 per year over a ten-year period. The responsibility for the undertaking was vested in a Committee of Management of seven members, four of whom were appointed by the Council, two by* The New York Times, *and the seventh (editor in chief) by the other six. Allen Johnson, historian and Yale professor, was chosen editor in chief in March 1925, and he established editorial offices in Washington in February 1926. Scribners jumped the gun by submitting its first* *proposal to Jameson in June 1924 before the project's organizational structure and financial backing were in place. This second proposal raised the original royalty offer to 15 percent from the start but also offered the possibility of a contract based on an even division of profits.*

Dear Sirs:

We submit the following proposals for the publication of the Dictionary of American Biography.

1. To manufacture the work at our own expense and to pay for the exclusive right of publication a royalty of 15% on the published price, to guarantee the sale of 3000 sets of the Dictionary, which according to the present estimate would comprise 60,000 volumes, and if we figure the retail price of each volume at $10, (and it could hardly be less) this would amount to $90,000.

2. The second proposal is based not upon royalty, but upon a division of the profits. Under this plan we propose that, after we have been reimbursed for all costs and expenses of manufacture, publication, and sale, the profits be equally divided between the proprietors and the publishers. There would have to be as clear an understanding as possible of exactly what expenses should be charged against the work. There should be, of course, a suitable provision for determining the financial condition of the enterprise at regular intervals.

Whichever of these plans would be acceptable, the publishers agree to manufacture the work in the manner acceptable to the proprietors, and to promote the distribution, and put the whole strength of the house behind the work. The proprietor would agree to give to the publishers the exclusive right of publication in all countries during the terms of the copyright, to deliver, without charge to the publishers, complete manuscript for each volume at reasonable intervals and become responsible for the proof-reading.

There should be some provisions covering such items as excess costs of corrections, protection of copyright, protection of publishers against suits of libel, protection of the proprietor against the volumes being allowed to go out of print. Such matters as these have been so standardized that we are certain they will present no difficulty in the language to be employed in the contract.

We are not sure which of those proposals would be the better for you; it depends upon so many conditions. A profit-division agreement would make certain that you received a just share of the profits and these would be determined by the success of the work. The return to you might be long delayed; it would depend upon the reception of the Dictionary by the public, upon the vigor with which the preparation and sale of the work were pushed — a delay in volumes would mean, of course, a corresponding delay in returns. We have the greatest confidence in the success of the Dictionary but the degree of success cannot be measured at this time. In the end, the sharing of the profits might yield a larger return to you but under a royalty contract the return is sure and proportionate to the sale; there can be no misunderstanding and the profits are easily determined.

As to the method of sale, we would agree that there should be in the name of the learned societies a very wide appeal for subscriptions as soon as an offer to the public can be made. These societies should, in our opinion, be kept to the front in all advertising and circularization. If we are so fortunate as to be chosen as the publishers of the Dictionary, we are prepared to spend liberally in every way to promote the enterprise and to bring to it all the publishing facilities of our house.

Our Scribner Press on 43rd Street, thoroughly equipped, can manufacture the work under our control — the composition, the electrotyping, the printing, and the binding. Our Trade organization can reach the Booksellers of the United States and Canada. Our Subscription department by dividing the country into sections can make an appeal through its canvassing agents the homes of every section. As an illustration, we have just completed the sale of one thousand sets of the Roosevelt Memorial Edition in 24 volumes, although the books were not all issued at the time the sale was made. We sold also a limited edition of 1000 sets of Stevenson (26 volumes) before a quarter of the work was published. We have sold successfully in this way the "Hastings Dictionary of the Bible," in 5 volumes, and also through our Subscription Department about 75,000 sets of the Encyclopedia Britannica, we being the first to sell that work in this country.

Our Retail Store has a following of patrons to whom this work would make a notable appeal; our Mail Order Department with many thousands of addresses of booklovers and book buyers can make a wide appeal to members of societies and organizations of all kinds; our Library Department can reach Public and Private Libraries.

Our Magazine one of the great advertising mediums can bring the work regularly and continuously to the attention of the public who would be considered likely purchasers of the Dic-

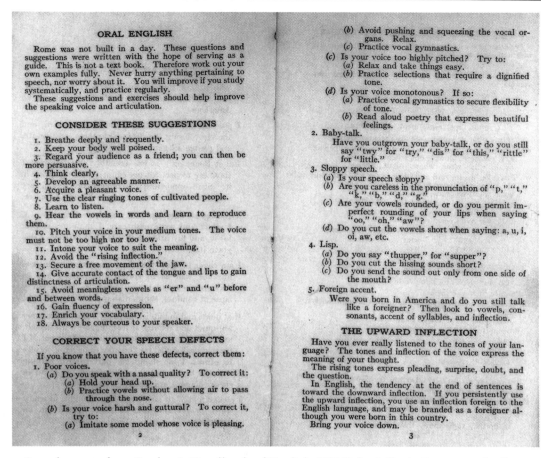

ORAL ENGLISH

Rome was not built in a day. These questions and suggestions were written with the hope of serving as a guide. This is not a text book. Therefore work out your own examples fully. Never hurry anything pertaining to speech, nor worry about it. You will improve if you study systematically, and practice regularly.

These suggestions and exercises should help improve the speaking voice and articulation.

CONSIDER THESE SUGGESTIONS

1. Breathe deeply and frequently.
2. Keep your body well poised.
3. Regard your audience as a friend; you can then be more persuasive.
4. Think clearly.
5. Develop an agreeable manner.
6. Acquire a pleasant voice.
7. Use the clear ringing tones of cultivated people.
8. Learn to listen.
9. Hear the vowels in words and learn to reproduce them.
10. Pitch your voice in your medium tones. The voice must not be too high nor too low.
11. Intone your voice to suit the meaning.
12. Avoid the "rising inflection."
13. Secure a free movement of the jaw.
14. Give accurate contact of the tongue and lips to gain distinctness of articulation.
15. Avoid meaningless vowels as "er" and "u" before and between words.
16. Gain fluency of expression.
17. Enrich your vocabulary.
18. Always be courteous to your speaker.

CORRECT YOUR SPEECH DEFECTS

If you know that you have these defects, correct them:
1. Poor voices.
   (a) Do you speak with a nasal quality? To correct it:
      (a) Hold your head up.
      (b) Practice vowels without allowing air to pass through the nose.
   (b) Is your voice harsh and guttural? To correct it, try to:
      (a) Imitate some model whose voice is pleasing.

2

   (b) Avoid pushing and squeezing the vocal organs. Relax.
   (c) Practice vocal gymnastics.
   (c) Is your voice too highly pitched? Try to:
      (a) Relax and take things easy.
      (b) Practice selections that require a dignified tone.
   (d) Is your voice monotonous? If so:
      (a) Practice vocal gymnastics to secure flexibility of tone.
      (b) Read aloud poetry that expresses beautiful feelings.
2. Baby-talk.
   Have you outgrown your baby-talk, or do you still say "twy" for "try," "dis" for "this," "rittle" for "little."
3. Sloppy speech.
   (a) Is your speech sloppy?
   (b) Are you careless in the pronunciation of "p," "t," "k," "b," "d," "g."
   (c) Are your vowels rounded, or do you permit imperfect rounding of your lips when saying "oo," "oh," "aw"?
   (d) Do you cut the vowels short when saying: a, u, i, oi, aw, etc.
4. Lisp.
   (a) Do you say "thupper," for "supper"?
   (b) Do you cut the hissing sounds short?
   (c) Do you send the sound out only from one side of the mouth?
5. Foreign accent.
   Were you born in America and do you still talk like a foreigner? Then look to vowels, consonants, accent of syllables, and inflection.

THE UPWARD INFLECTION

Have you ever really listened to the tones of your language? The tones and inflection of the voice express the meaning of your thought.

The rising tones express pleading, surprise, doubt, and the question.

In English, the tendency at the end of sentences is toward the downward inflection. If you persistently use the upward inflection, you use an inflection foreign to the English language, and may be branded as a foreigner although you were born in this country.

Bring your voice down.

3

Sample pages from Student's Handbook of English *(1925) by Julia A. Spencer, a Scribner Educational Department publication for use by students in grades seven through nine (courtesy of Josephine Fincken). Beyond providing rules of grammar, spelling, capitalization, and punctuation, the slim pocket-size volume included suggestions for speech improvement, lists of synonyms and vocabulary words, the titles of "one hundred interesting books," and poems ("memory selections") for recitation.*

tionary. Our Educational Deparment with offices and representatives in all sections of the country in constant touch with the colleges, universities, and public schools, can reach the great body of teachers and administrators. Our office in London can give us a publishing outlet in England and on the Continent and would be extended and adjusted to the distribution of the work.

These facilities we offer as a publishing unit to print and to distribute the product of your efforts, equal to that of any publisher in any one of these directions, and unequalled in inclusiveness and potentiality for a publication of this nature.

Very truly yours,
[Charles Scribner II]

The final contract, dated 3 June 1927, followed proposal number one. The first volume was pub-

lished on 8 November 1928; two to three volumes were published annually thereafter. The completed project of twenty text volumes—volume twenty appeared on 10 December 1936—totaled 12,685 pages, containing 13,633 articles submitted by 2,243 contributors.

LETTER:

Letter from Scribner editor W. C. Brownell to CS II, 30 October 1926.

*Hired by CS II in 1888 as an editor and literary adviser, Brownell had authored over the years critical works—*Victorian Prose Masters *(1901),* American Prose Masters *(1909),* Criticism *(1914),* Standards *(1917), and* The Genius of Style *(1924)—that had earned him a distinguished reputation beyond the editorial floor at*

MARK SULLIVAN

October 27, 1927.

Dear Mr. Scribner:

Your letter was characteristic of yourself and of your house. If my time were not so completely mortgaged by other things to write, I should like some time to write a celebration of Scribner's as one of the more nearly unchanging institutions in a much too rapidly changing world. I suspect not many other publishing houses, and probably no other business, retains, in its relations with authors and otherwise, a quality of combined dignity and courtesy which we like to think was an outstanding characteristic of the publishing business of say twenty-five to sixty years ago.

I think your expectations about the book will be justified by the public reception of it. As many persons as have already read it seem to like it, almost extravagantly--all of them saying it is as good as the first volume, and a decided number, including some quite competent ones, saying it is better.

I think that one way or another America is being turned back to pride and affection for its own, for the things that are traditionally and characteristically American. To what extent "Our Times" is a cause of that, and to what extent a beneficiary, I should not undertake to judge. But I am satisfied it will go on, and equally satisfied that it is a wholesome thing for America.

Sincerely yours,

Mark Sullivan

Letter by Mark Sullivan to Arthur H. Scribner written the day after publication of the second volume of Our Times: The United States, 1900–1925. *Volume one was the #4 nonfiction best-seller of 1926.*

Scribners. In his seventies at the time of this letter, he had relinquished his role as editor in chief to Maxwell Perkins but still came to work almost every day.

Dear Scribner,

The decision to give up altogether my work at the office, which I think I must relinquish, easy as it has been made for me, has been hard to reach and is hard to communicate. I can't help feeling I am somehow failing you, though I have no illusions as to the practical importance of my help latterly. That, too, has had its share in the dejection I have felt. I can't, however, think that any compromise would in my case fit the bill, and am reasonably sure that my wisest course would be the radical one. The fewer the demands on my remaining supply of strength the longer it should last, and the less serious should prove the special troubles so largely with me dependent on general condition.

Every other consideration than that of health weights the other scale:

(1) The proverbially dangerous rupture of routine by the aged is complicated by a homesickness for this office which I already feel in advance. It is still a second home for one and, having been for so many years my only one, has abiding memories. Should I miraculously happen to feel much more efficient in six months or a year, I should certainly have regrets. But I certainly can't count on that. My present incapacity and distaste for work requiring any concentration seem clearly symptomatic of a state that has already lasted long enough to make it

only prudent to devote what energy I have to improving it if possible.

(2) Financially, (though I think I am justified, and am also conscious that my affairs would give me less concern with more leisure to attend to them) I feel a certain timidity in depending wholly on investments—on which so much more now depends for me, and in which I have not always been fortunate.

(3) The standing conferred by my connection with the house has always been a matter of pride with me, and I am correspondingly reluctant to have it lapse. Nor shall I be likely ever to forget what I have always had abundant reason to bear in mind regarding your cordial forwarding by every encouragement the outside work that under other circumstances I should hardly have been able to accomplish. That, too, seems approaching its terms, and, without looking ahead to anything further, I shall consider myself lucky if I ever manage to finish the particular task I undertook so long ago and have so long now been unable to go on with [*Democratic Distinction in America,* published in 1927]. Not that it matters very much either; I do care for the subject, but everyone interested has my measure by this time, such as it is. What does matter is that henceforth I shall be out of touch with things.

I should like my withdrawal to cause no inconvenience, and with the editorial force as adequate as it is at present I can foresee none. It may not be logical, after what I have said, to suggest lingering so long, but I don't want to be or seem abrupt, and there would be a (perhaps fanciful and sentimental) fitness in lasting out the 39th year of my connection, which began in January 1888. Just as you think, of course, as to that. I only make the suggestion tentatively. Whenever I go, now or later, it will be a wrench you can't exaggerate, even if you can appreciate it. Don't forget me, or fail to remember how much I have wished really to be of the help which you said you needed when I came.

Affectionately yours,
W. C. Brownell

Brownell did not actually resign from Scribners until 1 January 1928.

ARTICLE:
Alfred S. Dashiell, "Two Rules Only for Scribner's Writers," *Author & Journalist,* Vol. XI, No. 11 (November 1926), pp. 5–9.

Associate editor of Scribner's Magazine *at the time of this article, Dashiell succeeded Robert Bridges as managing editor in 1930.*

The first admonition I would give those who wish to break into *Scribner's Magazine* is—be yourself. Forget that you are writing for one of the quality group. Don't try to be literary. Do your subject enthusiastic and complete justice by honest workmanship.

What shall your subject be? Let us examine the magazine itself. Because of the fact that we publish only twelve times a year and have only 128 pages of editorial contents each month, we cannot hold out great promise of a steady income to any one writer. We receive more than twelve thousand manuscripts a year and buy about one hundred. Approximately twenty per cent of the magazine is devoted to fiction.

In those pages we strive to present the writer who is vigorous and original, who has something to say and the power to say it. *Scribner's Magazine* is a special field for the new writer, due to our policy of buying for quality and not for the name attached to the manuscript. Many of the best known writers today had their first stories published in *Scribner's.* Since we publish only three or four stories a number (with the exception of the August Fiction Number and the Christmas Number, when we publish six or eight) we strive for variety. There is no "*Scribner* type" of story. Many writers, because they see a certain story in the magazine, conclude that we specialize in stories of that sort. They construct one on a similar pattern and are surprised and hurt when the well-known self-addressed envelope comes galloping home. We do not want the inspiration to come from anything you see in the Magazine. We want it to come from you, your knowledge, your experience. We do not demand the "happy ending," nor do we go in for the slaughterhouse school of fiction. Most of our stories are written by comparatively new writers who have not yet fallen victim to the spell of typewriter keys but still have time to live and observe.

We rarely publish stories with foreign settings unless they are written by one who has lived abroad and knows his terrain well. We do not go in for plot for plot's sake, nor art for art's sake. Both are, as a rule, pretty barren. What we want is stories that have the atmosphere of reality and the breath of life in them. That doesn't mean necessarily drab realism. The back-stairs and hall-bedroom story has been written. This doesn't imply that fancy and imagination are ruled out, but

Proof

*Dear Will:—
this one I am sending
Have you & Contributors
Have you any suggestions?
AJ*

DICTIONARY OF AMERICAN BIOGRAPHY

Suggestions to Contributors

The following fictitious sketch has been patched together to illustrate the typographical forms and usages which will be followed in the *Dictionary*. If contributors will observe the use of capitals, figures, and citations here suggested, they will spare the editorial staff much labor in the preparation of copy for the press. Obviously this sketch is not designed to serve as a model of literary style. A biographical article need not be annalistic to be accurate and informing. A merely chronological account of events does not reveal personality or explain achievements. The art of concise statement and interpretation is well exemplified in the articles on Jane Austen, Samuel Crompton, John Constable, and Thomas Brassey, in the *Dictionary of National Biography*.

DOE, JOHN (March 3, 1801–Sept. 6, 1863), lawyer, author. Among the passengers on the ship *Adventure* which entered the port of Philadelphia Nov. 15, 1793, were Timothy Doe, a native of Coventry, England, and his wife Mary (*Genealogy of the Doe Family*, p. 13). * * * John, the second of these three sons, was born at Pottstown in Montgomery County, Pennsylvania. * * * He attended a school conducted by Friends but his naturally contentious disposition seems not to have been affected by his environment. * * * In spite of his father's stubborn opposition, John entered the University of Pennsylvania. From his mother, a woman of superior intelligence and character, he received more encouragement. * * * In a constituency which had been staunchly Democratic hitherto, Doe won by a handsome majority of 7,500 in a total vote of 135,000 (*Whig Almanac*, 1840). He took his seat in the House on Dec. 4, 1841, and five days later made his first speech on the apportionment bill then before Congress (*Cong. Globe*, 25 Cong., 1 Sess., pp. 215 ff.). * * * Of his career in the Mexican War little need be said except that he served acceptably but without distinction as colonel of the 21st Pennsylvania Regiment which was part of the Sixth Corps. * * * His play *The Modern Hamlet*, produced at the Empire Theater in the autumn of 1849, was the outcome of these experiences. * * * His warm friendship with the Attorney-General led to the offer of the post of minister to Venezuela. His letter to the President declining the honor is an interesting revelation of his personality (*Works*, III, p. 254). * * * On the advice of his physician he sought rest and recreation by a leisurely journey over the Alleghany Mountains. His impressions of life in the Middle West are recorded in his *Travels in the Ohio Valley* (1854). * * * It was on one of these excursions that he met Richard Roe, then judge of the court of common pleas in Washington County. * * * Referring to this memorable meeting, Roe said in after years, "It was the beginning of that personal animosity which had such dire consequences for us both" (*My Legal Controversies*, p. 67). * * * The famous trial of *Doe* v. *Roe* (5 *Wallace*, 810) was followed with intense popular interest and was fully reported in the local newspapers (see files of the *Philadelphia Press*, 1859). * * * Doe now resigned from the Senate, but he never lost his keen zest for politics. His last speech was an impassioned plea for the Constitution and the Union. His death occurred just as the Southern Confederacy collapsed.

[The chief source of information about John Doe is his *Autobiography*, 2 vols. (1865), but confidence in its credibility has been shaken since the publication of *My Legal Controversies* (1893) by Richard Roe. It now appears that Doe is not the author of *A Day in Court* (1845). The question of authorship is thoroughly discussed by Thomas Usher in his paper on "A Great Plagiarist," in the *Transactions of the New Jersey Historical Society*, vol. XXI, p. 4. His work as a playwright has been appraised by Booth Barrett in the *Theater Magazine*, July, 1895. *The Works of John Doe*, 5 vols. (1873-79) have been edited by John Marshall Story. A sketch of his life appeared in *Some Great American Lawyers*, vol. II, chap. VII. Obituary notices were published in the *New York Times*, Sept. 7, 1863, and in the *Philadelphia Press*, Sept. 8, 1863.]

Asterisks have been used in this copy simply to indicate that no attempt has been made to present a complete biography.

Proof of style sheet sent to contributors of the Dictionary of American Biography, *annotated in the corner by editor in chief Allen Johnson. "Will" is Scribner editor Will D. Howe.*

it does mean that such stories must have a quality of reality which will carry the reader into the world of the story and keep him there. It means that there must be executions as well as conception. There is romance and high adventure in life and in real places—more of it than most of us can ever put into a mythical kingdom or a South Sea isle.

So much for fiction. It must be grounded in fact or idea. It must be sincerely worked out without particular regard for pattern or formula. It must have the feeling of reality and possibility about it.

We have three departments in the magazine: "As I Like It," by William Lyon Phelps; "The Field of Art," by Royal Cortissoz, and "The Financial Situation," by Alexander Dana Noyes. These men write their entire departments and are not looking for contributions, although Mr. Phelps enjoys and uses a great deal of comment from readers. These departments take care of books, art and finance. Notable additional articles on this subject, recently published, are: "The Writing of Fiction," by Edith Wharton; "A Critical Credo," by Mary Colum, and "A Leader in New Japanese Art," by Caroline Singer. They all, of course, have particular points to recommend them. Other departments in the magazine are: "Behind the Scenes," notes on authors contributing to the number; "What You Think About It," a forum for readers; "The Club Corner," a department of reference and program suggestions for clubs, which has recently included a new feature, "Interesting Things that Women Are Doing," short articles on unusual activities of women's organizations. The first department is written by a member of the staff and there is no remuneration for contributions to the other two. "The Club Corner" is announcing in the October number a Creative Work of America Contest open to members of clubs affiliated with the General Federation of Women's Clubs. Several prizes will be awarded.

I have left to the last the discussion of the most important part of the magazine. Each month we publish ten or more articles on topics of general interest. Here is, for the writer, a fertile field not offered by the magazines devoted entirely to fiction. Often the writer of fiction has valuable material which will not resolve itself into a story. He should not forget that there is a market for interesting short articles on many subjects. We work several months in advance and require that an article be as good six months from the time it is accepted as it is on the day it is written. We are not a current events magazine, but we are interested in articles commenting upon the more permanent phases of our civilization. We can not handle the usual type of travel article. That went out of date with the Grand Tour. The journalistic essay, based on passing observation, say, of Indian customs, had better be sent elsewhere. But there is a place for the article which you have perhaps always wanted to write, founded upon knowledge of conditions and places where your roots are deepest, pointing to something significant in our life today.

Many of our articles are written by authorities. I may mention such scientists as George Ellery Hale, Robert A. Millikan, Michael Pupin, and Edwin Grant Conklin, such statesmen and politicians as Senator Borah, Senator Bruce, and James Kerney, such engineers and adventurers as John Hays Hammond, such scholars as President Little of Michigan and President Hopkins of Dartmouth.

Nevertheless, the magazine is always spiced with articles written by persons who are perhaps hitherto unknown, articles presenting a new point of view about familiar subjects, done briefly and pointedly. Perfect examples are furnished by two men who have been literary sensations in recent years: Will James, a cowboy who writes of the range, of horses and men, in the cowboy lingo, and Captain John W. Thomason, Jr., of the Marine Corps, whose crashing war narratives have stirred both soldiers and critics. James writes "Western stuff," but it is "Western stuff" of a different sort. It is so real that it causes cattlemen and cowboys to write, sometimes in cramped, illiterate hand, telling us that here is the first man who writes of the range as it really is. Thomason writes "war stuff," which was supposed to be taboo. But when "Fix Bayonets!" appeared in the magazine we received a flood of letters from service men singing the praises of the fighting marine who at last had written the real story of the war. Critics cheered, and men in the street chuckled because here was a regular fellow who beat the literary birds at their own game.

Thomason and James derived their material from the pulsing life about them and worked hard to make words and pictures say what they felt. We may include in this group also Will Rose, editor of the newspaper in Cambridge Springs, Pa., a town of 1600. His work is less exciting, perhaps, but more amusing and nearer to the experience of most of us. He is writing a highly successful series of small-town articles. We have already published "The Small-Town Newspaper Divorces Its Party," "Small-Town Banker Puts on Knickers," and "Small-Town Gastronomy." In the October number appears "The Passing of the Country Store." In a short time will appear an article telling why he, a Cornell graduate with several years' experience in metropolitan advertising and newspaper experience, deliberately selected a small town in which to live and work. We have also purchased from him two short-stories built around the people he knows.

N. D. Marbaker, a Pennsylvania country doctor, has written "Leaves From a Country Doctor's Notebook," which is in reality a group of poignant short-stories done in five hundred words or so. We are publishing five of them in the October number.

George S. Brooks, a police reporter, has done some exceedingly interesting crime stories in a new way. They are based on fact and have neither a master criminal nor a master detective as the hero.

Kyle Crichton, who books a few shows as a side line to his regular job as representative of the Albuquerque Civic Center, has written "Who Says the Road Show Is Dead?" Mr. Crichton has also written an excellent biographical sketch of the picturesque Zebulon Pike. The manager of an old-time "Opr'y house" contributes "The Passing of the One-Night Stand." A professor's wife writes "Mr. and Mrs. Professor Look for a Job." Another tells of "The Professor and His Wife." The lady of manse writes of life with a parson. Dorothy Pratt, a Providence newspaper woman, stirred by a reference to the disappearing clambake in Will Rose's article on gastronomy, hastened to testify that the Rhode Island clambake was still flourishing. We do not usually buy an article written in answer to one which appeared in the magazine, largely because we cannot publish it until several months after the original. "What You Think About It" is for all such disputes. This article, however, could stand on its own feet and was interesting whether the reader had seen Rose's article or not.

A minister who resigned his pulpit as a result of the fundamentalist furor looked back over his years of preaching and wrote two interesting articles: "Is the Preacher a Professional?" and "Is the Minister a Student?" A young chap conceived the idea that real estate developments were leading to religious tolerance and put it into a brief article.

These instances will give you an idea of the sort of material we can use. The field is almost limitless. The articles spring out of thought or experience. They are well-written and have humor and the human touch. I shall crib a phrase of Mr. Rose's to clinch the point. A young friend asked him how to become a magazine writer. Rose answered, "Do your stuff and pray hard." Consider the "your" italicized. We want your stuff, not something done because someone else has sold something like it. The very fact that we have published one article on a subject may keep us from buying another on the same subject.

The manuscripts mentioned came in unsolicited and the authors were hitherto unknown to us. Many people wonder whether a manuscript submitted in the usual routine way is read. We can assure you—and the cases cited prove it—that it is. A few write a letter outlining the idea first. Sometimes this will save you trouble, for we can tell you that such an article would not interest us at this time. But we never order an article sight unseen. Much the best plan, it seems to me, is to write the article in the way you think it should be written and submit it.

The second admonition to all who would write for *Scribner's* is—be brief. We publish at most only one serial a year. We rarely buy two- or three-part stories. We have only published plays by such people as Galsworthy, Meredith and Rachel Crothers. If we use several articles by the same author each must be a complete unit without reference to others in the group.

We cannot publish stories of more than seven thousand words. Some of our best articles run to only twenty-five hundred or so. Four or five thousand is a good limit. Since our text matter is published solid and not continued through the advertising, these limits are necessary. No padding is required. State your case pungently, briefly, concisely, then come to a full stop.

Copy-book maxims to the contrary, persistency as such is not rewarded in editorial offices. We have too many manuscripts to read. Unfortunately, some of our most prolific would-be contributors never achieve publication. Although editors try to be impartial, you know that if you had read fifty sloppily-written stories from the same pen, showing no originality and no development, you would not be eager to read the fifty-first.

Too many people are writing who should be in some useful trade, such as brick-laying. We have to give all submitted manuscripts a fair reading. Oftentimes, this flood of manuscripts prevents us from writing the author of some better-than-average contribution an encouraging note. However, we do not pretend to be a literary bureau. We have to remember that we are reading manuscripts for the purpose of buying articles and stories for the magazine. Hence the ordinary rejection slip. Therefore, if you value our friendship, don't flood us with manuscripts.

As to the mechanical requirements, we ask only that the manuscript be typewritten with double space and that a self-addressed envelope and sufficient postage be enclosed for its return. We keep a careful record of all manuscripts received, and give as prompt a reading as possible, although that sometimes means two weeks or so. We do not read manuscripts submitted a second time, and we should, as a tip to the author, suggest that it be not too battered and shop-worn by the time it reaches us. We realize that we are near the end of the alphabet, but we should prefer to have first chance at an offering. We like to think that the author knows us by more than a name and knows something of the sort of material we publish.

Well then, you ask, what is your editorial policy? This is what Robert Bridges, the editor, said recently:

"In editing *Scribner's* it is not only our effort to present the best fiction, poetry, and essays, by the best writers, but also to give an adequate picture of big events by big actors in the events. Good articles can be made by clever reporters who interview and write about great men. But the article that is part of history is written by the great man himself. No second-hand account can supersede it. *Scribner* articles are first-hand stories. The reader is brought in close contact with directing minds. To be constantly on the alert for entertainment and instruction that will meet the needs of an audience very much alive to all modern movements that reflect our civilization—that is the reason-to-be of Scribner's."

We have no sacred cows. We belong to no clique or school. We have no pet ideas to put over, no creed to defend. We are animated by a belief that there are a great many intelligent people in this country who want the best that is being thought and said, no matter whether they happen to agree with the writer or not. We are conservative in the best sense of the word. We are not out to praise for the sake of praise, not to blame for the storm it will arouse.

Articles of a critical nature frequently find their way into our columns. Among recent ones have been: "How Free Is Free Speech?" by Judge Robert W. Winston of the Supreme Court of North Carolina; "The Juror's Part in Crime," by Judge Charles C. Nott, Jr., of the Court of General Sessions, New York; "Bigoted and Bettered

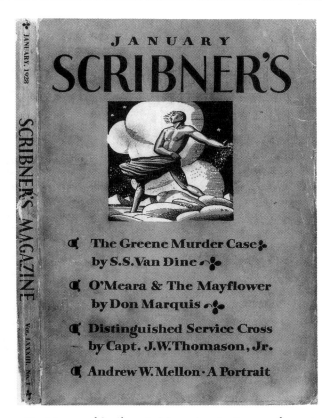

First issue of Scribner's Magazine *in its new format*

Pictures," by William C. de Mille; "Rubber-Stamp Parole," by Boyden Sparkes; "The Mating Season of Co-Education," by Professor Frank R. Arnold; "The Last Taboo," by Albert Guerard; "What Price Organization?" by Jesse Rainsford Sprague; "The Organization Complex in our Colleges," by Ruth Steele Brooks.

All these articles have been free of sensation-mongering. They have been sincerely put forward and substantiated by evidence.

Although we cannot handle the superficial journalistic interview, we are interested in well-rounded portraits of outstanding people. James Kerney did one of Al Smith for our September number. Silas Bent has written for us "Two Souls at War in General Dawes." Van Wyck Brooks has done "The Cassandra of New England," and I have mentioned Mr. Crichton's "Zebulon Pike." We are interested chiefly in people alive and important today, but likewise are looking for living portraits of the picturesque of other days.

Since *Scribner's* is the only illustrated general magazine in its field, we are always interested in good pictures. The time has passed, however, when we can take an article because of its illustra-

Acknowledgment from the New York Public Library to Scribners for its gift of a special, limited edition copy of volume one of the Dictionary of American Biography. *John Finley was a member of the American Council of Learned Societies' Committee of Management, which was overseeing the publishing project.*

tions. The rotogravure sections, the travel magazines, and picture newspapers cover the field of photography. We usually go elsewhere. We learned of Thomason first through his pictures. Then we discovered that he could write as well as he could draw. We publish photographs, but only when they accompany an important article.

I hope you may have gained a picture of the needs of the editors of *Scribner's Magazine* from the foregoing. Again I repeat the two fundamental requirements:

Be yourself
Be brief

If you follow them we shall be glad to read carefully anything you may send in.

ARTICLE:

"Behind the Scenes: Notes on the New Scribner's and Informal Glimpses of Contributors to This Number," *Scribner's Magazine*, 83, no. 1 (January 1928): 134a.

After many months of preparation the great day has finally arrived, and we usher in 1928 with the new SCRIBNER'S MAGAZINE. It was an interesting job, and it brought a lot of experts into consultation. Some of those who worked on the new Magazine are here presented, along with the contributors to the first number.

The cover was arranged by Gordon Aymar, art-director of the J. Walter Thompson Co. If, by some chance, you have never heard of the company, you have none the less been influenced by it, for you have read advertisements written by members of its staff—Fleischmann's Yeast, for example, and the Davey tree surgeons, and the Rand-McNally maps. Mr. Aymar is a graduate of Yale and combines the qualities of artist and art-director. He is recognized as one of the most brilliant men in advertising circles.

Rockwell Kent, who drew the decoration of the cover and will do a series of them for us, is a leader in modern art. He studied under William M. Chase, Robert Henri, Hayes Miller, and Abbot Thayer. His apprenticeship served, he began to attract attention by his strong designs and his work with both figure and landscape. His pictures hang in the Metropolitan Museum, New York; Art Institute, Chicago; Brooklyn Museum; and other American museums. He has exhibited widely here and abroad. He is likewise the author of two books, "Wilderness" and "Voyaging," done with his own illustrations. Mr. Kent has lately become the American editor of *Creative Art,* now published by A. & C. Boni. He has also illusrated a special edition of Voltaire's "Candide," the first book to bear the imprint of the new Random House.

The new type-face—Granjon—of the Magazine has never before been used in a periodical in this country. Paul Beaujon, type expert, says of Granjon, which is a modern adaptation of a sixteenth-century French type: "There has been no unwise attempt to produce a facsimile. The lightness and condensation of the lower-case gives the authentic spirit of the sixteenth-century letter; only an instructed designer, working from personal convictions, could so successfully have avoided the heaviness of most revivals from inked impressions. The capitals have been subdued by narrowing, and so improved."

The new editorial policy of SCRIBNER'S will express to an even greater degree a critical appreciation of American life. Many writers new to SCRIBNER'S audience will be introduced. We shall preserve continuity of purpose while presenting variety in treatment. A new political portrait will appear in each number, following those of Smith, Dawes, Ritchie, Hoover, and Mellon.

President Hopkins of Dartmouth appears in the next number with a courageous statement of the function of the American college. President Little of Michigan, Dean Gauss of Princeton, Dean Walters of Swarthmore, will follow with other pertinent articles.

Bishop Fiske's "Confessions" in the Christmas number have brought him and us a flood of letters. He will follow up with "Saving Souls Through Church Suppers" to appear soon. Other discussions of religious topics will follow.

W. O. McGeehan, sports writer extraordinary, will be a new contributor. Gerald Carson, advertising man, will contribute "Business Men of Letters."

New writers of fiction to rival those introduced last year will appear. And there will be stories by Zona Gale, Ernest Hemingway, Conrad Aiken, George S. Brooks, Louise Saunders, and others already known to our readers.

In this number, we present a varied and versatile group of authors and artists.

Among the contributors in this "new" issue were the English writer John Galsworthy, American novelist and storywriter Edith Wharton (with a poem), and "S. S. Van Dine," a mystery writer (Willard Huntington Wright) whose identity had not yet been guessed or revealed.

George McKay Schieffelin (1905–1988), eldest grandson of CS II, had the longest association with the firm of any Scribner family member. Joining in 1928 as assistant to the manager of Scribner Press, Schieffelin rose through the management to become executive vice president in 1963; elected as chairman of the board in 1970, he served as a director of the Scribner Book Companies from 1978 to 1984.

CS II DIARY ENTRY:
Wednesday 25 July 1928

Bridges and I go to Williamstown for funeral of Brownell & get back at ten

W. C. Brownell, Scribner editor and literary adviser, began with the firm in 1888 and retired on 1 January 1928 after forty years of service. He died seven months later.

ARTICLE:
"First Volume Ready of Great Biography," *New York Times,* 11 November 1928, II, pp. 1-2.

The American Council of Learned Societies will give a dinner to a group of several hundred distinguished scholars and historians at the Hotel Roosevelt on Tuesday night to celebrate the publication under its auspices of the first volume of the Dictionary of American Biography.

Dr. Joseph P. Chamberlain, Professor of Public Law at Columbia, will preside. Dr. John H. Finley, associate editor of THE NEW YORK TIMES, will be toastmaster. The speakers will include the German ambassador, Baron Friedrich Wilhelm von Prittwitz-Gaffron; Dr. J. Franklin Jameson, head of the Department of History in the Library of Congress and Chairman of the Committee of Management for the Dictionary; Dr. Allen Johnson, editor-in-chief of the dictionary and former Professor of American History at Yale, and Dr. William A. Neilson, President of Smith College.

The guests will include persons prominent in American letters, journalism, science, education,

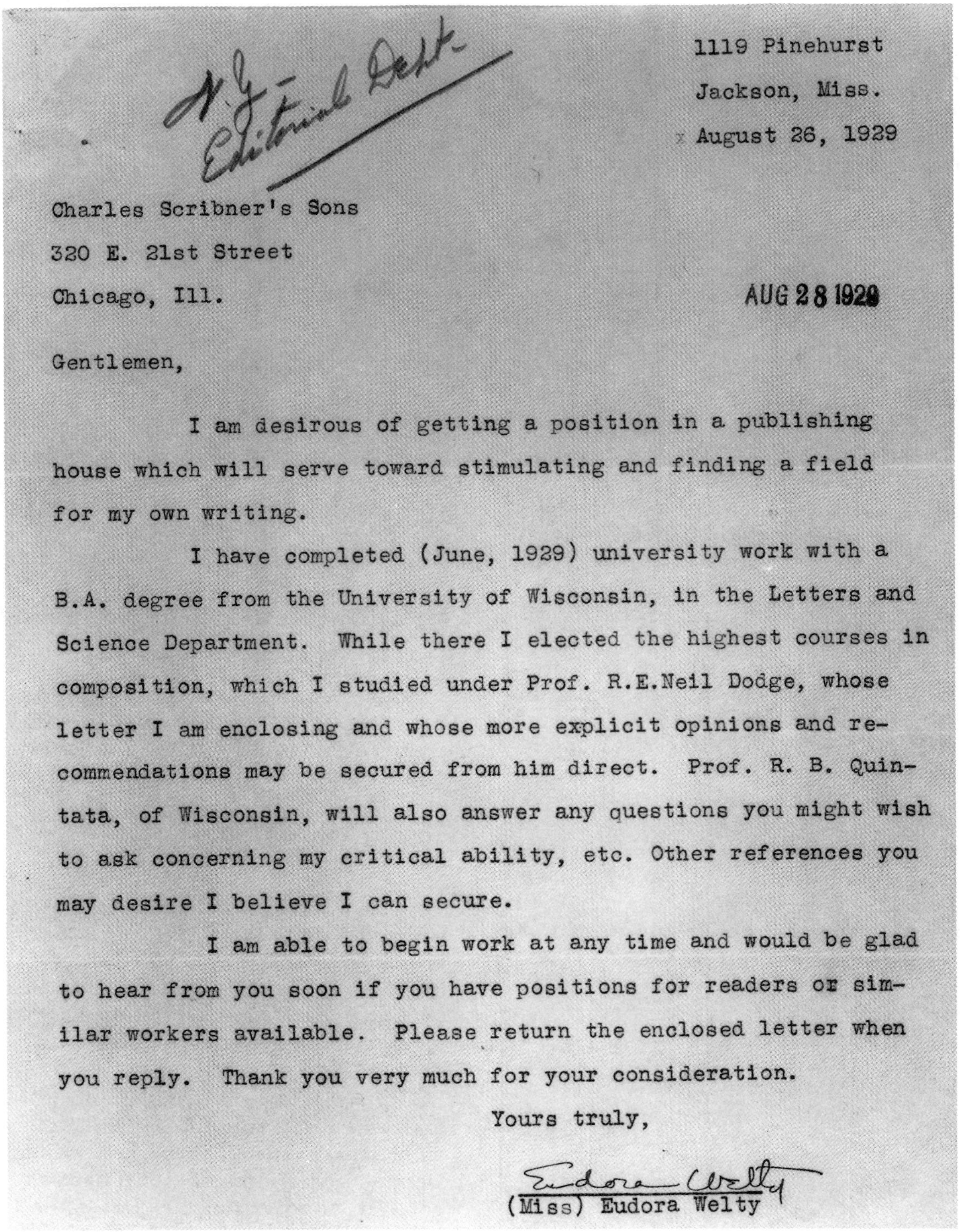

N.Y.
Editorial Dept.

1119 Pinehurst
Jackson, Miss.
August 26, 1929

Charles Scribner's Sons
320 E. 21st Street
Chicago, Ill.

AUG 28 1929

Gentlemen,

    I am desirous of getting a position in a publishing house which will serve toward stimulating and finding a field for my own writing.

    I have completed (June, 1929) university work with a B.A. degree from the University of Wisconsin, in the Letters and Science Department. While there I elected the highest courses in composition, which I studied under Prof. R.E.Neil Dodge, whose letter I am enclosing and whose more explicit opinions and recommendations may be secured from him direct. Prof. R. B. Quintata, of Wisconsin, will also answer any questions you might wish to ask concerning my critical ability, etc. Other references you may desire I believe I can secure.

    I am able to begin work at any time and would be glad to hear from you soon if you have positions for readers or similar workers available. Please return the enclosed letter when you reply. Thank you very much for your consideration.

        Yours truly,

        Eudora Welty
        (Miss) Eudora Welty

Job-hunting letter by Eudora Welty, who later became a distinguished southern storywriter and Pulitzer Prize–winning novelist. Sent mistakenly to the Chicago branch office, the letter was eventually forwarded to New York. Unfortunately, Maxwell Perkins replied, Scribners had no openings. The firm missed another opportunity with Welty several years later when she offered it a book of photographs showing "the types, economic conditions, and social and living habits of Negroes in Mississippi" (4 April 1936). Some of these were on exhibition at the time in New York City. And, she wrote, she was just about to have her first short stories published.

philanthropy, finance and public life, together with members of the diplomatic corps and foreign scholars now in the United States. There will be delegations from the Carnegie Corporation, the Carnegie Endowment, the General Education Board, the Laura Spelman Rockefeller Memorial, the Rockefeller Foundation, the Commonwealth fund, the Russell Sage Foundation, the National Research Council, the American Association for the Advancement of Science and other organizations devoted to the arts and sciences.

Second Volume on the Press.

The dictionary will consist of twenty volumes when completed. The first volume has just been published simultaneously in New York and London. The second volume is now on the press and will be published soon. At least three volumes a year will be published until the set is complete. Supplementary volumes will be published later to include the lives of distinguished persons who die during the publication of the dictionary, as no living persons are included.

Some idea of the magnitude of the undertaking may be obtained from the fact that the editorial work in preparation of the dictionary has been under way since the beginning of 1926, nearly three years ago, and that nearly ten years will have elapsed since that time before the final volume is published. The first volume includes the lives of 660 persons in alphabetical order from Cleveland Abbe, scientist, to Maurice Barrymore, actor, and the complete set will embrace about 15,000 lives, related in a total of something like 12,000,000 words.

First Such Work in America.

It is the first time that such an enterprise has been attempted in the field of American biography, although the desirability of such a work has long been realized among American scholars, librarians and university people. On this subject the introduction published in the first volume says:

"The lack of an authoritative dictionary of national biography has often been deplored by American scholars. Encyclopedias and dictionaries of biography abound, but none are comparable in either scope or scholarship to the British Dictionary of National Biography edited by Sir Leslie Stephen and Sir Sidney Lee. It was this need that moved the newly organized American Coun-

cil of Learned Societies to appoint a committee in 1922 to consider such a project. . . ."

Selection of Names Big Task.

After the financial problem was solved, the selection of names offered the greatest single task in the preparation of the dictionary.

"The very term American is not free from ambiguities," says the introduction. "To restrict the term to persons resident in the original Colonies and to citizens of the United States by birth or naturalization would exclude many individuals of foreign birth who have identified themselves with the country and contributed notably to its history. The Committee of Management decided against any such limitation.

"Three other restrictions, however, were adopted: First, that no living persons should have biographies in the dictionary; second, that no person who has not lived in the territory now known as the United States should be eligible, and third, that no British officers serving in America after the Colonies had declared their independence should appear in the dictionary." . . .

Reflects Whole National Life.

The dictionary, therefore, will reflect the whole American scene in its most significant aspects, from the old agricultural and frontier civilization of Colonial days to the technical culture of the twentieth century. As each individual biographical article attempts to analyze the contribution of its subject to the development of America, so the complete work will seek to interpret the history and progress of civilization in the United States as mirrored in the lives and careers of its leaders in government, war, religion, literature, art, science, engineering, industry, commerce, finance, social service, &c. Both in conception and treatment, it has been sought, without neglecting those who built the nation in Revolutionary and Civil War days, to make the dictionary modern in tone, and to make it conform in spirit to the changes wrought by the industrial revolution, scientific progress, and the machine age.

Achievement was made the test of inclusion . . .

Articles Are Independent.

The contributors were instructed to prepare fresh, original and independent articles, and not to be content with mere compilation of preceding sketches. They were also asked to give precise in-

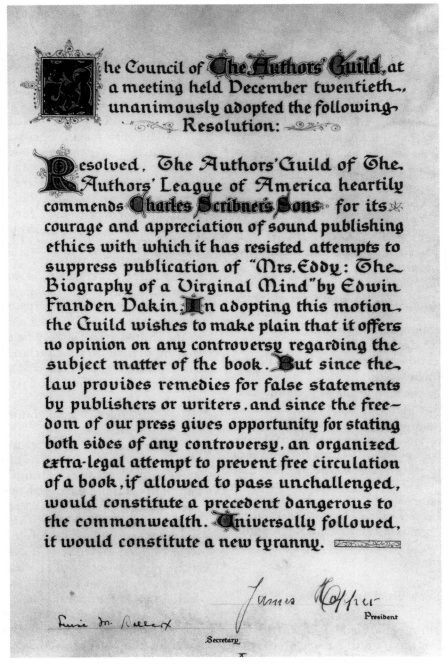

The Council of The Authors' Guild, at a meeting held December twentieth, unanimously adopted the following Resolution:

Resolved, The Authors' Guild of The Authors' League of America heartily commends Charles Scribner's Sons for its courage and appreciation of sound publishing ethics with which it has resisted attempts to suppress publication of "Mrs. Eddy: The Biography of a Virginal Mind" by Edwin Franden Dakin. In adopting this motion, the Guild wishes to make plain that it offers no opinion on any controversy regarding the subject matter of the book. But since the law provides remedies for false statements by publishers or writers, and since the freedom of our press gives opportunity for stating both sides of any controversy, an organized extra-legal attempt to prevent free circulation of a book, if allowed to pass unchallenged, would constitute a precedent dangerous to the commonwealth. Universally followed, it would constitute a new tyranny.

James Hopper
President

Luise M. Ballot
Secretary

Illuminated parchment copy of resolution adopted (20 December 1929) by the Authors' Guild in response to the extra-legal actions of Christian Scientists to suppress Edwin Franden Dakin's book about their church's founder, Mrs. Eddy: The Biography of a Virginal Mind. As with most censorship activities, related press coverage of this controversy only attracted public attention and interest to it. To accompany and promote its February 1930 publication of a cheaper, "popular" edition of the book, Scribners issued a sixteen-page pamphlet, The Blight That Failed, detailing the history of the whole affair—from Dakin's unsolicited submission of his manuscript in 1928 and the firm's enthusiastic acceptance, announcement, and publication (16 August 1929) of it, through the national campaign by Christian Scientists against booksellers (70% effective at one point) and libraries to stop selling/displaying/circulating it, to the crescendo of editorial comment in the press, such as that in the Saturday Review of Literature, *the* Christian Advocate, *and the* New Republic, *supporting free press and congratulating Scribners on its refusal to be intimidated.*

formation based on original sources and to list their authorities in brief bibliographies, which are published at the end of each article, so that the reader may check up for himself upon the accuracy of the statements made or consult the sources for additional information.

Space allotments were made for each article on the basis of the importance and nature of the subject's career, the amount of material available and the completeness of previous biographies. . . .

Set Will Cost $250.

The complete set will cost $250, which will be paid by instalments over the period of publication. Charles Scribner's Sons, the publishers, report a lively interest on the part of libraries and others to whom the dictionary appeals as a reference work. The set is being published in England with the imprint of the Oxford Press.

Scribner's has emphasized the fact that every volume issued will be published on rag paper. It is not a case of a special edition so published. The use of rag paper was requested by librarians for the sake of permanency. Newspapers published on ordinary newsprint fifteen years ago are going to pieces unless kept in a moist atmosphere. Librarians are concerned over the prospect of pulp paper books, and even Government records all over the country are going the same way.

In form as in substance, the dictionary is a notable contribution to American scholarship and letters. It is handsomely bound in durable buckram, and the size of the type, the width of the columns and the flexibility of the bindings have been specially selected to make the volumes easy to open and easy to read.

ARTICLES AND LETTER:
Though Scribners anticipated some puritanical reaction to Hemingway's A Farewell to Arms, *Boston's ban of the book's serialization in* Scribner's Magazine *only heightened his editor's and publisher's feeling that certain words should not and could not appear in the book version: they would prejudice people even more and detract attention from his great achievement in the work.*

• "Boston Bans *Scribner's Magazine,* Superintendent Acts on Objections to Ernest Hemingway's Serial, 'Farewell to Arms,'" *New York Times,* 21 June 1929, p. 2.

BOSTON, Mass. June 20—The June issue of Scribner's Magazine was barred from book-

stands here yesterday by Michael H. Crowley, Superintendent of Police, because of objections to an instalment of Ernest Hemingway's serial, "A Farewell to Arms." It is said that some persons deemed part of the instalment salacious.

The action of the Police Department, however, was similar to locking the stable door after the horse has been stolen, because the June issue of Scribner's has been on sale since May 25.

Mr. Crowley would not say where the complaints originated which resulted in the banning of the magazine. The story concerns the experiences of an American ambulance driver with the Italian army.

Charles Scribner's Sons issued this statement yesterday:

"The very fact that Scribner's Magazine is publishing 'A Farewell to Arms' by Ernest Hemingway is evidence of our belief in its validity and its integrity. Mr. Hemingway is one of the finest and most highly regarded of the modern writers.

"The ban on the sale of the magazine in Boston is evidence of the improper use of censorship which bases its objections upon certain passages without taking into account the effect and purpose of the story as a whole. 'A Farewell to Arms' is in its effect distinctly moral. It is the story of a fine and faithful love, born, it is true, of physical desire.

"If good can come from evil, if the fine can grow from the gross, how is a writer effectually to depict the progress of this evolution if he cannot describe the conditions from which the good evolved? If white is to be contrasted with black, thereby emphasizing its whiteness, the picture cannot be all white.

"A dispatch from Boston emphasized the fact that the story is anti-war argument. Mr. Hemingway set out neither to write a moral tract nor a thesis of any sort. His book is no more anti-war propaganda than are the Kellogg treaties.

"The story will continue to run in Scribner's Magazine. Only one-third of it has as yet been published."

• "Boston Bans Scribner's for July," *New York Times,* 29 June 1929, p. 8.

BOSTON, June 28 (AP)—The July issue of Scribner's Magazine will not appear on Boston news stands, a representative of the New England News Company, Greater Boston distributors, said today. The ban, which started with the June issue at the request of Superintendent of Police Michael Crowley, is because of the continuation of the serial "A Farewell to Arms," by Ernest Hemingway.

• Letter from Scribner editor Maxwell Perkins to Ernest Hemingway, 12 July 1929.

Dear Ernest:

... We considered taking the Boston ban to court, but all advice was that this could accomplish nothing in the specific instance, and probably nothing in a general sense. Their law is such that intelligent people in Massachusetts oppose it, but have not yet been able to get it changed.- Irish Catholics rule the town. There was, and there is still, considerable anxiety for fear of the federal authorities being stirred up. They seem to take curious activity of late, and if the post office should object, we would be in Dutch.-The thing could be fought out, but it would take so much time as to be very serious.-But we do not have to cross any such bridges as that until we come to it. The question does, however, affect the book in this way:-it has been immensely admired, but also it has aroused fierce objection. This means that when the book appears it will be scrutinized from a prejudiced standpoint, and this taken with everything else, did make us conclude, what we had always felt anyhow, that the three words we have talked so much about, could not be printed, or plainly indicated. . . . Anyhow, we went over this thing with the strongest inclination to play the game to the limit with you, and we felt that if we got in trouble in just a matter of words like this, you would be in the least defensible position, because they could easily be defined as indecent and impure, etc., etc. They would from a technical point, and they would arouse prejudice. This point of prejudice I think is hard for you to understand, but there is no question about the fact of it. Anyhow, that is the way the thing worked out after I had talked with Mr. Scribner [CS II] at great length about it. Everything else in the book goes, of course, as you have put it, exactly. . . .

Ever yours,
[Maxwell Perkins]

The book version of A Farewell to Arms, *published on 27 September 1929, did not contain the three problematic words:* cocksucker, fucking, *and* balls.

OBITUARY:
"Death of Charles Scribner," *Publishers' Weekly,* 26 April 1930, pp. 2212–2214.

Though full unexpected, CS II's death clearly marked the end of an era. The Depression was beginning, and world uneasiness was apparent in the headlines. Writers like Galsworthy would soon be in disfavor. For the House of Scribner, however, the transition would be almost seamless, for the next generation (CS III) was already at work in the firm.

On Saturday, April 19th, Charles Scribner died suddenly of heart disease at his home, 9 East 66th Street, New York. He had gone to his office as usual on Thursday, but on Friday he had a fainting spell and died the next day. He is survived by his widow, Louise Flagg Scribner; a daughter, Mrs. George R. R. Schieffelin of New York; a son Charles Scribner, Jr., of Far Hills, N.J., vice president of the firm; and a brother Arthur H. Scribner of New York, who three years ago succeeded to the presidency of Charles Scribner's Sons, while Charles Scribner remained chairman of the Board of Directors. The impressive services at Saint Bartholomew's on Tuesday saw an outpouring of friends and associates. The National Association of Book Publishers, to whose activities Mr. Scribner gave continuing support, was officially represented by the heads of fifteen of the older firms.

Mr. Scribner was born in New York City, October 14, 1854, the son of Charles Scribner, founder of the publishing business, and Emma E. Blair Scribner. The Scribner family traces its American ancestry back to colonial Virginia and it is recorded that Matthew Scrivener was a member of the Council of the Virginia Colony. The name was changed to its present form in the middle of the eighteenth century. Mr. Scribner graduated from Princeton in 1875 and immediately joined the business of publishing which was then being conducted by his elder brother, J. Blair Scribner, his father, founder of the business, having died in 1871. In 1879 Blair Scribner died and Charles Scribner became the head of the business of Charles Scribner's Sons. He was soon joined in partnership by Arthur H. Scribner, five years his junior. To this business, built upon the strong foundations laid by his father, he brought an equipment and natural ability that leaves his name outstanding in American publishing. He studied publishing as a profession and knew its innermost details. He approached it as a lover of

THE NATIONAL ASSOCIATION OF BOOK PUBLISHERS
347 FIFTH AVENUE, NEW YORK
TELEPHONE
ASHLAND 1871-1872-1873

CHARLES SCRIBNER

In the passing of CHARLES SCRIBNER, the distinguished leader of the publishing house of Charles Scribner's Sons, and dean of the publishing profession in America, this Association has suffered an irreparable loss.

The traditions and standards of the House of Scribner, preserved and expressed so faithfully by Charles Scribner himself, have for more than half a century been the model and inspiration for scores of publishing houses.

Mr. Scribner's service to all authors and publishers by his activity as a member of the Association's Copyright Bureau and his prompt and wise attention to every trade crisis have been a continuing contribution to the progress of American book publishing.

Mr. Scribner's character and championship of the best in literature and in publishing may well serve as a guide to all our members.

RESOLVED, that our sympathy and deep sense of loss be expressed to Mr. Scribner's family and to his associates, and be recorded on the minutes of the Association.

By order of the Board of Directors

Frederick A. Stokes, Chairman
George P. Brett
Edward A. Bristol
Irving Putnam

May 7, 1930

Resolution adopted by the National Association of Book Publishers upon the death of CS II, signed by the special committee members who prepared it

23 Bedford Square, London: home of the English branch of Charles Scribner's Sons. The firm moved here in September 1930.

books, with firm convictions as to the material he published, establishing warm friendships with the authors with whom he was in contact. He approached it with a general pride in the industry and gave liberally of his time to the trade's larger problems. He developed an unusual insight into the tendencies of the business which made for the rapid growth of the house of Scribner into the varied fields of publishing. The details of book production always interested him and the standard of the Scribner output was high, and since the establishment of the Scribner Press he has kept it to the best levels of American book production.

His knowledge of the details of the business was always evident at gatherings of publishers where Mr. Scribner could be relied upon to give wise estimates of every new project in publishing. His appreciation of literature was broad and discerning and as a publisher he could give full understanding to a Meredith, Stevenson or Henry James, or to a Scott Fitzgerald or an Ernest Hemingway.

In his contributions to the industry, he was one of the hardest workers for international copy-right, and in the famous struggle that led to our first international copyright measure of 1891 he worked side by side with Major Putnam and others, and it was Mr. Scribner who, with William Appleton and Robert Underwood Johnson, stood in President Harrison's office when this momentous bill was signed on March 4, 1891. Again, when the book trade was at a crisis in 1900 owing to the spread of price-cutting, Mr. Scribner was among the most active in facing the situation and organizing the American Publishers' Association. He served that organization as president, and helped in the handling of the famous legal suit to which this effort for trade betterment led. Only two weeks before his death Mr. Scribner attended the meeting of the copyright committee of the Publishers' Association of which he had been for years a member, to discuss the new copyright bill and lend his experience in pointing ways to progress in this important legislation.

In the manufacture of books the Scribner imprint has always evidenced Mr. Scribner's love of a fine book, and this love of the fine things in bookmaking is also seen in the firm's proclivity toward books on art among which so many of the finest of recent years have borne the Scribner imprint.

The Scribner catalog as it stands today is the real monument to Mr. Scribner, and the extent and variety of the firm's activities have been exceptional. As general publishers, there is no field of fiction or non-fiction into which this house has not entered with distinction. A highly organized subscription department with its staff of representatives all over the country, publishing and distributing the standard sets of many authors, is a separate department of the business. There has always been a special department of music books, both imported and American. The religious department also has separate organization and the output has always been large and significant. From earliest years the firm has had close relationship with England, maintained an office in London and has brought to this country each year many fine editions which could not be printed on this side. The firm has also represented Baedeker in America for many years. No record of the special departments would be complete without reference to the children's books that have been a leading specialty for many years, including such books as Howard Pyle's "Robin Hood" and "King Arthur" and the series of illustrated classics with pictures by Wyeth, Parrish and others. Early in the firm's history it became an agent in America for the *Encyclopedia Britannica,* and its

October 23, 1930

May I congratulate Scribner's on having published, not long ago, two of the most superb novels seen in America these many years? They are Mr. Hemingway's "A Farewell to Arms," and Mr. Thomas Wolfe's "Look Homeward, Angel." I wonder if they are going on selling? If they are, our country, especially that renowned Younger Generation, may be cheerful enough about the American development to forget even the radio and the panic.

Sinclair Lewis

Public statement given by Sinclair Lewis. In his letter to Maxwell Perkins accompanying it Lewis wrote: "I'm rather often asked to boost new novels. Generally I don't. So it gives me so much the more pleasure once in a coon's age to write something like the enclosed which, if you can use it, if it isn't untimely and in general too pontifical, you are welcome to use it as you see fit" (23 October 1930).

ability to handle the larger problems of distributing reference works has been later evidenced by the publication of such books as Hasting's *Dictionary of the Bible* and the *Dictionary of American Biography,* now in process of publication. The growth of the Scribner educational list has recently been very rapid, and the imprint is one of the best known in American educational circles. Besides these many departments, Mr. Scribner found time to direct the growth of a large retail business for both new and rare books, which moved from one beautiful store on lower Fifth Avenue to another still more beautiful store near 48th Street. Still further expanding the facilities of the firm, he organized the Scribner Press, a fourteen-story building on 38th Street which provides for book production in all its details. *Scribner's Magazine* as first founded in 1870 was sold and became the *Century Magazine,* but in 1886 Mr. Scribner entered the field again with the success evidenced by the present prosperity of the periodical.

Mr. Scribner had also shown a rare genius for recognizing publishing and editorial ability, and from the beginning had distinguished associates. W. C. Brownell, critic and writer, was for many years editorial director of the house, Robert Bridges has long been editor of *Scribner's Magazine* and consultant on other enterprises, Maxwell Perkins in recent years has added fresh viewpoints to the editorial staff, and more recently still John Hall Wheelock. In double relations with the editorial aspects of trade and educational departments Dr. Will D. Howe joined the firm ten years ago. Frank N. Doubleday gained his first experience in publishing with the Scribner house and Edward Bok was at one time with the firm.

Two years ago, when Mr. Scribner relinquished some of his responsibilities, Arthur H.

Scribner, who had been for so many years closely associated with his brother, took the presidency of the company, while Charles Scribner, Jr., who had been steadily rounding out his knowledge of publishing since his graduation from Princeton, became more and more active in the direction of the firm's affairs.

Mr. Scribner was a most loyal alumnus of Princeton, and when his alma mater awarded him the honorary degree of L.L.D. in 1925 the citation said, "He stands today a symbol for whatever is most courteous, honorable and fruitful in American endeavor. In his half century since graduation the head of the house has given every year to labor and love for Princeton. . . ." That Mr. Scribner gave of his publishing experience as well as of his time to his college is shown by the fact that he was in 1900 one of the organizers of the Princeton Publishing Co., which issued the *Alumni Weekly,* and in 1905 the organizer and president of the Princeton University Press, to whom he later gave the beautiful and well-equipped building which it now occupies. It was in connection with the development of these two ideas that he came into contact with Whitney Darrow, then graduating, who has represented Mr. Scribner in many of his Princeton contacts. Mr. Darrow is now director of sales and promotion of the firm. Mr. Scribner had been president of the Princeton Club in New York, as is his brother today, and was at one time president of the Graduate Council of Princeton.

PAMPHLET:

"Charles Scribner's Sons, 23 Bedford Square, London," an eight-page booklet, illustrated with photographs of interior and exterior views, dated July 1931. The branch had actually moved the previous September.

CHARLES SCRIBNER'S SONS, their London house having outgrown its quarters in Regent Street, have moved to twenty-three Bedford Square where they are occupying one of the old Adam houses, the lease of which they have purchased from the Bedford estate. The property is situated on the north side of the Square and ex-

tends through to Gower Mews in the rear, being unique in that respect and fortunately so as under the restrictions of the Bedford lease no business involving either dispatch or receipt of freight or parcels through the Bedford Square entrance is permitted. To meet this difficulty an entirely new modern building containing general offices, shipping and stock room, with access to the Mews, has been constructed, leaving the original fine Georgian house, which is devoted to executive offices, intact and in its original condition.

The reception-room with its Adam fireplace, together with the doorways, ceilings, and mantels, have all been maintained in perfect condition and are in the finest architectural tradition of the period. Their beauty will be strikingly apparent to all lovers of good architecture and here the many friends of the House, both English and American, will be most cordially welcome.

Bedford Square, a block or two from the British Museum, is the new publishing centre in London, a number of leading English and American publishing houses having recently moved to the Square itself or to the immediate neighborhood. For nearly seventy-five years the Scribners have maintained close relations with the London literary and publishing world, having been first represented by Charles Welford, the son of a London bookseller but long a resident on this side of the water; later by L. W. Bangs, after years of service in the importing and retail departments of the New York House. Since 1920 the present manager, Charles Kingsley, a graduate of Yale and experienced in American publishing, has been in charge, with John W. Carter of King's College, Cambridge, as his assistant and bibliographical expert, and supported by an efficient office and sales force. The business, formerly limited to the purchase of English editions for the American market and of fine and rare individual books, which have always been a feature of the retail store here, has been extended into the book publishing and magazine field in conjunction with the home House, and Charles Scribner's Sons are now well established as publishers in London with a prosperous and growing business.

SCRIBNER AUTHORS

N. C. Wyeth (1882 – 1945)

N. C. Wyeth (self-portrait in August 1928 issue of Scribner's Magazine*)*

Wyeth is probably the best-known American book illustrator of the twentieth century, primarily for his work in the Scribner Illustrated Classics, a literary adventure series that began in 1911 with his illustrated edition of Robert Louis Stevenson's *Treasure Island*. The oldest of four brothers, Wyeth attended (1902–1904) Howard Pyle's famous art school—spending winters in Pyle's Wilmington, Delaware, studio and summers in nearby Chadds Ford, Pennsylvania—and began his commercial work by illustrating magazine stories for *Leslie's Popular Monthly, Metropolitan, Saturday Evening Post, Scribner's Magazine*, and *Success*. A commission from Scribners in 1904 to illustrate Arthur Stanwood Pier's *The Boys of St. Timothys* inaugurated his career as a book illustrator and his thirty-five-year relationship with the publishing firm. Wyeth provided the illustrations in the majority of the Illustrated Classics—eighteen in all, most of which are still in print. Though advertised and promoted for children, the Classics were extremely popular with readers of all ages because of the dynamic storytelling quality of his richly colored illustrations, which present a heroic interpretation of diverse historical periods—from the Middle Ages (*The Boy's King Arthur*) to the Depression (*The Yearling*)—and even include science fiction (*The Mysterious Island*). His preference for oil painting on a large canvas led him to paint murals for the First National Bank of Boston, for several other banks and insurance companies, and for the Missouri state capitol in Jefferson City. As father-in-law of Peter Hurd and father-teacher of Andrew Wyeth, contemporary acclaimed artists, Wyeth's artistic legacy continues in his family.

Scribner Books Illustrated by Wyeth

Only Scribner books with the <u>first published appearance</u> of Wyeth's illustrations are listed.

1904	*The Boys of St. Timothy's* by Arthur Stanwood Pier
1906	*Whispering Smith* by Frank H. Spearman
1911	*Treasure Island* by Robert Louis Stevenson*
1912	*The Sampo: Hero Adventures from the Finnish Kalevala* by James Baldwin
1913	*Kidnapped: The Adventures of David Balfour* by Robert Louis Stevenson*
1916	*Nan of Music Mountain* by Frank H. Spearman

	The Black Arrow: A Tale of the Two Roses by Robert Louis Stevenson*
1917	The Boy's King Arthur: Sir Thomas Malory's History of King Arthur and His Knights of the Round Table, edited for boys by Sidney Lanier*
1918	The Mysterious Island by Jules Verne*
1919	The Last of the Mohicans: A Narrative of 1757 by James Fenimore Cooper*
1920	Westward Ho!; or, The Voyages and Adventures of Sir Amyas Leigh, Knight, of Burrough, in the County of Devon—In the Reign of Her Most Glorious Majesty Queen Elizabeth by Charles Kingsley*
1921	The Scottish Chiefs by Jane Porter, edited by Kate Douglas Wiggin and Nora A. Smith*
1922	Poems of American Patriotism chosen by Brander Matthews*
1924	David Balfour by Robert Louis Stevenson*
1925	The Deerslayer; or, The First War-Path by James Fenimore Cooper*
1927	Michael Strogoff: A Courier of the Czar Alexander II by Jules Verne*
1928	Drums by James Boyd*
1930	Jinglebob by Philip Aston Rollins*
1931	The Little Shepherd of Kingdom Come by John Fox Jr.*
	Lesby by Elizabeth Willis
1939	The Yearling by Marjorie Kinnan Rawlings*

* A Scribner Illustrated Classic (Wyeth's Robin Hood and Robinson Crusoe were added to the series later but had been issued originally by other publishers)

TRIBUTE:

Tribute by N. C. Wyeth in Joseph Hawley Chapin 1869–1939: Artist, Art Director, Friend, limited edition, "made by and for the friends of Joseph Hawley Chapin" (New York: Scribners, 1939), unpaginated.

In this reminiscence about Scribner art editor Joseph Hawley Chapin, Wyeth makes a small factual error: "The Moose Call" appeared in the October 1906 issue of Scribner's Magazine. Prior to that he had illustrated several stories by others for the magazine and had contributed a self-illustrated article on a typical Western cattle roundup, based on his own experiences in the West in the fall of 1904. Chapin was Scribner art editor from 1897 till 1936.

In the early summer of 1904, fresh from my studies under Howard Pyle, I made my first sale of a creative painting. It was Joe Chapin who bought it. This picture, which I had named "The Moose Call," appeared that autumn in Scribner's Magazine.

Early in this summer, just thirty-five years later, Chapin and I began the exciting task of building the new Pulitzer Prize Illustrated Edition of "The Yearling" by Marjorie Kinnan Rawlings. My art-editor friend did not live to see this book emerge finished from the press.

Thus came to a close a span of thirty-five years during which Joe Chapin as Art Editor and myself as illustrator worked together on many special and elaborate editions of famous stories, notably the series known to the trade as Scribner's Illustrated Classics. Besides these, we worked out many pages in color and black-and-white for Scribner's Magazine, and frontispieces for numerous other books.

Under Chapin's stimulating interest and his watchful eye, I painted about three hundred works. The accomplishment of this amount of work represents a great deal of intense, sympathetic and sustained co-operation, and I can happily assert that in every particular dealing, and in every situation, our work was a delightful experience. I wish that we had it to do over again.

The story of every serious-minded art student's career, from his first day in the art classes to his final initiation into the world of "practical illustration" (as Howard Pyle used to call it) is an odyssey in itself. It is a long, thrilling, harassing period of hopes raised high and dashed low; of trial and failure over and over again. One might well say that this kind of experience prevails throughout an artist's life; but the youth has no background against which to measure these violent fluctuations of the new adventure, and they continue to the climactic event where he launches forth to seek a market for the product of his years of laborious and painstaking study.

Who of us will ever forget those exciting but wearisome days of plodding the streets of New York, through driving wind and rain perhaps, overladen with prodigiously awkward and ungainly bundles of drawings and paintings (not quite dry!), going from publisher to publisher, climbing long flights of stairs, or begging our way into crowded elevators, and finally wheedling a pass from the calm but cautious secretary, and so, if fortunate, walk into the lair and the majestic presence of the Art Editor!

Most of us have done all of this, and those who have not have missed an unforgettable and colorful chapter of apprenticeship.

Forty years ago, in the pleasant retirement of the quiet city of Wilmington in Delaware, a sizable group of earnest students of illustration were working under the magnificent teaching and wise counsel of Howard Pyle. As the years of study rolled by we more and more often cast wistful glances into the northeastern horizon toward that illustrators' Eldorado, New York City! As we approached maturity under Pyle's magic leadership we became more and more restive and eager to do battle in that distant and shining city of promise. We were like so many impatient race horses, caged at the barrier, each awaiting his release, his signal from the master to "Go!"

I received such a release the day I completed the afore-mentioned painting "The Moose Call." I had at last created a picture which won the master's approval and the award of freedom to try my luck with the criterions of the illustrating profession—the art editors.

In those days, the shining lights of the publishing world (from the illustrator's point of view at least) were *Scribner's, Harpers* and *Century.* These mighty names were, to us, adorned and crowned with the illustrious names of their art editors. Chapin of *Scribner's!* Drake of *Century!* Wills of *Harpers!*

Of course there were other magazines and many other publishers whose presses were restricted to books; but the Big Three were glamorous! They were doing, by popular acclaim, the best in reproduction and were demanding the best

of the illustrator's art. They were our dream and our goal.

For one reason or another, the name of *Scribner's* had always been to me one to especially conjure with. Principally I believe, because it was the favorite periodical to come into my boyhood home. At any rate, my dreams and ambitions had been for a long time to paint pictures good enough to be used in *Scribner's.*

That day of trial came at last and the evening before the venture I sought the advice of Howard Pyle as to where it would be well to submit my painting. "Wyeth," he said, "always go to the very best publishers first."

The next day found me in the great city facing the small door at number 153 Fifth Avenue, and it was with fear and trembling that I was eventually ushered into the presence of Joseph Chapin, famed Art Director for Charles Scribner's Sons.

Joe Chapin's appearance was much the same then as in the last year he lived. Of course his hair had not silvered and his cropped moustache was not a pastel gray, but his manner remained always the same. On that fateful day he impressed me as at once benevolent and austere, friendly yet somewhat remote. As he sat behind his desk he made me think of King Edward VII. His greeting was quietly pleasant and brief, and he promptly asked to see what I had ardently brought in to show. So I opened the hinged box in which the small painting was fastened and placed it in the most favorable light of that office of most strange and tangled lighting. He looked at the canvas in silence, tipping his head to right and left in critical consideration. No change of expression; no words. There was an interval of exasperating and unrelated fussing with letters on his desk. My heart sank.

Suddenly, and rather tersely, he remarked that he would like to show the painting to Mr. Scribner. In ten minutes he returned, sat down again behind his desk and after a long pause said, "We'll be glad to buy your picture and can offer seventy-five dollars for it. We might run it in one of the fall issues of the magazine."

There is no use in my trying to describe the overwhelming sense of joy, gratitude and triumph I felt in that moment! Even to this day I can recapture some of the ecstasy of the adventure of that rainy morning in Chapin's office in that old building. And it is a fact of which I am reasonably proud, that this spirit of delightful tension, a blend of trepidation, anticipation, and a little tri-

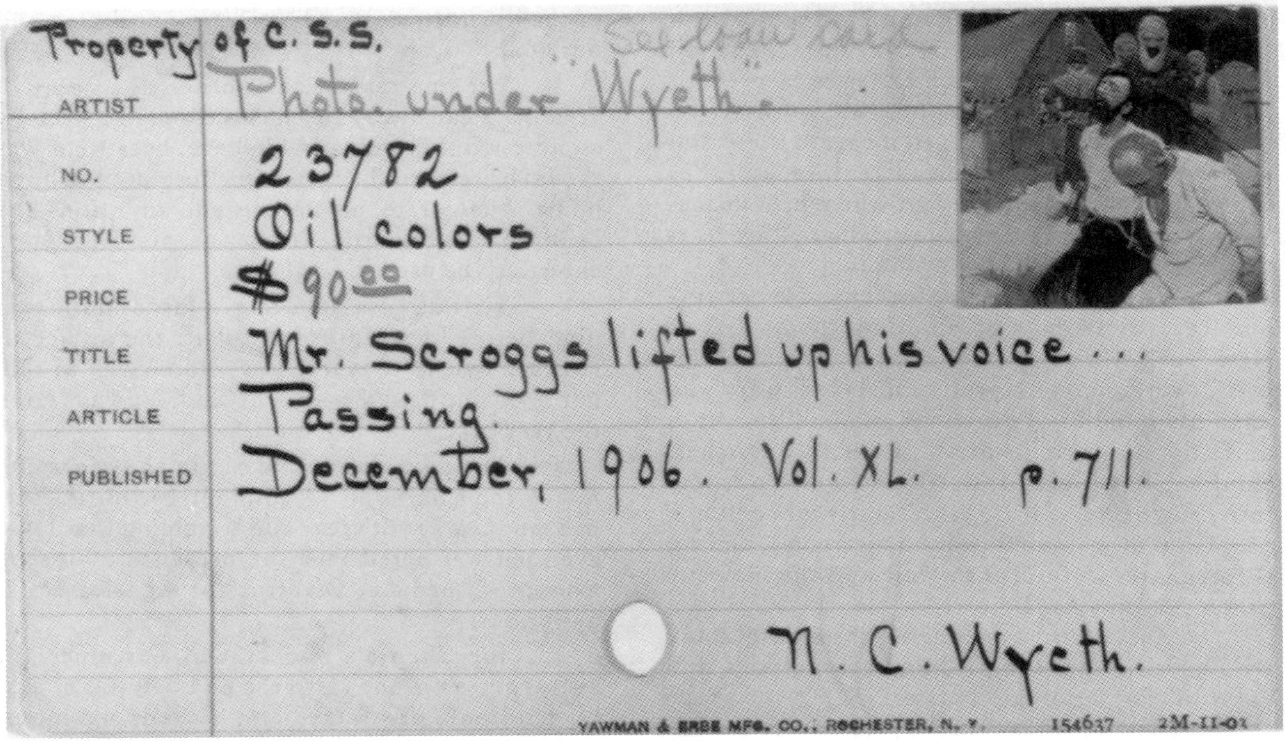

Property of C.S.S.

Set loan card

ARTIST   Photo. under "Wyeth".

NO.   23782

STYLE   Oil colors

PRICE $90.00

TITLE   Mr. Scroggs lifted up his voice...

ARTICLE   Passing.

PUBLISHED   December, 1906. Vol. XL.   p. 711.

N. C. Wyeth.

YAWMAN & ERBE MFG. CO., ROCHESTER, N. Y.   154637   2M-11-02

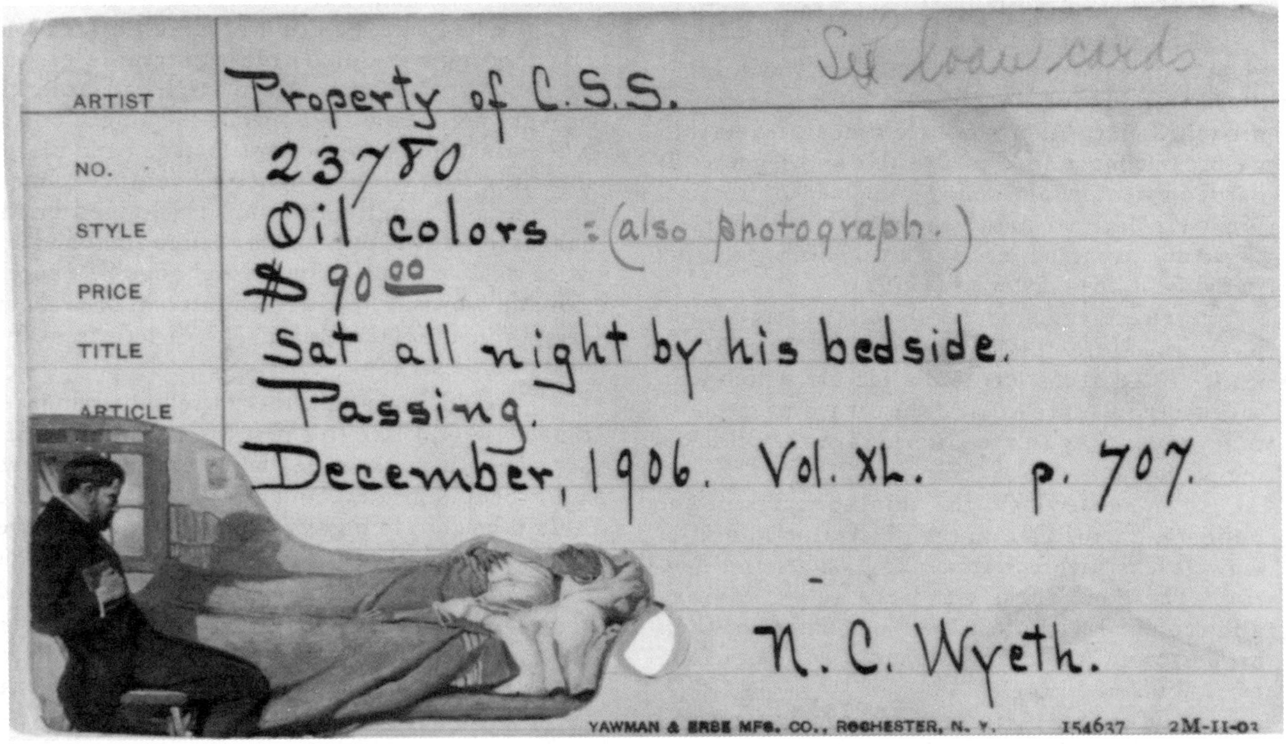

ARTIST   Property of C.S.S.   *Set loan cards*

NO.   23780

STYLE   Oil colors = (also photograph.)

PRICE $90.00

TITLE   Sat all night by his bedside.

ARTICLE   Passing.

December, 1906. Vol. XL.   p. 707.

N. C. Wyeth.

YAWMAN & ERBE MFG. CO., ROCHESTER, N. Y.   154637   2M-11-02

Scribner Art Department file cards for several of Wyeth's drawings (courtesy of the Brandywine River Museum). Until Westward Ho! (1920), Scribner owned Wyeth's book illustrations and offered the original paintings for sale.

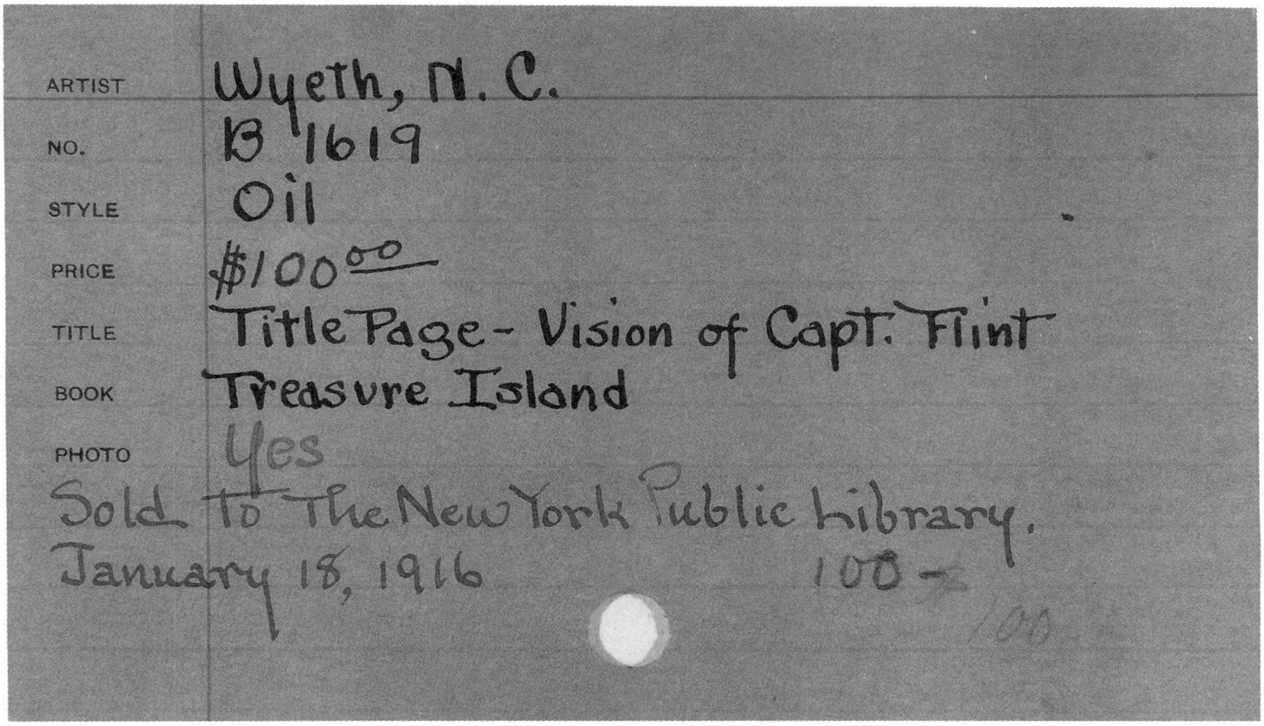

ARTIST Wyeth, N. C.

NO. B 1619

STYLE Oil

PRICE $100⁰⁰

TITLE Title Page - Vision of Capt. Flint

BOOK Treasure Island

PHOTO Yes

Sold to The New York Public Library.
January 18, 1916   100 -
                                        100

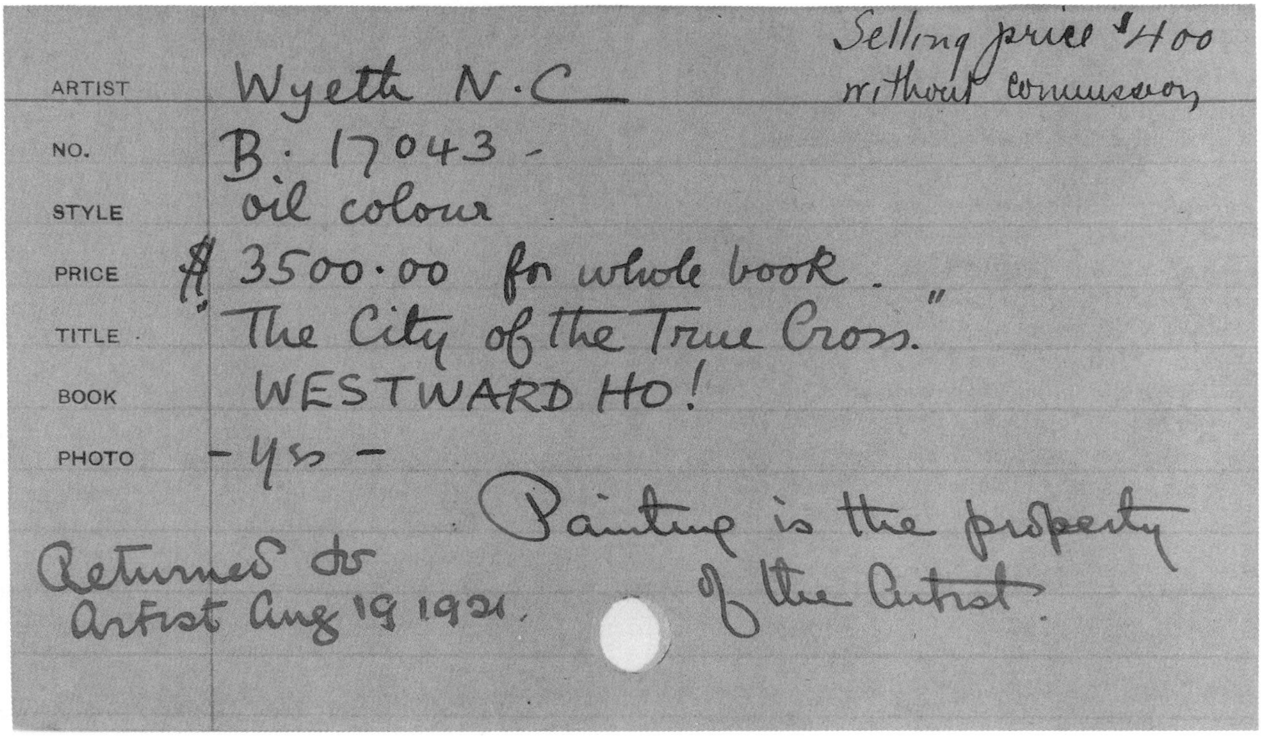

ARTIST Wyeth N·C   Selling price $400
                                 without commission

NO. B· 17043 -

STYLE oil colour

PRICE $ 3500·00 for whole book -

TITLE "The City of the True Cross."

BOOK WESTWARD HO!

PHOTO - Yes -

                              Painting is the property
Returned to   of the Artist.
Artist Aug 19 1921.

umph perhaps, definitely survived into my last conference with my editor friend.

This spirit of sympathetic co-operation, consistently and quietly held over so long a period of years, is the measure of the man I shall always cherish. Quite different in character and temperament from me, who am apt to be explosive and garrulous in my enthusiasms, yet we complemented each other in the work we had to do. Joe Chapin's long identification with the life in New York appeared to have removed him from the background and the traditions of his native New England, but this mutual heritage of ours seemed always to come to life in our dealings and became a common source of inspiration.

With the passing of this eminent editor, we have lost the last of that distinguished group of individuals who happily prevailed in America's more notable period of book and magazine illustration and decoration. Chapin was never a slave to fickle fashions nor a servant to narrow politics; therefore he was never inclined to over-direct the artist. He continually sought out, and successfully found, an unusual number of individual talents, and these he invariably met with discriminating sympathy and understanding. Many of us can count that day a blessing when we came to his notice.

LETTER:
Letter from Wyeth to Joseph Hawley Chapin [November 1912].

Encouraged by the success of Wyeth's illustrated Treasure Island, *Scribners was eager to follow it up with another classic.* Kidnapped, *also by Robert Louis Stevenson, was chosen and offered to Wyeth. At the time of this letter an exhibition of Wyeth's landscapes and other illustrations, including some from* Treasure Island, *was in progress at the Philadelphia Sketch Club. The "Gibbon story" he mentions was "Madame Robin" by Perceval Gibbon; it appeared, with Wyeth's illustrations, in the March 1913 issue of* Scribner's Magazine.

My dear Chapin:
We've certainly arrived at the point where I can call you <u>Chapin</u> and I'm proud of it!

Your letter this morning affected me greatly and I am delighted. I want you to know that I have the greatest hopes, and unless I outclass Treasure Island I want you to cancel the entire scheme!

The exhibition is compelling flattering attention, but it has given me a severe jolt, and I am getting a stern lesson out of it. I enclose one of many articles appearing in Phila. newspapers. The rest are slushy but this one hits straight from the shoulder.

Return this if you think of it please.

The Gibbon story is coming right along and will be done very soon.

With kindest regards
Wyeth

P.S. Will write regarding "Kidnapped" in a few days.

LETTER:
Letter from Wyeth to Joseph Hawley Chapin, 11 November 1919.

With this letter Wyeth wrought two concessions from Scribners: the freedom to illustrate one book per year for another publisher and the right to receive his original drawings and paintings back, which he could then sell for additional profit. In the process of explaining his situation to Chapin he describes the current financial opportunities available in commercial illustration.

My dear Chapin:
I have been reluctant to write at length for various reasons, the main reason being that I've been in such a quandary myself.

Since my return in September I've done little else than out-door painting, and in two canvasses at least I have surprised myself with the real progress made. Those, of capable judgement who have seen this work urge me to send them to the winter shows. However, I'm not sufficiently satisfied to let them go—facility and power fall too far short to warrant my making a debut just now. But I am greatly encouraged.

In the meantime opportunities in the illustrating field have piled in beyond anything I ever experienced, particularly from the advertising houses. To-date I have turned down <u>all</u> the latter with the exception of a single painting for the Winchester Rifle. In a sense it has been somewhat of an ordeal, for in several cases (three, to be accurate) the price has been 1500^{00} for single drawings.

I believe that most of my friends, were they to know this would say, "How foolish!" To me it is <u>not</u> foolish, even though it may be impractical. Heaven knows! I've none too much <u>idealism</u>, and what little I've got must be applied. So it

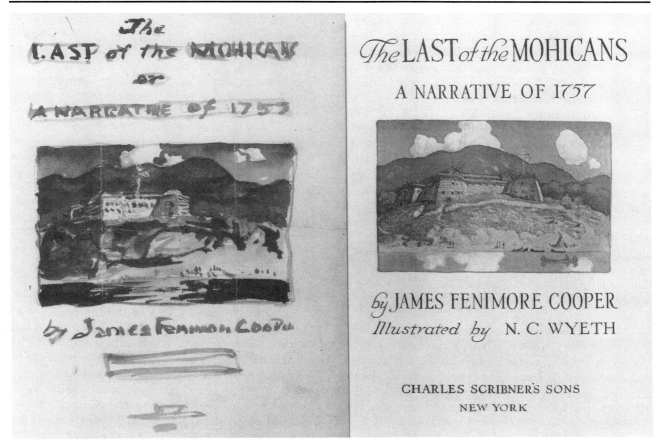

Wyeth's preliminary watercolor sketch contrasted with the final result on the title page of the Scribner Illustrated Classic edition of James Fenimore Cooper's The Last of the Mohicans.

is that I am resolved not to be inundated with a character of work which is such a insidious antidote to the qualities within my nature which are struggling for expression. The miserable failure of the older men of my generation in illustration to advance to higher forms of artistic expression, stands as an obvious and mighty lesson, and not to make an effort to avoid their errors would be the height of weakness.

Advertising art has indeed progressed remarkably and on the whole is much more interesting to look at than the illustrated story section of most periodicals, but that does not justify it to the artist by any means, for the demands of the advertiser are far more confining and far more artificial than the demands of an author. The big prices offered are blinding and it is so <u>dammed</u> easy not to see the danger.

Magazine illustration has become a very unsatisfying job. The pay in most instances is liberal enough, but presentation to the public is so <u>rotten</u>! One must needs work abortively to help the engraver, thus ruining the finer pleasure in making the pictures, and then one gets a bad re-

production anyway. I'm saying this of periodicals who are paying 300⁰⁰ and 400⁰⁰ a drawing. I'm telling you confidentially that I am offered $500⁰⁰ an illustration for Ladies Home Journal. Work for such publishers would indeed be financially satisfying, but that's about all there is in it—and I'm not going to do it if possible.

Coincident with all this are the book offers, and it is to this field that I must turn.

It has not been hard for me in the last eight years to turn down the many offers of other publishers, and with the exception of the McKay book [Paul Creswick's *Robin Hood* illustrated for David McKay in 1917], have been true to my word. But now the offers are beyond refusal and I cannot afford to confine myself to one book a year.

Perhaps it would interest you to hear that Hugh Walpole made the trip here to see my work and is already urging Conrads publishers to "<u>tie me up</u>"—this will never be done, but when the time comes I shall certainly do one or two of his books. A list of eight titles have been offered to me by four different publishing houses. The prices in some cases amounting to <u>double</u> of that received for the Cooper book [*The Last of the Mohicans*], with <u>originals back</u>. This latter arrangement is of valuable importance to me, and I was foolish not to have insisted on this arrangement with Scribners three years ago.

I am telling you all this at length, so that you will see exactly my position. From the standpoint of sentiment it is devilish hard to put these things down. I hate like everything to disturb arrangements which have gone on so long. They have been particularly pleasant and I trust will continue to be.

The alternative is to turn to commercial work to bolster up my finances as I said, and I have determined not to do it. Two juvenile books this year and next are my plans. Yours, if you decide to let me have it—and another. In any case I am going to ask for my originals back.

I have read "Westward Ho!" and am in the second reading. It is a great book, perhaps the richest one yet! I had never read it so went ahead irrespective of the possibility that you might substitute something else. I've already laid out my scheme, so for <u>once</u> feel that I will be ready.

In regard to the Cooper plates, I will confess they almost made me sick and I have not yet thrown off the gloom when I think of that book appearing.

In no sense do I blame you for the poor results, but am exasperated beyond measure at my own inability in not getting the pictures to you weeks before I did.

It does seem to me though, that ill-advised <u>economy</u> is playing a harmful role in Chas. Scribners Sons, and is squeezing out a certain buoyancy and spontaneity which goes to make expanding success. Certainly <u>I</u> have never grumbled around after extra dollars much, but I must confess to a growing sense of tightness which signifies stagnation rather than business sagacity.

I know I'm damned impertinent!
With best regards
Wyeth

Wyeth went to work on Charles Kingsley's West-ward Ho!, *which Scribners published in its Illustrated Classics series in October 1920.*

LETTER:
Letter from Wyeth to Joseph Hawley Chapin, "Tuesday morning 6:15" [1921].

Working on his illustrations for The Scottish Chiefs *by Jane Porter, Wyeth responds to proofs he has been receiving of already-completed drawings. These were often a disappointment to him, for the printing work seldom did justice, in his opinion, to the originals. His grandfather's house in Needham, Massachusetts, which he mentions having just bought, proved to be only a temporary residence; moving his family there in the fall, he realized Needham had changed a great deal since he was a boy growing up there, and his own children missed Chadds Ford, Pennsylvania. In 1923 all moved back to Chadds Ford.*

My dear Chapin:
I have been putting such long hours in at the studio and the remaining time has been so full of other distractions (three children with the whooping cough!) that letter writing has had to go by the board.

By this time, without much doubt, you have three more of the "Scottish Chiefs" drawings. More will follow soon. I hope that these come somewhere near your expectations. I am trying to keep a greater freshness of color and spontaneity of rendering, and still present considerable detail. The sea picture represents my second attempt at that motive. The first one took me four days, the one you have, a day and a half.

The proofs arrived O.K. and certainly give evidences of success. Bowker is assuredly getting a richness of color and strength of values which are uncommon. He has attained brilliant greens and blues in the same proof which I have always been told were impossible. One tendency which we must correct is that rawness of red—almost a bloody red as in the face and hands of Wallace seated under the tree.

The book lining is the least satisfactory. The weight and structural force of the castle has been sacrificed for the attainment of a delicate blue sky. i.e. I wish he had used a heavier blue and retained the strength of the castle and foreground and had let the sky come in whatever gray or dull blue it would.

The title-page seems good, and do you know I am very fond of that illuminated letter you put on it. I hope you will reconsider, and keep this feature. The page looks quite dull and stupid without it.

Covers from four reissued editions of Wyeth's Scribner Illustrated Classics

The cover design mounted on a black book board looks striking. I think Bowker has done very well with these plates.

————

I would like so much to have a chat with you at this time. Whenever I am working out new plans for my future I feel a desire to talk them over with three or four substantial friends, and I number you as one of these.

I have considered running up to see you, but time is so valuable and means so much in the making of your book that I have had to discourage myself of the idea. A day spent in New York isn't so much, but it usually takes me two to three days to re-adjust myself and get back to a really normal basis of working.

You will be surprised to know that I have bought my grandfather's homestead in Needham. It adjoins my father's property and like it fronts on the Charles River. It is an old New England house and apart from its historic beauty, is replete in personal meaning to me having been practically "raised" there. Apart and added to all this however, is the most practical advantages which we as a family will enjoy, advantages which we seriously miss here. Schools for the children, and the companionship of sympathetic and helpful townspeople, besides being within a few miles of Boston and its forceful influence.

Personally speaking, an outstanding event for me will be the arrangements already made to devote about 1/3 of my time to study under George Noyes (an obscure painter but a marvelous colorist). I need this help beyond words! Mural work is looming up importantly and I need to know, more definitely, the science of color:— this knowledge added to certain instructiive feelings I have regarding it should mean much.

I am paying 12000⁰⁰ for the property and by Sept. 1ˢᵗ fully expect to clean up the debt without having to mortgage this place (which I shall hold for several years) nor touch any of my investments. I am telling you this because I want very much to arrange if possible to get the lump sum of $3000⁰⁰ which will be due me on "Scottish Chiefs" by the above date. Do you think this can be done?

Now, as you see I am not going to Boston this summer so the correction of proofs must be done at long range. However, if at any time you think it necessary for me to come to N.Y. I shall gladly do so.

With best regards
Sincerely
Wyeth

Wyeth shipped the last illustration to Chapin on 12 August and wrote: "With reasonably good color plates, this series should take its place with the best I have done." In fact, he was so inspired with the results that he asked Chapin to send him to Scotland to gather material for illustrating five or six Sir Walter Scott novels—but such a trip did not develop. The Wyeth edition of The Scottish Chiefs *was published on 14 October 1921.*

LETTER:
Letter from Wyeth to Joseph Hawley Chapin, "12³⁰ Sat. night" [late 1921?].

The Studio: An Illustrated Magazine of Fine and Applied Art *began in 1893, published in London by John Lane. Here, Wyeth's suggestion that Scribners pursue an opportunity to publish it, perhaps prompted by the fact that the firm had taken over* Architecture *magazine in 1917, was not followed. The "virile"* Ladies' Home Journal *story Wyeth mentions illustrating was probably* Vandemark's Folly *by Herbert Quick, which was serialized in the magazine from October 1921 through February 1922.*

My dear Chapin:
To-day I enjoyed a most pleasant visit with Christian Brinton [American art critic] during which he let drop something about Mr. John Lane [English publisher] being in this country for the purpose of disposing of his magazine "The Studio".

Since returning home the thought has grown stronger and stronger in my mind that the only place for the publication is with Charles Scribner's Sons.

You must think me devilishly presuming to even mention this but I yearn so for a real rounded magazine, containing real art and artistic features (something we have absolutely nothing of in this country) that you must pardon me for my zeal.

There isn't a finer title for a magazine in the world. "The Studio" is smart, it is broadly significant and embraces the field of all arts. To broaden its scope into the literary field, that field in which Scribners excels preeminently combined with the best procurable from the painters, sculptors, architects, wood carvers, textile men etc. etc. would fill a most serious need and I feel certain would make a tremendous hit and could not but be a financial success. Just as Walter Hampden [popular American actor] is proving on the stage, a bang up <u>art</u> magazine will prove in the

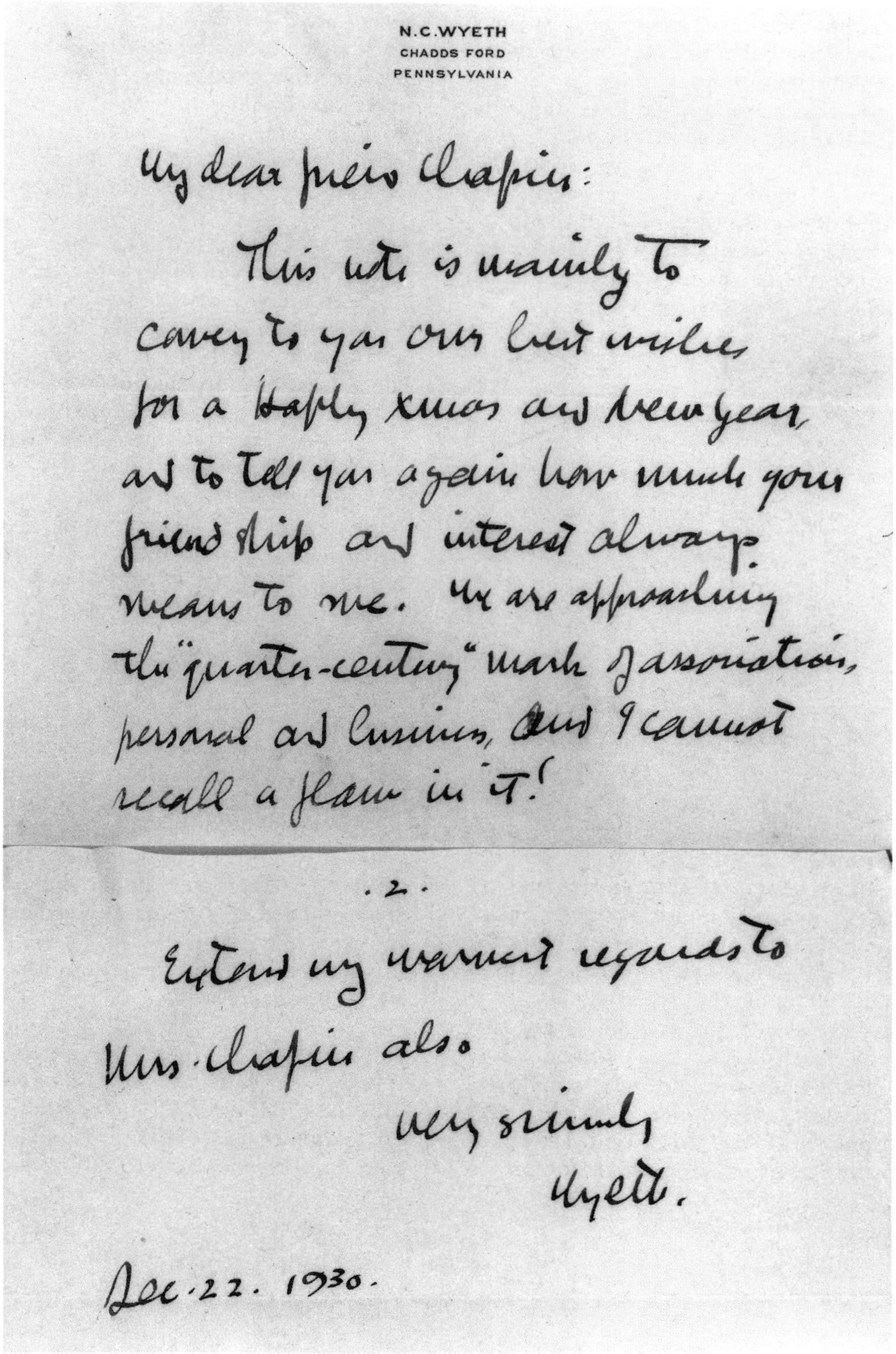

N.C.WYETH
CHADDS FORD
PENNSYLVANIA

My dear Mr. Chapin:

This note is mainly to
convey to you our best wishes
for a Happy Xmas and New Year
and to tell you again how much your
friendship and interest always
means to me. We are approaching
the "quarter-century" mark of association,
personal and business, and I cannot
recall a flaw in it!

. 2 .

Extend my warmest regards to
Mrs. Chapin also.
very sincerely
Wyeth.

Dec. 22. 1930.

Holiday greetings from Wyeth to Joseph Hawley Chapin, head of the Scribner Art Department

publishing world. In my relatively small circle of acquaintances, hundreds are hungry for just such a periodical and I firmly believe that tens of thousands feel the same way about it.

I am illustrating an unusually strong, virile story in the Ladies Home Journal, and I wish you would read the letters they are receiving about my pictures. They (the pictures) are nothing wonderful, but compared to most of the Journal pictorial material, they strike a much more commanding note in their seriousness and thought. Now think what real art would do.

This is my last note from Chadds Ford. Leave for Needham on Tuesday.

Sincerely
Wyeth

LETTER:
Letter from Wyeth to Joseph Hawley Chapin, 19 August 1929.

During the summer of 1929, Wyeth's daughter Henriette married the artist Peter Hurd (June), and his father died (July). In addition to the stress caused by these personal "crises" he had artistic reasons for wanting to postpone his plans for illustrating an edition of Jonathan Swift's Gulliver's Travels *for the Scribner Illustrated Classics series.*

My dear Chapin:

I am directing this letter to you, though by rights, I suppose, it should go direct to Mr. Scribner. But somehow, after our 25 years of work together you are the first one I am inclined to talk to when any matter of concern comes up.

To avoid holding you in unnecessary suspense I'll come right to the matter on my mind.

For reasons pertaining purely to my present state of artistic transition I wish to "beg off" and so postpone "Gulliver" for a year. I shall, of course, do nothing else in competitive book illus-

tration in the meantime, but, in order to assure myself a necessary income, I shall select enough work from various opportunities (preferably a few advertising drawings). In my extra time (and I am resolved there shall be plenty of this!) I shall work furiously to emerge into a more complete solution of what I feel certain will be an important step in my progress as an illustrator and painter.

The effect of this present aggitation (which has in fact existed for several years and has been increased with great rapidity in the last ten months) has been to very much depress my ardor for any more book work for the present. There must be a deeper purpose and a more individual impulse behind the next book I do for you.

I realize how much I am disturbing your plans, but no more so than a set of perfunctory drawings which would result were I forced to go through the work. I have tried hard, ever since reading and planning the "Gulliver" series two months ago, to see my way clear to tackle them, but I cannot arouse sufficient spirit and enthusiasm.

Very sincerely
Wyeth

P.S. I am aware that the various crises of this summer have had considerable to do with my feelings as expressed above. Henriette's marriage, my father's recent death—and now the necessary disposal of our birthplace and homestead in Massachusetts. These have all contributed to my determination not to slump into a mere dependable and passable picture maker. I feel that I've got enough inside of me that should be expressed to warrant added effort.

N.C.W.

Wyeth never returned to his plans for Gulliver's Travels; *the subject for his next book illustration for Scribners was Philip Ashton Rollins's* Jinglebob, *published in the fall of the following year.*

Arthur Train (1875–1945)

Arthur Train, standing under the portrait (1923) of his fictional lawyer, Ephraim Tutt, by Gordon Stevenson

Drawing upon his years as a successful prosecutor of both criminal offenses and political corruption—first as assistant district attorney of New York City and later as a special deputy attorney general of New York State—Train became the leading author of legal fiction in his time and probably the best-known lawyer-author of pre–World War II America. His greatest tribute as a writer was to have his fictional lawyer with the stovepipe hat, Ephraim Tutt, accepted as a real character by an adoring public. Train's traditionally plotted stories about legal exploits, in which Tutt demonstrated in an ingenuous manner his deep understanding of the law and his profession, received a wide circulation in *The Saturday Evening Post;* over a dozen collections of them were published by Scribners. Some law schools made *Mr. Tutt's Case Book* required reading. In addition, Train wrote popular novels that chronicled the American scene and nonfiction books about true crimes and the administration of criminal justice. He cofounded (1911) the Authors' League of America for the purpose of safeguarding the rights of authors. In 1941 he was elected president of the National Institute of Arts and Letters and was reelected to that post one week before his death.

Scribner Books by Train

1905	*McAllister and His Double*
1906	*The Prisoner at the Bar: Sidelights on the Administration of Criminal Justice*
1908	*True Stories of Crime from the District Attorney's Office*
1909	*The Butler's Story: Being the Reflections, Observations and Experiences of Mr. Peter Ridges, of Wapping-on-Velly, Devon, Sometime in the Service of Samuel Carter, Esquire, of New York*, illustrated by F. C. Yohn
1911	*Confessions of Artemas Quibble: Being the Ingenuous and Unvarnished History of Artemas Quibble, Esquire, One-Time Practitioner in the New York Criminal Courts, Together with an Account of the Divers Wiles, Tricks, Sophistries, Technicalities, and Sundry Artifices of Himself and Others of the Fraternity, Commonly Yclept "Shysters" or "Shyster Lawyers"*

1912	*Courts, Criminals and the Camorra*
1917	*The World and Thomas Kelly*
1918	*The Earthquake*
1920	*Tutt and Mr. Tutt*
1921	*By Advice of Counsel: Being Adventures of the Celebrated Firm of Tutt & Tutt, Attorneys and Counsellors at Law*
	The Hermit of Turkey Hollow: The Story of an Alibi, Being an Exploit of Ephraim Tutt, Attorney & Counsellor at Law
1923	*His Children's Children*
	Tutt, tut! Mr. Tutt
1924	*The Needle's Eye*
1925	*On the Trail of the Bad Men*
	The Lost Gospel
1926	*The Blind Goddess*
	Page Mr. Tutt
1927	*High Winds*
	When Tutt Meets Tutt
1928	*Ambition*
	The Horns of Ramadan
1929	*Illusion*
1930	*The Adventures of Ephraim Tutt, Attorney and Counsellor-at-Law*
	Paper Profits
1931	*Puritan's Progress: An Informal Account of Certain Puritans & Their Descendants from the American Revolution to the Present Time, Their Manners & Customs, Their Virtues & Vices, Together, with Some Possibly Forgotten Episodes in the Development of American Social & Economic Life During the Last One Hundred & Fifty Years*
1932	*Princess Pro Tem*
1933	*No Matter Where*
1934	*Tutt for Tutt*
1935	*Jacob's Ladder*
1936	*Manhattan Murder*
	Mr. Tutt Takes the Stand
	Mr. Tutt's Case Book: Being a Collection of His Most Celebrated Trials as Reported and Compiled by Arthur Train
1938	*Old Man Tutt*
1939	*My Day in Court*
	From the District Attorney's Office: A Popular Account of Criminal Justice
1940	*Tassels on Her Boots*
1941	*Mr. Tutt Comes Home*
1943	*Yankee Lawyer: The Autobiography of Ephraim Tutt*
1945	*Mr. Tutt Finds a Way*
1961	*Mr. Tutt at His Best*, edited by Harold R. Medina

LETTER:
Letter from Train to Edward L. Burlingame, editor of *Scribner's Magazine*, 24 August 1905.

In this letter by Train—his first in the Scribner Archives—he reveals an interest in creating "a certain kind of gentleman" character. This man of "quality," who must be true to history and human nature, would be realized fourteen years later in his fictional Ephraim Tutt. Burlingame, however, rejected this early story, feeling Train's character was more of a type than a personality.

My dear Mr. Burlingame,—
I know that it is one of the rules laid down for embryonic authors: "Don't send a letter with your MS. The Publisher doesn't want to read it." I want however to tell you that the sketch I am sending you, "Randolph '63," is a conscientious attempt at character drawing (of a very modest kind) which I have mulled over for a long time. I have tried to show both sides of a shield that usually hangs broadside on and can't be seen around. Hence the purpose of my anti-climax,—the failure of my character to "do" anything, which perhaps the reader discovers (if he is not fast asleep long before that) with a trifle of disappointment. My wife laid down the story and said: "Your old Curtis is always saying what a fine fellow this Randolph was, but he never did anything to prove it!" To which I reply: "Precisely. He was a fine fellow, and if you can't see it without his doing something, the whole thing is a flat failure. Moreover you are privileged to see, a little more clearly than the rather sentimental old class-mate, just about how fine he was. He was 'quality.' He was just a certain kind of a gentleman that is usually played up in fiction in a way that is not quite true to history and to human nature."
All of which sounds monstrous sententious.
Faithfully yours
Arthur C. Train

LETTER:
Letter to Train from his Scribner editor, Maxwell Perkins, 22 October 1919.

Perkins's praise for Train's Tutt stories, which had been appearing regularly in The Saturday Evening Post, *shows the distance he has come in his development as a writer. Train thought his*

editor's publishing suggestions were helpful but disagreed on the selection of stories. Published on 9 April 1920, Tutt and Mr. Tutt *contained nine stories, but none of them (at least by title) were drawn from Perkins's list.*

Dear Mr. Train:
I have read the last four of the Tutt stories which you had sent to me - and with great enjoyment and considerable laughter. Certainly there were never any stories nor any other kind of writing, so far as I know, that gave such a picture of the legal life in and about the criminal courts and the district attorney's office, and that of the lawyers connected with them. And certainly Mr. Tutt is a very real and sympathetic character. I now think you were probably right in letting his character develop incidentally, and in not subordinating the stories to it, because in the aggregate they give you the character in a truer way than would be the case had <u>that</u> been made in every sense the main thing.
I do think that it would be well, though, to have some stories that would be chiefly concerned in exhibiting his character; but when it comes to suggesting them, I am afraid I cannot help much. I have two very general ideas that might result in something: the kind of a case Tutt would not handle might furnish a story - a case for which rich clients wanted to retain him and in which, because of the great fee, he became involved up to a certain point, and then stuck upon the question of right and wrong and dropped it. Would this be plausible? The other, which would bring out the sympathy and sentiment of Mr. Tutt, might be based on one of those not uncommon incidents where a young man, or girl, comes to the city from the country and gets into ways of crime, or semi-crime, mainly through ignorance and greenness. I do not think you have referred to Tutt's origin, and it might be that the element of reminiscence - which has been rather overworked, it is true - by which a man's sympathy is engaged because he recalls his own first contact with the city, would be effectively evoked. In such a story might not Mr. Tutt ethically free the victim from the technicalities of law because of his conviction that his fault was due not to his nature but to his ignorance?
If we should select the stories, for a volume, from those we now have, I think a good list would be these:

"The People Against Angelo Seraphino"

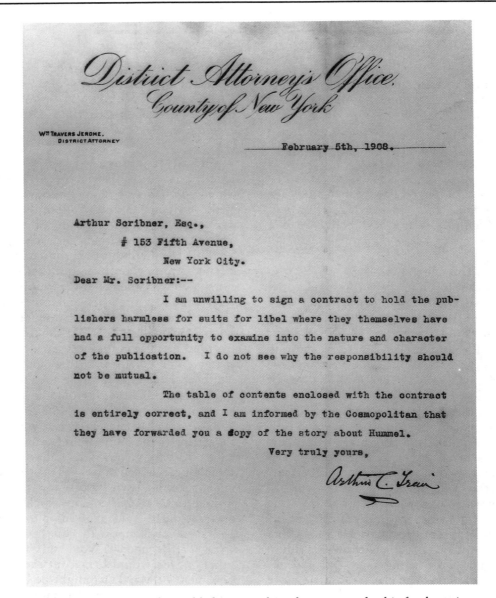

District Attorney's Office.
County of New York

Wᴹ TRAVERS JEROME.
DISTRICT ATTORNEY

February 5th, 1908.

Arthur Scribner, Esq.,
    # 153 Fifth Avenue,
        New York City.

Dear Mr. Scribner:--

I am unwilling to sign a contract to hold the publishers harmless for suits for libel where they themselves have had a full opportunity to examine into the nature and character of the publication. I do not see why the responsibility should not be mutual.

The table of contents enclosed with the contract is entirely correct, and I am informed by the Cosmopolitan that they have forwarded you a copy of the story about Hummel.

Very truly yours,

Arthur C. Train

Letter from Train to his publisher regarding the contract for his forthcoming book True Stories of Crime from the District Attorney's Office *(1908). At the time he was assistant district attorney for New York County in the reform administration of William Travers Jerome.*

"Case No. 2"
"Case No. 5"
"People vs. Appleboy"
"Contempt of Court"
"Hocus-pocus"

These alone would amount to almost 68,000 words, which would be enough for a book although a story or two more could be added. In making this selection I have left out some of the best stories, such as "Ways That Are Dark," "In Re Misella," "Sweet Land of Liberty." I have also omitted the sequel to the Barrows story, that is, "Barrows vs. Horses' Neck Extension Co." You also thought of doing a sequel story to "Case No. 5" about McFee. I was going on the theory of a second volume which should be as good as the first, but I thought it a good move to have that slight connection between the two volumes which there would be if certain stories in the second volume reached back to the first.

As to the advisability of publishing this

Spring, it seems to me we should strike while the iron is hot. Serialization in big papers in a disadvantage generally, but we should make it an advantage for the moment by publishing in book form while serialization is still going on.

Sincerely yours,
[Maxwell Perkins]

MEMORANDUM:
Memorandum by Train to Scribners, undated [1922?].

MEMORANDUM OF WHAT MR. TRAIN WOULD LIKE FROM CHARLES SCRIBNER'S SONS.

1. A practically unlimited free list on those of his books for which there is no steady demand to meet the constant applications from libraries, charities and individuals and to facilitate the getting of gratuitous information which must be recognized by the author or publisher in some polite way.

2. A dozen copies annually of such books as are in more or less demand for the same purpose, same to be delivered at 113 East 73rd Street each November.

3. Co-operation on the part of Charles Scribner's Sons in procuring books out of print and books in print which may be necessary for a working library in any subject on which Mr. Train is writing a novel to be published by Charles Scribner's Sons, the cost of said books to be shared equally between the publisher and the author, such books are for example: Ferrero's "Ancient Rome and Modern America," Tugot's "Essays on Economic Subjects Translated into English," translation of "Les Miserables," various works on political economy and the distribution of wealth by Sumner, Seligman &c.

Penciled responses next to each section are, respectively, "no," "no," and "Discount."

RELATED LETTERS:
Letter from Train to Maxwell Perkins, 17 December [1934], and Perkins's reply, dated the same day.

As a lawyer Train carefully scrutinized all of his publishing contracts with Scribners, and the following exchange regarding a clause in the contract for his novel Jacob's Ladder *(1935) was*

typical. Arthur Atwater Kent, whom he mentions, was an inventor who became extremely successful in mass-producing and selling high-quality radio receivers in the 1920s. Train's postscript refers to a gift of an antique bullfighting knife he had sent to Ernest Hemingway via Scribners. At this time Train was trying to convince Hemingway to accept his nomination to become a member of the National Institute of Arts and Letters.

Dear Max,—

While all goes well here for the time being I cannot safely—or in justice to you—make a long date ahead, until after the holidays.

Meantime—re contract—why should I guarantee you (¶ 2) against frivolous suits—any more than you should guarantee my immunity [?] from crazy or crafty people? It seems to me that the author and publisher are embarking on a joint adventure and should take an equal risk—except, where the supposed libel is within the author's knowledge alone or he has been negligent. Certainly there isn't the slightest reason why the author should reimburse the publisher for his expenses in an unjustifiable, malicious or wanton legal proceeding simply because some lunatic imagines he has been libelled. I thought that this clause had been recast long ago. You can easily see that—under it—if Atwater Kent, for example—took it into his head to bring a suit against Scribner's on the ground that all rich industrialists had been held up to ridicule in Jacob's Ladder—you can call on me to pay the bill! The author's liability should not extend beyond contributing to the final award and costs when a bona fide suit has been prosecuted to appeal. You must agree that this is so.

Affy
Arthur

P.S.
Did you ever send Hemingway that bull fighter's knife?

Dear Arthur:

I am quoting from a letter just received from Ernest: "Didn't Arthur Train ever get the letter I wrote him from Havana care of Scribner's? I must write him again if he didn't get it, to thank him. The dagger is a puntilla, for killing the bull once he has gone to his knees. As near as I can figure it belonged to Curro Cuchares who died in Havana the fourth of December 1868 of yellow fever while he was making a tour of Cuba and Mexico in the off season. He was one of the greatest matadors that ever lived. I prize it very much

TUTT AND MR. TUTT

BY
ARTHUR TRAIN

ILLUSTRATED

NEW YORK
CHARLES SCRIBNER'S SONS
1920

"I wonder, Mr. Tutt, if you would be willing to take a criminal case where there wouldn't be any prospect of a fee, simply to prevent a possible miscarriage of justice?"

Title page and frontispiece in the first edition of Tutt and Mr. Tutt, *Train's first volume chronicling the legal cases of Ephraim Tutt*

and appreciate it being given to me and feel badly that Mr. Train never heard from me about it.

"About the Institute of Arts and Sciences: please tell him I would not accept but appreciate the offer. Believe me I'm a little young and unsettled to become an academician."

We have no recollection of the letter he refers to, but if we did receive it, it may have been lost in the course of being forwarded to you in Europe. When I tell him this he will certainly write you.

I can see your point about the danger from cranks and crafty people, but the truth is that only the author can know of the dangers that reside in a book. The publisher could never investigate books to the degree that would make him able to insure himself against loss. Any author might put into a book some character whom the publisher thought entirely fictional, or some material which the publisher would never have enough personal knowledge to know was damaging, and so get the publisher into a bad scrape. It happens fairly often, and it is almost always due

to the carelessness of the author. The Author's League, and all literary agents recognize the propriety of this clause, and I never saw a publisher's contract which did not contain it.

Always yours,
[Maxwell Perkins]

The clause was kept in the contract. In 1941, as newly elected president of the National Institute of Arts and Letters, Train again tried (and failed) to make Hemingway a member.

LETTER:
Letter to Train from Maxwell Perkins, 22 July 1937.

At work on a book of reminiscences he tentatively called "The Odyssey of an American Writer" and, later, "That's Why I Write," Train asked Perkins to supply some topics which he felt ought to be covered in it. Here, in his reply, Perkins touches upon several of the most significant changes he has observed in the publishing business—and in

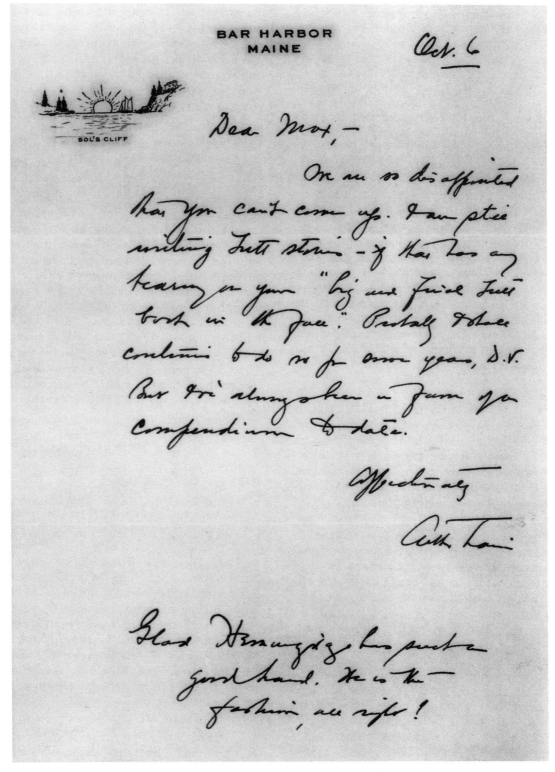

Letter (1929) from Train to his editor, Maxwell Perkins, written from his palatial summer home in Maine. His postscript refers to the popularity of Ernest Hemingway's A Farewell to Arms, *which Scribners had published less than ten days before.*

writing—in recent years. The book was published in 1939 under the title My Day in Court.

Dear Arthur:

I have been trying to put down some topics. I'll keep the list by me and add to it whenever I can. I am enclosing herewith an article by Ford Madox Ford. It might suggest something to you, and it relates to one topic that I think important. While Ford makes some ridiculous misstatements, there is much truth in what he says,- that publishing has become a racket, and a mad pursuit of the best seller. This seems to have happened quickly, in the last six years say. But I think it is probably due at bottom to the profound changes in ways of life, because it seems also to be true of England. But Ford does overlook one of its chief immediate causes here,- the Book of the Month Club. I think that has been very ably managed, and that the man at the head of it feels a public responsibility and intends to serve his subscribers well. He has made something of an institution of the Club. At the same time, its most conspicuous effect on publishing is to concentrate the attention of the entire public on one book a month.- I think that this is very harmful, particularly to that very class of craftsman in writing about whom Ford is especially worried. When people had to find their own books, they followed their own taste, but now, with the American tendency to follow fashion, they satisfy themselves with just the best sellers.- And the newspapers' policy of playing up the best sellers, works in the same way.

Another topic worth discussion is the literary conscience. Mrs. [Mary] Colum wrote a paper on this called "The Two Consciences." One of them is the one we all have, but the writer, the artist, has another which compels him in the same way not to shrink from revealing life, however unpleasant it is, and however offensive his writing is to important elements in the public. He is often looked upon as being immoral on account of the frankness of his expression, or the material he uses, when he would regard himself as immoral if he softened his words or misrepresented his material to conform to the conventions. You may think that the literary conscience is something of an affectation, but it is a good topic anyhow, and leads into a discussion of frankness and the use of unpleasant words, etc. You might point out that good writers like Hemingway sacrifice sales by their frankness, and know it.

Another topic should be the economic and literary effects on the writer, of the great popular magazines which are built up on advertising.- I think on this you have done some writing.

Your own methods of work, and how you reconcile them with social life,- how many hours you write,- should be covered. And I think this would be very interesting because as Kipling did, you got a great deal from talking to people, so that social life has furthered your work instead of hindering it as it does with some writers.

This might lead to a discussion of how a writer gets his characters,- to what extent he does or should use real people. In recent years writers have used real people directly to a much greater degree, I think, than ever was done before,- although it is said that almost all of Tolstoi's characters in "War and Peace" were members of his own family, and recognizable. The influence on you of other writers, and which ones, etc., would be very interesting. And the writer's relations to his public, and how he can gauge the response to his books, apart from sales.- This would bring in what you wrote about fan mail. I read that and thought the letters were excellent for the purpose.

The general scheme of your book is narrative so that I think it would be better if the topics were worked into the narrative rather than discussed separately.

Always yours,
[Maxwell Perkins]

RELATED LETTERS:
Letter from Train to Maxwell Perkins, 23 June 1939, enclosing a letter he had received from Robert Williams Wood, 20 June 1939.

In 1915 Train and Wood had co-authored a science-fiction work, The Man Who Rocked the Earth, *that Doubleday, Page had published. Now, on the eve of World War II, parts of their fiction were about to come true. Perkins, however, thought it would be too difficult to revive the book unless the experiments Wood was referring to "resulted in something sensational," and so the republication idea was dropped.*

Dear Max,—

I enclose a letter from R. W. Wood, the famous Johns Hopkins physicist, who wrote "The Man Who Rocked the Earth" and "The Moon Makers" with me. I think his idea a good one. It is 1914 all over again now, with the new slant on uranium added. Both stories could be printed in one volume. I think, if Scribner's doesn't care to, that Harpers, Farrar & Rhinehart, or S & S.

CHARLES SCRIBNER'S SONS

PUBLISHERS

597 FIFTH AVENUE   NEW YORK, N.Y.

Ephraim Tutt can be said to exist only in the same sense as Sherlock Holmes, Mr. Pickwick, and Don Quixote. Arthur Train is the author of YANKEE LAWYER, and a good deal of the autobiography is based on his own experiences. The idea was simply that Mr. Tutt has become so living a figure through Arthur Train's stories, that it seemed suitable to have it appear that he was now telling his own. An article which originally appeared in The Saturday Evening Post and is now a chapter in MR. TUTT FINDS A WAY tells the whole story of the origin of the book and of Mr. Tutt.

Very truly yours,

Following its publication of Yankee Lawyer: The Autobiography of Ephraim Tutt *(1943), Scribners was inundated with letters by readers wanting to know if Tutt was an actual man or a creation of Train. Readers' confusion was shared by newspapers that listed the best-selling book under both fiction and nonfiction categories; and Scribners had to intervene to prevent the A. N. Marquis Company from including a biographical sketch of Tutt in* Who's Who in America. *Most believed he was real—or hoped that he was—and some even wanted to hire him to represent them in their own legal cases. This 1944 form letter helped the firm respond to those queries.*

$2.50

Mr. Tutt Comes Home
by ARTHUR TRAIN

Countless Mr. Tutt enthusiasts will know what to expect in these new and thoroughly entertaining adventures of the wise and wily old jurist. With his usual mastery of stories rich in reading enjoyment, Arthur Train has packed these new Tutt tales with humor and pathos, with sharp insights into the vagaries of human conduct, and with all the varied, exciting drama of the courts.

Mr. Tutt in Valley Fair, in the midst of a feud between two hot-blooded Southern families that reached its climax in the trial of Old Duke, a canine aristocrat charged with sheep-killing. . . .

Mr. Tutt on Edgar Street, New York's small, spice-scented version of the Near East, untangling the marital affairs of Kalil, the little, soft-eyed Syrian rug-peddler and his intended bride, Fatima. . . .

Mr. Tutt in Bangor, solving the strange case of Aunt Althea's mutilated will (and incidentally dispatching a forty-pound salmon to the White House). . . .

Mr. Tutt——in whatever scene or circumstance, and in stories as wholly absorbing as any Arthur Train ever wrote——is here presented at his best, as humorous and humane, kindly and resourceful as ever.

Dust jacket for Train's 1941 collection of Tutt stories

might easily do it. I think I wrote you that we have given up [going to] Europe.

As ever
A.T.

Dear "A.T."

Did you see in Sunday's Her. Trib. (or perhaps the Times, I've forgotten which) a long account stating that Joliot of Paris & his wife (Irene Curie) were actually starting experiments with a view of getting atomic energy out of <u>uranium</u>? The blast of "neutrons" that everyone is working with now causes the explosion of the uranium atom, and there is some excitement over the possibility of getting one atom to "set off" the others and get a terrific liberation of energy. The flying ring had a cylinder of <u>uranium</u> metal bombarded by the disintegrating ray, & in Labrador "Pax" bombarded a cliff of pitchblende (uranium ore). So we made a sort of Jules Verne, H. G. Wells prediction on this as well as on the Paris bombard-

ment from 75 miles. In view of the apparent demand for fantastic stories about rocket ships etc written for the pulp magazines by half educated authors, it occurred to me that a republication of the man who rocked the earth & the moon maker in a single volume, <u>properly advertised</u> as containing the prophecy of release of atomic energy from uranium etc might appeal to some publisher willing to take a chance. There is a new generation of callous boys ready to eat up stuff of this sort isn't there?

R.W.

LETTER:
Letter from CS III to John W. Davis, partner in the New York City law firm of Davis Polk Wardell Sunderland and Kiendl, 4 April 1944.

In the spring of 1944 a reader initiated a suit against Scribners regarding its publication of

Train's Yankee Lawyer: The Autobiography of Ephraim Tutt. *The complaint charged that the book had been misrepresented as fact though it was actually fiction. "Facts" cited as evidence by the reader included the book's copyright notice ("Copyright 1943 by Ephraim Tutt"), statements on the dust jacket ("Ephraim Tutt is undoubtedly the best known lawyer now alive"), and Train's introduction, in which he claimed to have been playing for years (in his stories about Tutt) the part of Boswell to Tutt's Johnson. Asserting that books of fiction retailed for no more than $3.00 and that Tutt's autobiography was being sold for $3.50, the reader sought to recover the cost of the book for himself and other purchasers and to force Scribners to stop selling it under false pretenses.*

Dear Mr. Davis:

Mr. Arthur Train came to see me this morning to tell me of the developments in the Ephraim Tutt suit which you have been so good as to agree to defend for Charles Scribner' Sons.

I gather that there would be a good chance that the Court would dismiss the suit if we made a motion asking for its dismissal. On the other hand this would rob it of any significance or publicity value. Personally I would like to see it come to trial, but as president of Charles Scribner's Sons it is naturally my duty not to involve the company in expenses that far outweigh the benefits. Mr. Train has always insisted in his authors contracts with us that we cancel the usual clause whereby the author agrees to reimburse the publisher for any legal costs or damages that may be incurred in the publication of a book. Also he has not inti-mated that he would agree to assume any share of the costs incurred by this firm in defending the suit, although any publicity that might come from it would be far more to his advantage than ours, inasmuch the play, and perhaps also a motion picture are still to be produced. Charles Scribner's Sons are willing to assume a moderate expense of perhaps two or three thousand dollars in fighting out in Court this interesting but on the whole academic question, but if our share is apt to far exceed this sum we would naturally prefer to see the case settled with the least possible cost.

Please forgive my writing frankly on this matter. I appreciate the personal interest you have shown in being willing to give your time to a case of this sort. I also know that you will be entirely reasonable in the fees you ask, but I know that your time is valuable and that it might well prove of greater value in drawing out this case than we thought it was worth. I neglected to say that inasmuch as Mr. Maxwell E. Perkins, who is also named in the complaint, is a member of Charles Scribner's Sons, we would expect to pay any costs involved in defending him.

Mr. Train suggested my seeing you, which I would be very glad to do, but I feel that a letter would save your time.

Sincerely yours
[Charles Scribner]

Davis felt the costs would not be great and proceeded with this unprecedented case. The Court dismissed the complainant's request for an injunction against Scribners, agreeing with the publisher that the facts did not warrant it. Whether or not the reader ever recovered any money is not known.

John Galsworthy (1867–1933)

John Galsworthy with Wolf, his German shepherd, at Bury House (frontispiece to H. V. Marrot's A Bibliography of the Works of John Galsworthy, London: Elkin Mathews & Marrot / New York: Charles Scribner's Sons, 1928)

The son of a prosperous English family, Galsworthy trained for the law but turned seriously to writing in the mid 1890s, encouraged by his future wife and an early association with Joseph Conrad. His plays and novels, treating social and moral themes, were enormously successful and established a reputation for him as a social critic and historian of contemporary social developments whose works actually effected social change in England. Today, he is viewed as perhaps the last major British writer born in the Victorian age, but his frankness in dealing with the power of sexuality and his evolutionary views probably accounted for his "modern" appeal to the younger generations of his time. He is best remembered as author of the three-generation English family epic *The Forsyte Saga* (1922). Since its inception in 1921, Galsworthy was president of the International P.E.N. Club, an organization dedicated to helping and protecting writers and their freedom of expression throughout the world. Several months before his death he was awarded the Nobel Prize for literature (1932). Undoubtedly, Galsworthy was Scribners' most prolific author: beginning in 1910, when the firm became his American publisher, and continuing for a quarter of a century, Scribners published several volumes of his work each year.

Scribner Books by Galsworthy

1910	*A Motley*
	Justice: A Tragedy in Four Acts
1911	*The Patrician*
	The Little Dream: An Allegory in Six Scenes
1912	*The Pigeon: A Fantasy in Three Acts*
	Moods, Songs, and Doggerels
	The Inn of Tranquility: Studies and Essays

	The Eldest Son: A Domestic Drama in Three Acts
1913	*Plays* (2nd series)
	The Dark Flower
	The Fugitive: A Play in Four Acts
1914	*The Mob: A Play in Four Acts*
	Plays (3rd series)
	The Country House
	Memories, illustrated by Maud Earl
1915	*The Little Man, and Other Satires*
	A Bit o' Love: A Play in Three Acts
	The Freelands
1916	*A Commentary*
	Fraternity
	The Island Pharisees (revised edition)
	Joy: A Play on the Letter "I" in Three Acts
	A Man of Property
	Plays (1st series)
	The Silver Box: A Comedy in Three Acts
	Strife: A Drama in Three Acts
	Villa Rubein
	A Sheaf
1917	*Beyond*
1918	*Five Tales*
1919	*Another Sheaf*
	Saint's Progress
	Addresses in America, 1919
1920	*Tatterdemalion*
	The Foundations (An Extravagant Play)
	The Skin Game (A Tragi-Comedy)
	Plays (4th series)
	In Chancery
	Awakening, illustrated by R. H. Sauter
1921	*To Let*
	Six Short Plays
1922	*The Forsyte Saga*
	A Family Man, in Three Acts
	Loyalties: A Drama in Three Acts
1922–1936	*The Collected Works of John Galsworthy* (Manaton Edition of 30 volumes)
1923	*Windows: A Comedy in Three Acts for Idealists and Others*
	Plays (5th series)
	The Burning Spear: Being the Experiences of Mr. John Lavender in Time of War
	Captures

1924	*The Forest: A Drama in Four Acts*
	Representative Plays
	The White Monkey
1925	*Old English: A Play in Three Acts*
	Caravan: The Assembled Tales of John Galsworthy
	The Show: A Drama in Three Acts
1926	*Plays* (6th series)
	The Silver Spoon
	Verses New and Old
1926–1929	*The Novels, Tales, and Plays of John Galsworthy* (Devon Edition of 22 volumes)
1927	*Castles in Spain and Other Screeds*
	Escape: An Episodic Play in Prologue and Two Parts
1928	*Two Forsyte Interludes: A Silent Wooing, Passers By*
	Swan Song
	Plays
1929	*The Compact Edition of John Galsworthy* (6 volumes)
	A Modern Comedy
1930	*Soames and the Flag*
	On Forsyte 'Change
1931	*The Roof: A Play in Seven Scenes*
	Maid in Waiting
1932	*Worshipful Society*
	Carmen by Georges Bizet, new English version by John and Ada Galsworthy
	Flowering Wilderness
1933	*Candelabra: Selected Essays and Addresses*
	Three Novels of Love
	One More River
1934	*End of the Chapter*
	The Collected Poems of John Galsworthy
	The Apple Tree
	Letters from John Galsworthy, 1900–1932, edited and with introduction by Edward Garnett
1935	*Forsytes, Pendyces, and Others*, with foreword by Ada Galsworthy

RELATED LETTERS:
Letter from James B. Pinker, literary agent for Galsworthy, to CS II, 2 February 1910; letter from CS II in reply, 25 February 1910.

Deciding at last to change his American publisher, Galsworthy approached Scribners directly, via his agent, by offering a volume of short stories, with a promise of a novel to follow.

Dear Mr. Scribner,

As I promised, I now write to let you know that Mr. Galsworthy has made up his mind to change his publisher in the United States. I told Mr. Galsworthy of our various conversations on the subject, and he has authorised me to

NEW YORK, January 16th, 190 6.

Gentlemen:-

I am sending you a story entitled THE MAN
OF PROPERTY.   The author's name is Galsworthy.   Mr.
Heinemann has very exceptional opinions about this book and he
thinks that you will be interested in it.   He is under an
agreement to publish it before April 1st, 1906.   Would you
have it looked at and see what you think?

I can sell it to you for a twelve and one
half per cent royalty increasing to fifteen per cent after
three thousand copies have been sold, and to twenty per cent
after twenty thousand copies have been sold.

Faithfully yours,

Paul R. Reynolds
P.

Messrs. Charles Scribner's Sons,
153 Fifth Avenue,
New York City.

AR

Letter from agent offering Scribners Galsworthy's novel The Man of
Property. *Observing protocol among U.S. publishers, Scribners refused
the manuscript because Putnam had already published this English
author. Four years later Scribners became Galsworthy's American
publisher and eventually purchased the rights to this and other
Galsworthy works that Putnam had published.* The Man
of Property *ultimately became the first part of
Galsworthy's trilogy,* The Forsyte Saga.

make the arrangements with you for the future.
The first book to come along will be a volume of
short stories, which Mr. Galsworthy is preparing
for publication probably in April of this year. His
new novel will be finished later in this year, in
time, probably, for publication quite early in
1911. That is as far ahead as Mr. Galsworthy's
plans are laid at present. We might, therefore,
make an agreement for the two books, leaving future books to be discussed as soon as we know
what Mr. Galsworthy's plans are. Mr. Galsworthy dislikes change, and therefore it is in the hope
that he will not again have to change his publisher
that he authorised me to come to you. Messrs.
Putnam held all their books under terminable
agreements, and sooner or later Mr. Galsworthy
will, I am sure, wish to transfer those books to
you. I will not suggest terms to you, but perhaps

you will consider it and let me know what your views are, and I will then discuss the details with Mr. Galsworthy. . . .

> Believe me,
> Yours very truly
> James B. Pinker

Dear Mr. Pinker:

As I said to you in London, we are interested in Mr. Galsworthy's work but do not wish to interfere in any way with his relations with the Putnams. If he is determined to leave them, for reasons of his own independent of any offer from us, we should of course be glad to negotiate with him. Under the conditions we are not disposed to make any extraordinary terms but I can let you know what I think would be fair. For royalty I would propose that we pay 15% on the first 5000 and 20% thereafter, paying for Canadian sales half-royalty. No doubt he will want some advance but, in the absence of all information as to how his books will sell, it is extremely difficult to say what that should be. I should think however that for a novel £100 would be fair and for a book of stories or essays £50. Please bear in mind that I am making this suggestion in the absence of any information as to what Putnam is doing. It may be that he is doing as well or better than I propose.

The question of taking over the older books could be determined later. Such transfers are always troublesome and it would be better to wait and see how we get on with his new books. . . .

> Yours sincerely
> [Charles Scribner]

Scribners began its relationship with Galsworthy by publishing this book of short stories, A Motley, *on 16 June 1910 while it tried to arrange with Putnam to take over his earlier publications. However, the two publishers could not reach a satisfactory monetary agreement. Learning that most of Galsworthy's contracts with Putnam had a seven-year limit, Scribners decided to wait until the expiration date arrived for the last book (March 1916) before it made a deal for the books' plates and remaining stock. Meanwhile, it continued to publish Galsworthy on a regular basis, with several new volumes each year, to Galsworthy's complete satisfaction:*

> October 23. 1915.

My dear Mr. Scribner

. . . It is a very great comfort & pleasure to me to be published by your firm—the best in America, and I am more than pleased with all you have done for my work in the States. I look forward to the day when the whole of my books will be in your hands. . . .

When the six-years-in-the-making deal was finally achieved, Galsworthy's reaction was not unexpected:

> May. 8. 1916.

Dear Mr. Scribner

I have been meaning for some weeks now to write, and tell you of my pleasure in seeing that all my books have come under your control. It is a great satisfaction to me; and I sincerely hope that you won't have cause to regret it. . . .

> Always sincerely yours
> John Galsworthy

LETTER:
Letter from William Heinemann, Galsworthy's English publisher, to CS II, 23 February 1912.

Part of the unofficial duties of a publisher . . .

My dear Scribner,

Galsworthy is sailing in the "Campania" tomorrow and reaches New York on the 2nd March. His name is not on the passenger list and he is most anxious to avoid interference and publicity. In order to be very quiet, I have told him to go to the Seville Hotel, and if you will go or send there, you will find him there some time on Saturday. He will be in New York to rehearse his play [*The Pigeon*], and as soon as that is produced he wants to go to Japan. I need not recommend him to you for any kindness you can show him; but will you commend Mrs. Galsworthy especially to Mrs. Scribner? She will probably be at a loose end while he rehearses, and I believe wants to find a quiet place in the country where she can go. She is a bit of an invalid at present and wants bracing and a rest, I think.

> Yours sincerely,
> Wm Heinemann

RELATED LETTERS:
Letter from CS II to Galsworthy, 24 December 1920; letter from Galsworthy to CS II in reply, 30 December 1920.

Reading galleys for the April installment of Galsworthy's novel To Let, *which would begin its serialization in the January issue of* Scribner's Magazine, *CS II found a troublesome sexual reference.*

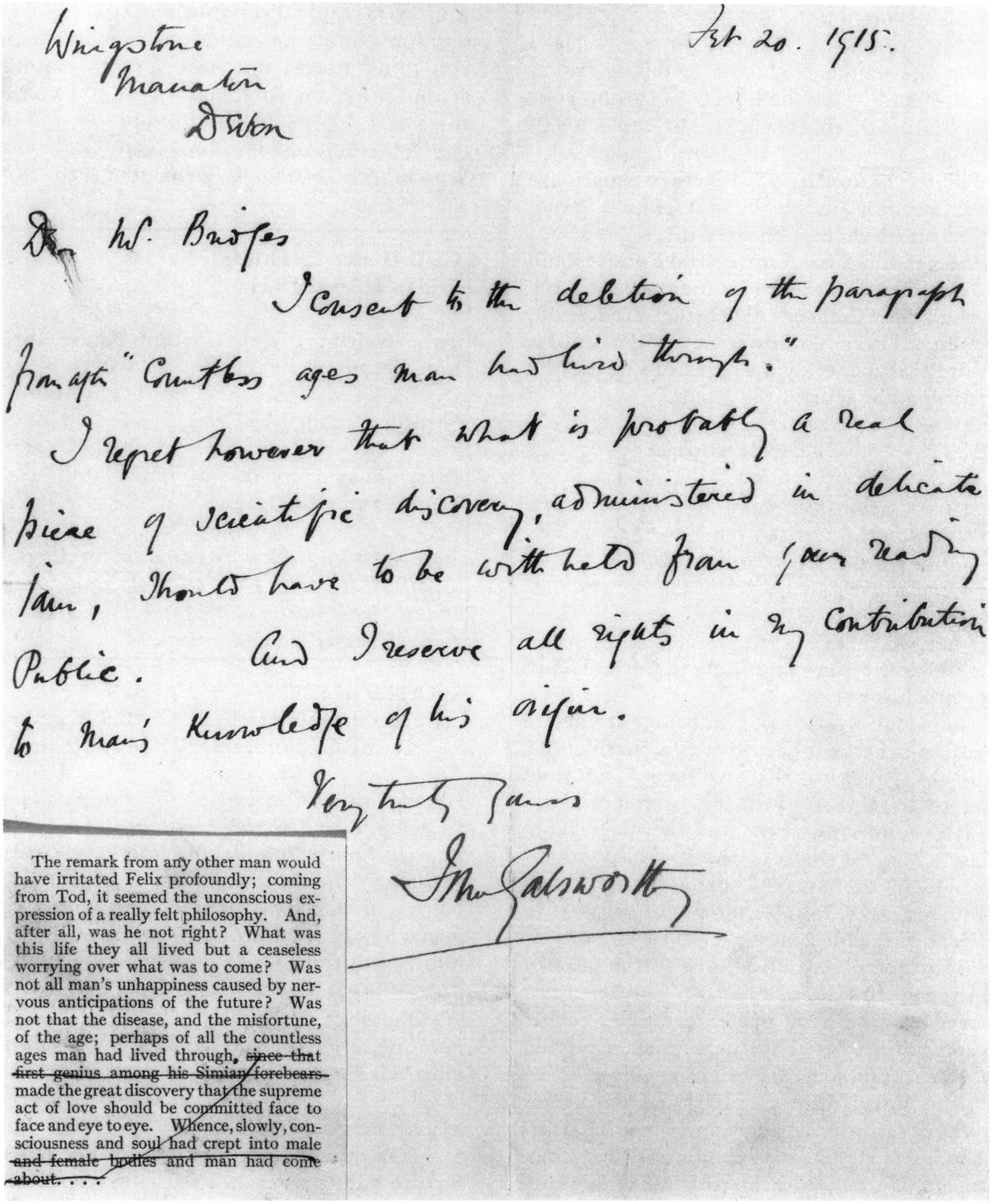

> Wingstone
> Manaton
> Dixon

> Feb 20. 1915.

> Dr Mr. Bridges

> I consent to the deletion of the paragraph from after "Countless ages man had lived through."

> I regret however that what is probably a real piece of scientific discovery, administered in delicate form, should have to be withheld from your reading Public. And I reserve all rights in my contribution to man's knowledge of his origin.

> Very truly yours

> John Galsworthy

The remark from any other man would have irritated Felix profoundly; coming from Tod, it seemed the unconscious expression of a really felt philosophy. And, after all, was he not right? What was this life they all lived but a ceaseless worrying over what was to come? Was not all man's unhappiness caused by nervous anticipations of the future? Was not that the disease, and the misfortune, of the age; perhaps of all the countless ages man had lived through, ~~since that first genius among his Simian forebears~~ made the great discovery that the supreme act of love should be committed face to face and eye to eye. Whence, slowly, consciousness and soul had crept into male ~~and female bodies~~ and man had come ~~about. . . .~~

Reviewing Galsworthy's novel The Freelands, *which had begun its serialization in the January issue of* Scribner's Magazine, *editor Robert Bridges suggested (8 February 1915) a deletion: "We are somewhat apprehensive about the effect of the enclosed paragraph on the general reader of the Magazine, and so frankly call it to your thoughtful consideration. The Magazine goes into a great many families where it has been for years accepted as appropriate reading for young and old. It also is used as collateral reading in some schools of both sexes. We fear that some of them would find this paragraph too frank for reading in public. It is not a question of morality or right intention—but of the standard by which it will be judged. We hope therefore that you may consent to omitting it. We shall appreciate very much your acquiescence in this." This is Galsworthy's reply, with the problematic paragraph bearing Bridges' censorship.*

Dear Mr. Galsworthy:

When reading the proof of the new serial I came upon one sentence which affected me rather unpleasantly and I take the liberty of calling your attention to it, for I am sure it will offend some of your readers. It is in Part II–II and reads as follows: "The river country was lovely in those days of her own month, and all the unappeased sexual instinct of June ached at its loveliness." It seems almost too Freudian for a novel and I understand that among scientists there is some reaction from the Freudian view that sexual cravings are responsible for almost every emotion. You will of course understand this is merely a suggestion passed on for what it may be worth.

Yours sincerely
[Charles Scribner]

Galsworthy's response came in an envelope marked "Personal," written from the San Ysidro Ranch, Santa Barbara, California, where he and his wife were staying:

My dear Mr. Scribner:

I have your letters of 22nd and 24th. Thank you very much for them.

Perhaps you would ask Mr. Bridges to delete the words "all the unappeased sexual instinct of" from the text, leaving the sentence "and June ached at its loveliness." I do this in deference to your wish. I am, however (quite apart from Freud's teaching—he is something of a monomaniac) convinced that starved sexual instinct is responsible for very much emotional vagary in many directions. This is however quite enough indicated in other places and ways in the case of June. So the elision doesn't matter. The Scientists are forever barging from one extreme to another on all such subjects. It gives them amusement and variety. I've just come from a dentist who tells me all his radio work [radiographs?] was wrong for fifteen years, and he is now convinced that his present work is right, as he then was. The scientists are as bad as the literary critics, who I suppose may in a sense be called Scientists. Never mind, we shall always have them with us.

A cold grey day today - the first. How charming Mr. & Mrs. Duane [friends of the Scribners] are!

Our very warm regards to you both
Sincerely yours
John Galsworthy

Scribner was grateful (19 January 1921): "Thank you for accepting my suggestion concerning the June paragraph. Probably you are right in your opinion about the sexual instinct but I am glad you think it was not necessary to emphasise it again, for I am sure many readers would have shied at it." *The serialization ran through the September issue, and the book was published on 2 September. Galsworthy dedicated it to CS II.*

CS II DIARY ENTRIES:
Friday 1 April 1921

Take Galsworthy to Custom House for shipping permit

Saturday 2 April 1921

Mrs. Galsworthy & . . . lunch at house with Louise and go to opera

Before he and his wife can sail for England (6 April), Galsworthy has to settle some American income tax matters. Meanwhile, CS II and his wife (Louise) aid and entertain.

RELATED LETTERS:
Letter from Galsworthy to CS II, 3 May 1921; letter by CS II in reply, 27 May 1921.

Having already arranged for the publication in September of the third volume (To Let) of his English family epic on the Forsytes, Galsworthy is already planning on how best to present the trilogy, which he feels will be his monument to posterity, to the public. In addition, plans for a limited edition of his complete works has begun. "Mr. Pinker" is Galsworthy's English literary agent, James B. Pinker; "Pawling" is Sydney S. Pawling, a partner in William Heinemann, Galsworthy's English publisher.

My dear Scribner

On my instructions Mr. Pinker has just cabled to you to ask you to discontinue all work on the issue of 'The Forsyte Saga' until you receive a letter from me. I have been thinking the matter over with him and with Mr. C. S. Evans of Heinemanns, and we are all agreed that far better than publishing it in three volumes this autumn would be to wait till next year and publish it then in one volume with a special preface and the pedigree. If printed on India, or other very thin paper, it will not be at all an unhandy book containing about 1150 pages. Heinemanns issued 'War & Peace' in one such quite moderate volume before the war

Some serialization instructions by Galsworthy for his novel The White Monkey, *which ran in nine installments (April–December 1924) in* Scribner's Magazine

containing over 1500 pages. Evans suggests that it should be a joint undertaking between yourselves and Heinemanns. The advantages are several. In the first place, it is far preferable, from my point of view, to have it as a sort of monumental single volume. In the second place, we think, people will, buy it far more freely as a single volume incorporating the whole chronicle than in three volumes which are, as it were, merely a replica of the three existing novels with the short stories thrown in. In the third place it gives the chance of making something very special of it, which will attract people. In the fourth place, it will not, if issued thus next year, interfere at all with the sale of 'To Let.' And, finally, with a year's interval the critics will take the single volume with fresh vim, whereas if it were issued in three volumes they would probably neglect it as being merely replica of volumes already issued.

I sincerely hope you will agree with me and proceed to arrange for its issue in conjunction with Heinemanns next year about June.

I have always been exceedingly set on having this long chronicle bound up in one volume, because it is emphatically my special book—the book by which I shall specially go down to posterity. I always hold that a writer goes down the ages identified with one book. Witness Cervantes, Goethe, Hugo, Hawthorne, Mark Twain. The attrition of time wears away his less monumental work. At my age I shall never do anything as big as this again, and I want to see it gathered up and bound in one tome as soon as possible. It is a much more coherent piece of work than the usual trilogy; and this binding of it up in one volume will take it out of that category. I would like it set in the type, and same size page as 'The Man of Property' all through of course. So much for that.

I am going to work to provide revised text of all my books, and a preface to the novels, a preface to the short stories, one for the essays, & one for the plays, by the end of this year, so that yourselves and Heinemanns may be able to bring out a complete limited edition of my work next year (in the summer, I hope for the first volumes). I trust you will be able to arrange for this with Pawling while he is over. I am anxious for it to come next year. There would be from twenty to twenty two volumes of uneven length. I should suggest at least 1250 sets for America, and 750 for England, and I should imagine it could be done for twenty guineas a set. I think it unwise to leave the bringing out of this limited edition later than next year.

My wife joins me in the heartiest wishes to Mrs. Scribner, all your circle, and your self.

Ever yours very sincerely
John Galsworthy

My dear Galsworthy:

Immediately on the receipt of Pinker's cablegram we suspended our preparations for the three-volume edition and now on receipt of your letter of May 3rd we have altogether given it up. The announcement was contained in the printed list of forthcoming publications and the proposed issue had been talked over with our salesmen. I think we could have done well with it and that the plan was a good one and did not at all make impossible the publication later of the one-volume book on thin paper as now proposed. You will see that we adjust ourselves to the change with a little reluctance but not because we do not thoroughly appreciate the importance of giving the greatest emphasis to the Forsyte Saga. What you write about the probability that this particular group of stories will be the one with which you as author will be particularly associated with in the future is strongly put and I join you in the determination to have them properly presented as a unity. We shall now see what can be done in the way of a single volume and how it will work out in cost. I don't know to what extent Heinemann will wish to join with us in the manufacture but I can see it will be an expensive book, as "In Chancery" and the additional stories will have to be reset, the other two volumes repaged, and the whole printed upon very thin paper which is always expensive. It will be evident that the page was not made for this particular edition, but a convenient and attractive book can be made, though the price will have to be very high.

As to the limited edition, I am prepared to join with Heinemann whenever they are ready. I spoke with Pawling of it but he seemed to wish to defer definite arrangements until the Stevenson edition was out of the way and perhaps until he knew how that edition would go. But my idea has always been an equal division—possibly of 1000 copies for each country—and it does not seem right that we should be expected to bear nearly two-thirds of the cost. Should we not also have some conference about the honorarium, as these editions are not usually published on a royalty basis. If nothing unexpected interferes I hope to be in England in August and these questions can then be discussed more fully. Please understand that I will do everything possible to advance the plan.

I was glad to hear of your comfortable voyage home and that you did not experience any great difficulty on account of the coal strike. We have now moved out to the country and are living very much as you will remember. Bishop Atwood was here yesterday and spoke of his interest in meeting you and particularly of your great game of tennis, an accomplishment of which I had not before heard. Yesterday I motored to Princeton to attend a meeting and must go there again tomorrow. That place takes up too much of my time but does oblige me to take holidays. We were all so distressed to hear of Barrie's loss.

Yours most sincerely
[Charles Scribner]

The one-volume edition of The Forsyte Saga *was published on 24 March 1922 at a price of $2.50. Later that fall, Scribners began issuing the first volumes of Galsworthy's collected works in a limited edition of 750 copies, named for the village (Manaton) where he and his wife moved in 1908.*

CS II DIARY ENTRY:
Wednesday 7 June 1922

Dine with Galsworthys &
theatre to see his play
Loyalties

While in England on business, Scribner visited a number of his English authors. Loyalties, *dealing with anti-Semitic prejudice, achieved both critical acclaim and wide popularity.*

I'm not surprised at Galsworthy's not being responsive to my stuff. I've found that if you don't respond to another man's writing the chances are it's mutual—and except for The Apple Tree and, oddly enough, Saints Progress he leaves me cold. I suspect he had some unfortunate iddylic love affair in his youth and whenever that crops into his work it comes alive to me. The subject matter of The Forsythe Saga seemed stuffy to me. I entirely "approve" of him though and liked him personally.

—F. Scott Fitzgerald in letter to Maxwell Perkins, [10 April 1926?]

LETTER:
Letter from Galsworthy to CS II, 17 September 1927.

Ostensibly about Canadian rights, Galsworthy's letter touches upon several other subjects of mutual interest. The sticky "Forsyte episode" is "A Silent Wooing," which appeared in the January 1928 issue of Scribner's Magazine. *His positive reaction to changes in the magazine derives from an announcement to the press of the features of a "new"* Scribner's Magazine *to begin in 1928: an editorial policy that will seek out writers "who are cutting individual paths in modern literature," a new cover designed by Rockwell Kent, a new typeface, a new method of illustration, and a new eggshell paper. (Galsworthy always preferred not to have his work illustrated.) In passing, Galsworthy mentions Charles Lindbergh, whose solo flight across the Atlantic had taken place in May, and J. M. Barrie, fellow English author of* The Admirable Crichton *and* Peter Pan.

My dear Scribner

I'm afraid you will not like this letter, but I earnestly trust you will see the difficulty and motives which cause me to write it.

I am on the Executive Committee of the London Authors Society and some months ago we received from the English Government through the Board of Trade a request that we of the Authors Society would do our best to assist Canadian publishers. We decided that it was our duty to do what we could. And I confess that personally I think the time has come to give them a chance, if they can prove themselves worthy of it, and this of course they cannot do unless they get from us the necessary material. I do not like to recommend to others what I will not do myself, and for these two reasons I feel that I am bound to give the Canadian rights of 'Swan Song' to a Canadian publisher. I do think, you know, considering the size and importance of Canada, that it is almost insulting to deny them a chance of making good with English works.

In view of the really big American sales of my last novels, and the comparatively small sale in Canada, this is really a matter of but little importance to you. Still I can't expect you to like the new departure, though I feel somehow that you will sympathize with my view, and recognize that an American would certainly do the same in a like case.

The Manaton Edition (1922–1936) of Galsworthy's works. In a letter (2 November 1922) to Maxwell Perkins, Ellery Sedgwick, editor of The Atlantic Monthly, *wrote: "The intervening days have enabled me to look through the initial volumes of your Galsworthy, and I can now write you with proper appreciation of their beauty — I might say perfection — as specimens of book-making. The work which the house of Scribner is doing for the art of making books is notable indeed. They are taking the leadership, relinquished long since, I am sorry to say, by Houghton Mifflin Company, and these Special Editions seem to me to mark a new standard of excellence for American books. I hope this large enterprise may be as successful financially as it is aesthetically. Incidentally, its general value to the prestige of your printing house must be great."*

I was very glad to get your letter of September 1 and to feel from it that you were in good health and spirits.

If only I can get that Forsyte episode written—somehow it sticks at present—you shall certainly have it for Scribner's Magazine. The news about that is admirable, and I entirely agree with your abandonment of illustration for fiction.

Lindbergh is a great young man. I like his unpretentiousness & refusal to be spoiled even better than his feats.

We have turned our faces toward Majorca for the extreme winter. We hope only to be away three months instead of six. But all de-

pends on Ada's health. We are assuming that dear Mrs. Charles is in the best of health.

Ada joins me in affectionate good wishes to you both.

Always your sincere friend
<u>John Galsworthy</u>

We have been staying for a few days with Barrie at Stanway, & found him pretty well. G

CS II replied (4 Ocotber 1927) that "Your decision respecting the Canadian publication of 'Swan Song' will be accepted in good spirit." He suggested, however, that Galsworthy deal directly with a Canadian publisher—otherwise Canadian branches of English publishers would

Dust jacket for Galsworthy's last work, completed shortly before his death. The novel became the #5 best-seller of 1933.

appropriate the market. However, Canadian publishers did not "show much energy," and no Canadian edition was published. As a result Scribners acquired the Canadian rights to many future Galsworthy works.

RELATED LETTERS:
Letter from Galsworthy to Maxwell Perkins, 8 May 1930; letter [excerpts] from Perkins in reply, 29 May 1930.

My dear Max

We were terribly sorry to hear of Charles Scribner's death, and I have just written to Charlie [CS III].

I hope you have safely received the signed sheets of 'Soames and the Flag.' Concerning the issue of that limited, and indeed of all my books limited or not, I would be very grateful if you would make it your personal business to make quite sure that your editions are published exactly on the same day as the English editions issued by Heinemanns. There have been cases in the past when the American edition has preceded the English, and this is altogether wrong because it sets collectors by the ears as to which is the real first, and complaints are made which are very embarrassing. May I rely on you in future. I have written to Evans [managing director of Heinemanns] in the same sense.

There is to be an American production of 'The Roof' by Charles Hopkins & his contract stipulates that the play shall not be issued in book form till after his production is launched.

I am telling Heinemanns, & the same applies to Scribners, that I don't wish any limited edition issued of 'On Forsyte 'Change' in view of the 'Four Forsyte Stories' & 'Soames & the Flag' limiteds.

—

Now for a very different matter. We would like to come to America again next winter, if it can be arranged by your firm that I should give say eight lectures at the end of March & beginning of April 1931, at say £250 a lecture which I calculated would just about give me the expenses of our trip. This is what I thought of as the programme.

We should arrive a few days before Xmas & go straight out to Arizona. Stay there till about March 20 & then go to San Francisco. Lecture there, say March 24. Thence to Chicago lecture say March 29. Thence Cincinnati lecture say

March 31. Thence <u>Washington</u> lecture say April 3. Thence <u>Philadelphia</u> lecture say April 4. <u>Pittsburgh</u> say April 6. <u>Boston</u> say April 8. <u>New York</u> say April 9. & sail thence.

That would be the very limit of my lecturing powers. I don't want to carry money out of this country, but I do want to make all our winter expenses. Incidentally this would give my nephew [the artist Rudolf Helmut Sauter] a chance to have a show at San Francisco in March & transfer it to New York for the beginning of April.

Now do you think Scribners can arrange this for me so that I get a fixed <u>nett</u> fee (after American income tax paid) for each lecture of say £250. (more of course if possible). Can you cable me whether the plan is feasible, because I must already begin to think ahead. I don't want to go to a lecture agent.

Till the matter is decided one way or the other, will you have it kept confidential.

We are at Bury [Bury House, Sussex] mostly now, which is getting very lovely with greenery & tulips. We all join in best greeting to you both.

Always yours
J.G.

Dear Mr. Galsworthy:

I was sorry not to have been able to answer your cable about the proposed lectures sooner, but it required a good deal of consideration. . . . I was sufficiently acquainted, personally, with two persons who knew the lecture field, to feel that I could trust them, and I consulted them confidentially on the general situation. Their report was as I cabled: that conditions in the last several years were adverse to lectures, relatively to five and ten years ago, and that the present business situation intensified the depression in this particular field;- that this would even apply to one who had greater appeal than perhaps any other man of letters, and

that the highest that one could count upon getting on an average of eight lectures, would be $1,000 each,- and that the expenses and commissions which would have to come out of this could not be reduced with any certainty to less than 20%. This seemed to be the way matters stood. . . At the same time it seemed to me that there was so much advantage to us as publishers in this plan, that we would wish to make it practicable, and that we ought to undertake some of the financial responsibility. But it was necessary for me to discuss this matter with Mr. Scribner, and that I was only just now able to do - everything has been thrown into confusion by violent price-cutting on the part of several publishers. We felt, immediately the matter was mentioned, that we wished to meet the agent's commission, and whatever the income tax might be;- and this would certainly enable you to net at least $1,000 a lecture.

If an agent were engaged, we should be able, in so far as you wished, to cooperate with him and deal with him in your behalf, in all matters of detail, of which there would be many, and to consult with him about, and indeed to print for him and supervise, what circular material might be needed, and so to take from you the burden of all these matters. . . .

We are extremely anxious that the plan may be feasible, also as publishers, for great indirect advantage should come from it; and we shall make the most of it in those respects in ways which you will not object.

Always yours,
[Maxwell Perkins]

Perkins arranged with Lee Keedick ("manager of the world's most celebrated lecturers") for the lecture tour, and Galsworthy gave eight lectures. Of the $8,000 he earned, Scribners contributed over 25 percent by paying Keedick's commission and Galsworthy's income tax.

Maxwell Struthers Burt (1882–1954)

Struthers Burt on his Wyoming ranch

Born and educated in the East, Burt gave his heart and most of his life to the West, particularly Wyoming. He moved to the Jackson Hole area in 1908 and with a partner began dude ranching—i.e., running a ranch for tourists—and in later life acquired his own property there. Much of his writing unites the beauty and romantic elements of the American West with the orderly and more refined society of the East Coast. While he was successful in several genres, notably essays, fiction, and poetry—and was a frequent and well-paid contributor of articles, reviews, and stories to the leading periodicals of the time—musings on religious, moral, literary, and political issues that dominate his fiction suggest that Burt was essentially an essayist. When he received a popular response to his work, and this was frequent, he told his Scribner editor, Maxwell Perkins, that he had caught the country's zeitgeist. In 1941 he authored the "American Authors' Manifesto" urging U.S. aid to England as a response against Hitler and totalitarianism, which was signed by one hundred writers. Burt's major publisher, Scribners, also published in later years novels by his wife, Katharine Newlin Burt, and fiction and poetry by his son, Nathaniel.

Scribner Books by Burt

1918	*John O'May, and Other Stories*
1920	*Songs and Portraits*
1921	*Chance Encounters,* with frontispiece by N. C. Wyeth
1924	*The Interpreter's House*
	The Diary of a Dude-Wrangler
1925	*When I Grew Up to Middle Age*
1927	*The Delectable Mountains*
1928	*They Could Not Sleep*
	The Other Side

1931	*Festival*
1933	*Entertaining the Islanders*
1935	*Malice in Blunderland, With Apologies to Lewis Carroll, Whose Name Has So Often Been Taken in Vain*
1936	*Escape from America*
1942	*Along These Streets*
	War Songs, with decorations by John C. Wonsetler

RELATED LETTERS:

Letter from Burt to Robert Bridges, editor of *Scribner's Magazine,* 14 January 1921; letter [excerpt] from Burt to Maxwell Perkins, his Scribner book editor, 2 February 1921.

Written from Santa Monica, California, where Burt and his wife are vacationing and enjoying "Hollywood," these two letters reflect, respectively, the different relationships he has established with his two Scribner editors. His story "Each in His Generation" appeared in the July 1920 issue of Scribner's Magazine. *"Whitney" is Whitney Darrow, Scribners' advertising manager.*

Dear Mr Bridges:

I suppose you have already heard that the story 'Each in His Generation' was awarded the first prize in the O. Henry Memorial Award of the Society of Arts and Sciences, but I thought I would write you if by any chance you hadn't. I have just now received word from the Society. I am particularly pleased that a story of that type should have got the prize; it seems rather un-American.

We are having a very amusing time out here. Last night we went to a dinner in honor of Charley Chaplin given at the Goldwyn Studios before the pre-view of his new picture 'The Kid.' I was delighted with Chaplin personally. Very much unlike the average movie-star. It was a sort of author–movie star dinner, there being present Gertrude Atherton, Rupert Hughes, Edward Knoblack, Gilbert Parker, and last but not least, Elinor Glyn: on the other side of production, were Chaplin, Will Roger, Mabel Normand and Elsie Ferguson.

I don't know how long we'll be here, probably a couple of months.

Did you see the interview with Scott Fitzgerald in this month's 'Shadowland.' I think he is trying to prove that the egg preceeds the chicken, or the other way about; at all events, I think he is trying to prove that writers create an era and are not of the era.

With many regards

Sincerely yours
Maxwell Struthers Burt

Dear Mr Perkins:

. . . But I mustn't ramble on—I will save my other [Hollywood] experiences until I see you.

I do wish that Mr Bridges could see his way to taking an occasional story from me at $500.00. That is a little less than half of what I get from every other magazine in the country except Harper's, and even they are willing to pay me $700.00. I would like to have a story every now and then in Scribner's, and would be willing to pocket a loss of $500.00, but as a mere matter of common sense I can't pocket a loss of $800.00, or over.

Strictly between you and myself, you and Whitney are the only people in your organization with whom I can talk business, and I know a whole lot of other writing people who say the same. I am devoted to Mr Bridges, but I find it irksome to be, as the years go by, treated always as a moderately bright young man whom he discovered and brought up by hand. I wrote him the other day telling him I had been awarded the O. Henry Memorial Prize, of the Society of Arts and Sciences, for the best story (in their opinion) written in 1920, a story that came out in your magazine.

I received in reply a letter from him, very nice, the import of which was that the prize was very pleasant and that he hoped it would 'encourage me to keep on at my novel.' Now, what does he mean? I may be able to write a novel, or I may not, but I don't feel that I need any particular encouragement to write one. At present, I have on file letters from Houghton, Mifflin; Doran; Harper's; Appleton; Small, Maynard, an English

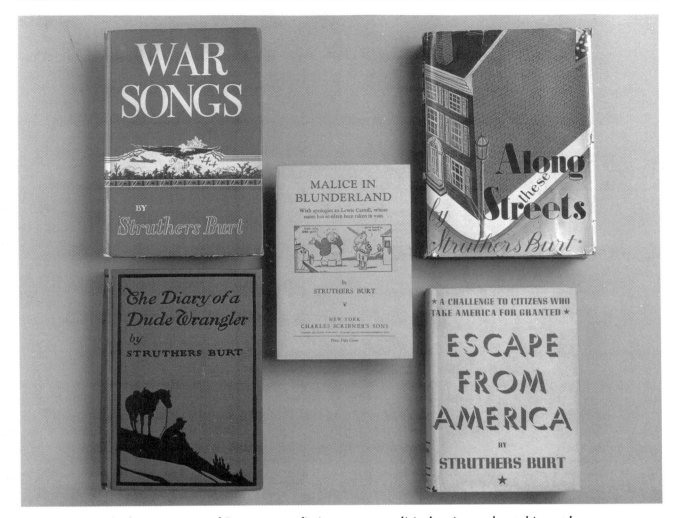

The literary range of Burt: essays, fiction, poetry, political satire, and autobiography

firm; and yourselves asking for a novel. Mr Bridges ought to realize that time passes and things grow. I have an abysmal contempt for the man who writes only for money, and will have always, but all things being equal, a man must live.

Please keep this entirely to yourself, with the exception, perhaps, of Whitney, although if it is possible to do so tactfully, I wish Mr Bridges could be jockeyed into the willingness to pay me $500.00 for a story now and then—that is, if he wants any at all.

With many regards
Faithfully yours
Maxwell Struthers Burt

I trust you will take this letter as it was meant; but I do think frankness is a good thing sometimes.

LETTER:
Letter from Burt to Maxwell Perkins, 31 May 1921.

Knowing Perkins would be a sympathetic reader, Burt sends poems he hopes to publish in Scribner's Magazine *to him first, thereby gaining an advocate for them with editor Robert Bridges.*

Dear Perkins:

I don't know whether this is what is called 'not going through military channels,' or not, but I am sending you these two poems directly for many reasons.

Please read them with the greatest of care and don't make up your mind about them until you've read them all through—perhaps twice.

The ordinary American magazine wouldn't touch them. In fact, I believe Scribner's is the only one which would, and yet in my humble opinion, 'When I Grew Up to Middle-Age' is the only thoroughly satisfactory poem I have ever written in my

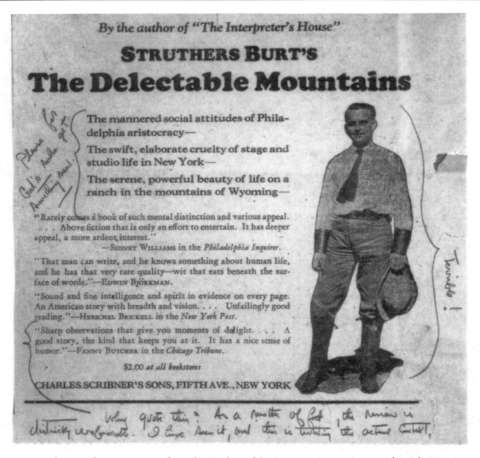

By the author of "The Interpreter's House"

STRUTHERS BURT'S
The Delectable Mountains

The mannered social attitudes of Philadelphia aristocracy—

The swift, elaborate cruelty of stage and studio life in New York—

The serene, powerful beauty of life on a ranch in the mountains of Wyoming—

"Rarely comes a book of such mental distinction and various appeal. . . . Above fiction that is only an effort to entertain. It has deeper appeal, a more ardent interest."
—SIDNEY WILLIAMS in the *Philadelphia Inquirer.*

"That man can write, and he knows something about human life, and he has that very rare quality—wit that eats beneath the surface of words."—EDWIN BJÖRKMAN.

"Sound and fine intelligence and spirit in evidence on every page. An American story with breadth and vision. . . . Unfailingly good reading."—HERSCHEL BRICKELL in the *New York Post.*

"Sharp observations that give you moments of delight. . . . A good story, the kind that keeps you at it. It has a nice sense of humor."—FANNY BUTCHER in the *Chicago Tribune.*

$2.00 *at all bookstores*

CHARLES SCRIBNER'S SONS, FIFTH AVE., NEW YORK

A Scribner advertisement for The Delectable Mountains *annotated with Burt's criticisms. In his accompanying letter (30 January 1927) to Maxwell Perkins, Burt wrote: "I should be glad if I could be advertised in as dignified a way as, let us say, Galsworthy and Hemingway. For instance, I think to print this picture of myself in ranch costume is absurd. I am not a Zane Gray, nor is The Delectable Mountains a cowboy romance." Scribners' advertising of his books was a constant source of irritation to Burt, leading him, in a long letter to CS III in 1934, to suggest that Scribners augment its advertising department by hiring a "liaison," particularly a* woman *with personality, imagination, and social contacts, to bridge the void between Scribner authors and reviewers—someone whose job it would be to keep in "intelligent touch" with authors. Much later, in a postscript to a letter (5 August 1942) to Burt, Perkins wrote: "We appear to be about to take your advice, of having a charming young woman to help with the publicity, etc."*

life. I may be deluded; but a great many other people think the same.

Now it is very long; I know that; and it belongs to a type of poetry that is completely understood in England and not at all in America, where only sonorous absurdities are ever spoken of as anything but 'verse,' but I'll wager, if you can find a way to slip it in, that you'll not regret it. It will be something quite new, anyway, and I think the story is sufficiently interesting to carry the length.

Moreover, the philosophy is not unneeded in America today, and Scribner's is the only magazine which has consistently stood for such philosophy. Urbane poetry is entirely misunderstood in America and yet a period of urbane poetry is surely coming, now that the nation is turning against the staccattoism of vers libre.

Please, please consider it, and get Bridges to consider it, very deeply.

This isn't merely a bit of verse I am trying to get published, it is a deeply laid philosophy both of life and poetry which chokes me for expression. Scribner's is the only magazine I know that doesn't strangle writers.

Faithfully yours
Maxwell Struthers Burt

Impressed with the poem, Bridges bought it for $100, though he could not guarantee an early use of it in the magazine because of its length. The poem appeared in the December 1921 issue and became the title poem of Burt's next collection, which Scribners published in 1925. Prior to that publication, Perkins wrote Burt (26 May): "I swear I do not know anybody writing poetry who gives the purely lyrical thrill you give in these poems of yours many times; and certainly there is nobody who has ever combined that quality with the homely sense of common humanity."

LETTER:
Letter from Burt to Maxwell Perkins, 24 January 1927.

Ten days after the publication of his novel The Delectable Mountains, *Burt is disappointed that reviewers miss both philosophically and technically what he is trying to do in his "modern" writing, which he relates to Hemingway's ("something new in English literature"), and wishes Scribners could help get the ideas across to the public. "Bernice" was Bernice Gilkyson, wife of Burt's friend Walter Gilkyson and a member of the* Scribner's Magazine *staff; Whitney Darrow and Wallace Meyer were members of the Scribner advertising and editorial staff.*

Dear Max:

Yes, The Times review wasn't bad, neither was The World. I am always glad to get the New York reviews over with as I rather dread them. Those boys up there are so hurried that they haven't time to read a long and closely written book, and they are always, of course, bitterly eager to impress their own personalities. I am beginning to get very enthusiastic letters from various people.

I wish it could be got over in some way, as I hinted in my last letter, that I am not merely writing books and verse, but that I am writing books and verse not only with a definite philosophical context but a very definite technical intention—the latter, of course, an attempt to express the former. Nobody seems to grasp this truth except a few people in Scribner's, and I think it a pity no one is given a lead. Incidentally, I think it a pity that you do not emphasize this is Heming-

way's book. You are losing a great opportunity. Outside of yourself and Bernice nobody seems to realize that Hemingway's book marks almost something new in English literature. It is not merely a good book, etc, etc, it is the emergence on the other side, into sense and beauty, of the gasping, ill directed efforts of a generation of Driesers, Gertrude Steins, Van Vechtens, and so on. I think Whitney and Meyer ought to be made to realize this and that Scribner's should capitalize properly such an event.

In my own humble way, and unconsiously, as is always the case, and more by the structure of the whole than by the structure of the whole plus sentence structure, I think to some extent I have done the same in some of my verse and The Delectable Mountains. I don't think these things are ever done with conscious deliberation. I think they are largely the result of being caught up by the seitgeist, but none the less they are done and can be viewed objectively afterwards.

You and I have discussed often the effect of relativity on writing, relativity of morals, point of view, etc, etc, but I think it is interesting to see it emerge in actual sentence structure and in the use of background. The very things that some critics balk at in The Delectable Mountains are the very things that make it modern. It is casual, for one thing, and it is meant to be casual. What The World man thinks are essays, are not essays at all, they are the casual thoughts of an intelligent man as he thinks them in this casual hardboiled but poignant period. Let me give an example.

Whatever the Victorian man may have done—and he fooled himself into doing many things by false sentiment—the modern man does this. Let us say he is in love, let us say, being in love, he walks from 52nd Street to 45th down 5th Avenue. Does he deliberately relate everything he sees and thinks to the object of his affection, as he was supposed to do according to former amoristic notions, and as he is supposed to do in 'well knit novels.' He does not. No matter how much in love he may be, if he is a thinking man, he reacts to a score of things in those seven blocks. But I think I make myself clear. It is the same thing in handling background. This is an extraordinary mobile world today; there is no longer any need to explain why your characters go to China—to plot it—they go because they go, in the way Hemingway's people go to Spain, or my people go to Mexico, or Europe. And so on, and so on.

But I wish that in some way these ideas could be formulated and made public. Authors can't do it themselves. I tried to some extent to do

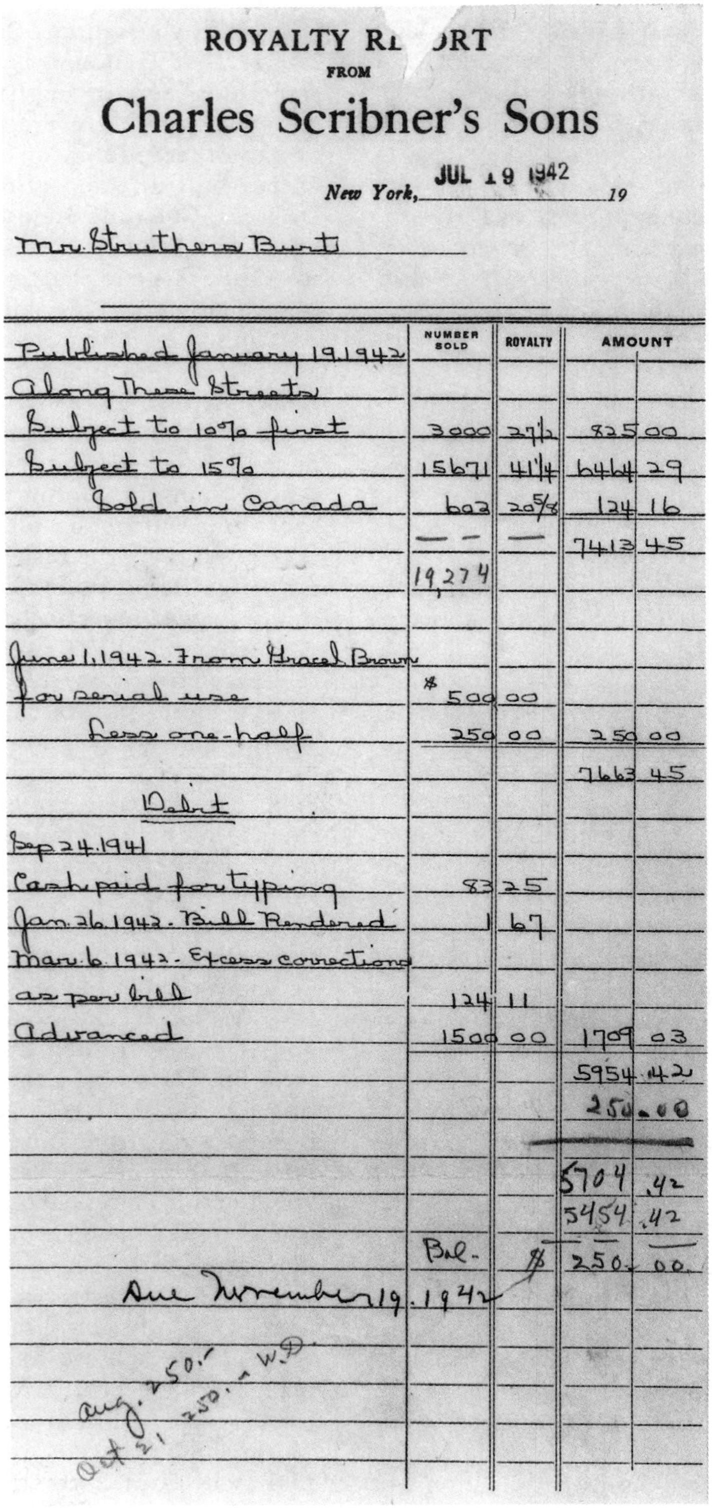

ROYALTY REPORT

FROM

Charles Scribner's Sons

New York, JUL 19 1942 _____ 19

Mrs. Struthers Burt _____

	NUMBER SOLD	ROYALTY	AMOUNT
Published January 19, 1942			
Along These Streets			
Subject to 10% first	3000	27½	825 00
Subject to 15%	15671	41¼	6464 29
Sold in Canada	602	20⅝	124 16
	— —	—	7413 45
	19,274		
June 1, 1942. From Gracel Brown			
for serial use	$ 500 00		
Less one-half	250 00		250 00
			7663 45
Debit			
Sep 24, 1941			
Cash paid for typing	83 25		
Jan. 26, 1942. Bill Rendered	1 67		
Mar. 6, 1942. Excess corrections			
as per bill	124 11		
Advanced	1500 00		1709 03
			5954 42
			250 00
			5704 42
			5454 42
	Bal.	$	250 00
Due November 19, 1942			

aug. 250. ∟ W.D.
Oct 21 250. ∟

First royalty report for Along These Streets *(1942)*

it in the introduction to When I Grew Up to Middle Age. On the whole I think that introduction, which cost me great sweat and did not say half of what I wanted, was more or less still born. It isn't an author's job, anyhow, to explain himself except in his books, and the public is so damned stupid that it requires a critic to explain things to it. In matters such as this a critic has more validity, anyhow.

Is this all nonsense? It doesn't seem so to me.
With many regards
S. B.

RELATED LETTERS AND TELEGRAM:
Letter from Burt to Maxwell Perkins, 27 June 1930; telegram and letter from Kyle S. Crichton, *Scribner's Magazine* staff member, 7 July 1930, in response.

Here Burt takes offense at the author's note accompanying his article "The Benefits of Prohibition," which was appearing in the current issue (July) of Scribner's Magazine.

Dear Max:

With all due respect to a great publishing house, whose editors, in my humble opinion, are the best in the country, I must again, in company with practically all your authors, raise my voice against your write-up men and publicity men—or women.

Who in hell is responsible for this patronizing little note? Why in hell shouldn't my mind be alert, even if I have reached the incredible age of forty seven? Why should I suddenly be elected the present 'dean of American letters'? Who does the writer behind the scenes think I am, Henry van Dyke? Furthermore, why can't Scribner's take the trouble to find out correctly what I am doing? My days as a rancher are not over. I am President of the Bar B.C. Ranches, inc. I do not sit, my dim eyes staring at the sun, on my terrace at Southern Pines [town in North Carolina]. I travel like the devil all over the country. Just at present, despite my great age, I am even starting a new ranch of my own—a little private ranch; once again buying horses, cows, spotting timber, running a saw mill, etc, etc. Extraordinary, isn't it, for a senile old fellow?

Finally—and most seriously—I am at great pains always to kill any rumor that Wyoming is no longer my home. It is and will be, I trust, for life. I have been a citizen out here for twenty two years and, god willing, will never be a citizen anywhere else. Southern Pines is merely my winter residence; Wyoming is my home. This is more important than it may seem. I am deeply involved in Wyoming politics of a kind and it would hamper me very greatly if the notice got abroad that I had deserted Wyoming. Wyoming is where my heart is and my deepest interests, and there they will always be.

I am writing a little note to the magazine for publication couched in more formal language.

. . . Golly this country is lovely. You must positively run out here next summer for as long as you can, when we get straightened out at this new little ranch. It is your duty as an editor and American citizen. . . .

With numerous regards, despite dimming faculties,

Your incredibly ancient friend,
Struthers Burt

Struthers Burt
Bar B.C. Ranch
Victor, Idaho

SHOULD LIKE VERY MUCH TO USE YOUR SWELL LETTER OF INDIGNATION IN OUR WHAT YOU THINK ABOUT IT DEPARTMENT STOP IT WOULD BE A COMPLETE VINDICATION OF YOUR YOUTH AND WOULD HELP US FILL THE LARGEST PAGE IN MAGAZINE HISTORY ON A HOT JULY DAY PLEASE WIRE COLLECT

Kyle S. Crichton

Dear Mr. Burt:

Thank God for that letter. There seems to be a feeling around Scribner's that an author—an established and swell author such as yourself—is something wrapped in moth balls. You aren't supposed to approach him unless with properly inclined backbone.

I'm a Westerner myself, New Mexico, and when I wrote that Southern Pines veranda bunk I gritted my teeth and asked myself what the world was coming to.

But it's all right by me. The last dope we had on you was six years old. Whether anybody ever had the nerve to ask for anything new or whether you had a saddle sore and couldn't write, I don't know. We have enough for an issue or two at any rate. . . .

Sincerely yours,
Kyle S. Crichton

Burt's indignant response, doctored for humorous effect, was used in the September issue's

"What You Think About It" department under the heading "That Ole Cowboy, Burt."

LETTER:

Letter from Burt to his publisher, Arthur H. Scribner, 7 August 1930.

When CS II died in April, the "mantle" passed to his younger brother, Arthur. In his recent letter Arthur had written Burt that a "novel by you of such importance and full length" (Festival) justified Scribners' pricing it at $2.50. Burt felt that a $2.00 price would increase sales.

Dear Mr Scribner:

Your letter has just reached me, and I shall be glad to abide utterly by your decision in regard to the price of "Festival." I can only hope the book lives up to your kind words about it.

It must be a great comfort and assurance to all authors devoted to the house of Scribner, as I am, to find you stepping so splendidly into the place left vacant by Mr Charles Scribner, and carrying forward his tradition of well-nigh perfect editorial letters, so that the author is neither unduly depressed nor unduly encouraged, but finds himself constantly urged to put forth his best efforts and finds, if such a thing be possible, his loyalty increased.

With many thanks,

Faithfully yours
Struthers Burt

LETTER:

Letter from Maxwell Perkins to Burt, 11 August 1930.

This is a representative letter by Perkins-as-editor, here suggesting in his tactful, encouraging way that Burt make deep cuts in the manuscript of his novel Festival.

Dear Struthers:

I greatly enjoyed reading the twenty-five galleys of "Festival,"- which I am now sending you with a few suggestions.- But take the suggestions not so much as being precise and specific, as indicating the direction toward which, it seems to me as a reader, you ought to work. This book too, does have the tendency to volubility. Whatever you say is good, but you think of too many things to say things about, and too many things to say about them. Your books are too full of most excellent table talk, so to speak.

I have tried hard to find lengthy cuts, and have refused when I did think I found them, to consider the intrinsic quality of the particular passages--and you ought to harden your heart too. I think more could be cut by you than I have been able to indicate, but it might require some re-writing.- I wanted to take out more, for instance, about Dee's bathroom, but there are paragraphs which could be taken out except for a few little things in them.- If those could be incorporated elsewhere, you could reduce that still further.

There is also the tendency you have to pass from the specific to the generality;- or rather to explain the implications of things, such as the increasing elegance in bathrooms as a symbol of American development. I think people will draw these general inferences for themselves, and that the effect of their doing this will be much greater than if you tell it to them.- Moreover, in a novel it is dangerous that the implications should be consciously carried outside the story.- But this is obvious, and it is only that you have such a gift for talking that you tend to overdo it.

Although your synopsis does tell me the outline of what I have not read of the story, at the same time, it is hard to know how truly important Dee and Elsie are to be when all is said and done. I rather think that they are relatively minor characters: the story is about Dawn and Delice. I think perhaps you could reduce Dee and Elsie further than I have suggested, because really they are very easily understood people, as you set them forth in what they say and do.- One needs to know very little of their past. They are excellently done,- particularly, I think, Dee. The fact is, I am sure you will run no danger of cutting out too much, so cut out what you think you can.

I had to be away for two weeks, and I had all sorts of domestic complications--not my own, but relative to a sister-in-law--and so I have not had much time for writing to anyone. Now do hurry the rest of the book as much as you can so that we may get out in as good season as possible.

Always yours,
[Maxwell Perkins]

Burt's response was one of gratitude: "You are a wise editor—the wisest I know, and I followed all of your suggestions but one, and did some extra cutting on my own . . . I think you will find the whole novel much tightened up" (20 August 1930). Festival was published on 23 January 1931 at $2.50. The Book League of America chose it as their February book, and the English

Book Society made it their November selection, one of only two American novels ever chosen (up to that time) for distribution to its members.

LETTER:

Letter from Burt to Maxwell Perkins, 4 September 1939, written from his ranch in Jackson Hole, Wyoming.

The day after Britain and France declared war on Germany and President Roosevelt in his radio talk stated that, although the nation does not seem neutral in thought, it must remain neutral in policy, Burt describes the effect the sudden beginning of World War II is having on him. He is in the midst of writing a new novel, Along These Streets. *He mentions two previous works,* Malice in Blunderland, *a political satire Scribners published in 1935, and* Powder River: Let'er Buck (1938), *a volume on the Wyoming-Montana river that he wrote for Farrar and Rinehart's Rivers of America series.*

Dear Max:

Well, it is here. What you and I, and everyone else with a modicum of vision, knew would happen but what the wish-fulfillment boys kept telling themselves was impossible. And what a monstrous and fantastic thing it seems in a country like this and at this particular time of year. More monstrous and fantastic even than it appears in more crowded places.

September in mountain valleys is peculiarly a time of fulfillment, a sort of golden period of quiet preparation for the cold. You turn most of your horses out after the hard work of summer, and all day, in pasture or on the range, they crop grass quietly and only very now and then raise their heads. You cut grain. And you know what that is. How quiet and golden with the bundles falling in swathes. The Canada geese begin to fly south. The elk begin to come down from their high summer meadows. Even the sun seems quiet and beginning to be a little remote. . . . And then this damned radio, every time you turn it on, flits across the world like a bat.

Well, there's one comfort. In a place like this you become aware that things go on imperturbably. Turkeys chase bugs. Coyotes howl at night. Mares take stallions, and the forests are undisturbed. You realize that nature takes little note of the suicidal folly of men. But it's damned hard on writing. . . . We've one radio on the place, and it's difficult to keep away from it. Our newspapers, even the Wyoming papers, get here four days late.

I'm right in the middle of the novel, and it was going well—about half done, and the latter part, to me, is always the easiest and goes the quickest. I'm going to keep right on—what else is there to do? I think by setting the time a year later I can make it and bring it up to the moment. And it considers all this stuff that is now in the minds of men.

But what a hell of a period for a novelist, as I have been saying for the past ten years! Galsworthy felt that so deeply in the last war.

My only hope is that this will be a short war. Let me make this prediction and I hope that this is not a wish-fulfillment too. Within six months a revolution in Germany and Louis Ferdinand Hohenzollern on the throne. The Germans have been too badly fooled not to be resentful; England, France and all the world is fighting for its life; Germany is only fighting for a regime. If they change that regime, they can have what they want; if they don't, they'll be smashed and this time terribly.

Will you send me a copy of "Malice in Blunderland"? I haven't one. For your own amusement you might read it over again. It is singularly apropos. You will notice that in it I say that Fascism and Communism are twin brothers. If I am not mistaken, I was among the very first to say that, but got no credit for it. I've been fighting that battle for years and the rich, vaguely pro-Fascist sneered at me, and the pro-Communistic were equally contemptuous. . . . But it spells the end of Communism in America. I am not so sure about Fascism. I have already talked to some of the rich, and God how the pocket-book can make well meaning folk compensate mentally! I have come to the conclusion that the pocket book warps the mind even more than poverty, which is saying a good deal.

I hope to stay here until October 10th, and then be in New York for a few days around the 15th. I also hope to get back to work again. I'll grit my teeth. "Powder River," incidentally, has helped my reputation enormously all over the country. I know that in dozens of ways I'll not burden you with, but it's a fact.

Don't sell any stock! Don't sell any stock! This country's going to be richer than it's been for years. Also Roosevelt is going to be re-elected. Also, if the war only lasts two years we won't be in it.

I feel like the Oracle of Delphi, and am probably one hundred per cent wrong, but I'm glad you're alive. Whenever I get too depressed I

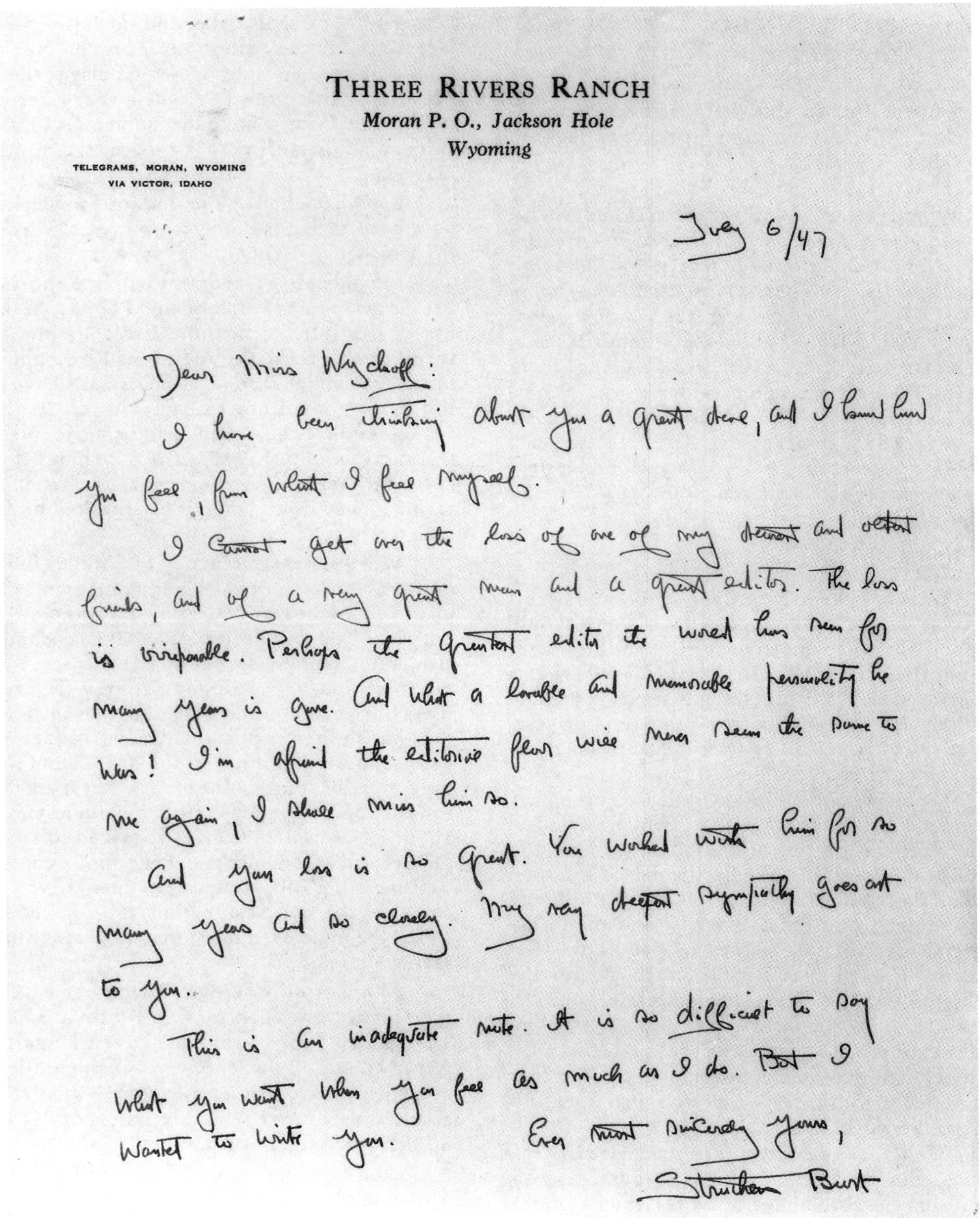

THREE RIVERS RANCH
Moran P. O., Jackson Hole
Wyoming

TELEGRAMS, MORAN, WYOMING
VIA VICTOR, IDAHO

July 6/47

Dear Miss Wyckoff:

I have been thinking about you a great deal, and I know how you feel, from what I feel myself.

I cannot get over the loss of one of my dearest and oldest friends, and of a very great man and a great editor. The loss is irreparable. Perhaps the greatest editor the world has seen for many years is gone. And what a lovable and memorable personality he was! I'm afraid the editorial floor will never seem the same to me again, I shall miss him so.

And your loss is so great. You worked with him for so many years and so closely. My very deepest sympathy goes out to you.

This is an inadequate note. It is so difficult to say what you want when you feel as much as I do. But I wanted to write you.

Ever most sincerely yours,
Struthers Burt

Condolence letter from Burt to Irma Wyckoff on the death of Maxwell Perkins. Wyckoff had been Perkins's secretary for his last twenty-seven years.

think about elk and the really fine, wise and good people I happen to know who are actually living.

Yours
Struthers

Incidentally, and I'm quite serious, should you run against any men of the Intelligence and Propaganda Service, and in your position you will, tell them to put me on their list should we by any foul chance in a long war get into it. I am over age for the active branches, but I have an honorable discharge from the last war, and I think now I rate a job in the Propaganda and I know damn well I could be useful. . . . I have ideas.

At all events, should by any foul chance we get into the war, I wish to know where to go and what to do at once. S. B.

One direct result of the war was Burt's return to writing poems—war ballads and songs—which he considered "good propaganda":

> *Must we in every age this dumb undoing learn?*
> . . . .
> *O God, make honest anger swift against this wrong,*
> *End it forever—it is over-long;*
> *Restore the dignity of men and song.*
> *(from "The Unknown Dead")*

Along These Streets *was not published till 19 January 1942, but it was followed in November by a collection of Burt's wartime verse,* War Songs.

LETTER:
Letter from Burt to Maxwell Perkins, 15 February 1947.

In December of 1944 Burt received an advance on his next novel, a historical work set in Cheyenne, Wyoming, in the 1880s which he tentatively titled Mrs. Phoenix. *Health problems and other interruptions ultimately gave way to writer's block. This is Burt's last letter to his editor: Perkins died four months later.*

Dear Max:

Thank you for your inevitably understanding and sympathetic letter. I am delighted to hear that your impression is that CLOSE PURSUIT [his wife's novel] is going well. There seem to be a good many enthusiastic letters.

You describe accurately my state of mind. It is pure hell, and makes you feel very angry with yourself, and the dismaying part is that it seems to linger so long. Just how I got into this state I don't know, but I think it is due to a long build-up, beginning with the desperate illness of my only sister last spring when we returned from California, followed by over-work and worry at the ranch last summer, and continuing, nagging pain I paid no attention to until it culminated in a minor, but painful operation. Anyway, until about three months ago, I was going strong so far as writing is concerned, and was very much interested in the novel. Then—bang—this happened, with the exact feelings you describe. And, of course, a vicious circle of worry begins.

If you are a writer, and writing is your life, and you can't write, you leave a vacuum for the devils of worry.

You worry about everything; in these days, finances no small part of them. There seems to be so many commitments, not the least the Income Taxes. Free-lancing seems such an uncertain business in the face of the uncertain times. You begin to sort of long for a routine job that brings in a regular salary, and all that sort of stuff. It makes you sick with yourself, as I've already said.

But no use continuing, it's tiresome.

Anyhow, I hope to come out of it soon. It is quite foreign to my usual hard-working, optimistic self. And I want so to write, but it doesn't flow as it should. . . .

With best of regards, and deep and renewed thanks,

Always yours,
Struthers

By January of 1948 he had pushed the historical fiction aside and begun a more contemporary novel that he called The Adamantine Spindle—*from Milton's poem "Arcades" ("And turn the adamantine spindle round / On which the fate of gods and men are wound"). Neither book could he finish before his death.*

F. Scott Fitzgerald (1896–1940)

F. Scott Fitzgerald (4 June 1937) in front of the Algonquin Hotel, New York City (photo by Carl Van Vechten)

A nongraduating member of the Princeton Class of 1917, Fitzgerald became famous almost overnight with the publication by Scribners of his first book, *This Side of Paradise* (1920). Set at Princeton, the novel captured the moods and manners of a new generation and the romance of the "Jazz Age," which, later, he claimed to have named. Thereafter, his stories became regular features of such magazines as *The Smart Set, The Saturday Evening Post,* and *Esquire.* Though Fitzgerald wrote some 160 stories, a play, and four novels, his fame rests primarily on *The Great Gatsby* (1925), his sensitive and symbolic treatment of contemporary life in pursuit of the "American dream." While the short novel never enjoyed great popular success during Fitzgerald's life, it has been Scribners' perennial best-seller since its introduction in 1960 in a paperback edition and its ubiquitous use by high-school and college teachers in their twentieth-century American literature classes and courses. The personal life of Fitzgerald and his wife, Zelda—their widely advertised spendthrift lifestyle and resultant emotionally and financially destitute ends—helped develop his status as both a cultural hero and a chronicler of his time: an identity that has become permanently established in American literary history. Fitzgerald was the youngest novelist published by Scribners, and still more books of his works have appeared posthumously as his literary reputation has increased.

Scribner Books by Fitzgerald

1920	*This Side of Paradise*
	Flappers and Philosophers
1922	*The Beautiful and Damned*
	Tales of the Jazz Age
1923	*The Vegetable; or, From President to Postman*
1925	*The Great Gatsby*

1926	*All the Sad Young Men*
1934	*Tender Is the Night: A Romance*, with decorations by Edward Shenton (revised edition, 1951)
1935	*Taps at Reveille*
1941	*The Last Tycoon: An Unfinished Novel, Together with The Great Gatsby and Selected Stories*, edited by Edmund Wilson
1951	*The Stories of F. Scott Fitzgerald: A Selection of 28 Stories*, with an introduction by Malcolm Cowley
1953	*Three Novels of F. Scott Fitzgerald: The Great Gatsby, Tender Is the Night, The Last Tycoon*
1960	*Babylon Revisited and Other Stories*
	Six Tales of the Jazz Age and Other Stories
1962	*The Pat Hobby Stories*, with an introduction by Arnold Gingrich
1963	*The Letters of F. Scott Fitzgerald*, edited by Andrew Turnbull
	The Fitzgerald Reader, edited by Arthur Mizener
1965	*Scott Fitzgerald: Letters to His Daughter*, edited by Turnbull, with an introduction by Frances Fitzgerald Lanahan
1971	*Dear Scott / Dear Max: The Fitzgerald–Perkins Correspondence*, edited by John Kuehl and Jackson R. Bryer
1973	*The Basil and Josephine Stories*, edited, with an introduction, by Bryer and Kuehl
1974	*Bits of Paradise: 21 Uncollected Stories by F. Scott and Zelda Fitzgerald*, selected by Matthew J. Bruccoli, with the assistance of Scottie Fitzgerald Smith
	The Romantic Egoists, edited by Bruccoli, Smith, and Joan P. Kerr; art editor, Margareta F. Lyons
1985	*F. Scott Fitzgerald on Writing*, edited by Larry W. Phillips
1989	*The Short Stories of F. Scott Fitzgerald: A New Collection*, edited and with a preface by Bruccoli
1994	*F. Scott Fitzgerald: A Life in Letters*, edited by Bruccoli, with the assistance of Judith S. Baughman

LETTER:
Letter from Sir Shane Leslie, the Irish writer, to CS II, 6 May 1918, written from Washington, D.C.

The Scribner author files for Fitzgerald begin with this letter, which is really a letter of introduction accompanying a manuscript. In the fall of 1917 Fitzgerald joined the army and was commissioned as a second lieutenant in the infantry; he began his novel, The Romantic Egotist, *while stationed at Fort Leavenworth, Kansas, and finished the first draft while on leave in Princeton during March 1918. Before reporting to Camp Sheridan, near Montgomery, Alabama, he put the manuscript in the hands of Leslie, a Scribner author who had befriended him while he was a student at* the Newman School in New Jersey and had encouraged his literary ambitions.

Dear Mr Scribner,

I am sending you the MS of a book by a Princeton boy a friend of mine and a descendant of the author of the Star spangled banner. He calls himself the descendant of Benedict Arnold in his autobiography in the approved style of modern youth! I have read it through and in spite of its disguises it has given me a vivid picture of the American generation that is hastening to war. I marvel at its crudity and its cleverness. It is naive in places, shocking in others, painful to the conventional and not without a touch of ironic sublimity especially toward the end. About a third of the book could be omitted without losing the impression

589 Summit Ave.
St. Paul, Minn.

1919?

Dear Mr. Perkins:

Thanks a lot for your letter. I feel I've certainly been lucky to find a publisher who seems so interested generally in his authors. Lord knows this literary game has been discouraging enough at times.

I'm enclosing a letter from Nathan I got this morning and a clipping from the Sun of two weeks ago. I wish you'd show 'em to Mr. Bridges too before you send them back. The story referred to by Nathan is Dalyrimple Goes Wrong and the play is a thing about a girl and a bath-tub called Porcelain and Pink.

My book plans have changed or rather enlarged. I'm going to obey my own mandate and write every book as if it were the last word I'd have on earth. I think Wells does that. So I think that the ms. I send you about next April or may will be rather a lively bolt!

As Ever

F Scott Fitzgerald.

You see I'm trying to make myself out as a poet and play-write, as well as a novelist and short story writer! Innocuous humor!

First Fitzgerald letter [early 1919?] in the Scribner Archives, written to Maxwell Perkins, who became his literary adviser and lifelong friend, in which he projects the completion of a new book manuscript in April or May. "Nathan" is George Jean Nathan, coeditor with H. L. Mencken of The Smart Set, *who had accepted Fitzgerald's story* "Dalyrimple Goes Wrong" *and* "Porcelain and Pink (A One-Act Play)" *for his magazine.*

that it is written by an American Rupert Brooke. I knew the poetic Rupert Brooke and this is a prose one, though some of the lyrics are good and apparently original. It interests me as a boy's book and I think gives expression to that real American youth that the sentimentalists and super patriots are so anxious to drape behind the canvas of the Y.M.C.A. tent. Though Scott Fitzgerald is still alive it has a literary value. Of course when he is killed it will also have a literary value. Before leaving for France he has committed it to me and will you in any case house it in your safe for the time? If you feel like giving a judgment upon it, will you call upon me to make any alterations or perform whatever duties accrue to a literary sponsor.

Without tying you down in any way, accept our best thanks in advance as well as my apology for intruding upon your good will yet again.

Yours faithfully
Shane Leslie

Scribners rejected the novel, but encouraged Fitzgerald to revise it and then resubmit it, which he did.

RELATED LETTERS:
Letters from Maxwell Perkins to Fitzgerald, 16 and 23 September 1919, accepting *This Side of Paradise* for publication and explaining the exigencies of the book publishing "seasons" to this young author.

Dear Mr. Fitzgerald:

I am very glad, personally, to be able to write to you that we are all for publishing your book, "This Side of Paradise". Viewing it as the same book that was here before, which in a sense it is, though translated into somewhat different terms and extended further, I think that you have improved it enormously. As the first manuscript did, it abounds in energy and life and it seems to me to be in much better proportion. I was afraid that, when we declined the first manuscript, you might be done with us conservatives. I am glad you are not. The book is so different that it is hard to prophesy how it will sell but we are all for taking a chance and supporting it with vigor. As for terms, we shall be glad to pay a royalty of 10% on the first five thousand copies and of 15% thereafter,- which by the way, means more than it use to now that retail prices upon which the percentage is calculated, have so much advanced.

Hoping to hear from you, we are,
Sincerely yours,
[Maxwell Perkins]

P.S. Our expectation would be to publish your book in the early spring. Now, if you are ready to have us do this, and have the time, we should be glad to have you get together any publicity matter you could for us, including a photograph. You have been in the advertising game long enough to know the sort of thing.

Fitzgerald had been working in a New York advertising agency earlier in the year.

Dear Mr. Fitzgerald:

I was very glad to get your letter of the 18th and to know that everything was ready with regard to "This Side of Paradise"; and we are now making an estimate upon the book preliminary to putting it in hand which we shall do within a short time if the printers strike does not make it impossible to put anything in hand.

It is this way about publishing before Christmas: there are two book seasons in the year and the preparations for each one are begun long before the season opens. The publishers travelers go out early in July and August over this country with trunks filled with dummies and samples of the Fall books, which are to have their greatest sale in the Christmas season. The advertisment department and the circularizing department get up their material in August and early September to make these books known considerably before publication and at the very time of publication. The advertising that is done from the first of September on is supposed to have its great effect in December, although the book may have appeared in August or September or October and may have sold considerably then. Now, if a book is accepted after all this preliminary work is done and comes out in November, as yours would have to do at the earliest, it must break its own way altogether: it will get no preliminary advertising; it will not be presented to the trade by salesmen on the basis of a dummy; and it will come to the book-seller, who is already nearly mad with the number of new books and has already invested all the money he can in them, as a most unwelcome and troublesome thing and will suffer accordingly. Even if it is a book by an author who has been selling well for years, it will be very considerably injured by this.

The next book publishing season is the Spring season. The moment the Christmas rush is ended, the travelers go out once more and see all the book-sellers, equipped with samples, etc. The book seller has made his money out of the previous season and is ready to begin afresh and to

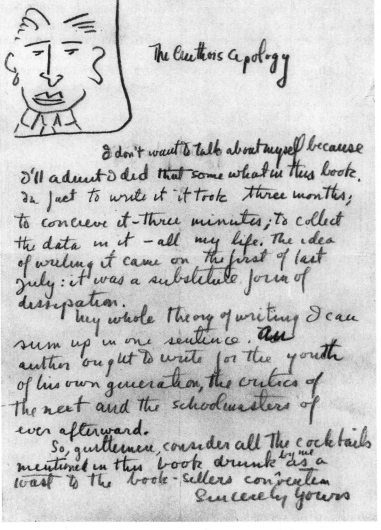

The Authors Apology

I don't want to talk about myself because
I'll admit I did that somewhat in this book.
In fact to write it it took three months;
to conceive it—three minutes; to collect
the data in it—all my life. The idea
of writing it came on the first of last
July: it was a substitute, form of
dissipation.

My whole theory of writing I can
sum up in one sentence. An
author ought to write for the youth
of his own generation, the critics of
the next and the schoolmasters of
ever afterward.

So, gentlemen, consider all the cocktails
mentioned in this book drunk by me as a
toast to the book-sellers convention.
Sincerely yours

"Authors's Apology" [1920] written by Fitzgerald for insertion in
This Side of Paradise, *distributed by Scribners at the American*
Booksellers Association meeting

stock up on new books. The Advertising and Circularizing departments have prepared their work on it and their accounts of the author, etc. and have advertised it in the trade magazines to reinforce the salesmen's selling arguement. Then, when the book does appear in February, March or April, the trade is ready for it and knows about it and it can be competently advertised because the publicity force of the house has become familiar with it.

These are the reasons why there is no question but it would damage your book exceedingly to try and rush it out before Christmas. Whether or not it can be printed in February we cannot yet say but it certainly can be published in that month or March and we shall remember that you want it to be as early as possible. . . .

Sincerely yours,
[Maxwell Perkins]

Though he was extremely anxious to have his book published by Christmas ["I have so many things dependent on its success—including of course a girl" (18 September)], Fitzgerald was convinced by Perkins's argument: This Side of Paradise *was published on 26 March 1920. Made famous almost overnight, he married the "girl," Zelda Sayre, a week later.*

LETTER:

Letter from Fitzgerald to Maxwell Perkins, 10 November 1920.

Fitzgerald questions Perkins's latest sales report for This Side of Paradise. *He mentions working on his second novel,* The Beautiful and Damned, *and also makes reference to the authors' night at the National Arts Club, to which he has been invited.*

Dear Mr. Perkins:

I thank you very much for the $1500.00. I thought as there have been 41,000 printed the sales would be more than <u>33,796</u> but I suppose there are about five thousand in stock and two thousand given away or sold at cost.

The novel goes beautifully. Done 15,000 words in last three days which is very fast writing even for me who write very fast. My record is still 12,000 words "The Camel's Back" begun eight o'clock one morning and finished at seven at night & then copied between seven & half past four & mailed at 5 in the morning. That's the story the O. Henry Memorial people are using in their second collection.

I'm awfully mixed on this Art Society thing. I remember they wrote me asking me to come on Thurs the 18th (I think) & I accepted. But I have a note in my note-book about the 11th & your letter says the seventeenth. I'd just as soon go twice if necessary but I sure am mixed up.

Sincerely
F. Scott Fitzgerald

Written in pencil at the bottom is this cautionary note by CS II: "This is an illustration of the danger of letting the author hear of every impression printed without warning him that that does not mean sold. Better not let him follow the printing this closely. CS"

LETTER:

Letter from Maxwell Perkins to Fitzgerald, 2 May 1921.

On the day before the Fitzgeralds sail to Europe for their first trip abroad, Perkins formalizes a line-of-credit policy with Fitzgerald by which he is free to get "reasonable" advances from Scribners even if his books have not yet earned them. Ultimately, the arrangement made the publisher Fitzgerald's personal banker, which created awkwardness for both author and editor, for Fitzgerald was continually in debt.

Dear Fitzgerald:

You left your copy of the contract [for *The Beautiful and Damned*] here and I enclose it with this letter as you ought to have it. I take this opportunity, in order that the thing may be set down in writing, that we are only not agreeing to any advance on the understanding that you are free to call on us to any reasonable extent against your general account with us. That is, we shall always be ready to advance, not only amounts equivalent to what your books have already earned, although the payments may not then be due, but amounts which may be considered reasonable estimates of what it may be anticipated that they will earn. In other words, the only reason why we are not making you a very handsome advance is that the figure is perhaps a little difficult to fix upon, but chiefly because we thought that in view of our previous association, an arrangement by which you were free to draw against your account here and reasonably in excess of it, would be more convenient and satisfactory.

I enclose also a letter to Galsworthy whom I hope you will see, and a letter to Mr. Kingsley [Scribners' agent in London] who may be able to help you one way or another.

I hope it will be a great trip both for you and your wife.

As ever,
[Maxwell Perkins]

CS II DIARY ENTRY:
Saturday 18 March 1922

<u>Luncheon</u> at home

Prof. Phelps	Scott Fitzgerald
Cortissoz	Bridges
Howe	Jesse Williams

Two weeks after the publication of his second novel, The Beautiful and Damned, *Fitzgerald joins several other Scribner authors (and staff) at the home of his publisher: William Lyon Phelps, Yale professor and author; Royal Cortissoz, art editor and critic; Will D. Howe, Scribner editor and director; Robert Bridges, editor of* Scribner's Magazine; *and Jesse Lynch Williams, playwright and storywriter.*

RELATED LETTERS:

Letter from Fitzgerald to CS II, 19 April 1922; letter by Arthur H. Scribner, 11 May 1922, in reply.

Memorandum of Agreement, made this twenty-second day of December 19 24

between F. SCOTT FITZGERALD ———————— hereinafter called "the AUTHOR,"

of

and CHARLES SCRIBNER'S SONS, of New York City, N. Y., hereinafter called "the PUBLISHERS." Said - - F. Scott Fitzgerald - - being the AUTHOR and PROPRIETOR of a work entitled:

THE GREAT GATSBY ————————

in consideration of the covenants and stipulations hereinafter contained, and agreed to be performed by the PUBLISHERS, grants and guarantees to said PUBLISHERS and their successors the exclusive right to publish the said work in all forms during the terms of copyright and renewals thereof, hereby covenanting with said PUBLISHERS that he is the sole AUTHOR and PROPRIETOR of said work.

Said AUTHOR hereby authorizes said PUBLISHERS to take out the copyright on said work, and further guarantees to said PUBLISHERS that the said work is in no way whatever a violation of any copyright belonging to any other party, and that it contains nothing of a scandalous or libelous character; and that he and his legal representatives shall and will hold harmless the said PUBLISHERS from all suits, and all manner of claims and proceedings which may be taken on the ground that said work is such violation or contains anything scandalous or libelous; and he further hereby authorizes said PUBLISHERS to defend at law any and all suits and proceedings which may be taken or had against them for infringement of any other copyright or for libel, scandal, or any other injurious or hurtful matter or thing contained in or alleged or claimed to be contained in or caused by said work, and pay to said PUBLISHERS such reasonable costs, disbursements, expenses, and counsel fees as they may incur in such defense.

Said PUBLISHERS, in consideration of the right herein granted and of the guarantees aforesaid, agree to publish said work at their own expense, in such style and manner as they shall deem most expedient, and to pay said AUTHOR, or - his - legal representatives, FIFTEEN (15) ———————— per cent. on their Trade-List (retail) price, cloth style, for the first forty thousand (40,000) copies of said work sold by them in the United States and TWENTY (20) per cent. for all copies sold thereafter. ——————— Provided, nevertheless, that one-half the above named royalty shall be paid on all copies sold outside the United States; and provided that no percentage whatever shall be paid on any copies destroyed by fire or water, or sold at or below cost, or given away for the purpose of aiding the sale of said work.

It is further agreed that the profits arising from any publication of said work, during the period covered by this agreement, in other than book form shall be divided equally between said PUBLISHERS and said AUTHOR.

Scribners' publishing contract with Fitzgerald for The Great Gatsby

Expenses incurred for alterations in type or plates, exceeding twenty per cent. of the cost of composition and electrotyping said work, are to be charged to the AUTHOR'S account.

The first statement shall not be rendered until six months after date of publication; and thereafter statements shall be rendered semi-annually, on the AUTHOR'S application therefor, in the months of February and August; settlements to be made in cash, four months after date of statement.

If, on the expiration of   five   years from date of publication, or at any time thereafter, the demand for said work should not, in the opinion of said PUBLISHERS, be sufficient to render its publication profitable, then, upon written notice by said PUBLISHERS to said AUTHOR, this contract shall cease and determine; and thereupon said AUTHOR shall have the right, at his option, to take from said PUBLISHERS, at cost, whatever copies of said work they may then have on hand; or, failing to take said copies at cost, then said PUBLISHERS shall have the right to dispose of the copies on hand as they may see fit, free from any percentage or royalty, and to cancel this contract.

Provided, also, that if, at any time during the continuance of this agreement, said work shall become unsalable in the ordinary channels of trade, said PUBLISHERS shall have the right to dispose of any copies on hand, paying to said AUTHOR – fifteen (15) – per cent. of the net amount received therefor, in lieu of the percentage hereinbefore prescribed.

In consideration of the mutuality of this contract, the aforesaid parties agree to all its provisions, and in testimony thereof affix their signatures and seals.

Witness to signature of
Charles Scribner's Sons

Witness to signature of
F. Scott Fitzgerald

[L. S.]

The Modern Library, begun by Boni & Liveright in 1917 and later sold to and expanded by Bennett Cerf and Donald S. Klopfer, was one of the most successful, inexpensive reprint series of twentieth-century publishing. Fitzgerald's suggestion to Scribners to begin their own similar series was a good one, but the firm did not think conditions were favorable. However, after the "revolution" brought about by cheap paperbacks, Scribners successfully launched the Scribner Library in 1960, drawing upon its own solid backlist. The first title in the series was Fitzgerald's The Great Gatsby.

Dear Mr. Scribner:

I am consumed by an idea and I can't resist asking you about it. It's probably a chestnut, but it might not have occurred to you before in just this form.

No doubt you know of the success that Boni and Liveright have made of their "Modern Library". Within the last month Doubleday Page & Company have withdrawn the titles that were theirs from Boni's modern library, and gone in on their own hook with a "Lambskin Library". For this they have chosen so far about 18 titles from their past publications—some of them books of merit (Frank Norris and Conrad, for instance) and some of them trashy, but all books that at one time or another have been sensational either as popular successes or as possible contributions to American literature. The Lambskin Library is cheap, bound uniformly in red leather (or imitation leather), and makes, I believe, a larger appeal to the buyer than the A. L. Burt reprints, for its uniformity gives it a sort of permanence, a place of honor in the scraggly library that adorns every small home. Besides that, it is a much easier thing for a bookseller to display and keep up. The titles are numbered and it gives people a chance to sample writers by one book in this edition. Also it keeps before the public such books as have once been popular and have since been forgotten.

Now my idea is this: The Scribner Company have many more distinguished years of publishing behind them than Doubleday Page. They could produce a list twice as long of distinguished and memorable fiction and use no more than one book by each author—and it need not be the book by that author most in demand.

Take for instance <u>Predestined</u> and <u>The House of Mirth</u>. I do not know, but I imagine that those books are kept upstairs in most bookstores, and only obtained when some one is told of the work of Edith Wharton and Stephen French Whitman.

They are almost as forgotten as the books of Frank Norris and Stephen Crane were five years ago, before Boni's library began its career.

To be specific, I can imagine that a Scribner library containing the following titles and selling for something under a dollar would be an enormous success:

1. The House of Mirth (or Ethan Frome) — Edith Wharton
2. Predestine — Stephen French Whitman
3. This Side of Paradise — F. Scott Fitzgerald
4. The Little Shepherd of Kingdom Come — John Fox, Jr.
5. In Ole Kentucky — Thomas Nelson Page
6. Sentimental Tommy — J. M. Barrie
7. Some Civil War book by — George Barr Cable [George Washington Cable]
8. Some novel by — Henry Van Dyke
9. Some novel by — Jackson Gregory
10. Saint's Progress — John Galsworthy
11. The Ordeal of Richard Feverell — George Meredith
12. Treasure Island — Robert Louis Stevenson
13. The Turn of the Screw — Henry James
14. The Stolen Story (Or The Frederick Williams Carrols) — Jesse Lynch
15. The Damnation of Theron Ware (I think Stone used to own this) — Harold Frederick
16. Soldiers of Fortune — Richard Harding Davis
17. Some book by — Mary Raymond Shipman Andrews
18. Simple Souls — John Hastings Turner

Doubtless a glance at your old catalogues would suggest two dozen others. I have not even mentioned less popular writers such as Burt and Katherine Gerould. Nor have I gone into the possibilities of such non-fiction as a volume of Roosevelt, a volume of Huneker, or a volume of Shane Leslie.

As I say, this is quite possibly an idea which has occurred to you before and has been dismissed for reasons which would not appear to me, an outsider. I am moved to the suggestion by the success of the experiments I have mentioned. They have been made possible, I believe, by the recent American strain for "culture" which expresses itself in such things as uniformity of bindings to make a library. Also the selective function of this library would appeal to many people in search of good reading matter, new or old.

One more thing and this interminably long letter is done. It may seem to you that in many cases

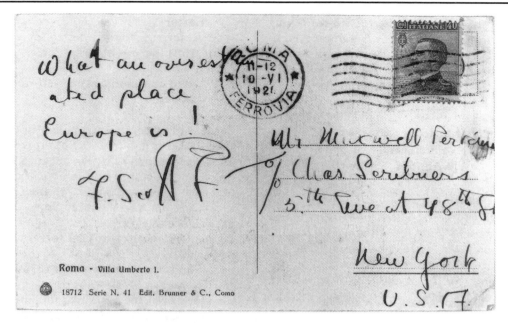

Postcard sent by Fitzgerald to Maxwell Perkins from Rome while on his second trip to Europe

I have chosen novels whose sale still nets a steady revenue at $1.75—and that it would be unprofitable to use such a property in this way. But I have used such titles only to indicate my idea - Gallegher (which I believe is not in your subscription sets of Davis) could be substituted for Soldiers of Fortune, the Wrong Box for Treasure Island, and so on in the case of Fox, Page and Barrie. The main idea is that the known titles in the series should "carry" the little known or forgotten. That is: from the little known writer you use his best novel, such as Predestined—from the well-known writer you use his more obscure, such as Gallegher.

I apologize for imposing so upon your time, Mr. Scribner. I am merely mourning that so many good or lively books are dead so soon, or only imperfectly kept alive in the cheap and severe impermanency of the A. L. Burt editions.

I am, sir,

Most sincerely,
F. Scott Fitzgerald

Dear Mr. Fitzgerald:

Your letter with its suggestion of a Scribner Library somewhat similar to Boni's Library and the one Doubleday, Page & Company are announcing has reached my desk in the absence of my brother, who is abroad, and a most interesting letter it is. One of our greatest difficulties is to keep even a very good book from falling out of mind and out of sight with the public after a comparatively limited period, which is growing shorter from year to year. Before Grosset & Dunlap, the predecessors of Burt, started their series a number of publishers had low-priced series of their own and we felt at the time that it was more desirable for those who had a large list to continue their own series rather than turn over their books to any other house. However, we were finally compelled to adopt the same course as others when these two series became so strong that we felt we could not do as well by our authors in any other way. Under these conditions I think that now the first low-priced sale of a leading book like your "This Side of Paradise" would do best in the hands of Grosset or Burt provided an adequate guarantee is secured, but their lists of titles have become so numerous and so many volumes are being continually added that even with them as a rule a book soon drops out of sight. Undoubtedly Burt and Grosset & Dunlap do not accomplish what you have in mind and I do think we should be able to make a successful series of our own which would keep certain books longer before the public and which could be made up in some cases of books which Grosset or Burt have already handled or of other books which do not especially appeal to them, for they are having so many titles submitted to them that they are more and more disposed to take up only what are called "high spots", which do not include in many instances novels which should make a better bid for a long sale. And as you say, a uniform and numbered library would have its advantages. We shall go into this more thoroughly and see if we cannot work out some scheme which promises success.

We received a letter from my brother the other day from Paris and a cable from Rome, reporting that he was having a most enjoyable trip.

Very sincerely yours,
[Arthur H. Scribner]

RELATED LETTERS:
The Great Gatsby was written in France, where the Fitzgeralds had gone in mid April 1924, and was revised in Rome later that winter. The following exchanges between author and editor document some of the growth of that masterpiece.

Great Neck [Long Island][April 1924]
Dear Max:

A few words more relative to our conversation this afternoon. While I have every hope & plan of finishing my novel in June you know how those things often come out. And even [if] it takes me ten times that long I cannot let it go out unless it has the very best I'm capable of in it or even as I feel sometimes, something better than I'm capable of. Much of what I wrote last summer was good but it was so interrupted that it was ragged & in approaching it from a new angle I've had to discard a lot ot it—in one case, 18,000 words (part of which will appear in the Mercury as a short story). It is only in the last four months that I've realized how much I've—well, almost <u>deteriorated</u> in the three years since I finished the Beautiful and Damned. The last four months of course I've worked but in the two years—over two years—before that, I produced exactly <u>one</u> play, <u>half a dozen</u> short stories and three or four articles—an average of about <u>one hundred</u> words a day. If I'd spent this time reading or travelling or doing anything—even staying healthy—it'd be different but I spent it uselessly, neither in study nor in contemplation but only in drinking and raising hell generally. If I'd written the B. & D. at the rate of one hundred words a day it would have taken me <u>4 years</u> so you can imagine the moral effect the whole chasm had on me.

What I'm trying to say is just that I'll have to ask you to have patience about the book and trust me that at last, or at least for the 1st time in years, I'm doing the best I can. I've gotten in dozens of bad habits that I'm trying to get rid of

1. Laziness
2. Referring everything to Zelda—a terrible habit, nothing ought to be referred to anybody until it's finished
3. Word consciousness & self-doubt
ect. ect. ect. ect.

I feel I have enormous power in me now, more than I've ever had in a way but it works so fitfully and with so many bogeys because I've <u>talked so much</u> and not lived enough within myself to develop the necessary self reliance. Also I don't know anyone who has used up so much personal experience as I have at 27. Copperfield and Pendennis were written at past forty, while This Side of Paradise was three books & the B. and D. was two. So in my new novel I'm thrown directly on purely creative work—not trashy imaginings as in my stories but the sustained imagination of a sincere yet radiant world. So I tread slowly and carefully & at times in considerable distress. This book will be a consciously artistic achievement & must depend on that as the 1st books did not.

If I ever win the right to any leisure again I will assuredly not waste it as I wasted this past time. Please believe me when I say that now I'm doing the best I can.

Yours ever,
Scott F—

In a letter to Perkins from St. Raphael, France, in August, Fitzgerald wrote: "The novel will be done next week. . . . I think my novel is about the best American novel ever written. It is rough stuff in places, runs only to about 50,000 words & I hope you won't shy at it . . ."

In another letter from St. Raphael, dated 27 October, Fitzgerald was able to report: "Under separate cover I'm sending you my third novel: <u>The Great Gatsby</u>. (I think that at last I've done something really my own), but how good 'my own' is remains to be seen."

November 20, 1924
Dear Scott:

I think you have every kind of right to be proud of this book. It is an extraordinary book, suggestive of all sorts of thoughts and moods. You adopted exactly the right method of telling it, that of employing a narrator who is more of a spectator than an actor: this puts the reader upon a point of observation on a higher level than that on which the characters stand and at a distance that gives perspective. In no other way could your irony have been so immensely effective, nor the reader have been enabled so strongly to feel at times the strangeness of human circumstance in a vast heedless universe. In the eyes of Dr. Eckleberg various readers will see different significances; but their presence gives a superb touch to the whole thing; great unblinking eyes, expressionless, looking down upon the human scene. It's magnificent!

I could go on praising the book and speculating on its various elements and meanings, but points of criticism are more important now. I think you are right in feeling a certain slight sagging in chapters six and seven, and I don't know how to suggest a remedy. I hardly doubt that you will find one and I am only writing to say that I think it does need something to hold up here to the pace set, and ensuing. I have only two actual criticisms:-

One is that among a set of characters marvelously palpable and vital--I would know Tom Buchanan if I met him on the street and would avoid him--Gatsby is somewhat vague. The reader's eyes can never quite focus upon his, his outlines are dim. Now everything about Gatsby is more or less a mystery, i.e. more or less vague, and this may be somewhat of an artistic intention, but I think it is mistaken. Couldn't he be physically described and distinctly as the others, and couldn't you add one or two characteristics like the use of that phrase "old sport",--not verbal, but physical ones, perhaps. I think that for some reason or other a reader--this was true of Mr. Scribner and of Louise--gets an idea that Gatsby is a much older man than he is, although you have the writer say that he is a little older than himself. But this would be avoided if on his first appearance he was seen as vividly as Daisy and Tom are, for instance;- and I do not think your scheme would be impaired if you made him so.

The other point is also about Gatsby: his career must remain mysterious, of course. But in the end you make it pretty clear that his wealth came through his connection with Wolfsheim. You also suggest this much earlier. Now almost all readers numerically are going to be puzzled by his having all this wealth and are going to feel entitled to an explanation. To give a distinct and definite one would be, of course, utterly absurd. It did occur to me though, that you might here and there interpolate some phrases, and possibly incidents, little touches of various kinds, that would suggest that he was in some active way mysteriously engaged. You do have him called on the telephone, but couldn't he be seen once or twice consulting at his

parties with people of some sort of mysterious significance, from the political, the gambling, the sporting world, or whatever it may be. I know I am floundering, but the fact may help you to see what I mean. The total lack of an explanation through so large a part of the story does seem to me a defect;- or not of an explanation, but of the suggestion of an explanation. I wish you were here so I could talk about it to you for then I know I could at least make you understand what I mean. What Gatsby did ought never to be definitely imparted, even if it could be. Whether he was an innocent tool in the hands of somebody else, or to what degree he was this, ought not to be explained. But if some sort of business activity of his were simply adumbrated, it would lend further probability to that part of the story.

There is one other point: in giving deliberately Gatsby's biography when he gives it to the narrator you do depart from the method of the narrative in some degree, for otherwise almost everything is told, and beautifully told, in the regular flow of it,- in the succession of events or in accompaniment with them. But you can't avoid the biography altogether. I thought you might find ways to let the truth of some of his claims like "Oxford" and his army career come out bit by bit in the course of actual narrative. I mention the point anyway for consideration in this interval before I send the proofs.

The general brilliant quality of the book makes me ashamed to make even these criticisms. The

---

'The Great Gatsby' seems to me a remarkably fine book. I was delighted with it, so was Katharine. I am astonished and pleased, and your predictions were, as usual, right. Scott has gone forward spiritually by leaps and bounds. He seems to me to have that super-American thing now that should, within the next fifty years, make American fiction the most important in the world—that full knowledge of life, the complete mastery of his craft (only recently an American acquirement) plus the spiritual quality which is now so purely American. The English have lost it—they don't believe in it anymore. Scott, out of the childish cynicism of extreme youth, has acquired it. That full knowledge of the sardonicism of life but with a mental reservation concerning its sweetness and mystery [and] pathos.

—Author Struthers Burt in a letter to Maxwell Perkins, 17 May 1925

Letter of gratitude by Fitzgerald to CS II, circa 10 June 1926

amount of meaning you get into a sentence, the dimensions and intensity of the impression you make a paragraph carry, are most extraordinary. The manuscript is full of phrases which make a scene blaze with life. If one enjoyed a rapid railroad journey I would compare the number and vividness of pictures your living words suggest, to the living scenes disclosed in that way. It seems in reading a much shorter book than it is, but it carries the mind through a series of experiences that one would think would require a book of three times its length.

The presentation of Tom, his place, Daisy and Jordan, and the unfolding of their characters is unequalled so far as I know. The description of the valley of ashes adjacent to the lovely country, the conversation and the action in Myrtle's apartment, the marvelous catalogue of those who came to Gatsby's house,- these are such things as make a man famous. And all these things, the whole pathetic episode, you have given a place in time and space, for with the help of T. J. Eckleberg and by an occasional glance at the sky, or the sea, or the city, you have imparted a sort of sense of eternity. You once told me you were not a natural writer--my God! You have plainly mastered the craft, of course; but you needed far more than craftsmanship for this.

As ever,
[Maxwell Perkins]

P.S. Why do you ask for a lower royalty on this than you had on the last book where it changed from 15% to 17½% after 20,000 and to 20% after 40,000? Did you do it in order to give us a better margin for advertising? We shall advertise very energetically anyhow and if you stick to the old terms you will sooner overcome the advance. Naturally we should like the ones you suggest better, but there is no reason you should get less on this than you did on the other.

Writing from Rome, Fitzgerald agreed with all of Perkins's criticisms, promised to "perfect" the book in the proofs, and wanted to change the royalty rate to make up for all the money he had been advanced by letting it pay "a sort of interest": "Anyhow I think (for the first time since *The Vegetable* failed) that I'm a wonderful writer and it's your always wonderful letters that help me go on believing in myself" [circa 20 December].

LETTER:
Letter [excerpt] from Fitzgerald to Maxwell Perkins, ca. 1 June 1925.

Fitzgerald quickly squashes a rumor that he may switch publishers.

Dear Max:

This is the second letter I've written you today—I tore my first up when the letter in longhand from New Cannan telling me about Liveright arrived. I'm wiring you today as to that rumor—but also it makes it necessary to tell you something I didn't intend to tell you.

Yesterday arrived a letter from T. R. Smith [editor at Boni and Liveright] asking for my next book—saying nothing against the Scribners but just asking for it: "if I happened to be dissatisfied they would be delighted," ect. ect. I answered at once saying that you were one of my closest friends and that my relations with Scribners had always been so cordial and pleasant that I wouldn't think of changeing publishers. That letter will reach him at about the time this reaches you. I have never had any other communication of any sort with Liveright or any other publisher except the very definite and explicit letter with which I answered their letter yesterday.

So much for that rumor. I am both angry at Tom [Thomas Boyd] who must have been in some way responsible for starting it and depressed at the fact that you could have believed it enough to mention it to me. Rumors start like this—

Smith (a born gossip): "I hear Fitzgerald's book isn't selling. I think we can get it, as he's probably blaming it on Scribners.

The Next Man: It seems Fitzgerald is dissatisfied with Scribners and Liveright is after him.

The Third Man: I hear Fitzgerald has gone over to Liveright.

Now, Max, I have told you many times that you are my publisher, and permanently, as far as one can fling about the word in this too mutable world. If you like I will sign a contract with you immediately for my next three books. The idea of leaving you has never for one single moment entered my head.

First. Tho, as a younger man, I have not always been in sympathy with some of your publishing ideas (which were evolved under the pre-movie, pre-high-literacy-rate conditions of twenty to forty years ago), the personality of you and of Mr. Scribner, the tremendous squareness, courtesy, generosity and open-mindedness I have always met there and, if I may say it, the special consideration you have all had for me and my work, much more than make up the difference.

Second. You know my own idea on the advantage of one publisher who backs you and not your work. And my feeling about uniform books in the matter of house and binding.

Third. The curious advantage to a rather radical writer in being published by what is now an ultra-conservative house.

Fourth (and least need of saying) Do you think I could treat with another publisher while I have a debt, which is both actual and a matter of honor, of over $3000?

If Mr. Scribner has heard this rumor please show him this letter. So much for Mr. Liveright & Co. . . .

With best wishes as always, Max,
Your Friend Scott

Perkins's response (13 June) seems prescient in view of Thomas Wolfe's break with Scribners in 1937: "I would not ever ask you to sign any permanent contract for the simple reason that it might be right for you sometime to change publishers, and while this would be a tragedy to me, I should not be so small as to stand in the way on personal grounds."

RELATED LETTERS:
Letter from Maxwell Perkins to Fitzgerald, 4 March 1926; letter from Fitzgerald in reply, [March 1926], from the French Riviera.

Dear Scott:

I just got your letter today asking for an income tax blank. I enclose one herewith. They issued corrections, due to the new law, in red, and we have had these pasted upon the blank, which will make it easier for you.

As for the sale of "All the Sad Young Men" which only came out last Friday, February 26th, we are already watching it very closely for reprinting. We have printed 10,100, and we have only about 300 on hand now, although of course many that are in the stores have not been sold. I feel no hesitancy in saying that you can count absolutely on a sale of 12,000, and the truth is the prospects are excellent. "The Great Gatsby" continues to be successful, markedly so.

I asked Arthur Train [lawyer and Scribner author] about an American who murders another American in France. He is treated as though he were a Frenchman. He is taken in charge by the French police and tried in the French courts by a French judge and jury. I hope this fact won't upset some plan you had for the novel. I asked Arthur if there were any possible way in which there might be some form of American intervention--an envoy of justice, or something, and he said only in case the murderer were in the diplomatic service. Otherwise, he would have the same status as a Frenchman.

I think "Our Type" is the best title. Would "Our Kind" be better? It was used by Louise [Perkins's wife] on a little one-act play, but that would make no difference.

As for Hemingway, whom I enjoyed very much, we have contracted to publish "Torrents of Spring" and the novel [*The Sun Also Rises*]. He was willing to give us options on other books, but I never thought well of that way of doing:--if a man does not like us after we have published two of his books, he ought not to be compelled to publish through us, and we do not want to publish for anyone who is not square enough to recognize that what we have done is good, if it is, and to give us the advantage over anybody else. If a writer can get better terms from another publisher on his third or fourth book, it is only fair that he can also demand better terms of us. The relations you have with an author cannot be satisfactory if they are absolutely cut and dried business relations, anyhow. I am extremely grateful to you for intervening about Hemingway. He is a most interesting chap about his bull fights and boxing. His admirable story, "Fifty Grand" was too long to be got into the magazine, and it has been declined by Colliers and the Post,- although Lorimer spoke highly of it. Liberty could not use it because of its length. I do not know exactly what to do with it now. I believe I could sell it to College Humor, but I do not know whether he would like that.

I think your idea about selections from your books of stories primarily for publication in England, is an excellent one; and I do not think there would be much difficulty in bringing it about. Curtis Brown, the agent who has placed your stories for us, could bring it about and would manage it well. Collins would not be in any position to make difficulties because he has sacrificed his opportunity by declining "Gatsby". The case is not the same as it was with Ring Lardner, where the publishers who had his books had not actually declined anything by him. There is no actual stipulation in the contracts by which you can acquire the rights to books, but it is a right that anybody would dispute in the case of books which are not active and which have not had much success. We could consult Curtis Brown for you confidentially, whenever you want. He does get a 10% commission, and we do take a 10% commission when the payment is made in your behalf.

I am mighty glad Zelda is better, I am getting off this series of facts as quickly as possible on account of the income tax, etc., but I will write you a <u>letter</u> soon.

As ever yours,
[Maxwell Perkins]

P.S. Tom Boyd has a job on the Atlanta Georgian,- I guess a pretty good job. He said he was not going to write another book right away. I agree with you about his power of radiocination, quite, but I should not have thought that he was lacking in emotion, and I thought there was great emotion implied throughout "Samuel Drummond" as well as that sensitiveness to the external world. But the total sale was only about five thousand copies.

Dear Max:

Thanks very much for your nice letter & the income blank. I'm delighted about the short story book. In fact with the play [of *The Great Gatsby*] going well & my new novel growing absorbing & with our being back in a nice villa on my beloved Rivierra (between Cannes and Nice) I'm happier than I've been for years. Its one of those strange, precious and all too transitory moments when everything in one's life seems to be going well.

Thanks for the Arthur Train legal advice.

I'm glad you got Hemmingway- I saw him for a day in Paris on his return & he thought you were great. I've brought you two successes (Ring & Tom Boyd) and two failures (Biggs [John Biggs] & Woodward Boyd)- Ernest will decide whether my opinions are more of a hindrance or a help.

Why not try College Humor for his story. They published one thing of mine.

Poor Tom Boyd! First I was off him for his boneheadedness. Now I'm sorry for him.

Your Friend Scott

I am out of debt to you for the first time in four years. . . .

Perkins's guarantee was good: sales of All the Sad Young Men *exceeded fifteen thousand. "Our Type" was a tentative, early title for what became* Tender Is the Night. *Nothing ever developed of Fitzgerald's plan for an English publication of his selected stories. Hemingway's story, "Fifty Grand," was not offered to* College Humor, *though it was rejected by other magazines before* The Atlantic Monthly *accepted it in 1927—after the success of* The Sun Also Rises—*paying Hemingway $350, the most he had yet earned for a short story.*

LETTER:
Letter from Maxwell Perkins to Fitzgerald, 12 April 1929.

Appreciative of Fitzgerald's tips regarding books by other authors that Scribners should attempt to acquire, Perkins offers Fitzgerald encouragement to finish his own book, Tender Is the Night, *which he had conceived in 1925 and would not finish until 1933.*

Dear Scott:

I was certainly glad to get a letter from you and I immediately wrote Madeline Boyd to see if she could get through Bradley, an option on the book about the escapes of aviators. The Chamson has got beautiful reviews, but so far has not sold much;- but we are bringing out "Roux le Bandit" in the fall, and shall follow it by the other. I think we shall get the right results in the end. Don't think that I do not--or that we do not--realize how much you have done for us apart from your own books. We fully appreciate it as a very great thing for us.- But the book we really want to publish is your book.

New $5000 Prize Contest Begins

SCRIBNER'S

NOVEMBER

ECHOES OF THE JAZZ AGE
by F. Scott Fitzgerald

& Features by Will Irwin, James Gould Cozzens, Owen Francis, Christian Gauss, Margaret Mead, etc.

Cover of November 1931 Scribner's Magazine showing Fitzgerald's obituary for the Jazz Age as its lead article. In a letter to Perkins from Lausanne, Switzerland, in May 1931, Fitzgerald had written: "The Jazz Age is dead. If Mark Sullivan is going on you might tell him I claim credit for naming it+ that it extended from the suppression of the riots on May Day 1919 to the crash of the stock market in 1929—almost exactly one decade." Scribners was in the process of publishing Sullivan's multivolume survey of the American scene, Our Times: The United States, 1900–1925; *the final volume would cover the Twenties.*

As for the last sentence of your letter [Fitzgerald's reference to his own whining], it ought not to have been written. You never did it so far as I know. You have always been to me the very model of courage.

Ever yours,
[Maxwell Perkins]

LETTER:
Letter [excerpt] from Thomas Wolfe to Maxwell Perkins, 1 July 1930, from Paris.

CONFIDENTIAL

March 19, 1934

Memorandum for Sales Department
from Mr. Charles Scribner

The arrival of the manuscript of Fitzgerald's "This Side of Paradise" will never be forgotten here. It was read by our editors with rising excitement. Its vitality, its astonishing display of varied talent inspired us all. We felt that its author was a man with genius in him, and it was a great disappointment to us that certain turns of fortune interrupted his production of novels. For instance, he was diverted to playwriting and lost a couple of years to the novel over "The Vegetable". But he followed this immediately with an almost perfect book, "The Great Gatsby" which nobody has ever forgotten. Thereafter circumstances put the author in a position where his financial requirement was so heavy as to force him to produce short story after story after story, under the most exhausting conditions. But even so, he at last finished "Tender Is the Night". My belief that Scott Fitzgerald has as magnificent a talent as a novelist as has appeared in the last quarter of a century, is fully confirmed by this brilliant, moving story;- and the following comments sent to him upon its appearance in serial form, and to the publishers, seem to support this view.

Charles Scribner

Draft of a confidential memo by CS III to prepare the Scribner sales department for the book publication of Fitzgerald's Tender Is the Night, *nearing the end of its serialization in* Scribner's Magazine

Wolfe's description of the first meeting between these two Scribner authors. Both have started work on new novels—Fitzgerald on Tender Is the Night, *Wolfe on* Of Time and the River—*neither of which will be finished for several years.*

Dear Mr. Perkins: I have a long letter under way to you, but I shall probably not send it until I have left Paris. The main news is that I have been at work for several weeks, and have worked every day except last Sunday, when I met Scott Fitzger-ald for the first time. He called me up at my hotel and I went out to his apartment for lunch: we spent the rest of the afternoon together talking and climbing—a good deal of both—and I finally left him at the Ritz Bar. He was getting ready to go back to Switzerland where he has been for several weeks, and had come up to close up his apartment and take his little girl back with him. He told me that Mrs. Fitzgerald has been very sick—a bad nervous breakdown—and he has her in a sanitarium at Geneva. He spoke of his new book and said he was working on it: he was very friendly and generous, and I liked him, and think he has a great deal of talent, and I hope he gets that book done soon. I think we got along very well—we had quite an argument about America: I said we were homesick people, and belonged to the earth and land we came from as much or more as any country I knew about—he said we were not, that we were not a country, that he had no feeling for the land he came from. "Nevertheless," as Galileo said, "it moves." We do, and they are all homesick or past having any feeling about anything. . . .

Faithfully yours,
Tom Wolfe

RELATED LETTERS:
Letter from Fitzgerald to Maxwell Perkins, 7 February 1934; letter from Perkins in reply, 9 February 1934.

Continuing a conversation he had apparently begun the previous night with Perkins while in New York working on the serial and book versions of Tender Is the Night, *Fitzgerald exhorts Scribners to take a "radical step" with* Scribner's Magazine: *reduce its emphasis on public affairs issues and make it primarily a vehicle for serializing several novels or long pieces of fiction at the same time.*

Dear Max:

The fear of being dependent again on the Saturday Evening Post promoted this idea and led me to a consideration of publishing in general; and, from that, the notion developed in the half-baked way that I told you. I began by thinking of the publishing devices of the early 18th century, with special reference to Dickens' Household Words.

Now, just as Scribner's magazine has changed its character several times between being primarily a fiction magazine, or primarily an Open Forum, so there is no reason in its tradition why it should not consider a radical step. I do not underestimate the value of the present Scribner's in the humanitarian way, but nowadays ventures must be self-sustaining, and competing journals can also muster the same quantity and quality of uneasy liberal thinking—viz Harper's and Atlantic Monthly. This innovationary policy has, of course, been exemplified in your regime, not only by encouraging the short novels, or novelettes, but also in this new departure about long novels. Pursuing this policy to its logical end, I am inclined to think that sooner or later you will be faced with the decision of choosing (temporarily

at least) between being a magazine of fiction or being a magazine of opinion, and that the opinions eventually must be yours. I am communist enough to distrust the idea of an "Open Forum," which usually means a forum in which a Roman citizen can appear and talk as much as he wants within the range of Roman opinion—in despite of the apparent radicalism of your publishing John Strachey.

By and large, I see the problems that confront you, yet I wonder whether you or I, or any of us, can really print a synthesis of opinions in the air as a policy; and in the same breath, I reiterate that in all common sense this tack will sooner or later amount to a compromise that like all compromises, will have neither force nor vitality. The other idea, on the contrary, has the following advantages: from the editorial point of view it would give you the opportunity of going into a specialization that, substituted for the somewhat vague economic views (and here I refer to the whole staff of Scribner's publishing house, from Charles [CS III] to the printer's devil, indeed, to all of us in so far as we are associated with you, with the accumulated taste embodied in the publishing house) would be a line for which you are perhaps better equipped than anybody in America.

A second argument in favor of the idea is that you have at your disposal almost anybody that you want. When you say, as you did the other night, that you cannot count on writers' deliver-

---

After all, Max, I am a plodder. One time I had a talk with Ernest Hemingway, and I told him, against all the logic that was then current, that I was the tortoise and he was the hare, and that's the truth of the matter, that everything that I have ever attained has been through long and persistent struggle while it is Ernest who has a touch of genius which enables him to bring off extraordinary things with facility. I have no facility. I have a facility for being cheap, if I wanted to indulge that. I can do cheap things. I changed Clark Gable's act at the moving picture theatre here the other day. I can do that kind of thing as quickly as anybody but when I decided to be a serious man, I tried to struggle over every point until I have made myself into a slow moving Behemoth (if that is the correct spelling), and so there I am for the rest of my life.

—F. Scott Fitzgerald in a letter to Maxwell Perkins, 4 March 1934

ing on time, God knows I understand, but you have so many good young writers, and I am counting on the idea attracting so many others who otherwise cannot publish except in book form. I think your difficulties, once the idea was launched, would be on the contrary, a question of deciding betwixt good things offered.

My idea, as I told you, would be a cover, which would say, for example: First part of Hemingway, Second part of Fleming, Third part of Fitzgerald, Fourth part of Wolfe. You would be dealing with two or three established authors and perhaps one newcomer that you happened to like, and the money that you paid out would serve to keep those people going. In these days any author would rather have a modest fee for his serial than not to serialize at all. In a sense, they would develop a feeling that they were partners in a corporate enterprise and I think that I can speak for many of us when I say that we would welcome the idea of a forum which is as open for long fiction as it is for the most casual opinionated shreds of political opinion.

A fourth point: while I don't know the mechanics of the magazine's make-up, this policy should not preclude the inclusion of a certain number of opinionated articles upon public affairs, used almost as editorials. From your experience you must have seen that out of a half dozen articles in Scribner's, or for that matter in any other quality magazine, about six a year have the value of what the Victorians would call essays and the rest is merely timely journalism, moribund almost with its appearance; after a few months how many of such articles are of more literary or humanitarian importance than the spreads in Hearst's Sunday supplement? And, practically, if the consumer can get the New York Sunday Times Book Review and Magazine Section what distinction can he make between that and a quality magazine except for the name and the colored jacket?

As I mentioned last night almost all the editorial magazine successes have depended on young men, if I can flatter you and Charles Scribner, me, Ernest, Tom Wolfe, as being young men. Crowninshield [Frank Crowninshield, editor of Vanity Fair] grows old and [Harold] Ross comes up with the New Yorker; The Literary Digest grows old and Time comes along; Lorimer [George Horace Lorimer, editor of The Saturday Evening Post], who has been for a long time my bread, Scribner's being considered the meat of my survival) is growing old, and then that bread will inevitably go stale.

It is not beyond the limits of imagination to suppose that this condition, in which only the choices of The Book of the Month get across big, may be a permanent condition. It is conceivable that the local book store, except as represented by such as yours and Brentano's, will become as obsolete as the silent picture. For one thing the chain-store buying and the job-lot-buying department stores seem to condemn the independent book stores to the situation that they have reached in Baltimore where, considering the outlay involved, they can only be compared to the fallow antique shops. There is also the library question, which, in a socializing world, will become bigger and bigger.

In resume, let me line up the elements for and against the idea:

Present procedure: Dignified presentation of a, perhaps, good book with sale of 3,000 copies, and not much profit to anybody.

Attitude toward the author's surrendering dramatic and movie rights correct in the 90's when conditions were different but now archaic.

Futility of issuing books that either from inefficiency in writing or being-over-the-heads-of-the-crowd, clutter up the remnants counter. Essentially this is not a service to writers as was the case in the past. Take for example, my recommendation to you, rather half-hearted, of Woodward Boyd's "The Love Legend." Why the hell should she have the right to publish a poor book? As things tighten up I think that more harm is done by encouraging inefficient amateurs than would be done if they were compelled to go through a certain professional apprenticeship. The one man or woman aspirant out of a hundred who has some quality of genius is another matter, but those who show "promise" had probably better be relegated immediately to doing other things in the world, or else working on their own guts for professional advancement, rather than be coddled along on the basis that they may eventually make a fortune for themselves and everybody concerned.

Therefore, a weariness in the reviewers, and, except for the presentation, no realistic cooperation.

Now to consider conditions as they are: there is first, the selection by the book leagues, whether we like it or not; there is the reprinting of either quality stuff in the Modern Library or drug-store stuff in the reprint houses, with the publishers frankly taking a share in other rights, specifically including movie rights.

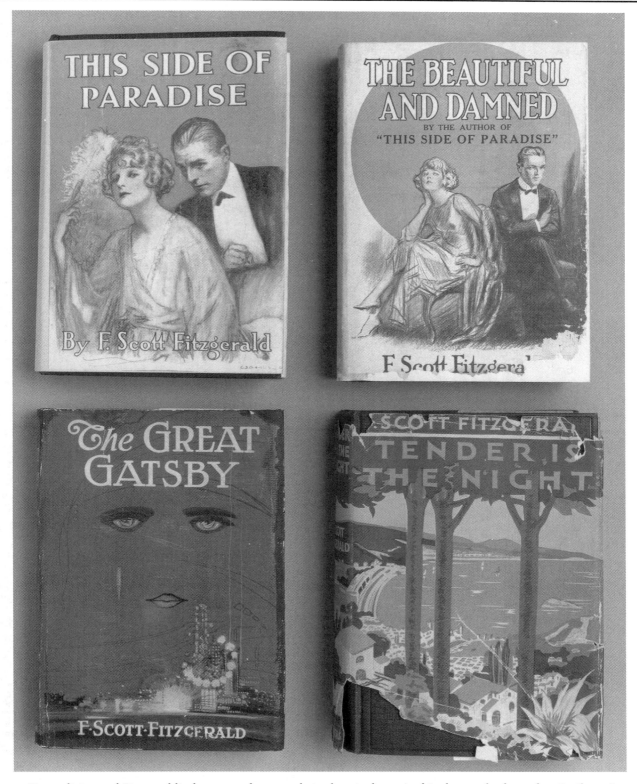

First editions of Fitzgerald's four complete novels in dust jackets. Archival records show that Scribners' advertising expenses were $2,308.58 for This Side of Paradise, *$11,675.88 for* The Beautiful and Damned, *$5,911.73 for* The Great Gatsby, *and $5,083.19 for* Tender Is the Night. *The huge jump in promotion for* The Beautiful and Damned *was the result of Maxwell Perkins's promise to "make a big campaign all around" for the second novel after Fitzgerald criticized Scribners' small-scale effort on his surprisingly popular first book.*

Now why shouldn't incipient writers have to prove themselves? Why shouldn't an issue of a book between boards be contingent upon the ability of the work to arouse interest? And isn't a magazine printing a cheaper and more advantageous test all around?

If this comes out at the proper end of the horn as the note I intended to blow when I blew, it reduces itself to the following propositions:

1. That Scribner's is much better equipped now to handle fiction, travel, etc. than to handle politics.

2. That, unless you have some big axe to grind, politics are of only transitory interest.

3. That traditionalism is, in this case, a policy to which one can fairly attach the odium of archaism, because just as an author's main purpose is "to make you see," so a magazine's principle purpose is to be read.

4. Perhaps I am the proverbial fool rushing in, and if it so appears to you simply forget the whole suggestion. However, I have a hunch that within a year somebody will adopt such a policy. And may I reiterate, that the idea was suggested originally by a policy which you have already inaugurated, and that this is simply a radical urge to hasten it toward what I think is an inevitable outcome, an effort to meet the entertainment business on its own predetermined grounds.

Ever yours,
F Scott Fitzgerald

Dear Scott:

I am enclosing your royalty report.

I won't say much, since I mean to see you next week, but in any event, I think you ought to be mighty near out of your economic difficulties. For instance, I believe that after the serialization of "Tender Is the Night" you could go to a popular magazine and get an advance of ten thousand dollars on a large price for such a serial as you spoke of. That could carry you through until the serial was done, and by that time you ought to be getting money for a movie sale. Surely this is not an unreasonable statement.

There are two other points I might speak of. It is not archaic to refrain from sharing in the author's picture rights. It is the other way round. Most publishers used to share. The Author's League made an issue of it, and most of them now do not share. All the organizations in the interests of authors have opposed the sale of rights, and I do not think it is openly done now, or only in special circumstances.

I agree with ever so much of what you say about magazine publishing,- particularly that of the economic and political article of the open forum type. When we changed the magazine it was intended to be a fiction and sort of human document magazine. It was supposed to contain imaginative and emotional literature. I'll show you the outline of policy I drew up for it, some day. But then the depression settled down and deepened and deepened, and people thought of nothing else, and it simply seemed impossible not to respond and to deal with it.- Particularly since when we did it, we could see the response to a particular economic or political article in the newsstands, immediately. You simply could not ignore the depression, and it became so enormously expensive to get subscriptions that the newsstand sale increased in importance. It was like the war. Nobody would read anything much except about the war while it was going on. Collier's Weekly was doing wonderfully before the war, and the editor of it refused for a long time to take any interest in the war, having done so well with the previous policy. He simply killed the magazine completely. The war could not be ignored, and the depression could not.

Another thing is that most of what you say is based on the assumption that there is going to be a permanent depression. You say that the bookstores are killed off, and it does look as if they might be. But it is only eighteen months since it was said that the railroads were done for and Henry Ford remarked that if we did not have them, we would not think of building them. Now the railroads are doing astonishingly, and are thought to be the best class of investment, which

> Feel awfully about Scott. I tried to write him (wrote him several times) to cheer him up but he seems to almost take a pride in his shamelessness of defeat. The Esquire pieces ["The Crack-Up" articles] seem to me to be so miserable. . . . It was a terrible thing for him to love youth so much that he jumped straight from youth to senility without going through manhood. The minute he felt youth going he was frightened again and thought there was nothing between youth and age. But it is so damned easy to criticize our friends and I shouldn't write this. I wish we could help him.
>
> —Ernest Hemingway in a letter to Maxwell Perkins, [7 February 1936]

may be temporary, but may not be. Before the depression, books were doing spendidly.

Ever yours,
[Maxwell Perkins]

Fitzgerald's suggestions were not tried. Scribner's Magazine continued to lose money, was sold in 1938, and died the following year.

LETTER:

Letter by Marjorie Kinnan Rawlings to Maxwell Perkins, 25 October [1936], about her first meeting with F. Scott Fitzgerald.

In July 1936 Fitzgerald broke his clavicle while diving and then was laid up for weeks with arthritis in his shoulder. Throughout the fall he recuperated at the Grove Park Inn in Asheville, North Carolina, while his wife was receiving treatment in a nearby sanitarium. Earlier in the year, he had published in Esquire *a series of confessional articles revealing his feelings of despair and inability to write, and Hemingway's reference to him as "wrecked" in his story "The Snows of Kilimanjaro" (published in* Esquire *in August) had further damaged his morale. In September the* New York Post *published an article called "The Other Side of Paradise," describing Fitzgerald as a defeated has-been. Rawlings was working hard on* The Yearling *in a mountain cabin near Banner Elk, North Carolina, when Perkins wrote her: "Are you near Asheville? If you are, I should like to have Scott Fitzgerald see you, for I think you would do him a great deal of good. He is in a very defeatist state of mind, has been for years . . ." (24 September). Only eighty-five miles away, Rawlings agreed to try.*

Dear Max:

I had a strange answer from Scott Fitzgerald, refusing my invitation to drive to the Pisgah Forest Pottery, but saying with what I could only take as sincerity, that he wanted to meet me and hoped I could make him a stop when I did go through Asheville. So Friday afternoon late I wired him that I'd be in Asheville at seven that night, and I barged along. I ran into the most beastly driving, storms and detours and those vicious mountain roads, and finally, thick fog for the last thirty miles into Asheville. I was all but babbling by the time I got in, alone, and I thought I'd have to climb in bed beside Fitzgerald and send for another psychiatrist. So it was almost with relief that first his nurse's voice, and then his own, very faint, informed me that his arthritis had been bad

and he had run a high temperature all day and couldn't see me. He was doubtful of his health the next day and I was very dubious about pressing the matter. But again I felt sure he really did care about a meeting. So the next morning I wrote him a very nice long note and said he needn't get out of bed if he felt badly but wanted a bit of chat, and I went along to the potter's and took care of my business there, came back to Asheville and telephoned him again at one o'clock. Something in the note must have hit right, for when he found I hadn't had luncheon, he insisted on my coming right over and having it with him in his room.

Max, we had a perfectly delightful time. Far from being depressing, I enjoyed him thoroughly, and I'm sure he enjoyed it as much. He was nervous as a cat, but had not been drinking—had had his nurse put his liquor away. We had only sherry and a table wine, and talked our head off. His reaction to the N.Y. Post story had been to go to New York and kill the German Jew, Mok, until he decided that would be a silly gesture with one arm disabled. He was terribly hurt about it, of course, for he had listened to a sob story from Mok, to let him in at all, and had responded to a lot of things the man told him—possibly spurious—about his own maladjusted wife, by talking more freely than he should have done. But he has taken the thing very gracefully and is not unduly bitter or upset about it. He was also more forgiving and reasonable than I think he should have been, about Hemingway's unnecessary crack at him in "The Snows of Kilimanjaro." We agreed that it was a part of Hemingway's own sadistic maladjustment, which makes him go around knocking people down. Scott said that Hemingway had written him very violently, damning him for his revealing self-searchings in Esquire, and Scott expressed the idea that it was just as legitimate to get one's grievances against life off the chest that way, as by giving an upper-cut to some harmless weakling. He resented Hemingway's calling him "ruined", and from other things he said, it was plain to me that he does not himself consider himself "ruined", by a long shot.

I am firmly convinced that the man is all right. I know just what his state of mind has been. The same kind of panic hits anyone like me, with no one dependent on me. With an ill and expensive wife, a child brought up to luxury, and then one thing after another going wrong—all on top of the inevitable revulsion, almost, against writing—"the times", as Hemingway wrote me, "when you can't do it"—it was natural enough for him to go into a very black mood. It lasted longer and he publicized it more, than with most of us—I am always ashamed to let anyone know about mine—but I should lay a heavy wager that he's safely on the way out.

We disagreed heartily about many things, of course. Principally as to what we expect of life. I expect the crest of the wave to have a consequent and inevitable trough, and whenever I'm at the bottom, I know there will be an up-turn sooner and later. Then when I'm at the top, I don't expect it to last indefinitely—he said that he did!—but know there will have to be less pleasant things coming along sooner or later.

He said, "You're not as much of an egotist as I am." Then he said and more or less correctly, too, that a writer almost had to be an egotist, to the point of megolomania, because everything was filtered through his own universe.

His point of view lets him in for much desperate unhappiness and disillusion, because he simply cannot expect the consistent perfection and magnificence of life that he does, frankly, expect. But as a writer, except for the times such as this one has been, when his misery holds him up too long, his masochism will not interfere with his work. We talked from a little after one, until five-thirty, when his nurse came back and fussed about his not resting, but we never reached talk of our plans for the future in any detail. He did say that he had a plan—and he spoke with every sign of the secret pleasure that is an indication of work in the brewing.

He spoke of the autobiographical thing, but said he could not do it with most of the people alive. That he could only do it now in a pleasant way, and it wouldn't be any fun without a little malice.

I wrote him that I felt he had a great gift as a social historian, and I do—that he had Thackeray's feeling for a period, but a finer literary style than Thackeray's, and that I thought he would some day do something very stirring as a record of our confused generation.

I feel I had no tangible help for him—he is in no truly desperate need of help—and our points of view are very different—but there is a most helpful stimulation in talk between two people who are trying to do something of the same thing—a stimulation I miss and do not have enough of, at Cross Creek. And I am sure that stimulation was good for him. I may be able to have another visit with him when I return to Pisgah Forest in a couple of weeks, if the dishes I ordered are ready before I drive home. He may go to a quiet place on one of the Florida coasts, this winter, and if he does, we shall have some good talks.

So certainly I can report that the contact was very pleasant. And I do not think you need to worry about him, physically or psychologically. He has thrown himself on the floor and shrieked himself black in the face and pounded his heels—as lots of us do in one way or another—but when it's over, he'll go back to his building blocks again. Have you ever felt what I call the cosmic despair? It's no joke. And if you slip a little too deep in it, as he did, it's one devilish job getting out again. But he's well on the way out and I think deserves lots of credit for getting himself so well in hand again. There will perhaps be relapses, but I don't think he feels the abyss so inescapably under him.

Marjorie

When we had our sherry, we lifted our glasses, as you might know, "To Max."

Perkins was grateful for her effort: " . . . thank you deeply for your fine long letter about Scott. I have known him so long, and have liked him so much that his welfare is very much a personal matter with me too. I would do anything to see him recover himself" [5 November].

LETTER:
Letter from Fitzgerald to Maxwell Perkins, 23 April 1938, written from the Garden of Allah Hotel, Hollywood. Marked "Personal and Confidential."

Working in Hollywood for M-G-M on various film scripts, Fitzgerald has learned that his first book is now out of print. With typical literary comment, he mentions other Scribner authors: Marjorie Kinnan Rawlings, Ernest Hemingway, and Thomas Wolfe (who had left Scribners for Harper & Bros.).

Dear Max:

I got both your letters and appreciate them and their fullness, as I feel very much the Californian at the moment and, consequently, out of touch with New York.

The Marjorie Rawlings' book [*The Yearling*] fascinated me. I thought it was even better than "South Moon Under" and I envy her the ease with which she does action scenes, such as the tremendously complicated hunt sequence, which I would have to stake off in advance and which would probably turn out to be a stilted business in the end.

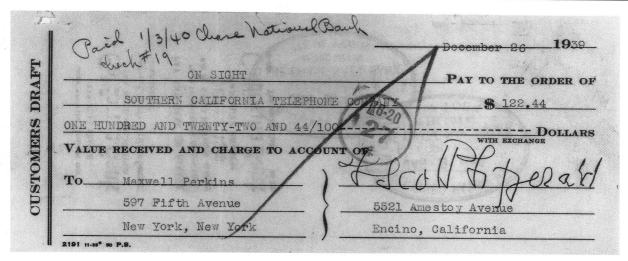

Drawing on his Scribner account, Fitzgerald used this bank draft to pay an overdue telephone bill.

Hers just simply flows; the characters keep thinking, talking, feeling and don't stop, and you think and talk and feel with them.

As to Ernest, I was fascinated by what you told me about the play [*The Fifth Column*], touched that he remembered me in his premonitory last word, and fascinated, as always, by the man's Byronic intensity. The Los Angeles Times printed a couple of his articles, but none the last three days, and I keep hoping a stray Krupp shell hasn't knocked off our currently most valuable citizen.

In the mail yesterday came a letter from that exquisitely tactful co-worker of yours, Whitney Darrow [Scribner business manager], or Darrow Whitney, or whatever his name is. I've never had much love for the man since he insisted on selling "This Side of Paradise" for a dollar fifty, and cost me around five thousand dollars; nor do I love him more when, as it happened the other day, I went into a house and saw someone reading the Modern Library's "Great Modern Short Stories" with a poor piece of mine called "Act Your Age" side by side with Conrad's "Youth," Ernest's "Killers" because Whitney Darrow was jealous of a copyright.

His letter informs me that "This Side of Paradise" is now out of print. I am not surprised after eighteen years (looking it over, I think it is now one of the funniest books since "Dorian Gray" in its utter spuriousness—and then, here and there, I find a page that is very real and living), but I know to the younger generation it is a pretty remote business, reading about the battles that engrossed us then and the things that were startling. To hold them I would have to put in a couple of abortions to give it color (and probably would if I was that age and writing it

again). However, I'd like to know what "out of print" means. Does it mean that I can make my own arrangements about it? That is, if any publisher was interested in reprinting it, could I go ahead, or would it immediately become a valuable property to Whitney again?

I once had an idea of getting Bennett Cerf to publish it in the Modern Library, with a new preface. But also I note in your letter a suggestion of publishing an omnibus book with "Paradise," "Gatsby" and "Tender." How remote is that idea, and why must we forget it? If I am to be out here two years longer, as seems probable, it certainly isn't advisable to let my name sink so out of sight as it did between "Gatsby" and "Tender," especially as I now will not be writing even the Saturday Evening Post stories.

I have again gone back to the idea of expanding the stories about Phillippe, the Dark Ages knight, but when I will find time for that, I don't know, as this amazing business has a way of whizzing you along at a terrific speed and then letting you wait in a dispirited, half-cocked mood when you don't feel like undertaking anything else, while it makes up its mind. It is a strange conglomeration of a few excellent over-tired men making pictures, and as dismal a crowd of fakes and hacks at the bottom as you can imagine. The consequence is that every other man is a charlatan, nobody trusts anybody else, and an infinite amount of time is wasted from lack of confidence.

Relations have always been so pleasant, not only with you but with Harold [Ober, his literary agent] and Lorimer's Saturday Evening Post, that even working with the pleasantest people in the industry,

Eddie Knopf and Hunt Stromberg, I feel this lack of confidence. . . .

I still feel in the dark about Tom Wolfe, rather frightened for him; I cannot quite see him going it alone, but neither can I see your sacrificing yourself in that constant struggle. What a time you've had with your sons, Max—Ernest gone to Spain, me gone to Hollywood, Tom Wolfe reverting to an artistic hill-billy.

Do let me know about "This Side of Paradise." Whitney Darrow's, or Darrow Whitney's letter was so subtly disagreeable that I felt he took rather personal pleasure in the book being out of print. It was all about buying up some second-hand copies. You might tell him to do so if he thinks best. I have a copy somewhere, but I'd like a couple extras.

Affectionately always,
Scott

Perkins wrote back (24 May) that publishing the three novels in one "omnibus" volume now, "in as deep a depression as we ever saw," would waste its possibilities:

> What's more, I think it is a little too soon anyway. There comes a time, and it applies somewhat now to both "Paradise" and "Gatsby," when the past gets a kind of romantic glamour. We have not yet reached that with "Tender Is the Night" and not to such a degree as we shall later even with "Paradise" I think. But unless we think there never will be good times again—barring a war there will be better times than ever, I believe—we ought to wait for them.

The book finally appeared in 1953. This Side of Paradise *was not reprinted by Scribners until 1951 and never appeared in the Modern Library.*

LETTER:
Last letter from Fitzgerald to Maxwell Perkins, 13 December 1940, from Hollywood.

Working well on his Hollywood novel, Fitzgerald reveals himself to be, as always, very much concerned with contemporary writers, their work, and their influences.

Dear Max:

Thanks for your letter. The novel progresses—in fact progresses fast. I'm not going to stop now till I finish a first draft which will be sometime after the 15th of January. However, let's pretend that it doesn't exist until it's closer to completion. We don't want it to become—"a legend before it is written" which is what I believe Wheelock [Scribner editor John Hall Wheelock] said about "Tender Is the Night". Meanwhile will you send me back the chapters I sent you as they are all invalid now, must be completely rewritten etc. The essential idea is the same and it is still, as far as I can hope, a secret.

Bud Shulberg, a very nice, clever kid out here is publishing a Hollywood novel with Random House in January [*What Makes Sammy Run?*]. It's not bad but it doesn't cut into my material at all. I've read Ernest's novel [*For Whom the Bell Tolls*] and most of Tom Wolfe's [*You Can't Go Home Again*] and have been doing a lot of ruminating as to what this whole profession is about. Tom Wolfe's failure to really explain why you and he parted mars his book but there are great things in it. The portraits of the Jacks (who are they?) Emily Vanderbilt are magnificent.

No one points out how Saroyan has been influenced by Franz Kafka. Kafka was an extraordinary Czechoslovakian Jew who died in '36. He will never have a wide public but "The Trial" and "America" are two books that writers are never able to forget.

This is the first day off I have taken for many months and I just wanted to tell you the book is coming along and that comparatively speaking all is well.

Ever your friend,
Scott

P.S. How much will you sell the plates of "This Side of Paradise" for? I think it has a chance for a new life.

Fitzgerald died suddenly eight days later from a heart attack. His unfinished novel was published by Scribners as The Last Tycoon *on 27 October 1941.*

> Thanks also for Scott's "Last Tycoon". I can't feel that the book would have been a triumph for him, but the notes are fascinating. As so often with him, the means by which he strove to arrive were more significant than the destination. The exception, of course, is "Gatsby" which I just re-read before my operation. I believe it's the best piece of writing we have produced between the wars.
>
> —Novelist James Boyd in a letter to Maxwell Perkins, 8 February 1942

Edward W. Bok (1863–1930)

Edward W. Bok

Bok is best known for his 1920s best-seller, *The Americanization of Edward Bok,* which was published by Scribners on the fiftieth anniversary of his immigration to the United States from the Netherlands at the age of six, and for his development and guidance of the *Ladies' Home Journal* as its seminal editor (1889–1919). He quit school at thirteen to become an office boy at the Western Union Telegraph Company, joined publisher Henry Holt and Company as a stenographer in 1882, and came to Scribners in 1884, where he worked first as a stenographer and later as the director of advertising for *Scribner's Magazine.* Throughout these years—on his own time—he worked on literary business projects, including the establishment in 1886 of the Bok Syndicate Press, whose feature articles attracted 137 subscriber newspapers and the attention of Cyrus H. K. Curtis, publisher of the Philadelphia-based *LHJ.* When Bok began as the magazine's editor, its paid circulation was 440,000; by February 1903 it had reached one million, the first American magazine to achieve that goal. During his long tenure he introduced innovative features on health and home geared to the American woman, maintained a high standard in the magazine's literary material, and promoted or originated discussion-provoking reforms. In his retirement Bok served charitable and cultural causes and offered a $100,000 prize, the American Peace Award (1923), for "the best practicable plan by which the United States may cooperate with other nations to achieve and preserve the peace of the world."

Scribner Books by Bok

1920	*The Americanization of Edward Bok: The Autobiography of a Dutch Boy Fifty Years After*
1921	*A Dutch Boy Fifty Years After,* edited, with an introduction, by John Louis Haney
1922	*Two Persons: An Incident and an Epilogue*
1923	*A Man from Maine*
1924	*The Boy Who Followed Ben Franklin,* edited, with an introduction, by John Louis Haney
1924–1925	Great Hollanders series edited by Bok:

Erasmus by J. Huizinga (1924)

William the Silent by Frederic Harrison (1924)

Vondel by A. J. Barnouw (1925)

1925   *Twice Thirty: Some Short and Simple Annals of the Road*

1926   *Dollars Only*

America, Give Me a Chance!, illustrated by Worth Brehm

1928   *Perhaps I Am*

REMINISCENCE:
Edward W. Bok, *The Americanization of Edward Bok* (New York: Scribners, 1920), pp. 108–112.

In his autobiography Bok describes—in the third person—how he joined Scribners, what his duties were, and what he learned from his five-year apprenticeship there in the publishing trade.

Edward had been in the employ of Henry Holt and Company as clerk and stenographer for two years when Mr. Cary [Clarence Cary, lawyer and family friend] sent for him and told him that there was an opening in the publishing house of Charles Scribner's Sons, if he wanted to make a change. Edward saw at once the larger opportunities possible in a house of the importance of the Scribners, and he immediately placed himself in communication with Mr. Charles Scribner, with the result that in January, 1884, he entered the employ of these publishers as stenographer to the two members of the firm and to Mr. Edward L. Burlingame, literary advisor to the house. He was to receive a salary of eighteen dollars and thirty-three cents per week, which was then considered a fair wage for stenographic work. The typewriter had at that time not come into use, and all letters were written in long-hand. Once more his legible handwriting had secured for him a position.

Edward Bok was now twenty-one years of age. He had already done a prodigious amount of work for a boy of his years. He was always busy.... If we are inclined to credit young Bok with an ever-willingness to work and a certain quality of initiative, the influences which played upon him must also be taken into account.

Take, for example, the peculiarly fortuitous circumstances under which he entered the Scribner publishing house. As stenographer to the two members of the firm, Bok was immediately brought into touch with the leading authors of the day, their works as they were discussed in the correspondence dictated to him, and the authors' terms upon which books were published. In fact, he was given as close an insight as it was possible for a young man to get into the inner workings of one of the large publishing houses in the United States, with a list peculiarly noted for the distinction of its authors and the broad scope of its books.

The Scribners had the foremost theological list of all the publishing houses; its educational list was exceptionally strong; its musical list excelled; its fiction represented the leading writers of the day; its general list was particularly noteworthy; and its foreign department, importing the leading books brought out in Great Britain and Europe, was an outstanding feature of the business. The correspondence dictated to Bok covered, naturally, all these fields, and a more remarkable opportunity for self-education was never offered a stenographer.

Mr. Burlingame was known in the publishing world for his singularly keen literary appreciation, and was accepted as one of the best judges of good fiction. Bok entered the Scribner employ as Mr. Burlingame was selecting the best short stories published within a decade for a set of books to be called "Short Stories by American Authors." The correspondence for this series was dictated to Bok, and he decided to read after Mr. Burlingame and thus get an idea of the best fiction of the day. So whenever his chief wrote to an author for permission to include his story in the proposed series, Bok immediately hunted up the story and read it.

Later, when the house decided to start *Scribner's Magazine*, and Mr. Burlingame was selected to be its editor, all the preliminary correspondence was dictated to Bok through his employers, and he received a firsthand education in the setting up of the machinery necessary for the publication of a magazine. All this he eagerly absorbed.

He was again fortunate in that his desk was placed in the advertising department of the house; and here he found, as manager, an old-time Brooklyn boy friend with whom he had gone to school: Frank N. Doubleday, to-day the senior partner of Doubleday, Page and Company. Bok had been attracted to advertising through his theatre programe and *Brooklyn Magazine* experience, and here was presented a chance to learn the art at first hand and according to the best tradition. So, whenever his stenographic work permitted, he assisted Mr. Doubleday in preparing and placing the advertisements of the house.

Mr. Doubleday was just reviving the publication of a house-organ called *The Book Buyer,* and, given a chance to help in this, Bok felt he was getting back into the periodical field, especially since, under Mr. Doubleday's guidance, the little monthly soon developed into a literary magazine of very respectable size and generally bookish contents.

The house also issued another periodical, *The Presbyterian Review,* a quarterly under the editorship of a board of professors connected with the Princeton and Union Theological Seminaries. This ponderous-looking magazine was not composed of what one might call "light reading," and as the price of a single copy was eighty cents, and the advertisements it could reasonably expect were necessarily limited in number, the periodical was rather difficult to move. Thus the whole situation at Scribners' was adapted to give Edward an all-around training in the publishing business. It was an exceptional opportunity.

Bok left Scribners on 13 October 1889 and became editor of the Ladies' Home Journal *the following week, a position he held for the next thirty years.*

RELATED LETTERS:
Letter from CS II to Bok, 28 September 1920; letter from Bok in reply, 29 September 1920.

Bok's book, The Americanization of Edward Bok, *was published several days before, on 24 September, at a price of five dollars.*

My dear Bok:

The copy of your book with the personal inscription was a surprise that was much appreciated.

When I first heard of the book I determined that if possible we should publish it, as it seemed such a fitting climax after our years of association.

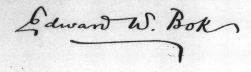

Last text page of The Americanization of
Edward Bok

How far off those years seem now! They were truly our golden days.

Your book itself has interested me greatly and is a worthy record of your career. It is interesting and sincere and I think it should be an encouragement to all young men. We hope for a decided success and should welcome any cooperation.

Yours sincerely
[Charles Scribner]

My dear Mr. Scribner:

Do let me thank you for your very cordial note of September twenty-eighth with regard to the book. It is one of the pleasantest experiences of my life to have this book come out with your imprint, and I only hope that the public may buy enough copies of it to justify your embarking upon it.

Believe me, with every good regard to you
Very sincerely yours,
Edward W. Bok

Soon afterward, commercial firms began soliciting Scribners for permission to reprint short sections of the inspirational work for their employees in their newsletters and periodicals, and in 1921 the book won the Pulitzer Prize for biography. Bok wanted it to reach a wider audience and argued successfully with Scribners for cheaper editions—in the three-dollar range. With their appearance the sales of the volume increased rapidly, keeping it on the nonfiction best-seller lists for 1922, 1923, and 1924. The book went through sixty printings over the next twenty years.

LETTER:

Letter from Bok to CS II, 18 August 1921, written from the Palace Hotel, Scheveningen, Netherlands.

With the exception of the United States most major countries adhered to the Bern Convention of 1887, which provided that literary material copyrighted in one signatory country automatically enjoyed copyright in all signatory countries. It was not until the Universal Copyright Convention was signed in Geneva in 1952 that the United States joined a general system of international copyright. As Bok describes in this letter, his work, The Americanization of Edward Bok, *fell victim to this copyright problem.*

My dear Scribner:

On arriving in the Netherlands I found that my book had been pre-empted by a man here who, with another, intends to start a publishing house and use my book to float it. This is due to the fact that the United States did not go into the Berne Convention and so there is no copyright relation between the two countries. Hence, I could only do the best under the circumstances, and fortunately the man who pre-empted the book turns out to be a distant member of my family. He has sold the book as a serial to begin immediately in a paper here called Het Vaderland, where it will run for sixty days. Then he is to publish it in the translated Dutch, but much abridged, in two editions, one with paper cover at three guldens, and the other in cloth at four guldens—these for popular consumption.

I did not particularly care for this sort of publication except that in these cheap forms the book would perhaps reach the young men and boys of the Netherlands, and so I made arrangements to have another edition, called a limited edition, of 175 copies exactly like the American edition only with the Dutch title-page and a special preface by me, published by Nijhoff, who is the leading publisher here, for 7.50 Guldens (about $2.75). Hence my cable for sheets, and as I don't want Nijhoff to get stuck, I want to pay for the sheets myself. I am to receive all that this edition may possibly make in the way of profits and on the other two editions I am to get 50% of any profits that may accrue after the expenses are paid.

Publishing in the Netherlands is an entirely different proposition from publishing in the United States, as you will see, and just as soon as I get back one of the first things that the new Netherlands-America Foundation will take up is to get a copyright between the two countries. As it is now, anybody can steal our books and we can steal their books, and that is not a condition to be tolerated in these days.

I hear the best reports from Darrow about the success of the book with you, but such figures are unheard of here.

Butterworth [his English publisher] writes me from London that he is printing the second edition, which pleases me very much.

I am having a wonderful but busy time here and am now off for Switzerland, where I hope to get more of a real vacation.

With every good wish, believe me,

Sincerely yours,

Edward W. Bok

RELATED LETTERS:

Letter from CS II to Bok, 23 July 1923; letter from Bok in reply, 26 July 1923.

This is a revealing exchange in which, for the most part, Scribner is soliciting suggestions from Bok, the retired editor of the Ladies' Home Journal, *for improving* Scribner's Magazine, *which has been steadily falling from its circulation heights of the early 1910s. What Bok had earlier suggested about Woodrow Wilson is unclear but probably had to do with serializing his political memoirs in the magazine.*

Dear Bok:

You and your work are continually in my mind but it is long since I have written. At my suggestion Darrow wrote about publicity the other day and I read your reply. The days go too quickly and I have never equipped myself for business work at home; I usually stay out Wednesday as well as Saturday and sometimes Watson brings the letters out and I manage some correspon-

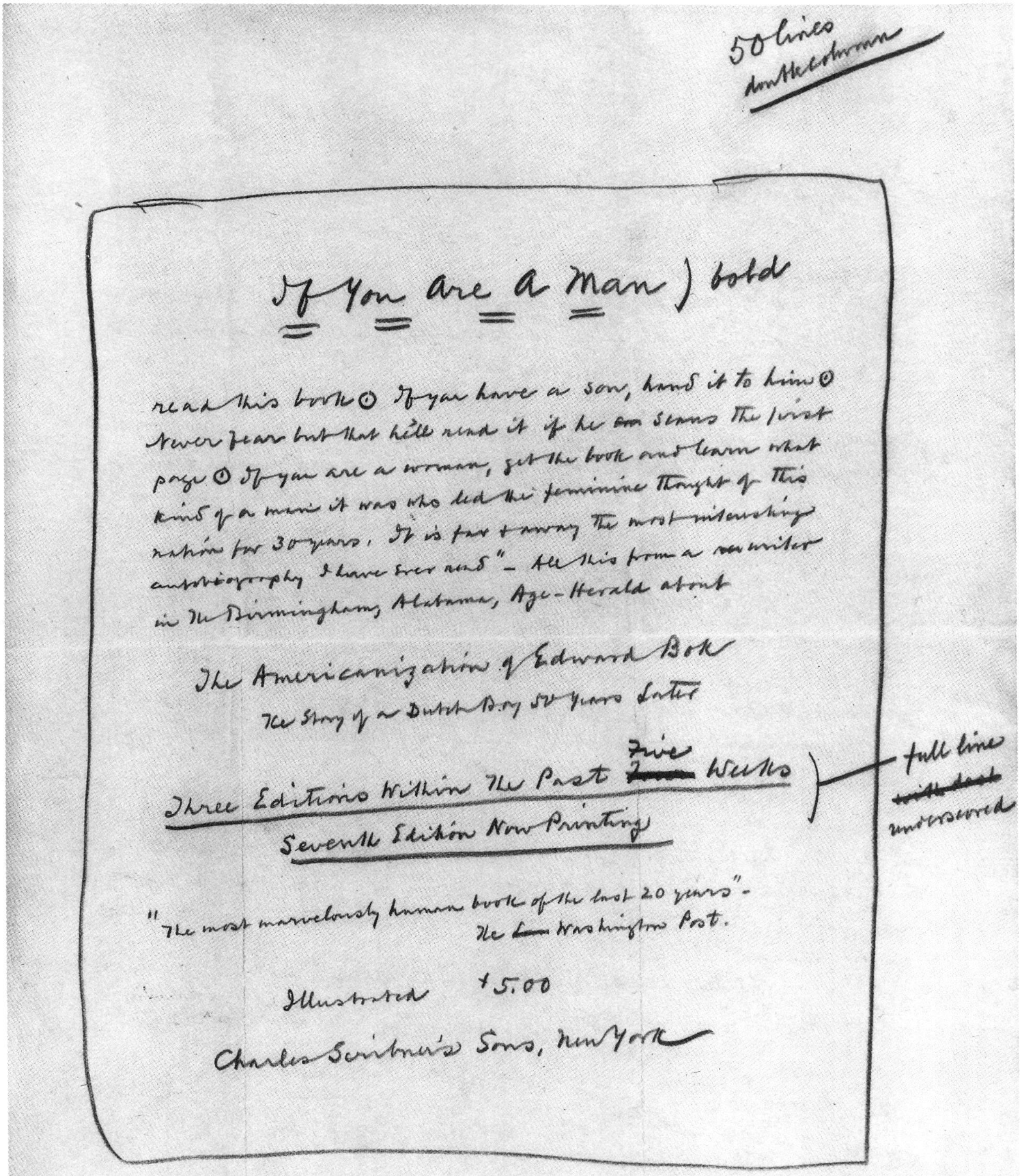

50 lines
dont hetchman

If You are a Man) bold

read this book ⊙ If you have a son, hand it to him ⊙
Never fear but that he'll read it if he can scans the first
page ⊙ If you are a woman, get the book and learn what
kind of a man it was who led the feminine thought of this
nation for 30 years, It is far + away the most interesting
autobiography I have ever read" — All this from a new writer
in the Birmingham, Alabama, Age—Herald about

The Americanization of Edward Bok

The Story of a Dutch Boy 50 years later

Three Editions within the Past ~~Two~~ *Five Weeks*   ) — *full line*
~~with dash~~
underscored

Seventh Edition Now Printing

"The most marvelously human book of the last 20 years"—
The ~~Sun~~ Washington Post.

Illustrated $5.00

Charles Scribner's Sons, New York

Promotional copy (1921) written by Bok for his own book, The Americanization of Edward Bok, *and used
by Scribners in Philadelphia newspapers*

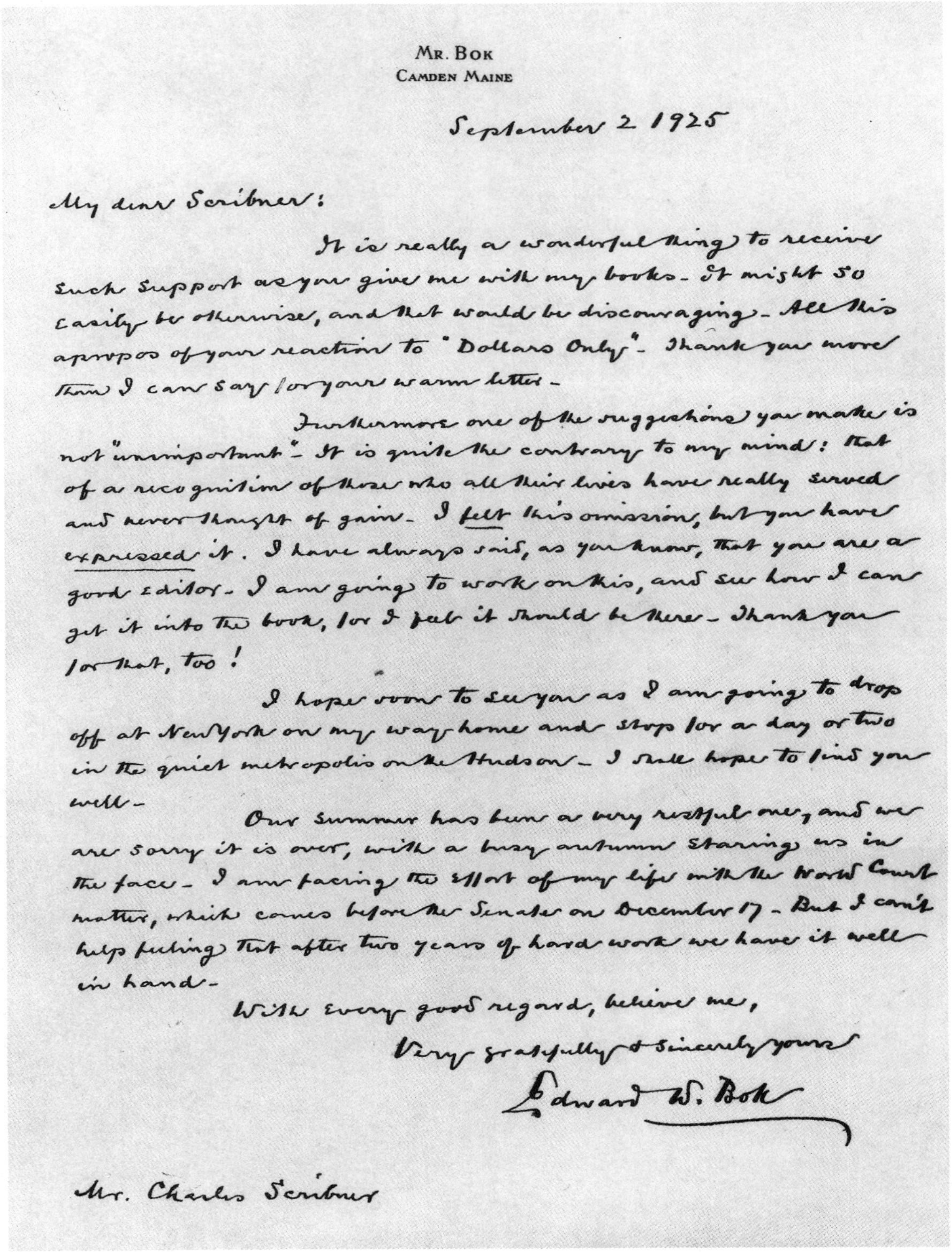

MR. BOK
CAMDEN MAINE

September 2 1925

My dear Scribner:

It is really a wonderful thing to receive such support as you give me with my books. It might so easily be otherwise, and that would be discouraging. All this apropos of your reaction to "Dollars Only". Thank you more than I can say for your warm letter.

Furthermore one of the suggestions you make is not "unimportant". It is quite the contrary to my mind: that of a recognition of those who all their lives have really served and never thought of gain. I _felt_ this omission, but you have expressed it. I have always said, as you know, that you are a good editor. I am going to work on this, and see how I can get it into the book, for I felt it should be there. Thank you for that, too!

I hope soon to see you as I am going to drop off at New York on my way home and stop for a day or two in the quiet metropolis on the Hudson. I sure hope to find you well.

Our summer has been a very restful one, and we are sorry it is over, with a busy autumn staring us in the face. I am facing the effort of my life with the World Court matter, which comes before the Senate on December 17. But I can't help feeling that after two years of hard work we have it well in hand.

With every good regard, believe me,

Very gratefully & sincerely yours

Edward W. Bok

Mr. Charles Scribner

Letter from Bok to CS II. Scribner's "unimportant" suggestion regarding Bok's current work, Dollars Only, *was that he qualify his definition of "service" by* <u>motive</u>: *some serve their communities to make money, but others only seek social recognition or public distinction. "Of course also your book takes no account of those whose lives by profession or choice have from the start been devoted to 'service'—who never wanted to make their pile—who might have first call for the kingdom of heaven" (31 August 1925). A vigorous supporter of the World Court movement, Bok also makes reference to an upcoming Senate vote regarding American participation in the Court.*

dence. There is always plenty to read—most of it rotten.

Sedgwick [Ellery Sedgwick, editor of *The Atlantic*] is an able fellow and a most likeable one. He found for the <u>Atlantic</u> an unoccupied field, has filled it well, and deserves his success. Sometimes the magazine falls off but he has the public hoodooed. It will be interesting to watch the reflex effect of his book publishing. The most successful periodicals, financially, are run entirely in their own interests.

I read all the news for the best world peace suggestion. The plan has stood up well under first criticism. I suppose organization is now going forward and do hope it will do good; you must not be disappointed if it fails of entire success. The farmers movement seems to absorb all political attention at the present and the President has certainly lost much ground. Apparently also the Republican Party is hopelessly split on the prohibition question and I am out of politics.

The popular edition of the "Americanization" looks right and should make a killing. I am keen to read your new manuscript but understand Perkins is to look it over first. All right, but I shall try to get an early view.

<u>Scribner's</u> goes on fairly well but of course I should like more circulation. The Phelps [William Lyon Phelps, author of "As You Like It" column in the magazine] articles have been fine and Cortissos [art critic and editor Royal Cortissoz] will be an improvement, but we need a large and more compelling program. The Wilson suggestion was rather Napoleonic but I doubt whether it is for us. I had more than a chance at some Myron Herrick [American ambassador to France] material but it did not much tempt me. I think Hendrick is making the book for Doubleday. Alexander Graham Bell's letters, in the hands of Grosvenor, of Washington, are now suggested but they don't seem very important to me—certainly not in a competitive way.

What value do you place upon magazine illustrations in our case? We have given up coated paper and the very high-priced artists, and there is no room any longer for descriptive articles. Illustrations sometimes tempt the editor into the acceptance of rather dull stuff but on the other hand there are some most desirable articles which require illustration. We cannot be an art magazine and perhaps we should settle down to using illustrations only when required, with the exception of sometimes brightening up stories.

My wife is making good progress. Next winter we must seek a good climate (probably Cali-

fornia) but after that I hope we may resume our normal existence.

Yours most sincerely
[Charles Scribner]

My dear Mr. Scribner:

It was good to get your letter, and particularly to hear that Mrs. Scribner was making good progress. That is fine. But why do you want to seek a good climate for her in California when there is Mountain Lake, Florida, unless you want the salt air? That's the only thing we haven't got there. We have everything else, though.

I was looking over the August number of Scribner's, in view of your letter, and I do not miss the coated paper at all. Of course, where you print on regular paper it calls for more careful over-laying and better printing. But with the proper distribution of pen and ink and wash drawings I see no reason why you should present a series of page illustrations. I used them, of course, in The Ladies' Home Journal very liberally because I had the large page, and they could be cut out and framed, but that is hardly true of the so-called standard magazine size.

After all, what you want to make a magazine go is good reading matter, and I quite agree with you that Scribner's ought to have a more compelling program. But then, you know, that does connote a compelling editor. If the Woodrow Wilson idea was too Napoleonic for you, why don't you work on my other suggestion to get Thomas Hardy to write his autobiography? I think that would be far more interesting than Alexander Graham Bell's material or the Myron Herrick stuff, unless the material in either case is exceptionally good. There isn't much allure to either of those names.

Of course, you know how I feel about the magazine, and that it ought to dominate its particular field, in which I class Harper's and The Century. Neither one of those two are filling the bill, and you seem to realize that yours is not. But yours can, and it should, and it is not difficult to do. It can hold on to all its traditions and its fine prestige, and yet get liver stuff. Once in a while you get it, as in the Pupin [physicist Michael Pupin] stuff, and this new series of Stevenson [Robert Louis Stevenson] letters is interesting.

It doesn't seem to me, however, that you are putting enough stress on the international viewpoint, which, to my mind, a magazine should do nowadays.

I think Darrow and Meyer and I can work out some publicity for the books in connection with the

Peace Award. I simply felt that with the work on my hands here I couldn't undertake it alone.

I am glad you like the popular edition of "The Americanization." I haven't seen it yet, nor have I had a glimpse of the library edition.

I am doing nothing about my new book. I haven't looked at the manuscript, in fact, because I wanted to get a good rest, and then of course The American Peace Award had to come out and break it all up. But that will die down now in the tremendous correspondence, and I shall soon let my mind turn toward the manuscript of the book.

The reaction of The American Peace Award has been really amazing in its unanimity of approval. I was quite prepared for a fifty-fifty reaction, because the subject is so debatable and so chuck-full of heat and dynamite. But, as Adolph Ochs from his watch-tower in The New York Times wrote me the other day, I should be mightily gratified at the reception of the idea, since, as he termed it, it is universally favorable. The conditions have just been published, as you have doubtless seen, and now they are working at the crux of the whole matter, i.e., the Jury of Award. There will either be five or nine on this Jury, and naturally a great deal depends on their selection. My first selection, whom everybody thought I couldn't get, I have just gotten, and with his acceptance almost any others are possible. So the road is opening for me there pretty clearly.

I suppose you will remain at Morristown during the summer, and I have been hoping to catch Arthur and his wife on their way up here, but thus far have not heard from them.

With every good regard, believe me,
Very sincerely yours,
Edward W. Bok

Bok's Jury of Award was announced on 17 September and included among its seven members Edward M. House, Elihu Root, and William Allen White.

RELATED LETTERS:
Letter from Bok to CS II, 16 October 1924; letter from CS II in reply, 21 October 1924.

Over twenty-two thousand plans were submitted for consideration by Bok's jury for the American Peace Award. In March 1924 Scribners published the twenty "most representative" of those submitted, including that of the winner, Charles H. Livermore, secretary of the New York Peace Society, in a volume called Ways to Peace, *edited by Esther Everett Lape. Now the more difficult work began: achieving something concrete by getting the plan*

approved by the Senate—hence, the need for continuing committee work.

My dear Scribner:

I don't know whether you met Miss Esther Everett Lape, the young woman who distinguished herself to such an extent with The American Peace Award before the Senate Committee. But I have asked her to call upon you to ask you to go upon my Committee in connection with the Award. I was very anxious last year that you should go on this Committee, but hesitated to ask you because I wanted the air of success around it first, as I don't want to lead my friends into doubtful things. Of course, now it is a success, and you and I have talked about this matter so thoroughly that you will be prepared, I hope, to tell Miss Lape that you will go on the Committee.

Of course, I need not say that personally I would love to have you associated with this lifework of mine, because nothing else counts so much as the matter of getting this whole question of peace over. And I am sure we can. So won't you listen favorably to Miss Lape when she comes to see you!

With every good regard, believe me,
Very sincerely yours,
Edward W. Bok

Dear Bok:

First, I must thank you for your telegram on the 18th [his birthday] which was much appreciated. As I grow older my friends become dearer to me and old friends are the best friends. I have not made much of a splash in the world but when I pass I should like to be thought well of by my old associates.

I have been embarrassed by your very complimentary suggestion that I go on the American Peace Award Committee. Miss Lape called upon me yesterday and I enjoyed meeting her, though I put her off with the statement that I would write to you today or to-morrow and also send her a note. The truth is I should like to be excused. As you know, I am still trying to conduct this business and find it a heavy job, sometimes regretting that I have taken upon myself so many outside duties. Princeton University and Skidmore College should have more time and thought than I find it possible to give them; and I cannot afford to give up my banking interests, for they keep me in touch with financial movements, with which it is necessary for me to be familiar. Besides all this I don't think I am very well qualified to serve on your Committee and should feel obliged to keep more abreast of foreign affairs. Please understand that I do

MR. BOK'S OFFICE
PACKARD BUILDING
PHILADELPHIA

October 17 1929

My dear Scribner:

Tomorrow you reach the dignified age of 75, and I want to be there to congratulate you - It ought to make you feel happy because to reach that age, is, I think, an achievement, since not so many men do - And I hope you reach it feeling well and happy and that the day may mean many good wishes for you -

I was 66 last week (think of your office boy at that age, if you can!) and my friends made a very happy day of it for me -

I *do* hope you will see many more returns of the day, and see each one happier and better in health -

My very best to you & believe me
Always devotedly
E.W.B.

Last letter from Bok (in the Scribner Archives) to CS II: a birthday greeting. The stock market crashed within two weeks. Both men were dead of heart attacks within six months, Bok in January and Scribner in April.

highly value the suggestion and should feel it an honor to be associated with your Committee but conditions make it almost impossible. I should be afraid to confess to my wife that I had accepted any additional responsibility. . . .

Yours sincerely
[Charles Scribner]

RELATED LETTERS:
Determined, at first, to fool the public by creating a pseudonymous work, Bok was gradually persuaded by editor Perkins that the advantages of publishing under his own name were more compelling. Bok compromised. Perhaps I Am *appeared under his name but carried this explanatory statement on the title page: "Based on the reflections and adventures*

of a retired business man who sent his story to Mr. Bok. The rewritten version of which Mr. Bok is 'perhaps' the author is given here."

June eighteenth Nineteen hundred and twenty-six

Dear Perkins:

I am determined that no new book over my name shall appear for some time to come, because I think they have been appearing quite actively of late, and I want to create a new desire, if I can, on the part of the public by keeping out of the market for a couple of years.

But it so happens that I have been collecting material for a new book, and I have some fifty or sixty thousand words which would make a very readable volume. It would consist of observations, experiences and impressions on a number of things: some humorous, some surprising, but all very popular and readable, unlike any of my books and really unlike any book that I know. The thought has occurred to me to create a fanciful writer who would follow my advice, and retire from business, devote a year or two to looking about and then write what he experiences. All the material could just as well be seen by another as by me, and I would write the book with the same care as if it were published over my own name. My idea of a title was "Your Fault, Mr. Bok," with some informal sub-title.

I have been thinking about this for some time, and could write the book this summer in Maine, if you and the house felt you could encourage me to do it. Naturally, I don't want to give the time to it if it doesn't seem possible. But I would really take a good deal of pleasure in writing a book of that sort and fooling the public.

I see it clearly, but do you and the powers-that-be?

Of course, I would not want it known that I wrote the book.

Do tell me what your reaction is to the idea.

I leave here on Sunday for Williamstown to see my boy graduate and to have a hood thrown across my shoulders, and then go to Camden, Maine, where I will arrive on Tuesday.

I hope a happy summer faces you and yours. With every good regard, believe me,
Very sincerely yours
[Edward W. Bok]

July 6, 1926

Dear Mr. Bok:

I had to go away at the end of last week on the day your letter came, in order to motor my family up to Vermont. I just got back, and just talked to C.S. about the plan for a new book and I shall write you at greater length about it soon. We think that the idea of your writing a book about, and ostensibly by, a business man who had retired in order to try the experiment you advocated, is an excellent one. We are all for it. We do not think that you could wisely present it under the title and with the introduction that you propose. These, however, seem to us to be details, and we think that they could be got around in such a way that the general effect would be very much the same. You would have to face the fact that sooner or later, in all probability, the authorship would be known. In fact, perhaps it

would be only fair to divulge it in the end. It seems to us it would certainly be known if we gave the introduction which is so distinctly after your manner of writing, and the title, that you suggest. But in the main we approve the idea thoroughly, and we only hope that there will be a great deal of direct narrative in the book, because few people have your ability to tell a story.
Very sincerely yours,
[Maxwell Perkins]

July 9 1926

Dear Perkins:

Your letter of the 6th, sent to Philadelphia, reaches me here to-day and I await the word from you which you say will come soon and go into the matter of the proposed book at greater length.

But I cannot help but feel that you will knock two important props from under the book by discarding the title, and the sketchy prologue and epilogue. I chose all three in order to make the book what I see it: absolutely informal and unique of its or any kind. If I write another kind of introduction or ending I will do something unnatural with me and make a mess of it. After all, my style, good or bad, is my style, and I can't get away from it. Besides, I felt this book would be so entirely different from my own that folk wouldn't associate it with me at all. There is to be nothing autobiographical or didactic in it: it will be very light, very readable, entirely composed of experiences that any one might have if he kept his eyes open, observations and anecdotes: the book would be largely humorous. All this is different from my books.

Then, too, I think that you are apt to mislead people more successfully by no attempt to disguise. After all, suppose, from the start, the public begins to say that I wrote the book, the result would be only a brisker sale from curiosity, and that wouldn't hurt.

At the same time, I want to see what is in your mind: how the title and the introduction and ending can be got around.

Remember one thing: this chap is not going into service directly after retirement: he is going to loaf for a year and it is what he sees, hears and reads that he is going to tell about. Nothing to make folk think: just to interest, entertain them and make them chuckle!

Let me hear from you—
Sincerely yours
E.W.B

With my prettiest bow I present this copy
To Charles Scribner
who in my later years as well as in my earlier
days has meant so much to me.-
Edward W. Bok
New Years Day 1925

Inscription to CS II in Bok's Twice Thirty

May 23, 1927

Dear Mr. Bok:

I found the manuscript which you left with me extremely attractive reading from beginning to end. It is different from any of your other books.- It lacks necessarily, some of their more weighty and substantial qualities, but they lack its discursive charm. It is quite a different sort of book even from "Twice Thirty," more literary and mellow, and I think it should appear in a smaller volume (its length is 60,000 words) characterized by some grace and delicacy of design with respect to the cover, and the typography, etc.

In spite of the individual impression which this book makes as a whole, and which distinguishes it from each of your other books, it is unmistakably the work of Edward Bok;- and for this we should certainly say "Thank Heaven" if it were not for your wish to publish it as if it were by someone else. It certainly has the stamp of your individuality upon it, and I do not think that anyone who knew your writings would fail to identify it as yours, unless he supposed that the author, having "Twice Thirty" always in mind, had become your imitator.- But I do not think any reviewer would be satisfied with this explanation. He would be sure to raise the question, I believe, of whether the author was not, in reality, you yourself.

We should therefore seriously consider the question of what it would signify if this book which came out as "Your Fault Mr. Bok" was thought in general to be actually your work. It seems to me that the result of this could not but be disadvantageous. It might even seem to some as though a document in evidence of your argument that a man should retire, had been seriously submitted, and that it was not a valid document.

But the book is of a light and genial character, and I doubt that it would be seriously regarded in this way. I think the chances are that the disguise would be so easily penetrated, that the attempt at concealment would seem rather feeble.

I put these points before you because they are important, and ought to be recognized. I would myself argue strongly against issuing the book under the name of Emory Mears solely for the sale of the book itself. I believe that the name of Edward Bok is a far more valuable one for it, and that the objections to using that name, such as that your books have come too rapidly upon the market, no longer apply. All of your books have been successful and the trade would be glad of another one, and so would the public.- Besides, while the book is distinctly yours in style, it is, as I said, a quite different one, of a more literary, casual, beguiling sort.

Therefore, even if there were no <u>disadvantages</u> in publishing the book under an assumed name, I would advocate issuing it under your name because of the strong advantages in doing so. This would simply mean that the very beginning and the very ending would have to be changed, and that there should be an introduction or preface in which you state that this book, written to reveal the experiences of a man of high ability and intelligence who retired at the age of fifty, was formed out of your own experience, observation, and the information you had gained from letters and interviews, of the experience of others, and that all this was presented under a sort of fictional title because while every part of it was true of somebody, not all of it was true of any one person. You would know just how to do such an introduction, and it would be an attractive one;- and the result would be an extremely entertaining, charming, and distinctive little book which would present the case for retirement more winningly than has ever been done in a book based on the experience of one only.

Most sincerely yours
[Maxwell Perkins]

Stark Young (1881–1963)

Stark Young

Young was the preeminent drama critic of the New York stage during its early twentieth-century renaissance. He became the theater critic and contributing editor of *The New Republic* (1922–1947) after establishing himself as a Southern man of letters on the faculty of the University of Texas, where he had founded the *Texas Review* (now called the *Southwest Review*) and a drama organization called the Curtain Club, and on the faculty of Amherst College in Massachusetts, writing essays and reviews for leading national journals. At the age of forty, he left the teaching profession and went to New York City to become a freelance writer on the arts. Scribners began as Young's publisher with a collection of his theater pieces, *The Flower in Drama,* and ended the relationship with a revised edition of the same work over thirty years later. In the intervening years Young received both critical and popular acclaim as a writer of Southern fiction associated with the Southern literary Renaissance. Though he never joined the group of Southern writers known as the "Fugitives" (later, the "Agrarians"), such as Allen Tate and Robert Penn Warren, his stories and novels anticipated their championing of the South's agrarian economy and its associated rural values, and were influential in the development of regionalism in Southern writing. That *So Red the Rose*—his best-selling 1934 novel set in Mississippi during the Civil War—remains in print testifies to the endurance of Young's personal interpretation of that tradition.

Scribner Books by Young

1923	*The Flower in Drama: A Book of Papers on the Theatre*
1924	*The Three Fountains*
1925	*Glamour: Essays on the Art of the Theatre*
1926	*Theatre Practice*
	Heaven Trees
1928	*The Torches Flair*
1929	*River House*

1930	*The Street of the Islands,* illustrated with woodcuts by Ilse Bischoff
1934	*So Red the Rose*
1935	*Feliciana*
1937	*Southern Treasury of Life and Literature,* selected by Young
1939	*The Sea Gull* by Anton Chekhov, translated by Young
1948	*Immortal Shadows: A Book of Dramatic Criticism*
1951	*The Pavilion: Of People and Times Remembered, Of Stories and Places*
1955	*The Flower in Drama & Glamour: Theatre Essays and Criticism* (revised edition)

RELATED LETTERS:
This is an early exchange of letters between Young and Scribner editor Maxwell Perkins. Having previously written books about the theater, Young is at work on his first novel.

January 12, 1926

Dear Max:

. . . I am hoping by next week to have some chapters of this Southern material ready for you to read, if you will kindly do it. It seems to me to come on very well and I am trying to keep it away from the novel form, and yet to have some of the plausibility of the novel. It will soon be as far as I can take it at any rate, and I think I will have it ready by February first.

I'll telephone up next week and see when you can come down to lunch.

With thanks again and every good wish and hopes for seeing you soon, I am

Yours,
Stark Young

I went down to Texas for the holidays and enjoyed seeing my family.

January 29, 1926

Dear Stark:

Of course "Heaven Tree" is lovely, and it has the note of authenticity. It has the charm and the pathos of that which was, long ago, and will never again be. The chapters are curiously and I judge artfully, cumulative in their effect, and as suggestions I thought to make at first came later to be superfluous, so a couple of points of question I still have, may vanish with the later chapters. May these come soon. I waited to write on account of the Magazine

to whom I showed some manuscript; but they have not read it. I shall write more later.

As ever,
[Maxwell Perkins]

Wednesday [February 1926]

Dear Max,

I didn't expect all that trouble, but I very much appreciate your letter. The fact is, however, I have been writing with much more confidence ever since I had that talk with you the other day. I very much appreciated your tact and understanding, and know what such a friend as you is worth—especially to me.

Merely speaking the same language is invaluable, so far as I'm concerned; there are times when the life around seems intolerable.

I've got settled on what the chronological plan of my book has to be, if it is to get the effect and sum I'm aiming at. And I've got forward considerably on the first chapters. Afterward I'm going through the whole thing and richen up the texture—after thinking of this element and that in relation to life, and to ideas, and to style in writing.

Thanks again, Max.

Yours sincerely
Stark Young

Robert Bridges, editor of Scribner's Magazine, *used a short chapter from Young's book in the August fiction issue.* Heaven Trees *was published on 11 September 1926.*

LETTER:
Letter from Maxwell Perkins to Young, 24 May 1926.

In 1920 Young befriended William Faulkner, a younger fellow Mississippian from Oxford,

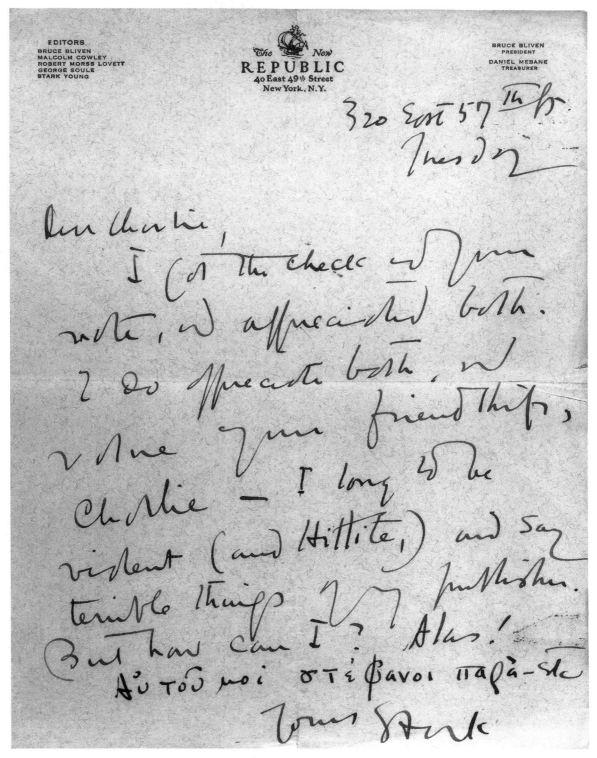

Letter of appreciation from Young to his publisher, CS III. His Greek quotation of Asclepiades (from The Greek Anthology) translates (roughly): "Abide here, my garlands . . ."

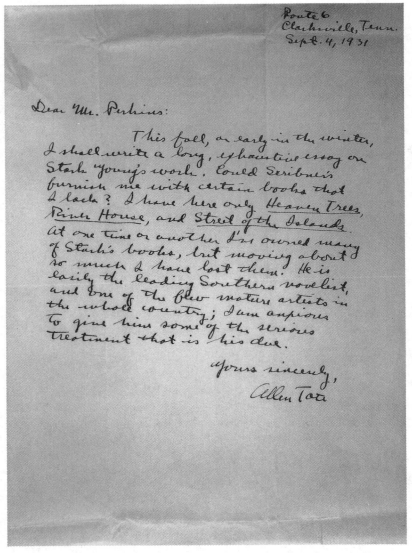

Route 6
Clarksville, Tenn.
Sept. 4, 1931

Dear Mr. Perkins:

This fall, or early in the winter, I shall write a long, exhaustive essay on Stark Young's work. Could Scribner's furnish me with certain books that I lack? I have here only *Heaven Trees*, *River House*, and *Street of the Islands*. At one time or another I've owned many of Stark's books, but moving about so much I have lost them. He is easily the leading Southern novelist, and one of the few mature artists in the whole country; I am anxious to give him some of the serious treatment that is his due.

Yours sincerely,
Allen Tate

Letter from poet Allen Tate to Maxwell Perkins, who was happy to supply him the needed books. Earlier in the year Tate had switched publishers—to Scribners.

where Young had lived as a teenager and university student: he put him up in New York and arranged a job for him as a clerk in the book department of Lord and Taylor's. Faulkner soon returned home, but the two men continued to share literary aspirations, and several years later Young attempted to interest Scribners in Faulkner's writing.

Dear Stark:

We sent you a lot more of the page proof [for *Heaven Trees*] today and I do hope you will have had all of it before you sail [for Italy].

As for "Sound and Fury"? I do not know exactly what to say. It has undoubted power. The man writes honestly and directly and he has observation and within certain limits understanding. I think that we should have declined this particular book, and I do not feel at all able to make any promise about its successor. Of course we should be glad to read it, and considerably hopeful of the result. Would it be better if I wrote directly to him? I will if you think so, and will tell me how to reach him. That would save you trouble anyhow.

As ever yours,
[Maxwell Perkins]

Though several of Faulkner's stories were accepted later by Scribner's Magazine, *the firm missed this early opportunity to become the publisher of this future Nobel Prize winner.* The Sound and the Fury *was published by Random House in 1929.*

LETTER:
Letter from Maxwell Perkins to Young, 5 November 1928.

Perkins writes to convince Young that Scribners is doing all it can (and should) to promote his fiction. His "building for the future" advertising logic proved prophetic, for Young's last novel, So Red the Rose *(1934), became a runaway best-seller.*

Dear Stark:

I am enclosing herewith a certain amount of statistical material and I am doing it with hesitation. I do not want to bother you about such details, and I think it is better that a writer--certainly one like you--should never bother about them. So if you agree on that point, you might just throw the enclosed documents away.

On the other hand, an author has no idea of the extent to which his books are advertised if they are advertised judiciously, which means in a considerable number of mediums upon most of which his eye never falls,--instead of in three or four mediums upon which his eye falls every week, and because it does. I do want you to see the extent of the advertising, and so I enclose a list of the mediums we have used for "Heaven Trees" and "The Torches Flare" and the dates on which the advertisements appeared.

Now I shall state the amount per copy we have spent in advertising "The Three Fountains," "Heaven Trees," and "The Torches Flare," but your way is to look at both sides of a thing, and so I have the somewhat unusual fear that you may be a little sensitive on our account. You certainly would be all wrong in this, because we have been playing with an eye to the future, always, and with a strong faith--and a mighty well founded one too--that your public would constantly grow, that your books would be increasingly understood and appreciated, and that our expenditures, where they exceeded the limits in particular instances, would be justified even in the most strictly business basis.- And in our opinion, our judgment is being justified.

On "Three Fountains" we spent 20¢ a copy in magazine and newspaper advertising;

on "Heaven Trees" 25¢ a copy; and on "The Torches Flare" 40¢ a copy. This is exclusive, of course, of all circularizing, in holiday lists, bookstore news, etc. On a strictly economic basis the amount spent on "The Three Fountains" is not much higher than justified, but in the case of "The Torches Flare" it is very much higher.- But as I say, in every case we have been building for the future, so that we are really justified in that way, in these expenditures. I only give you these figures in order that you may not think that we have not backed these books with as much advertising as the returns warranted.- In view of the admiration a number of us have here for them, we couldn't have done otherwise.

Forgive this statistical eruption. I understand the way you feel. But the whole situation may well be changed in a few weeks when you finish this novel [*River House*].

Ever yours,
[Maxwell Perkins]

LETTER:
Letter from Young to Maxwell Perkins, 3 May [1931], from Venice, Italy.

Young's reputation as a drama critic and scholar of the theater was international. While abroad lecturing in Italy, he writes Perkins about meeting the Italian dictator, Benito Mussolini, and his minister of foreign affairs, Dino Grandi. (Scribners had published Mussolini's autobiography in 1928.) Scribner's Magazine editor Alfred Dashiell was glad to have Young's article, "Echoes at Livarno: A Conversation on American Standards," when he finished it in the fall, and paid $175 for it. But it did not appear until the September 1934 issue.

Dear Max,

I have no secretary over here and many Italians letters to write, and so have done no letters home. Such is life. The lectures are supposed to have been a phenomenal success and there have been about two hundred things in the newspapers. The Ambassador—who has helped me a great deal and so has Mrs. Garrett [the ambassador's wife]—is much pleased with the way it has all turned out. The social people, the writers in the government have all been cordial and very hospitable. I saw Mussolini, who was very warm and very intelligent, and several times saw their remarkable Minister of Foreign Affairs, Grandi, who had me to dine and so on. I was warned to expect small audiences but

$2.50

So Red the Rose
by Stark Young

"'This is when Edward was seven,' Agnes said, taking up a small photograph from the mantel and handing it to General Sherman. 'That's his sister Lucy with him.'

"The picture showed a little boy with long trousers of some light, finely-striped cloth, a black silk jacket, and a linen collar turned down and tied with cord and tassels. He rested his arm on a table with a flowered cloth. Standing beside him was a little girl in a white dress to her ankles, with short, puffed sleeves and a sash of Roman silk. His eyes were large and looked straight at you with a sweet childish regard; her hair was parted in the middle and brushed smooth on her head; her eyes looked away, and the hands hung down at the sides against the little skirt.

"General Sherman held the picture, looking at it.

"'I always saw in Edward McGehee,' he said, 'hope for a gentleman and for a gallant soldier—in my mind's eye.'"

Dust jacket for Young's last novel, the #3 best-seller of 1934

every hall has been crowded and often people standing. I tried to make only a very discreet number of lectures, eleven in all, and in distinguished places only. Various editors asked to reprint articles, etc. So you'll be pleased.

I sail back June 9, and have a lot of writing, one of the things is the piece I promised you for the magazine. It's all sketched now and is called Echoes at Livarno. I look forward to some summer quiet in New York, and some good hours of work.

I hope your Florida visit [with Ernest Hemingway] was all to the good. You keep steadily to that desk at Scribners. Meanwhile you'd enjoy the magnificence of much of Italy, the style, the profundity of mind and the rich thought, that is expressed so frequently. The news of his racketeering, girl trapping, gangsters etcetera sounds very confusing at this distance. But the privacy of New York remains a fine thing.

I hope your family is well. Remember me to Mrs. Perkins. The season will be over and gone before we know it.

All good wishes. I was glad to have your note.

Stark

RELATED LETTERS:
Letter from Maxwell Perkins to Young, 10 August 1934; letter from Young in reply, 13 August, from Austin, Texas; letter from Young, 1 September 1934, from his home in New York City.

Published on 24 July 1934, Young's novel So Red the Rose *was immediately popular, but Perkins thought a staff member's suggestion could improve its reception.*

Dear Stark:
Everything goes on well. We had another order from Baker & Taylor for 500 today. Mr. Lord here, of the educational department, a great admirer of "So Red the Rose" did make a suggestion as the result of having been confused in the very first chapter by the number of characters, and by the different names that were applied to them. We thought that a page might be added just before the text which gave a list of the characters with some small amount of characterization, hardly anything, but just enough to designate each of the important

ones. This is often done. It is done especially in English books. It cannot do any harm, and I think it might very well be worthwhile. You can imagine that it might have been a great advantage in beginning "War and Peace" where he met about a score of characters immediately, to have had such a list. If you could prepare one, we should put it into the next printing.

Always yours,
[Maxwell E. Perkins]

P.S. I enclose a circular reprint of Ellen Glasgow's review which we are distributing widely.

Glasgow, a well-regarded Virginian writer, had called Young's novel "an artistic triumph": "The book is superb. There has never been a novel of the South in the Civil War that can compare with it."

Dear Max,

. . . I think the idea excellent for the characters in the first of the book, but I have no models to go by, and don't know quite how to do it. I am sending you two or three forms for the characters, and you can decide. I have absolute confidence in what you decide, but of course I hate to dump this work on you.

If I make too long a list, that will deter people. On the other hand, a list that is too short is of no help with the characters. I wish you would take the arrangement and cut out, or add to, or transfer as you see fit. I have arranged the list under the heads of the two houses, and then of people whom we meet at one or both houses who do not live there. Any shortening or rearrangement will be all right with me, of course. If I were only there, I could come in and settle the whole business in ten minutes. Please do as you think best. . . .

Yours,
Stark

Perkins chose to list the characters under the names of the two plantations which figure prominently in the novel.

Dear Max:

. . . The advertisment you sent and the ninth printing are all to the good. Thank you so much for sending them.

This gives me a chance to say to you that whenever I think of the book's success, my pleasure is partly made up of the thought of

---

A very extraordinary thing has happened. About two years ago Stark Young gave up heavy drinking for painting. He showed me some of his first pictures, and although I know less than nothing about painting, I do have some kind of instinct for it, and I thought they were amazingly good. They are as if a poet had made a picture instead of a poem, Poe for instance, or Coleridge as in "Kubla Khan". They are remarkable too in execution. There is one of flowers in jars on a balustrade, and the balustrade is as firm and solid as stone. I thought painters might say that he was doing things that painting should not. But even painters seem to admire them. They were exhibited, fifteen or sixteen of them, for the benefit of the friends of Greece, and ten of them were immediately sold, and others later.- And he has several orders for still more. They have a haunting enchantment to them. His landscapes have a little of that quality the El Greco's do, but they are absolutely Stark's pictures and nobody else's. I never knew such a thing to happen. . . .

— Maxwell Perkins in a letter to Ernest Hemingway, 11 June 1943

---

what a satisfaction it must give you. I could never have written it if you had not stood by me; and your gift for both encouragement and a sense of individual freedom has meant much more to me than I will ever put in words. I can only say that but for Scribner's in a secondary sense and you in a far fuller sense, this book of mine would not have been the same and might never have been written at all. The thought is so profoundly true that I must take all the greater pleasure in it, and I only wait for the time I begin my autobiography to make this clear as well as make it creative with regard to things and people and writing in general.

I hope all our good fortune keeps up. A man brought me the last copy of Publishers' Weekly. The cover looks corking and to see three book shops advertising for a first edition is a pleasant sensation.

Yours,
Stark

LETTER:
Letter from Young to CS III, [July 1947].

Perhaps writing on the day (12 July) he resigned from The New Republic, *Young consid-*

$2.50

FELICIANA
By
STARK YOUNG

Feliciana, Parlange, Terre Bonne, Lebanon, The Shadows, Seven Trees, Ascension, these are some of the lovely old parish and plantation names that live in the stories that Stark Young has written in this book. There are moments of Italy, and there are drawings out of Texas, recreated in literary forms that are original and complete. But the book returns always to that country of "So Red the Rose"—Louisiana and Mississippi: the Deep South is its refrain.

Stories like "Cousin Micajah," "Promise Land," or "Parlange" are not merely short stories. They have in them the same implications of life as in "So Red the Rose." They have echoes and tones that imply the same social elements that are found in the full-length novel. There is the same effect of real characters. Wherever one of the stories deals with the past, the quality is original and special. As one critic has said of "Shadows on Terre Bonne," "It is all as if it were reflected on water."

Feliciana is done with the glow, perception, hidden technical skill and depth of feeling that have made Stark Young not only the most famous delineator of the old South, but also a leader in contemporary American letters.

Dust jacket for Young's last fictional work, his second collection of short stories

ers a suggestion Scribner had made for a book of his dramatic criticism, which would be culled primarily from his twenty-five years' work with the journal. He mourns the loss of Maxwell Perkins, who had died in June.

Dear Charlie,

Thank you for such a letter. I really feel sorry for writers who have any publisher but Scribners—my whole relationship with Scribners has been well-bred, cordial and human—no highty-tighty nonsense but no crassness.

The idea of the theatre book may be a good one. I will think about it. I see Michael Straight [an editor at *The New Republic*] today to get the NR matter settled. They refuse to accept my resignation, go on sending the salary, etc. but this talk will be final. If I do

stay there will have to be, in writing, some very drastic changes. I can't believe that what I shall ask will be in tune with the paper's policy these days.

Alas, I can't agree with your final words—I am "convinced" about my painting ability, but not that I am a nice fellow. The distraction of the words nowadays makes it almost impossible to keep any center at all—"Milton, thou shouldst be living at this hour—England hath need of thee"—only it is not only England. Sta come torre firma, but how? Dante should be living at this hour—he would bite our heads off.

I still can't realize that Max is not there in his office. He was a marvellous combination of faults and virtues, and was profound in his understanding. And sweet in his nature, and aristocratic.

For sales notes

This is a book about places , which means the Deep South, with glimpses of London and Italy; and also about people.

Some of the people were dear to the author because of early associations and because of the stories that they represented, which appear in the book as they did Stark Young's novel SO RED THE ROSE , for which after seventeen years there is still some demand among bookbuyers. Besides his Cousin Charles Mc-Gehee, who was so like Byron, and Byram Ballou, the country Croesus , Miss Mary Cherry, Aunt Sally McGehee, Uncle Hugh and Billy McChedric, there are many other figures in and out of the story, as if they were in one of Stark Young's novel s.

this

who was a kind of

The general effect of the book is that of a painting in which we go from place to place, not bound by time.

The theatre enters in, with recollections of such a great figure as the famous Duse and her relation to this dramatic critic.

Literary memories and literary theories are scattered here and there. Sir Edmund Gosse especially and Henry James with the celebrated letter he wrote to Stark Young as a young reader and Henry James' recommendation as to which of his books should be read first .

The title of the book implies the deep love for the people and the part of the country that the author feels and conveys with the same touch that made such of his books as Heaven Trees, Feliciana, The Street of the Islands, The Three Fountains , River House , So Red the Rose widely read and translated into various foreign languages.

Ellen Glasgow said that So Red the Rose was the most profound novel she knew written about the Deep South. Margaret Mitchell, author of Gone With the Wind put So Red the Rose. William Faulkner once said that not only did the people in So Red the Rose live once in reality, they still exist in the South .

at the top of Southern novels.

In a letter (7 March 1951) to Young, Scribner editor John Hall Wheelock had asked for promotional help for Young's as-yet-untitled autobiographical book [The Pavilion]: "It has been my experience that an author likes to be consulted about the presentation of his book, about which he obviously knows more than anyone else and on which he can cast fresh light. If you will let me have two or three hundred words describing the book as you see it and indicating the points that you think should be emphasized, I will base my write-up on this." Young's responded with this memo.

Remember me to Mrs. Scribner—another aristocrat—and to young Charlie. Thank you again for your letter. I will certainly think on't.

Yours
Stark

Young soon warmed to the theater book idea: Immortal Shadows: A Book of Dramatic Criticism was published on 15 November 1948.

LETTER:
Letter from CS III to Young, 20 September 1948.

Scribner, as publisher, responds to the eternal author complaint that his work—in this case, Young's first book—is no longer in print.

Dear Stark:

I have been very much distressed (I use the word after due thought) that you should think we had let you down in not having kept THE FLOWER IN DRAMA in print. While I have always valued our relationship as author and publisher, our friendship and the goodwill you have ever shown towards Scribners means far more to me than merely acting as your midwife.

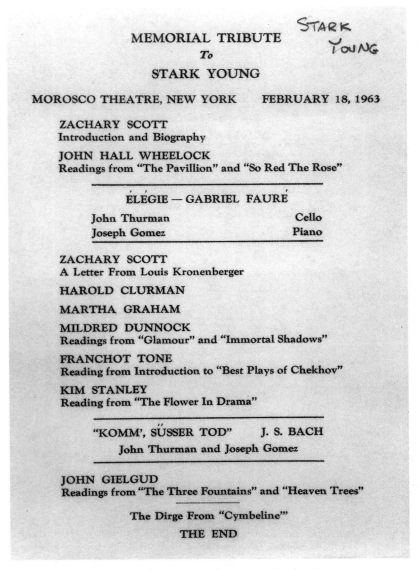

MEMORIAL TRIBUTE
To
STARK YOUNG

MOROSCO THEATRE, NEW YORK   FEBRUARY 18, 1963

ZACHARY SCOTT
Introduction and Biography

JOHN HALL WHEELOCK
Readings from "The Pavillion" and "So Red The Rose"

ÉLÉGIE — GABRIEL FAURÉ

| John Thurman | Cello |
| Joseph Gomez | Piano |

ZACHARY SCOTT
A Letter From Louis Kronenberger

HAROLD CLURMAN

MARTHA GRAHAM

MILDRED DUNNOCK
Readings from "Glamour" and "Immortal Shadows"

FRANCHOT TONE
Reading from Introduction to "Best Plays of Chekhov"

KIM STANLEY
Reading from "The Flower In Drama"

"KOMM', SÜSSER TOD"   J. S. BACH
John Thurman and Joseph Gomez

JOHN GIELGUD
Readings from "The Three Fountains" and "Heaven Trees"

The Dirge From "Cymbeline"
THE END

Program for the memorial service held for Young

If there is anyone for whom we would be prepared to lean backward, it would be you.

As fas as THE FLOWER is concerned, it was published while I was connected with the business management of Scribner's Magazine and before I knew you personally, and so I had to do a certain amount of research to learn the facts. From the records, it appears that our first edition of 2000 was sold out the end of 1925 and that early in 1926 we reprinted a small edition,—smaller than we could hope to print under present manufacturing conditions,—and that the copies of this second printing lasted us through 1940. I might add that between 1928 and 1940 the sale dropped to an average of about 15 copies a year. It is not practical to reprint or bind an edition of less than 500 of any book this size and 1,000 is as small an edition as we are normally prepared to order. You will see, therefore, that we would have an inventory stock of your book eating up its value for very many years to come. Such a policy if extended to other books would mean that we would soon be insolvent for lack of cash and then you would definitely have to look for another publisher.

You feel, I am led to understand, that the fact that this book is out of print robs you, as the author, of the distinction of having written it. On our part I see it somewhat differently:

this collection of articles which you wrote were, through book publication, given permanence. The book is undoubtedly in all of our principal libraries and universities. Therefore, it will be available for scholars and serious readers as long as our civilization lasts—very likely the Communists who follow us will burn it. There is also the hope that your new book, which I trust you will not withdraw, will arouse such interest in the earlier one as to make it feasible to carry them in stock again.

I felt you should know the facts and trust I have not stated them too bluntly. I do it solely in the hope of maintaining your goodwill. My friendship will continue to be yours whether or not you value it.

Sincerely,
[Charles Scribner]

Winston Churchill (1874–1965)

Sir Winston Churchill

A descendant of the renowned English military leader and diplomat of the early eighteenth century, the first Duke of Marlborough (John Churchill), Churchill became one of the leading world figures of the twentieth century. As a youth he enjoyed playing with toy soldiers; after an undistinguished school record, he was dispatched by his father on a military career, graduating from Sandhurst, the Royal Military Academy, in 1895. Thereafter, history provided the wars, and Churchill participated in them and wrote about them, serving as an observer in Cuba with Spanish forces (1895), in India (1897), in the Sudan (1898), and in South Africa (1899), where he was captured by Boers but escaped. As First Lord of the Admiralty (1911–1915), Churchill was responsible for accelerating Britain's naval program and coordinating naval strategy, and he directed the Antwerp expedition and the Dardanelles campaign of World War I. As Chancellor of the Exchequer (1924–1929), he accomplished the adjustment of war debt questions and national finance. Out of the government for ten years (1929–1939), he was called upon by Neville Chamberlain to become First Lord of the Admiralty again at the outbreak of World War II and was soon Prime Minister for its duration. His wartime leadership and resolve, aided by an ability to speak and write efffectively and stirringly, contributed heavily to the Allied victory. In 1953 he was awarded the Nobel Prize in literature. Though Scribners published Churchill's major pre–World War II writings, the firm did not have the resources to bid competitively for later works following his increased reputation after the war; sales of these works were enormous.

Scribner Books by Churchill

1923–1929	*The World Crisis* (5 volumes):
	The World Crisis, 1911–1914 (1923)
	The World Crisis, 1915 (1923)
	The World Crisis, 1916–1918 (2 volumes, 1927)
	The Aftermath (1929)
1930	*A Roving Commission: My Early Life*
1931	*The World Crisis: 1911–1918* (an abridged and revised 1-volume edition of the original first 4 volumes, reissued in 1992)
	The Unknown War: The Eastern Front

1932	*Amid These Storms: Thoughts and Adventures*
1933	*The River War: An Account of the Reconquest of the Soudan*
1933–1938	*Marlborough: His Life and Times* (6 volumes):
	Volume I, 1650–1688 (1933)
	Volume II, 1688–1702 (1933)
	Volume III, 1702–1704 (1935)
	Volume IV, 1704–1705 (1935)
	Volume V, 1705–1708 (1937)
	Volume VI, 1708–1722 (1938)
1939	*A Roving Commission: The Story of My Early Life,* a new American edition, with an introduction by Dorothy Thompson
1968	*Marlborough: His Life and Times* (4 volumes), abridged and with an introduction by Henry Steele Commager

RELATED LETTERS:

Letter from CS III to his parents (postmarked 9 February 1923), written while crossing the English Channel; letter from CS III to Churchill, 4 April 1923.

On a trip to Europe with his wife, CS III spent much of his time on publishing business, particularly in London, where the firm maintained its English office. Here the thirty-three-year-old publisher describes his first meetings with the forty-eight-year-old statesman Winston Churchill, whose World War I history, The World Crisis, *soon began to appear under the Scribner imprint.*

Dear Papa & Mama—

The last ten days have been so busy that I never seemed to have time to settle down to write a line. So now that I have a four hour trip alone across the channel from Ostend [in Belgium] to Dover I shall try to make up—provided the seas don't run too high for writing. . . . The most interesting thing in London was my two meetings with Winston Churchill. I don't know how much Kingsley [head of Scribners' London office] has written about them so I won't go into details.

It seems W.S.C. heard through Brown or Butterworth [Churchill's English agent and publisher] that I was in London so he had the office called up to make an appointment, and asked Kingsley to come too if he cared to. I was told by the two above (Brown & Butterworth) all of the intricacies of the situation and how difficult Churchill was on account of his enthusiasm and persuasiveness that made it hard to get over your

point of view. Also that Butterworth who is very nervous about the book naturally as he has so much at stake did not want to accept any title mentioned other than "The World Crisis" which he had thought of. He didn't feel like opposing Churchill strangely himself however, and hoped we could "pull it off" saving him as the last card. Churchill received us himself at the door of his sitting room in the Ritz and was so pleasant and unaffected that I felt immediately as much at home with him as if our positions in the world had been reversed. He offered us tea or whiskey and concurred heartily in my choice of the latter. He then asked me (as I was told to expect) to read the foreword of his book which starts off about the Great Amphibian etc., and a letter from the editor of the Times saying that there was no question but that that was the title for the book. Also that that had been his own original idea which he has given up but was now delighted to have confirmed. I simply remarked that that made it difficult for me and then went on to tell him that I did not think it a very fortunate choice as it would not be generally understood—that the fact he showed me the foreword & letter first showed that even he thought that it required explanation and how were we going to get over that explanation over to the public—that it was a hard word to handle—and that critics would naturally pick on it first in reviews so that there was danger that its prominence would distract attention from the text. We went on to joke a little about it together how they would picture him as the amphibian and he dropped it without a murmur. He then asked what we should prefer for U.S. and I said "The

World Crisis" while not perfect I felt sure would be the choice of those suggested. He pointed out his criticisms of this title as too pretentious for his book and embracing more than he attempted to cover as he only gave that part of the crisis in which he was himself an actor. I had to agree in part and we went on to drink, talk about hunting, and where I got my clothes etc., very congenially; then the idea "Sea Power, in (or, "and") The World Crisis" struck him. This limited it so as to cover the objections to the other; was reminiscent of Mahan which pleased him; and I agreed and said I felt sure it would be perfectly satisfactory to us and probably the best way out of our maze of difficulties. So we called up Butterworth; and B replied it would be felt sure [to] cause a big cut in his orders as being too narrow—in which we did not concur, but sympathised. There was then nothing to do after 2 hours but call it a day and arrange to meet Butterworth on the next day at Churchill's rooms. He was very gratious in helping with my coat etc. and took us himself down the hall to the lift.

Next day we went over the same ground with Butterworth there. Explained that it would cause all sorts of confusion to have different titles in the two countries and came to the conclusion that "The World Crisis" was the most generally satisfactory. Churchill bewailing that he had never yet had his way in anything so he was schooled in accepting other's judgement. On thinking things over however he waxed more enthusiastic and explained his difficulties in the II vol. now well underway. In it he planned to have a summary of say four chapters following Gallipoli (the theme over the vol and in his opinion the tragedy because of its failure of the war, which cost two years of unnecessary struggle and most of our present difficulties). He suggested that we might make a new agreement (on new terms) for a III vol. which it would be easy for him to write in another six months covering the last years and the conference resulting in the present difficulties which would be more sharply definited [defined?] he thought by the time he came to write it—this, he said would perhaps justify the title The World Crisis. B was silent but I said and thought that the idea certainly was interesting but could be decided on it better when he got on with his work—thinking to find some way to stall until we saw the reception of Vol I which I do not believe will be so startling as to pump the figures. Also I asked if that might not be planning pretty far ahead from his own point of view. He saw my question and assured me that he would not be

mixed up in anything that soon. Well this is all—as you know "Fateful Days" [another suggested title] has since come up while I was in Paris—with what result I have not heard yet. On the whole W.S.C. couldn't have been pleasanter and have treated what I say with seeming greater deference. I couldn't help wondering all the time where his strength came in, if it was not perhaps in the fact that he was big enough not to put on any aside [airs or affectation?]. He asked me to write when I got back and post him on how the book was going and wonders very much how it will—how many it will take us to get out of "our rash bargain ["] and was more than pleased when we told him (not B. who is upset about the length) that you had written that he had certainly fulfilled his part of the bargain. . . .

Your affectionate son
[Charles Scribner]

Dear Mr. Churchill:

We are mailing to you to-day two advance copies of the first volume of "The World Crisis" which is to be published here on April 6th. I hope that you will find its appearance all that you expected. The maps and diagrams are not, however, quite as clean cut as we should have liked them to be, due to the fact that we had to work from proofs of the British edition as copy, which naturally is not as easy to obtain good results from as originals.

I should also like to call your attention to the title-page. The years "1911 to 1915" properly follow your title "First Lord of the Admiralty" and I had understood that the years "1911–1914" would also appear as part of the title on this page and also on the spine of the cover, showing the scope of the particular volume and differentiating it from the second volume which would bear the date "1915". The final revised proof from Butterworth was followed however by our office and I trust it is in accordance with your wishes. On my own return from England it was too late to hold up on this point without causing delay, which we were anxious to avoid. If the present form is not correct it can be changed in the next edition.

There is little further that I can think of to say at present. The advance orders are not large but that is perhaps to be expected on such a high-priced book and will make no difference in the ultimate sale, if it "catches on". You may be assured that no effort will be spared on our part in advertising and other production work, and I shall keep you posted from time to time on how it is selling and will mail you reviews.

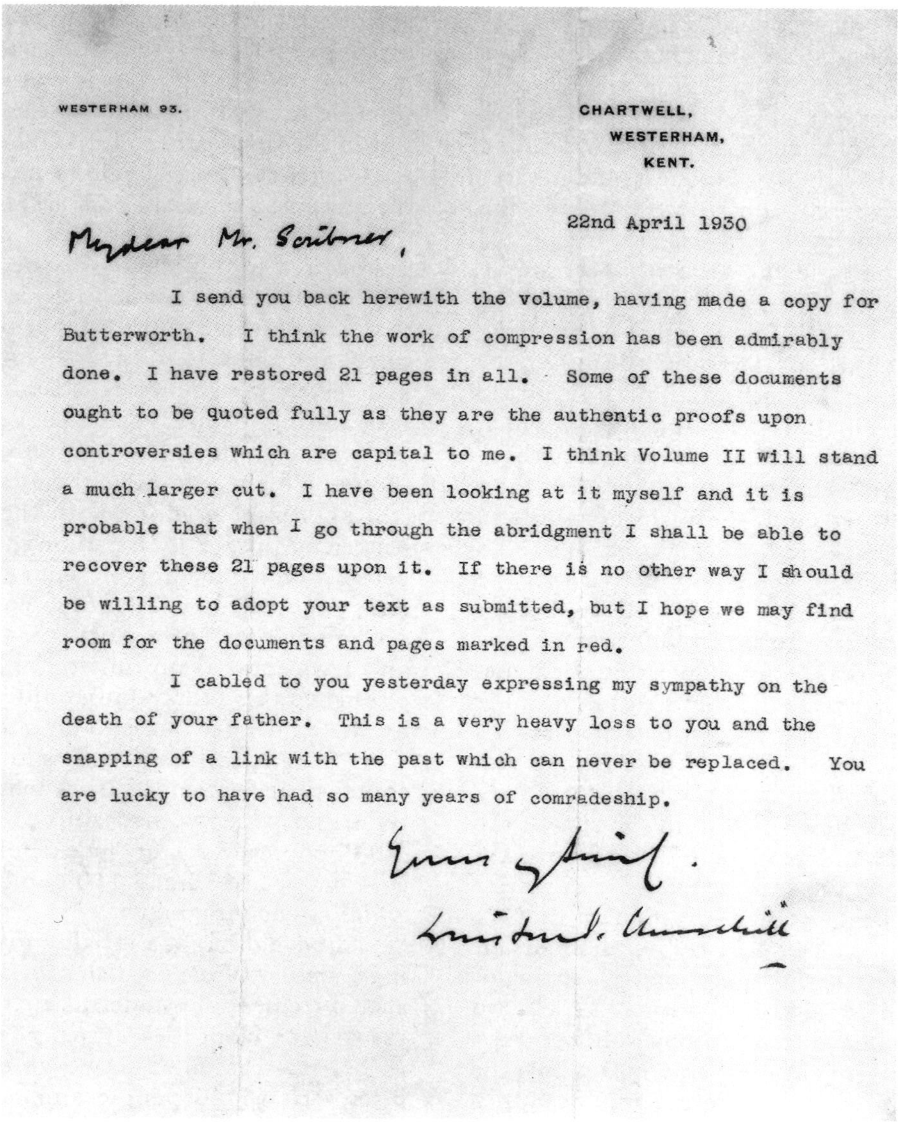

WESTERHAM 93.

CHARTWELL,
WESTERHAM,
KENT.

22nd April 1930

My dear Mr. Scribner,

    I send you back herewith the volume, having made a copy for Butterworth. I think the work of compression has been admirably done. I have restored 21 pages in all. Some of these documents ought to be quoted fully as they are the authentic proofs upon controversies which are capital to me. I think Volume II will stand a much larger cut. I have been looking at it myself and it is probable that when I go through the abridgment I shall be able to recover these 21 pages upon it. If there is no other way I should be willing to adopt your text as submitted, but I hope we may find room for the documents and pages marked in red.

    I cabled to you yesterday expressing my sympathy on the death of your father. This is a very heavy loss to you and the snapping of a link with the past which can never be replaced. You are lucky to have had so many years of comradeship.

Yours sincerely,

Winston S. Churchill

Letter from Churchill to CS III. He is at work on the abridged, one-volume edition of The World Crisis.

It was a great pleasure to have met you and I hope that our relationship of author and publisher may continue and prosper to our mutual advantage, so that I may have occasion to have other such pleasant afternoons in your company.

Very sincerely yours
[Charles Scribner]

Churchill followed up on his idea to continue his war history through the 1919 peace conference and its aftermath, which resulted in an additional three volumes. Exceeding his original word estimates would prove to be a pattern in his writing projects.

LETTER:
Letter from CS III to Churchill, 15 January 1930.

Scribner outlines his plan for creating an abridged, one-volume edition of The World Crisis, *for which his firm would do much of the editing. Churchill heartily approved of it, but more work was required than anticipated, and the volume did not appear until 6 February 1931.*

Dear Mr. Churchill:
    I have been intending to write to you for a long time but each time I got set to write I found that I had just missed a steamer so put off a week

to await the next ship. There is one matter that may interest you and if anything is to be done we had better start promptly, so here it is—

I have been thinking over a suggestion you made and the more I have thought of it and talked about it with others in our business, the greater its possibilities appear. It also offers to you the likelihood of securing a financial return out of proportion to the time and labor that would be entailed. To put it as briefly as possible—the three volumes of the "World Crisis" (omitting "The Aftermath") total about 550,000 to 575,000 words. If through the omission of the more technical portions and documents which could be paraphrased, or given in part, these books could be reduced to not more than 300,000, so that we could publish the whole in one volume at, say, $5.00, we might be able to do far more with it than we have done with any of the individual volumes. In fact, I believe that we might be justified in printing 10,000 copies as the first edition. My reason for suggesting the omission of "The Aftermath" is that I think that it is asking too much of you to try to compress this with the other volumes within the limits of a volume that we could afford to publish at not over $5.00 that would be attractive in the size of the type and bulk and have in general a popular appearance. Closing the volume with the armistice would be a natural ending, and the fact that we publish vol. IV ("The Aftermath") under a different title adds a further justification to omitting it. "The Aftermath" could then continue to sell as a companion volume with a prolonged life and the libraries and students of the war, who are now the principal purchasers of the present volumes I II & III, would still buy them in preference to the abridged edition.

A still further possibility is that if the new edition had a wide sale we could be justified going back and making a subscription set of the original volumes, adding "The Aftermath" and perhaps some illustrations to help agents in making a strong "selling talk".

As far as terms go, I find that the most royalty that such a volume could carry would be 15%, of which we would withhold 5% to be credited against the unearned advances on Volumes I and II, until these advances were met. In other words, we would from the start pay you 10% on the new one-volume edition, and in as much as only 5%, or one-third would be credited against the unearned advance on what would amount to approximately two-thirds of the new volume, I think you will appreciate that we are offering to you as attractive a proposal as you might reasonably expect. I don't think we should be held to making any advance but it would not be unreasonable for you to expect to earn $5,000 on the sale in the first year, and if 1600 copies were sold the former advances would be met and you would then receive a return of 15%. This 1600 would be reduced by sales of Vols I & II previous to the publication of this single volume.

I realize that you have a great many irons in the fire between politics, periodical contributions, and the Life of the Duke of Marlborough, and very likely you lack the time to do the necessary editing. If this is the case, I suggest that you let us do it in this office and submit our revision to you. This would have the advantage that the editing would be done with the interest of the American public as first thought, and would be better than having anyone aside from yourself attempt the cutting. Of course you may be doing such a book for Butterworth that we could use. In any case, there is no time to be lost if it is to be published this fall and it would have to be ready by September 1st for us to do our best with it.

"The Aftermath" has sold close on to 700 copies since September 7th when I rendered you a report of what we had sold previous to that— 5,047 copies. Each of the earlier books has also sold between 130 and 150 copies since Aug 1st, which is encouraging.

I have thought a lot about your idea of writing a history of the English speaking race, but it is such a tremendous undertaking that it is hard for me to get a clear idea of how it might be done. I rather fear that a large two-volume work would be apt to appall people and not have a really popular sale. Another difficulty is that unfortunately enough, from my point of view, the American people are becoming less and less of an Anglo Saxon race, and the Nordic tradition with England as the mother country of the USA is less popular in this country than one might expect. I can see a short history done from your own viewpoint without any great research, but I am, as is said, at sea on the larger proposition.

Our retail department tells me that the bound set of "The World Crisis" sent to your apartment before you sailed evidently was not delivered. It came back to us about a month or so later and we have been holding it here. Do you wish us to send it somewhere for you or would you prefer to have us take it over and cancel the charge to you?

I have enjoyed very much the articles you have contributed to the Telegraph on your trip

["What I Heard and Saw in America" during his 1929 visit]. They are the best of the kind I have ever read.

With all best wishes for 1930 and hoping you are making good progress with your biography,

Sincerely yours,
[Charles Scribner]

The biography mentioned above was published by Scribners in the fall as A Roving Commission: My Early Life.

LETTER:
Letter from CS III to Churchill, 19 June 1931.

Pressured by rumors and frustrated by half-information, CS III wants to know what other writing projects Churchill is contemplating or has begun. He is already under contract with Scribners for his history of The Unknown War: The Eastern Front *and his biography of the Duke of Marlborough.*

Dear Mr. Churchill:

So many rumors have come to me in the past week with regard to what you are planning to write that I feel I should address you personally and I cabled yesterday to that effect.

First, Mr. Kingsley [Charles Kingsley, head of Scribners' London office] arrived and told me of Butterworth's anxieties regarding a short history of the war which you are said to be contemplating. Then, yesterday I received a long "confidential" cable from another London publishing house asking us to join them in an offer for another book that you are also quoted as having planned. Therefore, at the risk of appearing to break confidence with these publishers, I think our publishing relations are such as warrants writing directly to you to make clear my own position and to ask you how matters actually stand.

With regard to the shortened history of the World War, if Scribners were not to have the book rights I should naturally oppose it to the limit, as it appears that it would have to closely parallel the "World Crisis". The publisher would therefore gain all the advantage of what we had spent in the way of promotion, since aside from the fact that the royalty advances have not been altogether met, we have spent to date over twenty thousand dollars on the series in advertising, not including circulars. As you can imagine, this leaves us no profit in the books to date, but we have done this with our eyes open and nothing to

complain of, as the quality of the books is such that we have confidence in their permanency. "A Roving Commission" coming when it did seemed to us to have such unusual possibilities of establishing your popularity among American readers before the publication of the one-volume "World Crisis" that we advertised it to the limit and further—practically $7,000. While conditions have been against us, I believe we made a dent which your visit to America in the fall should further.

I understand that the guarantee offered by an American publisher on this "popular" history is $50,000, and if this includes serial and syndicate rights I am not surprised, as a number of our authors receive such terms on these rights, although I would hesitate to give them an advance of $5,000 on book royalties. I am not keen myself to publish such a book at present, as it would kill the other volumes for the time, but I realise however that as a writer you cannot overlook such opportunities. My suggestion is that if such an organization as Hearst's has made the proposal, we could arrange with them without loss to you whereby they would be free on the serialization or syndication and the book would be ours. Otherwise, in conjunction with some other periodical publishers we might match their offer.

The second proposition is, I understand, a large one-volume history of the English speaking peoples, on the order of the book you talked to me about in New York that you thought of during the Army-Yale football game, and a further development of our suggestion that you write a history of the British Empire. The minimum offer expected from me was rather staggering, especially as they gave me little or no information. Also like our friend Butterworth they did not disclose whether they on their side were making any such advance for the British market. I have cabled Mr. John Carter of our London office to see them and, if they did not protest, to see you also. Naturally I should like to have the book, if you write it, and would do my best to meet any American offer—but at present it is like fencing with the air. I was surprised at the fact that it was to be published in 1933, as between finishing the Marlborough, lecturing in America, and all of the other calls on your time, this would scarcely seem possible. I remember when you talked to me of this book you placed it some three or four years after the Marlborough on account of the preparation that would be necessary to make it all that you conceived. I therefore have not mentioned it to you as I hoped we might have the two forthcoming books published, or at least practically fin-

MEMORANDUM OF AGREEMENT, made this twenty-ninth day of July 1930, between
WINSTON S. CHURCHILL, of London, England, hereinafter called "the
Author", and CHARLES SCRIBNER'S SONS, of New York City, U.S.A., hereinafter called "the Publishers", their successors and assigns; WHEREBY
it is mutually agreed as follows respecting a work by said Author
tentatively entitled MEMOIRS:

1. The Publishers shall, during the legal term of copyright and
renewals thereof, have the sole and exclusive right of publishing the
said work in volume form in the English language throughout the
United States of America and the Dominion of Canada. It is understood
that the Author retains the right of serial publication.

2. The Author guarantees to the Publishers that the said work is in
no way whatever a violation of any existing copyright and that it contains nothing of a libellous or scandalous character, and that he will
indemnify the Publishers from all suits, claims, and proceedings, damages
and costs, which may be made, taken or incurred by or against them on
the ground that the said work is an infringement of copyright or contains anything libellous or scandalous.

3. Said Publishers, in consideration of the right herein granted and
of the guarantees aforesaid, agree to publish said work at their own
expense, in such style and manner as they shall deem most expedient, and
to pay said Author the following royalties and moneys:

(a) A royalty of FIFTEEN (15) per cent. of the published price
on the first ten thousand (10,000) copies of said work sold
by them in the United States of America and TWENTY (20) per
cent. for all copies sold thereafter.

(b) A royalty of TEN (10) per cent. of the published price on
all copies of said work sold by them in the Dominion of Canada.

(c) Ten (10) per cent. of the sum received from the sale of any
copies of said work as a remainder. The Author shall first be
given the option for sixty days of purchasing such copies at
the price the Publishers reasonably expect to get in the open
market.

No royalties shall be payable upon any copies given
away for the purpose of review or in the interests of the sale,
or for the purpose of securing publicity for the said work.

(d) A total sum in advance and on account of said royalties of
Twenty-five Hundred Dollars ($2,500.00), payable on the date
of publication of said work.

4. The sum of Two Hundred Dollars ($200.00) shall be allowed by the
Publishers for author's alterations, to be remitted to said Author if
no author's alterations are made in the American edition of said work.

5. The first statement shall not be rendered until six months after
date of publication; and thereafter statements shall be rendered semi-
annually, in the months of February and August, settlements to be made in
cash four months after date of statement.

If the Publishers give notice at any time that, in their opinion,
the demand for said work has ceased, or if the said work be allowed to go
out of print and they neglect to issue a new edition within six months
of having received written notice thereof, then in any of these cases
all rights conveyed under this agreement shall revert to the Author without further notice.

Said Publishers shall have the right, when the sales of the full-
priced editions shall render it advisable, to publish a cheaper edition
of said work and shall pay a royalty of TEN (10) per cent. of the published price of such cheaper edition or editions, on every copy sold.

The Author shall receive on publication six presentation copies of
said work and shall be entitled to purchase further copies for personal
use at the lowest Trade price.

In consideration of the mutuality of this contract, the aforesaid
parties agree to all its provisions, and in testimony thereof affix their
signatures and seals.

Witness to signature of
Winston S. Churchill

Witness to signature of
Charles Scribner's Sons

*Scribners' publishing contract for Churchill's volume of
recollections, annotated by Churchill. The work was
published in 1930 under the title* A Roving
Commission: My Early Life.

CHURCHILL PROMOTION

Approximately 80 stores in 22 cities have been written with the offer to supplement their stock with consignment stock to tie up with Mr. Churchill's lecture in each city. About 30 stores have co-operated in ordering additional stock and making window displays, etc. With their orders have been shipped a set of 3 posters describing THE UNKNOWN WAR and measuring about 11 x 14, for window display.

About 500 Churchill books have been shipped at the request of various stores which is additional to the stock they already had on hand.

Three posters have been sent to either Mr. Churchill or a representative of the lecture bureau to arrive in time for Mr. Churchill's lecture in each city. These posters, measuring 11 x 17, announced "Books by Winston Churchill."

Ten thousand circulars have been imprinted and distributed to stores throughout the country as additional tie-up with his lecture itinerary.

Sterling Galt.

March 8, 1932.

Scribners' plan for promoting Churchill's books during his 1932 lecture tour in the United States

ished, before taking it up. I am certain you would write a magnificent history but the subject is so great as to rather stagger my mind, and without your giving some idea of your approach and treatment of it, I feel totally lost and do not know what to do or say.

You must think me rather squeamish in not mentioning the English publishers by name but although I am on the best of relations with them, they might not thank me for going direct to you, so I must use some decency—possibly they are merely sounding my resources and have no understanding with you, although they talk of having an option.

The sum of the whole matter is that we believe in your work and in its future, and we also believe that it would be very detrimental to your interests as well as our own if your American book rights were divided between two or more publishers. It has always worked out that neither publisher is then as keen to wholeheartedly push another's books, as his efforts may only result in bearing fruit for a rival and prevents combination in sets. I might add that if at any time you may wish £1000 we should be glad to advance it against your account, but naturally we would like some assurance that you will give us this option on your next book, provided we make terms satisfactory to you.

This I believe is by far the longest letter of my business career so I shall stop for breath before writing about the current books in which we are both interested.

With kindest regards
Sincerely yours
[Charles Scribner]

Churchill responded that nothing would be undertaken without "full consultation with you." Shortly afterward he offered Scribners a volume of his collected articles, which the firm published in 1932 as Amid These Storms: Thoughts and Adventures. *The idea for a one-volume "popular" history of World War I was never realized. CS III queried Churchill several more times in the 1930s regarding his plan on writing a history of the "English speaking race," but other writing projects and World War II intervened. The idea did not die, however, for in the 1950s Churchill published with Dodd, Mead a four-volume history on the subject, his last major work.*

RELATED LETTERS:
Scribners' 1929 contract with Churchill for a biography of the Duke of Marlborough specified a work consisting of no less than 200,000 nor more than 250,000 words. Churchill would receive an advance of $24,000 and a royalty of 20 percent of the published price on every copy sold. Complications arose when the work continued to balloon: before he was finished, Churchill wrote about 1,000,000 words. Volume I of the English edition was published by Scribners as two volumes in November 1933.

[telegram] Dec 2 – 1933
SCRIBNERS NEW YORK
VOLUMES RECEIVED CONGRATULATE YOU ON ADMIRABLE PRODUCTION
CHURCHILL

Dec.11, 1933
Dear Mr. Churchill:
It was very kind of you to have cabled congratulating us on the format of your book; publishers seldom receive compliments from authors and I can assure you that it was much appreciated. It will be January before we shall be able to give you any definite information regarding sales. Our first printing was 5000, of which we have bound up 4000 to date and I hope that we shall have practically disposed of this number. . . .
Sincerely yours
[Charles Scribner]

6th January 1934
My dear Charles Scribner,
. . . I have now reached a point in my work where its compass can be seen. I have no doubt that to do justice to the subject there ought to be a third volume. . . . I have been reflecting upon how this change would strike you. Originally our contract was $24,000 for 200,000 words. It will already be 400,000 for the same price. For the final volume I should like you to pay me $5,000 or £1250 at parity of exchange. . . . I am distressed that you have not made money out of my books like all my other publishers have done, and would not wish you to commit yourself to anything which was not sound business. But please send me a cable because your answer is necessary to my decision.
Yours sincerely
Winston S. Churchill

[telegram] January 19, 1934
CHURCHILL
THIRD VOLUME MARLBOROUGH WOULD INCREASE LIKELIHOOD OF WORK MEETING OUR ADVANCE AND HELP INSURE FUTURE ROYALTIES TO YOU STOP REGRET HOWEVER I DO NOT FEEL JUSTIFIED IN COMMITTING COMPANY TO YOUR PROPOSAL FOR INCREASED ADVANCE WRITING REGARDS
SCRIBNER

Oct.19, 1934
Dear Mr. Churchill:
. . . I hope to see you in England this winter, when we can talk over Volume III. I assure you that I have every wish to do the fair thing but you must remember that this work was contracted for before the depression and according to our contract it was to be only about a third the size, which in many ways would have been a more popular book with the general public in America.
With kindest regards
Sincerely yours
[Charles Scribner]

Volume II of the English edition was published by Scribners as two volumes in March of 1935.

23rd May 1936

Private

My dear Charles Scribner,

The inevitable has happened, and I am forced to spread Marlborough into a fourth volume. . . . In view of the fact that the American sales have been so disappointing I do not feel I can ask you to make any additional payments for the fourth volume, but I do hope you will agree with the new plan. . . . We shall publish here early in October Volume III. My hope is that Volume IV will be ready for April publication 1937. About one-third of that volume is already done, and the rest in full view.

With kind regards,
Believe me,
Yours sincerely,
Winston S. Churchill

June 4 1936

Dear Mr. Churchill:

Your letter of May 23rd is somewhat of a surprise as I had not guessed that the Marlborough would run into another volume. It is difficult to say whether we shall be the gainers or losers in America through having the added volume. We certainly cannot hope to do very much with the third and fourth volumes on publication, as the work has grown to a so much greater size than originally planned that it has lost all semblance of general popularity and has become more of a library set. Let us hope however that when it is completed we may be able to find some way of disposing of sets by subscription, emphasizing the fact that it is a history of England over a considerable period of years rather than the biography of a single character. I will have our London office follow the progress of the forthcoming volumes so that we may have the material promptly and be able to publish at the earliest possible date. There is always something of a gap, however, between American and English publication and if we are unable to publish before the end of October, we will probably have to hold volume III over until 1937 and hope to publish the fourth volume early in the Fall of that year.

It is a miracle to me that you found time to do so much work on your book, as you are quoted at length in the papers here once or twice a week, and your Parliamentary and newspaper work must take up a great portion of your time.

With kindest regards
Sincerely yours
[Charles Scribner]

Volume III of the English edition was published by Scribners in one volume in March of 1937; Volume IV appeared in October 1938, also as a single volume. By 1955, however, royalties had earned barely half of the 1929 advance.

RELATED LETTERS:
Letters from CS III to Churchill, 20 September 1945 (from New York) and 6 June 1946 (from London).

Admitting he no longer can bid competitively for Churchill's latest books in the postwar publishing boom era, Scribner offers to pursue selling the movie rights to Savrola (1900), Churchill's only attempt at full-length fiction, published almost fifty years before.

Dear Mr. Churchill:

For some months we have been owing you a cheque on your royalties, other than those which go through Curtis Brown [his early English agent]. I find that our Cashiers' Department held it up as they were not sure where it should be sent—previous reports having gone to the Macmillan Company [his wartime managing agent] and to the British Embassy in Washington. I am also including the payment on the August first report, due in December. I am sorry that these are not larger, and I hope to find some new means of stimulating the sale of your books, about which I shall write at another time.

A few months ago, I ran across a copy of your early novel Savrola, which I had not heard of before. You may not be too proud of it today, but it intrigued me as it brought back memories of Anthony Hope and George Barr McCutcheon [turn-of-the-century English and American novelists]. I wonder if it has occurred to you that you might sell the motion picture rights at a really high figure, in spite of the fact that the copyright does not seem to have been renewed in America. It would not only make a colourful story, but the plot of the great democrats overthrowing the dictator could be worked up in the scenario so that it would be most timely. Also, the fact that you wrote a story nearly fifty years ago, portraying a situation so parallel to one through which we have been living, would in itself make a great press story.

You may be interested in hearing that New York is alive with rumours and speculations about a book upon which it is assumed you are now at work. A number of agents and syndicates have asked me to join in offers, but nothing under

WESTERHAM 93.

CHARTWELL,
WESTERHAM,
KENT.

November 19, 1938.

My dear Charles Scribner,

Thank you very much for sending me the reviews of the last volume of Marlborough, which certainly are very complimentary.

I send you herewith ten inscribed pages for gift copies, which you would oblige me very much by sending to the addressees on the attached list. Will you let me know the cost of the extra copies beyond those to which I am entitled.

I hope indeed that the new volume will go well at the reduced price, and that the completion of the work may help to draw some of the earlier volumes.

I am very sorry that the book has not gone better in the United States, but we have had a very rough time, both in finance and foreign affairs. It is always a great satisfaction to me that this publication should be extant in the United States, and that I should have been associated in it with your famous firm.

Yours sincerely,

Winston S. Churchill

Charles Scribner Esq.

Letter from Churchill to CS III on receipt of the last volume of Marlborough: His Life and Times. *Scribner repaid Churchill's compliment: "It was very kind of you to say such pleasant things about Charles Scribner's Sons. On our part we have been very proud at having your name on our list, as we appreciate the fact that you are certainly one of the greatest English writers alive to-day, and it is a keen disappointment that we have not been able to sell your books as widely as they deserved" (5 December 1938).*

a hundred thousand dollars for American book rights appears of interest. In fact, it is said that one offer for book and syndicate rights totals a million; so, sadly enough for me, I fear it is getting beyond my depth. General MacArthur's prospective book is also getting a great deal of attention. In his case, the motion picture rights appear to be the principal drawing card.

Publishing in America has boomed during the past years, in spite of the scarcity of paper. I know that Scribner's has made (before taxes) double the amount of any of our ninety-seven previous years in business. I think this is very largely due to the fact that reading during the war years did not have the same competition from other forms of amusement, and we have yet to see whether those who bought a book for the first time will think well enough of it to wish to buy another.

You may have noticed that we published a short biography of you, based on the text of the three articles that appeared in "Life" magazine. It has done quite well, and I don't believe you would find anything objectionable in it.

It has been a great privilege to have been the publisher of so many of your books, and although their earnings may have been rather disappointing to you, they are certain to live and return a revenue for countless years.

    With every good wish,

        Faithfully yours,

        [Charles Scribner]

Dear Mr. Churchill,

    I arrived here Sunday evening and I am most disappointed that I am not bringing you an offer for "Savrola". I was certain that it would make an outstanding motion picture, not only because you were the author of the book, but also because it could be interpreted as a premonition you had in your youth of a role not unlike the one that you were destined to play in the world as the "great Democrat".

    I first made a polite "pass" at two or three of the principal companies which came to nothing. Then I was fortunate enough to meet Talbot Jennings, who wrote the scenario of "Mutiny on the Bounty" and many other outstanding pictures. He saw at once the possibilities that I had in mind, and was prepared to gamble his time for nothing to show just how it could be done—most producers are apparently not very imaginative. He felt however that he should first see if he could get any sign of a favourable reaction, and came back as disappointed as I am to say that the powers that be in Hollywood were not at all receptive at present, for more or less "Leftish" reasons. I don't think I need to elaborate on this. I still know it is a sound idea however and I am sure that sooner or later it will be produced.

    I am at the Savoy for two or three weeks. It may well be longer, as I am having a difficult time at the moment to arrange for passage home as there seem too few ships or planes on which the American Embassy can give priorities.

    It is rather frustrating to an American as most British publishers seem very adverse to seeing anyone without long standing appointments, whereas I have grown used to New York publishers and authors telephoning to ask if I would not be free in the next five or ten minutes. This avoids one's having to carry around a complicated engagement book.

    Please give my kindest regards to Mrs. Churchill.

        Very sincerely,

        [Charles Scribner]

In November, Churchill wrote back that he had disposed of the film rights to Savrola *himself (to London Film Productions), though no film ever resulted.*

RELATED LETTERS:

Letter from Churchill to CS III, 5 April 1949; letter from CS III to Churchill, 20 April 1949, in reply; letter from Churchill to CS III, 8 May 1949, in reply.

This exchange of letters—the last between the two men in the Scribner Archives—reveals the sincere and cordial tone on which their author/ publisher relationship ended.

My dear Charles,

    Thank you for your letter and for sending me a copy of the new one volume edition of THE WORLD CRISIS [a reissue of the 1931 edition]. I should be very glad indeed if you would send me a few more.

    I am glad to know that you plan a new edition of A ROVING COMMISSION. It would be quite wrong to add any parts of AMID THESE STORMS to such a volume, as there is no connection whatever between the two.

    In view of the increased publicity I now command it astonishes me that the books of which you hold the copyright have not had any sale worth speaking of in the United States during or since the war years.

    Thank you for your postscript. Let me know when you come to London.

    With kind regards

        Yours sincerely

        Winston S. Churchill

Dear Mr. Churchill:

    I appreciated very much your finding time to thank me for the new one-volume edition of THE WORLD CRISIS. Six more are being sent to you. Please don't hesitate to let me know if you should wish more, as I shall be only too glad to give them to you.

    I shall heed what you say and will not make any additions to the new edition of A ROVING COMMISSION. Perhaps a new wrap will be sufficient to draw attention to it. It seems a shame, however, that AMID THESE STORMS should be out of print and I must try to find a way of reviving it.

    What you say about the lack of sale of your earlier books, in view of your position in the world today as well as your great popularity in America, is hard to explain. My only answer is that you have moved at such a pace that the pub-

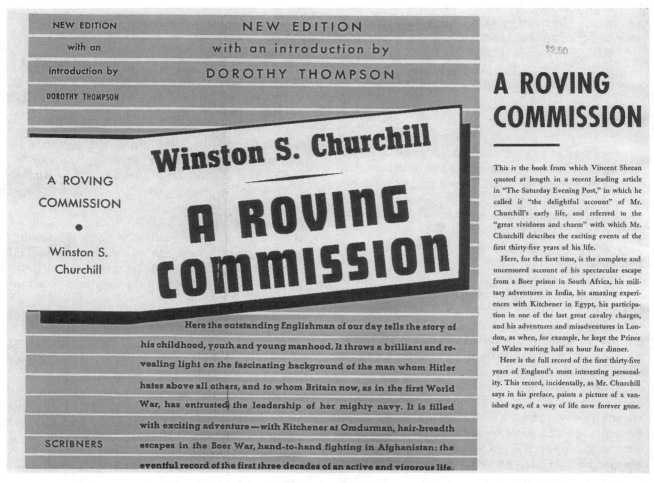

Dust jacket for the new American edition (1939) of Churchill's recollections of his early years

lic, in following you, have had little time to turn back to your earlier works. It is also far more a fact in America than in England that book stores tend to place their entire emphasis on an author's last book and will not carry earlier books in stock, even discouraging orders for them from customers.

It is very good of you to ask me to let you know when I come to London. Nothing could give me greater pleasure than to be able to be of some service to you. I feel reticent, however, of in any way imposing on your kindness as I know you must have to conserve your time for the many activities your are always engaged in.

With kindest regards,

Sincerely yours,

[Charles Scribner]

Dear Charles,

Thank you for your letter of April 20 and for sending me six more copies of your edition of THE WORLD CRISIS, which have now arrived safely and which I am glad to have.

Of course I understand all your difficulties. A publisher's task is not an easy one these days.

I send you herewith a copy of my latest volume, THEIR FINEST HOUR, which I have inscribed for you, with my good wishes.

Yours sincerely

Winston S. Churchill

Their Finest Hour *was the second volume of Churchill's six-volume history of World War II, which was being published by Houghton Mifflin Company.*

Thomas Boyd (1898–1935)

Thomas Boyd

Boyd began his career with Scribners as a novelist and finished it as a biographer. Born in Ohio, he left high school before graduating to join the marines to fight in World War I. He saw action with the Sixth Regiment at Verdun-sur-Meuse, Belleau Wood, Soissons, and Saint-Mihiel before effects from a gas-shell explosion at Blanc Mont in October 1918 ended his military career. Living in Saint Paul, Minnesota, in the early 1920s, he worked as literary editor of the *St. Paul Daily News* and was part owner of the Kilmarnock Bookshop, where he established close friendships with visiting writers, such as F. Scott Fitzgerald. The success of his first book, the war novel *Through the Wheat* (1923), and rapid acceptance and publication of subsequent fictional works, such as *Points of Honor* (1925), a collection of war stories, convinced him to devote his full time to writing. But he thereafter was frequently hard-pressed financially to afford the time to do the kind of writing he wanted and so began researching biographical subjects that sustained his historical and military interests. His biographies of two American Revolutionary War heroes, Generals Anthony Wayne and Henry Lee, established his reputation as an accomplished biographer who could create highly engaging narrative from fact. Though he never lived to write the best-selling historical novel his Scribner editor, Maxwell Perkins, thought he was destined to achieve, his first novel has become a classic of its genre.

Scribner Books by Boyd

1923	*Through the Wheat* (edition illustrated by John W. Thomason, 1927)
1924	*The Dark Cloud*
1925	*Points of Honor*
	Samuel Drummond
1928	*Shadow of the Long Knives: A Novel*

| 1929 | *Mad Anthony Wayne* |
| 1931 | *Light-Horse Harry Lee* |

RELATED LETTERS:

Letter from Scribner editor Maxwell Perkins to Boyd, 4 October 1922; letter from Boyd to F. Scott Fitzgerald [December 1922]; letter from Boyd to Perkins, 27 December 1922.

These letters document the initial rejection and subsequent acceptance by Scribners of Boyd's first book, Through the Wheat. *F. Scott Fitzgerald frequently visited Boyd's Saint Paul, Minnesota, bookstore during the winter of 1921–1922 and became a close friend. A successful Scribner author, Fitzgerald proved to be the catalyst for Boyd's reversal of fortune with Scribners. He considered Boyd's book to be the best war novel since Stephen Crane's* The Red Badge of Courage.

Dear Mr. Boyd:

I am returning "Through the Wheat," and I greatly admire it. You did not exactly submit it, but I did present it and saw to it that it was understood to be a remarkable piece of writing,- and as such it was considered, and discussed. But even when this, with all it implied, was insisted upon, we could not find encouragement to hope for an adequate sale as things are now. It is so utterly a war book,- a fighting book, and though it ends on a fine note, it is not (thank God!) uplifting.

But would not this material fall into some literary plan you have,- for no one could show this sensibility and power without having literary plans; and there is the chance that one is for a novel of which the war would be a part, and that the forty thousand words or so of "Through the Wheat" would fall into place, not of course without modification, but substantially as they are. And if this should be so, you would remove certain flaws in "Through the Wheat" which are now unavoidable. One is that in the natural and realistic way you have written it, Hicks does not become individualized for a long time,- of course I am thinking of him or some one like him as "hero" of the novel, and in that case he would be known as a character at the start of this part of the book. Then, the narrative at present would be, I think, even more effective if less continuously tense,- if there were more relief. Presumably, if

this were a part of a novel, there would be references between times to the hero's former life and so on. Of course, you couldn't, and you wouldn't, devise a novel around this just for the sake of putting this over: I am only hoping you have had a novel in mind of which it would form a really logical part.

I feel it is something of an impertinence in me to suggest this. I know how hard you work too. But I can't refrain from doing it because I can see such a book making a sensation, and making it on account of this fighting part too, if it could be published as a true novel and not as a picture of the front. It would be not unnatural if you had, or had had, a plan with which this would be compatible and if so I can hardly think you would not carry it out successfully.

There are incidents in "Through the Wheat" of most extraordinary quality: the scene in the forest where the branch falls and how it affects Hicks,- perhaps you saw it happen but it is equivalent to a stroke of genius; and the effect when released, of being pinned down by machine gun fire; and the discussion as to whether women of a certain sort could be "good"; and the scene of the road with the varied nationalities of troops streaming up and down; and the way the Moroccoans came through the wheat, and how they took their wounds. It is all very fine.

Sincerely,
[Maxwell Perkins]

In his letter of gratitude Boyd mentions Fitzgerald's new book of stories, Tales of the Jazz Age, *which Scribners had published in September. "Van" is Cornelius Van Ness, Boyd's bookstore partner. [Letter in F. Scott Fitzgerald Papers]*

Dear Scott:

To attempt to tell you of my honest gratitude would only show up my inability fully to express myself. When Scribner's turned down Through the Wheat I cried on reading the letter of rejection—as I also did when I wrote certain parts of the book. And besides, I felt that so long as it remained unpublished I could never write anything else: the best of which I am capable is in Through the Wheat, and to dam that would be to

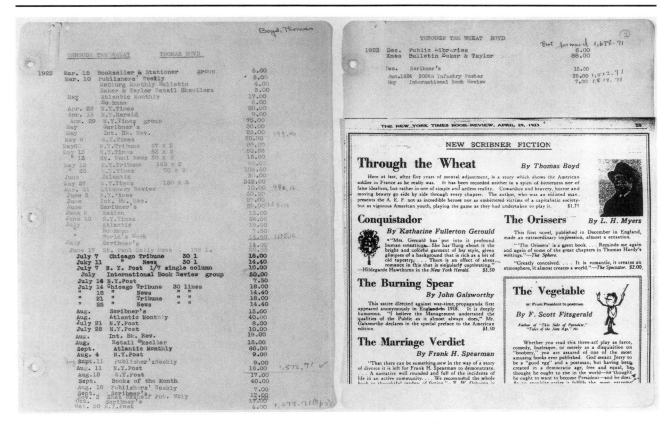

Scribners' advertising record for Through the Wheat, *shown with the first ad the firm placed for it after its publication on 27 April 1923*

dam all subsequent transcriptions of thoughts and experiences. I feel quite aware that it is only through you and your inexhaustable exuberance that Scribner's took the book. I hope for all of your sakes that it exhausts one edition. Strange, but I doubted that you would like it; why, I don't know. And when I sent it I did not believe that you intended doing with it. I thought you wanted only to read it. Well, it was a surprise. The wire came early in the morning over the telephone and getting me angrily out of bed at seven.—I had not planned to do anything with it for five or six more years. But while the m.s. was sunk my ambition was sunk also. You know how much I appreciate what you have done, don't you.

The book shop is moved under the womens city club. It now has spacious and luxurious quarters. Oliver Crosby [?] has died which has had no effect upon us. Did you read Peggy's review of The Jazz Age? Van and I sent you a book today and it is a Christmas remembrance. It went early for fear, if it didn't, it would arrive late.

Perkins doesn't want to publish my book until Fall. What do you counsel? If there ever is time in this Christmas rush I will write—

Love to Zelda

Tom

Peggy of course inundates you both with pleasurable feelings toward you.

Here, Boyd's reference to "Mrs. Boyd's book" is to his wife's first novel, The Love Legend, *which Scribners published in September under her pseudonym Woodward Boyd.*

Dear Mr. Perkins:

Your telegram threw me into a wild fit and my wits have lain dormant ever since. Rather a surprise to have a book accepted after one has composed himself with the thought of the book resting for years longer in inviolable obscurity. Of course I am glad. Also I am willing that some of the vulgarity be deleted. I never wanted merde to remain, and I've a notion that several of the oh Christ's and God damns may be scratched without detracting from the book. It never was my purpose to accentuate cursing.

Scott's suggestions of the make-up marine green with a white tab; sounds well—but please let the pages have a wide margin—as wide a margin as Crome Yellow [1921 Aldous Huxley novel] if that is practical.

You know, there is a chance of the book going. I hope so, for the plan of a book is forming in my mind and I want to begin to write it in the first of the year. It will take much longer to write than the other one and it may turn out to be fairly good. I am very eager to try it out: a novel method in form which is surprisingly simple. But in the first part there will be a great deal of documentation.

Just now I am praying that the publishing of the Boyd's will not result in the bankrupting of the Scribners. But, damn it, Mrs. Boyd's book ought to go well. I've sold 150 copies to people who have asked for it and they almost unanimously report themselves to be greatly taken with it.

Faithfully
Thomas Boyd

If I tried to thank you I would become thoroughly maudlin.

Published on 27 April 1923, Through the Wheat *was hailed by critics; it became a leader of the "new" war fiction that de-romanticized the horrors of war.*

RELATED LETTERS:
Boyd had second thoughts about the ending of Through the Wheat, *particularly its last sentence, which he hoped would be suggestive of the main character's surfeit of war. This exchange of letters (excerpts) with his editor follow his indecision about changing it, Perkins's suggestions for it, and the public's reaction to it as related by Perkins.*

[circa March 7, 1923]
Dear Mr. Perkins:
. . . I've made a few corrections in the enclosed proofs. Now as to the last line: if, after reading it over, you think it will make my meaning any clearer I wish you would make the sentence read: "Hicks was exalted: Gethsemaned." It comes nearer my meaning, for I did not intend that Hicks had become a full-fledged soldier, but rather that he had become so saturated with conflict that his soul, if I may use that word, could

stand no more. And so whatever consciousness he possesses rose above the scene.
Thomas Boyd
But I doubt it would make it any clearer.

[circa March 12, 1923]
Dear Mr. Perkins:
I know I'm an awful bother, but when one begins to change things he never stops. I wonder if you could catch the last paragraph of my book and cut the last sentence: "Hicks was exalted; lost in the absolute." and substitute for it the following sentence: The soul of Hicks was numb. . . .
Faithfully,
Thomas Boyd

March 16, 1923
Dear Mr. Boyd:
I think the last correction for the end of the book to the effect that Hick's soul was numb, is an improvement,- much better than your former suggestion which I had not followed. . . .
As ever yours,
[Maxwell Perkins]

June 20, 1923
Dear Boyd:
We are just ordering a third printing on "Through the Wheat"--the first was of three thousand, the second of two, and this third will be of three. Of course the number of copies printed runs far ahead of the number actually sold, but the situation is encouraging. This brings me to the point I have hesitated to raise about the end of the book. I find that it puzzles almost everyone as it stands, and while it makes no practical difference, it would be more satisfactory in the end if you could remove this uncertainty in any later editions. The whole book is so direct and definite that an indefinite ending is artistically disappointing. Many have told me that they thought the idea was that Hicks had gone "looney". Others say that their impression was that he was about to be killed and had a sort of foreknowledge of it. The general impression is a vague one that Hicks was finally killed. But very few, and nobody distinctly, understand the concluding psychology. As I say, I bring up this point purely upon artistic grounds for it does not affect the sale; it almost seems as if this book might become a sort of a classic and if this should happen, it would be better to have given an ending completely satisfying if it is possible to do it. I merely put this before you so that you will know of it and

perhaps you may strike upon an ending that would be exactly right. . . .

Yours as ever,
[Maxwell Perkins]

[circa June 23, 1923]

Mr. Perkins,

I don't know what to say about the ending of Through the Wheat. I'm afraid I can't improve it. Scott [Fitzgerald] hasn't written me about it—have you any suggestions? . . .

TB

Aug. 20, 1923

Dear Boyd:

. . . As for the ending of "Through the Wheat" I have nothing to suggest. I think the present ending is better than the first, and no ending that didn't come from yourself entirely would be right. Let the matter rest and if you ever strike one by inspiration that you think better, we could always add it. . . .

As ever,
[Maxwell Perkins]

And so the ending has remained.

RELATED LETTERS:

After completing his biography of the American Revolutionary War general Anthony Wayne, Boyd began to hunt for another suitable subject. "The Wrong Diana," mentioned in this first letter, was a contemporary novel he had finished in 1927 after Samuel Drummond *and which Perkins had recommended against publishing. It never was.*

Jan. 2, 1929

Dear Tom:

. . . Now I suppose you will soon be formulating plans for another book,- perhaps a novel. Do you think you will take up "The Wrong Diana" again? It had splendid things in it, and I think the fundamental conception from which it was written, if enlarged and deepened, was a fine, adequate one for a novel. It may not be wise though to take it up, simply because of the difficulty of working over material which has perhaps grown cold for you. Anyhow, I suppose you realize that your position as a writer is a strong one which commands the respect of critics, including those whose opinion has weight and value. This cannot be said of many writers. There are very few who have not written something specious or trivial. The "Mad Anthony" is certainly a very

fine piece of work, and all your work gives one a feeling of growth and increasing power.

Yours,
[Maxwell Perkins]

[early April 1929]

Dear Max:

I've not started another book yet, but I want to begin one shortly—perhaps by the last of May. And as I'm getting into that period and as I've no novel clamoring to be written I've thought quite seriously of a life of Alexander Hamilton, stirred perhaps by Claude Bower's Jefferson & Hamilton I read a month or so ago. What would you think of that? . . .

Yours
Tom

April 16, 1929

Dear Tom:

I would be all for your doing another biography. It does seem to me though, that Alexander Hamilton would be a most difficult subject for one, because although there was so much adventurous and romantic about him, there was also--and that the most important aspect of him--his political, constitutional, legal career. This would have to be treated fully and carefully, and I should think it would require an immense amount of special study.--And then there was the financial part of his career, which was almost equally important, and is also highly technical and abstruse. . . .

Ever yours,
[Maxwell Perkins]

[mid April 1929]

Dear Max:

What about Cornwallis? Do you think it would be possible for me to get the necessary material? He would be an excellent subject to follow Anthony Wayne. . . .

As ever
Tom

April 23, 1929

Dear Tom:

I think you are quite right in casting about for a subject of a biography in the Revolutionary period, and I am only raising all the objections to the ones you suggest in order that they may be surely considered;- though I could hardly think you would overlook them anyhow.

Cornwallis has much to recommend him, but the great difficulty is that the most important part of his life was the twenty-five years that followed the Revolution, when he was in India and there fought

THE SCRIBNER BOOKSTORE

The New Fiction

HALF–TOLD TALES, *by* HENRY VAN DYKE. $1.50

A new book by Henry van Dyke is always an event, and the publication of "Half-Told Tales" is especially noteworthy, as it is his first book of fiction in five years. His stories are known and loved wherever the English language is read, and have been translated into a score of foreign tongues—a treasured heritage of the whole world. Dr. van Dyke—philosopher, poet, essayist, spiritual teacher—is also a master teller of tales. The stories in this new volume are alive with the force, humanity, and spiritual beauty that have distinguished all the work of their famous author.

AND THEY LIVED HAPPILY EVER AFTER, *by* MEREDITH NICHOLSON, *author of* "*Broken Barriers,*" "*The Hope of Happiness,*" *etc.* $2.00

This is a dramatization of modern life with particular regard to the institution of marriage. The truth is set down with fearlessness and force, and brings a realization of how matters stand in this regard to-day.

THE PENCILED FROWN, *by* JAMES GRAY. $2.00

An amusing book. The frown is a world-weary, cynical fiction that decorates a smooth, fresh forehead, the forehead of one Timothy Wynkoop. For is he not dramatic critic of the leading paper of his city, a city in the Northwest? With him are shown up the desperate sophisticates of an American city.

SAMUEL DRUMMOND, *by* THOMAS BOYD. $2.00

This is the story of a man working upon nature, which he loves, to win her to yield prosperity to him and his family. The whole book is permeated with a deep sense of the reality of material things—an instinctive love of the rich soil turned by the plough, of wheat fields whipped by the wind, of the shambling cattle.

[7]

Announcement of Boyd's Samuel Drummond *included in the "new fall books" issue (September 1925) of* The Scribner Bookstore *periodical. In admiration of the book Maxwell Perkins had written to Boyd: "Judging the book intrinsically I hold it in very high estimation. For just one thing,- you've taken a man from youth to age with perfect consistency and veracity,- a living man every minute, and a developing and changing individual. A writer who does that is a <u>novelist</u> in the true, rare, lasting sense" (4 June 1925).*

brilliantly and successfully . . . There was also his work in Ireland . . .

The trouble with Arnold [Benedict Arnold] is his unpopularity, which would stand as a great obstacle to a sale.

I delayed answering this letter until I could talk to Mr. Scribner, who is also strongly in favor of your doing another biography, and in that period, if possible.

Ever yours,
[Maxwell Perkins]

[late April 1929]

Dear Max:

Well, it's all very depressing, though I suppose you're quite right. But as you and Mr. Scribner are both favorable to another biography I shall persevere and, so doing, offer the following names as possibilities: Ethan Allen (about whom you doubtless know more than I), Davy Crockett (who would be of a later time but a most picturesque and engaging character with, moreover, material covering him fairly plentiful), Light

Horse Harry Lee, possibly Francis Merion and that's about all. . . .

As I hope you've discovered, I'm glad to take advice. What I want now is the chance of getting at something serious and satisfying, but I don't want to overstep myself and get into a tangle with the elements of unfinished work, speeding time and vanishing money. I think a life of Allen would help me avoid all that—

As ever
Thomas Boyd

After more rehashing Boyd returned to his original idea, a biography of Alexander Hamilton, but with Perkins's help he planned one that would emphasize Hamilton's personal life. On that basis a contract was drawn up in June and a $1,000 advance was paid. However, circumstances prevented him from ever getting started (travel out West away from sources, family illness, short stories), and by February 1930 he decided instead to write a biography of Robert E. Lee's father, "Light-Horse Harry Lee." Completed in October, the book appeared on 20 March 1931.

LETTERS:

In these excerpts from letters by Maxwell Perkins to Boyd, the Scribner editor touches on changes in the publishing business, relates them to Boyd's writing abilities, and gently argues that he should attempt another novel. In an earlier letter to Perkins (circa 18 October 1930), Boyd had said on the completion of his biography of Light-Horse Harry Lee: "It has been very hard at times, but I feel the Revolution is a good field for me & I hope to start another biography this winter . . ."

Nov. 29, 1930

Dear Tom:

. . . You are right, I could not find much of anything about John Fitch [American steamboat inventor] except little mention of him, but I cannot believe that there would be a market for a book on him. You know how far, even when you had a bookstore, books sold on their outsides,--their titles and appearances. It is much more that way now because of greater competition, and however good a book may be intrinsically--however deserving it is of interest--it cannot seem to get a grip without some superficial salience. I do not think that John Fitch's name and all we could say about the book in advertising, could ever give it a proper chance. If there were very few biographical books out, it might, but nowadays there are too many.- Those with some

natural superficial advantage get the market to a very great degree.

As for the financial question, we would like to send a check for one thousand dollars simply as an advance against whatever you may do. What you do should be what you want to do, and so we ought not to try to drive you along any line you do not want to take. It seemed to me that in this interval when no large historical or biographical project appeals to you, you might do a novel. In "The Dark Cloud," "Samuel Drummond," and "Shadow of the Long Knives" you showed great sense of the past, and great feeling for it, and I think if you did a novel now of the Revolutionary period, after living in it through two books, you would be doing well. But it is purely a question for you,- whether after thinking it over, you feel inclined that way.

Yours,
[Maxwell Perkins]

Jan. 14, 1931

Dear Tom:

. . . I must say, I am worried about your plans for writing in future. You must do what you are moved to do, of course;- or at any rate you cannot do what you are not moved to do, just because it may be expedient. I understand that view and sympathize with it. At the same time I cannot think that you could hope to get a pecuniary return on the two books you spoke of which would be anywhere nearly in proper proportion to the work that would be entailed. I have thought about these plans many times since I saw you, and with every inclination to be persuaded to your opinion, but I cannot manage it. The commercial requirements in publishing have become more exacting, and the considerations of intrinsic value--such as that which would come from the historical importance of what you plan--less effective.--The market is so crowded with books, competition so acute, and people so much more inclined apparently, to travel in flocks even in their reading, that it is harder to get an adequate sale for books of the sort you speak of. On the other hand, you have a great gift for narratives of action, and this can be displayed both in biography and history, but hardly in the type you are considering. It can also be displayed in fiction, and perhaps it is best there. You have done very fine work in fiction too. You ought not to turn away from it altogether.

Yours,
[Maxwell Perkins]

Dear Max:

Thanks for your letter about my novel. However, I'm in just as much of a dilemma as ever. For one thing, Hicks is the character of the novel and the story fits in with *Through the Wheat*. Moreover, if this book is good I want to write a sequel to it — which would make, all told, a trilogy of Hicks. For that reason alone Scribners would be the logical publisher.

Also, I don't think there are any other houses quite as good as Scribners. I've had several letters from Harcourt, but I'm not sure that I'd like them even if they were very enthusiastic about the book.

In this state of affairs, I have a proposal to make. Not wanting to take time to copy the novel, I intend to bring it to New York. Now could you give it a personal reading while I'm down there and tell me your frank opinion of it? I think that would be the best arrangement all around — Scribners would have a fair shot at it and I would be satisfied either way the decision went.

I'm beginning the last chapter on Monday and expect to get down the first week in May — there might be a little waiting to do, but not much.

The title, by the way, is TRAMPLED GRAIN

as ever
Tom

Letter [April 1934] from Boyd to Maxwell Perkins concerning his recently completed novel and hopes beyond it. "Trampled Grain" appeared posthumously under the title In Time of Peace, *published by Minton, Balch.*

Aug. 31, 1931

Dear Tom:

. . . You notice that Scott Fitzgerald has announced that the Jazz Age ended with the stock market crash in 1929! Anyhow, the Jazz Age has ended, and I think this ought to be a good thing for you because you were never typical of it, I think, and the raucous qualities of it rather deafened people to qualities your writing had. This makes me think that if you can do a novel, it may stand out to more advantage now than it did in those days. . . .

Yours,
[Maxwell Perkins]

Around Christmas Boyd began work on a novel about a contemporary love story that he called A Wall Like China's *and submitted the finished work in September 1932. (In the meantime he had gotten another $1,000 advance.) The novel was rejected by Perkins on the grounds that the depressed book market demanded books that had "some particular salience"; Boyd's did not. In 1933 Boyd tried to interest Perkins in a book idea he titled* The Enemy Shore.

March 21, 1933

Dear Tom:

I find it hard to give you a very satisfactory answer. If we were to publish "The Enemy Shore" and so believed in its reasonable success, we could agree to disregard the present advance until after the sale of a certain number of thousand copies. This would mean that on the first few thousand copies sold you would receive full royalty. How would that seem to you?

You have always written very good narrative, and it seems to me that if you did such books as "Shadow of the Long Knives" you might establish yourself as a writer of semi-historical novels. You might be able to serialize them, and occasionally sell picture rights, and do well in that way through a period of years, assuming any sort of normal conditions. You have studied American history and you have a strong feeling for it, and I think a right sense of the life of the past. It seems to me the most likely line you could follow in order to attain a sort of stability. If you could get established in that way, you might later be able to do the kind of writing you prefer. . . .

Yours,
[Maxwell Perkins]

Boyd did not publish any more books with Scribners. At the time of his death, the $1,000 advance still had not been repaid by royalties earned on his other books.

RELATED LETTERS:
Letter from Maxwell Perkins to Boyd, 17 May 1934; letter from Boyd to Perkins, circa 20 August 1934.

Here Perkins, who initially rejected Boyd's first novel in 1922, finally rejects Boyd's last novel, tentatively called "Trampled Grain," which continues the story of the main character of Through the Wheat. *In his last letter (in the Scribner Archives), written several months later, Boyd credits his unpopularity to his point of view, which had become decidedly socialistic. Later that fall he ran as the Communist candidate for the Vermont governorship.*

Dear Tom:

I am terribly sorry, but we really do not think we could sell enough copies of this novel--and I agree with you that you have very much improved it--to warrant us in publishing it.- So there is no use arguing with myself or with you about it. I can only send it back.

Always yours,
[Maxwell Perkins]

Dear Max:

I've been meaning to write and thank you for your last letter; but there really isn't much more than that for me to say.

Whether I'll ever be able to write an historical novel or a biography that Scribner's will want to publish is one of those confounded questions. I was extremely disappointed when you rejected the novel—whether you were justified in your attitude has yet to be seen. I am now writing the Fitch biography for Putnam, who will publish the novel in January. Frankly I don't care much for Earle [Earl Balch] and Minton, but so long as they will publish my books I can't ask any more.

But no matter what happens, whether I get published or not, whether capitalism temporarily jerks out of the crisis or not, I'll never write again without a definite purpose and point of view. And that point of view must always be unpopular to people who can afford to buy books under present conditions. I never wanted much from the old set-up, but I was denied what little I did want. I'm glad that so far as I'm concerned it's gone, for I feel at last that I'm going forward, not retreating as I tried so long and so unsuccessfully to do

Yours
Tom

Boyd did not live to see his last two books published: in January 1935 he died of a cerebral hemorrhage. The biography, Poor John Fitch, Inventor of the Steamboat *(G. P. Putnam's Sons), and the novel,* In Time of Peace *(Minton, Balch), appeared later that year.*

RELATED LETTERS:
Letter from Elizabeth Boyd to Maxwell Perkins, 4 March 1943, written from Vassar College; letter from Perkins in reply, 10 March 1943.

Boyd divorced his first wife, Margaret Woodward Smith, a novelist who wrote under the name "Woodward Boyd" and, later, "Peggy Shane," in 1929. Elizabeth, their only child, was six at the time.

Dear Mr. Perkins:

I am writing a biography of my father, Thomas Boyd, for my senior thesis, and I would appreciate your help. I would like to know if Through the Wheat was a financial success, and if it made much of an impression when it came out; it is hard to tell from the reviews. I wonder if you could also give me some impression of what Daddy was like when you first met him, how he looked, and how he acted, and what he was thinking about?

I know you must be very busy, but I hope that you will have time to answer this; it would be immensely helpful.

Sincerely,
Betty Grace Boyd

Dear Miss Boyd:

I am sending you two pictures of your father around the time when we first knew him here. The smaller one may have been while he was still in the marine corps. The larger one is a much better likeness except that one would think it must have been touched up. It makes him almost pretty, which he was not. He was very masculine looking, and even somewhat rugged. But on the whole, that large picture is a very good likeness, and can tell you more than any description I could give. I can't tell you what color his eyes were, but I should think gray.- And his hair was light brown, and wavy. He was not much below six feet, strongly built but rather slender,- not spare. In his manner he was quiet until one knew him well, almost shy,- not one of those who put themselves forward in a conversation, especially when a number of people were present. But he was sympathetic, and made friends easily, even with those with whom he did not agree. He seemed to have no resentments against anyone, and I cannot remember his ever speaking badly of a person unless for reasons that nobody could dispute about. And yet he had strong feelings too, as a great deal of "Through the Wheat" will show,- for instance in the presentation of the General making the speech. And you can see that he was capable of great admiration for the simple, manly virtues of courage and leadership, in what he tells of his Major in that book.

In the first years that I knew him he was thinking mostly of literature, as in fact, he always was. That was his first interest. But he also talked a great deal about the economic situation and the injustices of capitalism. He was apparently in favor of some very considerable degree of socialism, though I don't think he would ever have called himself a socialist.

"Through the Wheat" was a very distinct success, and its influence and reputation were all out of proportion to its sale which was never very large,- 12,032 copies in the regular edition, and 1,390 copies in the edition illustrated by Lieut-Col John W. Thomason, Jr., who was a great admirer of the book. He also was in the marine corps, but he never knew your father.

If you wish to ask me any further questions, I should be very glad to try to answer them.

Ever sincerely yours,
[Maxwell Perkins]

Ring W. Lardner (1885–1933)

Ring Lardner at the Chicago Tribune, *1913*

The conversion of Lardner from a popular humorist to a serious voice in American fiction began with the publication of his first Scribner book in 1924, *How to Write Short Stories (With Samples)*, a gathering of his best fiction to date. Prior to that, he had worked as a sportswriter (1908–1913) who had followed baseball in its early years for the *Chicago Inter-Ocean, Tribune,* and *Examiner* newspapers; a writer of a daily column, "In the Wake of the News," for the *Tribune* (1913–1919); a weekly columnist for John N. Wheeler's Bell Syndicate, starting in 1919 (which he stopped in 1927); and the author (1922–1925) of the continuity for the *You Know Me Al* comic strip based on one of his baseball characters. During this period his publications included several baseball stories in *The Saturday Evening Post* and over ten books of humorous sketches and stories. However, Scribners' publication of Lardner's stories, which it followed the next year with a five-volume uniform edition of his works, brought him critical attention. The humorous voice that had uniquely captured the vernacular of small-town America finally began to receive recognition for the sardonic treatment of its subjects that Lardner had crafted into high-quality fiction. During the 1920s he extended the range of his satirical eye beyond baseball in his stories and also succeeded as a dramatist with *June Moon* (Broadway premiere, October 1929), a play adapted with George S. Kaufman from Lardner's story "Some Like Them Cold." Though the longer, sustained work which his Scribner editor, Maxwell Perkins, urged him to produce eluded Lardner, he remains one of the best-known and admired American story writers of the twentieth century.

Scribner Books by Lardner

1924	*How to Write Short Stories (With Samples)*
1925	*The Big Town: How I and the Mrs. Go to New York to See Life and Get Katie a Husband* (reprint with new preface)
	Gullible's Travels, Etc. (reprint)
	What of It? (reprint)

You Know Me Al: A Busher's Letters (reprint)

1926   *The Love Nest and Other Stories,* with an introduction by Sarah E. Spooldripper

1927   *The Story of a Wonder Man: Being the Autobiography of Ring Lardner,* illustrated by Margaret Freeman

1929   *Round Up: The Stories of Ring W. Lardner*

1930   *June Moon: A Comedy in a Prologue and Three Acts,* by Lardner and George S. Kaufman

1933   *Lose With a Smile*

1934   *First and Last,* edited by Gilbert Seldes

1957   *The Best Short Stories of Ring Lardner*

1961   *Haircut and Other Stories*

1962   *Shut Up, He Explained,* edited by Babette Rosmond and Henry Morgan

1963   *The Ring Lardner Reader,* edited by Maxwell Geismar

1976   *Some Champions,* edited by Matthew J. Bruccoli and Richard Layman

1992   *Ring Around the Bases: The Complete Baseball Stories of Ring Lardner,* edited, with an introduction, by Matthew J. Bruccoli

---

RELATED LETTERS:

In October 1922 F. Scott Fitzgerald became Lardner's neighbor in Great Neck, Long Island. Already an admirer of his work, Fitzgerald became a close friend and, soon, a one-man rooting section for Lardner's stories with his own editor at Scribners, Maxwell Perkins. These letters from Perkins clearly show the efforts each man (Fitzgerald and Perkins) contributed to get Lardner into the Scribner stable.

July 2, 1923

Dear Mr. Lardner:

I read your story "The Golden Wedding" with huge enjoyment. Scott Fitzgerald recommended it to me and he also suggested that you might have other material of the same sort which, with this, could form a volume. I am therefore writing to tell you how very much interested we should be to consider this possibility, if you could put the material before us. I would hardly have ventured to do this if Scott had not spoken of the possibility, because your position in the literary world is such that you must be besieged by publishers, and to people in that situation their letters of interest are rather a nuisance. I am certainly mighty glad to have the chance of expressing our interest though, if, as Scott thought, you would not feel that we were merely bothering you. Would you be willing to send on any material that might go with "The Golden Wedding" to form a volume, or to tell me where I might come at it in periodicals?

Very truly yours,
[Maxwell Perkins]

Feb. 1, 1924

Dear Mr. Lardner:

I hope Scott has told you that we have actually gone so far as to put your "How To Write Short Stories" into the spring list;- a rather irregular proceeding since you have never told us we could. But we were very much interested in the general idea and we felt that the best thing to do was to act immediately and get out a volume. If this seems right to you, we will pay a fifteen percent royalty from the start on this first book.

I am having a bad time getting together the stories though. I have a letter from McClure's saying that they haven't got the issue for August 1915, and the Post did not have any story in the issue of December 6, 1919. I sent Scott a list of the stories that the Cosmopolitan had and will copy for us. I can have the Post looked through in the library between 1914 and 1919--for after that the Post is indexed--and see what we find and I think we can arrange to have the stories copied out. We will do the same with McClure's for August 1915. If we get these stories we will have a good representative collection.

Sincerely yours,
[Maxwell Perkins]

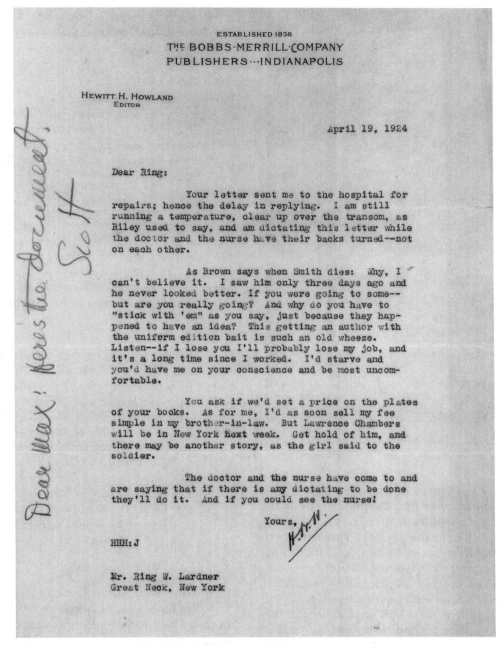

Letter to Lardner from his editor at Bobbs-Merrill on learning that Lardner wants to change publishers. Apparently sent the letter by Lardner, F. Scott Fitzgerald has penciled his forwarding note to Maxwell Perkins on the side.

March 17, 1924

Dear Mr. Lardner:

I have sent you some of the galley proof and will follow rapidly with the rest. Will you read it quickly?

We have had trouble with the wrap and called in Scott for consultation. Held [John Held, illustrator] fell down on the case, at least we thought so. But everything is going well now, I think. On the side of the cover we are going to reproduce your signature.

Now here is an idea. Reject it if you want to, of course, but do give it thought. We have always felt there was a little weakness in the title, that the intent of it was not strongly enough expressed in the book. It occurred to me that you might write a

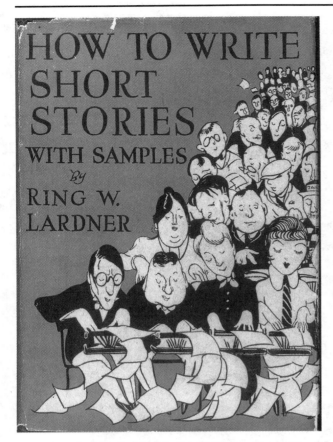

Dust jacket for Lardner's first Scribner book. The title was probably suggested by F. Scott Fitzgerald.

comment on each story, suiting the comment of course, to each story so that its quality would accordingly vary, but which would carry on the general spirit and idea of the preface. This comment might in some cases be only a couple of lines long and in none more than twenty lines. We would then precede each story with a half title page--a page normally blank except for the title. Under this title, probably in italics, would be printed this comment on the story which would represent each one, amusing and satirical as an illustration of short story writing. Maybe your idea of it would be different even if you did make the comment, but if you made it according to your idea I know it would add immensely to the interest of the book and would help immensely in the whole matter of publicity, etc. Please consider it.

My remembrances to Mrs. Lardner. I hope you are having a good time.

Sincerely,
[Maxwell Perkins]

On 9 May 1924 Lardner's How to Write Short Stories (With Samples) *appeared—barely ten*

months after Perkins's first letter. Each story was introduced, as Perkins had suggested, with a short, humorous commentary.

RELATED LETTERS:

Letter from Arthur H. Scribner, Scribners' vice president and brother of CS II, to David L. Chambers, vice president of The Bobbs-Merrill Company, 25 August 1924; letter from Chambers to Scribner in reply, 28 August 1924.

Following up on earlier letters from Lardner (author) and Maxwell Perkins (editor), Scribner (publisher) makes his formal pitch to acquire Lardner's supposedly inactive books. The firm's plan was to reissue Lardner's "old" books with his new, hoping to revitalize his career and stimulate the public's interest in his writing.

Dear Mr. Chambers:

You no doubt know of our having recently published "How to Write Short Stories", by Ring Lardner, whose books have previously been published by your house and Mr. Doran. The book came to us without solicitation on our part, but we now wish if feasible to secure the publication of his previous books with a view to a uniform edition. Would you consider transferring to us those published by you, and if so on what terms? Of course we would not write you about this were it not Mr. Lardner's wish as well as our own.

Yours sincerely,
[Arthur H. Scribner]

Dear Mr. Scribner:—

Your letter of the 25th is received.

We would part reluctantly with our Lardner books. They have had an honored place on our list and as we did everything we knew how to develop this author in the book field we would hope that some day he would return to the fold.

Of course we wouldn't want to stand in the way of his putting all his eggs in one basket if that is his wish and I would undertake to ask our people to find a satisfactory basis for putting the plates and stock at your disposal at a satisfactory price. Perhaps our actual investment figures will throw some light on what this price should be. If you think so, I'll get them together.

With kind regards, I am

Sincerely yours,
D. L. Chambers

Ca. 12/2/24

RING LARDNER
GREAT NECK, NEW YORK

December second.

Dear Max:-

I am tickled to death with your report on Scott's book. It's his pet and I believe he would take poison if it flopped.

Ellis and I have both read "Three Flights Up" and both liked the two middle stories best. My favorite is "Transatlantic." The last story is way over my head.

I think I am going to be able to sever connections with the daily cartoon early next month. This ought to leave me with plenty of time and it is my intention to write at least ten short stories a year. Whether I can do it or not, I don't know. I started one the other day and got through with about 700 words, which were so bad that I gave up. I seem to be out of the habit and it may take time to get back.

Don Stewart's "Mr. and Mrs. Haddock Abroad" was a blow to me. That is the kind of "novel" I had intended to write, but if I did it now, the boys would yell stop thief.

Five "articles" on the European trip are coming out in Liberty, beginning in January. I don't know whether or not they will be worth putting in a book.

I'm coming to town early next week to call on a dentist. As soon as I know when, I'll telephone you and try to make a date. Not that we don't want you in Great Neck, but I realize that it's no pleasure trip.

Sincerely,

R.W.L.

*Letter from Lardner to Maxwell Perkins. While he touches upon several topics—
F. Scott Fitzgerald's "book" (The Great Gatsby), which Perkins is enjoying reading
in draft form, and Sidney Howard's collection of stories,* Three Flights Up, *which
Scribners had just published—the most significant item is Lardner's announcement
of his intention to quit writing text for a daily comic strip based on Jack Keefe,
the semiliterate baseball character ("busher") from his* You Know Me Al. *This
step marked a turning point in his career, for afterward reviewers began to
think of him as a more serious literary artist.*

Acquiring the rights to Lardner's earlier works cost Scribners $2,500: $500 to the George H. Doran Company for You Know Me Al *and* Say It With Oil *and $2,000 to Bobbs-Merrill for* Gullible's Travels, Etc., My Four Weeks in France, Treat 'Em Rough, The Real Dope, Own Your Own Home, The Young Immigrunts, Symptoms of Being 35, *and* The Big Town. *This enabled the firm to issue a five-volume, uniform edition of Lardner's works, including much of the old with the new, the following spring.*

RELATED LETTERS:
Letter from Maxwell Perkins to Lardner, 16 March 1925; Lardner's reply, the next day.

Praise from Perkins for what has become Lardner's most anthologized story . . .

Dear Ring:

I read "Hair Cut" on Friday and I can't shake it out of my mind;- in fact the impression it made has deepened with time. There's not a man alive who could have done better, that's certain.

Everyone will tell you this, or something like it I guess, so there's little use in my doing it.- But it is a most biting and revealing story and I'd like to say so.

Yours,
[Maxwell Perkins]

Dear Max:—
Thanks.

R. W. L.

RELATED LETTERS:
Over the course of half a dozen years, Maxwell Perkins, as Lardner's editor, tried to get him to write something on a "larger scale"—either a long story or a novel—which he felt would broaden his appeal and increase his recognition.

Dec. 8, 1926
Dear Ring:

. . . I just read with great delight, in the Cosmo, the story "Sun Cure". But I think the best of the four is "The Jade Necklace" which is perfect. I wish though, that for the next book of stories, we could have one long one, and the longer the better. I know that while you are writing for the Cosmopolitan, this is impossible for periodical use, but couldn't you do one long one just for a book? If it were twenty or twenty-five thousand words, we would have something entirely new, and we could make ever so much of it, and we might be able to even get a financial return that would warrant the sacrifice of magazine publication. I do not mean, of course, that you should deliberately think up a story for this purpose, but you may well have one that you want to write, and could write best at that length. We could strike a new note for you then. It might be in the vein of "Champion", a sort of biography of a type of character. If you had an impulse to write a long story of this sort, I truly believe it would be a good thing to do, even if your agreement with the Cosmopolitan prevents its serial publication.

Yours,
[Maxwell Perkins]

April 6, 1927
Dear Ring:

. . . You always do everything your own way so perhaps you would rather not, but I wish I could sometime have a talk with you in the idea that you are now so much freer, that you might be willing to think of a book on a larger scale than you have done. The last thing I want to be is a nuisance, so if you would rather not, all right. . . .

Yours,
[Maxwell Perkins]

Nov. 3, 1928
Dear Ring:

. . . And I wish there were something I could do to compel you to write that 40,000 word story, or novel, or whatever it ought to be called. I do not know of any publishing news that would be more interesting than that such a book by you was to come out.

Yours always,
[Maxwell Perkins]

May 31, 1929
Dear Ring:

. . . If only you would do that 40,000 word story you thought of, now would be the time for it, with the great distribution of "Round Up" as a background.

Ever yours,
[Maxwell Perkins]

February 13, 1931.
Dear Max:—

My health hasn't been so good - I guess I am paying for my past - and I'm not averaging more than four short stories a year. None of the recent ones has been anything to boast of and I'm afraid there won't be enough decent ones to print by fall. Maybe I'll get more energetic or inspired or something in the next few months. . . .

Sincerely,
Ring Lardner

The **LITERARY GUILD** of **AMERICA**
INCORPORATED

CARL VAN DOREN — HENDRIK WILLEM VAN LOON   ELINOR WYLIE — JOSEPH KRUTCH — BURTON RASCOE

55 FIFTH AVENUE
New York

December 26,1928.

Chas. Scribner's Sons,
597 Fifth Avenue,
New York City.

Gentlemen: <u>Attention of Mr. Maxwell Perkins.</u>

This will confirm our understanding of the purchase
by the Literary Guild of an edition of Ring Lardner's Stories.
These stories embrace two previous books of Ring Lardner
and the third book in the course of preparation.

We agree to take an edition in a quantity sufficient
for our subscribers. This will be approximately 70,000 copies.

We agree to pay for this edition the sum of thirteen
thousand five hundred dollars ($13,500.00), the payment to be
made net within sixty (60) days from publication date.

You agree to publish the book during the first ten
days of April, May or June,1929. We will advise you of the
definite month of publication sixty days in advance.

We agree to use the books of our edition to send to
regular Guild subscribers and in no case to sell single copies.

This book is to be completely re-set in format for a
single volume embracing about 250,000 words and about 250 pages.

If your printing plant can meet the delivery date and
price of our printers we will be glad to have you deliver us printed
sheets from paper supplied by ourselves. Otherwise you agree
to furnish us with an extra set of plates at cost.

The composition and plate cost shall not be included
in figuring the cost of printing the Guild edition.

We are very anxious to cooperate with you in promoting
the trade sale of this book and urge you to make use of our
Publicity Department in any way which you feel will be of service to you.

If this agrees with your understanding will you be good
enough to sign and return the enclosed carbon copy for our files.

Very truly yours,

THE LITERARY GUILD OF AMERICA INC.,
Managing Director.

MJS.MC

*Letter from the Literary Guild explaining the terms by which it will purchase from
Scribners an edition of Lardner's stories. On the left side, CS II has written his
response, "Accepted."*

Feb. 16, 1931

Dear Ring:

I am sorry you have not been feeling well.- But spring is not so far off now, and that always, I find, brings a man up a good many notches. I wish you would take a year off from New York, and the theatre, etc., and quietly do a novel!

Always yours,
[Maxwell Perkins]

In these later years Lardner became preoccupied with music and the theater, collaborating with George S. Kaufman in the 1929 stage hit June Moon—*hence, Perkins's reference to the theater in this last letter. But now Lardner's poor health, the result of tuberculosis and heavy drinking dating from his newspaper days, prevented any kind of sustained composition. There would be no novel.*

LETTER:
Letter from Maxwell Perkins to Lardner, 27 December 1928.

In the spring of 1928 Perkins began planning for a new collection of Lardner stories, tentatively titled "And Other Stories," to be published by Scribners the following year. However, in the fall the Literary Guild approached the firm with an idea of putting out an "omnibus" edition of Lardner's stories, which would replace Scribners' plan. Perkins explains the advantages of the Guild's offer to Lardner in this letter.

Dear Ring:

This is to put on record with you what I said by telephone yesterday:-

The Literary Guild wishes to take for their book of the month for either April, May, or June (probably April, and almost certainly not June) a book of your stories to embrace those in "How to Write Short Stories," "The Love Nest," and those we have already in type for the book we had planned to publish this spring. They agree to pay $13,500, which we propose should be divided equally between you and ourselves.

The job is quite a big one, and we ought to get ahead immediately, and are even now making estimates on the printing so that we ought to know as soon as possible what stories you wish to omit.- But as the book is to be about 250,000 words, it would be undesirable to omit more than two or three stories anyhow. I hope you won't want to omit "The Facts" which is a light story but a very funny one, extremely well told. Another point to be considered is that the book should contain as large a proportion of the new stories as possible.

As to the general proposition, we think it highly advantageous because it will put a very fine book by you in the hands of some 70,000 people, to say nothing of those to whom we can sell copies through the regular trade. And so your public will be greatly enlarged. It will also lead, we think, to a re-estimation of you as a writer of stories, etc., in all the reviewing papers, which would also be most advantageous.

We of course, shall scrap "And Other Stories" entirely, only using the corrected proofs to reset that part of the new book.

This is the first book we have had with the Guild because we were unwilling to sell anything to them until they gave up cutting prices. I think they will give it rather special attention, certainly a great amount of publicity and advertising,- more than a publisher could afford to give to any one book.

Ever yours,
[Maxwell Perkins]

The new book was published as Round Up: The Stories of Ring W. Lardner *in April 1929. Lardner preferred the word* ensemble *to round up but stated his preference too late for the title change to be made.*

LETTER:
Letter from Lardner's wife to Maxwell Perkins, [September 1931].

In the midst of her family's own troubles, Ellis Lardner empathizes with those of their old friends, Scott and Zelda Fitzgerald. Zelda had been released recently from a Swiss sanatorium where she had been undergoing treatment following a nervous breakdown.

Dear Mr. Perkins:

Thank you for your letter. Ring is not much better and is still unable to do any work. I am rather discouraged about him because he worries so over not being able to work that the rest he is having does not do him the good it should.

I have been so sorry about Zelda and do hope they are still getting along all right. Do you suppose there is anyone left in the world who is well physically, mentally <u>and financially</u>?

Sincerely
Ellis Lardner

Lardner's third Scribner volume, published in 1926

LETTER:

Letter from Lardner to Maxwell Perkins, 3 February 1933.

This is Lardner's last letter in the Scribner Archives: he died in September. The rejected story was "Poodle," which was accepted finally by the Delineator *and published in its January 1934 issue.* Lose With a Smile, *a collection of baseball stories, was Lardner's last publication with Scribners during his lifetime; it appeared the next month, on 3 March.*

Dear Max:-

Some day I will probably realize that there is a depression. I wouldn't have asked you for any advance if I hadn't got into a sudden jam. The doctor and I decided that my place was the desert for a while, and not having done any real work since June, I was obliged to borrow money. I borrowed less than I needed, figuring I would sell a story to the Post. Once I wrote a complete story, "Alibi Ike," between 2 P.M. and midnight, with an hour off for dinner. This last one was begun in July and finished ten days ago, and the Post

turned it down just as promptly as it had accepted "Ike." Since then, Bill Lengel has said it was great (but he ain't the boss), Collier's has rejected it as too long and tenuous (It runs 7,500 words) and Mencken has told me it was too much of a domestica symphonica or something for the Mercury. Mr. Graeve (Delineator), suggested, perhaps sarcastically, by Mencken, now has it as a week-end guest and I have asked him to return it to my brother on the Times, who will give it to some poor author's agent to peddle. I have always scoffed at agents, but I am leaving tomorrow morning for La Quinta, California, to be gone till the money has disappeared. I have promised the doctor that I won't work on anything but a play which George Kaufman has been waiting for me to start for three years; of course, I will have to cheat a little, but I can't cheat much.

What I started to say is that the fiction story (really not bad, and just as really not a Pulitzer prize winner) has a great many local stops to make, and if I were to stay here and wait till the last possible purchaser had said no, I would die of jitters. Your loan has made it possible for me to get out of here before I am committed to Bellevue, and I am truly grateful. I won't need the "other" two hundred, and if the sale of "Lose With a Smile" never totals the amount you have advanced me, I will see to it that you don't lose. The agent can make the rounds much quicker than I could from 3,500 miles away.

This letter doesn't seem to be properly constructed or quite clear. That is a symptom of my state of mind, but the fact that I can laugh at the succession of turn-downs of a story which everybody but the Post has had a kind word for but no inclination to buy, makes me hopeful for the future. Maybe some day I can write a piece about the story's Cook's Tour—it is the first one I ever wrote that wasn't accepted by the first or second publication to which it was offered, and that either means go west old man or quit writing fiction or both.

Thanks again, and honestly I want you to forget the "balance" because I can easily get along without it.

Will you send me a couple of copies of "Lose With a Smile" when it is published? Yours, RWL

Will James (1892–1942)

Will James on his Montana ranch

With the sale of his first article, "Bucking Horses and Bucking Horse Riders," to *Scribner's Magazine* for $300 (March 1923), James began a prolific career with Scribners as a writer in the Western idiom and an illustrator in the tradition of Frederic Remington and Charles Russell. The unusual qualities in James—a storyteller with natural artistic talent and a real cowboy who wrote in his own, unaffected spoken language—combined to make him one of the most popular interpreters of the "authentic"—rough, open, and restless—West. His first novel, *Smoky, The Cowhorse,* which won the Newbery Medal as the best children's book for 1926, has become a classic. James's work was equally well received for the quality of his pen-and-ink illustrations of the "cow country" and life on the range, and he was particularly praised for his drawings of horses and cowboys in action. His nostalgic portrayal of the West also appealed to Hollywood, which produced several films based on his work. Throughout his life James developed and maintained a myth about himself. Born in Quebec, Canada, as Joseph Dufault, he changed his name and fictionalized his early years in his autobiography, *Lone Cowboy: My Life Story* (1930), fooling even his wife; the sham went unexposed until after his death.

Scribner Books by James
James illustrated all of his books.

1924	*Cowboys North and South*
1925	*The Drifting Cowboy*
1926	*Smoky, The Cowhorse*
1927	*Cow Country*
1929	*Sand*
1930	*Lone Cowboy: My Life Story*
1931	*Sun Up: Tales of the Cow Camps*
	Big-Enough

1932	*Uncle Bill: A Tale of Two Kids and a Cowboy*
1933	*All in the Day's Riding*
	The Three Mustangeers
1935	*In the Saddle with Uncle Bill*
	Young Cowboy
	Home Ranch
1936	*Scorpion, A Good Bad Horse*
1937	*Cowboy in the Making*
1938	*Look-See with Uncle Bill*
	The Will James Cowboy Book, edited by Alice Dalgliesh
	Flint Spears, Cowboy Rodeo Contestant
1939	*The Dark Horse*
1940	*My First Horse*
	Horses I've Known
1942	*The American Cowboy*
1951	*Book of Cowboy Stories*

RELATED LETTERS:

Encouraged by the success of James's first book, Scribners sought to help him continue developing his talents by suggesting the kind of book he should attempt for his next project. Increasingly, however, as the years passed and James's personal problems and Scribners' debt concerns mounted, these suggestions became a useful "program" to keep him focused on book writing and illustrating.

Dec. 5, 1924

Dear Mr. James:

I suppose you have seen enough reviews of "Cowboys North and South" to know with what enthusiasm the critics and literary observers have received it,- and as much on account of the text as the pictures.- I enclose a review that has just come from Struthers Burt [Wyoming author];- but the comments of the ordinary unliterary citizen who is the really important critic in the end, would probably interest you more, and if so, those I have heard would please you much. As for the sale, it goes well and promises to go better.

Anyhow, the outcome of the publication has already been such it seems to us, as to give you any assurance you may have wanted of marked success in book writing; I hardly think you could have had any doubts at all upon the matter of illustrating. I am therefore writing to suggest that you consider following this book with another, written in the same manner but different in design,- a continuous narrative with as much or as little plot as you thought best which would bring into the compass of a single story the adventures and incidents characteristic of a young cowboy's career, related in his own words. Really the book I have in mind -- for unsatisfactory as comparisons are, one can never altogether avoid them -- is "Huckleberry Finn". There was very little plot to it you probably remember. Its great interest was simply in the incidents and scenes of the trip on a raft down the Mississippi, told in the language of a boy. Of course, "Huckleberry Finn" is primarily a boy's book and it would be better if what you would do were not altogether that, but the great thing is that any such consecutive narrative would give you unquestionable talent for graphic human writing a chance beyond that which this book gave. And we suspect that it would show an equal skill in making types and characters realizable as individuals. Won't you consider this? We should then have a boook the novel size, to sell as a novel, and would be quite justified in having great expectations for it. We of course see it also as illustrated with your own pictures. I have talked to Mr. Chapin [head of Scribner Art Department] about this and he is in hearty accord with the plan.

Sincerely yours,
[Maxwell Perkins]

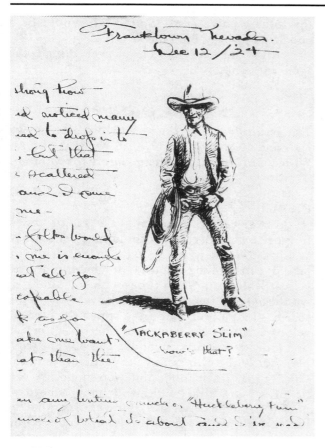

Ink drawing by James in his letter to Perkins of 12 December 1924: his response to "Huckleberry Finn"

Dec 12/'24

Dear Mr. Perkins—

I'd been wondering strong how my book was doing, and noticed many good reviews that happened to drop in to me from different parts, but that good letter of yours sure scattered my doubts four ways and I sure appreciate your telling me —

The fact that you folks would like another book from me is enough proof — and with what all you suspicion me of being capable of doing in such a book as you suggest is enough to make me want to wear a still bigger hat than the one I'm wearing now.

I've never read or saw any writing much on "Huckleberry Finn" but I have a strong hunch of what its about and I've read other things of Mark Twain's — so as it is, I'm pretty sure I know what kind of writing you suggested — nothing like "Huckleberry Finn" of course but something of the same interest. Its a mighty good idea, and I appreciate your interest in suggesting it —

The thing now, is wether I can do it — you seem to think I can and somehow I feel that I can

too. I hope so.— I have many ideas for novels such as you mention.— I was thinking of just letters of a cowboy to another cowboy with little sketches and taking in a year in a cowboy's life — I think I could make a mighty interesting thing out of that. And when you mentioned "Huckleberry Finn's" trip down the Mississippi — I thought of a trip I made myself once when the trapper that'd raised me dissapeared in the river one spring morning — that happened up in the prairie countries of Canada and I traveled over a thousand miles with two ponies leading back in the U.S.A. — I stopped and worked as I went and when I was tired of working I'd just catch up my ponies and go on again — I didn't hurt myself none on that trip, I took things mighty easy — and the different incidents that happened on the trail along with a little coloring to make them good reading — I think would tally up with Huckleberry on the Mississippi —

Would that work have to be fact or fiction or a little of both?

I think myself it'd make a heap better book than my first one and with the characters I could bring in that I knowed it would as you say five me a chance at 'em —

If I take it right, I think you mean that book should be wrote of my own talk and as if I was going thru the whole performance myself — which I would sure enough — but is that what you'd want? — I just want to make that plain — ...

I'll be thinking strong on the novel while I'm waiting to hear from you — and I'm pretty sure I can do the work — I feel it in my bones, like rheumatism, and like all of 'em that's afflicted that way I want to get it out of my system.

Many thanks for the good letter and review of Struther Burt's—

Sincerely —
Will James —

Smoky, the Cowhorse was the novel that resulted, published in 1926; Lone Cowboy: My Life Story *(1930) became the autobiographical work that contained a "little of both" fact and fiction.*

July 1, 1931

Dear Bill:

I am waiting impatiently for the rest of your manuscript [*Big-Enough*]. Now you have done with it, I'll tell you what my very simple plan is,- and I believe you could carry it out extremely well.- It is that you should write a book of about 30,000 words for small children, that is, for children between five and eight, or nine, and should illustrate it. It would be very easy to do. You would only have to imagine a couple of children who lived in a city or anyhow had never lived on a ranch, and who came to one and made friends with a horse wrangler, and the cowboys, and saw all the different regular things that happen on a ranch, and rode in the chuck wagon, etc. There really would not have to be any story to speak of,- not any more than that at the end of the summer they went back home. Almost everything that happens on a ranch would interest little children immensely, and you write very sympathetically for children, and they would adore the pictures of calves and horses, and all. I think it would be an extremely easy book for you to write, and it is short.- It would not sell in huge numbers in the first season, but it might easily end up by outselling everything you have done.

If you take up the notion, I can send you one or two books for little children, to show how people do them in a general way.- Though you would just naturally do it right, I believe.

Couldn't we dodge any danger about the Vee Cee brand [ranch brand used in *Big-Enough*] by putting the story into certain states where you knew there was no such brand? Anyhow, I think the risk is slight.

Always yours,
[Maxwell Perkins]

July 14, 1931

Dear Max:

I'm glad you liked the last part of the manuscript. You've long ago received my wire saying that I had the Vee Cee brand recorded to my name, so that in case anything comes up about it I have the first right to the brand.

This new story you suggested more than interests me. I feel sure that I can do it to your taste, and I've been using my head on it ever since I heard from you.

You didn't mention when you would like that book finished nor when you would expect to put it out. I don't expect it would be before spring anyhow, and I have an idea that that story would serialize pretty well. I was just wondering if I would have time to get it in a magazine first.

There is a little boy here on the ranch who is just at the right age to give me a lot of coaching on such a story. I had the honor of putting the name on him and you can guess what I picked, that's Clint. Before "Big Enuf" comes out, I wish you would see to it that that book is dedicated to Clint. Nobody needs to know wether Clint is this boy or the Clint in "Smoky", and I think that with

the folks who've read "Smoky" it would be a good tie-up with "Big Enuf".

All is fine here, and I hope everything is the same with you.

As Ever,
Bill

The resulting book, Uncle Bill: A Tale of Two Kids and a Cowboy *(1932), was the first of three "Uncle Bill" books that James wrote for children.*

Sept. 17, 1937

Dear Bill:

I have been thinking about a "major" book for you to consider, but without much success so far. It did occur to me though, that if driving a herd of cattle a long distance, or a herd of horses, was still done in your time--which I doubt--it would make a fine basis for a novel. Any book that has in it a journey during which the plot develops, has a strong element of interest.- A march or a journey interests anybody. There is one trouble, that Phil Rollins used the cattle drive in the '80s for his "Jinglebob",- but even so, no two cattle drives are alike. I think driving a herd of horses would be better still, if it was ever done for long distances, or was within your recollection. Maybe there is nothing in it for some such reason as that, but I thought I would propose it because of the great interest of the journey element in fiction, and the opportunity it would give to bring in all kinds of change and happenings.

Always yours,
[Maxwell Perkins]

Oct 4/'37

Dear Whit. [Whitney Darrow, Scribner business manager]

As I airmailed you a long letter yesterday I received yours of Sept 30 and answering today.

After thinking it over overnight I see that a major book on all-around rodeo is a very good idea — There's worlds of material I could put into that that could make many books — A book of the kind, as it comes to me, that's never been written and badly needs writing — Written in the right way I think would make a book that would be of interest to many — The rodeo is an established game now that very few people in the grandstands understand but are very glad to see,— Making that game understood would make them doubly glad, not only them who are fans but many others who sneer at the word Rodeo — Thinking it's only a Wild West show by paid performers, like actors, and that it's only a trick, the

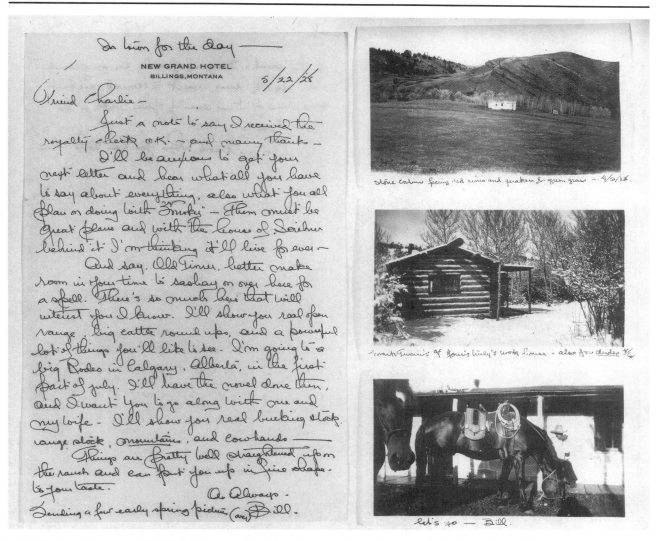

Letter from James to CS III with accompanying photographs of his ranch. Scribner loaned James the money to buy the ranch in 1926 but never visited it—despite many invitations; nor did Maxwell Perkins who received the same entreaties. Eight years later, James announced to Scribner: "You called it a white elephant, and Max said I'd get so interested in it I'd forget about my writing and suds. Well, I've decided and sold the ranch and got a fair price, considering the times, crickets and drougth . . . But I wish that while I'm here this year you could come and pay me a visit and see what a fine ranch I had" (20 July 1936).

animals all trained and so on — The life of the Rodeo contestant is very different than that of the circus performer — Like a good all around cowboy I know said once "No catch um no eat." In other words if he missed his steer in roping or bulldogging or didn't qualify in bronc riding that's his bad luck, also any broken bones he might have, then getting back to where he came is another problem, also the dwindling flour in the bin at his home on the range. Sometimes children to feed too and a winter coming on — And as you say, not a handbook giving these facts, but the story of the cowboy who competes

at these rodeos, which would give a real picture of the rodeo life in all of its details — I savvy —.

But I better stop here or I'll be starting on the story right now. I think I know the game from its start and can notice some things that even some of today's contestants don't notice or know.

Anyhow I think it would make a fine book and during these days would be the time to write it. It's a good idea that I shouldn't be too much illustrator in that book, only maybe a few small sketches here and there — and I know a professional Rodeo photographer, the best and

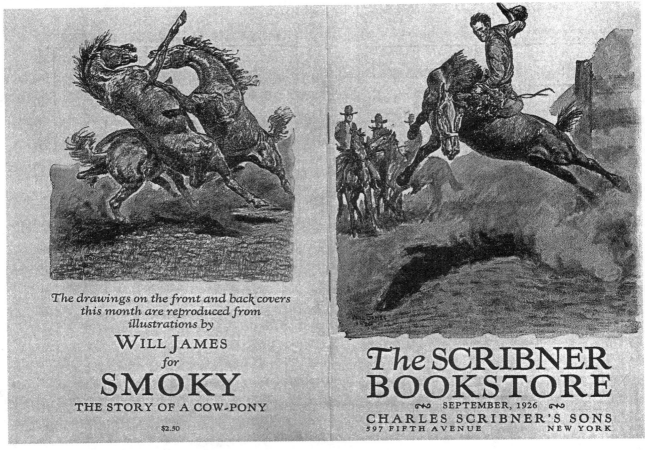

The drawings on the front and back covers
this month are reproduced from
illustrations by

WILL JAMES
for

SMOKY
THE STORY OF A COW-PONY

$2.50

The SCRIBNER BOOKSTORE
SEPTEMBER, 1926

CHARLES SCRIBNER'S SONS
597 FIFTH AVENUE   NEW YORK

Scribners actively promoted James's third book.

oldest in the game and does nothing else who can furnish the most unbelievable action photographs anybody could see — He's a very good friend of mine and I know he'd be more than glad to dig up his best for me and for such a book — It would make a much different book, too.

I thought some on the trail-herd subject which Max suggested, but got to thinking that that has been trailed to pieces, and <u>drags</u> as a trail herd does. . . .

But maybe Max would like this for another prospect — I thought of a cowboy camped way up in the northern Montana mountains, making a fire, a pitch pine chip is left by the dead fire afterwards, is washed down into a small mountain stream by a shower, then into a creek, on into a river that takes it all thru the West on down to the Gulf of Mexico —

That little chip, whirling in pools here and there, sometimes left high and dry or frozen into beaver ponds for the winter, drifting on by spring, would be a witness to many things on its way thru the cow country, camps, herds,

ranches, settlements and all kinds of goings on —

With the story, the cowboy who first left it at his fire would often cross the streams or ride along the rivers the chip went to finally lose one another when the Gulf of Mexico is reached.

. . . I also thought of another one which I would call "Has-Beens" or maybe some such name — Anyway it would have to do with a sort of one chapter biography (no real names mentioned) and in story form of different good cowboys' lives, cowboys who done things above the average and some away up. . . .

Then there's the horse story Westbrook [Elroy H. Westbrook, Montana friend and banker] reminded me of . . . and finally, with "Horses I've Known" I think there's mighty good prospects for these five as good major books without any trouble nor fixings, just to work on them. . . .

Now, while you and Max and Charlie figure out and decide which book I should get to work on out of the five I've listed for the next major book I'll be working on three short stories for "Horses I've Known", as to the program we've mapped out, then I'll make the major book this winter and should easy enough have it done by March or April, regarless of where I winter, for there's no more foolishness now.

I'm writing this letter to you, Whit and it's also in answer to Max's letter, but I know that you and him and Charlie will get your wise head on this anyway, so here it is and I hope it strikes you all well —

As ever,
Bill—

P.S. A fine snow is falling today, the first of the year. It has a very promising and prosperous look for the land, stockman and farmer, and I know that includes publishers and the poor writer.

The consensus of the group was for the rodeo book, which Scribners published the next fall as Flint Spears, Cowboy Rodeo Contestant. Horses I've Known *appeared in 1940.*

RELATED LETTERS:
Letter from James to CS III in envelope marked "personal," 7 June 1926, from Billings, Montana; letter from CS III in reply, 21 June 1926.

In soliciting CS III's financial help to buy a cattle ranch, James explains why and what he needs to settle down.

Dear Mr. Scribner

On account of me never hearing a word from you I just had to ask Mr Chapin if you'd broke your wrist — a quick answer to this will relieve me of that worry.

I dont know as you'll remember but while I was in New York you mentioned something one time about how you could help me get a place or home, that you hadn't got around to get your own yet, and so on.

Anyway, it's been hitting me pretty strong that thru running around living in town with writing folks etc. that I'm forgetting or beginning to forget some of the life I'm writing about. And since that's hit me I begin to get scared. And I'm wanting to get back to the places I tell of and the folks there. I've been doing too much running around, not enough work, and my mail's been having a hell of a time finding me.

All put in a nutshell, I need a place for steady headquarters, a place that'll pay for itself in time and where I can run stock so that I'll be right in the thick of what I'm drawing and writing about. A cow camp fitted up as a home — I'm had my mind on such a place for quite a long time and I sort of refused your offer while in New York on account I thought I could handle the buying of such a place without help.

I could, of course, if I waited long enough but I find sudden that I lose a lot by waiting — for one thing I'm unsettled, my stuff is scattered in four states, I have no real place to work and I'm away from the life.

Now just the other day I found the place I want, made to order looks like, in the heart of a cow country, on a injun reservation and where there's wild horses, and all kinds of real riders — the kind I used to ride with and know.

I can in time run plenty of cattle on the place, enough to pay for the place itself and a man to take charge so I won't be called away from my work. In the evenings I could ride out with my wife and stretch my rope in the same way I'd be writing about — I could have the chief of the crow injuns come and set on my porch after sundown and have him tell me of the early days and bronc riders and cowboys dropping by telling me what happened on the other side of the ridges — then you could come and bring a few friends and wade in the trout stream that runs thru the place or follow the bear that left a track on the bank of it.

We could talk over the book we might put out sometime "The riders of the World". And many other things. And I could have you set on a stock saddle and ride a cow horse, there's some yearlings here that's harder to get near than a fox. Then you could try your hand at corraling a few wild horses.

But getting down to bedrock. Would you help me get that place? If you could I'd sure like to have you come and see it. And I'd sure bet you'd never be sorry for coming. You'd have to come to Billings, Montana, only three days ride from N.Y. I'm staying in Billings now.

I want to get that place right away before the owner changes his mind or before somebody else gets it. It'll take eight or ten thousand dollars to get the land and build a house on it — and I'll need two thousand dollars to make the first payment and hold it.

As security for your money, I could give you first mortgage on the property or else sign a contract for more books with you. I plan to pay you back with the royalty from the books — or quicker if I can.

I'll need eight or ten thousand dollars all together — two thousand now and the rest later along in the fall.

1932 Christmas card sent by James to CS III

The place won't be so that it'll be any extra work on my hands. I'll be careful of that, and it will be a big help in many ways. Later on, and when the chance comes I'll want to get a little more land so as I'll have room for the stock which'll accumulate but I dont ever want to run over 300 head of cattle, a bunch of that size will give me all I want for every purpose and enough to pay for a man or two as grub and so on — then I'll be at home.

I'd sure appreciate your writing to me as soon as you can about this. I'm sort of afraid I might lose the place if I dont get it right away. So, if you believe in it and want to help me now, I'd sure like to have you send the $2,000 dollar check so I can plank it as first payment.

As ever sincerely
Will James
Bill

P.S. I was hoping you could come out this summer, I know of a place, seven miles from where I want to locate, where I could put you, amongst friends, fine folks and old timers, and real coun-try. I'll furnish you with a good saddle, horse, and whole outfit even bull Durham —

Dear James:

I returned from Europe the end of the week but it was not until to-day that I had a chance to attend to my mail as I found my two children were sick but fortunately not seriously so.

The following telegram which I sent in reply to your letters tells the whole story:

Received your letters. Scribners can advance you two thousand dollars at once on SMOKY royalties and I personally can loan you two thousand later, but have just purchased a farm and am about to build, so feel very poor at the moment. Writing for further particulars and will send money at once if you telegraph that four thousand is sufficient to help you out.

I wish that I could see my way to agreeing to lend you the eight or ten thousand that you say you need but I think that since you are in the same position, you will understand that with the purchase of a farm and the necessity of building myself a home, I am pretty well strapped for money and cannot see my way to lending a large amount at present. My fa-

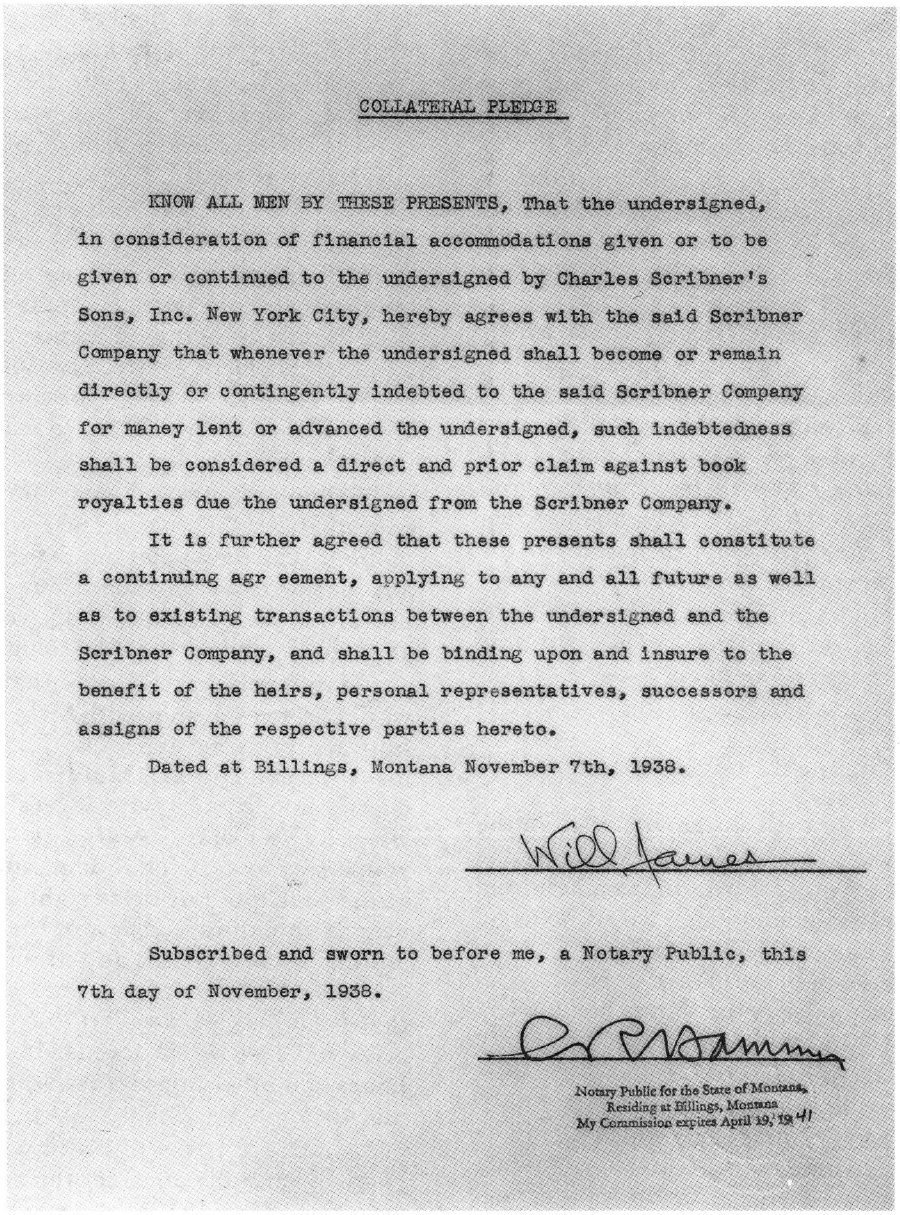

COLLATERAL PLEDGE

KNOW ALL MEN BY THESE PRESENTS, That the undersigned, in consideration of financial accommodations given or to be given or continued to the undersigned by Charles Scribner's Sons, Inc. New York City, hereby agrees with the said Scribner Company that whenever the undersigned shall become or remain directly or contingently indebted to the said Scribner Company for maney lent or advanced the undersigned, such indebtedness shall be considered a direct and prior claim against book royalties due the undersigned from the Scribner Company.

It is further agreed that these presents shall constitute a continuing agr eement, applying to any and all future as well as to existing transactions between the undersigned and the Scribner Company, and shall be binding upon and insure to the benefit of the heirs, personal representatives, successors and assigns of the respective parties hereto.

Dated at Billings, Montana November 7th, 1938.

Will James

Subscribed and sworn to before me, a Notary Public, this 7th day of November, 1938.

Notary Public for the State of Montana, Residing at Billings, Montana My Commission expires April 19, 19 41

Concerned that James might be forced to declare bankruptcy, Scribners sought, with this document, to protect itself from possible future claims on James's royalties by creditors.

ther and uncle are both away, so I did not have a chance to consult with them, but Perkins and I felt that we could make you an advance of $2,000. on SMOKY on our own responsibility. I really believe that the book has a chance for a big sale but one never can tell; it might conceivably pay for your whole place in a year's time but I do not wish to encourage you to count on such a dream.

You do not say in your letter how much the place will cost and how much you have to allow for building, also how much land is involved. On my personal loan of $2,000. I do not ask for any security and you can pay it out of your royalties as you can best afford to. You are therefore free to put a mortgage on the property, if you can arrange to do so, in order to build your house. I am uncertain if the four thousand I offer is enough for you to turn the corner on and have therefore asked you to wire in reply. . . .

With best wishes

Sincerely yours

[Charles Scribner]

Scribner's loan enabled James to buy a six-hundred-acre ranch for $4,500. However, the precedent had been established, and James continued to solicit the company for money to buy more acreage, to lease land, to construct buildings, to buy livestock, to pay help—thereby spending future royalties of books he had not even started to write.

LETTER:
Letter from Stephen Slesinger to Scribner editor Wallace Meyer, 12 February 1932.

The business of developing and promoting subsidiary rights related to the manufacture of novelties (games and toys) was in its infancy before World War II. Here, Slesinger, who already represented A. A. Milne, the English author of the Winnie-the-Pooh stories, and Hendrik Willem Van Loon, the Dutch American author (and artist) of historical works for children, suggests how he could make James marketable.

Dear Mr Meyer:

Please pardon me for not having communicated with you sooner.

As I explained to you when you were in the office, most of the original ideas I had for Milne were displaced by other ideas that came along later. However, I am giving you a list of items on which I believe I can utilize Will James.

(1) A series of board games, or possibly on cloth similar to the Winnie-the-Pooh and Van Loon games.
(2) A card game.
(3) A series of puzzles.
(4) A series of paint sets which would be divided among the following manufacturers whose items are non-conflicting.
   a. Transparent Drawing Slate.
   b. Artist's Easel.
   c. Paint Box Set.
   d. Paint Book.
(5) Lamp-shades; desk sets; waste paper baskets, etc. for a boy's room.
(6) A bare possibility of an adult wallpaper.
(7) In the event that a wallpaper is brought out — a printed drapery.
(8) A cowboy's A B C Book, which could probably consist of the drawings already used. This could be brought out by a publisher of toy books and toy novelties; you might wish to consider bringing this out yourself.
(9) Boy's stationery. There is a possibility of this appealing to some adults.
(10) A cowboy's calendar, for a boy. This would consist of twelve loose pages, one for each month, held together by a silk cord.
(11) Pencil sets for boys.

In addition to the above, there is always a possibility that one of my manufacturers, Community Plate for instance, might use a tray with a Will James drawing in connection with their $30.00 sets of silverware. You will recall from the conversation we had that possibilities continually arise for the use in a dignified way of my authors in innumerable fields.

I do not know and would not estimate the income that Mr. James might receive through my promotion; I can only point out that he is not receiving any income from the above sources at this moment nor are his books benefitting by the tremendous amount of publicity that they would be receiving.

I told you that the terms that I would suggest would be an even split with Mr. James. After carefully analyzing my expenses I find that my share is insufficient. You as a publisher no doubt have clauses in contracts with several of your authors whereby you share evenly any additional rights which may arise, even though you put forth little effort to dispose of these rights. My entire business as you know consists of the selling and promoting of these rights, and of the two the promotion takes up more of my time. The arrangements that I am making now are for the author to receive 25% of the proceeds. In the case of Will James and other important authors I would make this 40%.

I believe you will agree with my figures if you will carefully consider the nature of my business, remembering that all expenses in addition to overhead such as trade marks, design patents and other legal fees are paid by me. Remember, too, that the rights for which I ask are those which are dormant, and on which I propose to put in a considerable investment in time.

If any original work would be required of Mr. James that could be taken up separately and he could decide whether or not he wished to undertake it.

If any of the above is not clear to you, or if you wish to have me go into greater detail, please let me know.

Cordially yours,
Stephen Slesinger

Scribners and James agreed to this contract, though when it was canceled five years later, nothing had materialized and nothing had been earned.

RELATED LETTERS:

Letter from James to Maxwell Perkins, 17 March 1932, from Santa Barbara, Calif.; letter from CS III to James, 18 May 1932.

The dominant theme of the later James/Scribners correspondence is money—specifically, James's chronic lack of it and Scribners' attempts to recover its advances.

Dear Max:

I sure dont like to write this letter because I know I'm going to have to tell something that will disappoint you, and that's that I havent started on the story yet, only to scribble some notes down now and again that I will use.

Fact is I been trying to make some side money so I wouldn't have to bother Charlie so much. I managed to make some which cut out my demands on Charlie to about half. Sure been needing a lot of money last two months, everything seemed to come due.

Got things caught up now so I can breathe a little freer and expect to start on the story on monday the 21st. I'm going to get at it as hard as I can and if I dont have any interruptions I can easy have it done in a month's time. But I'm afraid I'm going to have interruptions.

I been illustrating some short stories I wrote, and now I went to work and sold LONE COWBOY to the movies. a good outfit I think. Paramount Corp. I sold the movie rights for $10.000. got the check and sent it to the bank. It reads in the contract that they want to play the book and not so much the actor, that they will make the picture as much as possible as it is in the book. It says a lot of things, and a lawyer said the contract was sure okay.

But I dont trust nobody down here in Hollywood, and there might be a flaw anywhere. It aint like dealing with Scribner's.

They're pretty sure of taking the picture on my ranch, along in June, and if they do I'll be hired to sort of be second director and advisor and see that everything is as it should be. I'd sure like that for the sake of the book, even tho they say they want to be true to it. Of course I'd get paid extra for that. — It would take about three weeks on the ranch.

I sure will try hard to get the book done before that time, that is, even with the interruptions I get from the Paramount. I get a wire pretty near every day asking me about this or that, and later on they'll want me in Hollywood for different things that goes with the starting or advertising of the picture.

They sure seem to be going at it strong and that makes me feel sort of good, specially when I get paid while I help, and the way they seem to want to go at it I dont think it'll at all hurt the book.

But I'm going to hang on to my horses a spell and watch out that there's no flaw where I might lose anything I make or the first price I got for the book.

So, with that and a few other things, Max you can guess a little how hard it is for me to start and stay with the book, but I sure cant overlook that picture money, and in the meantime I'm sure going to do my best to put out that book in good shape. I'd sure like to have it all done by the middle of may.—I remember one book, I think it was SAND, when you didn't get all the stuff till August and that book came out in the fall.

I guess this one will have to come out in the fall too, maybe early summer. Anyway you'll sure have it as early as I can make it and I'll send you some of the story soon as I get it lined out well.

Hope all is fine with you.

As ever,

Bill J.

P.S. There was no agent connected with the sale of LONE COWBOY, I done all the rustling myself. Am not drinking atall, sure cant afford it at this time.

The Paramount film of Lone Cowboy *(1934), starring Jackie Cooper, was narrated by James.*

Dear Bill:

I am delighted to hear that you are at least on the way back to your ranch. If you should show any signs of stampeding now I feel that I have two good boys in Snook and Snell [two of James's Billings, Montana, friends] who can round you up.

What I wished to write about is the fact that I hear you have had luck in selling your motion-picture rights. Would it not be a good thing if you used part of this money to cut down your mortgage that we hold? I know that it is annoying to you to

Dust jacket art by James for four of his books

have money clinking in your pockets and that it interferes with your work, but it certainly has not got that effect on me and my main job today is to round up what cash I can, as it is very scarce in the East. You would still be comfortably in debt to me so you would not have to worry about that, but I would not like to see you pass out of the picture leaving a ranch with a heavy mortgage and no cash in sight for Alice [James's wife]. You will also remember that when we loaned you the money there was no thought or expectation that it would be for more than a year or two, and if I had to help stake my other authors to country places I would certainly have to take over a bank.

I have not had a chance to read any of your new story but I am sure that it is good. I believe that Chapin [Scribner art director] is writing to ask you to do a half dozen more illustrations showing children, as you seem to be a little short on such pictures for a juvenile.

With best wishes

Sincerely yours

[Charles Scribner]

Though James agreed to apply future royalties directly to Scribners' mortgage loan, it was never retired because new debt was constantly being incurred; Scribners was able to transfer the mortgage to the Federal Farm Mortgage Corporation in 1934.

ATTACHMENT TO LETTER:
In a letter to CS III dated 12 July 1932, in which he describes his construction plans and asks for more advances, James writes: "I'm also enclosing the figures of what I done with what money I received so far this year and that'll maybe help some. It'll at least prove why I haven't paid up on the rest of the mortgage." This is his attachment:

1932

Money received from January first.

Charles Scribner's - $	2.500
Paramount Publix Corporation - - - - - - - - - - - - - - - - - - $	10.000
Two short short stories, American, Liberty - - - - - - - - - - $	1.415
Total $	13.915

Money spent from January first to July twelve.

On $53.000 life insurance - $	1.934.25
Automobile and ranch insurance on help - - - - - - - - - - - - $	160.00
Leases on land - $	459.00
Property and income taxes - $	908.70
Payment on land bought in 1931 - - - - - - - - - - - - - - - - - - $	500.00
Lawyer fees, Hollywood and Billings - - - - - - - - - - - - - - $	650.00
Bills. hardware, groceries, implements, general goods, final payment on 1931 truck for ranch, etc. - - - - - - - - - - $	2.200.00
Wages on ranch - $	900.00
Note on bank, paid. - $	1.000.00
Hollywood. Hotel, expenses, fare back home - - - - - - - - - - $	400.00
Bought 68 head of cattle, with expenses and time spent to buy, handling and getting them to the ranch. - - - - - - - - - - $	2.500.00
Santa Barbara, rent, living and general expenses from January first till middle of may, oil paints, shipping of oil paintings, trip to Los Angeles to autograph books and such like - $	2.125.00

I've figured pretty close in the above. There's some things a feller cant keep track of very well, such as a little entertainment, bull durham and dry socks. but the difference between what I received and what I've recorded as spent leaves me very little and I'm thinking I've spent wisely even if most all has gone for the ranch. I'm a little surprised that I done so good, after all this close figuring, and Alice [wife] will sure verify me on the figures above, her and me went over 'em careful and I can send the checks showing the payings if you want to be bothered looking 'em over.

As a summup it looks like there's there's an amount of around $178.05 that I've lost track of since January first. Such things as meeting Whitney [Whitney Darrow], entertaining him, taking him to the ranch and then having my truck take him back to the railroad has something to do with that.

Anyway, as close as I can figure, the above
sums up to - $ 13.736.95
Money received - $ 13.915.00
Unaccounted for, $178.05

In short, James had spent all of the money and was practically broke. Estimating royalties that were due James on 1 August, CS III sent him a check for $1,000—but with the warning that sales in 1932 had fallen off 50 percent from 1931: "don't spend a cent more than you need to." But James's spendthrift ways continued, compounded by a worsening drinking problem.

LETTER:
Letter from James to Maxwell Perkins, 10 January 1940, written from Rimrock Ranch, Billings, Montana.

James continued to write and draw and publish in the years following the sale (1936) of his beloved ranch, the Rocking R.

Dear Max:
Enclosed is the short story I wired you about, MY FIRST HORSE.

I think you'll agree with me that with about twenty pen illustrations it would make a dandy children's book. There's plenty of material in that story for twenty drawings, made especially for children.

Miss Dalgleish [Alice Dalgliesh, Scribner children's books editor] will like the story too, I think, and with working it over to her taste, as she did with the other books she done from my writing I know it will make a much better child's book than the others.

This is of the very earliest part of my life which was about skipped in LONE COWBOY.

This book would be something like the picture book Miss. Dalgleish suggested a couple of years ago, only with a more thru running story. I would make the illustrations in one or two colors, simple, and as the little copper-toed boot above—

I thought too that beside being on summer publication it would also make a dandy children's Christmas book, if boosted at that time, for the story has quite a bit of the Christmas doings in it.

I originally started this story to go into the major book of HORSES I'VE KNOWN, and it still can, as my opening story for that book, for, with Miss. Dalgleish work-over of the story for the children it would be changed some to the way I've got it.

If you all decide to make a children's book out of the story, for summer and Christmas publication I'll wait until Miss. Dalgleish revises the story and sends me the galleys before illustrating it. That will take a little time off the other stories for the major book but it'll be very much worth it, and I'll still have the major book done in good time.

I would make different illustrations again for the short story, MY FIRST HORSE, for the major book, and I think that for the children's booktitle that same one would be a good one, MY FIRST HORSE. It would sort of go well with THE DARK HORSE, and I could give the story another title for the major book.

As we are going to bring Smoky and Big-Enough in this book I thought they'd be good for the ending, along with another horse I now have which I raised at the ranch, Cortez, by name. His Majesty is another Smoky in brains

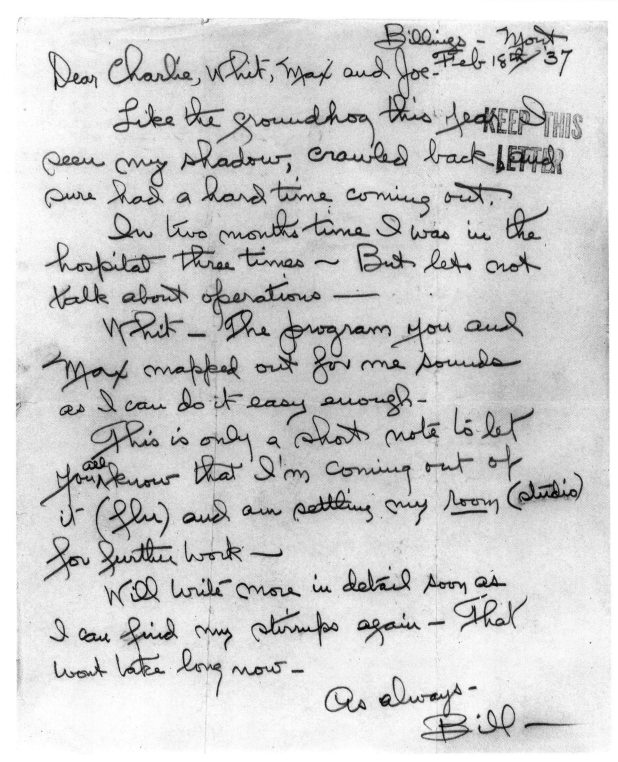

Billings – Mont
Feb 18th '37

Dear Charlie, Whit, Max and Joe –

Like the groundhog this week KEEP THIS LETTER seen my shadow, crawled back sure had a hard time coming out.

In two months time I was in the hospital three times ~ But lets not talk about operations —

Whit – The program you and Max mapped out for me sounds as I can do it easy enough –

This is only a short note to let you all know that I'm coming out of it (flu) and am settling my room (studio) for further work —

Will write more in detail soon as I can find my stumps again – That wont take long now –

As always –
Bill –

Letter from James addressed to his four Scribner "pardners": CS III (publisher), Whitney Darrow (business manager), Maxwell Perkins (book editor), and Joseph Chapin (art director). The program he mentions is the writing regimen Perkins and Darrow outlined for him to try to follow—another "Uncle Bill" book, a children's picture book like Young Cowboy, *and then a "major" book like* Scorpion—*in order to keep him out of trouble and financially out of the red.*

and all around, excepting color. I wouldn't take the amount the European War is costing, for him, as broke and in the red as I am.

As ever —
Bill

I'm going right on with the short horse stories —
No sales yet but it's still early —
I'm not fooling around no more, no fooling —
Jan 10/1940

My First Horse, *published (26 August) and marketed as a children's book, was not included in* Horses I've Known, *which quickly followed it (16 September). Next, James turned to developing the great American cowboy novel that he had had in his mind for several years, tentatively titled* The Saga of the American Cowboy, *a sweeping chronicle told through three generations of horsemen, each main character named Bill. The idea interested M-G-M Studios, so James went to Hollywood to write a preliminary treatment. But he failed to produce, and the project was dropped; instead, he started writing the book. Scribners published it in 1942 as* The American Cowboy. *Six months later, James died of alcoholic complications. He was fifty.*

James Boyd (1888–1944)

James Boyd

One of the best-known pre–World War II American writers of historical fiction, Boyd helped revitalize the genre with works distinguished for their psychological and historical realism. Born in Pennsylvania, he lived most of his life as a gentleman farmer in Southern Pines, North Carolina. He was a graduate of Princeton and earned a master's degree in English literature at Trinity College, Cambridge. He served with an ambulance corps in World War I; his unit participated in the Saint-Mihiel operation and the Meuse-Argonne offensive, and he was discharged in July 1919 following months of treatment for what would be a lifelong sinus condition. Settling in North Carolina, he vowed to spend five years as an apprentice writer: either he would succeed or change his vocation. In 1923, apparently encouraged by John Galsworthy, who was vacationing nearby, he shifted from short stories, some of which had been published, to the writing of a novel. *Drums,* which Scribners published in 1925, was critically acclaimed as the best novel of the American Revolution to date—and for years it was used as standard reading in high schools. Other successful novels on the Civil War, pre-Revolution days, and the western frontier followed. His strong literary reputation and friendship with many leading American writers enabled him to organize the Free Company in 1940 for the purpose of countering the threat of Nazi propaganda with the broadcasting of original radio plays that dramatized American civil liberties.

Scribner Books by Boyd

1925	*Drums* (edition illustrated by N. C. Wyeth, 1928)
1927	*Marching On*
1930	*Long Hunt*
1935	*Roll River*
1939	*Bitter Creek*
1944	*Eighteen Poems*

RELATED LETTERS:
Scribner book editor Maxwell Perkins had been following Boyd's literary development since his first story ("The Sound of a Voice") had been accepted by Robert Bridges, editor of Scribner's Magazine, *in 1920. When he heard of Boyd's novel-in-progress, he asked to see it as soon as possible. These letters begin Boyd's initiation into a twenty-year publishing relationship with Scribners.*

Jan. 19, 1924

Dear Mr. Boyd:

We have just finished reading the last part of your novel. We thought that before writing you we ought to have read all of it, but it has not been easy to refrain from speaking to you about it before, on the basis of the earlier parts. Of course we want to publish it and have written Mr. Paget [Boyd's literary agent] to say so and to make an offer. It seems to us a very unusual and important book,- to constitute an extraordinarily vivid and effective presentation of the times, and of that political and social evolution which created a nation. In this respect, which is the most important, it is at least emotionally a revelation to a reader. The latter part of the book where the realization of the Americans that they are an entity, that they are all the same people, however different and altogether separate from the English, is extremely moving. It seems to me that in this respect you have done something truly unique at any rate for America. It is a very large canvas and beautifully painted, and we have naturally found it a great pleasure to read.

I suppose Mr. Paget will write you immediately about the question of terms and I hope before so very long we may be approaching the time for publication.

Sincerely yours,
[Maxwell Perkins]

P.S. I am trying hard to think of a title. It seems to me it should express the self-realization of a distinct race of men,- the birth of a nation. I had thought of that passage in "Areopagitica" for instance, about the eagle mewing her mighty youth, but there was no phrase there. You may have thought of something anyway by now.

Jan 23 '24

Dear Mr. Perkins. I am naturally relieved & delighted to know that you want the novel; but if I had to choose between your acceptance of it & your comments on it I would take the latter. I can't tell you how pleased I am to learn from you that I have presented the central theme with clarity & force. That has all along been the question in my mind as I suppose it always is with anyone writing his first novel. Could I manage the larger canvass & avoid blurring or sprawling? I knew that many of the individual scenes were all right & a few of them really fine but that did not cheer me because I knew that if the anatomy of the book were wrong no number of brilliant spots could save it. Now, it is merely a question of finish, of revision. In this connection I should add that the copy you hold is extremely defective, the typist having made some 150 errors while I have made about the same number of minor changes. I am sending my revised copy to Paget today. I have already written him suggesting a very simple, & I believe effective scheme for serializing the novel which would reduce it to about 87,000 words.

Thanks again for your letter. With best wishes

Yours sincerely
James Boyd

P.S. Please keep on thinking about the title. I'm still absolutely stumped.

Bridges was against serialization of the novel because of its episodic nature, so Scribners proceeded with its plans for book publication. In November, Boyd's wife went up to New York with ideas on how to improve—with pine tree trunks and coonskin caps—the dust jacket design Scribners' art department had already created. Changes were made to incorporate them. By then Boyd's earlier title suggestion of "Drums" had been agreed upon.

Nov 28th, 1924.

Dear Mr. Perkins:—

. . . I understand the book is slated for February and that the title is to be "Drums". . . .

I suppose you feel towards young authors the way a head-master of a boarding-school does towards the parents who are putting their children under him for the first time—to wit: a weary tolerance tinged with Olympian humor. . . .

My wife reports that at her interviews she was scared and you were nice. I hope, of course, that your impression of the occasions was just the reverse.

Best wishes,

Yours sincerely,
James Boyd

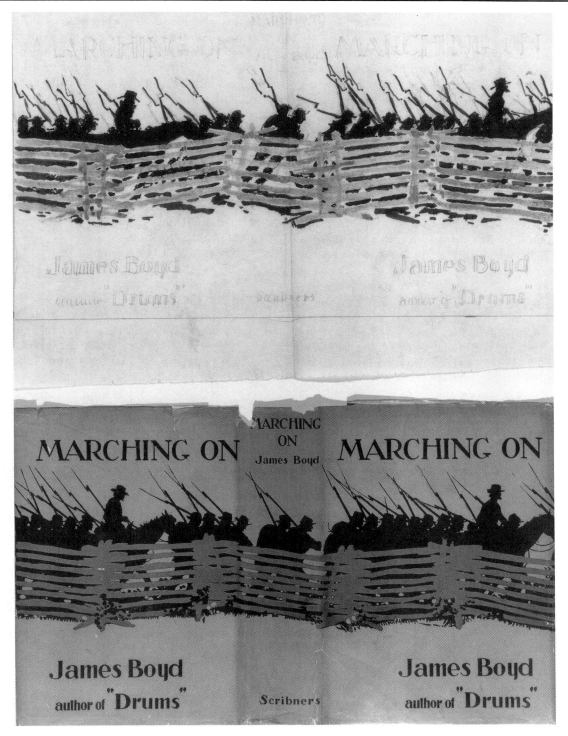

Dust jacket drawing by Boyd contrasted with the final jacket used for his novel. Not impressed with the preliminary drawing he had been sent, Boyd wrote to Perkins: "Notes on the jacket —color scheme & general idea bully! But the troops are not marching on. They are strolling. There is neither the mass nor the movement which make <u>momentum</u>. And momentum is the thing you feel when you see a division on the march. Also I'd like more made of the rail fence. . . . I send you a hasty & crude wash drawing which if not looked at too closely may give you an idea of what's in my mind. If the present artist can't do the trick I implore you to get one who can" (circa 23 January 1927).

Dec. 1, 1924

Dear Mr. Boyd:

... About young authors I do not feel in the least as you suggest. Far from it. It is with them that our great hopes lie. We know what the old authors can do and although some of them do admirably, they seldom surprise us. But the young writers may do anything,- at least several of them may, and you are certainly one of those several.

If Mrs. Boyd was "scared" it must have been of the formidable Miss DeVoy of the Art Department of whom I also am scared. But of me not even my own children are scared;- while I am still always scared when confronted by a charming young woman.- But don't tell anybody this because it is not a suitable characteristic for an editor.

Sincerely yours,
[Maxwell Perkins]

RELATED LETTERS:

Letter from Maxwell Perkins to Boyd, 8 December 1926; letter from Boyd to Perkins [December 1926], in reply.

While working on his second novel, Marching On, *Boyd clarifies his attitude toward Perkins's editorial role.*

Dear Jim:

The second section of the manuscript came today. I have looked over both of these sections a little and I tell you I cannot but think you are doing a splendid book;- not but what I should like to think this naturally, but I do try to be cautious in describing an unpublished manuscript for fear that it may lead the writer to expect too much. I see, for instance, how you have changed and to great effect, the encounters between James Frazer and the heroine....

Yours as ever,
[Maxwell Perkins]

Dear Max:

... You speak of fearing that criticism may confuse & trouble me. If you have such a fear it troubles me more than any criticism could. I have spent a lot of time trying to get intelligent criticism of my stuff. Of the many who have comment you seem to me to have a good deal of the most sense. So I beg you not to go back on me. On the other hand don't fear that my high opinion will over balance my independent judgement. It's my stuff & every decision must be mine. Thus when I thought, mistakenly it seems, that you advocated the addition of further characters to the caste of the army phase I objected. At the same time I admitted that the phase itself might need building up—but by different means. And again when you suggest a maturing of James I fully agree & will tackle that this week.

In a word whenever I can feel the force of your criticism I'll seize upon it avidly & use it without acknowledgement, & in any case when I can't, I will wrangle bitterly, denounce you passionately but all on purely professional grounds & without reference to the many vistas of juleps that lie before us.

So sing out loud & clear. Then we'll have something to work on—

As ever
Jim

RELATED LETTERS:

Letter from N. C. Wyeth to Arthur H. Scribner, 4 October 1927; letter from Scribner to Wyeth, 6 October 1927, in reply; letter from Wyeth to Boyd, 10 December 1927, which Boyd apparently sent to Perkins.

Much of the popularity and success of Scribners' series of illustrated classics was due to the quality of the artwork done for them by the Chadds Ford (Pa.) artist N. C. Wyeth. One of the leading figures in early-twentieth-century American art, Wyeth ultimately provided all the illustrations in eighteen volumes in the series. Here, he reacts to Scribner's invitation to illustrate Boyd's fictional work on the American Revolution.

My dear Mr. Scribner:

Let me say immediately that I am joyously surprised that you are to feature "Drums." Although different than R.L.S. Mr. Boyd achieves the same satisfying substance and spirit. Splendid in style, the vitality of the story properly submerges it, and one lives in those early stirring days along with John Frazer, Captain Flood, Paul Jones etc. accepting them all and their surroundings at once casually and intensely — the latter quality a rare treat in modern story telling where the machinery of dramatics and bizarre happenings makes such a din. But here, bless me—I am launching into a review!

More than this — in spite of a feeling of apathy which has stolen over me in the past few years, caused by the endless pageant of poor color-engraving and printing — I rise once more with renewed enthusiasm to greet this unusual opportunity. I thrill to the picture possibilities in

```
                                                          1.


                    THE DARK SHORE

                          By

                      James Boyd


                     SECOND PART
                      SYNOPSIS

        The childhood of Tommy Rand recalled in flashes; small

    tragedies, the circus, bicycle races, nurses, day-school.  His

    parents only dimly felt.  A bright glimpse of his Uncle Fitz-

    Greene.  His Aunt Clara.

        He leaves the world of women and goes to boarding

    school.  A chocolate brown institution, inculcating muscular

    Christianity, which he accepts.

        At Yale, the same process is continued.  His lack of

    prowess, physical or otherwise, precludes him from preferr-

    ment, but he accepts the system.  A party of drunken outlaw

    undergraduates at the Taft.  Women.

        On graduation, he goes to work in the coal business in

    Midian determined to make good in spite of the fact that his

    father had made Signet at Yale and he had not.  His father,
```

```
                                                          5.


        His aunt arrives.  They talk about the mystery of this

    world.  And then about the children.  It is agreed that they

    both will grow up to be splendid and happy.


                        THE END
```

First and last pages of Boyd's synopsis for the second part of his contemporary novel Roll River. *The first part was serialized in* Scribner's Magazine *(May–August 1934) under the title* The Dark Shore. *In his letter to Maxwell Perkins accompanying this plan, Boyd wrote: "My stories don't lend themselves to synopsis as you know & I write a bad synopsis at best. This could be filled in indefinitely until we had the completed novel. But as always happens with me it will be changed, perhaps radically while it develops. . . . I have no element of the master mind. A theme always but after that until my people start moving I can't guess what they'll do. Even then it is only a sort of higher reporting. . . . I feel the story shaping but it clears itself slowly as I write into it. Like a light fog" (5 May 1934).*

this story — I thrill to be associated with one of the precious few substantial and capable story-tellers — and as ever, I thrill to know that you again desire my contributions under your house imprint!

But we must get better color-plates and printing. I hate like fury to become a pest to you on this subject. But hardly a week goes by but I must suffer torture when I open new books from your shelves (books sent to me to be autographed — and I have drawn and written in hundreds!) and I gaze upon prints hardly recognizable for their false color, poor register or both. Only yesterday I returned a Scottish Chiefs and a Kidnapped to the sender unsigned, advising them to seek further for better printed copies.

And then the missing prints — those deleted. These can't cost 3 or 4 cents apiece, and for this saving a carefully worked out cycle of pictures is broken.

I have tried to think with you, that some improvement in the newer editions is evident; perhaps there is — a little — but not enough to make much difference.

I am not super-sensitive about this matter Mr. Scribner; in fact ordinarily I am quite resigned to the usual poor presentation of my work. But fortified by the constant expressions of many many known and unknown friends, expressions which at times amounts to indignation, and urged by the positive knowledge that this long and varied series which I have done for you in the last seventeen years comprises the best juvenile adventure pictures ever published (pray excuse my modesty this time) I must plead once more for better engraving and better printing.

You have control of the best I have ever done in illustration. I must always stand or fall by your presentation of it.

—

Some time, when Mr. Boyd is available in N.Y. I would like to talk over a scheme for illustrating "Drums" which is taking shape in my mind.

I have just completed the reading of the copy you sent me. Having read the novel when it was published I can say that I am more captivated by the book than ever.

Very respectfully yours
N. C. Wyeth

Dear Mr. Wyeth:

I am delighted that "Drums" especially appeals to you, as I felt sure it would, and I know that Boyd will be immensely pleased when he learns that you have been secured to illustrate it. I understand that he is to be in this neighborhood next week, and as soon as we have definite information I will telgeraph you to arrange for a meeting here some time convenient to you both. I realize more fully our responsibility in having in our keeping in a measure the presentaton of your illustrative work and shall be ready to go over this thoroughly with you when you are here. With a new book we have often suffered under the handi-

cap of being hurried at the last moment, and now that we are starting early, and I take it you are ready to begin almost at once, I hope that you can help us in this. We shall try to do our part.

Looking forward to seeing you, I am
Yours very sincerely,
Arthur H. Scribner

The following letter, written from Edenton, North Carolina, shows Wyeth already at work. Edenton, the scene of the "Edenton tea party" of 25 October 1774, in which fifty-one ladies signed a pact resolving not to drink tea or wear English clothing until the tea tax should be repealed, figured prominently in Boyd's book.

My dear Boyd:—

Some tower in the brilliant moonlight has just rung out the hour of two. I have tried to sleep, but the crowded hours of the day are racing through my mind at such a pace that sufficient composure for slumber seems out of the question. Perchance, this letter will invite sleep — if not to me, mayhap to you.

For the last two hours, lying by the open window, I have listened to the night sounds of this little town, with great interest, contrasting them with those Johnny Frazer heard so long ago, and by doing so have enjoyed certain revealments which for moments at a time became very poignant and very moving.

At this instant a dog is barking somewhere on the edge of the city, there is also the faint muffled staccato of a small power boat out on the sound. Occasionally the sudden angry grind of a Ford, new-starting in the cold, shatters the quiet. But the silence that follows becomes the more pregnant with echoes of the past.

I am actually not many feet from the cubic areas occupied by the young boy Johnny and his dad in their candle-lit room at Hornblowers. My window faces the harbor and I too can look upon "dim shapes of fences, walks, houses—" some of them identical, changed only in material of roof-covering. Dimly bulking against the glow of the full moon on the water I can see the angular shapes of these ware-houses just as Johnny Frazer saw them!

This afternoon was spent wandering in and about these gray relics of 1760. My heart went out to them, because Boyd, you have made them live for me. The oak timbers, whose adze-marked surfaces are still crisp on their protected sides and smoothed to gentle undulations where the sun and rain of years have touched them thrilled me like music.

Dust jackets for Boyd's first (and best-known) novel—from a later edition illustrated by N. C. Wyeth—and Boyd's posthumously published book. The illustration of the southern pine on the collection's cover was done by Boyd's son, Dan.

While I was sitting in one of those great empty storerooms with a sharply cut square of the sun-lit bay before me, one of the supporting timbers creaked — a slow weary creak as though it were trying to change its position. I was greatly moved. It was a privilege I thought, to have heard that. There was no wind, the sun was low, the old building was muttering to itself and I overheard. I have a feeling that I know what it said—which is one reason that I can't sleep. . . .

I arrived (very thankful to you for the use of your motor, and pleased with the careful but not dull driving of Calvin) at Plymouth [N.C.] Friday morning. . . . From Plymouth the passage lay over the rails to <u>Mackeys</u> where I shifted to the ferry, the better to sense Albemarle Sound from the deck-line of a boat. . . .

Approaching Edenton on the ferry, the waterfront became monstrously enlarged for a few moments, by a mirage — a "loom" as the Maine fisherman would say. It affected me queerly. It was as though the little port had stood up from a seated position, open eyed, to view with alarm the impertinent

coming of another artist to reveal her past, when the first artist had already accomplished the job! That no other one of the twenty or more passengers on the boat made comment on this phenomenon, I am convinced that it was <u>a personal matter</u>!

And now, if I do not sleep, I shall not be fit to meet some of your friends to-morrow. . . .

<u>To bed</u> — but not before I express my warmest thanks to you and Mrs. Boyd for your kindnesses. You have given me a wonderful start in the new adventure <u>Drums</u> and I do hope I succeed.

     Cordially
     Wyeth

Wyeth's illustrated edition of Drums *was published on 14 September 1928.*

LETTER:
Letter from Boyd to Maxwell Perkins, 1 August 1938.

As the artist who had created "decorations" for the current Scribner best-seller by Marjorie Kin-

nan Rawlings, The Yearling, *Edward Shenton seemed to Perkins a good choice for Boyd's novel of the western frontier, which was to be serialized in* The Saturday Evening Post. *At the time of this letter, Thomas Wolfe, whose illness is mentioned at the end, was hospitalized in Seattle with pneumonia (he died in September).*

Dear Max:

I spent an evening with Shenton when I was staying with Stuart Rise in Phila & I like him immensely & think his headings for the Yearling are fine. But I think it would be a mistake to have him do the novel. Such headings, amounting virtually to illustrations, inevitably mark the book as a juvenile. That's all right <u>after</u> a book has been established, as in the case of Drums, but I think it's an unwise lead-off for first pub. Then, above all, a writer is trying not so much to draw pictures himself as to give the reader an impulse to draw them for <u>himself</u>. Such pictures must inevitably vary depending on each reader's qualities & must therefore conflict with actual pictures that are presented to him at the same time. This sets up a conflict in the graphic image which is weakening to both elements particularly the writer's since, not only is the first impact of line stronger than that of words, but also it is easier, if less than satisfying in the end, for a reader to accept a ready-made image than to create one for himself out of his imaginative resources. The readers of children's books & of the Sat Eve Post, also a children's book, recognize this & make the concession in the interest of appeal to limited capacity. It is of course a principle, as well, of the more primitive forms of religion. But I think a writer, & no doubt a prophet, always likes first to see how much his followers can do for themselves. For inherently it is the art of rousing & satisfying their own capacities that he addresses himself.

But I have made for my own guidance a crude map of the imaginary country I describe & I should think it would be excellent to have Shenton use it as a basis for endpapers. In that case there is no conflict with the reader's conception of character. He might also be the man for the jacket. I'd like to see him get the work. I know he needs it & can do it & he is a man of singular integrity & good heart.

I called up The Chelsea [Wolfe's New York City hotel] again on my way back through N.Y. & learned of Tom's illness. Let me know his address when you have it & I'll write him.

The galleys & the 1st installment have come from the Post. And still no title. I've compiled a list of over 70 from which I cull the least impossible.

Let me hear. Good luck

Jim

Open Range
A Horse, A Gun
A Cloud on the Plains
West of Greasewood
Bitter Creek
Medicine Valley
The Only Maverick *
Wide and Starry Sky
High Country
Head West
Bury Me Not
* Adopted provisionally by Post.

Bitter Creek *was published on 20 March 1939 with map endpapers drawn by H. H. Gilmore.*

Thanks so much for James Boyd's BITTER CREEK. His writing is so strong and real, such a change from the pseudo-intellectual blather one reads lately. I'm getting not to like intellectuals. I don't think they wash enough; they don't sweep out corners, either. I've been in a few of their homes! But Mr. Boyd's writing is so firm and clear and full of vitality. I've got nearly everything he's written.

— Novelist Janet M. Reback [Taylor Caldwell] in a letter to Maxwell Perkins, 25 February 1939

RELATED LETTERS:
Letter from Boyd to Maxwell Perkins, 14 March 1940; letter from Perkins to Boyd, 29 March 1940, in reply.

The stimulus for this exchange of letters on the intellectual level and writing quality of current literature was a long quotation Perkins had sent Boyd from I Begin Again, *a book by Alice Bretz, who had become blind. Her test of a good book was to read it in braille, and having applied the test to Boyd's novel* Roll River, *felt it was an outstanding example of what a good book could be.*

Dear Max—

Thanks for your letter with its touching & satisfying quotation. If only more readers were blind: that is if only more were able to place themselves when reading in a state of isolation where what they read became for the time their only world. Then they would feel the subtler values of craftsmanship. I have an idea that these ideas meant more in the past where reading was the reader's other life & not mere broken interludes in the swift & shallow stream of innumerable distractions. Perhaps that sounds like [Charles] Lamb's "Then I shall write for antiquity." But I don't think we realize how low is the intellectual level of our time. In form & content political utterances here & in England are infantile compared with any period of the past. And in writing, which we have the great craftsman, Hem. [Hemingway] & two or three fine naturals their level of pure intelligence is low. That itself imposes on their style, however admirable within its field, a rigid limitation. The poets are our flower, a number of very good minors, and [Robert] Frost & [Edward Arlington] Robinson. I wonder if the terms of our life admit only the serial novel (whether in book form or not) wherein we pick up & lay down the successive episodes of Dick Tracy or some other, if they don't exclude any other habitable spirit world except for the blind. Or have we failed in how we tell our story? We can't simply say that the play was a great success but the audience a flop as [Oscar] Wilde more elegantly did.

We saw something of Mrs. Hemingway [2nd wife, Pauline] in Key West, as good a girl as I've met since I had sense to pick them. But he, as you know, was in Cuba.

Thanks for your letter. I'll write Mrs. Bretz.

As ever

Jim

Dear Jim:

I have often thought sadly along the lines of the idea you expressed in your letter.- But I do not know whether the difficulty has not been in the last decade, or almost that, rather the nature of the times. It seemed to me in the twenties that something wonderful was happening in regard to literature. Very notable writing was suddenly beginning to appear, and an eager public existed. I think there is still notable writing very much in evidence, but that the public's attention has been turned so much in the direction of economic worries and wars, that it has greatly deteriorated in respect to literature. If we can only get this war over in some decent fashion--and God knows it doesn't seem likely it can be done--we may see an-

other good day. Maybe this is nothing but wishful thinking. . . .

Always yours,
[Maxwell Perkins]

LETTERS:

As a reaction to the developing war in Europe, the U.S. Department of Justice asked Boyd to come to Washington in the fall of 1940 to advise it on a propaganda project that would make a "positive restatement in moving terms of our own ideals." The program would consist of a weekly series of thirty-minute radio broadcasts, each scripted by a different leading American writer and dealing with some aspect of American civil liberties. Boyd was very supportive of the idea and immediately began organizing a group of writers and meeting with the broadcasting companies. And he turned to Perkins for help.

Oct 3 '40

Dear Max—

I'm sending you a copy of this letter to Bob Sherwood as the easiest way of explaining what's afoot. Please return.

I'd like to know what you think of the scheme.

If favorably inclined what do you think of the chances of getting something from Hemingway?

Do you think we could use straight or adapt a dramatic passage from Tom Wolfe's work? I was thinking of the short piece he did for the New Republic on his journey out of Germany? Having him speak again from beyond the grave on the very theme that now engrosses us might be most impressive.

If we succeeded in getting the best writers to do original scripts would the collection interest a publisher as a commercial proposition?

I have to be in N.Y. next Thurs & Fri talking to the radio people & will see you then. Meanwhile be thinking it over & if any suggestions occur to you send me a line here.

As ever

Jim

Tentative list from which writers would be selected.
So far only Sherwood has been approached.

Maxwell Anderson	Sherwood
Millais	Sandburg
Hemingway	Marj. Rawlings
Saroyan	Sinclair Lewis

The Free Company

"I say there can be no salvation for These States . . . . . . without free tongues, and ears willing to hear the tongues." —Walt Whitman

Room 4409, 60 East 42nd Street, New York City, MU 2-5860

JAMES BOYD
National Chairman
Southern Pines, North Carolina

ROBERT SHERWOOD
Chairman, Writers' Division
630 Fifth Ave., New York City

BURGESS MEREDITH
Chairman, Actors' Division
9200 Wilshire Boulevard,
Beverly Hills, California

W. B. LEWIS
V. P., Columbia Broadcasting System
Chairman, Radio Division
485 Madison Ave., New York City

MAXWELL ANDERSON
SHERWOOD ANDERSON
STEPHEN VINCENT BENÉT
GEORGE M. COHAN
MARC CONNELLY
PAUL GREEN
ERNEST HEMINGWAY
ARCHIBALD MacLEISH
WILLIAM SAROYAN
ORSON WELLES

CHARLES VANDA
Producer

April 21, 1941

Maxwell Perkins, Esq.,
Charles Scribner's Sons,
597 Fifth Avenue,
New York City

Dear Max:

Thank you for your note. I rather expected it would turn out that way. There is a possibility that we may run another series next fall, in which case we will hold Hemingway to his promise. Meanwhile, thanks for your good offices.

I have been swamped with work and have had no chance to see you and would not know what to say if I did. I feel sickened by this black sickness of the world and just now see no light. There is nothing to do but stand as firm as we can by the best that we are able to believe in. I can only hold my breath and hope that there are enough of those who will do this to save some fragments from the cataclysm.

I have been here a few days and go South tomorrow night. Will be back again next week when I hope to have more leisure and see you.

As ever,

Jim

Letter from Boyd to Maxwell Perkins, written near the end of his group's eleven weekly radio broadcasts (23 February–4 May 1941). Despite his promise, Hemingway did not contribute a play for the series.

O'Neill
Steinbeck
Cather
Stephen Benet
Wilder

Elmer Rice
Kenneth Roberts

[*At the bottom, Perkins added the names of Walter D. Edmonds, Arthur Train, Sherwood Anderson, and James Truslow Adams.*]

Possible Subjects for the Treatment

Freedom of Speech
   "   " the Press

   "   in Teaching
Right of Assembly
   "   to Vote
   "   of Property
Religious Freedom
Economic   "
Racial Equality
Freedom for Thinkers Writers & Artists to
    Express Themselves
Trial by Jury
Search & Seizure
Due Process of Law

The Free Company, as Boyd's group was called (he became its national chairman), began its weekly broadcasts on the Sunday afternoon of 23 February 1941 with William Saroyan's play The People With Light Coming Out of Them. *Perkins tried to acquire the publishing rights to the series for Scribners, but some of the playwrights with connections to Dodd, Mead prevailed.*

March 17, 1941

Dear Jim:

I do, of course, fully understand your position, and respect your decision that it must be a completely impartial one in this matter. I do wish though, that I had understood when we had lunch that there was to be competition because I would have pointed out that the possibilities this book would have for prominence would depend largely on its being published by a house that had a very strong educational department,- which is not true of the house selected. I think that most of these authors regard that house as a prominent publisher of plays on account of the annual Burns Mantle anthology which they all like to appear in, though I understand they get no recompense for it. As a matter of fact, the publisher of the largest number of current plays is Random House, and they have specialized in that field. But we are distinctly the strongest house in plays published as literature, and have always been so.

Always yours,
[Maxwell Perkins]

Burns Mantle was the drama critic of the New York Daily News *at the time and edited* The Best Plays of . . . *and the* Year Book of the Drama in America, *published annually by Dodd, Mead. Later in 1941 the company published the collection of radio plays under the title* The Free Company Presents . . . A Collection of Plays About America.

Ernest Hemingway (1899–1961)

Ernest Hemingway at the Finca Vigía, his home in Cuba from 1939 until 1960 (photo by George Leavens)

Charles Scribner Jr.'s belief (expressed in a 1982 lecture) that Hemingway's books were the "foundation stones" of the firm's publishing reputation is understandable, for there has never been a more dynamic figure in American literary history than Hemingway, nor another twentieth-century writer who has had more of an influence on the course of modern American literature: publishing his books would seem to have been a privilege. Hemingway, in turn, was one of Scribners' most loyal authors, whose humorous, warm, kidding, and gently insulting letters to his publisher (1939–1952), CS III, almost outnumber those written to his editors, Maxwell Perkins (1925–1947), Wallace Meyer (1947–1957), and Harry Brague (1957–1961). Often called the leading spokesman of the "lost generation" between the two world wars, Hemingway is equally well-known for his wide-ranging adventures as a Red Cross ambulance driver wounded in Italy in World War I; a bullfighting afficionado running with the bulls in Pamplona, Spain; a deep-sea fisherman of the Gulf Stream's giant marlin; a big-game hunter on safari in Africa; a Loyalist-supporting war correspondent in the Spanish Civil War; and a World War II participant and reporter. This rugged lifestyle took its toll in serious wounds, concussions, broken bones, and mental strain but reflected his overriding view that life was a competition to enter and to win, whether the particular activity was boxing, marlin fishing, hunting lions, fighting wars—or writing. Early in his career Hemingway joked to Perkins that Scribners could make more money insuring him against accident and disease than publishing his books. His literary reputation rests firmly upon four novels—*The Sun Also Rises* (1926), *A Farewell to Arms* (1929), *For Whom the Bell Tolls* (1940), and *The Old Man and the Sea* (1952)—and frequently anthologized stories, including "Big Two-Hearted River," "The Killers," "The Short Happy Life of Francis Macomber," "A Clean Well-Lighted Place," and "The Snows of Kilimanjaro"—a body of work characterized by understatement and the spare use of dialogue, with strong characters exhibiting "grace under pressure." Hemingway's simple, direct writing style, which cumulates effects using compound clauses and prepositional phrases, also influenced the technique of modern fiction writing. For his achievement he was awarded the Nobel Prize for literature in 1954.

Scribner Books by Hemingway

1926   *The Torrents of Spring: A Romantic Novel in Honor of the Passing of a Great Race*

	The Sun Also Rises
1927	*Men Without Women*
1929	*A Farewell to Arms* (edition illustrated by Daniel Rasmusson, 1948)
1930	*In Our Time: Stories by Ernest Hemingway,* with an introduction by Edmund Wilson
1932	*Death in the Afternoon*
1933	*Winner Take Nothing*
1935	*Green Hills of Africa,* with decorations by Edward Shenton
1937	*To Have and Have Not*
1938	*The Fifth Column and the First Forty-Nine Stories*
1940	*The Fifth Column: A Play in Three Acts*
	For Whom the Bell Tolls
1950	*Across the River and Into the Trees*
1952	*The Old Man and the Sea* (edition illustrated by Raymond Sheppard and C. F. Tunnicliffe, 1960)
1953	*The Hemingway Reader,* selected, with a foreword and twelve brief prefaces, by Charles Poore
1954	*The Short Stories of Ernest Hemingway*
1964	*A Moveable Feast*
1967	*By-Line: Ernest Hemingway: Selected Articles and Dispatches of Four Decades,* edited by William White
1969	*The Fifth Column and Four Stories of the Spanish Civil War*
1970	*Islands in the Stream*
1972	*The Nick Adams Stories*
1974	*The Enduring Hemingway: An Anthology of a Lifetime in Literature,* edited, with an introduction, by Charles Scribner Jr.
1981	*Ernest Hemingway: Selected Letters, 1917–1961,* edited by Carlos Baker
1984	*Hemingway on Writing,* edited by Larry W. Phillips
1985	*The Dangerous Summer,* with an introduction by James A. Michener
	Dateline, Toronto: The Complete Toronto Star *Dispatches, 1920–1924,* edited by William White
1986	*The Garden of Eden*
1987	*The Complete Short Stories of Ernest Hemingway*
1996	*The Only Thing That Counts: The Ernest Hemingway/Maxwell Perkins Correspondence, 1925–1947,* edited by Matthew J. Bruccoli, with the assistance of Robert Trogdon

ADDRESS:
"Publishing Hemingway," address given by Charles Scribner Jr. (CS IV) at the Hemingway Conference at Northeastern University, 22 May 1982.

Hemingway's long association with Scribners began in February of 1926 when he met with Maxwell Perkins—his future editor—in the publishing company's offices on Fifth Avenue in New York. The two men hit it off from the start, and their meeting resulted in Hemingway's accepting a contract covering both his novella *The Torrents of Spring* and the unfinished novel which would later be published under the title *The Sun Also Rises.*

For Perkins, that contract was the successful upshot of a long campaign to bring the talented

Hemingway (right) with Maxwell Perkins in Key West, Florida, 1935

young author onto the Scribner list. A year earlier, upon the strenuous urging of Scott Fitzgerald, he had written to Hemingway in Europe asking him to submit his work to Scribners. But by the time the Perkins letter reached Hemingway in Paris, the writer had already signed up with the firm of Boni and Liveright in New York. It was they who published Hemingway's first book-length collection of short stories under the title *In Our Time*. Hemingway's contract with Boni and Liveright gave them an option on his second book; and, if they accepted that, on his third. As it turned out they published neither, for they turned down *The Torrents of Spring* when he submitted it to them. It was too clearly a parody of their famous author Sherwood Anderson. This dilemma was a particularly painful one for Horace Liveright, who must have felt that he had earned the right to be Hemingway's publisher. He undoubtedly regarded *The Torrents of Spring* as a contract-breaker. But what could he do?

To Perkins, on the other hand, it was an unexpected reversal of fortune. He was now able to sign up a very promising writer at the cost of publishing a relatively minor work.

As it turned out, he was also taking on an extremely loyal author, for Hemingway remained on the Scribner list from the time of that first meeting until his death 35 years later. Today, when so many writers change publishers with as

little hesitation as they might change accountants, Hemingway's loyalty seems all the more extraordinary.

In the course of Hemingway's association with Scribners, three generations of the family served as heads of the company. The succession began with my grandfather, who was a son of the founder. He was followed by my father in 1931. I became president a generation later when my father died in 1952. That's a great many Scribners for one author to put up with, but Hemingway took them as they came. There was also a succession of editors who worked with Hemingway during the same period. The relationship with Scribners covered virtually his entire career as a writer.

Much of what I shall say this morning is likely to be familiar to you as students of Hemingway's life and work. Given all that has been published on the subject, it could hardly be otherwise. But I think that this may be the first time that a member of the Scribner family has testified on the experience of publishing Hemingway. For me it is an opportunity to pay a debt of gratitude to him that is long overdue. To the extent that what I have to say may give some of you a greater sense of the kindness and loyalty of that extraordinary man, I shall have achieved my purpose.

During the first twenty years or so of his association with Scribners, Max Perkins was his principal contact within the company. It was to Perkins that he wrote continually about his writing projects, his books, his travels, his ideas, his family, and his finances. Perkins was wholly devoted to Hemingway as a writer, and an entirely trustworthy friend and confidant as well. At the same time, he was able to maintain, when necessary, a degree of personal detachment which Hemingway preferred to a more effusive or solicitous approach. They were both shy men, although their shyness took on very different forms. In a situation where Hemingway might become boisterous and exuberant, Perkins would be more likely to withdraw into his shell. Of course, Perkins was also hard of hearing—an affliction that is not entirely a handicap for a book editor.

During the Thirties and Forties, Hemingway came to know other members of Scribners' editorial team. After the deaths of Perkins and of my father, Wallace Meyer became his primary contact at Scribners. Hemingway got along well with his editors. On the other hand, he tended to distrust individuals belonging to the sales or business side of the company. He imagined that they did not understand or appreciate his writings and that they were not wholly committed to promoting his books. He later admitted to me that most writers seem to have eye defects when it comes to seeing advertisements for their books.

During the same period, a close friendship developed between Hemingway and my father. Their relationship was strengthened by occasional luncheons and dinner parties in New York and Paris, and by visits of the Scribners to Cuba. It was during a visit to Finca Vigía that my father first had the chance to read in manuscript large portions of *For Whom the Bell Tolls*. Later—and with perhaps a trace of irony in his deference—Hemingway asked my father to check the passages about horses in the first part of the novel. It was important to him that all such details be technically accurate. Later, he wrote my father a letter filled with details of horse anatomy so minute that it would have astonished a veterinarian. He insisted on being the expert.

From then on, he continually teased my father for being so wrapped up in horses. On one occasion, he tried to horrify him by filling a letter with the gory details of how he had run over a horse in an automobile. How much of that incident was horse feathers I shall leave to others to determine. It made a good story.

Although my father did not pretend to be a man of letters, Hemingway valued his naturally sound literary perceptions and his consistently active common sense. My father slipped easily into the role of Hemingway's main contact at Scribners when Perkins died in 1947. Indeed, the two men entered almost at once into a voluminous correspondence in which they kidded and insulted each other in a way that bespoke a deep mutual affection. For example, my father would write: "I have just received your cheerful but rather vulgar letter"—or would say to his famous author: "I had hoped you might have matured more over the years."

Because so many accounts of Hemingway's behavior depict him as churlish or capricious, I'd like to comment on his amiability toward Max Perkins and my father. Before Ernest admitted anyone into the inner circle, he needed to trust them to an almost abnormal degree, and they had to adhere unswervingly to his image of them. In dealing with individuals he wasn't sure of, he was prone to truculence in self-protection. He did not like or dislike anyone half-heartedly.

I joined Scribners in 1946—the year in which it was celebrating its one-hundredth anniversary. Max Perkins was still editor in chief, and I was fortunate to have almost a year in which to see him in action before his death.

Although I had been put in charge of publicity and advertising, my father and Max had a way of giving me other publishing chores which I was usually unqualified to handle. At that time, Scribners espoused the sink-or-swim method of instruction, and it was not always easy to stay afloat.

One of my special assignments was to supervise the production of an illustrated edition of *A Farewell to Arms*. It is still not entirely clear to me why that item was placed on my plate, but there were difficulties about the book, the greatest and simplest difficulty being that Hemingway did not care for the illustrations. Perhaps it was believed that this hot potato might do less damage to an innocent newcomer like myself, who was not responsible for its conception.

In any case, I set about proofreading the text and performing other routine tasks, little realizing that I was dealing with a potential *casus belli*. When the time came, I wrote to our famous author and gave him a deadline for the introduction he had agreed to write for the book. In due course he sent it to me. The Introduction was written in an "*O tempora, o mores*" vein, denouncing war. As for the illustrations by Daniel Rasmusson, he scarcely mentioned them at all except to describe the disappointment they caused him. He made no bones about that and spoke wistfully about how he would have preferred an artist like Winslow Homer or Cezanne.

In his accompanying letter to me he brushed aside any worries I might have about publishing his introduction. I was not to worry about the feelings of the illustrator; illustrators have no right to have feelings. They rank little higher than photographers. I was also not to worry that what he wrote was politically subversive. His folks had been around a long time. They had all done their duty in time of war. Hemingway was not a pen name. He could take an oath that he had never been a member of the Communist Party. He was not being snotty, he added—just kidding rough the way he did with my old man.

It was vintage Hemingway—a grand mixture of wild hyperbole and sweeping decrees. It was fun to read, and I also felt the implicit friendliness in Hemingway's writing to me in the same confiding vein that he used with my father.

I did not hear from Hemingway again until four years later when he wrote to me about my father's sudden death. I had been called back into the Navy and was stationed in Washington at the time. In his letter, Hemingway wanted me to know how badly he felt about having been away

Memorandum of Agreement, *made this* **fifteenth** *day of* **February** 1926

between **ERNEST HEMINGWAY** — — — — — —
of **Paris, France,** — — — — *hereinafter called* "the AUTHOR,"
and CHARLES SCRIBNER'S SONS, *of New York City, N. Y., hereinafter called* "the
PUBLISHERS." *Said* — — **Ernest Hemingway** — — *being the* AUTHOR
and PROPRIETOR *of a work entitled:* **two works entitled:**

The Torrents of Spring
The Sun Also Rises

*in consideration of the covenants and stipulations hereinafter contained, and agreed to be per-
formed by the* PUBLISHERS, *grants and guarantees to said* PUBLISHERS *and their successors the
exclusive right to publish the said work in all forms during the terms of copyright and renewals
thereof, hereby covenanting with said* PUBLISHERS *that he is the sole* AUTHOR *and*
PROPRIETOR *of said work.*

Said AUTHOR *hereby authorizes said* PUBLISHERS *to take out the copyright on said
work, and further guarantees to said* PUBLISHERS *that the said work is in no way whatever a
violation of any copyright belonging to any other party, and that it contains nothing of a scandalous or libelous character; and that he and* **his** *legal representatives shall and will hold
harmless the said* PUBLISHERS *from all suits, and all manner of claims and proceedings which
may be taken on the ground that said work* **are** *is in such violation or contains anything scandalous or
libelous; and he further hereby authorizes said* PUBLISHERS *to defend at law any and all
suits and proceedings which may be taken or had against them for infringement of any other copyright or for libel, scandal, or any other injurious or hurtful matter or thing contained in or
alleged or claimed to be contained in or caused by said work, and pay to said* PUBLISHERS *such
reasonable costs, disbursements, expenses, and counsel fees as they may incur in such defense.*

Said PUBLISHERS, *in consideration of the right herein granted and of the guarantees
aforesaid, agree to publish said work at their own expense, in such style and manner as they
shall deem most expedient, and to pay said* AUTHOR, *or* — **his** — *legal representatives,*
FIFTEEN (15) — — *per cent. on their Trade-List (retail) price, cloth style, for
all copies of said works sold by them.*

*Provided, nevertheless, that one-half the above named royalty shall be paid on all copies sold out-
side the United States; and provided that no percentage whatever shall be paid on any copies
destroyed by fire or water, or sold at or below cost, or given away for the purpose of aiding the
sale of said work.*

*It is further agreed that the profits arising from any publication of said work, during
the period covered by this agreement, in other than book form shall be divided equally between
said* PUBLISHERS *and said* AUTHOR.

Scribners' first publishing contract with Hemingway, covering The Torrents of Spring *and* The Sun Also Rises

Expenses incurred for alterations in type or plates, exceeding twenty per cent. of the cost of composition and electrotyping said work, are to be charged to the AUTHOR's account.

The first statement shall not be rendered until six months after date of publication; and thereafter statements shall be rendered semi-annually, on the AUTHOR's application therefor, in the months of February and August; settlements to be made in cash, four months after date of statement.

If, on the expiration of **five** years from date of publication, or at any time thereafter, the demand for said work should not, in the opinion of said PUBLISHERS, be sufficient to render its publication profitable, then, upon written notice by said PUBLISHERS to said AUTHOR, this contract shall cease and determine; and thereupon said AUTHOR shall have the right, at **his** option, to take from said PUBLISHERS, at cost, whatever copies of said work they may then have on hand; or, failing to take said copies at cost, then said PUBLISHERS shall have the right to dispose of the copies on hand as they may see fit, free from any percentage or royalty, and to cancel this contract.

Provided, also, that if, at any time during the continuance of this agreement, said work shall become unsalable in the ordinary channels of trade, said PUBLISHERS shall have the right to dispose of any copies on hand, paying to said AUTHOR **fifteen (15)** per cent. of the net amount received therefor, in lieu of the percentage hereinbefore prescribed.

Said Publishers shall pay to said Author the sum of fifteen hundred dollars ($1,500.) as an advance on royalty account, said amount to be reimbursed to said Publishers from the first monies accruing under said royalties.

In consideration of the mutuality of this contract, the aforesaid parties agree to all its provisions, and in testimony thereof affix their signatures and seals.

Witness to signature of
Ernest Hemingway

Witness to signature of
Charles Scribner's Sons

and out of touch when my father died. Since he had to die, at least he had gotten it over with. As for himself, I did not have to write him letters or have him on my mind.

I cannot imagine a kinder expression of condolence or a more delicate assurance of loyalty. And in the lovely phrase of Dickens, he was better than his word. For the next nine years of his life, he was as easy to work with as any author I have ever known. Let me describe some of the highlights of our publishing association during that period.

I was released from active duty in the Navy a month or so after my father's death, and returned to Scribners as president of the company. At that time, Wallace Meyer was still Hemingway's editor. All of us were looking forward to publishing *The Old Man and the Sea*. We had no doubt of its virtuosity.

I was proceeding with a plan to bring all of Hemingway's books back onto the Scribner list. At that time, most of the titles had been licensed for hardcover reprints by the Modern Library or Grosset and Dunlap, or for paperback reprints by Bantam Books or others.

I had a master plan, and wrote the following letter outlining it to Hemingway:

> I have asked for a complete report on the publishing status of all your titles because I wanted to be certain that nothing was sold on a reprint basis that might be sold by us on terms conceivably more remunerative to you.
>
> Frankly I am attempting to provide for the effects that the publication of *The Old Man and the Sea* could have on all of your earlier works. We anticipate a wonderful reception to this as would have to follow the publication of something so magnificent. Furthermore I feel that your books are, in any case, the foundation stones of our publishing reputation in this country. I believe that we must be continually self-critical with respect to operations on them.

I do not think that my crystal ball is better than that of any other publisher, but I must admit that it was never so helpful as on that occasion. Hemingway endorsed my plan wholeheartedly even though it called for the cancellation of Modern Library editions for which he had strong sentimental feelings. Over the next few years we reissued all his books—at first in hardcover editions, and then in paperback for school and college use. We redesigned the bindings, reset some of the older books, and redid almost all the jackets.

Hemingway was delighted by this deliberate revival of his books. He differed from our suggestions only once or twice, and then only in the most tactful manner. For example, he took exception to a drawing of a bullfighter for the jacket of *Death in the Afternoon*, and wrote me as follows: "It has this against it, Charlie: the bullfighter is a Mexican, an Indian, and he looks almost as though he were suffering from leprosy in the peculiar swellings of his face." We scrapped that jacket and afterwards managed to have an ectochrome photograph taken of the original of the Roberto Domingo poster at the Finca.

Another time one of our book designers thought it would be a good idea to print the interchapter pieces of *In Our Time* in red ink instead of in italics. Hemingway was very doubtful about that idea: "My mother at one time had some theory about transcribing music into color but I never subscribed to it."

A few weeks ago I reread the correspondence between Hemingway and myself. Those letters now belong to Princeton and are on deposit in the Firestone Library [they are open to researchers now]. Before I did so, I had the recollection that Hemingway had been very kind to me as a young man from the time of our first contacts over thirty years before. But that impression did not prepare me for the extraordinary warmth and kindness of his letters. I am much older now, and have a better idea of the value of kindness.

The Hemingway that I dealt with professionally was as magnanimous as any man I ever met. Most of my letters were written in a practical vein and involved business matters. I did not feel it would be appropriate for me to seek or to expect the easy footing of a personal friendship of the sort that had existed between Hemingway and Perkins, or between Hemingway and my father. I think he understood that and was all the more gracious.

I suppose the greatest strain on our relation was in connection with an introduction I asked him to write for a paperback collection of his stories. This was in 1959 and Hemingway worked very conscientiously in Spain during May and June.

When his Introduction came in, I was shocked by its contents and tone. It would have been a disservice to his reputation to publish it for student use and I saw no alternative but to bite the bullet and tell him so. I now suspect that there may have been an earth tremor in that part of Spain when my letter arrived. On July 3rd, I received a cable ordering me to stop work on the anthology and on all similar projects. It had been a big mistake that he would not make again, he added ominously.

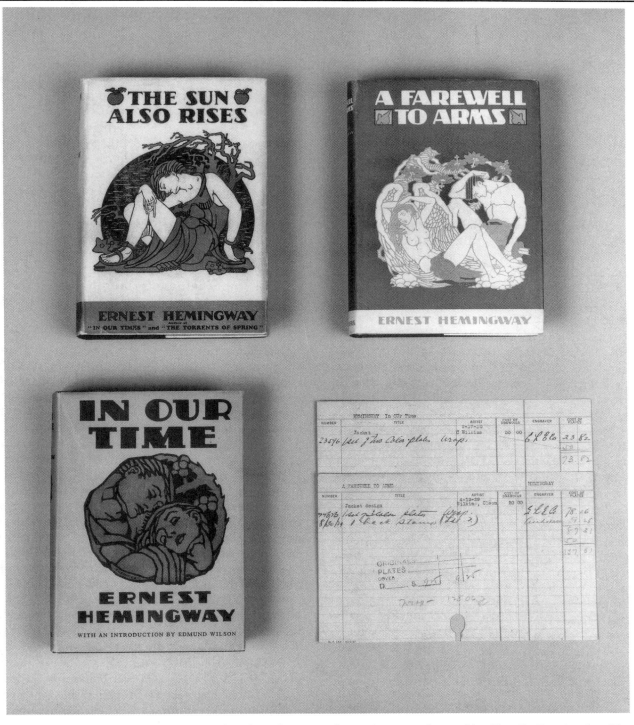

First editions of the three Hemingway titles whose distinctive dust jackets were designed by Cleonike Damianakes (Mrs. Ralph Wilkins), with the firm's "artist cards" for two of them. "About the jacket [A Farewell to Arms]; I think both the title of the book and the name of the author have been sacrificed to Mr. Miss or Mrs. Cleon's artistic [sic] conception. . . . The Cleon drawing has a lousy and completely unattractive decadence i.e. Large, misplaced breasts etc. About it which I think might be a challenge to anyone who was interested in suppressing the book.Altho on the other hand it is probably very fine and supposedly classical and I a damned fool. But at least I cannot admire the awful legs on that woman or the gigantic belly muscles. I never liked the jacket on the Sun but side by side with this one The Sun jacket looks very fine now. So maybe this one is fine too" (Hemingway to Maxwell Perkins, 4 October 1929). Damianakes also designed Scribner jackets for F. Scott Fitzgerald's All the Sad Young Men *and Zelda Fitzgerald's* Save Me the Waltz.

Although the cable ended with "kind regards" I was terribly worried that I had ruined my relationship with Hemingway.

But a month later he wrote to me again, saying he was sorry about the school project not coming off. He had really taken it seriously and tried to write something valid that would counteract the type of teaching children were getting on the short story. He was happy to have me try the alternative plan I had outlined and went along with me completely as stated in my letter. With the confidence he had in me as a publisher, he said, that was a very easy decision to make.

During the years I corresponded with Hemingway, we did not meet more than four or five times and all those meetings were in New York City. The first was in June of 1953 when my wife Joan and I went to the dock to see Ernest and Mary off on the *Flandre* on the first leg of their trip to France, Spain, and Africa.

We waited for them rather self-consciously in their stateroom together with some other visitors whom we knew only by name. Ominous bells and horns were sounding continually and it seemed likely that the ship would set sail with us on board and not the Hemingways.

We had almost given up hope when the cabin door burst open and in plunged Hemingway with a large retinue of men and women bringing up the rear. There was now no room to turn around and the air turned blue with four-letter words and Hemingwayisms.

Ernest's lawyer Alfred Rice had brought some important documents that needed to be signed but Hemingway pretended to brush them off as trivialities. He was delighted by the wisecrack he had heard that Hollywood was going to change the name of the Spencer Tracy film from *The Old Man and the Sea* to *The Old Jew and the Lake*.

It seemed certain now that the last call for visitors to go ashore had long since been given. But with all the loud talking no one could have heard it.

In the midst of this confusion Hemingway even took time out to inscribe for me a copy of the limited edition of his novella with the slogan "*Il faut d'abord durer.*" Although we finally did disembark in New York and not in Le Havre, our visit made me realize the appropriateness of Hemingway's slogan. It was no small feat to survive the strain of many such performances. Nothing in his letters had given me an inkling of the frenzied pace of those parts of his life.

I did not see Hemingway again until six years later, in November of 1959. He had just returned to New York on the *Liberté* and was staying for a few days in a borrowed apartment on the East Side. His friend George Plimpton called me at my office and said, "Your famous author is in town and wants to see you." I hurried over.

It was the briefest of meetings, mostly filled with small talk. I do not drink, and when I declined a highball, Ernest suggested a vermouth and soda water. It was virtually not drinking, he said, but it does light a little fire. I found that an appealing phrase, but I stuck to ginger ale.

One of the difficulties of visiting Hemingway in New York was that he was almost always accompanied by a number of well-wishers. Each of them appeared to believe that he or she had the special responsibility of protecting Ernest from all the others. As result, a fair degree of tension was often generated. It was also difficult to conduct a serious conversation.

Because our friendship had been created almost entirely through letters, it was probably natural that I at least had a stronger sense of meeting a stranger than I might have had upon meeting him for the first time, and with no prior correspondence.

A few days later he delivered to me, kindness of A. E. Hotchner, some first drafts of his "Paris Sketches," which we were to publish posthumously under the title *A Moveable Feast*. Naturally we read them at once, and because we were so positively impressed by them, I called Ernest immediately to tell him so. I was astonished to hear him respond like a diffident young writer having a book accepted for the first time. He was obviously delighted. "I thought you'd be willing to lend me money on the strength of this," he said. Of course we would gladly have lent him all the money he wished, but he never borrowed any. That was just his way of expressing his pleasure.

The next meeting with him was in the apartment on 62nd Street that the Hemingways had rented. Our editor Harry Brague and I went over to see him and find out when he wished to publish the "Paris Sketches." Hemingway's health was very poor and he agonized over the question in a way that made me feel sad. I wished that we had not raised the matter. He worried about the effect on his eyes from having to work on a book. How would he be able to shoot a gun if he couldn't see? Would he have to learn to shoot by ear?

As it turned out, these "Paris Sketches" were the first of six posthumous works, all of which were received in a way that would have filled Hemingway with joy.

At the end of that visit, he gave me a battered valise to take back to the office and hold for him under lock and key. He mentioned that it contained his will. "Don't lose it," he told me. I knew he had some terrible experiences with lost suitcases in the past, so I reassured him as well as I could.

Very early the next morning, Ernest appeared at Scribners. He wanted to look something up among the papers he had given me. I opened the locked filing cabinet outside my office and watched him rummaging around in the valise. Of course I realized that he had come to Scribners to make sure I hadn't lost it.

Then he came into my office full of cheer. To put me at my ease, he sat down in my chair. I stood there quite at a loss, not knowing where to sit and feeling wholly disoriented. A man's desk becomes part of him, as you all know.

We offered him some coffee, and one of the secretaries brought him in a cup with a great sense of mission.

"Would you like some cream?" we asked.

"Just enough to change the color," he replied with characteristic precision.

Although we exchanged letters afterwards, that was the last time I ever saw Ernest.

But I never forgot his instructions for pouring in the cream. Only Hemingway would have thought out a specific formula for performing such a routine task. In a way, it was a tiny example of his whole approach to life.

RELATED LETTERS:
The story of how Hemingway became a Scribner author reveals interesting sidelights: the scouting role of F. Scott Fitzgerald, who had already been instrumental in bringing Thomas Boyd and Ring Lardner into the Scribner stable; the protocol among publishers vying for new authors and the contracts they created to keep them; and the diplomatic efforts of Scribner editor Maxwell Perkins to gain Hemingway's confidence and to persuade his conservative publishing house to take a risk on this "modern" writer.

St. Raphael, France [October 1924?]
Dear Max:

The royalty was better than I'd expected. This is to tell you about a young man named Ernest Hemmingway, who lives in Paris (an American), writes for the *Transatlantic Review* and has a brilliant future. Ezra Pount published a collection of his short pieces in Paris, at some place like the Egotist Press. I haven't it here now but it's remarkable and I'd look him up right away. He's the real thing. . . .
Scott

Feb. 21, 1925
Dear Mr. Hemingway:

I have just read "in our time" published by the Three Mountain Press. I had heard that you were doing very remarkable writing and was most anxious to see it and after a great deal of effort and correspondence, I finally did manage to get this book which seems not to be in circulation in this country. At all events I could not find it. I was greatly impressed by the power in the scenes and incidents pictured, and by the effectiveness of their relations to each other, and I am venturing to write to you to ask whether you have anything that would allow us to consider as publishers. I am bound to say at the same time that I doubt if we could have seen a way to the publication of this book itself, on account of material considerations;- it is so small that it would give the booksellers no opportunity for substantial profit if issued at a price which custom would dictate. The trade would therefore not be interested in it. This is a pity because your method is obviously one which enables you to express what you have to say in very small compass, but a commercial publisher cannot disregard these factors. It occured to me, however, that you might very well be writing something which would not have these practical objections and in any sense, whatever you are writing, we should be most interested to consider.
Sincerely yours,
[Maxwell Perkins]

Paris April 15, 1925
Dear Mr. Perkins:

On returning from Austria I received your letter of February 26 inclosing a copy of a previous letter which unfortunately never reached me. About ten days before your letter came I had a cabled offer from Boni and Liveright to bring out a book of my short stories in the fall. They asked me to reply by cable and I accepted.

I was very excited at getting your letter but did not see what I could do until I had seen the contract from Boni and Liveright. According to its terms they are to have an option on my next three books, they agreeing that unless they exercise this option to publish the second book within 60 days of the receipt of the manuscript their option shall lapse, and if they do not publish the second book they relinquish their option on the third book.

So that is how matters stand. I cannot tell you how pleased I was by your letter and you must know how gladly I would have sent Charles Scribner's Sons the manuscript of the book that is to come out this fall. It makes it seem almost worth while to get into Who's Who in order to have a known address.

I do want you to know how much I appreciated your letter and if I am in a position to send you anything to consider I shall certainly do so.

I hope some day to have a sort of Daughty's Arabia Deserta of the Bull Ring, a very big book with some wonderful pictures. But one has to save all winter to be able to bum in Spain in the summer and writing classics, I've always heard, takes some time. Somehow I don't care about writing a novel and I like to write short stories and I like to work at the bull fight book so I guess I'm a bad prospect for a publisher anyway. Somehow the novel seems to me to be an awfully artificial and worked out form but as some of the short stories now are stretching out to 8,000 to 12,000 words may be I'll get there yet.

The In Our Time is out of print and I've been trying to buy one to have myself now I hear it is valuable; so that probably explains your difficulty in getting it. I'm awfully glad you liked it and thank you again for writing me about a book.

Very sincerely,
Ernest Hemingway

Telegram to Scribners from Paris, 8 January 1926:

YOU CAN GET HEMINGWAYS FINISHED NOVEL PROVIDED YOU PUBLISH UNPROMISING SATIRE HARCOURT HAS MADE DEFINITE OFFER WIRE IMMEDIATELY WITHOUT QUALIFICATIONS
FITZGERALD

Jan. 13, 1926

Dear Scott:

. . . I thought Hemingway's stories astonishingly fine and so does everyone who reads them. It seems strange that Liveright has put so little behind them. I speak of this on the assumption that for some reason he is not to publish any more for Hemingway. Otherwise your cable would not have come. I did my best with that cable, but there was a fear that this satire [*The Torrents of Spring*]- although in the hands of such a writer it could hardly be rightly so upon any theory- might

be suppressible. In fact we could tell nothing about it of course in these respects and it is not the policy obviously of Scribners to publish books of certain types. For instance, if it were even Rabelasian to an extreme degree, it might be objected to. It was only this point that prevented me from wiring you without any qualification because these stories are as invigorating as a cold, fresh wind.

I am afraid though that the qualification was fatal.- But in any case, I think it was bully of you to have acted in our behalf in that way. I was much pleased that you did it. As for Harcourt, I think him an admirable publisher and I haven't any criticism of him. But I believe that as compared with most others, Hemingway would be better off in our hands because we are absolutely true to our authors and support them loyally in the face of losses for a long time, when we believe in their qualities and in them. It is that kind of publisher that Hemingway probably needs, because I hardly think he could come into a large public immediately. He ought to be published by one who believes in him and is prepared to lose money for a period in enlarging his market.- Although he would certainly, even without much support, get recognition through his own powers.

I have not tried to communicate with him because I did not know how far I ought to go, particularly after getting your second telegram. The fact is that we would publish the satire however certain it might be of financial failure because of our faith in him,- and perhaps also because of the qualities of the work itself, of which I cannot speak.

As ever yours,
[Maxwell Perkins]

Released from his Boni and Liveright contract when the firm rejected his satire, Hemingway made a quick trip to New York, signing a contract with Scribners, dated 15 February 1926, for the publication of both The Torrents of Spring *and* The Sun Also Rises, *which was still unfinished.*

May 18, 1926

Dear Mr. Hemingway:

"The Sun Also Rises" seems to me a most extraordinary performance. No one could conceive of a book with more life in it. All the scenes, and particularly those when they cross the Pyrenees and come into Spain, and when they fish in that cold water, and when the bulls are sent in with the steers, and when they fought in the arena, are of

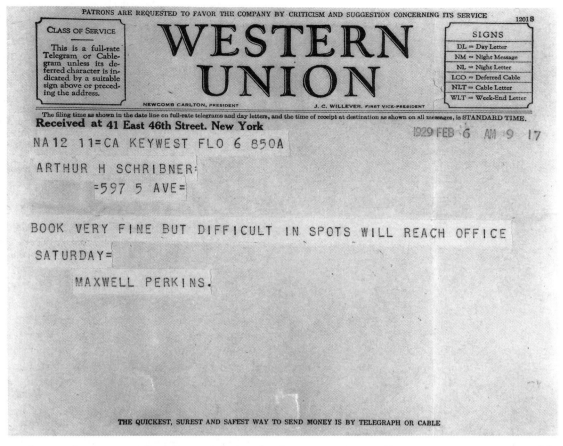

Telegram from Maxwell Perkins to Arthur Scribner reporting on Hemingway's manuscript of A Farewell to Arms, *which he has been reading in Key West, Florida*

such quality as to be like actual experience. You have struck our pet phrase, "pity and irony," to death so I can't use it; but the humor in the book and the satire - especially expressed by Gorton, and by the narrator,- are marvelous; and not in the least of a literary sort. But in connection with this there is one hard point - a hard one to raise too, because the passage in question comes in so aptly and rightly. I mean the speech about Henry James. I swear I do not see how that can be printed. It could not by any conception be printed while he was alive, if only for the fear of a lawsuit; and in a way it seems almost worse to print after he is dead. I am not raising this you must believe, because we are his publishers. The matter referred to is peculiarly a personal one. It is not like something that a man could be criticized for,- some part of his conduct in life and which might therefore be considered open for comment. I want to put this before you at the very beginning. There are also one or two other things that I shall bring up in connection with the proof, but there is no need to speak of them here.

The book as a work of art seems to me astonishing, and the more so because it involves such an extraordinary range of experience and emotion, all brought together in the most skillful manner - the subtle ways of which are beautifully concealed - to form a complete design. I could not express my admiration too strongly.

As ever yours,
[Maxwell Perkins]

May 27th 1926

Dear Charley [CS III]:-

You wanted to know the decision on Hemingway: we took it,- with misgiving. In the course of the debate I argued that the question was a crucial one in respect to younger writers;- that we suffered by being called "ultra-conservative" (even if unjustly & with malice) & that this would become our reputation for the present when our declination of this book should, as it would, get about. That view of the matter influenced our decision largely. Wheelock [John Hall Wheelock, poet and Scribner editor] was called in, with a curious result: I thought he had been so much out of the world on that balcony of his, & in his generally hermit like life, as to be out of touch with modern tendencies in writing & therefore over sensitive;- but to my amazement he thought there was no question whatever but that we should publish. There was of course a great one. I simply thought in the end that the balance was slightly in favor of acceptance, for all the worry & general misery involved.- But you won't see Hemingway: he's in Spain, Bull fighting I suspect. . . .

Sincerely Yours
Maxwell E. Perkins

LETTER:
Letter from Maxwell Perkins to CS II, dated 14 February 1929.

In his "editor's report" on Hemingway's book, Perkins provides a rare insight into his interpretation of the work.

Dear Mr. Scribner:

I'd meant to write you the moment I got back from Key West- after a splendid, refreshing week of sunshine and outdoors- but found an accumulation of little time-taking troubles.- And I thought it better to wait perhaps till Mr. Bridges and Dashiel had read, "A Farewell to Arms."

This title is a bitter phrase: war taints and damages the beautiful and the gallant, and degrades everyone;- and this book which is a <u>farewell</u> to it, as useless and hateful, would be only grim reading if it were not illuminated with the beauty of the world, and of the characters, even though damaged, of some people, and by love; and if it were not also lively with incident and often, in spots, amusing. Its quality is that of "The Sun", though its range is much larger and its implications consequently more numerous and widely scattered. Its story in outline is not objectionable but many words and some passages in it are: we can blank the words and the worst passages can be revised.- The reading of the book will still be a violent experience because of the force, directness, and poignance of the writing. We wired Hemingway yesterday naming a price of $16,000 and the first instalment is being set.

The story begins after a year or so of war, with some such phrase as, "That summer we were in the mountains." You get the idea of a place of charm and beauty hurt and saddened by war; of troops and guns passing up and down, and of a fatigued, raw-nerved group of men in the officer's mess,- one of whom, the narrator, an American boy, named Henry, is in charge of an ambulance section. A likable, dissolute surgeon named Rinaldi, persuades him to go to a hospital to see a "lady English". She is a tall, 'tawny' beauty. Henry who has frankly been all over the place with all sorts of girls approaches her like one of them;- but this approach is somewhat resented and he feels the cheapness of it. He goes to the front with a little "St. Anthony" she gives him for luck around his neck.-There while eating cheese with his men in a dugout, he is wounded in the legs by a shell.- All this is fiercely vivid, sharp, and painful.- It almost happens to the reader.

A couple of days after, he arrives at the hospital- certain disagreeable physiological aspects in the care of him having been frankly described- Katherine Barker arrives. The moment they meet Henry discovers that he is in love.- He had not meant to fall in love, his idea had been quite different, but he finds that he has, and it is a wholly new experience in spite of all of his amorous adventures. She is a gallant, winning girl, and she also has fallen in love. And though not his nurse, she manages, by taking on more than her share of undesired night work, to stay with him at night. And as he recuperates, they go to hotels once or twice together. He wants her to marry him, but if she does this she will be sent home on account of regulations, and will be separated from him, and she keeps saying that she already is his wife,- that a ceremony is a mere technicality. At the same time he is worried, and before he goes back to the front he knows that he has cause to be. He gets back in time to be part of the great Caparetto retreat. This is a magnificent episode in the book. It is the account of the experience of several individuals,- Henry, and his companions, ambulance drivers. The episode as described differs from conventional descriptions of a retreat in much the same way as Stendhal's account of Waterloo differs from conventional accounts of battles. Henry gets loose from the great column of retreat which is constantly blocked, loses his cars in mud on a side road, loses one man by desertion, and another by a bullet, an Italian one too, finds himself at one time among detachments of Germans, finally rejoins the column at night as it approaches a river. On the other side of the river is a group of officers with battle police. They are flashing lights to the column and calling out officers from it. Two police come and seize Henry. He finds that all officers separated from their men are instantly shot. This is happening on the spot. He is indignant because he has behaved manfully throughout and has been true in every sense, and yet he knows he will be shot. He will be thought to be a German in Italian uniform. He breaks away, dives into the river, and with the help of a timber escapes. He is through with the Italian army.- He knows that they will finish him off if they get him anyhow. He gets civilian clothes from a friend, makes his way to a lake near the Swiss border where he hears that Katherine is, and is with her in the hotel there when late on a stormy night his friend the bar man tells him a squad has come to arrest him. He and Katherine get into a row boat and row up the lake in the storm with the help of the wind (a fine episode) until in the morning they have crossed the Swiss line. The rest of the book is most beautiful. It records the life of Katherine and Henry in Switzerland throughout the fall and the winter. It has the pathos of a happy time that is tinged with sorrow because those having it feel that it must end soon, tragically. That sense of the beauty of nature and of its permanence, in contrast to the brevity and fluidity of an individual's affairs, pervades it. It is beautiful and affecting reading.

Henry tries several times to persuade Katherine to marry him, but she will not do it now because she says she looks too "matronly". They will get married later in America, when this is over with.- The reader knows by the tone of the narrative that when it is over with, Henry will have nobody to marry.

The last twenty pages of the book tell of the birth of the child which results in her death,- and rather fully, although not naturalistically. The reason it is recounted is to show what a brave, gallant person Katherine is. It is most painful and moving reading because of her bravery in suffering.

Mr. Bridges thinks the book a very strong one and its motif- a revelation of the tragic degradation of war, of which this love affair is a part- a fine one. Dashiel is very enthusiastic and regrets that even a word must be changed. I do not think that given the theme and the author, the book is any more difficult than was inevitable. It is Hemingway's principle both in life and literature never to flinch from facts, and it is in that sense only, that the book is difficult. It is not at all erotic, although love is represented as having a very large physical element.

I had a splendid eight days in Key West, and formed a very high opinion of Hemingway's character. Nobody could be more altogether healthy and decent in every sense, and no household could be more natural and simple than his, with his wife and sister and two children. We spent almost all of every day on the water fishing. Hemingway was determined I should get a tarpon, although I had considerable doubts of my ability to land one after quite exhaustive struggles even with barracudas. At the very last possible moment, on my last day, it was Hemingway, and not I, who hooked a tarpon. He instantly wanted me to take his rod and was so violently insistent that I did it, and after about fifty fine and quite exhausting minutes made more exciting by a sudden storm which kept the spray flying over us all the time, and, added to the strength of the tarpon, kept me staggering all over the boat, we landed him. In view of the rarity of tarpons, and the value set upon them by sportsmen, I think this was a remarkably generous thing of Hemingway to do.

Everything here seems to be going very well. Merritt is delighted with the returns he has got on the circular, and from the advertising, of the Compact edition of Galsworthy.

Every sincerely yours,
Maxwell E. Perkins

P.S.

I was somewhat constrained in bringing out the difficult points in "A Farewell" by dictating this to Miss Wykoff, but I thought your familiarity with Hemingway's way would sufficiently supplement what I have said. MEP

LETTERS:
Hemingway's letters (1925–1947) to his first and major editor, Maxwell Perkins, reflect the many moods of his creative life. Here are some excerpts:

•[circa 20 August 1928] "Writing whether you want it or not is competitive—most of the time you compete against time and dead men— sometimes you get something from a living (contemporary) competitor that is so good it jars you—as the story of Esteban in Thornton's last book [Thornton Wilder's *The Bridge of San Luis Rey*]. But as you read them dead or living you unconsciously compete—I would give 6 mos. of my life to have written it. You know the ones you have no chance against and the others that, with luck, you can beat living and dead. Only never tell this to anyone because they might call it the megalomania or simply swollen head."

•[7 December 1932] "Will you come out here and meet me at Memphis on December 15 to shoot ducks for a week from the houseboat Walter Adams—anchored in the Arkansas river at Watkins Ark. If you cant stay a week stay as long as you can. You dont need to bring anything but some warm clothes. I have everything else and have made the reservation and paid for you in advance. We could talk over everything and have the finest duck shooting in the world. . . . I know of course that business and your family affairs absolutely forbid it but I need to see you and you need to get away and we will have the sort of shooting our grandfathers and great grandfathers had. . . . Please come Max and if you dont have a better time than you ever had will push you back to N.Y. in a wheelbarrow." *Perkins went.*

• [30 April 1934] "I rushed a book last year [*Winner Take Nothing*] because I had taken an advance. It was no fault of yours. I felt the obligation to get it out although my best judgement told me it needed another story of the kind I knew it needed to have people think they were getting their moneys worth. It is not enough to just give them their two dollars worth, anybodys two dollars worth, if they will read them over. You have to give them just ten times more than anybody else ever gives them for the same amt. of money. And I had kidded myself that you didn't. [new paragraph] But I am a careerist, as you can read in the papers, and my idea of a career is never to write a phony line, never fake, never cheat, never be sucked in by the y.m.c.a. movements of the moment, and to give them as much literature in a book as any son of a bitch has ever gotten into the same number of words. But that isn't enough. If you want to make a living out of it you have to, in addition every so often, without faking, cheating or deviating from the above give them something they understand and that has a story—not a plot—just a story that they can follow instead of simply feel, the way most of the stories are. The story is there but I dont tell it to them in so many words. I knew it then, too. But because I had taken the damned advance I thought what the hell—that's good enough for them and more—they won't know it is—but what the hell. [new paragraph] But I am a professional and professionals learn by their mistakes instead of justifying them. So that won't happen again."

• [10 May 1939] "The book [*A Farewell to Arms*] goes fine. Am going over it from the start all the time and working slowly and steadily and not rushing and still am averageing between 700 and 1000 words a day and have to hold down not to do more. Keep on wishing me luck. Have really good working conditions for first time in a long time. No telephone, get mail twice a week, and

work hard every day and on nothing else, play tennis and swim when am through and go out in the gulf stream saturday and Sunday. I wish you could see it but I think it is bad business and bad luck to show or talk about it while you are still doing it. Thing to do with a novel is to finish it; just like with a war to win it. We've lost everything else in two years and I want to win with this. But christ it is hard not to rush when every day things are going like they are going. But am trying to write as well as I can absolutely without any hurry or sense of hurry so that no matter what happens will have this book. It ought to be done around July or early august. . . . Here work in a joint on top of a hill so that no matter where the wind is from, even south, it is cool—or seems so compared to what am used to. It is wonderful to be working steadily at your trade again. Nothing, really, makes you happier. I find, too, I know a lot more than I used to know and that is a help. . . . If I would read this over would get impression that think I am pretty terrific but it is just that when you go good writing you go good every way—or think you do anyway."

• [10 June 1943] "Max please dont get sore at me. I need your sound advice, your judgement and your help—If Charley Scribner ever wants to pick a fight with me because I am insufficiently respectful or more bother than I am worth, or simply for any good reason at all that is okay— but dont <u>you</u> pick any fights because you are my most trusted friend as well as my god damned publisher and dont get yourself confused in your mind with too many institutions or I wont be able to speak ill of Harvard, Connecticut, the Confederate Army, Scribners, god or god knows what without being accused of imputive skunkhood and will only be able to curse women and still be your pal. Which I still hope I am."

• [14 April 1945] "Since then [visit of his sons] have been death lonely but have put in my time getting in shape, sweating the liquor out on the tennis court, running mornings, and not drinking in the nights nor in the mornings. The usual preliminary training, for me, before writing. But it is very tough doing it alone. Hope won't have to for very long. I don't mind missing the end of the war at all. I didn't leave until I knew we had beaten the Germans. Until then anything I could do seemed necessary and useful. After that it seemed only ornamental and self indulgent. The hardest thing for me to do in this world is write a fine book and that is what I have to do now. Every time it is tougher. But don't worry.

Will get in shape, not worry and do it. But it may take a while to get in shape. But have several good fights left in me yet. Though last year was a son of a bitch. Nothing to put a writer through."

LETTER:
Letter from Maxwell Perkins to Hemingway, 11 June 1931.

Hemingway had gone to Spain for the summer bullfighting season to work on his nonfiction book, Death in the Afternoon.

Dear Ernest:

I hope you are going safely through revolutionary Spain. I doubt if this letter will reach you except after great delay,- unless it is held in Paris.

. . . In a letter you pointed out the disappointing fact that books do not hold up as well as you had thought from year to year. We know that well enough. It is increasingly true. And the chief reason for it is the short-sightedness and avariciousness of publishers. They were such fools years ago as to let Grosset & Dunlap, and such reprint houses, get going, and the result was that many people got in the habit of not buying books until they came down to a dollar, or seventy-five cents as it then was. This led to Doubleday, for the sake of their printing which is the big end of their business, starting a dollar library, and this led to other cheap libraries.

At the start, all the publishers refrained from putting in books into these libraries until two years after they had appeared,- which was too long a time for people to just wait until the price came down. But as new, and sometimes low-grade, publishers came into the business--people who were thinking of nothing but quick profit-the time limit was cut down more and more, until now people actually sell editions to printing houses and libraries as shortly after publication as six months, and generally, even, after a year. It was the most short-sighted and selfish policy. It takes a year or eighteen months for a book to get known outside of the centres, and often its biggest sale in the old days came after a year or eighteen months.- But now people generally find what books they want to read in dollar series by that time. That is the great reason why books do not hold up as they did in the old days, and as they ought to do.

Another reason, of course, is the greatly increased number of publishers, and of books, whose pressure on the trade is such as to compel the bookseller practically to give all his emphasis to new books. He is so hard pressed by salesmen that he finds all his capital for a season has gone into current orders, and that he has little left with which to order old books for stock.- His inclination is to order them only when people ask for them,- and then of course, he tries to sell them some new book instead. It is an unhealthy situation for literature and an unsound one for publishers. Maybe the present discouraging state of business will end by improving things,- for those who come through.

Send me a picture postcard if you get a chance, to say that everything is all right, if it is. I hope to Heaven it is. So many disasters have fallen upon people connected with me lately that I am on edge for bad news. Send me good news if you can.

Always your friend,
[Maxwell Perkins]

LETTER:
Letter from Maxwell Perkins to Everett R. Perry, City Librarian of Los Angeles, 17 January 1933.

Perkins presents his viewpoint on censorship of literary work—and the function of a publisher—in response to a librarian's objection to certain words in Hemingway's Death in the Afternoon.

Dear Sir:

We were very glad to receive your letter of the 12th with regard to Mr. Hemingway's "Death in the Afternoon" because we are naturally quite aware of your work and position, and respect your judgment. We are certainly very far from regarding your views as old-fashioned: in fact it is easy for us to sympathize with your objection to the words you refer to.

It seems to me though, that a publisher--unless he choose to be a purely personal one, and so

> Max if I ever sound rude in a letter please forgive it. I am naturally a rude bastard and the only way I know not to be is always to be formally polite. You stopped me doing that when you asked me to un-mister you. So please remember that when I am loud mouthed, bitter, rude, son of a bitching and mistrustful I am really very reasonable and have great confidence and absolute trust in you.
>
> —Ernest Hemingway in a letter to Maxwell Perkins, 27 April [1931]

not to fulfill the larger functions of publishing--must take a very different attitude from that of personal preference or taste;- that is an attitude according to which he may serve as a medium for what is alive and important in the literature of his day. He may, and in fact is sure sometimes to make a mistake of judgment; but if he finds his view is supported by a very important public which includes those who must be recognized as excellent judges, it seems to us that he is fulfilling this function. As a publisher he is not a censor of taste, or of morals, though as a man he is likely to have the common human impulse of wishing that his own ideas of taste could be generally imposed.

The fact that this book has received the support, both in England and in this country, of a very large public composed, to judge by all available evidence, of those of the higher levels of education and taste, does not prove, of course, that your view of the book is not the right one. But does it not indicate a sufficient body of important opinion on the other side to leave the question open to doubt, and to sustain the publisher in his judgment? After all, it is historically true that the most enlightened ages have been the most free-spoken;- that the Eighteenth Century, generally regarded as the greatest of all in taste and intellect, was the very one in which there was the greatest freedom in respect to literary expression.

Your objection is perhaps only to specific words, and we suppose that you would argue that the publisher should simply strike out these words from the text;- but the fact is that no genuine writer will allow a publisher to exercise this kind of censorship over him. The true artist has always insisted upon making his work what he wanted it, and it is our opinion that it would be an extremely bad thing for literature if real writers did allow themselves to be censored by their publishers.

You have, of course, every right to question whether Mr. Hemingway is such a writer; but we as publishers can hardly question it in light of statements concerning him from the highest sources in this country, England, France and Germany; most of the leading critics and writers in those countries have testified to their admiration of him in extreme terms.

In short, we are far from maintaining that your view is not the right one. Our position is that no absolute decision, but a purely personal one, can be made on that point; and that when a publisher believes in the literary importance of a writer, and finds his beliefs supported by an imposing body of literary opinion, he is compelled in the exercise of his professional function to publish him to the very best of his powers.

Very truly yours,
[Maxwell Perkins]

LETTER:
Letter from Hemingway to Maxwell Perkins, 17 January 1934.

This is Hemingway's first letter to his editor from Africa, where he had gone on a much-anticipated safari. Hemingway's hunting experiences proved to be rich and useful sources for some of his memorable fiction; Philip Percival, whom he mentions, was the partial model for the white hunter Robert Wilson in the short story "The Short Happy Life of Francis Macomber" (1936).

Dear Max:

Thanks for your two letters enclosing royalty reports statistics for income tax etc.

I am afraid I do not understand your remark about "What business advice!" I gave Franklin [Sidney Franklin, bullfighter friend of Hemingway]. In order to aid you I went over his translation [*Shadows of the Sun*], 2 weeks of steady work, got him a jacket, explained every point to him that you asked me to, and showed him just why and how the contract you offered him was just. If you were unwilling or unable to advertize this last book as you have former books is no reason to act as though I were working against your interests with Franklin. If you knew the number of times I have explained to him that he could trust you absolutely you would not write in that tone.

Another thing you might remember is that there is a time in every mans life, if he is worth a damn, when he has to be unpopular. The only writers who survived the war were the ones who did not believe in it. You have to believe in writing. I am against and outside this present damned YMCA economic hurrah business and you will find, when it is over, that I will be neither old fashioned, nor behind the times. I will be the same as always, only better, because I will have stuck to my job and will know a damned sight more. But when a publishing organization seems unable to keep up a pretense of believing in you—How is the public expected to respond.

Have seen 83 lion—I've shot 2 bull buffalo—excellent heads of Eland, Roan antelope, record Impala, good Grant and Robertsi gazelle, Bushbuck and water buck. Also a very big leopard. And 2 cheetah. Charles [Hemingway's friend

Charles Thompson] has killed a fine lion and a marvellous buffalo—and has some fine heads.

He and Pauline [Hemingway's second wife] are very well. I have had Tropical dysentery for last two weeks. Hunted every day but 2 with it But those 2 were <u>something</u>. OK. Now. Passed as much as a pint and 1/2 of blood a day. Flew in here [Nairobi, Kenya] about 400 miles yesterday over Ngorongoro Crater, Rift Escarpment to Arusha, then here, to get some injections Rejoining the safari on the 21st at the Crater. It takes them 5 days to get there from where I got the plane. We hunt Rhino then greater and lesser Kudu and Sable. Have killed every thing, including <u>Buffalo</u>, with the Springfield 30-06 and the little Mannlicher. Ordered the Plane from Victoria Nyanza (Mumbashi think the station is)

Took the plane in to ease my ass and get the dysentery injections. That's a hell of a lousy disease. Your whole damn intestine tries to come out. Feels as though you were giving birth to a child. Will fly back out to meet the outfit. Dr. says am through the worst of it. Had really very light case.

This is the finest country I've ever been in. Believe we will settle out here. Wonderful people and splendid climate. Pauline is mad about it.

Come out of the bush on Feb 20—go down to a little island off <u>Lamu</u> at the mouth of the <u>Tana</u> river where have hired an empty Arab house to fish for swordfish—They report them 18 feet long (Probably bunk) Young Alfred Vanderbilt is going too and Philip Percival (who we've been hunting with) is going down to fish with us. He's the man who got Roosevelt his lions and is a wonderful bird. But would rather fish than do anything. Have had a wonderful time with him. Have heard some marvelous stories.

Well so long Max.
You would be crazy about this country.
    Best luck,
    Ernest/

LETTER:
Letter from Marjorie Kinnan Rawlings to Maxwell Perkins, 18 June [1936].

A few months before she actually began the writing of her classic, The Yearling, *Rawlings had an opportunity to meet Hemingway, which Perkins—in his role as their editor—had suggested. Here is her description of the meeting of these two Scribner authors.*

Thanks for the message from Ernest. I'd like to see him too and I always think of my friendship with him as being one of the high spots of life. But I still believe that such things have a mortality, perhaps in reaction to their very excessive life, and that we will never again see very much of each other.

—F. Scott Fitzgerald in a letter to Maxwell Perkins, 15 April 1935.

Dear Max:
    . . . I was glad to meet Hemingway, and wished we could have had time for more than a brief talk. My hostess, Mrs. Oliver Grinnell, was the former president of the Salt Water Anglers of America, and she still works with people like Zane Grey and Hemingway on conservation. He came to call on her on her yacht, and she was privately furious that he talked far more about literary things than fishing! The man astonished me. I should have known, from your affection for him, that he was not a fire-spitting ogre, but I'd heard so many tales in Bimini of his going around knocking people down, that I half-expected him to announce in a loud voice that he never accepted introductions to female novelists. Instead, a most lovable, nervous and sensitive person took my hand in a big gentle paw and remarked that he was a great admirer of my work. He is immensely popular with the anglers, and the natives adore him. The day before I left, he battled six hours and fifty minutes with a 514-lb. tuna, and when his "Pilar" [Hemingway's own boat] came into the harbor at 9:30 at night, the whole population turned out to see his fish and hear his story. There was such a mob on the rotten dock that a post gave way, and his Cuban mate was precipitated into Bimini Bay, coming to the surface with a profanity that was intelligible even to one who speaks no Spanish. A fatuous old man with a new yacht and a young bride had arrived not long previously, announcing that tuna-fishing, of whose difficulties he had heard, was easy. So as the "Pilar" was made fast, Hemingway came swimming up from below-decks, gloriously drunk, roaring, "Where's the son of a bitch who said it was easy?" The last anyone saw of him that night, he was standing alone on the dock where his giant tuna hung from the stays— using it for a punching bag.

A story, told and re-told in Bimini, is of Hemingway's knocking down a man named Platt, for calling him a big fat slob. "You can call me a slob," Hemingway said, "but you can't call me a big fat slob," and he laid him out. Now the natives have a song which they will sing to you if they are sure Hemingway isn't about—"The big fat slob's in the harbor."

There is, obviously, some inner conflict in Hemingway which makes him go about his work with a chip on his shoulder, and which makes him want to knock people down. He is so great an artist that he does not need to be ever on the defensive. He is so vast, so virile, that he does not need ever to hit anybody. Yet he is constantly defending something that he, at least, must consider vulnerable. It seems to me that there is a clue to it in the conflict between the sporting life and the literary life; between sporting people and the artist. That life on the water, with its excitement, which almost nothing that I have experienced can equal, is a self-containing entity. When you are a part of it, nothing else seems valid. Yet occasionally a knife would go through me, and I became conscious of treachery to my own, and when I put it behind me, I felt a great guilt. The sporting people are delightful. They lave your soul. You feel clean and natural when you are with them. Then when you leave them, you are overcome with the knowledge that you are worlds away from them. You know things they will never know. Yet they wear an armor that is denied you. They are somehow blunted. It is not so much their money, for some of them are not unduly prosperous, but their reaction to living. They enjoy life hugely, yet they are not sensitive to it.

Hemingway is among these people a great deal, and they like and admire him—his personality, his sporting prowess, and his literary prestige. It seems to me that unconsciously he must value their opinion. He must be afraid of laying bare before them the agony that tears the artist. He must be afraid of lifting before them the curtain that veils the beauty that should be exposed only to reverent eyes. So, as in "Death in the Afternoon," he writes beautifully, and then immediately turns it off with a flippant comment, or a deliberate obscenity. His sporting friends would not understand the beauty. They would roar with delight at the flippancy. They are the only people who would be pleased by the things in his work that distress all the rest of us. He injects those painfully foreign elements, not as an artist, but as a sportsman, and a sportsman of a particular type.

. . . I couldn't have liked anyone as much as I liked Hemingway, without his liking me a little. . . .

Always with my best,
Marjorie

LETTER:
Letter from Hemingway to Maxwell Perkins, 28 October [1938], from Paris.

Hemingway's The Fifth Column and the First Forty-Nine Stories *was published on 14 October. Instead of impressing the critics with its play/short story combination, the book received mixed reviews. In a typical response Hemingway suggested that Scribners emphasize in its promotion the physical dimensions of the writing, the number of words and pages, which were the "sound points." At almost six hundred pages, the longest of his works, the book was a "very good bargain." He was about to return to Spain, where the civil war was nearing its conclusion.*

Dear Max;

I should have written you a long time ago how sorry I was about old Tom [Tom Wolfe, who had died in September]. But I knew you would know and it never does any good to discuss casualties. You must have had a hell of a time with it all. That was a good letter he wrote. Everybody writes you fond letters when they think they are going to die. You ought to get quite a collection. Hope I'll write you a lot of them in the next fifty years.

Well we thought we had something pretty unbeatable in that book didn't we? But you can't beat those guys. They can gang up to play it down. You know Max I think I'll still be around and going pretty good when there is a whole new generation of critics. You see those guys all buried me and it is awkward and difficult for them to see you rising like Lazarus. I always thought Lazarus must have been awkward to have around myself. What was it they said "Lord he stinketh."

I don't give a shit about any of it except the aspect of interfering with my livelihood. When I got the book and saw all those stories I knew I was all right as a sort of lasting business if I kicked off tomorrow. Which, by the way,—oh well let us neither talk nor write balls.

Pauline wrote that on the day the book came out there wasn't a copy visible in the window. But I'm sure there must be a mistake. Is there any connection with the size of the reviews and the size of the ads? I can see how a large ad could <u>not</u> get a large review. But a small ad might be used as an indication of size of review. Must be quite a racket.

Think you might emphasise in the advertising that there is 185 pages of hitherto unpublished material. Give the length of the new stories.

Mention that Up in Michigan is only obtainable in a book which now sells for $350. a copy. and emphasize the size and number of words in the book.

Those seem to me to be sound points.

There is enough new stuff in the book to make a book a good deal longer than Of Mice and Men say.

Mention that. I think you will have to push it to sell it with those kind of reviews. But I do think, truly, that you offer a very good bargain and that it can be sold if the strong points are emphasized.

I worked like a bastard right up until that Wednesday. Thought maybe it would be last chance ever to write and wrote well. Did two long stories. One was just unfinished when the war was called off. Finished it afterwards. Since, in the mess everything's in, the sort of let down and carnival of treachery and rotten-ness that's going on, coupled with being upset about the damn book (not hearing anything and then everything I hear being bad) it's been hard to work. But I have two Chapters done on the novel [*For Whom the Bell Tolls*]. Look like will be back pretty soon now. Ask Pauline to show you the copy of one of the stories I sent her—Night Before Battle. It is ten thousand some words long.

Will work again on the novel today. Writing is a hard business Max but nothing makes you feel better.

. . . I haven't written the napoleonic story yet. But will. Going to look in on Barcelona next week before comeing home. Max I am a little gloomy so I will terminate this.

Remember if anything ever happens to me I think just as much of you as Tom Wolfe even if I can't put it so well.

So long Max.
Ernest

Cable me the sale when you get this. Garritus Paris

Perkins cabled that 6,350 copies had been sold and that prospects were good. Total sales were about 15,000.

LETTERS:
Written in a very free, no-holds-barred manner, Hemingway's letters (1939–1952) to his publisher, CS III, were usually devoid of business talk and often contained observations on writing and his work and reflections on life—in short, they were letters from a friend. These are typical excerpts:

•[24 February 1940] "Don't worry about the words [his habit of counting his daily word production]. I've been doing that since 1921. I always count them when I knock off and am drinking the first whiskey and soda. Guess I got in the habit writing dispatches. Used to send them from some places where they cost a dollar and a quarter a word and you had to make them awful interesting at that price or get fired. Then I kept it up when started writing stories etc. I don't know as many words as a guy like Tom Wolfe and so it is a hell of a thing for me to get anything over five hundred of them down in a day. Then at the end of the week I always add them up so that I can think, even if I am a no good son of a bitch I wrote, say, 3500 words this week. It's wonderful to be a writer. You ought to try it. . . . Charlie there is no future in anything. I hope you agree. That is why I like it at a war. Every day and every night there is a strong possibility that you will get killed and not have to write. I have to write to be happy whether I get paid for it or not. But it is a hell of a disease to be born with. I like to do it. Which is even worse. That makes it from a disease into a vice. Then I want to do it better than anybody has ever done it which makes it into an obsession. An obsession is terrible. Hope you haven't gotten any. That's the only one I've got left. Well I better try to do a little of it now instead of talking about it."

•[7 August 1941] "Marty [Martha Gellhorn] says you wrote a very funny letter, and sound as though you were going to live. This makes me very happy as it would be an awful nuisance having to get used to a completely new publisher after all these years. Try and survive, if possible, because your boy is still a little young . . . I still think there's a definite place for you in Scribner's, so don't try to die on us. [new paragraph] Hope the pain eases up. That's the worst part of it in anything. And then when I have nothing else to worry about in the night, I think, 'Well, Charlie will probably become a dope head, if this disease keeps up long enough.' What will that make me being published by? Will not show this to Martha as she will probably think I kid too roughly. But the idea of this letter is: delighted that you are on the mend and going to be around for awhile. Everything is very quiet here."

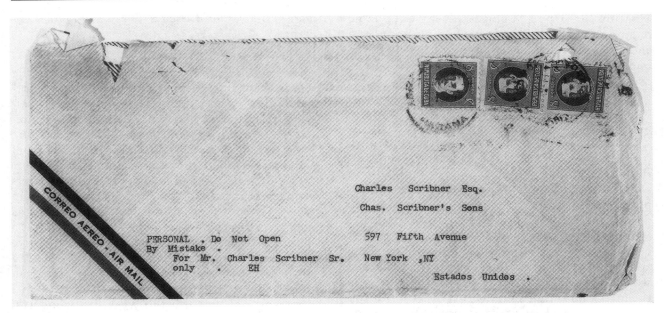

Envelope for one of Hemingway's personal letters to CS III, written from Cuba

•[28 June 1947] "Don't worry about me kid. You have troubles enough without that. I didn't write you after I cabled because what the hell can you say. We don't need to talk wet about Max [Maxwell Perkins] to each other. The bad was for him to die. I hadn't figured on him dying; I'd just thought he might get so completely damn deaf we'd lose him that way. Anyway for a long time I had been trying to be less of a nuisance to him and have all the fun with him possible. . . . Max had a lot of fun, anyway I know we had a lot of fun together, but useing up all his resistance that way by not takeing some lay offs to build up is a good lesson to us and don't you get to overworking now, at least until young Charlie [CS IV] gets to know the business for quite a long time because I want to be able to see your alcohol ravaged face when I come in the office for at least the next twenty two years to help me feel someone in N.Y. has a worse hang-over than I have. . . . If it would do any good you might let it be known that while Max was my best and oldest friend at Scribners and a great, great editor he never cut a paragraph of my stuff nor asked me to change one. One of my best and most loyal friends and wisest counsellors in life as well as in writing is dead. But Charles Scribners Sons are my publishers and I intend to publish with them for the rest of my life."

• [10 July 1949] "I am awfully glad the firm is doing well and that you are getting good new kids. That is really the most important thing as a young ball team is something that you can back while an aging ball team is simply a collection of individuals you must get rid of. Some of us old timers will be able to serve long after the young ones have cracked up for various reasons. But you must always build on youth and get them as young as possible. If they do not come through with a second book, possibly due to too much forcing, would advise hanging on to an option as they may simply be unable to produce the second book and still have a good book in them given proper time. Don't know who you have handling your stable of writers now so only offer these suggestions which you probably have already assimilated, discarded and reclassified. [new paragraph] Most writers are only one book writers anyway. They have one story to tell which is the thing that impressed them, themselves, as terrifically important and once they have succeeded in expressing it fully they are at a loss for anything further to write; consequently, they start some sort of mechanical project and that is the usual second book. [new paragraph] This is enough of this sort of drivel for you to read on a hot day so will close."

•[4 September 1950] "Don't know that I can agree on the value of the various blood sports and the Things of Life. Think you are pretty sound though. I love so many things it is hard to give them priorities. We omitted painting; which I love; architecture; the same; music too. Fighting I love but it is so expensive and so hard on other people and it takes so much out of you. Writing is more fun than anything but hard to do. And all the lovely sports; baseball to play; tennis to play; rideing, shooting, fishing of every kind, sailing to win; sailing for fun, flying in airplane (fast); reading; drinking; fucking; learning, above all learning; meteorology, trying to bring your kids up, training and teaching, navigation. What a lovely world to have to get the hell out of when you just get to know your way around. Raiseing and training fighting chickens is good fun. Drinking with the worthless characters at White's; gambling on things you know about; or sometimes just gambling. Being rude to shits; ski-ing; drinking at the top; driveing a good car well and fast. Plenty things to do Charlie beside read the clippings."

•[14 March 1951] "Have found this great secret that if you love two people, neither of whom you are worthy of, you just work twice as hard. In the end this should be useful to your publisher. [new paragraph] This would be hard to explain to the critics and will not try it. But would like to write a book that would be so wonderful that it would put them all out of business. They will probably say the book is worthless. But maybe I can write a book they <u>can't</u> say is worthless. . . . Am trying to write very well, Charlie, and wish me luck. A man can always use plenty of it." *Hemingway had just recently completed what would become a classic:* The Old Man and the Sea.

LETTER:
Letter from Hemingway to Maxwell Perkins, 15 November 1941, from Sun Valley, Idaho.

When F. Scott Fitzgerald died from a heart attack in Hollywood on 21 December 1940, he left behind an unfinished novel with an outline and notes for completing it. Scribners published the work-in-progress under the title The Last Tycoon: An Unfinished Novel, Together with The Great Gatsby and Selected Stories, *edited by the critic Edmund Wilson, Fitzgerald's friend from Princeton days. Here, Hemingway unsentimentally criticizes his old friend's last work.*

Dear Max,

First, about business. It is o.k. to let Robert Warren reprint "The Killers." I agree with you about the importance of having it in the school books, no matter how hard it is on the poor students. Anyhow it is more interesting than "A Dog of Flanders" and the stuff we had to read as short stories when we were kids. I'll never forget how sick I was of "A Piece of String" and "The Neck-

lace" of de Maupassant. But I suppose they couldn't put his good ones in the school books.

I read all of Scott's book and I don't know whether I ought to tell you what I truly think. There are very fine parts in it, but most of it has a deadness that is unbelievable from Scott. I think Bunnie Wilson did a very credible job in explaining, sorting, padding and arranging. But you know Scott would never have finished it with that gigantic, preposterous outline of how it was to be. I thought the part about Stahr was all very good. You can recognize Irving Thalberg, his charm and skill, and grasp of business, and the sentence of death over him. But the women were pretty preposterous. Scott had gotten so far away from any knowledge of people that they are very strange. He still had the technique and the romance of doing anything, but all the dust was off the butterfly's wing for a long time even though the wing would still move up until the butterfly was dead. The best book he ever wrote, I think, is still "Tender Is the Night" with all of its mix-up of who was Scott and Zelda and who was Sara and Gerald Murphy. I read it last year again and it has all the realization of tragedy that Scott ever found. Wonderful atmosphere and magical descriptions and none of the impossible dramatic tricks that he had outlined for the final book.

Scott died inside himself at around the age of thirty to thirty-five and his creative powers died somewhat later. This last book was written long after his creative power was dead, and he was just beginning to find out what things were about.

I read over the stories and I think Bunnie Wilson made a very poor selection. "The Rich Boy" if you read it, is really profoundly silly. "The Diamond As Big As The Ritz" is simply trash. When you read in "The Rich Boy" about his gradual decay and suddenly see that Scott has given twenty-eight as the age for this oldness setting in, it is hardly credible that he could write that way.

I am happy the book had such a fine review by J. Donald Adams in the Sunday Times with such a good picture of Scott. I think that should please Scotty [Fitzgerald's daughter] very much and be very good for her because she never really knew how good Scott was. But J. Donald Adams is not really a very intelligent man, and to someone who knew Scott truly well and is in the same trade, the book has that deadness, the one quality about which nothing can be done in writing, as though it were a slab of bacon on which mold had grown. You can scrape off the mold, but if it has

Ernest Hemingway

Don't lose This For Christ's Sake. 8/26
C 14

Memorandum on corrections of proof For Whom The Bell Tolls
These corrections may not have been made on this set of galleys due to lack of space .They
are uniform and each word and usage should be checked throughout all the galleys .

Throughout the book use Heinkel for planes —never Henkel .

It is Golz —— never Goltz

It is Estremadura - never Extremadura .

Rafael is the gypsy - never the Gypsy (except at the beginning of a sentence)

Maria is referred to as guapa — not Guapa (except at the beginning of
a sentence .)

Maria is referred to as rabbit — not Rabbit (except at beginning of
a sentence .)

It is viejo (l.c.) never Viejo (except at the beginning of a sentence .)

It should be máquina — never machina

In Qué va the accent aigu should be used in every instance .

~~Guerrilleros should be in italics and~~
guerrillero should be in italics throughout the book .

partizan should be italics and in l.c. through the book .

It should be Agustín throught the book— never Augustin

In some places the Sierra de Gredos is referred to as the Gredos

(Robert Jordan always refers to them thus) Sordo and Pablo would simply say Gredos
. Follow my corrected galleys on this without querying them . I have checked all usage
carefully .

Since I have cut chapter three into chapters three and four the numeration
of all subsequent chapters should be advanced by one . Check this carefully .

Please check with some one who is familiar with Russian names as to
whether Kashkeen should be spelled Kashkin . (I do not have my Russians here)
If it should be spelled Kashkin correct the spelling to this through-out the book .

I will wire you the name of a proper cavalry regiment to insert in the blank
left in galley 9I

The dedication is to read :

This book is for Martha Gellhorn .

Check carefully my corrections on the passage from Donne . In the
galleys it was full of errors which I have corrected from the original .

*With his 26 August 1940 letter to Maxwell Perkins, Hemingway included this sheet of instructions for
editing* For Whom the Bell Tolls.

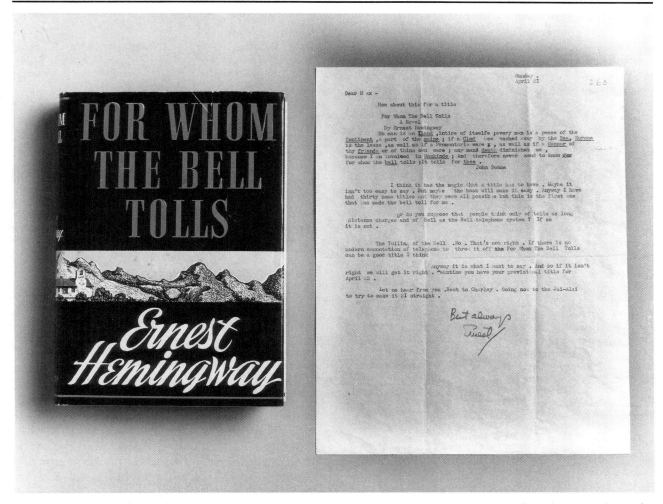

First-edition copy of For Whom the Bell Tolls *with the letter Hemingway sent to Maxwell Perkins supplying the title. "After UARCO had perfected rubber plate printing, book publishers adopted our methods and the first book published from rubber plates was by Scribner and Sons, 'For Whom the Bells Toll,' by Ernest Hemingway. UARCO made the rubber printing plates for Scribner and Sons and a UARCO pressroom foreman went to their plant and helped run them" (letter from UARCO to Scribners, 17 April 1961).*

gone deep into the meat, there is nothing that can keep it from tasting like moldy bacon.

When you wrote Martha [Martha Gellhorn, Hemingway's third wife], you said that Hollywood had not hurt Scott. I guess perhaps it had not because he was long past being hurt before he went there. His heart died in him in France, and soon after he came back, and the rest of him just went on dying progressively after that. Reading the book was like seeing an old baseball pitcher with nothing left in his arm coming out and working with his intelligence for a few innings before he is knocked out of the box.

I know you're impressed by all the stuff about riding in aeroplanes on account of you not doing that and Scott had done it so recently that it impressed him too and he got something of the old magic into it. But in the things between men and women, the old magic was gone and Scott never really understood life well enough to write a novel that did not need the magic to make it come alive.

This sounds gloomy and critical, but I know you want me to write what I really thought about it. You've had three guys. Scott, Tom Wolfe and me. Two of them are already dead, and no one can say what will happen to the third one. But I think it is best to criticize strongly so when you get the new ones that will come along afterwards, you can talk to them truly.

. . . That's all I know about to write now. Please excuse this long letter, and if I sound deprecatory about Scott, remember I know how good he is and was only criticizing Wilson's selections and the posthumous work.

Best to you always,
Ernest/

$12,000⁰⁰/₁₀₀   N.Y. March 2 1942

On demand   after date I promise to pay
to the order of Charles Scribner Sons
Twelve thousand ⁰⁰/₁₀₀   Dollars
Payable at
Value received with interest @ 2%

No.   Due   Ernest Hemingway

Gibsons 536 Plain   U.S. Bond.

Hemingway's IOU to Scribners. Explaining his need for the loan, Hemingway wrote to Maxwell Perkins on 22 February 1942: "About the loan for the tax money, the reason that I wanted this as a loan rather than an advance is because if I take a bigger advance than I would be taking ordinarily it indicates a larger income than I truly have. It is not a tax evasion in any way, nor any attempt to evade taxes. It is just insane to borrow money to pay a tax and then pay a tax on the money you are borrowing as though it were income. In another year, when I make money, I can repay the loan to you as I did the other loan and the money which I earn will be taxable but I will not be paying income tax on a loan." Hemingway's large income from the success of For Whom the Bell Tolls *pushed him into a high tax bracket, which sapped much of his earnings from the book. He had put aside $86,000 toward his 1941 income tax bill, but almost $104,000 was due.*

LETTER:

Letter from Maxwell Perkins to Hemingway, 13 September 1945.

In his proposal to include a Hemingway novel in the first publications of a new reprint company—Bantam Books, Inc., of which Scribners owns a small share—Perkins acknowledges that the twenty-five-cent book is here to stay.

Dear Ernest:

You may be shocked at the proposal that I am making, as I know how you feel about small royalties. The fact of the matter is that a new twenty-five cent book company, "Bantam Books, Inc." wishes to include one of your books among its first publications.

Bantam Books is owned 42% by Grosset & Dunlap, 40% by the Curtis Publishing Company, who will do the distributing, and the remainder by Ian Ballantine who is Manager. This is one of the projects that the Book of the Month, Harper's, Random House, Little Brown and Scribner's had in mind when we [jointly] purchased Grosset. Very likely we shall start other subsidiary companies within the next year or two, to insure the fact that there will be an open market for our books in every form and at every price. . . .

I believe, that with the backing of the Curtis Publishing Company which is the strongest distributing agency in the United States, Bantam Books can match, and, I think, do better with twenty-five cent books than other publishers.

The plan is to publish twenty books at one time, about the first of the year, and to follow this up with a regular schedule of four books a month. Bantam has been able to secure an excellent list of titles, and while a book by you would be the greatest feature, you would not find yourself in bad company. The rates paid are the same as are paid by Pocketbooks—one cent a copy on the first hundred and fifty thousand, and a cent and a half thereafter. The minimum printing is two hundred and fifty thousand, and there is every indication that the sale of the better titles will reach the million mark; this is based on the experience that Ballantine had as Manager of Penguin Books, where the titles did not compare with those that we have already contracted for, and it is also the experience of Pocketbooks.

Bantam Books would be delighted to arrange to sell a twenty-five cent edition for a three year period of one of your novels or of a volume of stories, and would pay an advance of $5000. I neglected to say that this advance and the royalties are divided between author and publisher, which, you know, is the accepted procedure, the only exception I know of being in the case of "For Whom the Bell Tolls." If you are interested, I would suggest "Farewell to Arms", as there are still cheap editions running for selections from your stories and "For Whom the Bell Tolls" is still selling too well in higher priced editions. . . .

Well, this is the story; you can turn it down or not as you think best. I would not pass it up without due thought, as twenty-five cent books are here to stay, and the best books will sooner or latter be offered in this form. Scribner's interest in Bantam Books is only 6% so you will realize that it is not of any great importance to us from a financial viewpoint, and I am not in any wise urging you to give Bantam a book for any personal desire to help that Company to make money. It may not seem very profitable to you to earn a fraction of a cent on the sale of a book, but I believe that wide circulation, while it not only brings you a certain income, is far more important than letting your books dry up at the higher prices. Keeping the titles alive and moving is, after all, the best insurance for their future, as well as bringing your name to new readers who could not be reached in any other way.

As ever,
[Maxwell Perkins]

Hemingway liked the look of Bantam editions once he saw them, but felt the financial terms of these reprints were unfair. However, he finally agreed that there were more than monetary advantages to the wide distribution of cheap paperbacks: For Whom the Bell Tolls *appeared on the Bantam list in the spring of 1951.*

RELATED LETTERS:
Letter from CS III to Hemingway in Paris, 3 December 1949; letter from Hemingway in reply, 10 December 1949, from the Ritz Hotel.

Ten years—and a world war—passed between Hemingway novels. The gap created a pent-up curiosity and demand for his work. In this booming, postwar economic climate, Hemingway was able to sell the serial rights for Across the River and Into the Trees *to* Cosmopolitan *for an unheard-of figure of $85,000. Expectations, of critics, the public, and Hemingway himself—and the deadlines and formatting required of serialization—created unusual pressure for the author. In the meantime Perkins had died, and CS III had assumed an "editorial" role.*

Dear Ernest—

I was truly delighted to find your letter from Paris when I returned from Nantucket yesterday. What gave me the pleasure was that it indicated that you had caught your breath and cooled out a bit. Any one, who has driven himself relentlessly as you, must ease up or go into a tail-spin. Like a good thoroughbred, who has given his all, you are probably not yet completely cooled out inside so may break out again. Therefore do take it easy, and argue amicably with "Hotshot" [A. E. Hotchner, *Cosmopolitan* editor] over what you have in writing and what or what-not our great conveyor of culture, the Cosmo, can print with impunity.

. . . I realize both our fathers would probably think us wise to make a sure bet (if it could be arranged in advance) with a book club—but to hell with them—that means new dead lines and I am far happier for your book to keep you as free as air. Clubs are only the result of the average American's lack of personal culture—just like a Simon Shuster ad—"You have got to read this as all your neighbors are reading it" (no mention of what the damn book is about). Well for better or worse they have got to read the new Hemingway—but how I personally hate regimentation?—I failed to read many best-sellers just because I was expected to have read the damned books.

Well "Hotshot" is with you now. I like him ever so much personally. Dont envy him—you made a hell of a good deal with Cosmo. Your book (I might say) is ok but how in hell is one to cut four or five pictures out of one photograph. I dont envy the guy. But all this has nothing to do with CS sons. It is the book which counts and where on your record lies. If I am any good as your publisher this book should earn an income like a bond issue for 56 years or however long is the copyright. When you left you were to send the M.S. from Havre. I have a good sample page & 3 machines to go to work in 24 hours. But to hell with that if you can fix up the original M.S. with Hotshot.

What I want to do is to set your M.S. in type (while you do nothing) then send it to you and you can cut it to ribbons when you see it in a different form or say it is your best—all authors alterations I will assume and send revised galleys. Do let's take our time and make this book your best—you have slaved too hard over it not to have the right to balance it anew with a fresh eye. My father in the old days had three popular writers: Thomas Nelson Page, John Fox and Peter Dunn: all of which rewrote their books on the margins of the galleys—very hard for the typographers = Page had married a rich wife so not dependant, but I hear Fox say to Dunn: "I'm bust and must get an advance from CS (Sr) do you think I could sell him on the title 'The Trail of the Lonesome Pine'" "Hell" said Peter Dunn "Any bastard could sell him on that but I haven't time to think of a title until I have my advance set."—They were tough guys and knew as well as you all your four letter words but in their time the words were unprintable. Dunn (Mr. Dooley), although my father's age, was one of my closest friends and advisers until his death. A lazy Irish man who drank too much but with wonder philosophy and insight into the future. I remember his telling me that "The Killers" was one of the very few really great stories in the English language—he followed it up as you might have done in his place "E. H. is a great writer, always remember that Charlie, but some day he may have remorse for the sins that made him great. Drop him then Charlie unless you are just collecting Davis's, Fox's & Pages like your father" Well your present M.S. is certainly not of the Victorian era.

I am happy that you took no offense at my suggestions regarding earlier thoughts of the girl in your novel—in fact that you had already thought of it yourself. She is at the core of the story and any building of her is what I believe your readers will welcome. Perhaps that is what you intended, but she is still primarily only a rather dumb, but beautiful, sounding board for the Colonel. She is so complacent—if she only expressed some real like or dislike for anything it would give her character. The Col. I appreciate is rather ashamed of some of the finer things he says to her and therefore ends them—with what shall I say—a decided off color remark (I am not telling you) but I do think this is at times over done. As I read the story the Col not only loves her for her physical looks but loves her with a certain respect as a true lady—not a whore or bitch—who has of her will well broken with her way of life to give her all to him. I know the way you talk to Vera [CS III's wife], your wife and other women you respected and why should you make the Col so much tougher than you. In the actual love scenes I admire your great restraint.

Well I dont want to presume to give the Old Master indigestion with my ideas. I know that it will all come right—but you have slaved too hard and too long. I have reread all your earlier books and honestly Ernest you have not yet put all the cutting and refining into this book that you put into them—This is your most important book so

take your time—get mad at me if you wish but I am your personal friend. As a publisher I could publish anything over your name and hope to make money but believe me that is secondary to the pride of being your publisher.

Do think over some of the venomish accusations you make of some "high brass" by name—the girl would scarcely know their names and we trust your book will outlive their names. Dont make it necessary for me at the age of 90 to edit an edition with footnotes explaining who everyone is.

I believe in your creed that an author should draw on his own experiences and, if truthful, should only write from that well of personal experience but I believe he should distill his experiences into generalities and not like Tom Wolfe—because a girl has a mole on the left side of her mouth refuse to move it in fiction to the right side of her mouth.

Well you are probably angry at me now so I wont touch on the Col's burying that 1500 lira note with a turd—perhaps your favorate incident—but just crap to me—I can still teach you new 4 letter words—if desired will send you forty = My every best to you & Mary—have a good time—dont worry & all will be for the best—see you perhaps in Feb.—Best Charlie

Dear Charlie:

I am terribly sorry about your aunt's death. Your run on the blacks really should be over.

Finished first draft of book and am naturally beat to the wide. Will take time and make all the necessary bettering where bettering can be made. Hotch cried, Mary [Hemingway's 4th wife] cried, Pete's wife cried, now the old woman who copied it cried. Wish to Christ I had Marlene [Marlene Dietrich, the actress] her to make her cry. If you don't choke-up I give you your god-damn money back.

What I need now is not to think of it until I am far enough away to be able to see it completely detached.

Thanks for all the criticism and suggestions. You are the owner, no, the publisher, so you can say anything to me. But since am both horse and jockey will make my own ride as I always have. As publisher, naturally, you have a right to refuse to publish anything I write. I truly appreciate all suggestions. But judge my finished product. Not first drafts turned out under pressure. You made me one good suggestion once and one that am not sure yet whether was good or not; although told you it was good on first thought in my last letter.

Most of the other Hemingway titles published by Scribners

But you have been reading an un-cut, un-rewritten mss. and I'm the cutter and re-writer. Why wouldn't it seem un-cut and un-rewritten alongside a book I wrote the last chapter of 42 times? But what a pace you bastards set and you should be fucking glad your horse could win and still be alive. It reminded me of the time I raced the streamliner that Averell runs from Green River to Rawlings, Wyo. Had to hold over ninety all the time with Mary sitting by me watching for the Streamliner to show. And she always showed. That was best race I ever had until this one.

Now race over. Can correct all errors, see it again, eliminate and add if necessary. Plenty work. But have to take a breather first.

. . . Don't worry about book. Give me any of your bright ideas but never expect me to act on

them unless they are better than mine. Will not act on them just because they are different than mine. Write them down; save them up and get them to me with the proof. Will give them all practical consideration and act on any that I think are good. Max never made a change (or maybe he did) but then I never worked at the pace you two characters imposed for a while.

Have also written two poems since here, while cooling out, both good.

But do not want to hear of, or about this book again until I hit it again once more and want an exact and precise deadline. Know you will keep in touch and work things out with Hotchner and give it to me.

Don't get worried about four letter words; nor tell me you know more of them than me. I never used one uselessly on paper. But know them in four languages and can command in all four. This is not a myth nor a legend.

. . . Respect Peter Dunne and the best writings of the other late characters you mentioned. But no one of them really played in the big league; not one. That is where you have to do it perfectly and for all time and with that you make the consequent mistakes. Nobody bats 1000 but am going to have a life time average that will spook you. Cheer up mon vieux. What is a critic more or less. If they get out on a limb we simply saw it off.

As you can see from this have the beautiful confidence of a son of a bitch with reserves who has learned to handle same.

I expect you, naturally, to bring the book out anonymously, or with somebody else's name on it, or with the title spelled backwards and refuse to offer it to the trade because it might be surruptitious. But we will still win.

Will attempt not to offend any of your brass. . . . But have no plans for being gelded either. Anyplace I say a General was a shit will make it jerk; when say jerk will make it a character. Remember it was an intelligent former general officer speaking who was intelligent _and_ bitter.

What do you think it sounds like when a 50 year old former General officer talks with a girl of 19? That they should exchange reminiscences of old days at Fort Riley or Leavenworth? She simply wanted to know about his trade to share it with him.

Lillian Ross [friend on _The New Yorker_] asked me if it was really true that people joke with waiters in high class hotels. I assured her that it was; if they were well enough brought up; not snobs; and knew the language.

For instance at Plymouth in the small bar of the first class on the Ile [_Île de France_ ocean liner], after the passport and currency examination all the passport, m5s and currency and other British gestapo came into the bar where was haveing a drink. All, except one of them who gave a quick look and retractable grin, in case he were wrong, started to talk about everything they shouldn't on the assomption that I was a foreigner, or displaced person, (bearded etc.) and consequently as inoffensive to talk in front of as a waiter. Was wearing an old blue sweater and had come from the gym. I said, "We all speak English here you know." One unfortunate rose to the bait and said, "But perhaps with a different accent." Bowler-hatted type.

"My brand's as good as yours and I pay your wages," I tossed it back if he wanted to play.

But the retractable grin character in an old Burberry got up and said, "It's been quite a long time."

We both knew where it had been a long time since, when, and the type of air-craft had been the new big Hamilcar gliders.

So we bought the bowler hat-man a drink and he had to drink it because he had never worn the blue clothes of the disinherited of this earth, nor translated Ad Astra Per Aspera as To The Stars The Hard Way, nor eaten the cold potato pan-cakes of the poor after missions when the mess and the bar were both closed. I didn't rub it in at all except, perhaps, with my elbow. Was extremely polite and even solicitous.

The faded and worn Burberry coat man and I were both very happy.

Why should I write this well for nothing? . . .

Thanks for everything.

Ernest

Wish you were here Town full of good drink, food, beautiful womens. When they finish at Auteuil [French racetrack] will go south. EH.

Across the River and Into the Trees, _published on 7 September 1950, greatly disappointed the critics, who felt Hemingway's work seemed out of fashion, a parody of his former style. Yet the novel was the #3 best-seller of the year._

RELATED LETTERS:
Letter from Hemingway to Scribner editor Wallace Meyer, 4 and 7 March 1952; letter from Meyer in reply, 13 March 1952.

Hemingway's letter to Scribners accompanying his submission of The Old Man and the Sea.

Dear Wallace:

Thank you very much for your letter. You could not have written one explaining more clearly the whole picture nor one that gave me the details I needed to know about Charlie's death. I've had to write many letters about how people died and how good and well loved they were. But usually you have to be so careful about how they died in the letter that it is worthless. I thank you very much for the letter.

With this letter I am sending you an uncorrected typescript of The Old Man and The Sea. I do not want to correct it nor attempt to retitle it until I have done the two weeks of the second part

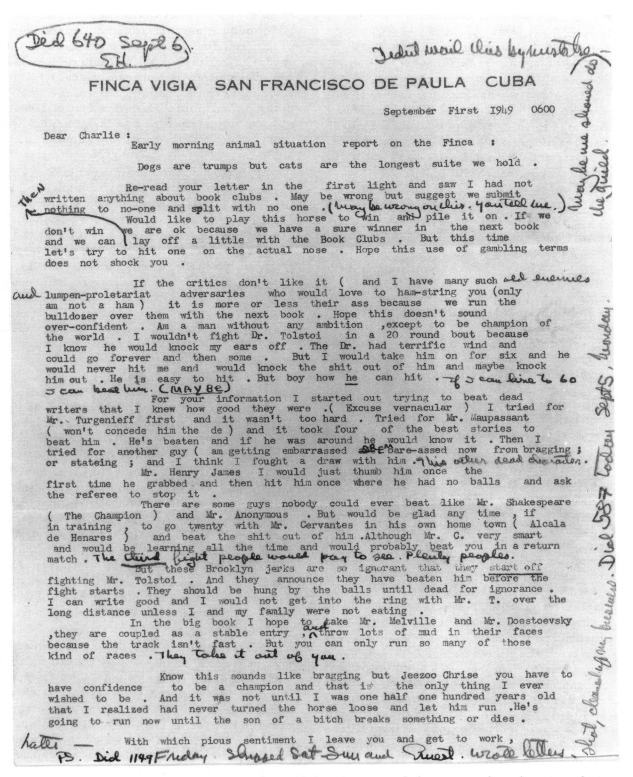

FINCA VIGIA   SAN FRANCISCO DE PAULA   CUBA

September First 1949   0600

Dear Charlie :

Early morning animal situation report on the Finca :

Dogs are trumps but cats are the longest suite we hold .

Re-read your letter in the first light and saw I had not written anything about book clubs . May be wrong but suggest we submit nothing to no-one and split with no one . (may be wrong on this . you tell me.)
Would like to play this horse to win and pile it on . If we don't win we are ok because we have a sure winner in the next book and we can lay off a little with the Book Clubs . But this time let's try to hit one on the actual nose . Hope this use of gambling terms does not shock you .

If the critics don't like it (and I have many such old enemies lumpen-proletariat adversaries who would love to ham-string you (only am not a ham) it is more or less their ass because we run the bulldozer over them with the next book . Hope this doesn't sound over-confident . Am a man without any ambition ,except to be champion of the world . I wouldn't fight Dr. Tolstoi in a 20 round bout because I know he would knock my ears off . The Dr. had terrific wind and could go forever and then some . But I would take him on for six and he would never hit me and would knock the shit out of him and maybe knock him out . He is easy to hit . But boy how he can hit . if I can live to 60 I can beat him. (MAYBE)
For your information I started out trying to beat dead writers that I knew how good they were .(Excuse vernacular) I tried for Mr. Turgenieff first and it wasn't too hard . Tried for Mr. Maupassant (won't concede him the de) and it took four of the best stories to beat him . He's beaten and if he was around he would know it . Then I tried for another guy (am getting embarrassed been bare-assed now from bragging ; or stateing ; and I think I fought a draw with him . this other dead character.
Mr. Henry James I would just thumb him once the first time he grabbed and then hit him once where he had no balls and ask the referee to stop it .
There are some guys nobody could ever beat like Mr. Shakespeare (The Champion) and Mr. Anonymous . But would be glad any time , if in training , to go twenty with Mr. Cervantes in his own home town (Alcala de Henares) and beat the shit out of him .Although Mr. C. very smart and would be learning all the time and would probably beat you in a return match . The third fight people would pay to see. Plenty peoples.
But these Brooklyn jerks are so ignorant that they start off fighting Mr. Tolstoi . And they announce they have beaten him before the fight starts . They should be hung by the balls until dead for ignorance . I can write good and I would not get into the ring with Mr. T. over the long distance unless I and my family were not eating .
In the big book I hope to take Mr. Melville and Mr. Doestoevsky ,they are coupled as a stable entry , and throw lots of mud in their faces because the track isn't fast . But you can only run so many of those kind of races . They take it out of you.

Know this sounds like bragging but Jeezoo Chrise you have to have confidence to be a champion and that is the only thing I ever wished to be . And it was not until I was one half one hundred years old that I realized had never turned the horse loose and let him run .He's going to run now until the son of a bitch breaks something or dies .

later — With which pious sentiment I leave you and get to work,

PS. Did 1149 Friday. Sh.... Sat. Sun. and fiesta. wrote letters.

"Situation report" sent by Hemingway to his publisher, CS III—including count of words written during the past few days—while working on Across the River and Into the Trees

of the austerity vacation Mary and I are going to under-take next week. But it is [in] such shape that you will know what you think about it. Please do not let anyone outside of the office nor anyone not of your complete confidence read it.

It is 26,531 words in length. It may be impossible to publish a book of this length. But I know that in the history of publishing there have been books of this length which have had an extraordinary and continued sale. I will not try to point out to you what virtues or implicaciones (mis-spelled) it has. But I know that it is the best I can write ever, for all of my life I think, and that it destroys good and able work by being placed alongside of it. I'll try to write better but it will be tough. Please do not think that I am haveing a rush of conceit to the head. I am a professional writer and I know something about this piece of work. It is not a short story nor a novella. I would rather have your opinion of it than to try to sound off with what I know about it.

So far I only showed it to Charlie and his wife and to various friends of mine including the boy who edits Cosmopolitan. It had a very strange effect on all of them. It effected all of them in a stronger way than anything that I have ever written. While I was writing it you can more or less imagine the effect it had on me after you have read it. It is the epilogue to my long book. But it is a complete unit in its-self. Actually, the book, when properly finished, does not need an epilogue. But this can always be republished as such; or as an epilogue to all my writing and what I have learned, or tried to learn, while writing and trying to live. This sounds grandiose. It will go at the end of the book where it belongs.

Leland Hayward [theatrical producer and former literary agent], who has read it while here in Havana on vacation, suggests that it could be published in a single issue of LIFE. I don't know whether that would be better than publication in a single issue of THE NEW YORKER. Of course neither of them might want it. The editor of Cosmopolitan wanted to publish it in a single number but his budget only allowed him to pay $10,000 for it and I told Charlie that I did not think that was worthwhile compensation for the loss of surprise and shock of anyone comeing on it suddenly in a book.

But now I think it should be a separate book and be published this fall if your schedule permits. It could be moderately priced and would not take too much paper for costs.

You will know what you think of it when you read it. Tactically publishing it now will get rid of the school of criticism that maintains that I am through as a writer. It will destroy the school of criticism that claims I can write about nothing except myself and my own experiences. That would give us, in the long run, a great strategical advantage. These martial terms are extremely tedious. But no more than always hearing Generals talk in terms of foot-ball a game I always thought you could get tired of without even playing it.

I am tired of not publishing anything. Other writers publish short books. But I am supposed to always lay back and come in with War and Peace or Crime and Punishment or be considered a bum. This is probably very bad for a writer and I will bet it did more to wreck poor old Scott [Fitzgerald] than anything except Zelda [his wife], himself and booze. I know Max would have been happy with a truly good and sound book from Scott. But Scott tried to be a better writer than he was and he threw the ball over the grandstand. (Where I must throw this typewriter if it isn't over-hauled)

I would like to publish this book now. Publish the next book that I have worked so damned hard on next and keep on like that. This book comes out again with the other as added value. The other one, long, is a hell of a good book and this comes after as a million dollar postscript.

On the practical side books that have had no size and sold in great amounts were (not to make comparisons but only speaking technically) Dicken's Christmas Carol, The Story of the Other Wise Man [by Henry van Dyke], Mary Raymond Shipman Andrew's story [The Perfect Tribute] about the Gettysburg Address (May have author's and characters mixed on this) and The Man Without a Country [by Edward Everett Hale]. Your researchers would turn up more and give you the figures on these.

I know that my own dislike of Jones book [James Jones's From Here to Eternity], which was a wonderful selling volume, aside from it being psychopathic and Over-The-Hilly was its weight and length. There is always the certainty that the tide turns. People, possibly, might like to handle a good non-overweight book where a man shows what a human being is capable of and the dignity of the human soul without the word soul being capitalized. . . .

Good luck Wallace. I hope I am bringing you a victory instead of makeing you trouble and worry.

Ernest

FINCA VIGIA, SAN FRANCISCO DE PAULA, CUBA

February 25 1952

Dear Charlie :

It would seem strange to call your father Charlie and then address you as Mr. Scribner . But I can do it if you would prefer and if it makes things any simpler .

Please know how badly I felt to be away and out of touch when your father died . We must have left the harbor about an hour before he felt ill from what Wallace Meyer and Rice wrote me and Mary brought word of his death the following Saturday evening . From down the coast we tried to write your mother how Mary and I felt about him . But I do not even know if she received the letter as it had to be sent inland to be posted .

I won't try to write to you how much he meant to me as a friend and as a publisher . He was the best and closest friend that I had and it seems impossible that I will never have another letter from him . It does not do any good to talk about it and there is nothing to say that makes it any easier . Since he had to die at least he has gotten it over with

If there is anything practical I can do please let me know . After the March 15 income tax, has been paid I will plan to draw nothing more on my loan account except for the four payments of $750 that Rice figures must be made against 1952 tax . Please cancel the monthly payment of $100. a month to Gregory Hemingway as of March First ie. make no payment on March First. As soon as the money is paid me for the cinema rights to Across The River and Into the Trees I I will pay something to reduce my loan account . There is $25,000 in escrow as an advance against ten percent of the gross in that picture deal . But the motion picture people still have to fulfil certain requirements before it is paid . When I talked to Rice on the phone he was optomistic about them raising all their money . This is the first time he has been optomistic and told me this is the type of deal that cannot be hurried . It is a good property and there is no sense in makeing a forced sale when it is possible to wait .

I will try and not worry you about finances nor about anything else . You don't have to write me letters nor have me on your mind in any way . I know what a terribly tough job you have now with Navy ,Estate and the House of Scribner to look after . They shouldn't do that to any human being . Please take it as easy as you can and feel free to call on me in any way that I can be of help . If there is anything Mary and I can do for your Mother please let us know . She likes Mary and she likes the sea and to fish and she might like to come down some time and stay with us and get some fishing with Mary .

I plan to pick up the vacation where we left it and not worry about anything nor think of things that can't be helped and keep on getting in the best of shape to hit the book again . On the boat we were getting to bed at nine ,sleeping well , getting up at daylight and fishing all forenoon and reading and loafing in the afternoon . I could feel the batteries re-chargeing every day . It is not fair to anyone not to keep in shape to do your best work and I am going to get in the best shape I can now no matter what other things have to second priority for the necessary time . We over-worked for 18 months .

This is not a good letter ,Charlie . But I still feel too sad to write a good one .

your friend

Ernest Hemingway.

Am sorry I don't know your rank so address this as a civilian. EH

Letter of condolence on the death of CS III sent by Hemingway to CS IV

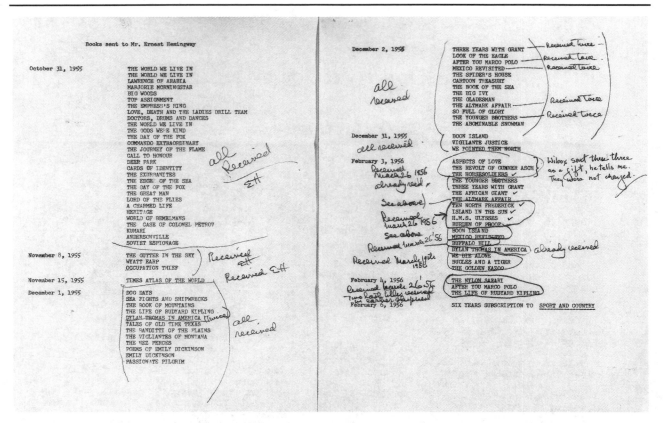

List of books sent by Scribners to Hemingway in Cuba with his annotations. A voracious reader, Hemingway often received complimentary copies of new books the firm published that Maxwell Perkins or CS III felt might interest him, and he also ordered many others from the Scribner bookstore, charging them to his account.

Dear Ernest:

I waited until Tuesday evening to read the manuscript, for I wanted to be alone and absolutely sure against interruptions. I don't know that I can tell you how it moved me. All I can say is that a man is never the same after he has read anything like that—and it happens only a very few times in a lifetime. Every time I woke up in the night it was with me. And I hope it won't seem presumptuous if I say that I was deeply proud of you, and proud to think that for twenty-five years—more than that, I guess—I had been working somewhere on the fringe of the creative activity of a man who, in the fourth decade of his writing career, could produce a thing like that. Finer for me, Ernest, than anything you have ever done. Everything is in it. Next day at the office it was wonderful to see the other editors take it up, one after another, and to see their eyes shine as it began to take hold. By noon four of us had read it, and then I cabled you how we all felt about it. It is a perfect thing in its length. You could not have got the full effect with anything less, and it needs nothing more. By all means it should go into one of the weeklies—Life or The New Yorker—where

it will not be divided, and for a very good price. There is also the advantage of flexibility in having four issues a month and the ability to synchronize magazine publishing and book publishing dates. The Book-of-the-Month Club idea in your letter should be a certainty for a dual selection, and perhaps for a single selection. I should think that the quality of it would completely override any consideration of length.

It is hard to be silent about something that you feel so deeply about, but we who have read it are keeping still about it, even here in the house, until you get back from your trip and we can be in close touch with you and get our signals straight. . . .

Hope you are having good weather for the trip.

Best,
[Wallace Meyer]

The public presentation of The Old Man and the Sea *was the biggest publishing feat of its time:* Life *magazine ran it complete in one issue (1 September); Scribners published the book on 8 September; and the Book-of-the-Month Club, using it as one of its dual selections for October, began*

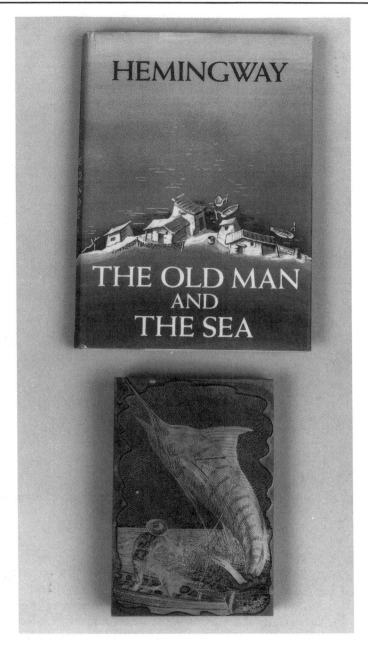

A first-edition copy (1952) and one of the original plates used in the 1960 illustrated edition of The Old Man and the Sea. *One of Hemingway's earliest mentions of the story was in a letter to Maxwell Perkins, dated 7 February 1939, when he was considering getting out a book of stories later that fall: "And three very long ones I want to write now. . . . One about the old commercial fisherman who fought the swordfish all alone in his skiff for 4 days and four nights and the sharks finally eating it after he had it alongside and could not get it into the boat. That's a wonderful story of the Cuban coast. I'm going out with old Carlos in his skiff so as to get it all right. Everything he does and everything he thinks in all that long fight with the boat out of sight of all the other boats all alone on the sea. It's a great story if I can get it right. One that would make the book." There is considerable disagreement about the chronology of the composition of the story, but he completed it in 1951, astonishing himself at the ease and speed with which he wrote it down. Hemingway dedicated the book to "Charlie Scribner and to Max Perkins." The dust jacket, designed by his Italian friend Adriana Ivancich, won the National Arts Club's award as the best book jacket of the year.*

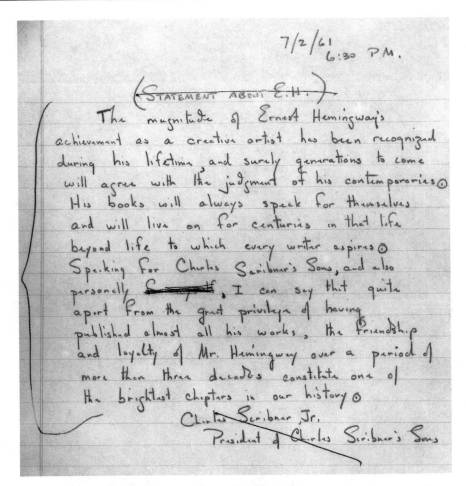

*Draft of the statement issued by CS IV to the press after hearing of
Hemingway's death by suicide*

distributing its copies the next day. A very popular work—the book was the #7 best-seller of 1952—The Old Man and the Sea was also critically acclaimed, winning the Pulitzer Prize for fiction in 1953.

LETTER:
Letter from Wallace Meyer to Hemingway in
    Paris, 6 December 1956.

This sales report from Hemingway's editor confirms that CS IV's "master plan," undertaken in 1952 to bring all of Hemingway's titles back to the Scribner list by not renewing reprint licenses, was continuing to show remunerative results.

Dear Ernest:

I've been wanting to give you a report on the way the books are selling. I have figures now up through November 20, and I'm not likely to have

any more up-to-date ones before the first of the year. The Royalty department has all it can do to hold the pace in these few weeks, and they are not likely to be able to report to us until the rush is over. I think the best way to give you a representative idea of the way the books are going is to cite sales in the ten days between November 10 and November 20.

THE OLD MAN AND THE SEA still holds the lead, and its sale in the beginning of the fifth year of its life is really amazing. In those ten days it sold 534 copies, and when next we get a full report, the total sale will be over 145,000 copies. This is still the original edition at $3.00. Charlie has in reserve a format and a type style for a lower-priced edition, very attractive indeed, but as we study the sales, we continually come back to the view that the time is not yet. A new edition at a lower price may well step up the sale, but from your point of view and from our own as well it would probably be a mistake to make the move until the sale needs stimulation. It isn't as if the book were being withheld from its public by the present price—that clearly isn't the case. I've been observing the sales of books for 35 years, and I've never seen anything to equal the vitality, five years after publication, of THE OLD MAN AND THE SEA. I hope that same vitality is being shown by foreign-language editions all over the world.

I'll list below the other titles with the sales for those ten days. They all show steady progress. I don't think there is another writer in the world today whose books can show equal performance. The real veterans in the list are as good as the younger ones, but they all have life.

Title	November 10–November 20
TO HAVE AND HAVE NOT	69
THE GREEN HILLS OF AFRICA	62
A FAREWELL TO ARMS	134
THE SUN ALSO RISES	58
THE HEMINGWAY READER	127
THE COLLECTED SHORT STORIES	191
IN OUR TIME	57
MEN WITHOUT WOMEN	54
WINNER TAKE NOTHING	61
ACROSS THE RIVER AND INTO THE TREES	77
DEATH IN THE AFTERNOON	103
FOR WHOM THE BELL TOLLS	133

Several of these titles still have the competition of reprints in the paper-back field, but these contracts have all been terminated on expiration, and by next August all your books will be out of the paper-back field. I think the figures show that Charlie's policy in this respect is sound in your interest.

Perhaps six weeks ago Harvey Breit [assistant editor of *The New York Times Book Review* and Hemingway friend] called me by telephone about something, and I learned then where you and Mary were during your days in New York. It was a secret well kept, and you both must have enjoyed the privacy it gave you. Charlie and I were sorry not to be here to see you, but there would have been no official business to take up and the result must have been a few days of real freedom for you. We're hoping for the new book of stories for the fall of 1957.

Africa should be good to you this time, with no mishaps, and I hope it lives up to expectations in every way.

My very best to you both.
[Wallace Meyer]

Hemingway's poor health prevented him from continuing on to Africa as he had planned; he came home aboard the Île de France *the next month.*

LETTER:
Letter from CS IV to Hemingway in Ketchum, Idaho, 30 January 1961.

Suffering from high blood pressure, hypertension, and depression, Hemingway secretly flew to the Mayo Clinic in Rochester, Minnesota, on 30 November for tests, the results of which were essentially negative, though they revealed "mild diabetes mellitus." He received a course of shock treatments, from which he seemed to respond well, and was discharged on 22 January.

Dear Ernest:

This is just a note to say that we've all been thinking about you and hoping that if you are not already home you will be soon. It was awfully wise to have a check-up like this and I am simply delighted at the reports you have given Harry [his Scribner editor Harry Brague]. You once inscribed THE OLD MAN AND THE SEA for me with the words "D'abord il faut durer." It's pretty clear to us that you're going to be following your own advice for a great many years to come!

Please don't hesitate to let me or Harry know if there is anything we can do for you here. Nothing would give either of us greater pleasure.

All the very best regards to you both.
Yours ever,
[Charles Scribner]

Willard Huntington Wright (1888–1939)
("S. S. Van Dine")

Willard Huntington Wright ("S. S. Van Dine") in the late 1930s (photo from John Loughery's Alias S. S. Van Dine, *New York: Scribners, 1992)*

Wright is best known as a writer of detective fiction under the pseudonym S. S. Van Dine and the creator of the urbane and scholarly master sleuth Philo Vance. This was actually his second career, for he had already established a name as a writer on art and as art critic of *Forum* (1915–1916), *International Studio* (1916–1917), *San Francisco Bulletin* (1918–1919), and *Heart's International Magazine.* He also had played a leading role in organizing the seminal Forum Exhibition of Modern American Painters, held at the Anderson Galleries in New York City in March 1916, an important event in the development of modern art in the United States. In 1923 Wright suffered a severe nervous breakdown and was confined to bed for a couple of years. While he was forbidden by his physician to do any "serious" reading, Wright was permitted to relax with detective novels. These he collected and analyzed by the hundreds, eventually deciding he could master the technique himself. Mapping out three novels, he brought his ten-thousand-word synopses to Scribner editor Maxwell Perkins, whom he had known as a fellow student at Harvard: his success was immediate with the publication of *The Benson Murder Case* (1926). Wright's well-written, intricately plotted murder mysteries reinvigorated the genre and attracted a devoted, sophisticated reading public—several were true bestsellers, though all proved popular and were translated around the world. Hollywood produced movies based on the books, with William Powell as the best-known Philo Vance.

Scribner Books by Wright

1926	*The Benson Murder Case: A Philo Vance Story*
1927	*The "Canary" Murder Case: A Philo Vance Story*
	The Great Detective Stories: A Chronological Anthology, compiled and edited, with an introduction, by Wright
1928	*The Greene Murder Case: A Philo Vance Story*

S. S. Van Dine Detective Library (6 volumes), selected and prefaced by Wright

1929   *I Used to Be a Highbrow, But Look at Me Now* (pamphlet)

The Bishop Murder Case: A Philo Vance Story

1930   *The Man of Promise*

The Scarab Murder Case: A Philo Vance Story

1933   *The Kennel Murder Case: A Philo Vance Story*

The Dragon Murder Case: A Philo Vance Story

1934   *The Casino Murder Case: A Philo Vance Story*

1935   *The Garden Murder Case: A Philo Vance Story*

1936   *Philo Vance Murder Cases*

The Kidnap Murder Case: A Philo Vance Story

1938   *The Gracie Allen Murder Case: A Philo Vance Story*

1939   *The Winter Murder Case: A Philo Vance Story*

LETTERS:

The scheme for his detective novels that Wright had previously outlined to Perkins over lunch met with swift approval at Scribners. Here Perkins relays the publishing terms to get the "project" rolling.

March 23, 1926

Dear Wright:

The sooner you get to work the better we shall be pleased. I immediately talked over the arrangement we outlined at lunch and met with full approval. I am therefore having the contract prepared for the publication of "The Benson Murder Case" and "The Whipporwill Murder Case" on the basis of 15% straight royalty with the other conditions we outlined. But we hereby further agree to pay an advance of nine hundred dollars to apply against this royalty on "The Benson Murder Case" in three installments of three hundred dollars each, the first installment to be paid on April first, the second on May first, and the third on June first, and we understand that the completed manuscript will be in our hands by July first. I think the whole layout is extraordinarily good and expect a great deal of pleasure in the working out of the project. You can certainly count on warm support from our entire force.

Yours as ever,
[Maxwell Perkins]

Wright delivered the first manuscript on schedule.

July 7, 1926

Dear Wright:

I think the story altogether admirable. It gets better all the time up to the end. It is an extremely able, skillful piece of work. Everyone in it takes on a definite personality and is given form and appearance. As for Van Dine [Wright's pseudonym], he is a great boy. I have no important changes to suggest, but as I read, certain little questions came into my mind, the merest trifles, which I might point to in the galleys for your consideration.

I am sure nobody would identify the criminal except by merest chance.-

- So I put the ms. in hand with orders to rush through.

Yours as ever,
[Maxwell Perkins]

The book was published on 8 October under the pseudonym S. S. Van Dine, and the first printing of forty-nine hundred sold out within two weeks. In the November issue of Scribner's Magazine, *using his own name, Wright presented his ideas about the genre in an essay titled simply "The Detective Novel"—hence seeking to keep his identity as a crime novelist hidden.*

RELATED LETTERS:

The sale of second serial rights—for example, the rights covering the postpublication syndication of novels in newspapers—was an important financial consideration to novelists such as Wright during the 1920s. The following letters illustrate how

SCRIBNER'S MAGAZINE
January 1928
VOL. LXXXIII   NO. I

The Greene Murder Case

A PHILO VANCE STORY

BY S. S. VAN DINE
Author of "The Benson Murder Case" and "The 'Canary' Murder Case"

ACCORDING to the foremost critics of both England and America, "The 'Canary' Murder Case" (which ran serially in this magazine last year) set a new standard in detective-mystery fiction. "A model of everything a detective story should be—a monument, a cathedral amongst detective stories," wrote Arnold Palmer in the London *Sphere;* and Robert John Bayer, in the Chicago *Post,* said it proved that "the writing of such a novel can be raised to high art." These two comments reflected the consensus of critical sentiment evoked by the book. Perhaps not in our generation has any other novel of this *genre* been so extensively read and so highly praised.

We are happy, therefore, to be able to present to the readers of SCRIBNER'S MAGAZINE Mr. Van Dine's latest book, "The Greene Murder Case." This new Philo Vance story, telling of the mysterious criminal tragedy that befell the strangely assorted household of the old Greene mansion, more than meets, in dramatic narrative interest and literary quality, the standard set by the author's previous work.

THE EDITOR.

The Greene Mansion, New York, as it appeared at the time of the notorious Greene murder case. From an old woodcut by Lowell L. Balcom.

Frontispiece and first page of the January 1928 Scribner's Magazine, the inaugural issue of the magazine's "new" format (typeface, cover design, editorial policy), beginning the serialization of Wright's latest Philo Vance story. The true identity of S. S. Van Dine, which allegedly was a pseudonym compounded from the abbreviation for steamship and an old family name (Van Dyne), was not generally known at that time.

this market dramatically declined during the Depression.

May 14, 1928

Dear Mr. Perkins:

This will confirm our verbal agreement to the effect that we are to have the newspaper rights in the United States and Canada to THE GREENE MURDER CASE by S. S. Van Dine. We agree to pay you for this $3,000.00 the payment to be made not later than July 1, 1928.

I am assuming that this date is all right and I expect to pay you before that but as I explained to you on the telephone it will be a little while before money begins coming in from the sale of the book and we would appreciate it if you could agree to this. If this is not satisfactory please let me know and we will handle it on whatever basis you wish. . . .

I assume you will give us a chance to look over the next Van Dine book although I would not want to consider this present agreement a precedent as it is very unusual to make such a guarantee on a serial these days.

Yours sincerely,
Henry M. Snevily
[a representative of the
Bell Syndicate]

June 3, 1930

Dear Mr. Wheeler [president of the Bell Syndicate]:

On "The Greene Murder Case" you paid us $3,000, and on "The Bishop" $2,000. There seems to be a very great demand for "The Scarab" although I have not yet invited any bids except from you. I shall have to write to these various syndicates and ask them to submit bids, and then I shall have to give it to the highest bidder. If you think your bid is all right, all right, but if somebody else bids $2,500 or $3,000, you can see that I shall have to give it to them, and I would get into no end of trouble if I took offers and then went back to you for a counter offer. In the circumstances we would rather you had the book, and in fact we have always found it pleasant to deal with you anyway, and I wished to inform you how the situation looked in advance, if only to enable you to understand it if we gave the book to someone else.

Ever sincerely yours,
[Maxwell Perkins]

The Bell Syndicate increased its bid to $2,500, which was the highest.

April 29, 1933

Dear Willard:

I have tried all the syndicates. I can get from none of them any offer with a guarantee attached.- Only a fifty-fifty division [of net profits]. In view of this, unless you do not want to syndicate at all, I think that it would be best to give it [*The Kennel Murder Case*] to the Bell which is the most efficient and reliable of the lot, barring the N.E.A. which would only run first-run serials and so is not interested.

Always yours,
[Maxwell Perkins]

Wright insisted on, and received, a fifty-fifty division of gross returns from the Bell Syndicate.

November 11, 1933

Dear Mr. Perkins:

. . . Can you not, just to try us out, let us have the story [*The Dragon Murder Case*] on a 50/50 basis with a guarantee of $1000. This is the most we have ever had to guarantee any one serial novel in the whole history of the syndicate. . . .

A great sales advantage that we can offer you is our practice of recanvassing on each big serial year after year. This month we are selling serials that we announced ten years ago.

Do give us a trial at this new release of my favorite detective-story writer, Mr. Wright.

Very sincerely yours,
J. E. Watkins
[manager of the
Ledger Syndicate]

Oct. 30, 1936

Dear Mr. Graves [Ralph H. Graves, a literary rights agent]:

I think if you can give the five hundred dollar guarantee on "The Kidnap Murder Case" you can count upon having it, because the Bell did not give us a guarantee on the last previous book, and I think I would be justified in taking a better offer than their regular division. Before the depression we got as high guarantees on Van Dine as three thousand, but conditions are different now. . . .

Sincerely yours,
[Maxwell Perkins]

Feb. 15, 1937

Dear Mr. Perkins:

. . . I realize that the result was disappointing in contrast to sales in the old days but the serial market has materially changed. You now pretty nearly have to have a story written especially for newspaper publication with short installments deliberately planned with a climax at the end of each installment. At least we have found this to be the case with our papers. It was for this reason that when you telephoned about the last Van Dine serial I did not feel we ought to take it on because I felt that the results would be disappointing. . .

Yours sincerely,
Henry M. Snevily

LETTERS:
Telegram from Wright to Maxwell Perkins, 22 July 1931; letter from Wright to Perkins, 16 September 1932.

Of the many favors asked of Perkins by Scribner authors, these two by Wright were among the more reasonable since they related directly to his work.

DEAR MAX WILL YOU BE GOOD ENOUGH TO SEND ME TO LOSANGELES IMMEDIATELY THE EARLY CERAMIC WARES OF CHINA BY HETHERINGTON AND THE LATER CERAMIC WARES OF CHINA BY HOBSON STOP I NEED BOTH OF THESE BOOKS AS SOON AS POSSIBLE FOR DATA WHICH I AM USING IN THE KENNEL MURDER CASE STOP I AM GETTING MY WORK PRETTY WELL IN SHAPE HERE AND IT WONT BE MORE THAN A COUPLE OF WEEKS BEFORE I WILL BE ABLE TO RE-

TO THE LITERARY EDITOR: The following signed article by Mr. Van Dine may be used, either as a whole or in part, on or after May 10th.

Charles Scribner's Sons.

LITERARY SLEUTHING

The Creator of Philo Vance Sets Down Twenty Rules for Writing Detective Stories

By S. S. VAN DINE
AUTHOR OF "THE GREENE MURDER CASE"

The detective story is a kind of intellectual game. It is more,—it is a sporting event. And the author must play fair with the reader. He can no more resort to trickeries and deceptions and still retain his honesty than if he cheated in a bridge game. He must outwit the reader, and hold the reader's interest, through sheer ingenuity. For the writing of detective stories there are very definite laws—unwritten, perhaps, but none the less binding; and every respectable and self-respecting concocter of literary mysteries lives up to them. Herewith, then, is a sort of Credo, based partly on the practice of all the great writers of detective stories, and partly on the promptings of the honest author's inner conscience. To wit:

1. The reader must have equal opportunity with the detective for solving the mystery. All clews must be plainly stated and described.

2. No wilful tricks or deceptions may be placed on the reader other than those played legitimately by the criminal on the detective himself.

3. There must be no love interest. The business in hand is to bring a criminal to the bar of justice, not to bring a lovelorn couple to the hymeneal altar.

4. The detective himself, or one of the official investigators, should never turn out to be the culprit. This is bald trickery, on a par with offering some one a bright penny for a five-dollar gold piece. It's false pretenses.

5. The culprit must be determined by logical deductions—not by accident or coincidence or unmotivated confession. To solve a criminal problem in this latter fashion is like sending the reader on a deliberate wild-goose chase, and then telling him, after he has failed, that you had the object of his search up your sleeve all the time. Such an author is no better than a practical joker.

6. The detective novel must have a detective in it; and a detective is not a detective unless he detects. His function is to gather clews that will eventually lead to the person who did the dirty work in the first chapter; and if the detective does not reach his conclusions through an analysis of those clews, he has no more solved his problem than the schoolboy who gets his answer out of the back of the arithmetic.

7. There simply must be a corpse in a detective novel, and the deader the corpse the better. No lesser crime than murder will suffice. Three hundred pages is far too much pother for a crime other than murder. After all, the reader's trouble and expenditure of energy must be rewarded.

8. The problem of the crime must be solved by strictly naturalistic means. Such methods for learning the truth as slate-writing, ouija-boards, mind-reading, spiritualistic séances, crystal-gazing, and the like, are taboo. A reader has a chance when matching his wits with a rationalistic detective, but if he must compete with the world of spirits and go chasing about the fourth dimension of metaphysics, he is defeated *ab initio*.

9. There must be but one detective—that is, but one protagonist of deduction—one *deus ex machina*. To bring the minds of three or four, or sometimes a gang of detectives to bear on a problem, is not only to disperse the interest and break the direct thread of logic, but to take an unfair advantage of the reader. If there is more than one detective the reader doesn't know who his co-deductor is. It's like making the reader run a race with a relay team.

10. The culprit must turn out to be a person who has played a more or less prominent part in the story—that is, a person with whom the reader is familiar and in whom he takes an interest.

11. Servants must not be chosen by the author as the culprit. This is begging a noble question. It is a too easy solution. The culprit must be a decidedly worth-while person—one that wouldn't ordinarily come under suspicion.

12. There must be but one culprit, no matter how many murders are committed. The culprit may, of course, have a minor helper or co-plotter; but the entire onus must rest on one pair of shoulders: the entire indignation of the reader must be permitted to concentrate on a single black nature.

13. Secret societies, camorras, mafias, *et al.*, have no place in a detective story. A fascinating and truly beautiful murder is irremediably spoiled by any such wholesale culpability. To be sure, the murderer in a detective novel should be given a sporting chance; but it is going too far to grant him a secret society to fall back on. No high-class, self-respecting murderer would want such odds.

14. The method of murder, and the means of detecting it, must be rational and scientific. That is to say, pseudo-science and purely imaginative and speculative devices are not to be tolerated in the *roman policier*. Once an author soars into the realm of fantasy, in the Jules Verne manner, he is outside the bounds of detective fiction, cavorting in the unchartered reaches of adventure.

15. The truth of the problem must at all times be apparent—provided the reader is shrewd enough to see it. By this I mean that if the reader, after learning the explanation for the crime, should reread the book, he would see that the solution had, in a sense, been staring him in the face—that all the clews really pointed to the culprit—and that, if he had been as clever as the detective, he could have solved the mystery himself without going on to the final chapter. That the clever reader does often thus solve the problem goes without saying.

16. A detective novel should contain no long descriptive passages, no literary dallying with side-issues, no subtly worked-out character analyses, no "atmospheric" preoccupations. Such matters have no vital place in a record of crime and deduction. They hold up the action, and introduce issues irrelevant to the main purpose, which is to state a problem, analyse it, and bring it to a successful conclusion. To be sure, there must be a sufficient descriptiveness and character delineation to give the novel verisimilitude.

17. A professional criminal must never be shouldered with the guilt of a crime in a detective story. Crimes by house-breakers and bandits are the province of the police departments—not of authors and brilliant amateur detectives. A really fascinating crime is one committed by a pillar of a church, or a spinster noted for her charities.

18. A crime in a detective story must never turn out to be an accident or a suicide. To end an odyssey of sleuthing with such an anti-climax is to hoodwink the trusting and kind-hearted reader.

19. The motives for all crimes in detective stories should be personal. International plottings and war politics belong in a different category of fiction—in secret-service tales, for instance. But a murder story must be kept *gemütlich*, so to speak. It must reflect the reader's everyday experiences, and give him a certain outlet for his own repressed desires and emotions.

20. And (to give my Credo an even score of items) I herewith list a few of the devices which no self-respecting detective-story writer will now avail himself of. They have been employed too often, and are familiar to all true lovers of literary crime. To use them is a confession of the author's ineptitude and lack of originality. (*a*) Determining the identity of the culprit by comparing the butt of a cigarette left at the scene of the crime with the brand smoked by a suspect. (*b*) The bogus spiritualistic séance to frighten the culprit into giving himself away. (*c*) Forged finger-prints. (*d*) The dummy-figure alibi. (*e*) The dog that does not bark and thereby reveals the fact that the intruder is familiar. (*f*) The final pinning of the crime on a twin, or a relative who looks exactly like the suspected, but innocent, person. (*g*) The hypodermic syringe and the knockout drops. (*h*) The commission of the murder in a locked room after the police have actually broken in. (*i*) The word-association test for guilt. (*j*) The cipher, or code letter, which is eventually unravelled by the sleuth.

Scribners' promotional use of Van Dine's "famous" twenty rules for writing detective stories, circulated to trade journals and newspapers after the publication of The Greene Murder Case *in the spring of 1928*

TURN EAST STOP MY VERY BEST WISHES AND SINCEREST REGARDS ALWAYS=
WILLARD HUNTINGTON WRIGHT.

Dear Max,

Here's the passage. Please have it put in perfectly swell high-class academic German—the kind a professor of criminology would write. It must be done by a German professor—not an American-German—as the series of books from which this passage is supposed to be taken is written by pundits. It is not absolutely necessary that the German is a literal translation, as Vance is supposed to read it from the original at sight, and therefore certain liberties are permissible, but the German text should follow as closely as possible the passage I am enclosing.

Could I get this within a week? . . .

As ever,
Willard

Perkins had a professor at Barnard College translate the passage and returned it five days later.

RELATED LETTERS:
Letter from Douglas M. Hoffecker to Scribners, 28 February 1932; letter from Maxwell Perkins, 29 February 1932, in reply.

Perkins agrees with a reader's theory that the success of Wright's detective novels is due to their quality, but he also associates Wright with the younger, relevant authors who "have struck the note" to which the public can respond in this time of rapidly changing values.

Gentlemen:

Could you advise me the approximate volume of sales of "The Benson Murder Case" by S. S. Van Dine (both exclusive and inclusive of reprint sales, if possible)?

Also, is it not correct that this story was not serialized in any magazine?

I'm doing an article on detective fiction and wish to establish that good work will sell in large volume irrespective of whether the author be known and irrespective of whether he has had any previous publicity, such as serialization. "Benson Murder" was Van Dine's first detective novel and at that time his identity as W. H. Wright was unknown to the reading public, yet his book had a deservedly good sale. To be sure, he had written previous works, but not under his newly assumed pseudonym.

Your book shop representative informed me yesterday afternoon (Saturday) that they felt sure you would be glad to furnish this data and suggested that I write, inasmuch as your office was closed when I called.

Thanking you in advance for your courtesy, I am

Very truly yours,
Douglas M. Hoffecker

Dear Mr. Hoffecker:

"The Benson Murder Case" by S. S. Van Dine was never serialized. Its sale was approximately 150,000 copies.- But that is a smaller sale than any of his other books, and very much smaller than the sale of "The Greene Murder Case" and "The Canary Murder Case." It is also true that a large proportion of "The Benson" sale came after the appearance of "The Canary," which was what we counted on.

At the same time, your main argument is sound, in my opinion. In recent years-although the old-time writers like Tarkington [Booth Tarkington], who got established twenty years ago or more, still outsold most of the new ones in actual volume-the recent big sellers have been of first novelists' who had nothing to go on at all but the quality of their work.- And not a few of them have had a greater success with their first novels than with later ones. I think though, that this was not so true in the old days when conditions were more static. But in recent, rapidly changing years when all values were being revalued, the older ones have rapidly become irrelevant in respect to their subject and their philosophy, and the younger ones have been those who struck the note to which the public responded, because their reactions were to life as it is today and were consequently relevant to life as it is lived by people today.

Ever truly yours,
[Maxwell Perkins]

LETTER:
Letter from Maxwell Perkins to Frederic A. Burlingame, a partner in the legal firm that handled Scribners' affairs, 14 April 1938.

Wright's last fully embellished Philo Vance story was an unusual attempt to utilize the characters of two well-known radio personalities, Gracie Allen and George Burns—to incorporate their professional personae—in his detective fiction. This experiment required careful legal review.

PARAMOUNT FAMOUS LASKY CORPORATION

Paramount Pictures

WEST COAST STUDIOS · 5451 MARATHON STREET

HOLLYWOOD · CALIFORNIA

October 13, 1928.

Dear Max:

They have me working day and night here, with hardly enough time to sleep and eat, but we'll be through in a week or two and then I'll get that rest I came three thousand miles to take.

I couldn't finish reading the proof of the Bishop on the train. It was in terrible condition and I had to go through it almost letter by letter. Some time next week, however, I'll clean it up and send it to you. I know you're in no great rush for it so it won't make much difference.

This is a wild, febrile life and I'll thank my various tutelary gods when the picture is, according to the Hollywood venacular, 'in the sack'. Incidentally, you may be interested to know that it is a damn good picture -- much better than I imagined possible. Everyone here, including myself, thinks it will be a great success. I am helping out on the dialogue and this is what takes my time. Otherwise, I'm feeling much better -- the work is a change from my regular routine and, like golf and mendicancy, it keeps one out in the open.

Give my best to Jack and tell Darrow I'll drop him a line as soon as I get a breathing spell.

This note is being dictated between shots.

My warmest regards always.

Sincerely,

Willad

Letter from Wright to his editor, Maxwell Perkins, while working in Hollywood on the film version of his detective novel The "Canary" Murder Case. *The "Bishop" is a reference to his most recently completed Philo Vance novel,* The Bishop Murder Case, *which Scribners would publish in February 1929.*

Dear Fred:

Our friend S. S. Van Dine has left with me the two enclosed permissions in reference to a book he intends to write under the title of "The Gracie Allen Murder Case." It is later going to be made into a motion-picture play, in which she is to appear, but this does not concern us.

The clause that concerns us is No. 2 which seems to me to be just the normal lawyers wording and only refers to their <u>personal</u> characters, not their professional characters. If you have ever heard Gracie Allen over the radio you will realize that in her professional character she does hold herself up to public ridicule, in being a ridiculously stupid girl, and in the book she naturally would be impersonated in the same way.

The question seems to me to be whether in accepting these consents some covering letter ought to be attached explaining that Van Dine understands that while nothing should appear that would be libellous, etcetera, to them personally, he understands that their consent gives him permission to portray them in the same general farcical manner that their professional radio programs are carried out.

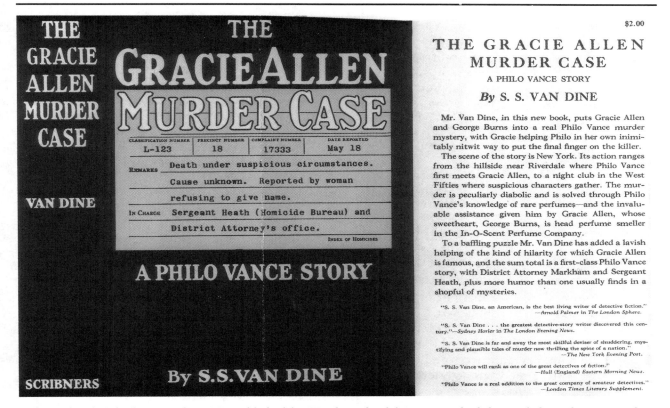

$2.00

THE GRACIE ALLEN
MURDER CASE

A PHILO VANCE STORY

By S. S. VAN DINE

Mr. Van Dine, in this new book, puts Gracie Allen and George Burns into a real Philo Vance murder mystery, with Gracie helping Philo in her own inimitably nitwit way to put the final finger on the killer.

The scene of the story is New York. Its action ranges from the hillside near Riverdale where Philo Vance first meets Gracie Allen, to a night club in the West Fifties where suspicious characters gather. The murder is peculiarly diabolic and is solved through Philo Vance's knowledge of rare perfumes—and the invaluable assistance given him by Gracie Allen, whose sweetheart, George Burns, is head perfume smeller in the In-O-Scent Perfume Company.

To a baffling puzzle Mr. Van Dine has added a lavish helping of the kind of hilarity for which Gracie Allen is famous, and the sum total is a first-class Philo Vance story, with District Attorney Markham and Sergeant Heath, plus more humor than one usually finds in a shopful of mysteries.

"S. S. Van Dine, an American, is the best living writer of detective fiction."
—Arnold Palmer in *The London Sphere.*

"S. S. Van Dine . . . the greatest detective-story writer discovered this century."—Sydney Horler in *The London Evening News.*

"S. S. Van Dine is far and away the most skilful deviser of shuddering, mystifying and plausible tales of murder now thrilling the spine of a nation."
—*The New York Evening Post.*

"Philo Vance will rank as one of the great detectives of fiction."
—Hull (England) *Eastern Morning News.*

"Philo Vance is a real addition to the great company of amateur detectives."
—*London Times Literary Supplement.*

Dust jacket for the last novel (1938) published by Wright in his lifetime, in which he used the radio personalities of the popular husband-and-wife comic team of Gracie Allen and George Burns

I would not bother you personally with all this but Van Dine has gotten himself all worked up about it.

Yours sincerely,
[Maxwell Perkins]

PREFACE:

Draft of the preface Maxwell Perkins wrote for Wright's posthumously published *The Winter Murder Case.*

It was characteristic of Willard Huntington Wright, known to the great public as S. S. Van Dine, that when he died suddenly on April 11, 1939, he left "The Winter Murder Case" in the stage in which it is published, complete to the last comma. Everything he ever did was done that way, accurately, thoroughly, and with consideration for other people. It was so with the entire series of the Philo Vance mysteries.

He has himself told the story in an article called, "I Used to Be a Highbrow, and Look at Me Now"- how he had worked as a critic of literature and art, and an editor, since he left Harvard in 1907. And this he had done with great distinction, but with no material reward to speak of,- certainly no accumulation of money. When the war came it seemed to him that all he had believed in and was working for was rushing into ruin,- and now, twenty-five years later, can anyone say he was wrong? There were other influences at work on him perhaps, but no one who knew Willard and the purity of his perceptions in art, and his devotion to what he thought was the meaning of our civilization as expressed in the arts, can doubt that the shattering disillusionment and the ruin of the war was what brought him at last to a nervous breakdown which incapacitated him for several years. He would never have explained it so, or any other way. He made no explanations, or excuses, ever, and his many apologies were out of the kindness of a heart so concealed by reticence that only a handful ever knew how gentle it really was. So at last all that he had done and aimed to do seemed to have come to ruin, and he himself too.

Only a gallant spirit could have risen up from that downfall, and gallantry alone would not have been enough. But Willard had also intellect-even despair could not suppress it-which worked on anything at hand. One might believe that if his fate had been solitary confinement he would have emerged with some biological discovery based on the rats that infested his cell. Anyhow, his doctor finally conceded to his demands for literature, that he could read mysteries, which he had never done before. The result was, that as he had studied painting, literature and philosophy, he now involuntarily studied and then consciously analyzed, the mystery story. And when he recovered he had mastered it.

He was then heavily into debt, but he thought he saw the possibility of freeing himself from obligations a nature of his integrity could not ignore, or in fact endure, by what he had learned in his illness. He wrote out at some ten thousand words each, the plots of his first three murder cases, thought through to the last detail, footnotes and all, and brought them to the Century Club to a lunch with an editor of the publishing house that put all of them before the public.

This editor knew little about mystery stories, which had not been much in vogue since Sherlock Holmes, but he knew Willard Wright. He knew from far back in Harvard that whatever this man did would be done well, and the reasonable terms-granting the writer's talent-that Willard proposed were quickly accepted.

It is now Thirteen years since Philo Vance stepped out into the world to solve the Benson Murder Case, and with that and the eleven others that followed, to delight hundreds of thousands of readers, hard pressed by the anxieties and afflictions of a tragic decade. Each of these famous cases began, as the first three began, with a long synopsis-about ten thousand words-letter perfect and complete to that point in its development. After the first three of these, the publisher never saw any, nor wanted to, for he knew beyond peradventure that the finished book would be another masterpiece in its kind. Nor did he ever see the second stage of development, but only the third, the final manuscript,- and that he read with the interest and pleasure of any reader, and with no professional anxieties. But this second stage in the infinitely painstaking development of the story was some 30,000 words long, and it lacked only the final elaboration of character, dialogue, and atmosphere. "The Winter Murder Case" represents this stage in S. S. Van Dine's progress to completion, and if the plot moves faster to its culmination than in the earlier books, it is for that reason.

They say now that Philo Vance was made in the image of S. S. Van Dine, and although Willard smoked not regies but denicotined cigarettes, there were resemblances. Both were infinitely neat in dress, equally decorous and considerate in manners, and Vance had Willard's amazingly vast and accurate knowledge of a thousand arts and subjects, and his humorously skeptical attitude toward life and society. But in fact the resemblance would stand for only those with a superficial knowledge of Willard Huntington Wright. Vance in so far as he was Wright, was perhaps the form under which a gallant, sensitive, gentle man concealed a spirit almost too delicate and sensitive for an age so turbulent and crude as this. Willard was not one to wear his heart upon his sleeve;- but there were daws enough to pick, as there always are, and they found it where his friends always knew it to be, near the surface, and quick to respond.

At the request of Wright's widow, reflecting what she believed would be his wish, The Winter Murder Case *was published on Friday the 13th (October 1939).*

Thomas Wolfe (1900–1938)

Thomas Wolfe at the door of his mother's boardinghouse at 48 Spruce Street in Asheville, North Carolina, made famous as "Dixieland" in his first novel, Look Homeward, Angel

With the publication of his story "Angel on the Porch" in the August 1929 issue of *Scribner's Magazine,* the house announced the arrival of a "new writer about whom much will be heard." In the remaining nine years of his life, Wolfe fulfilled that expectation with the millions of words he organized into four highly autobiographical novels: *Look Homeward, Angel* (1929) and *Of Time and the River* (1935)—with the legendary and controversial help, guidance, and support of his Scribner editor, Maxwell Perkins—and, posthumously, *The Web and the Rock* (1939) and *You Can't Go Home Again* (1940), edited by Edward Aswell at Harper. Wolfe was brought up in his mother's boardinghouse, "My Old Kentucky Home," in Asheville, North Carolina, the youngest of eight (six surviving) children. He entered the University of North Carolina at the age of sixteen; upon graduation in 1920, he studied playwriting under George Pierce Baker in the famous 47 Workshop in the Harvard Graduate School, receiving an M.A. in English in 1922. Unsuccessful with his plays, he began writing his first novel in England in 1926, while abroad on the second of seven European trips. Yet, however much Wolfe traveled, himself, his family, his friends, his childhood town, and his America remained the preoccupation of most of his writing. He has been called the Walt Whitman of fiction for his egocentric "song"—and likened to Dostoyevsky for his brooding depths and to Dickens for the passionate spirit and vivid portraiture of his narrative. With F. Scott Fitzgerald and Ernest Hemingway, Wolfe completes the triad of geniuses that Scribners nurtured in the Twenties upon whose fiction most of its twentieth-century publishing laurels rest.

Scribner Books by Wolfe

1929	*Look Homeward, Angel: A Story of the Buried Life* (edition illustrated by Douglas W. Gorsline, 1947)
1935	*Of Time and the River: A Legend of Man's Hunger in His Youth*
	From Death to Morning

1936   *The Story of a Novel*

1939   *The Face of a Nation: Poetical Passages from the Writings of Thomas Wolfe*, decorations by Edward Shenton

1943   *Thomas Wolfe's Letters to His Mother, Julia Elizabeth Wolfe*, edited with an introduction by John Skally Terry

1945   *A Stone, A Leaf, A Door: Poems by Thomas Wolfe*, selected and arranged in verse by John S. Barnes, with a foreword by Louis Untermeyer

1956   *The Letters of Thomas Wolfe*, collected and edited, with an introduction and explanatory text, by Elizabeth Nowell

1961   *The Short Novels of Thomas Wolfe*, edited, with an introduction and notes by C. Hugh Holman

1962   *The Thomas Wolfe Reader*, edited, with an introduction and notes, by Holman

1965   *Of Time and the River: Young Faustus* [and] *Telemachus*, with an introduction by Holman

1987   *The Complete Short Stories of Thomas Wolfe*, edited by Francis E. Skipp, foreword by James Dickey

---

LETTER:

"Note for the Publisher's Reader," which Wolfe wrote to accompany the submission of his recently completed novel, "O, Lost" (*Look Homeward, Angel*) to a publisher, [March 1928].

This book, by my estimate, is from 250,000 to 280,000 words long. A book of this length from an unknown writer no doubt is rashly experimental, and shows his ignorance of the mechanics of publishing. That is true: this is my first book.

But I believe it would be unfair to assume that because this is a very long book it is too long a book. A revision would, I think, shorten it somewhat. But I do not believe any amount of revision would make it a short book. It could be shortened by scenes, by pages, by thousands of words. But it could not be shortened by half, or a third, or a quarter.

There are some pages here which were compelled by a need for fullness of expression, and which had importance when the book was written not because they made part of its essential substance, but because, by setting them forth, the mind was released for its basic work of creation. These pages have done their work of catharsis, and may now be excised. But their excision would not make a short book.

It does not seem to me that the book is overwritten. Whatever comes out of it must come out block by block and not sentence by sentence. Generally, I do not believe the writing to be wordy, prolix, or redundant. And separate scenes are told with as much brevity and economy as possible. But the book covers the life of a large family intensively for a period of twenty years, and in rapid summary for fifty years. And the book tries to describe not only the visible outer lives of all these people, but even more their buried lives.

The book may be lacking in plot but it is not lacking in plan. The plan is rigid and densely woven. There are two essential movements—one outward and one downward. The outward movement describes the effort of a child, a boy, and a youth for release, freedom, and loneliness in new lands. The movement of experience is duplicated by a series of widening concentric circles, three of which are represented by the three parts of the book. The downward movement is represented by a constant excavation into the buried life of a group of people, and describes the cyclic curve of a family's life—genesis, union, decay, and dissolution.

To me, who was joined so passionately with the people in this book, it seemed that they were the greatest people I had ever known and the texture of their lives the richest and strangest; and discounting the distortion of judgment that my nearness to them would cause, I think they would seem extraordinary to anyone. If I could get my magnificent people on paper as it were, if I could get down something of their strangeness and richness in my book, I believed that no one would object to my 250,000 words; or, that if my pages swarmed with this rich life few would damn an inept manner and accuse me of not knowing the technique for making a book, as practiced by Balzac, or Flaubert, or Hardy, or Gide. If I have failed to get any of this opulence into my book, the fault lies not in my people—who could make an epic—but in me.

But that is what I wanted to do and tried to do. This book was written in simpleness and nakedness of soul. When I began to write the book twenty months ago I got back something of a child's innocence and wonder. You may question this later when you come to the dirty words. But the dirty words can come out quickly—if the book has any chance of publication, they will come out without conscience or compunction. For the rest, I wrote it innocently and passionately. It has in it much that to me is painful and ugly, but, without sentimentality or dishonesty, it seems to me, because I am a romantic, that pain has an inevitable fruition in beauty. And the book has in it sin and terror and darkness—the dark, the evil, the forbidden. But I believe it has many other things as well, and I wrote it with strong joy, without counting the costs, for I was sure at the time that the whole of my intention—which was to come simply and unsparingly to naked life, and to tell all of my story without affectation or lewdness —would be apparent. At that time I believed it was possible to write of all things, so long as it was honestly done. So far as I know there is not a nasty scene in the book,—but there are the dirty words, and always a casual and unimpeded vision of everything.

When I wrote the book I seized with delight everything that would give it color and richness. All the variety and madness of my people—the leper taint, the cruel waste, the dark flowering evil of life I wrote about with as much exultancy as health, sanity, joy.

It is, of course, obvious that the book is "autobiographical." But, in a literal sense, it is probably no more autobiographical than Gulliver's Travels. There is scarcely a scene that has its base in literal fact. The book is fiction—it is loaded with invention: story, fantasy, vision. But it is a fiction that is, I believe, more true than fact—a fiction that grew out of a life completely digested in my spirit, a fiction which telescopes, condenses, and objectifies all the random or incompleted gestures of life—which tries to comprehend people, in short, not by telling what people did, but what they should have done. The most literal and autobiographical part of the book, therefore, is its picture of the buried life.

First page of Wolfe's first appearance in a major magazine (Scribner's Magazine, August 1929). *This story was part of* Look Homeward, Angel, *published two months later.*

The most exact thing in it is its fantasy—its picture of a child's soul.

I have never called this book a novel. To me it is a book such as all men may have in them. It is a book made out of my life, and it represents my vision of life to my twentieth year.

What merit it has I do not know. It sometimes seems to me that it presents a strange and deep picture of American life—one that I have never seen elsewhere; and that I may have some hope of publication. I do not know; I am very close to it. I want to find out about it, and to be told by someone else about it.

I am assured that this book will have a good reading by an intelligent person in a publishing house. I have written all this, not to propitiate you, for I have no peddling instinct, but entreat you, if you spend the many hours necessary for a careful reading, to spend a little more time in giving me an opinion. If it is not a good book, why? If parts are good and parts are bad, what are

Memorandum of Agreement, made this — ninth — day of **January** 19 29

between THOMAS WOLFE

of **New York City, N.Y.,** — — hereinafter called "the AUTHOR,"

and CHARLES SCRIBNER'S SONS, of New York City, N. Y., hereinafter called "the PUBLISHERS." Said — — **Thomas Wolfe** — — being the AUTHOR and PROPRIETOR of a work entitled: ~~O LOST~~ *published as → LOOK HOMEWARD, ANGEL*

in consideration of the covenants and stipulations hereinafter contained, and agreed to be performed by the PUBLISHERS, grants and guarantees to said PUBLISHERS and their successors the exclusive right to publish the said work in all forms **in the United States and Canada after first serialization** during the terms of copyright and renewals thereof, hereby covenanting with said PUBLISHERS that he is the sole AUTHOR and PROPRIETOR of said work.

Said AUTHOR hereby authorizes said PUBLISHERS to take out the copyright on said work, and further guarantees to said PUBLISHERS that the said work is in no way whatever a violation of any copyright belonging to any other party, and that it contains nothing of a scandalous or libelous character; and that he and **his** legal representatives shall and will hold harmless the said PUBLISHERS from all suits, and all manner of claims and proceedings which may be taken on the ground that said work is such violation or contains anything scandalous or libelous; and he further hereby authorizes said PUBLISHERS to defend at law any and all suits and proceedings which may be taken or had against them for infringement of any other copyright or for libel, scandal, or any other injurious or hurtful matter or thing contained in or alleged or claimed to be contained in or caused by said work, and pay to said PUBLISHERS such reasonable costs, disbursements, expenses, and counsel fees as they may incur in such defense.

Said PUBLISHERS, in consideration of the right herein granted and of the guarantees aforesaid, agree to publish said work at their own expense, in such style and manner as they shall deem most expedient, and to pay said AUTHOR, or — **his** — legal representatives, **TEN (10)** — per cent. on their Trade-List (retail) price, cloth style, for **the first Two Thousand (2000) copies of said work sold by them in the United States and FIFTEEN (15) per cent. for all copies sold thereafter.** Provided, nevertheless, that one-half the above named royalty shall be paid on all copies sold outside the United States; and provided that no percentage whatever shall be paid on any copies destroyed by fire or water, or sold at or below cost, or given away for the purpose of aiding the sale of said work.

It is further agreed that the profits arising from any publication of said work, during the period covered by this agreement, in other than book form shall be divided equally between said PUBLISHERS and said AUTHOR.

Scribners' publishing contract with Wolfe for his first book, Look Homeward, Angel, *showing his original title ("O lost, and by the wind grieved, ghost, come back again")*

Expenses incurred for alterations in type or plates, exceeding twenty per cent. of the cost of composition and electrotyping said work, are to be charged to the AUTHOR's account.

The first statement shall not be rendered until six months after date of publication; and thereafter statements shall be rendered semi-annually, on the AUTHOR's application therefor, in the months of February and August; settlements to be made in cash, four months after date of statement.

If, on the expiration of **five** *years from date of publication, or at any time thereafter, the demand for said work should not, in the opinion of said PUBLISHERS, be sufficient to render its publication profitable, then, upon written notice by said PUBLISHERS to said AUTHOR, this contract shall cease and determine; and thereupon said AUTHOR shall have the right, at* **his** *option, to take from said PUBLISHERS, at cost, whatever copies of said work they may then have on hand; or, failing to take said copies at cost, then said PUBLISHERS shall have the right to dispose of the copies on hand as they may see fit, free from any percentage or royalty, and to cancel this contract.*

Provided, also, that if, at any time during the continuance of this agreement, said work shall become unsalable in the ordinary channels of trade, said PUBLISHERS shall have the right to dispose of any copies on hand paying to said AUTHOR — **fifteen (15)** — *per cent. of the net amount received therefor, in lieu of the percentage hereinbefore prescribed.*

Said Publishers shall pay to said Author the Sum of FIVE HUNDRED ($500.) DOLLARS (the receipt of which is hereby acknowledged) as an advance payment on the royalty account, said amount to be reimbursed to said Publishers from the first monies accruing under said royalties.

All monies due under this contract shall be paid to Mrs. Ernest Boyd, 131 East 19th Street, New York City, as representative of said author, and her receipt shall be a valid discharge for all said monies.

In consideration of the mutuality of this contract, the aforesaid parties agree to all its provisions, and in testimony thereof affix their signatures and seals.

Witness to signature of
Thomas Wolfe

Madeline Boyd

Thomas Wolfe

Witness to signature of
Charles Scribner's Sons

W. D. Watson

Charles Kingsley
G. Charles Scribner
Chairman

{L. S.}

they? If it is not publishable, could it be made so? Out of the great welter of manuscripts that you must read, does this one seem distinguished by any excellence, interest, superior merit?

I need a little honest help. If you are interested enough to finish the book, won't you give it to me?

Aline Bernstein, Wolfe's married lover, undertook to show the novel to publishers for him. The book was rejected outright by Boni and Liveright and by an attorney for Harcourt, Brace before Madeleine Boyd, wife of the writer and critic Ernest Boyd, offered to be its agent, for she was starting her own literary agency. She first submitted it to Covici, Friede, who also rejected it—because of its size. Discouraged, Wolfe went abroad, leaving the marketing of the manuscript in Mrs. Boyd's hands.

RELATED LETTERS:

Oct. 22, 1928

Dear Mr. Wolfe:

Mrs. Ernest Boyd left with us some weeks ago, the manuscript of your novel, "O Lost." I do not know whether it would be possible to work out a plan by which it might be worked into a form publishable by us, but I do know that setting the practical aspects of the matter aside, it is a very remarkable thing, and that no editor could read it without being excited by it, and filled with admiration by many passages in it, and sections of it.

Your letter that came with it shows that you realize what difficulties it presents, so that I need not enlarge upon this side of the question. What we should like to know is whether you will be in New York in a fairly near future, when we can see you and discuss the manuscript. We should certainly look forward to such an interview with very great interest.

Ever truly yours,
[Maxwell Perkins]

Vienna, Saturday Nov 17, 1928

Dear Mr. Perkins:

Your letter of October 22 which was addressed to Munich, was sent on to me here. I have been in Budapest for several weeks and came back last night. I got your letter at Cook's this morning.

Mrs Ernest Boyd wrote me a few weeks ago that she was coming abroad, and said that you had my book. I wrote her to Paris but have not heard from her yet.

I can't tell you how good your letter has made me feel. Your words of praise have filled me with hope, and are worth more than their weight in diamonds to me. Sometimes, I suppose, praise does more harm than good, but this time it was badly needed, whether deserved or not.—I came abroad over four months ago determined to put the other book out of my mind, and to get to work on a new one. Instead, I have filled one notebook after another, my head is swarming with ideas—but I have written nothing that looks like a book yet. In Munich I did write thirty or forty thousand words, then I got my head and my nose broken, and began to have things happen thick and fast with a great many people, including the police. I have learned to read German fairly well, and have learned something of their multitudinous books. But I had indigestion from seeing and trying to take in too much, and I was depressed at my failure to settle down to work. Now I feel better. I have decided to come back to New York in December, and I shall come to see you very soon after my arrival.

I have not looked at my book since I gave a copy to Mrs. Boyd. At the time I realized the justice of all people said—particularly the impossibility of printing it in its present form and length. But at that time I was "written out" on it—I could not go back and revise. Now I believe I can come back to it with a much fresher and more critical feeling. I have no right to expect others to do for me what I should do for myself, but, although I am able to criticize wordiness and over-abundance in others, I am not able practically to criticize it in myself. The business of selection and of revision is simply hell for me—my efforts to cut

> I'm still jogging on with 'Look Homeward, Angel'. It strikes me, & strikes me hard not as a novel, hardly as a book but as a great inchoate bellow of the human soul. I don't know where he'll end but I have an uneasy feeling that the little fellows had better move over for this bird. But whether I mean the little fellows on Parnassus or on Blackwell's Island I don't yet know. I only know somebody's got to move. And on personal grounds there's no writer I'd rather move over or down for myself. Although there will be no question of volunteering. It will be a case of the brewer's big horses.
>
> — Novelist James Boyd in a letter to Maxwell Perkins, 25 November 1929

out 50,000 words may sometimes result in my adding 75,000.

As for the obscene passages and the dirty words, I know perfectly well that no publisher could print them. Yet, I swear to you, it all seemed to me very easy and practical when I wrote them. But already I have begun to write a long letter to you, when all I should do is to thank you for your letter and say when I am coming back. Then the other things can come out when I see you.

But your letter has given me new hope for the book—I have honestly always felt that there are parts of it of which I need not be ashamed, and which might justify some more abiding form. I want you to know that you have no very stiff-necked person to deal with as regards the book—I shall probably agree with most of the criticisms, although I hope that my own eagerness and hopefulness will not lead me into a weak acquiescence to everything.

I want the direct criticism and advice of an older and more critical person. I wonder if at Scribners I can find someone who is interested enough to talk over the whole huge Monster with me—part by part. Most people will say "it's too long," "it's got to be cut," "parts have to come out," and so on—but obviously this is no great help to the poor wretch who has done the deed, and who knows all this, without always knowing how he's going to remedy it.

I am sorry that Mrs Boyd sent you the letter that I wrote for the reader. She said it was a very foolish letter, but added cheerfully that I would learn as I grew older. I wish I had so much faith. I told her to tear the letter out of the binding; but if it indicated to you that I did realize some of the difficulties, perhaps it was of some use. And I realize the difficulties more than ever now.

I am looking forward to meeting you, and I am still youthful enough to hope that something may come of it. It will be a strange thing indeed to me if at last I shall manage to make a connection with such a firm as Scribners which, in my profound ignorance of all publishing matters, I had always thought vaguely was a solid and somewhat conservative house. But it may be that I am a conservative and at bottom a very correct person. If this is true, I assure you I will have no very great heartache over it, although once it might have caused me trouble. At any rate, I believe I am through with firing off pistols just for the fun of seeing people jump—my new book has gone along for 40,000 words without improprieties of language—and I have not tried for this result.

Please forgive my use of the pencil—in Vienna papers and pen and ink, as well as many other things that abound in our own fortunate country, are doled out bit by bit under guard. I hope you are able to make out my scrawl—which is more than many people do—and that you will not forget about me before I come back.

Cordially yours
Thomas Wolfe

Jan. 8, 1929

Dear Mr. Wolfe:

This is to tell you that we have formally considered "O Lost" and shall be delighted to publish it on the basis of 10% royalty on the first 2,000 copies and of 15% thereafter;- and as soon as we hear that the terms suit you, we shall send a cheque for five hundred dollars as an advance. The question of terms would naturally be taken up with Mrs. Boyd who brought us the book and acts as literary agent. I'd be glad to get into touch with her if she's in New York, or you might do it;- or if she's out of reach, we could make the terms dependent on her approval, which I hardly doubt she would give, and send you the advance immediately. You could simply give us a note accepting provisionally.

Ever sincerely yours,
[Maxwell Perkins]

Harvard Club [New York City] Jan 9, 1929
Dear Mr. Perkins:

I got your letter this morning and I have just come from a talk with Mrs Madeleine Boyd, my literary agent.

I am very happy to accept the terms you offer me for the publication of my book, O Lost. Mrs Boyd is also entirely satisfied.

I am already at work on changes and revisions proposed in the book, and I shall deliver to you the new beginning some time next week.

Although this should be only a business letter I must tell you that I look forward with joy and hope to my connection with Scribner's. To-day—the day of your letter—is a very grand day in my life. I think of my relation to Scribner's thus far with affection and loyalty, and I hope this marks the beginning of a long association that they will not have cause to regret. I have a tremendous lot to learn, but I believe I shall go ahead with it, and I know that there is far better work in me than I have yet done.

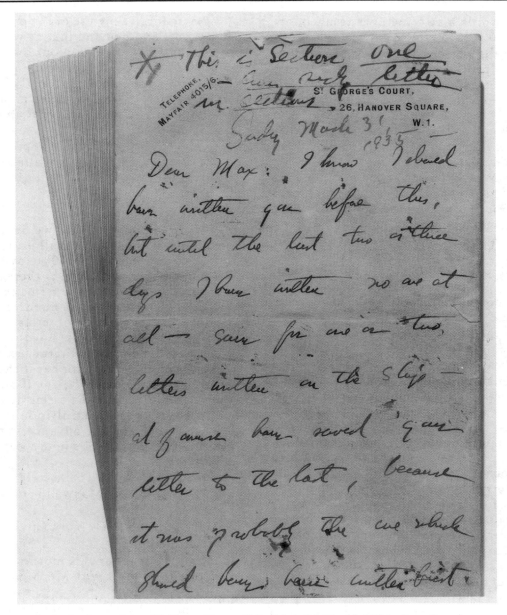

Lengthy letter from Wolfe to Maxwell Perkins, 31 March 1935, from London. Written over the course of a week and mailed in sections, the letter, filling both sides of sixty-six pages of stationery (shown in this half-inch-high stack), expresses Wolfe's gamut of emotions, particularly anxiety, despair, worry, and anger, over the completion and early reception of Of Time and the River. He concludes: "Forget these wild and whirling words—you are the friend I honor and respect more than anyone else."

If you have any communication for me before I see you next, you can reach me at 27 West 15th Street (2nd Floor Rear).

> Faithfully yours,
> Thomas Wolfe

Look Homeward, Angel *was published on 18 October 1929, eleven days before the stock market crashed.*

LETTER:
Letter to Wolfe from Maxwell Perkins, 18 December 1929.

To support himself while writing his second book, Wolfe, at Perkins's suggestion, applied

5 Montague Terrace, Brooklyn,
New York, December 15, 1933.

Mr. Maxwell Perkins
Charles Scribner's Sons
Fifth Avenue @ 48th Street
New York City

Dear Max:

I was pretty tired last night when I delivered that last batch of manuscript to you and could not say very much to you about it. There is not much to say except that today I feel conscious of a good many errors, both of omission and commission and wish I had had more time to arrange and sort out the material, but think it is just as well that I have given it to you even in its present shape.

I don't envy you the job before you. I know what a tough thing it is going to be to tackle, but I do think that even in the form in which the material has been given to you, you ought to be able to make some kind of estimate of its value or lack of value and tell me about it. If you do feel that on the whole I can now go ahead and complete it, I think I can go much faster than you realize. Moreover, when all the scenes have been completed and the narrative change to a third person point of view, I think there will be a much greater sense of unity than now seems possible in spite of the mutilated, hacked-up form in which you have the manuscript, and I do feel decidedly hopeful, and hope your verdict will be for me to go ahead and complete the first draft as soon as I can, and in spite of all the rythms, chants--what you call my dithyrambs--which are all through the manuscript, I think you will find when I get through that there is plenty of narrative--or should I say when you get through-- because I must shame-facedly confess that I need your help now more than I ever did.

You have often said that if I ever gave you something that you could get your hands on and weigh in its entirety from beginning to end, you could pitch in and help me to get out of the woods. Well, now is your chance. I think a very desperate piece of work is ahead for both of us, but if you think it is worth doing and tell me to go ahead, I think there is literally nothing that I cannot accomplish. But you must be honest and straightforward in your criticism when you talk about it, even though what you say may be hard for me to accept after all this work, because that is the only fair way and the only good way in the end.

I want to get back to work on it as soon as I can and will probably go on anyway writing in the missing scenes and getting a complete manuscript as soon as I can. I wanted to write you this mainly to tell you that I am in a state of great trepidation and great hope also. Buried in that great pile of manuscript is some of the best writing I have ever done. Let's see to it that it does not go to waste.

Yours always,
Tom Wolfe

Letter from Wolfe to Maxwell Perkins after delivering the last batch of manuscript for Of Time and the River. *On a separate page, as a postscript, Wolfe added: "Max, I think the total length of the manuscript I gave you is around 500,000 words." Thirteen months later, Perkins would write Wolfe about his experience spent working with him: "But the plain truth is that working on your writings, however it has turned out, for good or bad, has been the greatest pleasure, for all its pain, and the most interesting episode of my editorial life" (21 January 1935).*

for a Guggenheim Fellowship in December 1929. However, since the fellowships were not awarded until March (even if he were to win one), Scribners offered to subsidize him.

Dear Mr. Wolfe:

We are deeply interested in your writing, and have confidence in your future, and we wish to cooperate with you so far as possible toward the production of a new novel. We think you would be able to write it to much better advantage if you were free from the necessity of earning money at the same time, and we should be glad to undertake to pay you, as an advance on the earnings of the next novel, forty-five hundred dollars ($4500) in installments, at the rate of two hundred and fifty dollars ($250) a month, beginning with February first.

We should be glad to draw up a contract with regard to yur next novel whenever you desire, but presumably about February first, which would embody this agreement. We only defer drawing this contract because it is unnecessary so far as we are concerned, since this letter is binding, and also because when February first comes there may be some reason why you would rather have the arrangement made different in some respect. For the present, however, this letter may stand as a definite agreement.

Ever sincerely yours,
[Maxwell Perkins]

On the strength of this letter, Wolfe resigned from his teaching position at New York University's Washington Square College and began drawing upon his monthly subsidy in February. By June, earnings from Look Homeward, Angel *and $2,500 from the Guggenheim Foundation enabled him to discontinue the arrangement.*

LETTER:
Letter from Wolfe to poet and Scribner editor John Hall Wheelock, 24 June 1930, on stationery of the "Writing Room" of the Guaranty Trust Company of New York in Paris.

Wolfe sailed for Europe in May and eventually settled down in Paris, where he began writing sections of a long novel, part of which became Of Time and the River. *Recognizable scenes from it are evident in this letter to Wheelock, who had been following Wolfe's work with a poet's interest and had provided emotional support.*

Written above the letterhead in Wolfe's hand: "Everything moves, everything moves, goes on from place to place, except the women and the everlasting earth"

Dear Jack:

Thanks very much for your fine letter—I can't tell you how touched and grateful I was. I'm not going to write you a long one now—I'll do that later when things have settled a little more. Briefly, this has happened: I have been in Paris almost all the time since I landed, with the exception of a few days in Rouen—this not because I love Paris, but after two weeks of casting around, moving from one hotel to the other, I suddenly decided that we spend too much of our lives looking for ideal conditions to work in, and that what we are after is an ideal condition of the soul which almost never comes. So I got tired and disgusted with myself went to a little hotel—not very French, I'm afraid, but very touristy—and set to work. I've been doing five or six hours a day for almost two weeks now—the weather is hot and sticky, but I sweat and work—its the only cure I've found for the bloody hurting inside of me. Dear Jack, its been so bad I can't tell you about it: I feel all bloody inside me—but have faith in me, everything's going to be all right. What do you know about it? I am writing a book so filled with the most unspeakable desire, longing, and love for my own country and ten thousand things in it—that I have to laugh at times to think what the Mencken [H. L. Mencken, editor of *The American Mercury*] crowd and all the other crowds are going to say about it. But I can't help it—if I have ever written anything with utter conviction it is this—dear Jack, I <u>know</u> that I know what some of our great woe and sickness as a people is now, because that woe is in me—it is rooted in myself, but by God, Jack, I have not written a word directly about myself yet God knows what Maxwell Perkins will say when he sees it, but I've just finished the first section of the first part—it is called <u>Antaeus</u>, and it is as if I had become a voice for the experience of a race: It begins "Of wandering forever and the earth again"— and by God Jack, I believe I've got it—the two things that haunt and hurt us—the eternal wandering, moving, questing, loneliness, homesickness, and the desire of the soul for a home, peace, fixity, repose. In Antaeus, in a dozen short scenes, told in their own language, we see people of all sorts <u>constantly in movement</u>, going somewhere, haunted by it—and by God, Jack, its the <u>truth</u> about them—I saw it as a child, I've seen it here in their poor damned haunted eyes: Well there are these scenes—a woman telling of the river—the ever-moving river —coming through the levee at night, and of the crippled girl clinging to the limb of the oak, and of then how she feels the house break loose and go with the tide, then of living on the roof-top with 7 women and the children, and of other houses and people—tragedy, pity, humor, bravery, and the

Letter from Wolfe to Maxwell Perkins accompanying his manuscript of "A Portrait of Bascom Hawke." Perkins entered it immediately in the second Scribner's Magazine contest for best long story/short novel, the deadline for which was 1 February. Wolfe shared the $5,000 award with John Herrmann; the story appeared in the magazine's April 1932 issue.

CHARLES SCRIBNER'S SONS

PUBLISHERS, IMPORTERS AND BOOKSELLERS

597 Fifth Avenue
NEW YORK

YOUR ORDER No.

No.

DATE September 25, 1935.

CLAIMS FOR DAMAGES OR SHORT-
AGES MUST BE MADE IMMEDIATELY
ON RECEIPT OF GOODS.

TERMS: NET CASH
PAYABLE WITH EXCHANGE ON
NEW YORK

Sold To   Mr. Thomas Wolfe

No.

Sent Per

QUANTITY	DESCRIPTION	EDUCATIONAL	TRADE	TOTAL
	To excess cost of author's alterations on:			
	<u>OF TIME AND THE RIVER</u>			
	Cost of composition and electrotyping	2479.06		
	Cost of corrections		1676.41	
	Allowance according to agreement - 20% of $2479.06		495.81	$1180.60

Charges to Wolfe for excess alterations in Of Time and the River. *A standard clause in Scribner author contracts specified: "Expenses incurred for alterations in type or plates, exceeding twenty per cent of the cost of composition and electrotyping said work, are to be charged to the AUTHOR'S account." Once text had been set in type, changes were expensive; this bill shows that so many late changes were made that the cost was two-thirds that of the original composition.*

great wild savagery of American nature; then the pioneer telling of "the perty little gal" he liked, but moving on because the wilderness was getting too crowded; then the hoboes waiting quietly at evening by the water tower for the coming of the fast express; then a rich American girl moving on from husband to husband, from drink to dope to opium, from white lovers to black one, from New York to Paris to California; then the engineer at the throttle of the fast train; then a modest poor little couple from 123rd St—the woman earning living by painting lampshades, the man an impractical good-for-nothing temporarily employed in a filling station—cruising in their cheap little car through Virginia and Kentucky in the autumn—all filled with details of motor camps, where you can get a shack for $1.00 a night, and of "lovely meals" out of cans—whole cost $0.36—etc; then a school teacher from Ohio taking University Art Pilgrimage No. 36 writing back home "— didn't get your letter till we got to Florence . . . . stayed in Prague 3 days but rained whole time we were there, so didnt get to see much, etc" . Then Lee coming through Virginia in the night on his great white horse; then the skull of a pioneer in the desert, a rusted gun stock and a horses skull, then a Harry's New York Bar American saying "Jesus! What a country! I been back one time in seven years, that was enough . . . . Me, I'm a Frenchman. See?" But talking, talking, cursing, until he drinks himself into a stupor—then a bum, a natural wanderer who has been every where; then a Boston woman and her husband who have come to France to live—"Francis always felt he wanted to do a little writing . . . . . we felt the atmosphere is so much better here for that

To

MAXWELL EVARTS PERKINS

A GREAT EDITOR AND A BRAVE AND HONEST MAN, WHO STUCK TO
THE WRITER OF THIS BOOK THROUGH TIMES OF BITTER HOPELESS-
NESS AND DOUBT AND WOULD NOT LET HIM GIVE IN TO HIS OWN
DESPAIR, A WORK TO BE KNOWN AS "OF TIME AND THE RIVER" IS
DEDICATED WITH THE HOPE THAT ALL OF IT MAY BE IN SOME WAY
WORTHY OF THE LOYAL DEVOTION AND THE PATIENT CARE WHICH
A DAUNTLESS AND UNSHAKEN FRIEND HAS GIVEN TO EACH PART OF
IT, AND WITHOUT WHICH NONE OF IT COULD HAVE BEEN WRITTEN

Wolfe's dedication to Maxwell Perkins in Of Time and the River

kind of thing; then a Jew named Greenberg, who made his pile in New York and who now lives in France having changed his name to Montvert, and of course feels no homesickness at all, save what is natural to 4000 years of wandering—and more, and more, and more! Then amid all this you get the thing that does not change, the fixed princi-ple, the female principle—the earth again—and by God, Jack, I know this is true also. They want love, the earth, a home fixity—you get the mother and the lover—as the book goes on, and you see this incessant change, movement, unrest, and the great train with the wanderers rushing through the night, outside you get the eternal silent wait-ing earth that does not change, and the two women, going to bed upon it, working in their gardens upon it, dreaming longing, calling for men to return upon it. And down below in the mighty earth, you get the bones of the pioneers, all of the dust now trembling to the great train's wheel, the dust that loved, suffered, died, and is now buried, pointing 80 ways across 3000 miles of earth—and deeper than all, eternal and endur-ing, "the elm trees thread the bones of buried lov-ers" Through it all is poetry—the enormous rivers of the nation drinking the earth away at night, the vast rich stammer of night time in America, the lights, the swells, the thunder of the train—the savage summers, the fierce winters, the floods, the blizzards—all, all! and finally the great soft galloping of the horses of sleep! Mr Perkins may say that the first part is too much like a poem—but Jack, I've got it loaded with these sto-

ries of the wanderings of real people in their own talk, and by God, Jack, a real unified single story opens up almost at once and gathers and grows from then on. The chapter after Antaeus is called at present Early October, and begins "October is the richest of the seasons"—it tells about great barns loaded with harvest, the mown fields, the burning leaves, a dog barking at sunset, the smell of supper cooking in the kitchen—Oct is full of richness, a thousand things, then a section begins 'October is the time for all returning'—(which is true, Jack)—it tells how exiles and wanderers think of home again, of how the last tourists come back on great ships, of how the old bums shiver in their ragged collars as the newspaper behind the Public Library is blown around their feet, and of how they think of going South; it tells of the sum-mer girls who have gone back home from the re-sorts; of the deserted beaches; of people lying in their beds at night thinking "Summer has come and gone—has come and gone"—then in the frosty dark and silver, they hear the thunder of the great train. Then the October of a persons life—the core, the richness, the harvest, and the sadness of the end of youth.

By God, Jack, I'm just a poor bloody home-sick critter, but when I think of my book some-times I have the pride of a poet and a master of man's fate. Don't sigh and shake your head and think this is a welter of drivel—I've slapped these things down wildly in haste but I tell you, Jack, this book is not incoherent—it has a beautiful plan and a poetic logic if I am only true to it. I

Dust-jacketed first editions of the four Wolfe volumes published by Scribners during his lifetime

have not told you the thousandth part of it, but I hope you can see and believe in the truth and worth of it—and then if you do, please pray for me, dear Jack, to do my best and utmost, and to write the kind of book I want to write. In case you should doubt my condition, I am perfectly sober as I write this, it is a hot day, and I am now going back to my little room to work like hell. I have really not told you about my book—all this has been coming in the sweat and heat of the last few days, and this letter, however crazy, has made this clearer for me. I shall not leave Paris until I finish that first section—then I'm going like a shot to Switzerland, I think. I wont waste time moving about—I have a horror of moving now at all. Reeves [A. S. Frere-Reeves of William Heinemann], the English publisher was here, took me around to see Aldington [Richard Aldington], Michael Arlen, and other lit. lights—I was so unhappy at the time I have not been back since—although they were very nice. Reeves wants me to come to England and stay with him, the book is coming out there next month, but I've a horror of reading more reviews—I don't want to do anything more about it. Hope and pray for me, dear Jack—write me soon and talk to me. I've said nothing about you, forgive me, I'll write you a regular letter later.

With love and best wishes to everyone.
Tom Wolfe

Write me here—the mail will be sent on
Dear Jack—I'm sending this on a day or two later—I guess I'm really started—six hours a day, kid

June 24, 1930

This is my schedule if you can make a way of living a schedule—up at noon, to Bank for mail, write letters have lunch (and bottle of wine!), buy a book—go home and work from four or five until 10 at night. Then out to eat, walk—back at midnight or one 'oclock read—work until three or four

Judging from the tone of Wolfe's long letter, Wheelock wrote back: "I know that a great book is in process . . ." (23 July 1930). However, Wolfe's spirit was soon broken by reviews of the English edition of Look Homeward, Angel. *Later, after a period of aimless travel, Wolfe spent the winter in London, in a flat that his English publisher had found for him. When he set sail for the United States in late February 1931, as his Guggenheim year neared its end, he was carrying with him six large bookkeeping ledgers filled with about two hundred thousand words of manuscript.*

Tom Wolfe is the only man I've met here who isn't sick or hasn't sickness to deal with. You have a great find in him—what he'll do is incalculable. He has a deeper culture than Ernest [Hemingway] and more vitality, if he is slightly less of a poet that goes with the immense surface he wants to cover. Also he lacks Ernest's quality of a stick hardened in the fire—he is more susceptible to the world. John Bishop [poet friend] told me he needed advice about cutting etc., but after reading his book I thought that was nonsense. He strikes me as a man who should be let alone as to length, if he has to be published in five volumes. I liked him enormously.

— F. Scott Fitzgerald in a letter to Maxwell Perkins, circa 1 September 1930

Fitzgerald ran into Wolfe while in Geneva, Switzerland, keeping near his wife, Zelda, who was being treated for a nervous breakdown in a sanatorium in Prangins.

LETTER:
Letter from Wolfe to Maxwell Perkins, 18 August 1930, from Geneva, Switzerland.

Written during a period of depression following the English publication (14 July) of Look Homeward, Angel *and more criticism of the novel . . .*

Dear Mr Perkins:

Will you please have Mr Darrow send me, at his convenience, a statement of whatever money is due me? I shall not write any more books, and since I must begin to make other plans for the future, I should like to know how much money I will have. I want to thank you and Scribners very sincerely for your kindness to me, and I shall hope someday to resume and continue a friendship which has meant a great deal to me.

I hope this finds you well, and entirely recovered from the trouble that took you to Baltimore. Please get a good vacation and a rest away from the heat and confusion of New York.

Yours faithfully,
Tom Wolfe

RELATED LETTERS:
Letters from Maxwell Perkins to A. S. Frere-Reeves, a director of William Heinemann,

Glad about what you wrote of Tom Wolfe. He was awfully nice. He is like a great child and you must remember that. Geniuses of that sort I guess are always children. Children, as you may have observed, Mr. Poikins, are a hell of a responsability. I liked him very, very much.

— Ernest Hemingway in a letter to Maxwell Perkins [late January 1933]

Perkins had arranged for the two Scribner authors to meet in New York City several weeks earlier.

Ltd., Wolfe's English publisher; letter from Perkins to Ernest Hemingway.

Perkins's monumental work in editing Of Time and the River *is indirectly revealed in these letters to his English colleague at William Heinemann, who was eager to put another Wolfe novel before the English public before they had forgotten him, and to Hemingway who was trying to lure him down to Key West, Florida, for some fishing.*

Sept. 25, 1933

Dear Frere-Reeves:

The Tom Wolfe problem is a very difficult one, but I think I shall get a very large part of his manuscript this week (he has promised it) and then I shall have something to begin work on, with the idea of a book in early 1934.

I am sorry now that we did not publish a book of his stories a year ago, but he was very much averse to it, and so was our sales department. But I do not think it could be done now, particularly as the best ones that have appeared, the last three, are really out of the new book. They could not be published in a collection therefore, and the public would be disappointed if one came out without them.

The trouble with Tom is not that he does not work, for he does, like a dog. It is that everything grows and grows under his hands, and he cannot seem to control that. He takes up an episode which is to be part of the book, and a small part, and by the time he is through with it it is big enough to make a volume by itself. I know, and he knows, that his manuscript will have to be cut greatly, and it will mean a couple of months work,- as indeed was the way with his first book. After I get hold of this large part of the manuscript, I shall write you in detail how the matter looks, for that will enable me really to estimate the possibilities. I think he himself means to write to you.- I think he said he had had a letter from you.

[Maxwell Perkins]

Jan. 18, 1934

Dear Frere-Reeves:

This is just a line to tell you that I have Tom Wolfe's manuscript except for certain unfilled gaps which he is working on, and that we see nothing that can prevent its being published in book form in the early fall. The manuscript comes at present to 344,000 words. There is a great deal of cutting to be done, but the probability is that it won't be shorter than 300,000 words, and might be longer. I shall let you know exactly when I know.

[Maxwell Perkins]

March 23, 1934

Dear Frere:

. . . We have had another struggle here over the book and the result is that I alone am to go through it all with a blue pencil, and the argument is to come later. . . .

[Maxwell Perkins]

June 28, 1934

Dear Ernest:

. . . I cannot come down now. I cannot leave as long as I can keep Tom going well, as he is doing now. We have over half the book finished, except for a little touching up on another reading. We have got a good system now. We work every evening from 8:30 (or as near as Tom can come to it) until 10:30 or 11:00, and Tom does actual writing at times, and does it well,- where pieces have to be joined up. We are organizing the book.- that is the best part of the work we are doing. It will be pretty well integrated in the end, and vastly more effectively arranged. The fact is, Tom could do the work but his impulse is all away from the hard detailed revision. He is mighty ingenious at times, when it comes to the organization of material. The scheme is pretty clear in his own head, but he shrinks from the sacrifices which are really cruel often. A couple of nights ago I told Tom that a whole lot of fine stuff he had in simply ought to come out because it resulted in blurring a very important effect. Literally, we sat here for an hour thereafter without saying a word, while Tom glowered and pondered and fidgeted in his chair. Then he said, "Well, then will you take the responsibility?" And I said, "I have simply got to take the responsibility. And what's more," I said, "I will be blamed either way." But he did it, and in the end he knew he was right. . . .

[Maxwell Perkins]

Sept. 5, 1934

Dear Frere:

The struggle with Tom goes on. The present stage is that one hundred galleys of the book have been set up, about half. Tom has had them for quite a long time, and I cannot get him to give them up, but expect to in the end, which should not be far distant. There are still gaps in the book which should be filled in with about 5,000 words each, but for one of them Tom has supplied copy to the extent of 70,000 words. You can guess how it all goes on. We quarrel furiously, but the after-effects of the quarrels on Tom are generally good. . . .

[Maxwell Perkins]

September 14th.1934

Dear Max,

Thank you for the latest communiqué from the battle-front with Tom. I am sorry that I cannot help laughing when you say that when asked for five thousand words to fill in a gap he weighs in with seventy thousand.

Just as you are within sight of an armistice and the job looks like being done, I hope you will let me know because I still have the problem of putting Tom over to the British public, who by now may have forgotten him. . . .

Yours as ever,
Frere [A. S. Frere-Reeves]

Oct. 31, 1934

Dear Frere:

I have sent you 195 galleys of Tom Wolfe's book. We hope it will not run beyond 300 galleys, but it won't run less. Maybe you can do more cutting, and it would be an advantage. I think I have done all that is possible at this end, although I cannot be sure until Tom reads the proof,- which he is very dilatory about doing. The rest of the galleys will follow soon. Tom threatens to tear everything to pieces and put in a few hundred thousand more words, but I rather think the book will stand about as it is, though you won't, of course, set up from this proof.- Later we shall send you page proof.

[Maxwell Perkins]

Dec. 18, 1934

Dear Frere,

. . . After Tom had carried his proofs about for weeks without reading them, we finally told him that whatever came, we were going to send back twenty galleys a day to be put into pages. We therefore got not far from the end of the book, where something had to be done, and for the last week he has been writing. I do not know what the result is going to be, but I suppose it will mean a very long passage which will need cutting.- But it seems as though we ought to be able to send you complete page proof by the end of this month, or early in the next.

[Maxwell Perkins]

Jan. 16, 1935

Dear Frere:

I was delighted to receive your note of the 7th. The battle seems nearly over, and I am still alive. I am sending you 766 pges in foundry, with the rest to follow soon. Tom is writing a preface, but I think whether that should be in the English edition ought to be up to you. It may not go in the American edition, but what I have heard of it over the telephone was filled with life and interest. We shall send it to you so that you can consider the matter.

I have got to go down next week to see a manuscript of Ernest Hemingway's [*Green Hills of Africa*]. I want to see the manuscript very much, but as soon as I have got it read, if not sooner, he will put me to hard labor pulling whales out of the ocean where I would just as soon they stayed.

[Maxwell Perkins]

Feb. 6, 1935

Dear Frere:

We got Tom to leave out the introduction. It had good points, but would have been harmful. Had quite a time about it. I am sending you now a complete set of sheets, but if you have begun to set from the foundry you will be safe.

Had a fine eight days in Key West and caught a sailfish.

[Maxwell Perkins]

March 11, 1935

Dear Frere:

. . . I shall try to pick up a first edition for you and get Tom to sign it when he gets back here. I may not be able to do it though. We have printed five editions. The reviews have been magnificent. I cannot remember a novel that created such a sensation at the moment of publication.

[Maxwell Perkins]

Of Time and the River, running to 912 pages, was published on 8 March 1935. It was immediately popular and became the #3 best-seller of the year's fiction.

LETTER:
Letter from Maxwell Perkins to the "Collector of Internal Revenue," 18 June 1934.

Dear Sir:

I am writing in behalf of Thomas Wolfe, of 5 Montague Terrace, Brooklyn. He neglected to pay the second installment of his 1933 income tax which amounted to $13.07, on the 15th. We therefore suppose that he is obliged now to pay the entire balance for the year, and we therefore enclose a check for the total amount.

We feel responsible for Mr. Wolfe's failure to pay on the 15th. He is a novelist, and not so constituted that he is able to look after matters of this kind,- which is often the case with writers. We have therefore taken the responsibility of reminding him, but in this instance we failed to do it. If any information is desired about the matter I should be glad to give it at any moment.

Very truly yours,
[Maxwell Perkins]

RELATED LETTERS:
Letter from CS III to Alfred Harcourt, 11 September 1934; letter from Donald Brace, 13 September 1934, in reply.

Objecting to what he perceives as a breach of protocol by another publishing house, Scribner reaffirms the sanctity of the author/publisher relationship.

Dear Mr. Harcourt:

I have just learned of an incident in connection with your house that so surprised and shocked me that I do not feel that I can let it pass without taking it up with you personally.

According to the word I received one of your representatives made an appointment with Tom Wolfe and told him that he understood that he was considering severing relations with Scribners. Of course one hears all sorts of rumors, so I am not altogether surprised at this. What does seem to me to be unpardonable, however, is that when Wolfe assured him that this was not in any way the case your representative went on to tell Wolfe that if it had been he was authorized to offer him as an advance on a new novel either $10,000 or

$250.00 a month up to three years while he was writing one.

This seems to me to be about as subtle a method of attempting to build up discontent between author and publisher as I have heard of, and if it is to be the custom then it seems that in the future it will be everyone for himself and the end of any cordial feelings between houses.

I trust that your man may be able to explain that there was some possible misunderstanding in this instance, as I have always held your house in the highest regard and this is the first time that any such attack has been made on our list that has come to my attention since I have been in the business.

Sincerely yours
[Charles Scribner]

Dear Mr. Scribner:

I have been much distressed by your letter of September 11th, and so has Mr. Pearce, to whom of course I have shown it. I am glad, however, that you wrote so promptly and frankly about it. Your letter is addressed to Harcourt, but he left the night before last to be away for two weeks.

Mr. Wolfe and Mr. Pearce met at the latter's home Tuesday night and spent some three hours together. The more I have heard about their talk, the more convinced I am that it does not justify any such serious interpretations as you have given it. As might be expected of a conversation continuing until 2:30 in the morning between a young author and a young man in the publishing business, they talked a great deal about books and publishing and about their personal problems. It is definitely not true, however, that our representative was authorized to make any offer whatever, either directly or subject to any contingency. And it is equally not true, I am convinced, that he said that he was, or would be, authorized to make any offer. Mr. Pearce, who has been deeply disturbed at the interpretation put upon the incident, has spoken to Mr. Wolfe on the telephone, and Mr. Wolfe assures him he thought of their talk as being purely friendly and personal and did not interpret it in any way as being in the realm of "offers."

It is now and always has been our policy to refrain from disturbing or attempting to disturb existing publishing relations between authors and other publishers. I know this is your policy, too. Both Harcourt and I have always felt and repeatedly expressed the highest regard for your house and your imprint, and certainly our general policy is particularly emphatic in respect to your firm.

Mr. Pearce, I may say, understands all this and agrees with it.

I wish I could report the same freedom from attacks on our list that you have found in the case of yours. Our authors are frequently being sought by offers of big advances, high royalties, and other inducements from many other American publishers, though not, I am happy to say, from Scribner's. As for Mr. Wolfe, we are not in any sense "after" him, and if the interview I have described has in any way caused difficulty, I am deeply sorry.

Yours sincerely,
Donald Brace

LETTER:
Letter from Aline Bernstein to Maxwell Perkins, 17 October 1934.

Dear Mr. Perkins —

Some time ago, when Tom Wolfe went abroad on his Guggenheim Fellowship, he gave me as a present the handwritten manuscript of "Look Homeward Angel." I have been very ill in hospital for some time, and unable to work at my own profession. I plan to go to California to rest, and very likely we will rent or sell our house in the Country.

I want to give you the manuscript, if you care to have it, on the condition that you will never, under any circumstances, return it to Tom. If you do not want it, I will destroy it before I leave, as I do not care to have it fall into other hands than yours or mine.

While I do not claim any part in the creation of the book, I believe that my love and friendship for Tom at the time of its writing was a source of strength and comfort to him.

I shall be grateful if you will let me know at once whether or not you want the manuscript. I will be at the Hotel Gotham where a letter will reach me after Sunday. I have to go to get it from my house, and if you choose to have it, will send it by express wherever you say, as it is bulky and almost impossible to deliver by hand. I shall be leaving for the West some time between the 10" & 15" of November. —

Sincerely Yours
Aline Bernstein

*Perkins's generous offer to hold it for safekeeping was accepted. However, Wolfe later pressured Bernstein to sell it, perhaps thinking he would thereby clear his debt to her. She donated the manuscript to a charity auction held for the Span-*ish Loyalists in 1936, where it was bought by Gabriel Wells, an antiquarian book dealer, for $1,750 and presented to Harvard.

RELATED LETTERS:
Letter from Maxwell Perkins to Wolfe, 22 April 1936; letter from Wolfe in reply, 23 April 1936.

Perkins's concession and Wolfe's apology bring about a temporary reconciliation between the editor and author, whose relationship is beginning to show strain. The Story of a Novel *has just been published (21 April) at $1.50.*

Dear Tom:

I am giving directions to reckon your royalties on "The Story of a Novel" at 15% from the start. The difference in what you will receive if 3,000 copies are sold, between the ten and fifteen percent royalty, will be $225.00. We certainly do not think that we should withhold that sum of money if it is going to cause so much resentment, and so much loss of time and disquiet for us all.

I would rather, simply agree to do this and say nothing further, but I should not have the right to do it without telling you that the terms as proposed on the $1.50 price are just, and that if the matter were to be looked upon merely as business, we should not be justified as business men in making this concession. You are under a misapprehension if you think that when we suggested a reduction of royalty--such as in similar cases have been freely made by writers of the highest rank, at least in sales--we were basing the suggestion on the question of price. I do remember that the price of $1.25 was mentioned as a desirable one, or a probable one, but the idea of the royalty was not dependent on that. We could not at that time know what the price would have to be. We found that the price had to be higher because of the question of basic costs which have come into every phase of the handling, advertising, promoting, and making of a book. Many of these basic costs do not vary at all because of the size of the book. We do not want to put our prices any higher than we are compelled to, and in fact more than most publishers, have tried to keep them low. We put them up only because we have to. The terms we proposed were therefore in my opinion just.

You return to the question of the excess corrections which were, I believe, $1100.00. If I gave you the impression that I thought this was unfair, it came from my dread of the resentment I knew you would feel to have them deducted from your royalties even though they have always been taken into account in every publisher's contract, and generally at only half the percentage we allow for them. I once said to you in Charles Scribner's presence that you had a good technical argument for not paying these corrections. This would be true, since you did not read your proof, but if you had done so, is there any doubt but what these corrections would have been much larger? They were almost wholly unavoidable corrections, like the change from the first to third person, and the changing of names. They were therefore rightly author's corrections and why should the author not pay for them? I think we began wrong by making no charge in the case of excess corrections on the "Angel", which amounted to seven hundred dollars, so that this charge came to you as a surprise.- And the truth is that many authors do resent being charged for such corrections because they cannot be got to consider them in advance. But if the author does not pay for this cost, after the publisher has paid the 20% allowance himself, the publisher will have to pay that too. Why should he have to do it?

As to the other matter you speak of, your freedom to do whatever you think is to your best interests in business, nobody could ever deny it, and I have often said that we did not. I certainly would not wish you to make what you thought was a sacrifice on my account, and I would know whatever you did would be sincerely believed to be right by you,- as I know that you sincerely believe the contentions you make in this letter to me, to be right. I have never doubted your sincerity and never will. I wish you could have felt that way toward us.

Always yours,
[Maxwell Perkins]

Dear Max:

I got your letter this morning and I just want to write you back now to tell you that everything is settled so far as I am concerned, so let's forget about it.

Now that you have told me that you would restore my old royalty rate of 15%, I want to tell you that I don't want it and want to stick to the contract I signed. That goes for all my other obligations as well. I really made up my mind to this yesterday and that was the reason I called you up last night and went around to see you.

I wanted to tell you and I am afraid I didn't succeed telling you very well that all the damn contracts in the world don't mean as much to me as your friendship means, and it suddenly occurred to me yesterday that life is too short to quarrel this way with a friend over something that matters so little. But I do want to tell you again just how genuinely and deeply sorry I am for boiling over the way I did the other night. We have had fireworks of this sort before and I am afraid it may occur again, but every time they do, I say something to a friend that is unjust and wrong and sweat blood about it later. So just help me along with this by forgetting all about it, and lets look forward to the future.

I suppose it is a good thing for me to have had this experience in the last year but there is something a little grotesque and tragic in the fact that the success I wanted and looked forward to having as a child, should have brought me so much trouble, worry, bewilderment and disillusion, but I am going to try to add the whole experience to the sum of things I have found out about all through my life and I hope that I will be able to make use of it, instead if letting it make use of me.

I see know what a terribly dangerous thing a little success may be because it seems to me the effort of an artist must always aim at even greater concentration and intensity and effort of the will where his work is concerned and anything that tends to take him away from that, to distract him, to weaken his effort is a bad thing.

I am now started on another book. I need your friendship, and support more than I ever did, so please forget the worse mistakes I have made in the past and lets see if I can't do somewhat better in the future.

Sincerely,
Tom

LETTER:
Letter from Scribner author Marjorie Kinnan Rawlings to Maxwell Perkins, [June 1936], regarding Wolfe's critical examination of his writing recorded in *The Story of a Novel*.

Dear Max:—
Wolfe's "Story of a Novel" is unbearable. I have just finished it. It's unbearable—its honesty,—its fierceness,—its beauty of expression. And for another writer—.

There is no damnation for such a man. Don't be concerned—I know you are not—that he goes "completely off the reservation." He is his own torment and his own strength.

He is so young! When a little of this torment has expended itself, you will have the greatest artist America has ever produced.

My thanks and my gratitude for autographing the book as you did.

When all of us are done for, the chances are that literary history will find you the greatest—certainly the wisest—of us all.

Marjorie

RELATED LETTERS:
Wolfe's break with Scribners had numerous sources. Several of the more obvious were Scribners' desire to settle a lawsuit brought by people who thought Wolfe had libeled them in his story "No Door"; a quarrel with Perkins over the royalty rate for The Story of a Novel; *Perkins's opposition to Wolfe's writing about people at Scribners, as in his story "No More Rivers"; and, a major irritant, Bernard De Voto's article about Wolfe, "Genius Is Not Enough," which appeared in* The Saturday Review of Literature *(25 April 1936). De Voto admitted that Wolfe had genius but argued that genius in any art must be supported by craftsmanship to impart shape to material—and that the only one exhibiting any organizing ability in Wolfe's work was Maxwell Perkins. Wolfe was torn between his strong friendship with Perkins and the need to demonstrate a more creative independence.*

November 12, 1936

Dear Max:

I think you should now write me a letter in which you explicitly state the nature of my relation with Chas. Scribner's Sons. I think you ought to say that I have faithfully and honorably discharged all obligations to Chas. Scribner's Sons, whether financial, personal or contractual, and that no further agreement or obligation of any sort exists between us.

I must tell you plainly now what you must know already, that, in view of all that has happened in the last year and a half, the differences of opinion and belief, the fundamental disagreements that we have discussed so openly, so frankly, and so passionately, a thousand times, and which have brought about this unmistakable and grievous severance, I think you should have written this letter that I am asking you to write long before this. I am compelled by your failure to do so to ask you, in simple justice, to write it now. . . .

Sincerely yours,
Tom Wolfe

Nov 17th, 36

Dear Tom:

I haven't time to write today- we have a meeting that often lasts till five and my late P.M. and evening are full too. I can say this though, I never knew a soul with whom I felt I was in such fundamentally complete agreement as you. What's more, and what has to do with it, I know you would not ever do an insincere thing, or anything you did not think was right. I don't fully understand your letter, but I'll answer it as best I can. You must surely know, though, that any publisher would leap at the chance to publish you.

Always yours,
[Maxwell Perkins]

Nov. 18, 1936

Dear Tom:

With this is a more formal letter which I hope is what you want. This is to say that on my part there has been no "severance." I can't express certain kinds of feelings very comfortably, but you must realize what my feelings are toward you. Ever since "Look Homeward, Angel" you work has been the foremost interest in my life, and I have never doubted for your future on any grounds except, at times, on those of your being able to control the vast mass of material you have accumulated and have to form into books. You seem to think I have tried to control you. I only did that when you asked my help and then I did the best I could. It all seems very confusing to me but, whatever the result, I hope you don't mean it to keep us from seeing each other, or that you won't come to our house.

Max

Nov. 18, 1936

Dear Tom:

You ask me to explicitly state the nature of your relations with Charles Scribner's Sons. To begin with, you have faithfully and honorably discharged all obligations to us, and no further agreement of any sort exists between us with respect to the future. Our relations are simply those of a publisher who profoundly admires the work of an author and takes great pride in publishing whatever he may of that author's writings. They are not such as to give any sort of rights, or anything approaching that, over that author's future work. Contrary to custom, we have not even an option which would give us the privilege of seeing first any new manuscript.

We do not wholly understand parts of your letter, where you speak of us as putting you in a position of denying an obligation that does not exist, for we do not know how we have done that; or where you refer to "exerting control of a man's future," which we have no intention of doing at all, and would not have the power or right to do.

There are other phrases, in that part of your letter, that I do not understand, one of which is that which refers to us as being absolved from any commitments of any kind, "should the author fail." If this and these other phrases signify that you think you should have a contract from us if our relations are to continue, you can certainly have one. We should be delighted to have one. You must surely know the faith this house has in you. There are, of course, limits in terms beyond which nobody can go in a contract, but we should expect to make one that would suit you if you told us what was required.

Ever sincerely yours
[Maxwell Perkins]

Wolfe answered each of Perkins's letters, the "personal" one and the "business" one, separately. His answer to the personal one reached twenty-eight typewritten pages, from which the following is excerpted:

December 15, 1936 [mailed 10 January 1937]
Dear Max:

. . . First of all, let me tell you that for what you say in your own two personal letters of November 17th and November 18th I shall be forever proud and grateful. I shall remember it with the greatest happiness as long as I live. I must tell you again, no matter what embarrassment it may cause you, what I have already publicly acknowledged and what I believe is now somewhat understood and known about in the world, namely, that your faith in me, your friendship for me, during the years of doubt, confusion and distress, was and will always be one of the great things in my life.

. . . In one sense, my whole effort for years might be described as an effort to fathom my own design, to explore my own channels, to discover my own ways. In these respects, in an effort to help me discover, to better use, these means I was striving to apprehend and make my own, you gave me the most generous, the most painstaking, the most valuable help. But that kind of help might have been given to me by many other skilful people — and of course there are other skilful people in the world who could give such help — although none I know of who could give it so skilfully as you.

But what you gave me, what in my acknowledgment I tried to give expression to, was so much more than this technical assistance — an aid of spiritual sustenance, of personal faith, of high purpose, of profound and sensitive understanding, of utter loyalty and staunch support, at a time when many people had no belief at all in me, or when what little belief they had was colored by serious doubt that I would ever be able to continue or achieve my purpose, fulfill my "promise"—all of this was a help of such priceless and incalculable value, of such spiritual magnitude, that it made any other kind of help seem paltry by comparison. And for that reason mainly I have resented the contemptible insinuations of my enemies that I have to have you "to help me write my books." As you know, I don't have to have you or any other man alive to help me with my books. I do not even have to have technical help or advice, although I need it badly, and have been so immensely grateful for it. But if the worst came to the worst — and of course the worst does and will come to the worst — all this I could and will and do learn for myself, as all hard things are learned, with blood-sweat, anguish and despair. . . .

Sincerely yours,
Tom Wolfe

The following rough draft was found in Wolfe's files after his death—it was never mailed [Houghton Library, Harvard University].

[December 1936?]
Dear Charles [CS III]:

I have upon this present date written a letter to Maxwell Perkins in which I told him that the firm of Charles Scribner's Sons are no longer, for any publication save those which have previously been published by Charles Scribner's Sons, my publisher. It is a painful and chastising experience to renounce an agreement that does not exist, an understanding for the future that, however undefined, was mine alone, and in my mind alone; but in order that there may be no misunderstanding of my purpose, or of the meaning of this letter, I do state here and now that you are no longer my publisher, that you will never again be my publisher for anything that I may ever write, that I hereby renounce, abjure, abrogate, deny, and terminate any requests, claims, offers, inducements, obligations, commitments, or persuasions which you have made formerly, shall make now, or in the future make.

Faithfully and sincerely yours
T. Wolfe

A year passed before Wolfe actually found a new publisher and editor: Edward Aswell of Harper and

Brothers. The spring of 1938 was among his most productive, during which he rethought, reorganized, and rewrote material he had been working on with Perkins. However, in the summer he caught pneumonia while on a Western trip, which aggravated an old tubercular condition in a lung; tubercles were released as a result, and Wolfe died quickly in September from tuberculosis of the brain. From the manuscript Wolfe left behind, Harpers published three works: The Web and The Rock, You Can't Go Home Again, *and* The Hills Beyond. *In Wolfe's will, Perkins was named executor of his estate and administrator of all his literary affairs, and, therefore, he had a significant role in all of Wolfe's Harper publications.*

CHARACTER PORTRAIT:

"The Fox," excerpt from Chapter 28 of Wolfe's *You Can't Go Home Again* (New York: Harper & Brothers, 1940), pp. 437-438, 442-443.

Foxhall Edwards, the editor of George Webber, the protagonist of Wolfe's two posthumous novels, is an obvious characterization of Maxwell Perkins—even down to the man's deafness, custom of wearing his hat indoors, and family of five daughters. Only the name has been changed.

DURING ALL THESE DESPERATE YEARS IN BROOKLYN, WHEN GEORGE LIVED and worked alone, he had only one real friend, and this was his editor, Foxhall Edwards. They spent many hours together, wonderful hours of endless talk, so free and full that it combed the universe and bound the two of them together in bonds of closest friendship. It was a friendship founded on many common tastes and interests, on mutual liking and admiration of each for what the other was, and on an attitude of respect which allowed unhampered expression of opinion even on those rare subjects which aroused differences of views and of belief. It was, therefore, the kind of friendship that can exist only between two men. It had in it no element of that possessiveness which always threatens a woman's relations with a man, no element of that physical and emotional involvement which, while it serves nature's end of bringing a man and a woman together, also tends to thwart their own dearest wish to remain so by throwing over their companionship a constricting cloak of duty and obligation, of right and vested interest.

The older man was not merely friend but father to the younger. Webber, the hot-blooded Southerner, with his large capacity for sentiment and affection, had lost his own father many years before and now had found a substitute in Edwards. And Edwards, the reserved New Englander, with his deep sense of family and inheritance, had always wanted a son but had had five daughters, and as time went on he made George a kind of foster son. Thus each, without quite knowing that he did it, performed an act of spiritual adoption.

So it was to Foxhall Edwards that George now turned whenever his loneliness became unbearable. When his inner turmoil, confusion, and self-doubts overwhelmed him, as they often did, and his life went dead and stale and empty till it sometimes seemed that all the barren desolation of the Brooklyn streets had soaked into his very blood and marrow—then he would seek out Edwards. And he never went to him in vain. Edwards, busy though he always was, would drop whatever he was doing and would take George out to lunch or dinner, and in his quiet, casual, oblique, and understanding way would talk to him and draw him out until he found out what it was that troubled him. And always in the end, because of Edwards' faith in him, George would be healed and find himself miraculously restored to self-belief.

What manner of man was this great editor and father-confessor and true friend—he of the quiet, shy, sensitive, and courageous heart who often seemed to those who did not know him well an eccentric, cold, indifferent fellow—he who, grandly christened Foxhall, preferred to be the simple, unassuming Fox?

. . .

A man of five and forty years, not really seeming younger, yet always seeming something of the boy. Rather, the boy is there within that frame of face, behind the eyes, within the tenement of flesh and bone—not imprisoned, just held there in a frame—a frame a little worn by the years, webbed with small wrinkles round the eyes—invincibly the same as it has always been. The hair, once fair and blond, no longer fair and blond now, feathered at the temples with a touch of grey, elsewhere darkened by time and weather to a kind of steel-grey—blondness really almost dark now, yet, somehow, still suggesting fair and blond. The head well set and small, boy's head still, the hair sticking thick and close to it, growing to a V in the center of the forehead, then back straight and shapely, full of natural grace. Eyes pale blue, full of a strange misty light, a kind of far weather of the sea in them, eyes of a New England sailor long months outbound for

China on a clipper ship, with something drowned, sea-sunken in them.

The general frame and structure of the face is somewhat lean and long and narrow—face of the ancestors, a bred face, face of people who have looked the same for generations. A stern, lonely face, with the enduring fortitude of granite, face of the New England seacoast, really his grandfather's face, New England statesman's face, whose bust sits there on the mantel, looking at the bed. Yet something else has happened on Fox's face to transfigure it from the primeval nakedness of granite: in its essential framework, granite still, but a kind of radiance and warmth of life has enriched and mellowed it. A light is burning in the Fox, shining outward through the face, through every gesture, grace, and movement of the body, something swift, mercurial, mutable, and tender, something buried and withheld, but passionate—something out of his mother's face, perhaps, or out of his father's, or his father's mother's—something that subdues the granite with warmth—something from poetry, intuition, genius, imagination, living, inner radiance, and beauty. This face, then, with the shapely head, the pale, far-misted vision of the eyes, held in round bony cages like a bird's, the strong, straight nose, curved at the end, a little scornful and patrician, sensitive, sniffing, swift-nostriled as a hound's—the whole face with its passionate and proud serenity might almost be the face of a great poet, or the visage of some strange and mighty bird.

ARTICLE:

Maxwell Perkins, "Scribner's and Tom Wolfe," *Carolina Magazine*, LXVIII (October 1938), pp. 15–17.

When I knew that Tom Wolfe had died, as I knew he must after the day of his operation at Johns Hopkins—and before that it had seemed inconceivable that one so vibrant with life could die young—a line kept recurring in my mind as a kind of consolation: "He hates him that would upon the rack of this tough world stretch him out longer." For he was on the rack almost always, and almost always would have been—and for one reason. He was wrestling as no artist in Europe would have to do, with the material of literature—a great country not yet revealed to its own people. It was not as with English artists who revealed England to Englishmen through generations, each one accepting what was true from his predecessors, in a gradual accretion, through centuries. Tom knew to the uttermost meaning of the literatures of other lands and that they were not the literature of America. He knew that the light and color of America were different, and its people, were; that the smells and sounds that were so much to us were; and the structure and dimensions of our continent. It was with this that he was struggling, and it was that struggle alone that, in a large sense, governed all he did. How long his books may last as such, no one can say, but the trail he has blazed is now open forever. American artists will follow, and widen it to express the things Americans only unconsciously know, to reveal America and Americans to Americans. That was at the heart of Tom's fierce life.

It was a gigantic task, and Tom was a giant in energy and in power of feeling as well as in physique. His too great dimensions seemed to represent the difficulties that almost drove him mad: he could not fit a book to the conventional length, nor produce one in the usual space of time. He was not proportioned to these requirements, but neither was his subject, the vast, sprawling, lonely, unruly land.

His books are formless, it is said, but I do not think he lacked a sense of form. Is it wanting, for instance, in "The Web of Earth"? In a large way he knew where he was going, and given twenty years and many volumes, I often thought, he might have fully achieved a proper form. But as he had to fit his body to the doorways, vehicles, and furniture of smaller men, so he had to fit his expression to the conventional requirements of a space and time that were as surely too small for his nature as they were for his subject.

Four years after the publication of "Look Homeward, Angel" about Christmas time in 1933, he brought me the huge manuscript, two feet high, of "Time and the River." And he was desperate. Time, his old enemy, the vastness and toughness of his material, the frequent and not always sympathetic inquiries of people about his progress toward another book, and financial pressure too—all were closing in on him. I thought, "This book has to be done," and we set to work. I, who thought Tom a man of genius, and loved him too, and could not bear to see him fail, was almost as desperate as he—so much there was to do. But the truth is that if I did him a real service—and in this I did—it was in keeping him from losing his belief in himself, by believing in him. What he most needed was comradeship and understanding in a long crisis, and those things I could give him then.

After I had read the manuscript and marked it up, we began a year of nights of work. The book was far from finished. It was in great fragments, and they were not in order. Large parts were missing. It was all disproportioned. Tom, who knew all this, would come in at eight or so, and I would point these things out, part by part. But I could tell Tom nothing, if it were right, that he did not easily see, and perhaps had already seen. But his whole natural impulse was outward, not inward—to express, not compress, or organize, and even though he realized that something had to be cut, as extrinsic, or otherwise superfluous, he could not easily bear to have it done. So every night we worked and argued in my boxstall of an office on Fifth Avenue, often accomplishing nothing, and strewed the floor with cigarettes and papers—and the night-watchman and the scrub-woman forgave us, because there was that in Tom that established a fellowship with all good sound people. And there was his humor too, always, except in the mortal struggle with his material.

Once I argued for a big deletion, late on a hot night, and then sat in silence. I knew he must agree to it for the reasons were strong. Tom tossed his head about, and swayed in his chair, and his eyes roved over the office. I went on reading in the manuscript for not less than fifteen minutes, but I was sure of Tom's movements—aware at last that he was looking fixedly at one corner of the office. In that corner hung a winter hat and overcoat, and down from under the hat, along the coat hung a sinister rattlesnake skin with seven rattles—a present from Marjorie Rawlings. I looked at Tom. He was eyeing that group of objects, and the rattlesnake stood out. He waved his hand at them: "Aha," said Tom, "the portrait of an editor." He worked no more that night. After the laughter we went to the Chatham Garden which Tom loved—and where the waiters all knew him as a brother—and talked and argued for an hour under the summer stars.

Such cutting was one thing, but there were the gaps, and Tom filled some of them in there and then, writing in his huge, heavy scrawl, on the corner of my desk. When we came to the point where Eugene's father died, I said that it must be told about, but that since Eugene was away at Harvard, Tom need only tell of the shock of the news, and of Eugene's return for the funeral—a matter of perhaps five thousand words. And Tom agreed.

The next night he came in with some thousands of words about the life of the doctor who attended Gant. I said, "This is good, Tom, but what has it to do with the book? You are telling the story of Eugene, of what <u>he</u> saw and experienced. We can't waste time with all this that is outside it." Tom fully accepted this, but still, the next night, he brought in a long passage about Eugene's sister Helen, and her thoughts while shopping in Altamont, and then at night in bed when she heard the whistle of the train. I said, "How in God's name will you get this book done this way, Tom? You have wasted two days already, and instead of reducing the length and doing what is essential, you are increasing it and adding what doesn't belong here."

Tom was penitent. He did not argue back as he almost always had done. He promised he would write only what was needed—and yet the next night he brought in thousands of words about Gant's illness, all outside of what I thought was wanted. But it was too good to let go. I said so. It was wrong, but it was right, and Tom went on, and the death of Gant is one of the finest things he ever wrote. Thank God I had sense enough to see that early, even though it seemed to me to violate the principle of form. But I do not think I could have stopped Tom anyhow. He had agreed that I was right, but underneath he knew what he was doing and had to do it.

All this perhaps sounds grim and desperate—and it should, for that it often was—but it gives no picture of Tom. It presents him as he was in the heat of struggle. After "Look Homeward, Angel" was published he was happy, and after the great success of "Of Time and the River," when he came home from Europe, and before he began the next long battle that ended last May when he set out (The Far Wanderer) on the tour of the Northwest that ended in his fatal illness. In that last interval he lived on First Avenue off Forty-ninth Street, and we had a house two blocks away, on Forty-ninth. Then we had many happy times before the struggle with his new book grew too fierce. The block between us and First Avenue was almost slum like. Boys played some exciting adaptation of baseball, and then of football, in the street, and the sidewalks were crowded with children. They all knew Tom. When he went by in his long, slow, country stride, looking at everything, they would call out, "Hello Mr. Wolfe." And the police all knew him too. Once my wife said, "A flowerpot has disappeared from one of our window boxes. I can't understand how it happened." The window box was too high for anyone to reach, you would think, and who would want a geranium? Long afterward, one night Tom said: "I meant to tell you, I took one of your geraniums. I was coming in but the house was dark so I just took a flower pot, and a cop saw me and said,—What are you doing?' I said,—I'm taking it

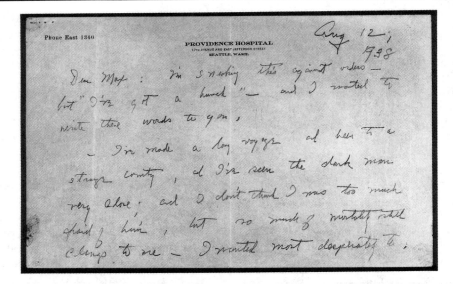

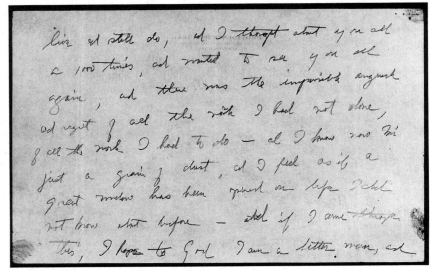

Last letter from Wolfe, addressed to Maxwell Perkins from his hospital bed in Seattle, Washington (by permission of the Houghton Library, Harvard University). He died on 15 September.

At the time of Perkins's death in 1947, he was working on an article on Wolfe for an issue of the Harvard Library Bulletin *marking William B. Wisdom's gift of his Thomas Wolfe collection to Harvard. The following excerpt from a Perkins manuscript, describing that Fourth of July referenced in Wolfe's letter, may be from an early draft of that memorial piece; however, the posthumous article printed in the* Bulletin *(volume 1, pp. 269–277) does not include it.*

Once, some three months after the triumphant publication of "Of Time and the River" Tom landed from a steamer on a blazing hot Fourth of July, and I met him. For all his good times abroad, his overwhelming reception in Germany, no child could have been more happy to be home, more eager to see all of New York at once. And that afternoon and night we did range from the floating restaurant on the East River at 55th Street, to the roof of the Prince George Hotel in Brooklyn where the whole shining city and the harbor were spread out. In the course of our wanderings we passed a doorway somewhere near Tenth Street close to Third Avenue. Tom caught me by the shoulder, swung me round and pointed to the top of a house. "There," he said, "is where a young man, six years ago began to write his first novel in an attic." And he added eagerly, "Let's go up and see it." But when we got to the top floor under its low ceiling and Tom knocked, and then rattled the door, no one was within. Meanwhile I was looking out a rear window, I saw that by going up one fire escape and down another, you could enter the so-called attic. I said, "Tom if we want to see the eyrie where the young eaglet mewed his mighty youth we can do it," and we did. Maybe it was burglary but the window was open and the statute of limitations must now obtain. There it was that he had begun to write "Look Homeward, Angel" and it was an attic but a comfortable one, and in the spacious dimensions of Thomas Wolfe himself.

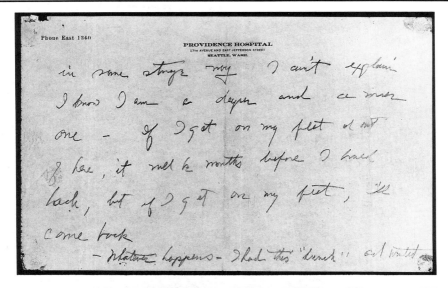

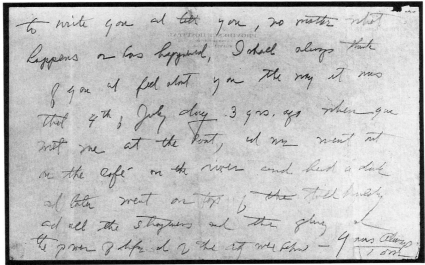

home to water it.' He just laughed." This was New York. Was the cop afraid of Tom and his great size? No, he knew him, and understood him: that human quality in Tom had made him friends with everyone around, and they knew he was one of them.

Tom was always one of them, the regular people, and he liked them most. His talk was beyond any I ever heard when he was not in the torment of his work. He would tell you of the river Cam in Cambridge, England, and the mist over it, so that you knew the magic Tennyson felt; or of the tulip fields in Holland, or the paintings he liked in the galleries of Europe so that if you knew them you saw them again and afresh; or of that ruined monastery, Fountain Abbey near York, in its old forest—and you knew it as it was when it was still alive. He could have talked to anyone about anything he had touched at all—but what he wanted, or thought he did, was to be one of the regular people. He was lonely. He inspired fellow feeling, but it could not embrace him enough. He wanted the simple, hearty life of Gant in his best times, the wife and the children, and coming home for lunch, and the fire roaring up the chimney. (No door!) . . .

Cumulative Index

Dictionary of Literary Biography, Volumes 1-183
Dictionary of Literary Biography Yearbook, 1980-1996
Dictionary of Literary Biography Documentary Series, Volumes 1-16

Cumulative Index

DLB before number: *Dictionary of Literary Biography,* Volumes 1-183
Y before number: *Dictionary of Literary Biography Yearbook,* 1980-1996
DS before number: *Dictionary of Literary Biography Documentary Series,* Volumes 1-16

A

Abbey Press DLB-49

The Abbey Theatre and Irish Drama,
1900-1945 . . . . DLB-10

Abbot, Willis J. 1863-1934 . . . . DLB-29

Abbott, Jacob 1803-1879 . . . . DLB-1

Abbott, Lee K. 1947- DLB-130

Abbott, Lyman 1835-1922 . . . . DLB-79

Abbott, Robert S. 1868-1940 . . . . DLB-29, 91

Abe, Kōbō 1924-1993 . . . . DLB-182

Abelard, Peter circa 1079-1142 . . . . . DLB-115

Abelard-Schuman DLB-46

Abell, Arunah S. 1806-1888 . . . . . . DLB-43

Abercrombie, Lascelles 1881-1938 . . . . DLB-19

Aberdeen University Press
Limited DLB-106

Abish, Walter 1931- DLB-130

Ablesimov, Aleksandr Onisimovich
1742-1783 . . . . DLB-150

Abraham à Sancta Clara
1644-1709 . . . . DLB-168

Abrahams, Peter 1919- DLB-117

Abrams, M. H. 1912- DLB-67

Abrogans circa 790-800 . . . . DLB-148

Abschatz, Hans Aßmann von
1646-1699 . . . . DLB-168

Abse, Dannie 1923- DLB-27

Academy Chicago Publishers DLB-46

Accrocca, Elio Filippo 1923- DLB-128

Ace Books DLB-46

Achebe, Chinua 1930- DLB-117

Achtenberg, Herbert 1938- DLB-124

Ackerman, Diane 1948- DLB-120

Ackroyd, Peter 1949- DLB-155

Acorn, Milton 1923-1986 . . . . DLB-53

Acosta, Oscar Zeta 1935?- DLB-82

Actors Theatre of Louisville DLB-7

Adair, James 1709?-1783? DLB-30

Adam, Graeme Mercer 1839-1912 . . . . DLB-99

Adame, Leonard 1947- DLB-82

Adamic, Louis 1898-1951 . . . . DLB-9

Adams, Alice 1926- Y-86

Adams, Brooks 1848-1927 . . . . DLB-47

Adams, Charles Francis, Jr.
1835-1915 . . . . DLB-47

Adams, Douglas 1952- Y-83

Adams, Franklin P. 1881-1960 . . . . . DLB-29

Adams, Henry 1838-1918 . . . . . DLB-12, 47

Adams, Herbert Baxter 1850-1901 . . . . DLB-47

Adams, J. S. and C.
[publishing house] DLB-49

Adams, James Truslow 1878-1949 . . . . DLB-17

Adams, John 1735-1826 . . . . . . DLB-31, 183

Adams, John 1735-1826 and
Adams, Abigail 1744-1818 . . . DLB-183

Adams, John Quincy 1767-1848 . . . . DLB-37

Adams, Léonie 1899-1988 . . . . DLB-48

Adams, Levi 1802-1832 . . . . DLB-99

Adams, Samuel 1722-1803 . . . . . DLB-31, 43

Adams, Thomas
1582 or 1583-1652 . . . . DLB-151

Adams, William Taylor 1822-1897 . . . DLB-42

Adamson, Sir John 1867-1950 . . . . . DLB-98

Adcock, Arthur St. John
1864-1930 . . . . DLB-135

Adcock, Betty 1938- DLB-105

Adcock, Betty, Certain Gifts DLB-105

Adcock, Fleur 1934- DLB-40

Addison, Joseph 1672-1719 . . . . . . DLB-101

Ade, George 1866-1944 . . . . . . DLB-11, 25

Adeler, Max (see Clark, Charles Heber)

Adonias Filho 1915-1990 . . . . DLB-145

Advance Publishing Company DLB-49

AE 1867-1935 . . . . DLB-19

Ælfric circa 955-circa 1010 . . . . . . DLB-146

Aeschines circa 390 B.C.-circa 320 B.C.
. . . . DLB-176

Aeschylus
525-524 B.C.-456-455 B.C. DLB-176

Aesthetic Poetry (1873), by
Walter Pater DLB-35

After Dinner Opera Company Y-92

Afro-American Literary Critics:
An Introduction DLB-33

Agassiz, Jean Louis Rodolphe
1807-1873 . . . . DLB-1

Agee, James 1909-1955 . . . . . DLB-2, 26, 152

The Agee Legacy: A Conference at
the University of Tennessee
at Knoxville Y-89

Aguilera Malta, Demetrio
1909-1981 . . . . DLB-145

Ai 1947- DLB-120

Aichinger, Ilse 1921- DLB-85

Aidoo, Ama Ata 1942- DLB-117

Aiken, Conrad 1889-1973 . . . . . DLB-9, 45, 102

Aiken, Joan 1924- DLB-161

Aikin, Lucy 1781-1864 . . . . . . DLB-144, 163

Ainsworth, William Harrison
1805-1882 . . . . DLB-21

Aitken, George A. 1860-1917 . . . . . . DLB-149

Aitken, Robert [publishing house] DLB-49

Akenside, Mark 1721-1770 . . . . DLB-109

Akins, Zoë 1886-1958 . . . . DLB-26

Akutagawa, Ryūnsuke
1892-1927 . . . . DLB-180

Alabaster, William 1568-1640 . . . . . . DLB-132

Alain-Fournier 1886-1914 . . . . DLB-65

Alarcón, Francisco X. 1954- DLB-122

Alba, Nanina 1915-1968 . . . . DLB-41

Albee, Edward 1928- DLB-7

Albert the Great circa 1200-1280 . . . . DLB-115

Alberti, Rafael 1902- DLB-108

Albertinus, Aegidius
circa 1560-1620 . . . . DLB-164

Alcaeus born circa 620 B.C. DLB-176

Alcott, Amos Bronson 1799-1888 . . . . . DLB-1

Alcott, Louisa May
1832-1888 . . . . . . DLB-1, 42, 79; DS-14

Alcott, William Andrus 1798-1859 . . . DLB-1

Alcuin circa 732-804 . . . . DLB-148

Alden, Henry Mills 1836-1919 . . . . . DLB-79

Alden, Isabella 1841-1930 . . . . DLB-42

Alden, John B. [publishing house] DLB-49

Alden, Beardsley and Company DLB-49

Aldington, Richard
1892-1962 . . . . . . DLB-20, 36, 100, 149

Aldis, Dorothy 1896-1966 . . . . DLB-22

Aldiss, Brian W. 1925- DLB-14

Aldrich, Thomas Bailey
1836-1907 . . . . DLB-42, 71, 74, 79

Alegría, Ciro 1909-1967 . . . . DLB-113

Alegría, Claribel 1924- DLB-145

Aleixandre, Vicente 1898-1984 . . . . . DLB-108

Aleramo, Sibilla 1876-1960 . . . . DLB-114

Alexander, Charles 1868-1923 . . . . . DLB-91

Alexander, Charles Wesley
[publishing house]. DLB-49

Alexander, James 1691-1756 . . . . . . DLB-24

Alexander, Lloyd 1924- DLB-52

Alexander, Sir William, Earl of Stirling
1577?-1640 . . . . DLB-121

Alexie, Sherman 1966- DLB-175

Alexis, Willibald 1798-1871 . . . . . . DLB-133

Alfred, King 849-899 . . . . DLB-146

Alger, Horatio, Jr. 1832-1899 . . . . . DLB-42

Algonquin Books of Chapel Hill. . . . DLB-46

Algren, Nelson 1909-1981 . . . . . DLB-9; Y-81, 82

Allan, Andrew 1907-1974 . . . . DLB-88

Allan, Ted 1916- DLB-68

Allbeury, Ted 1917- DLB-87

Alldritt, Keith 1935- DLB-14

Allen, Ethan 1738-1789 . . . . DLB-31

Allen, Frederick Lewis 1890-1954 . . . . DLB-137

Allen, Gay Wilson
1903-1995 . . . . DLB-103; Y-95

Allen, George 1808-1876 . . . . DLB-59

Allen, George [publishing house]. DLB-106

Allen, George, and Unwin
Limited DLB-112

Allen, Grant 1848-1899 . . . . . DLB-70, 92, 178

Allen, Henry W. 1912- Y-85

Allen, Hervey 1889-1949 . . . . DLB-9, 45

Allen, James 1739-1808 . . . . DLB-31

Allen, James Lane 1849-1925. . . . . . . DLB-71

Allen, Jay Presson 1922- DLB-26

Allen, John, and Company. DLB-49

Allen, Paula Gunn 1939- DLB-175

Allen, Samuel W. 1917- DLB-41

Allen, Woody 1935- DLB-44

Allende, Isabel 1942- DLB-145

Alline, Henry 1748-1784 . . . . DLB-99

Allingham, Margery 1904-1966. . . . . . DLB-77

Allingham, William 1824-1889 . . . . . . DLB-35

Allison, W. L.
[publishing house]. DLB-49

The *Alliterative Morte Arthure* and
the *Stanzaic Morte Arthur*
circa 1350-1400 . . . . DLB-146

Allott, Kenneth 1912-1973 . . . . DLB-20

Allston, Washington 1779-1843 . . . . . DLB-1

Almon, John [publishing house]. DLB-154

Alonzo, Dámaso 1898-1990 . . . . DLB-108

Alsop, George 1636-post 1673 . . . . . DLB-24

Alsop, Richard 1761-1815 . . . . DLB-37

Altemus, Henry, and Company DLB-49

Altenberg, Peter 1885-1919 . . . . DLB-81

Altolaguirre, Manuel 1905-1959. . . . . DLB-108

Aluko, T. M. 1918- DLB-117

Alurista 1947- DLB-82

Alvarez, A. 1929- DLB-14, 40

Amadi, Elechi 1934- DLB-117

Amado, Jorge 1912- DLB-113

Ambler, Eric 1909- DLB-77

*America: or, a Poem on the Settlement of the
British Colonies* (1780?), by Timothy
Dwight. DLB-37

American Conservatory Theatre. DLB-7

American Fiction and the 1930s DLB-9

American Humor: A Historical Survey
East and Northeast
South and Southwest
Midwest
West. DLB-11

The American Library in Paris Y-93

American News Company DLB-49

The American Poets' Corner: The First
Three Years (1983-1986). Y-86

American Proletarian Culture:
The 1930s. DS-11

American Publishing Company. DLB-49

American Stationers' Company. DLB-49

American Sunday-School Union DLB-49

American Temperance Union DLB-49

American Tract Society. DLB-49

The American Trust for the
British Library Y-96

The American Writers Congress
(9-12 October 1981) Y-81

The American Writers Congress: A Report
on Continuing Business Y-81

Ames, Fisher 1758-1808. . . . . DLB-37

Ames, Mary Clemmer 1831-1884 . . . . DLB-23

Amini, Johari M. 1935- DLB-41

Amis, Kingsley 1922-1995
. . . . DLB-15, 27, 100, 139, Y-96

Amis, Martin 1949- DLB-14

Ammons, A. R. 1926- DLB-5, 165

Amory, Thomas 1691?-1788 . . . . . . DLB-39

Anaya, Rudolfo A. 1937- DLB-82

Ancrene Riwle circa 1200-1225 . . . . . DLB-146

Andersch, Alfred 1914-1980 . . . . . . DLB-69

Anderson, Margaret 1886-1973 . . . . DLB-4, 91

Anderson, Maxwell 1888-1959. . . . . . DLB-7

Anderson, Patrick 1915-1979 . . . . . . DLB-68

Anderson, Paul Y. 1893-1938 . . . . . DLB-29

Anderson, Poul 1926- DLB-8

Anderson, Robert 1750-1830 . . . . . DLB-142

Anderson, Robert 1917- DLB-7

Anderson, Sherwood
1876-1941 . . . . . . DLB-4, 9, 86; DS-1

Andreae, Johann Valentin
1586-1654 . . . . DLB-164

Andreas-Salomé, Lou 1861-1937 . . . . DLB-66

Andres, Stefan 1906-1970 . . . . DLB-69

Andreu, Blanca 1959- DLB-134

Andrewes, Lancelot
1555-1626. . . . . DLB-151, 172

Andrews, Charles M. 1863-1943 . . . . DLB-17

Andrews, Miles Peter ?-1814 . . . . . DLB-89

Andrian, Leopold von 1875-1951 . . . . DLB-81

Andrić, Ivo 1892-1975 . . . . DLB-147

Andrieux, Louis (see Aragon, Louis)

Andrus, Silas, and Son DLB-49

Angell, James Burrill 1829-1916 . . . . DLB-64

Angell, Roger 1920- DLB-171

Angelou, Maya 1928- DLB-38

Anger, Jane flourished 1589. . . . . . DLB-136

Angers, Félicité (see Conan, Laure)

Anglo-Norman Literature in the
Development of Middle English
Literature. DLB-146

The Anglo-Saxon Chronicle
circa 890-1154 . . . . DLB-146

The "Angry Young Men" DLB-15

Angus and Robertson (UK)
Limited. DLB-112

Anhalt, Edward 1914- DLB-26

Anners, Henry F.
[publishing house] DLB-49

Annolied between 1077
and 1081. . . . . DLB-148

Anselm of Canterbury
1033-1109 . . . . DLB-115

Anstey, F. 1856-1934. . . . . DLB-141, 178

Anthony, Michael 1932- DLB-125

Anthony, Piers 1934- DLB-8

Anthony Burgess's *99 Novels:*
An Opinion Poll. Y-84

Antin, David 1932- DLB-169

Antin, Mary 1881-1949. . . . . Y-84

Anton Ulrich, Duke of Brunswick-Lüneburg
1633-1714 . . . . DLB-168

Antschel, Paul (see Celan, Paul)

Anyidoho, Kofi 1947- DLB-157

Anzaldúa, Gloria 1942- DLB-122

Anzengruber, Ludwig
1839-1889 . . . . DLB-129

Apess, William 1798-1839 . . . . DLB-175

Apodaca, Rudy S. 1939- DLB-82

Apollonius Rhodius third century B.C.
. . . . DLB-176

Apple, Max 1941- DLB-130

Appleton, D., and Company DLB-49

Appleton-Century-Crofts DLB-46

Applewhite, James 1935- DLB-105

Apple-wood Books DLB-46

Aquin, Hubert 1929-1977 . . . . DLB-53

Aquinas, Thomas 1224 or
1225-1274 . . . . DLB-115

Aragon, Louis 1897-1982 . . . . DLB-72

Aralica, Ivan 1930- DLB-181

Aratus of Soli circa 315 B.C.-circa 239 B.C.
. . . . DLB-176

Arbor House Publishing
Company DLB-46

Arbuthnot, John 1667-1735 . . . . . . DLB-101

Arcadia House DLB-46

Arce, Julio G. (see Ulica, Jorge)

Archer, William 1856-1924 . . . . DLB-10

Archilochhus mid seventh century B.C.E.
. . . . DLB-176

The Archpoet circa 1130?-? DLB-148

Archpriest Avvakum (Petrovich)
1620?-1682 . . . . DLB-150

Arden, John 1930- DLB-13

Arden of Faversham DLB-62

Ardis Publishers Y-89

Ardizzone, Edward 1900-1979 . . . . . DLB-160

Arellano, Juan Estevan 1947- DLB-122

The Arena Publishing Company DLB-49

Arena Stage DLB-7

Arenas, Reinaldo 1943-1990 . . . . . . DLB-145

Arensberg, Ann 1937- Y-82

Arguedas, José María 1911-1969 . . . . DLB-113

Argueta, Manlio 1936- DLB-145

Arias, Ron 1941- DLB-82

Arishima, Takeo 1878-1923 . . . . . . DLB-180

Aristophanes circa 446 B.C.-circa 446 B.C.-
circa 386 B.C. DLB-176

Aristotle 384 B.C.-322 B.C. DLB-176

Ariyoshi, Sawako 1931-1984 . . . . . . DLB-182

Arland, Marcel 1899-1986 . . . . DLB-72

Arlen, Michael
1895-1956 . . . . DLB-36, 77, 162

Armah, Ayi Kwei 1939- DLB-117

Der arme Hartmann
?-after 1150 . . . . DLB-148

Armed Services Editions DLB-46

Armstrong, Richard 1903- DLB-160

Arndt, Ernst Moritz 1769-1860 . . . . . DLB-90

Arnim, Achim von 1781-1831 . . . . . DLB-90

Arnim, Bettina von 1785-1859 . . . . . DLB-90

Arno Press DLB-46

Arnold, Edwin 1832-1904 . . . . DLB-35

Arnold, Edwin L. 1857-1935 . . . . . . DLB-178

Arnold, Matthew 1822-1888 . . . . DLB-32, 57

Arnold, Thomas 1795-1842 . . . . DLB-55

Arnold, Edward
[publishing house] DLB-112

Arnow, Harriette Simpson
1908-1986 . . . . DLB-6

Arp, Bill (see Smith, Charles Henry)

Arpino, Giovanni 1927-1987 . . . . . . DLB-177

Arreola, Juan José 1918- DLB-113

Arrian circa 89-circa 155 . . . . DLB-176

Arrowsmith, J. W.
[publishing house] DLB-106

Arthur, Timothy Shay
1809-1885 . . . . . . DLB-3, 42, 79; DS-13

The Arthurian Tradition and Its European
Context DLB-138

Artmann, H. C. 1921- DLB-85

Arvin, Newton 1900-1963 . . . . DLB-103

As I See It, by
Carolyn Cassady DLB-16

Asch, Nathan 1902-1964 . . . . DLB-4, 28

Ash, John 1948- DLB-40

Ashbery, John 1927- DLB-5, 165; Y-81

Ashendene Press DLB-112

Asher, Sandy 1942- Y-83

Ashton, Winifred (see Dane, Clemence)

Asimov, Isaac 1920-1992 . . . . . DLB-8; Y-92

Askew, Anne circa 1521-1546 . . . . . DLB-136

Asselin, Olivar 1874-1937 . . . . DLB-92

Asturias, Miguel Angel
1899-1974 . . . . DLB-113

Atheneum Publishers DLB-46

Atherton, Gertrude 1857-1948 . . . . DLB-9, 78

Athlone Press DLB-112

Atkins, Josiah circa 1755-1781 . . . . . DLB-31

Atkins, Russell 1926- DLB-41

The Atlantic Monthly Press DLB-46

Attaway, William 1911-1986 . . . . . . DLB-76

Atwood, Margaret 1939- DLB-53

Aubert, Alvin 1930- DLB-41

Aubert de Gaspé, Phillipe-Ignace-François
1814-1841 . . . . DLB-99

Aubert de Gaspé, Phillipe-Joseph
1786-1871 . . . . DLB-99

Aubin, Napoléon 1812-1890 . . . . . . DLB-99

Aubin, Penelope 1685-circa 1731 . . . . DLB-39

Aubrey-Fletcher, Henry Lancelot
(see Wade, Henry)

Auchincloss, Louis 1917- DLB-2; Y-80

Auden, W. H. 1907-1973 . . . . . DLB-10, 20

Audio Art in America: A Personal
Memoir Y-85

Audobon, John Woodhouse
1812-1862 . . . . DLB-183

Auerbach, Berthold 1812-1882 . . . . . DLB-133

Auernheimer, Raoul 1876-1948 . . . . . DLB-81

Augustine 354-430 . . . . DLB-115

Austen, Jane 1775-1817 . . . . DLB-116

Austin, Alfred 1835-1913 . . . . DLB-35

Austin, Mary 1868-1934 . . . . DLB-9, 78

Austin, William 1778-1841 . . . . DLB-74

Author-Printers, 1476–1599 . . . . . . DLB-167

The Author's Apology for His Book
(1684), by John Bunyan DLB-39

An Author's Response, by
Ronald Sukenick Y-82

Authors and Newspapers
Association DLB-46

Authors' Publishing Company DLB-49

Avalon Books DLB-46

Avancini, Nicolaus 1611-1686 . . . . . DLB-164

Avendaño, Fausto 1941- DLB-82

Averroëó 1126-1198 . . . . DLB-115

Avery, Gillian 1926- DLB-161

Avicenna 980-1037 . . . . DLB-115

Avison, Margaret 1918- DLB-53

Avon Books DLB-46

Awdry, Wilbert Vere 1911- DLB-160

Awoonor, Kofi 1935- DLB-117

Ayckbourn, Alan 1939- DLB-13

Aymé, Marcel 1902-1967 . . . . DLB-72

Aytoun, Sir Robert 1570-1638 . . . . . DLB-121

Aytoun, William Edmondstoune
1813-1865 . . . . DLB-32, 159

B

B. V. (see Thomson, James)

Babbitt, Irving 1865-1933 . . . . DLB-63

Babbitt, Natalie 1932- DLB-52

Babcock, John [publishing house] . . . DLB-49

Babrius circa 150-200 . . . . DLB-176

Baca, Jimmy Santiago 1952- DLB-122

Bache, Benjamin Franklin
1769-1798 . . . . DLB-43

Bachmann, Ingeborg 1926-1973 . . . . DLB-85

Bacon, Delia 1811-1859 . . . . DLB-1

Bacon, Francis 1561-1626 . . . . DLB-151

Bacon, Roger circa
1214/1220-1292 . . . . DLB-115

Bacon, Sir Nicholas
circa 1510-1579 . . . . DLB-132

Bacon, Thomas circa 1700-1768 . . . . . DLB-31

Badger, Richard G.,
and Company. DLB-49

Bage, Robert 1728-1801. . . . . DLB-39

Bagehot, Walter 1826-1877 . . . . DLB-55

Bagley, Desmond 1923-1983 . . . . DLB-87

Bagnold, Enid 1889-1981 . . . . . . DLB-13, 160

Bagryana, Elisaveta 1893-1991 . . . . . DLB-147

Bahr, Hermann 1863-1934 . . . . . DLB-81, 118

Bailey, Alfred Goldsworthy
1905- DLB-68

Bailey, Francis
[publishing house]. DLB-49

Bailey, H. C. 1878-1961 . . . . DLB-77

Bailey, Jacob 1731-1808. . . . . DLB-99

Bailey, Paul 1937- DLB-14

Bailey, Philip James 1816-1902 . . . . . DLB-32

Baillargeon, Pierre 1916-1967 . . . . . . DLB-88

Baillie, Hugh 1890-1966 . . . . DLB-29

Baillie, Joanna 1762-1851 . . . . DLB-93

Bailyn, Bernard 1922- DLB-17

Bainbridge, Beryl 1933- DLB-14

Baird, Irene 1901-1981 . . . . DLB-68

Baker, Augustine 1575-1641 . . . . . . DLB-151

Baker, Carlos 1909-1987 . . . . DLB-103

Baker, David 1954- DLB-120

Baker, Herschel C. 1914-1990 . . . . . DLB-111

Baker, Houston A., Jr. 1943- DLB-67

Baker, Samuel White 1821-1893 . . . . DLB-166

Baker, Walter H., Company
("Baker's Plays") DLB-49

The Baker and Taylor
Company DLB-49

Balaban, John 1943- DLB-120

Bald, Wambly 1902- DLB-4

Balde, Jacob 1604-1668 . . . . DLB-164

Balderston, John 1889-1954 . . . . . . DLB-26

Baldwin, James
1924-1987 . . . . DLB-2, 7, 33; Y-87

Baldwin, Joseph Glover
1815-1864 . . . . DLB-3, 11

Baldwin, Richard and Anne
[publishing house] DLB-170

Baldwin, William
circa 1515-1563 . . . . DLB-132

Bale, John 1495-1563 . . . . DLB-132

Balestrini, Nanni 1935- DLB-128

Ballantine Books. DLB-46

Ballantyne, R. M. 1825-1894 . . . . . DLB-163

Ballard, J. G. 1930- DLB-14

Ballerini, Luigi 1940- DLB-128

Ballou, Maturin Murray
1820-1895 . . . . DLB-79

Ballou, Robert O.
[publishing house] DLB-46

Balzac, Honoré de 1799-1855 . . . . . DLB-119

Bambara, Toni Cade 1939- DLB-38

Bancroft, A. L., and
Company DLB-49

Bancroft, George
1800-1891 . . . . DLB-1, 30, 59

Bancroft, Hubert Howe
1832-1918 . . . . DLB-47, 140

Bangs, John Kendrick
1862-1922 . . . . DLB-11, 79

Banim, John
1798-1842. . . . . . . DLB-116, 158, 159

Banim, Michael 1796-1874 . . . . . DLB-158, 159

Banks, John circa 1653-1706 . . . . . DLB-80

Banks, Russell 1940- DLB-130

Bannerman, Helen 1862-1946 . . . . . DLB-141

Bantam Books. DLB-46

Banti, Anna 1895-1985 . . . . DLB-177

Banville, John 1945- DLB-14

Baraka, Amiri
1934- DLB-5, 7, 16, 38; DS-8

Barbauld, Anna Laetitia
1743-1825 . . . . . DLB-107, 109, 142, 158

Barbeau, Marius 1883-1969 . . . . . . DLB-92

Barber, John Warner 1798-1885 . . . . DLB-30

Bàrberi Squarotti, Giorgio
1929- DLB-128

Barbey d'Aurevilly, Jules-Amédée
1808-1889 . . . . DLB-119

Barbour, John circa 1316-1395 . . . . DLB-146

Barbour, Ralph Henry
1870-1944 . . . . DLB-22

Barbusse, Henri 1873-1935 . . . . . . DLB-65

Barclay, Alexander
circa 1475-1552 . . . . DLB-132

Barclay, E. E., and Company DLB-49

Bardeen, C. W.
[publishing house] DLB-49

Barham, Richard Harris
1788-1845 . . . . DLB-159

Baring, Maurice 1874-1945 . . . . . . DLB-34

Baring-Gould, Sabine 1834-1924 . . . . DLB-156

Barker, A. L. 1918- DLB-14, 139

Barker, George 1913-1991 . . . . . . DLB-20

Barker, Harley Granville
1877-1946 . . . . DLB-10

Barker, Howard 1946- DLB-13

Barker, James Nelson 1784-1858 . . . . DLB-37

Barker, Jane 1652-1727 . . . . . . DLB-39, 131

Barker, Lady Mary Anne
1831-1911 . . . . DLB-166

Barker, William
circa 1520-after 1576 . . . . DLB-132

Barker, Arthur, Limited DLB-112

Barkov, Ivan Semenovich
1732-1768 . . . . DLB-150

Barks, Coleman 1937- DLB-5

Barlach, Ernst 1870-1938 . . . . . DLB-56, 118

Barlow, Joel 1754-1812 . . . . DLB-37

Barnard, John 1681-1770 . . . . DLB-24

Barne, Kitty (Mary Catherine Barne)
1883-1957 . . . . DLB-160

Barnes, Barnabe 1571-1609 . . . . . . DLB-132

Barnes, Djuna 1892-1982 . . . . . DLB-4, 9, 45

Barnes, Jim 1933- DLB-175

Barnes, Julian 1946- Y-93

Barnes, Margaret Ayer 1886-1967 . . . . DLB-9

Barnes, Peter 1931- DLB-13

Barnes, William 1801-1886 . . . . . . DLB-32

Barnes, A. S., and Company. DLB-49

Barnes and Noble Books DLB-46

Barnet, Miguel 1940- DLB-145

Barney, Natalie 1876-1972 . . . . DLB-4

Barnfield, Richard 1574-1627 . . . . . DLB-172

Baron, Richard W.,
Publishing Company DLB-46

Barr, Robert 1850-1912. . . . . . . DLB-70, 92

Barral, Carlos 1928-1989 . . . . DLB-134

Barrax, Gerald William
1933- DLB-41, 120

Barrès, Maurice 1862-1923 . . . . . . DLB-123

Barrett, Eaton Stannard
1786-1820 . . . . DLB-116

Barrie, J. M. 1860-1937 . . . . DLB-10, 141, 156

Barrie and Jenkins DLB-112

Barrio, Raymond 1921- DLB-82

Barrios, Gregg 1945- DLB-122

Barry, Philip 1896-1949 . . . . DLB-7

Barry, Robertine (see Françoise)

Barse and Hopkins DLB-46

Barstow, Stan 1928- DLB-14, 139

Barth, John 1930- DLB-2

Barthelme, Donald
1931-1989 . . . . DLB-2; Y-80, 89

Barthelme, Frederick 1943- Y-85

Bartholomew, Frank 1898-1985 . . . . DLB-127

Bartlett, John 1820-1905 . . . . DLB-1

Bartol, Cyrus Augustus 1813-1900 . . . . DLB-1

Barton, Bernard 1784-1849 . . . . . . DLB-96

Barton, Thomas Pennant
1803-1869 . . . . DLB-140

Bartram, John 1699-1777 . . . . DLB-31

Bartram, William 1739-1823 . . . . . . DLB-37

Basic Books DLB-46

Basille, Theodore (see Becon, Thomas)

Bass, T. J. 1932- Y-81

Bassani, Giorgio 1916- DLB-128, 177

Basse, William circa 1583-1653 . . . . . DLB-121

Bassett, John Spencer 1867-1928 . . . . . DLB-17

Bassler, Thomas Joseph (see Bass, T. J.)

Bate, Walter Jackson
1918- DLB-67, 103

Bateman, Christopher
[publishing house] DLB-170

Bateman, Stephen
circa 1510-1584 . . . . DLB-136

Bates, H. E. 1905-1974 . . . . DLB-162

Bates, Katharine Lee 1859-1929 . . . . . DLB-71

Batsford, B. T.
[publishing house] DLB-106

Battiscombe, Georgina 1905- DLB-155

The Battle of Maldon circa 1000 . . . . . DLB-146

Bauer, Bruno 1809-1882 . . . . DLB-133

Bauer, Wolfgang 1941- DLB-124

Baum, L. Frank 1856-1919 . . . . DLB-22

Baum, Vicki 1888-1960 . . . . DLB-85

Baumbach, Jonathan 1933- Y-80

Bausch, Richard 1945- DLB-130

Bawden, Nina 1925- DLB-14, 161

Bax, Clifford 1886-1962 . . . . . . DLB-10, 100

Baxter, Charles 1947- DLB-130

Bayer, Eleanor (see Perry, Eleanor)

Bayer, Konrad 1932-1964 . . . . DLB-85

Baynes, Pauline 1922- DLB-160

Bazin, Hervé 1911- DLB-83

Beach, Sylvia 1887-1962 . . . . . DLB-4; DS-15

Beacon Press DLB-49

Beadle and Adams DLB-49

Beagle, Peter S. 1939- Y-80

Beal, M. F. 1937- Y-81

Beale, Howard K. 1899-1959 . . . . . . DLB-17

Beard, Charles A. 1874-1948 . . . . . . DLB-17

A Beat Chronology: The First Twenty-five
Years, 1944-1969 . . . . DLB-16

Beattie, Ann 1947- Y-82

Beattie, James 1735-1803 . . . . DLB-109

Beauchemin, Nérée 1850-1931 . . . . . DLB-92

Beauchemin, Yves 1941- DLB-60

Beaugrand, Honoré 1848-1906 . . . . . DLB-99

Beaulieu, Victor-Lévy 1945- DLB-53

Beaumont, Francis circa 1584-1616
and Fletcher, John 1579-1625 . . . . DLB-58

Beaumont, Sir John 1583?-1627 . . . . . DLB-121

Beaumont, Joseph 1616–1699 . . . . . DLB-126

Beauvoir, Simone de
1908-1986 . . . . DLB-72; Y-86

Becher, Ulrich 1910- DLB-69

Becker, Carl 1873-1945 . . . . DLB-17

Becker, Jurek 1937- DLB-75

Becker, Jurgen 1932- DLB-75

Beckett, Samuel
1906-1989 . . . . DLB-13, 15; Y-90

Beckford, William 1760-1844 . . . . . . DLB-39

Beckham, Barry 1944- DLB-33

Becon, Thomas circa 1512-1567 . . . . DLB-136

Bećković, Matija 1939- DLB-181

Beddoes, Thomas 1760-1808 . . . . . DLB-158

Beddoes, Thomas Lovell
1803-1849 . . . . DLB-96

Bede circa 673-735 . . . . DLB-146

Beecher, Catharine Esther
1800-1878 . . . . DLB-1

Beecher, Henry Ward
1813-1887 . . . . DLB-3, 43

Beer, George L. 1872-1920 . . . . . . DLB-47

Beer, Johann 1655-1700 . . . . DLB-168

Beer, Patricia 1919- DLB-40

Beerbohm, Max 1872-1956 . . . . DLB-34, 100

Beer-Hofmann, Richard
1866-1945 . . . . DLB-81

Beers, Henry A. 1847-1926 . . . . . . DLB-71

Beeton, S. O.
[publishing house] DLB-106

Bégon, Elisabeth 1696-1755 . . . . . . DLB-99

Behan, Brendan 1923-1964 . . . . . . DLB-13

Behn, Aphra
1640?-1689 . . . . DLB-39, 80, 131

Behn, Harry 1898-1973 . . . . DLB-61

Behrman, S. N. 1893-1973 . . . . . DLB-7, 44

Belaney, Archibald Stansfeld (see Grey Owl)

Belasco, David 1853-1931 . . . . DLB-7

Belford, Clarke and Company DLB-49

Belitt, Ben 1911- DLB-5

Belknap, Jeremy 1744-1798 . . . . . DLB-30, 37

Bell, Clive 1881-1964 . . . . DS-10

Bell, Gertrude Margaret Lowthian
1868-1926 . . . . DLB-174

Bell, James Madison 1826-1902 . . . . . DLB-50

Bell, Marvin 1937- DLB-5

Bell, Millicent 1919- DLB-111

Bell, Quentin 1910- DLB-155

Bell, Vanessa 1879-1961 . . . . DS-10

Bell, George, and Sons DLB-106

Bell, Robert [publishing house] DLB-49

Bellamy, Edward 1850-1898 . . . . . . DLB-12

Bellamy, John [publishing house] DLB-170

Bellamy, Joseph 1719-1790 . . . . . . DLB-31

Bellezza, Dario 1944- DLB-128

La Belle Assemblée 1806-1837 . . . . . DLB-110

Belloc, Hilaire
1870-1953 . . . . . DLB-19, 100, 141, 174

Bellow, Saul
1915- DLB-2, 28; Y-82; DS-3

Belmont Productions DLB-46

Bemelmans, Ludwig 1898-1962 . . . . . DLB-22

Bemis, Samuel Flagg 1891-1973 . . . . . DLB-17

Bemrose, William
[publishing house] DLB-106

Benchley, Robert 1889-1945 . . . . . . DLB-11

Benedetti, Mario 1920- DLB-113

Benedictus, David 1938- DLB-14

Benedikt, Michael 1935- DLB-5

Benét, Stephen Vincent
1898-1943 . . . . DLB-4, 48, 102

Benét, William Rose 1886-1950 . . . . . DLB-45

Benford, Gregory 1941- Y-82

Benjamin, Park 1809-1864 . . . . DLB-3, 59, 73

Benlowes, Edward 1602-1676 . . . . . DLB-126

Benn, Gottfried 1886-1956 . . . . . . DLB-56

Benn Brothers Limited DLB-106

Bennett, Arnold
1867-1931 . . . . . . DLB-10, 34, 98, 135

Bennett, Charles 1899- DLB-44

Bennett, Gwendolyn 1902- DLB-51

Bennett, Hal 1930- DLB-33

Bennett, James Gordon 1795-1872 . . . . DLB-43

Bennett, James Gordon, Jr.
1841-1918 . . . . DLB-23

Bennett, John 1865-1956 . . . . DLB-42

Bennett, Louise 1919- DLB-117

Benoit, Jacques 1941- DLB-60

Benson, A. C. 1862-1925 . . . . DLB-98

Benson, E. F. 1867-1940 . . . . . DLB-135, 153

Benson, Jackson J. 1930- DLB-111

Benson, Robert Hugh
1871-1914 . . . . DLB-153

Benson, Stella 1892-1933 . . . . . DLB-36, 162

Bent, James Theodore
1852-1897 . . . . DLB-174

Bent, Mabel Virginia Anna ?-? DLB-174

Bentham, Jeremy
1748-1832 . . . . DLB-107, 158

Bentley, E. C. 1875-1956 . . . . DLB-70

Bentley, Richard
[publishing house] DLB-106

Benton, Robert 1932- and Newman,
David 1937- DLB-44

Benziger Brothers DLB-49

Beowulf circa 900-1000
or 790-825 . . . . DLB-146

Beresford, Anne 1929- DLB-40

Beresford, John Davys
1873-1947 . . . . DLB-162; 178

Beresford-Howe, Constance
1922- DLB-88

Berford, R. G., Company DLB-49

Berg, Stephen 1934- DLB-5

Bergengruen, Werner 1892-1964 . . . . . DLB-56

Berger, John 1926- DLB-14

Berger, Meyer 1898-1959 . . . . DLB-29

Berger, Thomas 1924- DLB-2; Y-80

Berkeley, Anthony 1893-1971 . . . . . . DLB-77

Berkeley, George 1685-1753 . . . . DLB-31, 101

The Berkley Publishing
Corporation DLB-46

Berlin, Lucia 1936- DLB-130

Bernal, Vicente J. 1888-1915 . . . . . . DLB-82

Bernanos, Georges 1888-1948 . . . . . . DLB-72

Bernard, Harry 1898-1979 . . . . DLB-92

Bernard, John 1756-1828 . . . . DLB-37

Bernard of Chartres
circa 1060-1124? DLB-115

Bernari, Carlo 1909-1992 . . . . DLB-177

Bernhard, Thomas
1931-1989 . . . . DLB-85, 124

Bernstein, Charles 1950- DLB-169

Berriault, Gina 1926- DLB-130

Berrigan, Daniel 1921- DLB-5

Berrigan, Ted 1934-1983 . . . . DLB-5, 169

Berry, Wendell 1934- DLB-5, 6

Berryman, John 1914-1972 . . . . DLB-48

Bersianik, Louky 1930- DLB-60

Berthelet, Thomas
[publishing house] DLB-170

Berto, Giuseppe 1914-1978 . . . . . . DLB-177

Bertolucci, Attilio 1911- DLB-128

Berton, Pierre 1920- DLB-68

Besant, Sir Walter 1836-1901 . . . . . . DLB-135

Bessette, Gerard 1920- DLB-53

Bessie, Alvah 1904-1985 . . . . DLB-26

Bester, Alfred 1913-1987 . . . . DLB-8

The Bestseller Lists: An Assessment Y-84

Betham-Edwards, Matilda Barbara (see Edwards,
Matilda Barbara Betham-)

Betjeman, John 1906-1984 . . . . . DLB-20; Y-84

Betocchi, Carlo 1899-1986 . . . . . . DLB-128

Bettarini, Mariella 1942- DLB-128

Betts, Doris 1932- Y-82

Beveridge, Albert J. 1862-1927 . . . . . DLB-17

Beverley, Robert
circa 1673-1722 . . . . DLB-24, 30

Beyle, Marie-Henri (see Stendhal)

Bianco, Margery Williams
1881-1944 . . . . DLB-160

Bibaud, Adèle 1854-1941 . . . . DLB-92

Bibaud, Michel 1782-1857 . . . . DLB-99

Bibliographical and Textual Scholarship
Since World War II Y-89

The Bicentennial of James Fenimore
Cooper: An International
Celebration Y-89

Bichsel, Peter 1935- DLB-75

Bickerstaff, Isaac John
1733-circa 1808 . . . . DLB-89

Biddle, Drexel [publishing house] DLB-49

Bidermann, Jacob
1577 or 1578-1639 . . . . DLB-164

Bidwell, Walter Hilliard
1798-1881 . . . . DLB-79

Bienek, Horst 1930- DLB-75

Bierbaum, Otto Julius 1865-1910 . . . . . DLB-66

Bierce, Ambrose
1842-1914? DLB-11, 12, 23, 71, 74

Bigelow, William F. 1879-1966 . . . . . . DLB-91

Biggle, Lloyd, Jr. 1923- DLB-8

Bigiaretti, Libero 1905-1993 . . . . . . DLB-177

Biglow, Hosea (see Lowell, James Russell)

Bigongiari, Piero 1914- DLB-128

Billinger, Richard 1890-1965 . . . . . . DLB-124

Billings, John Shaw 1898-1975 . . . . . DLB-137

Billings, Josh (see Shaw, Henry Wheeler)

Binding, Rudolf G. 1867-1938 . . . . . DLB-66

Bingham, Caleb 1757-1817 . . . . DLB-42

Bingham, George Barry
1906-1988 . . . . DLB-127

Bingley, William
[publishing house] DLB-154

Binyon, Laurence 1869-1943 . . . . . . DLB-19

Biographia Brittanica DLB-142

Biographical Documents I Y-84

Biographical Documents II Y-85

Bioren, John [publishing house] DLB-49

Bioy Casares, Adolfo 1914- DLB-113

Bird, Isabella Lucy 1831-1904 . . . . . . DLB-166

Bird, William 1888-1963 . . . . . . DLB-4; DS-15

Birken, Sigmund von 1626-1681 . . . . DLB-164

Birney, Earle 1904- DLB-88

Birrell, Augustine 1850-1933 . . . . . . DLB-98

Bisher, Furman 1918- DLB-171

Bishop, Elizabeth 1911-1979 . . . . DLB-5, 169

Bishop, John Peale 1892-1944 . . . DLB-4, 9, 45

Bismarck, Otto von 1815-1898 . . . . . DLB-129

Bisset, Robert 1759-1805 . . . . DLB-142

Bissett, Bill 1939- DLB-53

Bitzius, Albert (see Gotthelf, Jeremias)

Black, David (D. M.) 1941- DLB-40

Black, Winifred 1863-1936 . . . . DLB-25

Black, Walter J.
[publishing house] DLB-46

The Black Aesthetic: Background DS-8

The Black Arts Movement, by
Larry Neal DLB-38

Black Theaters and Theater Organizations in
America, 1961-1982:
A Research List DLB-38

Black Theatre: A Forum
[excerpts] DLB-38

Blackamore, Arthur 1679-? DLB-24, 39

Blackburn, Alexander L. 1929- Y-85

Blackburn, Paul 1926-1971 . . . . DLB-16; Y-81

Blackburn, Thomas 1916-1977 . . . . . . DLB-27

Blackmore, R. D. 1825-1900 . . . . . . DLB-18

Blackmore, Sir Richard
1654-1729 . . . . DLB-131

Blackmur, R. P. 1904-1965 . . . . . . DLB-63

Blackwell, Basil, Publisher DLB-106

Blackwood, Algernon Henry
1869-1951 . . . . DLB-153, 156, 178

Blackwood, Caroline 1931- DLB-14

Blackwood, William, and
Sons, Ltd. DLB-154

Blackwood's Edinburgh Magazine
1817-1980 . . . . DLB-110

Blair, Eric Arthur (see Orwell, George)

Blair, Francis Preston 1791-1876 . . . . . DLB-43

Blair, James circa 1655-1743 . . . . . . DLB-24

Blair, John Durburrow 1759-1823 . . . . DLB-37

Blais, Marie-Claire 1939- DLB-53

Blaise, Clark 1940- DLB-53

Blake, Nicholas 1904-1972 . . . . . . DLB-77
(see Day Lewis, C.)

Blake, William
1757-1827 . . . . DLB-93, 154, 163

The Blakiston Company DLB-49

Blanchot, Maurice 1907- DLB-72

Blanckenburg, Christian Friedrich von
1744-1796 . . . . DLB-94

Blaser, Robin 1925- DLB-165

Bledsoe, Albert Taylor
1809-1877 . . . . DLB-3, 79

Blelock and Company DLB-49

Blennerhassett, Margaret Agnew
1773-1842 . . . . DLB-99

Bles, Geoffrey
[publishing house] DLB-112

Blessington, Marguerite, Countess of
1789-1849 . . . . DLB-166

The Blickling Homilies
circa 971 . . . . DLB-146

Blish, James 1921-1975 . . . . DLB-8

Bliss, E., and E. White
[publishing house] DLB-49

Bliven, Bruce 1889-1977 . . . . DLB-137

Bloch, Robert 1917-1994 . . . . DLB-44

Block, Rudolph (see Lessing, Bruno)

Blondal, Patricia 1926-1959 . . . . DLB-88

Bloom, Harold 1930- DLB-67

Bloomer, Amelia 1818-1894 . . . . . . DLB-79

Bloomfield, Robert 1766-1823 . . . . . DLB-93

Bloomsbury Group DS-10

Blotner, Joseph 1923- DLB-111

Bloy, Léon 1846-1917 . . . . DLB-123

Blume, Judy 1938- DLB-52

Blunck, Hans Friedrich 1888-1961 . . . . DLB-66

Blunden, Edmund
1896-1974 . . . . DLB-20, 100, 155

Blunt, Lady Anne Isabella Noel
1837-1917 . . . . DLB-174

Blunt, Wilfrid Scawen
1840-1922 . . . . DLB-19, 174

Bly, Nellie (see Cochrane, Elizabeth)

Bly, Robert 1926- DLB-5

Blyton, Enid 1897-1968 . . . . DLB-160

Boaden, James 1762-1839 . . . . DLB-89

Boas, Frederick S. 1862-1957 . . . . . DLB-149

The Bobbs-Merrill Archive at the
Lilly Library, Indiana University Y-90

The Bobbs-Merrill Company DLB-46

Bobrov, Semen Sergeevich
1763?-1810 . . . . DLB-150

Bobrowski, Johannes 1917-1965 . . . . . DLB-75

Bodenheim, Maxwell 1892-1954 . . . DLB-9, 45

Bodenstedt, Friedrich von
1819-1892 . . . . DLB-129

Bodini, Vittorio 1914-1970 . . . . . . DLB-128

Bodkin, M. McDonnell
1850-1933 . . . . DLB-70

Bodley Head DLB-112

Bodmer, Johann Jakob 1698-1783 . . . . DLB-97

Bodmershof, Imma von 1895-1982 . . . DLB-85

Bodsworth, Fred 1918- DLB-68

Boehm, Sydney 1908- DLB-44

Boer, Charles 1939- DLB-5

Boethius circa 480-circa 524 . . . . . . DLB-115

Boethius of Dacia circa 1240-? DLB-115

Bogan, Louise 1897-1970 . . . . . DLB-45, 169

Bogarde, Dirk 1921- DLB-14

Bogdanovich, Ippolit Fedorovich
circa 1743-1803 . . . . DLB-150

Bogue, David [publishing house] DLB-106

Böhme, Jakob 1575-1624 . . . . DLB-164

Bohn, H. G. [publishing house] DLB-106

Bohse, August 1661-1742 . . . . DLB-168

Boie, Heinrich Christian
1744-1806 . . . . DLB-94

Bok, Edward W. 1863-1930 . . . DLB-91; DS-16

Boland, Eavan 1944- DLB-40

Bolingbroke, Henry St. John, Viscount
1678-1751 . . . . DLB-101

Böll, Heinrich 1917-1985 . . . . . Y-85, DLB-69

Bolling, Robert 1738-1775 . . . . DLB-31

Bolotov, Andrei Timofeevich
1738-1833 . . . . DLB-150

Bolt, Carol 1941- DLB-60

Bolt, Robert 1924- DLB-13

Bolton, Herbert E. 1870-1953 . . . . . DLB-17

Bonaventura DLB-90

Bonaventure circa 1217-1274 . . . . . DLB-115

Bonaviri, Giuseppe 1924- DLB-177

Bond, Edward 1934- DLB-13

Bond, Michael 1926- DLB-161

Bonnin, Gertrude Simmons (see Zitkala-Ša)

Boni, Albert and Charles
[publishing house] DLB-46

Boni and Liveright DLB-46

Robert Bonner's Sons DLB-49

Bonsanti, Alessandro 1904-1984 . . . . DLB-177

Bontemps, Arna 1902-1973 . . . . . DLB-48, 51

The Book Arts Press at the University
of Virginia Y-96

The Book League of America DLB-46

Book Reviewing in America: I Y-87

Book Reviewing in America: II Y-88

Book Reviewing in America: III Y-89

Book Reviewing in America: IV Y-90

Book Reviewing in America: V Y-91

Book Reviewing in America: VI Y-92

Book Reviewing in America: VII Y-93

Book Reviewing in America: VIII Y-94

Book Reviewing in America and the
Literary Scene Y-95

Book Reviewing and the
Literary Scene Y-96

Book Supply Company DLB-49

The Book Trade History Group Y-93

The Booker Prize Y-96

The Booker Prize
Address by Anthony Thwaite,
Chairman of the Booker Prize Judges
Comments from Former Booker
Prize Winners Y-86

Boorde, Andrew circa 1490-1549 . . . . DLB-136

Boorstin, Daniel J. 1914- DLB-17

Booth, Mary L. 1831-1889 . . . . DLB-79

Booth, Philip 1925- Y-82

Booth, Wayne C. 1921- DLB-67

Borchardt, Rudolf 1877-1945 . . . . . . DLB-66

Borchert, Wolfgang
1921-1947 . . . . DLB-69, 124

Borel, Pétrus 1809-1859 . . . . DLB-119

Borges, Jorge Luis
1899-1986 . . . . DLB-113; Y-86

Börne, Ludwig 1786-1837 . . . . DLB-90

Borrow, George
1803-1881 . . . . DLB-21, 55, 166

Bosch, Juan 1909- DLB-145

Bosco, Henri 1888-1976 . . . . DLB-72

Bosco, Monique 1927- DLB-53

Boston, Lucy M. 1892-1990 . . . . . . DLB-161

Boswell, James 1740-1795 . . . . DLB-104, 142

Botev, Khristo 1847-1876 . . . . DLB-147

Bote, Hermann
circa 1460-circa 1520 . . . . DLB-179

Botta, Anne C. Lynch 1815-1891 . . . . . DLB-3

Bottomley, Gordon 1874-1948 . . . . . DLB-10

Bottoms, David 1949- DLB-120; Y-83

Bottrall, Ronald 1906- DLB-20

Boucher, Anthony 1911-1968 . . . . . . DLB-8

Boucher, Jonathan 1738-1804 . . . . . . DLB-31

Boucher de Boucherville, George
1814-1894 . . . . DLB-99

Boudreau, Daniel (see Coste, Donat)

Bourassa, Napoléon 1827-1916 . . . . . DLB-99

Bourget, Paul 1852-1935 . . . . DLB-123

Bourinot, John George 1837-1902 . . . . DLB-99

Bourjaily, Vance 1922- DLB-2, 143

Bourne, Edward Gaylord
1860-1908 . . . . DLB-47

Bourne, Randolph 1886-1918 . . . . . . DLB-63

Bousoño, Carlos 1923- DLB-108

Bousquet, Joë 1897-1950 . . . . DLB-72

Bova, Ben 1932- Y-81

Bovard, Oliver K. 1872-1945 . . . . . . DLB-25

Bove, Emmanuel 1898-1945 . . . . . . DLB-72

Bowen, Elizabeth 1899-1973 . . . . DLB-15, 162

Bowen, Francis 1811-1890 . . . . . . DLB-1, 59

Bowen, John 1924- DLB-13

Bowen, Marjorie 1886-1952 . . . . . . DLB-153

Bowen-Merrill Company DLB-49

Bowering, George 1935- DLB-53

Bowers, Claude G. 1878-1958 . . . . . DLB-17

Bowers, Edgar 1924- DLB-5

Bowers, Fredson Thayer
1905-1991 . . . . DLB-140; Y-91

Bowles, Paul 1910- DLB-5, 6

Bowles, Samuel III 1826-1878 . . . . . DLB-43

Bowles, William Lisles 1762-1850 . . . . DLB-93

Bowman, Louise Morey
1882-1944 . . . . DLB-68

Boyd, James 1888-1944 . . . . . . DLB-9; DS-16

Boyd, John 1919- DLB-8

Boyd, Thomas 1898-1935 . . . . . DLB-9; DS-16

Boyesen, Hjalmar Hjorth
1848-1895 . . . . DLB-12, 71; DS-13

Boyle, Kay
1902-1992 . . . . . DLB-4, 9, 48, 86; Y-93

Boyle, Roger, Earl of Orrery
1621-1679 . . . . DLB-80

Boyle, T. Coraghessan 1948- Y-86

Božić, Mirko 1919- DLB-181

Brackenbury, Alison 1953- DLB-40

Brackenridge, Hugh Henry
1748-1816 . . . . DLB-11, 37

Brackett, Charles 1892-1969 . . . . . . DLB-26

Brackett, Leigh 1915-1978 . . . . . DLB-8, 26

Bradburn, John
[publishing house] DLB-49

Bradbury, Malcolm 1932- DLB-14

Bradbury, Ray 1920- DLB-2, 8

Bradbury and Evans DLB-106

Braddon, Mary Elizabeth
1835-1915 . . . . DLB-18, 70, 156

Bradford, Andrew 1686-1742 . . . . DLB-43, 73

Bradford, Gamaliel 1863-1932 . . . . . DLB-17

Bradford, John 1749-1830 . . . . DLB-43

Bradford, Roark 1896-1948 . . . . DLB-86

Bradford, William 1590-1657 . . . . DLB-24, 30

Bradford, William III
1719-1791 . . . . DLB-43, 73

Bradlaugh, Charles 1833-1891 . . . . . DLB-57

Bradley, David 1950- DLB-33

Bradley, Marion Zimmer 1930- DLB-8

Bradley, William Aspenwall
1878-1939 . . . . DLB-4

Bradley, Ira, and Company DLB-49

Bradley, J. W., and Company DLB-49

Bradstreet, Anne
1612 or 1613-1672 . . . . DLB-24

Bradwardine, Thomas circa
1295-1349 . . . . DLB-115

Brady, Frank 1924-1986 . . . . DLB-111

Brady, Frederic A.
[publishing house] DLB-49

Bragg, Melvyn 1939- DLB-14

Brainard, Charles H.
[publishing house] DLB-49

Braine, John 1922-1986 . . . . . DLB-15; Y-86

Braithwait, Richard 1588-1673 . . . . DLB-151

Braithwaite, William Stanley
1878-1962 . . . . DLB-50, 54

Braker, Ulrich 1735-1798 . . . . DLB-94

Bramah, Ernest 1868-1942 . . . . . . DLB-70

Branagan, Thomas 1774-1843 . . . . . DLB-37

Branch, William Blackwell
1927- DLB-76

Branden Press DLB-46

Brant, Sebastian 1457-1521 . . . . . DLB-179

Brassey, Lady Annie (Allnutt)
1839-1887 . . . . DLB-166

Brathwaite, Edward Kamau
1930- DLB-125

Brault, Jacques 1933- DLB-53

Braun, Volker 1939- DLB-75

Brautigan, Richard
1935-1984 . . . . . . DLB-2, 5; Y-80, 84

Braxton, Joanne M. 1950- DLB-41

Bray, Anne Eliza 1790-1883 . . . . . . DLB-116

Bray, Thomas 1656-1730 . . . . . . DLB-24

Braziller, George
[publishing house] DLB-46

The Bread Loaf Writers'
Conference 1983 . . . . Y-84

The Break-Up of the Novel (1922),
by John Middleton Murry DLB-36

Breasted, James Henry 1865-1935 . . . . DLB-47

Brecht, Bertolt 1898-1956 . . . . . DLB-56, 124

Bredel, Willi 1901-1964 . . . . DLB-56

Breitinger, Johann Jakob
1701-1776 . . . . DLB-97

Bremser, Bonnie 1939- DLB-16

Bremser, Ray 1934- DLB-16

Brentano, Bernard von
1901-1964 . . . . DLB-56

Brentano, Clemens 1778-1842 . . . . . DLB-90

Brentano's DLB-49

Brenton, Howard 1942- DLB-13

Breton, André 1896-1966 . . . . DLB-65

Breton, Nicholas
circa 1555-circa 1626 . . . . DLB-136

The Breton Lays
1300-early fifteenth century DLB-146

Brewer, Warren and Putnam DLB-46

Brewster, Elizabeth 1922- DLB-60

Bridge, Horatio 1806-1893 . . . . . . DLB-183

Bridgers, Sue Ellen 1942- DLB-52

Bridges, Robert 1844-1930 . . . . . DLB-19, 98

Bridie, James 1888-1951 . . . . DLB-10

Bright, Mary Chavelita Dunne
(see Egerton, George)

Brimmer, B. J., Company DLB-46

Brines, Francisco 1932- DLB-134

Brinley, George, Jr. 1817-1875 . . . . DLB-140

Brinnin, John Malcolm 1916- DLB-48

Brisbane, Albert 1809-1890 . . . . . . DLB-3

Brisbane, Arthur 1864-1936 . . . . . . DLB-25

British Academy DLB-112

The British Library and the Regular
Readers' Group Y-91

The British Critic 1793-1843 . . . . . . DLB-110

The British Review and London
Critical Journal 1811-1825 . . . . . DLB-110

Brito, Aristeo 1942- DLB-122

Broadway Publishing Company DLB-46

Broch, Hermann 1886-1951 . . . . DLB-85, 124

Brochu, André 1942- DLB-53

Brock, Edwin 1927- DLB-40

Brockes, Barthold Heinrich
1680-1747 . . . . DLB-168

Brod, Max 1884-1968 . . . . DLB-81

Brodber, Erna 1940- DLB-157

Brodhead, John R. 1814-1873 . . . . . DLB-30

Brodkey, Harold 1930- DLB-130

Broeg, Bob 1918- DLB-171

Brome, Richard circa 1590-1652 . . . . DLB-58

Brome, Vincent 1910- DLB-155

Bromfield, Louis 1896-1956 . . . . DLB-4, 9, 86

Broner, E. M. 1930- DLB-28

Bronk, William 1918- DLB-165

Bronnen, Arnolt 1895-1959 . . . . . . DLB-124

Brontë, Anne 1820-1849 . . . . DLB-21

Brontë, Charlotte 1816-1855 . . . . DLB-21, 159

Brontë, Emily 1818-1848 . . . . . . DLB-21, 32

Brooke, Frances 1724-1789 . . . . . DLB-39, 99

Brooke, Henry 1703?-1783 . . . . . . DLB-39

Brooke, L. Leslie 1862-1940 . . . . . DLB-141

Brooke, Margaret, Ranee of Sarawak
1849-1936 . . . . DLB-174

Brooke, Rupert 1887-1915 . . . . . . DLB-19

Brooker, Bertram 1888-1955 . . . . . . DLB-88

Brooke-Rose, Christine 1926- DLB-14

Brookner, Anita 1928- Y-87

Brooks, Charles Timothy
1813-1883 . . . . DLB-1

Brooks, Cleanth 1906-1994 . . . . DLB-63; Y-94

Brooks, Gwendolyn
1917- DLB-5, 76, 165

Brooks, Jeremy 1926- DLB-14

Brooks, Mel 1926- DLB-26

Brooks, Noah 1830-1903 . . . . . DLB-42; DS-13

Brooks, Richard 1912-1992 . . . . . . DLB-44

Brooks, Van Wyck
1886-1963 . . . . DLB-45, 63, 103

Brophy, Brigid 1929- DLB-14

Brossard, Chandler 1922-1993 . . . . . DLB-16

Brossard, Nicole 1943- DLB-53

Broster, Dorothy Kathleen
1877-1950 . . . . DLB-160

Brother Antoninus (see Everson, William)

Brougham and Vaux, Henry Peter
Brougham, Baron
1778-1868 . . . . DLB-110, 158

Brougham, John 1810-1880 . . . . . . DLB-11

Broughton, James 1913- DLB-5

Broughton, Rhoda 1840-1920 . . . . . DLB-18

Broun, Heywood 1888-1939 . . . . DLB-29, 171

Brown, Alice 1856-1948. . . . . DLB-78

Brown, Bob 1886-1959 . . . . DLB-4, 45

Brown, Cecil 1943- DLB-33

Brown, Charles Brockden
1771-1810. . . . . DLB-37, 59, 73

Brown, Christy 1932-1981 . . . . DLB-14

Brown, Dee 1908- Y-80

Brown, Frank London 1927-1962 . . . . DLB-76

Brown, Fredric 1906-1972 . . . . DLB-8

Brown, George Mackay
1921- DLB-14, 27, 139

Brown, Harry 1917-1986 . . . . DLB-26

Brown, Marcia 1918- DLB-61

Brown, Margaret Wise
1910-1952 . . . . DLB-22

Brown, Morna Doris (see Ferrars, Elizabeth)

Brown, Oliver Madox
1855-1874 . . . . DLB-21

Brown, Sterling
1901-1989. . . . . DLB-48, 51, 63

Brown, T. E. 1830-1897 . . . . DLB-35

Brown, William Hill 1765-1793 . . . . DLB-37

Brown, William Wells
1814-1884. . . . . DLB-3, 50, 183

Browne, Charles Farrar
1834-1867 . . . . DLB-11

Browne, Francis Fisher
1843-1913 . . . . DLB-79

Browne, Michael Dennis
1940- DLB-40

Browne, Sir Thomas 1605-1682 . . . . DLB-151

Browne, William, of Tavistock
1590-1645 . . . . DLB-121

Browne, Wynyard 1911-1964 . . . . . DLB-13

Browne and Nolan DLB-106

Brownell, W. C. 1851-1928 . . . . . . DLB-71

Browning, Elizabeth Barrett
1806-1861 . . . . DLB-32

Browning, Robert
1812-1889 . . . . DLB-32, 163

Brownjohn, Allan 1931- DLB-40

Brownson, Orestes Augustus
1803-1876 . . . . DLB-1, 59, 73

Bruccoli, Matthew J. 1931- DLB-103

Bruce, Charles 1906-1971 . . . . DLB-68

Bruce, Leo 1903-1979 . . . . DLB-77

Bruce, Philip Alexander
1856-1933 . . . . DLB-47

Bruce Humphries
[publishing house] DLB-46

Bruce-Novoa, Juan 1944- DLB-82

Bruckman, Clyde 1894-1955 . . . . . . DLB-26

Bruckner, Ferdinand 1891-1958 . . . . DLB-118

Brundage, John Herbert (see Herbert, John)

Brutus, Dennis 1924- DLB-117

Bryant, Arthur 1899-1985 . . . . DLB-149

Bryant, William Cullen
1794-1878 . . . . DLB-3, 43, 59

Bryce Echenique, Alfredo
1939- DLB-145

Bryce, James 1838-1922 . . . . DLB-166

Brydges, Sir Samuel Egerton
1762-1837 . . . . DLB-107

Bryskett, Lodowick 1546?-1612 . . . . . DLB-167

Buchan, John 1875-1940 . . . . DLB-34, 70, 156

Buchanan, George 1506-1582 . . . . . DLB-132

Buchanan, Robert 1841-1901. . . . . DLB-18, 35

Buchman, Sidney 1902-1975 . . . . . . DLB-26

Buchner, Augustus 1591-1661. . . . . DLB-164

Büchner, Georg 1813-1837 . . . . DLB-133

Bucholtz, Andreas Heinrich
1607-1671 . . . . DLB-168

Buck, Pearl S. 1892-1973. . . . . . DLB-9, 102

Bucke, Charles 1781-1846 . . . . DLB-110

Bucke, Richard Maurice
1837-1902 . . . . DLB-99

Buckingham, Joseph Tinker 1779-1861 and
Buckingham, Edwin
1810-1833 . . . . DLB-73

Buckler, Ernest 1908-1984 . . . . DLB-68

Buckley, William F., Jr.
1925- DLB-137; Y-80

Buckminster, Joseph Stevens
1784-1812 . . . . DLB-37

Buckner, Robert 1906- DLB-26

Budd, Thomas ?-1698 . . . . DLB-24

Budrys, A. J. 1931- DLB-8

Buechner, Frederick 1926- Y-80

Buell, John 1927- DLB-53

Buffum, Job [publishing house]. DLB-49

Bugnet, Georges 1879-1981. . . . . . DLB-92

Buies, Arthur 1840-1901 . . . . DLB-99

Building the New British Library
at St Pancras Y-94

Bukowski, Charles
1920-1994 . . . . DLB-5, 130, 169

Bulatović, Miodrag 1930-1991. . . . . DLB-181

Bulger, Bozeman 1877-1932. . . . . . DLB-171

Bullein, William
between 1520 and 1530-1576. . . . DLB-167

Bullins, Ed 1935- DLB-7, 38

Bulwer-Lytton, Edward (also Edward Bulwer)
1803-1873 . . . . DLB-21

Bumpus, Jerry 1937- Y-81

Bunce and Brother DLB-49

Bunner, H. C. 1855-1896 . . . . . DLB-78, 79

Bunting, Basil 1900-1985 . . . . DLB-20

Bunyan, John 1628-1688 . . . . DLB-39

Burch, Robert 1925- DLB-52

Burciaga, José Antonio 1940- DLB-82

Bürger, Gottfried August
1747-1794 . . . . DLB-94

Burgess, Anthony 1917-1993 . . . . . . DLB-14

Burgess, Gelett 1866-1951 . . . . DLB-11

Burgess, John W. 1844-1931 . . . . . . DLB-47

Burgess, Thornton W.
1874-1965 . . . . DLB-22

Burgess, Stringer and Company DLB-49

Burick, Si 1909-1986. . . . . DLB-171

Burk, John Daly circa 1772-1808 . . . . DLB-37

Burke, Edmund 1729?-1797. . . . . . DLB-104

Burke, Kenneth 1897-1993 . . . . . DLB-45, 63

Burlingame, Edward Livermore
1848-1922 . . . . DLB-79

Burnet, Gilbert 1643-1715 . . . . DLB-101

Burnett, Frances Hodgson
1849-1924. . . . . DLB-42, 141; DS-13, 14

Burnett, W. R. 1899-1982 . . . . DLB-9

Burnett, Whit 1899-1973 and
Martha Foley 1897-1977 . . . . . . DLB-137

Burney, Fanny 1752-1840 . . . . DLB-39

Burns, Alan 1929- DLB-14

Burns, John Horne 1916-1953. . . . . . Y-85

Burns, Robert 1759-1796 . . . . DLB-109

Burns and Oates. DLB-106

Burnshaw, Stanley 1906- DLB-48

Burr, C. Chauncey 1815?-1883 . . . . . DLB-79

Burroughs, Edgar Rice 1875-1950. . . . DLB-8

Burroughs, John 1837-1921. . . . . . . DLB-64

Burroughs, Margaret T. G.
1917- DLB-41

Burroughs, William S., Jr.
1947-1981 . . . . DLB-16

Burroughs, William Seward
1914- DLB-2, 8, 16, 152; Y-81

Burroway, Janet 1936- DLB-6

Burt, Maxwell Struthers
1882-1954 . . . . DLB-86; DS-16

Burt, A. L., and Company. DLB-49

Burton, Hester 1913- DLB-161

Burton, Isabel Arundell
1831-1896 . . . . DLB-166

Burton, Miles (see Rhode, John)

Burton, Richard Francis
1821-1890 . . . . DLB-55, 166

Burton, Robert 1577-1640 . . . . DLB-151

Burton, Virginia Lee 1909-1968 . . . . . DLB-22

Burton, William Evans
1804-1860 . . . . DLB-73

Burwell, Adam Hood 1790-1849 . . . . DLB-99

Bury, Lady Charlotte
1775-1861 . . . . DLB-116

Busch, Frederick 1941- DLB-6

Busch, Niven 1903-1991 . . . . DLB-44

Bushnell, Horace 1802-1876 . . . . DS-13

Bussieres, Arthur de 1877-1913 . . . . . DLB-92

Butler, Juan 1942-1981 . . . . DLB-53

Butler, Octavia E. 1947- DLB-33

Butler, Robert Olen 1945- DLB-173

Butler, Samuel 1613-1680 . . . . . DLB-101, 126

Butler, Samuel 1835-1902 . . . . DLB-18, 57, 174

Butler, William Francis
1838-1910 . . . . DLB-166

Butler, E. H., and Company DLB-49

Butor, Michel 1926- DLB-83

Butter, Nathaniel
[publishing house] DLB-170

Butterworth, Hezekiah 1839-1905 . . . . DLB-42

Buttitta, Ignazio 1899- DLB-114

Buzzati, Dino 1906-1972 . . . . DLB-177

Byars, Betsy 1928- DLB-52

Byatt, A. S. 1936- DLB-14

Byles, Mather 1707-1788 . . . . DLB-24

Bynneman, Henry
[publishing house] DLB-170

Bynner, Witter 1881-1968 . . . . DLB-54

Byrd, William circa 1543-1623 . . . . . DLB-172

Byrd, William II 1674-1744 . . . . DLB-24, 140

Byrne, John Keyes (see Leonard, Hugh)

Byron, George Gordon, Lord
1788-1824 . . . . DLB-96, 110

C

Caballero Bonald, José Manuel
1926- DLB-108

Cabañero, Eladio 1930- DLB-134

Cabell, James Branch
1879-1958 . . . . DLB-9, 78

Cabeza de Baca, Manuel
1853-1915 . . . . DLB-122

Cabeza de Baca Gilbert, Fabiola
1898- DLB-122

Cable, George Washington
1844-1925 . . . . DLB-12, 74; DS-13

Cabrera, Lydia 1900-1991 . . . . DLB-145

Cabrera Infante, Guillermo
1929- DLB-113

Cadell [publishing house] DLB-154

Cady, Edwin H. 1917- DLB-103

Caedmon flourished 658-680 . . . . . DLB-146

Caedmon School circa 660-899 . . . . DLB-146

Cafés, Brasseries, and Bistros DS-15

Cahan, Abraham
1860-1951 . . . . DLB-9, 25, 28

Cain, George 1943- DLB-33

Caldecott, Randolph 1846-1886 . . . . DLB-163

Calder, John
(Publishers), Limited DLB-112

Calderón de la Barca, Fanny
1804-1882 . . . . DLB-183

Caldwell, Ben 1937- DLB-38

Caldwell, Erskine 1903-1987 . . . . DLB-9, 86

Caldwell, H. M., Company DLB-49

Calhoun, John C. 1782-1850 . . . . . DLB-3

Calisher, Hortense 1911- DLB-2

A Call to Letters and an Invitation
to the Electric Chair,
by Siegfried Mandel DLB-75

Callaghan, Morley 1903-1990 . . . . . DLB-68

Callahan, S. Alice 1868-1894 . . . . . DLB-175

Callaloo Y-87

Callimachus circa 305 B.C.-240 B.C.
. . . . DLB-176

Calmer, Edgar 1907- DLB-4

Calverley, C. S. 1831-1884 . . . . . . DLB-35

Calvert, George Henry
1803-1889 . . . . DLB-1, 64

Cambridge Press DLB-49

Cambridge Songs (Carmina Cantabrigensia)
circa 1050 . . . . DLB-148

Cambridge University Press DLB-170

Camden, William 1551-1623 . . . . . DLB-172

Camden House: An Interview with
James Hardin Y-92

Cameron, Eleanor 1912- DLB-52

Cameron, George Frederick
1854-1885 . . . . DLB-99

Cameron, Lucy Lyttelton
1781-1858 . . . . DLB-163

Cameron, William Bleasdell
1862-1951 . . . . DLB-99

Camm, John 1718-1778 . . . . DLB-31

Campana, Dino 1885-1932 . . . . . . DLB-114

Campbell, Gabrielle Margaret Vere
(see Shearing, Joseph, and Bowen, Marjorie)

Campbell, James Dykes
1838-1895 . . . . DLB-144

Campbell, James Edwin
1867-1896 . . . . DLB-50

Campbell, John 1653-1728 . . . . . . DLB-43

Campbell, John W., Jr.
1910-1971 . . . . DLB-8

Campbell, Roy 1901-1957 . . . . . . DLB-20

Campbell, Thomas
1777-1844 . . . . DLB-93, 144

Campbell, William Wilfred
1858-1918 . . . . DLB-92

Campion, Edmund 1539-1581 . . . . DLB-167

Campion, Thomas
1567-1620 . . . . DLB-58, 172

Camus, Albert 1913-1960 . . . . DLB-72

The Canadian Publishers' Records
Database Y-96

Canby, Henry Seidel 1878-1961 . . . . DLB-91

Candelaria, Cordelia 1943- DLB-82

Candelaria, Nash 1928- DLB-82

Candour in English Fiction (1890),
by Thomas Hardy DLB-18

Canetti, Elias 1905-1994 . . . . . . DLB-85, 124

Canham, Erwin Dain
1904-1982 . . . . DLB-127

Canitz, Friedrich Rudolph Ludwig von
1654-1699 . . . . DLB-168

Cankar, Ivan 1876-1918 . . . . DLB-147

Cannan, Gilbert 1884-1955 . . . . . . DLB-10

Cannell, Kathleen 1891-1974 . . . . . DLB-4

Cannell, Skipwith 1887-1957 . . . . . DLB-45

Canning, George 1770-1827 . . . . . DLB-158

Cannon, Jimmy 1910-1973 . . . . . . DLB-171

Cantwell, Robert 1908-1978 . . . . . DLB-9

Cape, Jonathan, and Harrison Smith
[publishing house] DLB-46

Cape, Jonathan, Limited DLB-112

Capen, Joseph 1658-1725 . . . . DLB-24

Capes, Bernard 1854-1918 . . . . . . DLB-156

Capote, Truman 1924-1984 . . DLB-2; Y-80, 84

Caproni, Giorgio 1912-1990 . . . . . DLB-128

Cardarelli, Vincenzo 1887-1959 . . . . DLB-114

Cárdenas, Reyes 1948- DLB-122

Cardinal, Marie 1929- DLB-83

Carew, Jan 1920- DLB-157

Carew, Thomas
1594 or 1595-1640 . . . . DLB-126

Carey, Henry
circa 1687-1689-1743 . . . . DLB-84

Carey, Mathew 1760-1839 . . . . . DLB-37, 73

Carey and Hart DLB-49

Carey, M., and Company DLB-49

Carlell, Lodowick 1602-1675 . . . . . DLB-58

Carleton, William 1794-1869 . . . . . DLB-159

Carleton, G. W.
[publishing house] DLB-49

Carlile, Richard 1790-1843 . . . . DLB-110, 158

Carlyle, Jane Welsh 1801-1866 . . . . DLB-55

Carlyle, Thomas 1795-1881 . . . . DLB-55, 144

Carman, Bliss 1861-1929 . . . . DLB-92

Carmina Burana circa 1230 . . . . . DLB-138

Carnero, Guillermo 1947- DLB-108

Carossa, Hans 1878-1956 . . . . DLB-66

Carpenter, Humphrey 1946- DLB-155

Carpenter, Stephen Cullen ?-1820? . . . DLB-73

Carpentier, Alejo 1904-1980 . . . . . DLB-113

Carrier, Roch 1937- DLB-53

Carrillo, Adolfo 1855-1926 . . . . DLB-122

Carroll, Gladys Hasty 1904- DLB-9

Carroll, John 1735-1815 . . . . DLB-37

Carroll, John 1809-1884 . . . . DLB-99

Carroll, Lewis
1832-1898 . . . . DLB-18, 163, 178

Carroll, Paul 1927- DLB-16

Carroll, Paul Vincent 1900-1968 . . . . . DLB-10

Carroll and Graf Publishers DLB-46

Carruth, Hayden 1921- DLB-5, 165

Carryl, Charles E. 1841-1920 . . . . . . DLB-42

Carswell, Catherine 1879-1946 . . . . . DLB-36

Carter, Angela 1940-1992. . . . . DLB-14

Carter, Elizabeth 1717-1806 . . . . . . DLB-109

Carter, Henry (see Leslie, Frank)

Carter, Hodding, Jr. 1907-1972 . . . . . DLB-127

Carter, Landon 1710-1778 . . . . DLB-31

Carter, Lin 1930- Y-81

Carter, Martin 1927- DLB-117

Carter and Hendee DLB-49

Carter, Robert, and Brothers. DLB-49

Cartwright, John 1740-1824 . . . . DLB-158

Cartwright, William circa
1611-1643 . . . . DLB-126

Caruthers, William Alexander
1802-1846. . . . . DLB-3

Carver, Jonathan 1710-1780 . . . . . . DLB-31

Carver, Raymond
1938-1988. . . . . DLB-130; Y-84, 88

Cary, Joyce 1888-1957 . . . . . . DLB-15, 100

Cary, Patrick 1623?-1657 . . . . DLB-131

Casey, Juanita 1925- DLB-14

Casey, Michael 1947- DLB-5

Cassady, Carolyn 1923- DLB-16

Cassady, Neal 1926-1968 . . . . DLB-16

Cassell and Company DLB-106

Cassell Publishing Company DLB-49

Cassill, R. V. 1919- DLB-6

Cassity, Turner 1929- DLB-105

Cassius Dio circa 155/164-post 229
. . . . DLB-176

Cassola, Carlo 1917-1987 . . . . DLB-177

The Castle of Perseverance
circa 1400-1425 . . . . DLB-146

Castellano, Olivia 1944- DLB-122

Castellanos, Rosario 1925-1974 . . . . . DLB-113

Castillo, Ana 1953- DLB-122

Castlemon, Harry (see Fosdick, Charles Austin)

Čašule, Kole 1921- DLB-181

Caswall, Edward 1814-1878 . . . . DLB-32

Catacalos, Rosemary 1944- DLB-122

Cather, Willa
1873-1947. . . . . . . DLB-9, 54, 78; DS-1

Catherine II (Ekaterina Alekseevna), "The
Great," Empress of Russia
1729-1796 . . . . DLB-150

Catherwood, Mary Hartwell
1847-1902 . . . . DLB-78

Catledge, Turner 1901-1983. . . . . . DLB-127

Cattafi, Bartolo 1922-1979 . . . . DLB-128

Catton, Bruce 1899-1978 . . . . DLB-17

Causley, Charles 1917- DLB-27

Caute, David 1936- DLB-14

Cavendish, Duchess of Newcastle,
Margaret Lucas 1623-1673 . . . . DLB-131

Cawein, Madison 1865-1914 . . . . . . DLB-54

The Caxton Printers, Limited DLB-46

Caxton, William
[publishing house] DLB-170

Cayrol, Jean 1911- DLB-83

Cecil, Lord David 1902-1986 . . . . . DLB-155

Celan, Paul 1920-1970 . . . . DLB-69

Celaya, Gabriel 1911-1991. . . . . . . DLB-108

Céline, Louis-Ferdinand
1894-1961 . . . . DLB-72

The Celtic Background to Medieval English
Literature. DLB-146

Celtis, Conrad 1459-1508 . . . . DLB-179

Center for Bibliographical Studies and
Research at the University of
California, Riverside Y-91

The Center for the Book in the Library
of Congress. Y-93

Center for the Book Research. Y-84

Centlivre, Susanna 1669?-1723 . . . . . DLB-84

The Century Company. DLB-49

Cernuda, Luis 1902-1963 . . . . DLB-134

Cervantes, Lorna Dee 1954- DLB-82

Chacel, Rosa 1898- DLB-134

Chacón, Eusebio 1869-1948 . . . . . . DLB-82

Chacón, Felipe Maximiliano
1873-? DLB-82

Chadwyck-Healey's Full-Text Literary Data-bases:
Editing Commercial Databases of
Primary Literary Texts Y-95

Challans, Eileen Mary (see Renault, Mary)

Chalmers, George 1742-1825 . . . . . DLB-30

Chaloner, Sir Thomas
1520-1565 . . . . DLB-167

Chamberlain, Samuel S.
1851-1916 . . . . DLB-25

Chamberland, Paul 1939- DLB-60

Chamberlin, William Henry
1897-1969 . . . . DLB-29

Chambers, Charles Haddon
1860-1921 . . . . DLB-10

Chambers, W. and R.
[publishing house]. DLB-106

Chamisso, Albert von
1781-1838 . . . . DLB-90

Champfleury 1821-1889 . . . . DLB-119

Chandler, Harry 1864-1944 . . . . . . DLB-29

Chandler, Norman 1899-1973. . . . . DLB-127

Chandler, Otis 1927- DLB-127

Chandler, Raymond 1888-1959 . . . . . DS-6

Channing, Edward 1856-1931 . . . . . DLB-17

Channing, Edward Tyrrell
1790-1856 . . . . DLB-1, 59

Channing, William Ellery
1780-1842 . . . . DLB-1, 59

Channing, William Ellery, II
1817-1901. . . . . DLB-1

Channing, William Henry
1810-1884 . . . . DLB-1, 59

Chaplin, Charlie 1889-1977. . . . . . . DLB-44

Chapman, George
1559 or 1560 - 1634 . . . . . DLB-62, 121

Chapman, John DLB-106

Chapman, William 1850-1917 . . . . . DLB-99

Chapman and Hall DLB-106

Chappell, Fred 1936- DLB-6, 105

Chappell, Fred, A Detail
in a Poem DLB-105

Charbonneau, Jean 1875-1960 . . . . . DLB-92

Charbonneau, Robert 1911-1967 . . . . DLB-68

Charles, Gerda 1914- DLB-14

Charles, William
[publishing house]. DLB-49

The Charles Wood Affair:
A Playwright Revived Y-83

Charlotte Forten: Pages from
her Diary DLB-50

Charteris, Leslie 1907-1993 . . . . . . DLB-77

Charyn, Jerome 1937- Y-83

Chase, Borden 1900-1971. . . . . DLB-26

Chase, Edna Woolman
1877-1957 . . . . DLB-91

Chase-Riboud, Barbara 1936- DLB-33

Chateaubriand, François-René de
1768-1848 . . . . DLB-119

Chatterton, Thomas 1752-1770 . . . . DLB-109

Chatto and Windus DLB-106

Chaucer, Geoffrey 1340?-1400 . . . . . DLB-146

Chauncy, Charles 1705-1787 . . . . . . DLB-24

Chauveau, Pierre-Joseph-Olivier
1820-1890 . . . . DLB-99

Chávez, Denise 1948- DLB-122

Chávez, Fray Angélico 1910- DLB-82

Chayefsky, Paddy
1923-1981 . . . . DLB-7, 44; Y-81

Cheever, Ezekiel 1615-1708. . . . . . . DLB-24

Cheever, George Barrell
1807-1890 . . . . DLB-59

Cheever, John
1912-1982 . . . . . . DLB-2, 102; Y-80, 82

Cheever, Susan 1943- Y-82

Cheke, Sir John 1514-1557 . . . . . . DLB-132

Chelsea House DLB-46

Cheney, Ednah Dow (Littlehale)
1824-1904 . . . . DLB-1

Cheney, Harriet Vaughn
1796-1889 . . . . DLB-99

Cherry, Kelly 1940- Y-83

Cherryh, C. J. 1942- Y-80

Chesnutt, Charles Waddell
1858-1932 . . . . DLB-12, 50, 78

Chester, Alfred 1928-1971 . . . . DLB-130

Chester, George Randolph
1869-1924 . . . . DLB-78

The Chester Plays circa 1505-1532;
revisions until 1575 . . . . DLB-146

Chesterfield, Philip Dormer Stanhope,
Fourth Earl of 1694-1773 . . . . . DLB-104

Chesterton, G. K. 1874-1936
. . . . . DLB-10, 19, 34, 70, 98, 149, 178

Chettle, Henry
circa 1560-circa 1607 . . . . DLB-136

Chew, Ada Nield 1870-1945 . . . . . DLB-135

Cheyney, Edward P. 1861-1947 . . . . DLB-47

Chiara, Piero 1913-1986 . . . . DLB-177

Chicano History DLB-82

Chicano Language DLB-82

Child, Francis James
1825-1896 . . . . DLB-1, 64

Child, Lydia Maria
1802-1880 . . . . DLB-1, 74

Child, Philip 1898-1978 . . . . DLB-68

Childers, Erskine 1870-1922 . . . . . DLB-70

Children's Book Awards
and Prizes DLB-61

Children's Illustrators,
1800-1880 . . . . DLB-163

Childress, Alice 1920-1994 . . . . . . DLB-7, 38

Childs, George W. 1829-1894 . . . . . DLB-23

Chilton Book Company DLB-46

Chinweizu 1943- DLB-157

Chitham, Edward 1932- DLB-155

Chittenden, Hiram Martin
1858-1917 . . . . DLB-47

Chivers, Thomas Holley
1809-1858 . . . . DLB-3

Chopin, Kate 1850-1904 . . . . . . DLB-12, 78

Chopin, Rene 1885-1953 . . . . DLB-92

Choquette, Adrienne 1915-1973 . . . . DLB-68

Choquette, Robert 1905- DLB-68

The Christian Publishing
Company DLB-49

Christie, Agatha 1890-1976 . . . . . DLB-13, 77

Christus und die Samariterin
circa 950 . . . . DLB-148

Chulkov, Mikhail Dmitrievich
1743?-1792 . . . . DLB-150

Church, Benjamin 1734-1778 . . . . . DLB-31

Church, Francis Pharcellus
1839-1906 . . . . DLB-79

Church, William Conant
1836-1917 . . . . DLB-79

Churchill, Caryl 1938- DLB-13

Churchill, Charles 1731-1764 . . . . . DLB-109

Churchill, Sir Winston
1874-1965 . . . . DLB-100; DS-16

Churchyard, Thomas
1520?-1604 . . . . DLB-132

Churton, E., and Company DLB-106

Chute, Marchette 1909-1994 . . . . . DLB-103

Ciardi, John 1916-1986 . . . . . . DLB-5; Y-86

Cibber, Colley 1671-1757 . . . . DLB-84

Cima, Annalisa 1941- DLB-128

Čingo, Živko 1935-1987 . . . . DLB-181

Cirese, Eugenio 1884-1955 . . . . . . DLB-114

Cisneros, Sandra 1954- DLB-122, 152

City Lights Books DLB-46

Cixous, Hélène 1937- DLB-83

Clampitt, Amy 1920-1994 . . . . . . DLB-105

Clapper, Raymond 1892-1944 . . . . DLB-29

Clare, John 1793-1864 . . . . DLB-55, 96

Clarendon, Edward Hyde, Earl of
1609-1674 . . . . DLB-101

Clark, Alfred Alexander Gordon
(see Hare, Cyril)

Clark, Ann Nolan 1896- DLB-52

Clark, C. M., Publishing
Company DLB-46

Clark, Catherine Anthony
1892-1977 . . . . DLB-68

Clark, Charles Heber
1841-1915 . . . . DLB-11

Clark, Davis Wasgatt 1812-1871 . . . . DLB-79

Clark, Eleanor 1913- DLB-6

Clark, J. P. 1935- DLB-117

Clark, Lewis Gaylord
1808-1873 . . . . DLB-3, 64, 73

Clark, Walter Van Tilburg
1909-1971 . . . . DLB-9

Clark, William (see Lewis, Meriwether)

Clarke, Austin 1896-1974 . . . . . DLB-10, 20

Clarke, Austin C. 1934- DLB-53, 125

Clarke, Gillian 1937- DLB-40

Clarke, James Freeman
1810-1888 . . . . DLB-1, 59

Clarke, Pauline 1921- DLB-161

Clarke, Rebecca Sophia
1833-1906 . . . . DLB-42

Clarke, Robert, and Company DLB-49

Clarkson, Thomas 1760-1846 . . . . . DLB-158

Claudius, Matthias 1740-1815 . . . . . DLB-97

Clausen, Andy 1943- DLB-16

Claxton, Remsen and
Haffelfinger DLB-49

Clay, Cassius Marcellus
1810-1903 . . . . DLB-43

Cleary, Beverly 1916- DLB-52

Cleaver, Vera 1919- and
Cleaver, Bill 1920-1981 . . . . . . DLB-52

Cleland, John 1710-1789 . . . . DLB-39

Clemens, Samuel Langhorne
1835-1910 . . . . . DLB-11, 12, 23, 64, 74

Clement, Hal 1922- DLB-8

Clemo, Jack 1916- DLB-27

Cleveland, John 1613-1658 . . . . . . DLB-126

Cliff, Michelle 1946- DLB-157

Clifford, Lady Anne 1590-1676 . . . . DLB-151

Clifford, James L. 1901-1978 . . . . . DLB-103

Clifford, Lucy 1853?-1929 . . . . . DLB-135, 141

Clifton, Lucille 1936- DLB-5, 41

Clode, Edward J.
[publishing house] DLB-46

Clough, Arthur Hugh 1819-1861 . . . . DLB-32

Cloutier, Cécile 1930- DLB-60

Clutton-Brock, Arthur
1868-1924 . . . . DLB-98

Coates, Robert M.
1897-1973 . . . . DLB-4, 9, 102

Coatsworth, Elizabeth 1893- DLB-22

Cobb, Charles E., Jr. 1943- DLB-41

Cobb, Frank I. 1869-1923 . . . . DLB-25

Cobb, Irvin S.
1876-1944 . . . . DLB-11, 25, 86

Cobbett, William 1763-1835 . . . . DLB-43, 107

Cobbledick, Gordon 1898-1969 . . . . DLB-171

Cochran, Thomas C. 1902- DLB-17

Cochrane, Elizabeth 1867-1922 . . . . DLB-25

Cockerill, John A. 1845-1896 . . . . . DLB-23

Cocteau, Jean 1889-1963 . . . . DLB-65

Coderre, Emile (see Jean Narrache)

Coffee, Lenore J. 1900?-1984 . . . . DLB-44

Coffin, Robert P. Tristram
1892-1955 . . . . DLB-45

Cogswell, Fred 1917- DLB-60

Cogswell, Mason Fitch
1761-1830 . . . . DLB-37

Cohen, Arthur A. 1928-1986 . . . . . DLB-28

Cohen, Leonard 1934- DLB-53

Cohen, Matt 1942- DLB-53

Colden, Cadwallader
1688-1776 . . . . DLB-24, 30

Cole, Barry 1936- DLB-14

Cole, George Watson
1850-1939 . . . . DLB-140

Colegate, Isabel 1931- DLB-14

Coleman, Emily Holmes
1899-1974 . . . . DLB-4

Coleman, Wanda 1946- DLB-130

Coleridge, Hartley 1796-1849 . . . . . . DLB-96

Coleridge, Mary 1861-1907 . . . . . DLB-19, 98

Coleridge, Samuel Taylor
1772-1834 . . . . DLB-93, 107

Colet, John 1467-1519 . . . . DLB-132

Colette 1873-1954 . . . . DLB-65

Colette, Sidonie Gabrielle (see Colette)

Colinas, Antonio 1946- DLB-134

Collier, John 1901-1980 . . . . DLB-77

Collier, Mary 1690-1762 . . . . DLB-95

Collier, Robert J. 1876-1918 . . . . . . DLB-91

Collier, P. F. [publishing house] DLB-49

Collin and Small DLB-49

Collingwood, W. G. 1854-1932 . . . . DLB-149

Collins, An floruit circa 1653 . . . . . DLB-131

Collins, Merle 1950- DLB-157

Collins, Mortimer 1827-1876 . . . . DLB-21, 35

Collins, Wilkie 1824-1889 . . . DLB-18, 70, 159

Collins, William 1721-1759 . . . . . . DLB-109

Collins, William, Sons and
Company DLB-154

Collins, Isaac [publishing house] DLB-49

Collyer, Mary 1716?-1763? DLB-39

Colman, Benjamin 1673-1747 . . . . . . DLB-24

Colman, George, the Elder
1732-1794 . . . . DLB-89

Colman, George, the Younger
1762-1836 . . . . DLB-89

Colman, S. [publishing house] DLB-49

Colombo, John Robert 1936- DLB-53

Colquhoun, Patrick 1745-1820 . . . . DLB-158

Colter, Cyrus 1910- DLB-33

Colum, Padraic 1881-1972 . . . . DLB-19

Colvin, Sir Sidney 1845-1927 . . . . . DLB-149

Colwin, Laurie 1944-1992 . . . . Y-80

Comden, Betty 1919- and Green,
Adolph 1918- DLB-44

Comi, Girolamo 1890-1968 . . . . . . DLB-114

The Comic Tradition Continued
[in the British Novel] DLB-15

Commager, Henry Steele
1902- DLB-17

The Commercialization of the Image of
Revolt, by Kenneth Rexroth DLB-16

Community and Commentators: Black
Theatre and Its Critics DLB-38

Compton-Burnett, Ivy
1884?-1969 . . . . DLB-36

Conan, Laure 1845-1924 . . . . DLB-99

Conde, Carmen 1901- DLB-108

Conference on Modern Biography Y-85

Congreve, William
1670-1729 . . . . DLB-39, 84

Conkey, W. B., Company DLB-49

Connell, Evan S., Jr. 1924- DLB-2; Y-81

Connelly, Marc 1890-1980 . . . . . DLB-7; Y-80

Connolly, Cyril 1903-1974 . . . . DLB-98

Connolly, James B. 1868-1957 . . . . . DLB-78

Connor, Ralph 1860-1937 . . . . DLB-92

Connor, Tony 1930- DLB-40

Conquest, Robert 1917- DLB-27

Conrad, Joseph
1857-1924 . . . . DLB-10, 34, 98, 156

Conrad, John, and Company DLB-49

Conroy, Jack 1899-1990 . . . . Y-81

Conroy, Pat 1945- DLB-6

The Consolidation of Opinion: Critical
Responses to the Modernists DLB-36

Constable, Henry 1562-1613 . . . . . DLB-136

Constable and Company
Limited DLB-112

Constable, Archibald, and
Company DLB-154

Constant, Benjamin 1767-1830 . . . . DLB-119

Constant de Rebecque, Henri-Benjamin de
(see Constant, Benjamin)

Constantine, David 1944- DLB-40

Constantin-Weyer, Maurice
1881-1964 . . . . DLB-92

Contempo Caravan: Kites in
a Windstorm Y-85

A Contemporary Flourescence of Chicano
Literature Y-84

The Continental Publishing
Company DLB-49

A Conversation with Chaim Potok Y-84

Conversations with Editors Y-95

Conversations with Publishers I: An Interview
with Patrick O'Connor Y-84

Conversations with Publishers II: An Interview
with Charles Scribner III Y-94

Conversations with Publishers III: An Interview
with Donald Lamm Y-95

Conversations with Publishers IV: An Interview
with James Laughlin Y-96

Conversations with Rare Book Dealers I: An
Interview with Glenn Horowitz Y-90

Conversations with Rare Book Dealers II: An
Interview with Ralph Sipper Y-94

Conversations with Rare Book Dealers
(Publishers) III: An Interview with
Otto Penzler Y-96

The Conversion of an Unpolitical Man,
by W. H. Bruford DLB-66

Conway, Moncure Daniel
1832-1907 . . . . DLB-1

Cook, Ebenezer
circa 1667-circa 1732 . . . . DLB-24

Cook, Edward Tyas 1857-1919 . . . . DLB-149

Cook, Michael 1933- DLB-53

Cook, David C., Publishing
Company DLB-49

Cooke, George Willis 1848-1923 . . . . DLB-71

Cooke, Increase, and Company DLB-49

Cooke, John Esten 1830-1886 . . . . . . DLB-3

Cooke, Philip Pendleton
1816-1850 . . . . DLB-3, 59

Cooke, Rose Terry
1827-1892 . . . . DLB-12, 74

Cook-Lynn, Elizabeth 1930- DLB-175

Coolbrith, Ina 1841-1928 . . . . DLB-54

Cooley, Peter 1940- DLB-105

Cooley, Peter, Into the Mirror DLB-105

Coolidge, Susan (see Woolsey, Sarah Chauncy)

Coolidge, George
[publishing house] DLB-49

Cooper, Giles 1918-1966 . . . . DLB-13

Cooper, James Fenimore
1789-1851 . . . . DLB-3, 183

Cooper, Kent 1880-1965 . . . . DLB-29

Cooper, Susan 1935- DLB-161

Cooper, William
[publishing house] DLB-170

Coote, J. [publishing house] DLB-154

Coover, Robert 1932- DLB-2; Y-81

Copeland and Day DLB-49

Ćopić, Branko 1915-1984 . . . . DLB-181

Copland, Robert 1470?-1548 . . . . . DLB-136

Coppard, A. E. 1878-1957 . . . . . . DLB-162

Coppel, Alfred 1921- Y-83

Coppola, Francis Ford 1939- DLB-44

Copway, George (Kah-ge-ga-gah-bowh)
1818-1869 . . . . DLB-175, 183

Corazzini, Sergio 1886-1907 . . . . . DLB-114

Corbett, Richard 1582-1635 . . . . . . DLB-121

Corcoran, Barbara 1911- DLB-52

Corelli, Marie 1855-1924 . . . . . DLB-34, 156

Corle, Edwin 1906-1956 . . . . Y-85

Corman, Cid 1924- DLB-5

Cormier, Robert 1925- DLB-52

Corn, Alfred 1943- DLB-120; Y-80

Cornish, Sam 1935- DLB-41

Cornish, William
circa 1465-circa 1524 . . . . DLB-132

Cornwall, Barry (see Procter, Bryan Waller)

Cornwallis, Sir William, the Younger
circa 1579-1614 . . . . DLB-151

Cornwell, David John Moore
(see le Carré, John)

Corpi, Lucha 1945- DLB-82

Corrington, John William 1932- DLB-6

Corrothers, James D. 1869-1917 . . . . . DLB-50

Corso, Gregory 1930- DLB-5, 16

Cortázar, Julio 1914-1984 . . . . DLB-113

Cortez, Jayne 1936- DLB-41

Corvinus, Gottlieb Siegmund
1677-1746 . . . . DLB-168

Corvo, Baron (see Rolfe, Frederick William)

Cory, Annie Sophie (see Cross, Victoria)

Cory, William Johnson
1823-1892 . . . . DLB-35

Coryate, Thomas
1577?-1617 . . . . DLB-151, 172

Ćosić, Dobrica 1921- DLB-181

Cosin, John 1595-1672 . . . . DLB-151

Cosmopolitan Book Corporation DLB-46

Costain, Thomas B. 1885-1965 . . . . . DLB-9

Coste, Donat 1912-1957 . . . . DLB-88

Costello, Louisa Stuart 1799-1870 . . . DLB-166

Cota-Cárdenas, Margarita
1941- DLB-122

Cotter, Joseph Seamon, Sr.
1861-1949 . . . . DLB-50

Cotter, Joseph Seamon, Jr.
1895-1919 . . . . DLB-50

Cottle, Joseph [publishing house] DLB-154

Cotton, Charles 1630-1687 . . . . DLB-131

Cotton, John 1584-1652 . . . . DLB-24

Coulter, John 1888-1980 . . . . DLB-68

Cournos, John 1881-1966 . . . . DLB-54

Cousins, Margaret 1905- DLB-137

Cousins, Norman 1915-1990 . . . . . . DLB-137

Coventry, Francis 1725-1754 . . . . . . DLB-39

Coverdale, Miles
1487 or 1488-1569 . . . . DLB-167

Coverly, N. [publishing house] DLB-49

Covici-Friede DLB-46

Coward, Noel 1899-1973 . . . . DLB-10

Coward, McCann and
Geoghegan DLB-46

Cowles, Gardner 1861-1946 . . . . . . DLB-29

Cowles, Gardner ("Mike"), Jr.
1903-1985 . . . . DLB-127, 137

Cowley, Abraham
1618-1667 . . . . DLB-131, 151

Cowley, Hannah 1743-1809 . . . . . . DLB-89

Cowley, Malcolm
1898-1989 . . . . DLB-4, 48; Y-81, 89

Cowper, William
1731-1800 . . . . DLB-104, 109

Cox, A. B. (see Berkeley, Anthony)

Cox, James McMahon
1903-1974 . . . . DLB-127

Cox, James Middleton
1870-1957 . . . . DLB-127

Cox, Palmer 1840-1924 . . . . DLB-42

Coxe, Louis 1918-1993 . . . . DLB-5

Coxe, Tench 1755-1824 . . . . DLB-37

Cozzens, James Gould
1903-1978 . . . . DLB-9; Y-84; DS-2

Crabbe, George 1754-1832 . . . . DLB-93

Crackanthorpe, Hubert
1870-1896 . . . . DLB-135

Craddock, Charles Egbert
(see Murfree, Mary N.)

Cradock, Thomas 1718-1770 . . . . . . DLB-31

Craig, Daniel H. 1811-1895 . . . . . . DLB-43

Craik, Dinah Maria
1826-1887 . . . . DLB-35, 136

Cranch, Christopher Pearse
1813-1892 . . . . DLB-1, 42

Crane, Hart 1899-1932 . . . . DLB-4, 48

Crane, R. S. 1886-1967 . . . . DLB-63

Crane, Stephen 1871-1900 . . . . DLB-12, 54, 78

Crane, Walter 1845-1915 . . . . DLB-163

Cranmer, Thomas 1489-1556 . . . . . . DLB-132

Crapsey, Adelaide 1878-1914 . . . . . . DLB-54

Crashaw, Richard
1612 or 1613-1649 . . . . DLB-126

Craven, Avery 1885-1980 . . . . DLB-17

Crawford, Charles
1752-circa 1815 . . . . DLB-31

Crawford, F. Marion 1854-1909 . . . . DLB-71

Crawford, Isabel Valancy
1850-1887 . . . . DLB-92

Crawley, Alan 1887-1975 . . . . DLB-68

Crayon, Geoffrey (see Irving, Washington)

Creamer, Robert W. 1922- DLB-171

Creasey, John 1908-1973 . . . . DLB-77

Creative Age Press DLB-46

Creech, William
[publishing house] DLB-154

Creede, Thomas
[publishing house] DLB-170

Creel, George 1876-1953 . . . . DLB-25

Creeley, Robert 1926- DLB-5, 16, 169

Creelman, James 1859-1915 . . . . . . DLB-23

Cregan, David 1931- DLB-13

Creighton, Donald Grant
1902-1979 . . . . DLB-88

Cremazie, Octave 1827-1879 . . . . . . DLB-99

Crémer, Victoriano 1909?- DLB-108

Crescas, Hasdai
circa 1340-1412? DLB-115

Crespo, Angel 1926- DLB-134

Cresset Press DLB-112

Cresswell, Helen 1934- DLB-161

Crèvecoeur, Michel Guillaume Jean de
1735-1813 . . . . DLB-37

Crews, Harry 1935- DLB-6, 143

Crichton, Michael 1942- Y-81

A Crisis of Culture: The Changing Role
of Religion in the New Republic
. . . . DLB-37

Crispin, Edmund 1921-1978 . . . . . . DLB-87

Cristofer, Michael 1946- DLB-7

"The Critic as Artist" (1891), by
Oscar Wilde DLB-57

"Criticism In Relation To Novels" (1863),
by G. H. Lewes DLB-21

Crnjanski, Miloš 1893-1977 . . . . . . DLB-147

Crockett, David (Davy)
1786-1836 . . . . DLB-3, 11, 183

Croft-Cooke, Rupert (see Bruce, Leo)

Crofts, Freeman Wills
1879-1957 . . . . DLB-77

Croker, John Wilson
1780-1857 . . . . DLB-110

Croly, George 1780-1860 . . . . DLB-159

Croly, Herbert 1869-1930 . . . . DLB-91

Croly, Jane Cunningham
1829-1901 . . . . DLB-23

Crompton, Richmal 1890-1969 . . . . DLB-160

Crosby, Caresse 1892-1970 . . . . DLB-48

Crosby, Caresse 1892-1970 and Crosby,
Harry 1898-1929 . . . . DLB-4; DS-15

Crosby, Harry 1898-1929 . . . . DLB-48

Cross, Gillian 1945- DLB-161

Cross, Victoria 1868-1952 . . . . DLB-135

Crossley-Holland, Kevin
1941- DLB-40, 161

Crothers, Rachel 1878-1958 . . . . . . DLB-7

Crowell, Thomas Y., Company DLB-49

Crowley, John 1942- Y-82

Crowley, Mart 1935- DLB-7

Crown Publishers DLB-46

Crowne, John 1641-1712 . . . . DLB-80

Crowninshield, Edward Augustus
1817-1859 . . . . DLB-140

Crowninshield, Frank 1872-1947 . . . . DLB-91

Croy, Homer 1883-1965 . . . . DLB-4

Crumley, James 1939- Y-84

Cruz, Victor Hernández 1949- DLB-41

Csokor, Franz Theodor
1885-1969 . . . . DLB-81

Cuala Press DLB-112

Cullen, Countee 1903-1946 . . . . DLB-4, 48, 51

Culler, Jonathan D. 1944- DLB-67

The Cult of Biography
Excerpts from the Second Folio Debate:
"Biographies are generally a disease of

English Literature" – Germaine Greer, Victoria Glendinning, Auberon Waugh, and Richard Holmes Y-86

Cumberland, Richard 1732-1811 . . . . . DLB-89

Cummings, Constance Gordon 1837-1924 . . . . DLB-174

Cummings, E. E. 1894-1962 . . . . . DLB-4, 48

Cummings, Ray 1887-1957 . . . . DLB-8

Cummings and Hilliard. DLB-49

Cummins, Maria Susanna 1827-1866 . . . . DLB-42

Cundall, Joseph [publishing house] DLB-106

Cuney, Waring 1906-1976 . . . . DLB-51

Cuney-Hare, Maude 1874-1936 . . . . . DLB-52

Cunningham, Allan 1784-1842. . . . . DLB-116, 144

Cunningham, J. V. 1911- DLB-5

Cunningham, Peter F. [publishing house]. DLB-49

Cunquiero, Alvaro 1911-1981 . . . . . . DLB-134

Cuomo, George 1929- Y-80

Cupples and Leon DLB-46

Cupples, Upham and Company DLB-49

Cuppy, Will 1884-1949 . . . . DLB-11

Curll, Edmund [publishing house] DLB-154

Currie, James 1756-1805 . . . . DLB-142

Currie, Mary Montgomerie Lamb Singleton, Lady Currie (see Fane, Violet)

Cursor Mundi circa 1300 . . . . DLB-146

Curti, Merle E. 1897- DLB-17

Curtis, Anthony 1926- DLB-155

Curtis, Cyrus H. K. 1850-1933 . . . . . DLB-91

Curtis, George William 1824-1892 . . . . DLB-1, 43

Curzon, Robert 1810-1873 . . . . . . DLB-166

Curzon, Sarah Anne 1833-1898 . . . . . DLB-99

Cynewulf circa 770-840 . . . . DLB-146

Czepko, Daniel 1605-1660. . . . . . . DLB-164

D

D. M. Thomas: The Plagiarism Controversy. Y-82

Dabit, Eugène 1898-1936 . . . . DLB-65

Daborne, Robert circa 1580-1628 . . . . DLB-58

Dacey, Philip 1939- DLB-105

Dacey, Philip, Eyes Across Centuries: Contemporary Poetry and "That Vision Thing". DLB-105

Dach, Simon 1605-1659 . . . . DLB-164

Daggett, Rollin M. 1831-1901 . . . . . DLB-79

D'Aguiar, Fred 1960- DLB-157

Dahl, Roald 1916-1990 . . . . DLB-139

Dahlberg, Edward 1900-1977. . . . . . DLB-48

Dahn, Felix 1834-1912. . . . . DLB-129

Dale, Peter 1938- DLB-40

Daley, Arthur 1904-1974 . . . . DLB-171

Dall, Caroline Wells (Healey) 1822-1912. . . . . DLB-1

Dallas, E. S. 1828-1879 . . . . DLB-55

The Dallas Theater Center DLB-7

D'Alton, Louis 1900-1951. . . . . DLB-10

Daly, T. A. 1871-1948 . . . . DLB-11

Damon, S. Foster 1893-1971 . . . . . . DLB-45

Damrell, William S. [publishing house]. DLB-49

Dana, Charles A. 1819-1897 . . . . . DLB-3, 23

Dana, Richard Henry, Jr. 1815-1882 . . . . DLB-1, 183

Dandridge, Ray Garfield DLB-51

Dane, Clemence 1887-1965 . . . . DLB-10

Danforth, John 1660-1730 . . . . DLB-24

Danforth, Samuel, I 1626-1674 . . . . . DLB-24

Danforth, Samuel, II 1666-1727 . . . . . DLB-24

Dangerous Years: London Theater, 1939-1945 . . . . DLB-10

Daniel, John M. 1825-1865 . . . . DLB-43

Daniel, Samuel 1562 or 1563-1619 . . . . DLB-62

Daniel Press DLB-106

Daniells, Roy 1902-1979 . . . . DLB-68

Daniels, Jim 1956- DLB-120

Daniels, Jonathan 1902-1981 . . . . . DLB-127

Daniels, Josephus 1862-1948 . . . . . . DLB-29

Dannay, Frederic 1905-1982 and Manfred B. Lee 1905-1971 . . . . . DLB-137

Danner, Margaret Esse 1915- DLB-41

Danter, John [publishing house]. DLB-170

Dantin, Louis 1865-1945 . . . . DLB-92

Danzig, Allison 1898-1987 . . . . DLB-171

D'Arcy, Ella circa 1857-1937 . . . . . DLB-135

Darley, George 1795-1846 . . . . DLB-96

Darwin, Charles 1809-1882 . . . . . DLB-57, 166

Darwin, Erasmus 1731-1802 . . . . . . DLB-93

Daryush, Elizabeth 1887-1977 . . . . . DLB-20

Dashkova, Ekaterina Romanovna (née Vorontsova) 1743-1810 . . . . DLB-150

Dashwood, Edmée Elizabeth Monica de la Pasture (see Delafield, E. M.)

Daudet, Alphonse 1840-1897 . . . . . DLB-123

d'Aulaire, Edgar Parin 1898- and d'Aulaire, Ingri 1904- DLB-22

Davenant, Sir William 1606-1668 . . . . DLB-58, 126

Davenport, Guy 1927- DLB-130

Davenport, Robert ?-? DLB-58

Daves, Delmer 1904-1977 . . . . DLB-26

Davey, Frank 1940- DLB-53

Davidson, Avram 1923-1993. . . . . . . DLB-8

Davidson, Donald 1893-1968. . . . . . DLB-45

Davidson, John 1857-1909 . . . . DLB-19

Davidson, Lionel 1922- DLB-14

Davie, Donald 1922- DLB-27

Davie, Elspeth 1919- DLB-139

Davies, Sir John 1569-1626 . . . . DLB-172

Davies, John, of Hereford 1565?-1618. . . . . DLB-121

Davies, Rhys 1901-1978. . . . . DLB-139

Davies, Robertson 1913- DLB-68

Davies, Samuel 1723-1761 . . . . DLB-31

Davies, Thomas 1712?-1785. . . . DLB-142, 154

Davies, W. H. 1871-1940. . . . . . DLB-19, 174

Davies, Peter, Limited DLB-1,12

Daviot, Gordon 1896?-1952 . . . . . . DLB-10 (see also Tey, Josephine)

Davis, Charles A. 1795-1867. . . . . . . DLB-11

Davis, Clyde Brion 1894-1962. . . . . . DLB-9

Davis, Dick 1945- DLB-40

Davis, Frank Marshall 1905-? DLB-51

Davis, H. L. 1894-1960 . . . . DLB-9

Davis, John 1774-1854 . . . . DLB-37

Davis, Lydia 1947- DLB-130

Davis, Margaret Thomson 1926- DLB-14

Davis, Ossie 1917- DLB-7, 38

Davis, Paxton 1925-1994 . . . . Y-94

Davis, Rebecca Harding 1831-1910 . . . . DLB-74

Davis, Richard Harding 1864-1916 . . . . DLB-12, 23, 78, 79; DS-13

Davis, Samuel Cole 1764-1809 . . . . . DLB-37

Davison, Peter 1928- DLB-5

Davys, Mary 1674-1732 . . . . DLB-39

DAW Books DLB-46

Dawson, Ernest 1882-1947 . . . . . . DLB-140

Dawson, Fielding 1930- DLB-130

Dawson, William 1704-1752 . . . . . . DLB-31

Day, Angel flourished 1586. . . . . . . DLB-167

Day, Benjamin Henry 1810-1889 . . . . DLB-43

Day, Clarence 1874-1935. . . . . DLB-11

Day, Dorothy 1897-1980 . . . . DLB-29

Day, Frank Parker 1881-1950 . . . . . . DLB-92

Day, John circa 1574-circa 1640 . . . . . DLB-62

Day, John [publishing house] DLB-170

Day Lewis, C. 1904-1972 . . . . . DLB-15, 20 (see also Blake, Nicholas)

Day, Thomas 1748-1789 . . . . DLB-39

Day, The John, Company DLB-46

Cumulative Index

Day, Mahlon [publishing house] DLB-49

Dazai, Osamu 1909-1948 . . . . DLB-182

Deacon, William Arthur
1890-1977 . . . . DLB-68

Deal, Borden 1922-1985 . . . . DLB-6

de Angeli, Marguerite 1889-1987 . . . . DLB-22

De Angelis, Milo 1951- DLB-128

De Bow, James Dunwoody Brownson
1820-1867 . . . . DLB-3, 79

de Bruyn, Günter 1926- DLB-75

de Camp, L. Sprague 1907- DLB-8

The Decay of Lying (1889),
by Oscar Wilde [excerpt] DLB-18

Dedication, Ferdinand Count Fathom (1753),
by Tobias Smollett DLB-39

Dedication, The History of Pompey the Little
(1751), by Francis Coventry DLB-39

Dedication, Lasselia (1723), by Eliza
Haywood [excerpt] DLB-39

Dedication, The Wanderer (1814),
by Fanny Burney. DLB-39

Dee, John 1527-1609. . . . . DLB-136

Deeping, George Warwick
1877-1950 . . . . DLB 153

Defense of Amelia (1752), by
Henry Fielding DLB-39

Defoe, Daniel 1660-1731 . . . . DLB-39, 95, 101

de Fontaine, Felix Gregory
1834-1896 . . . . DLB-43

De Forest, John William
1826-1906 . . . . DLB-12

DeFrees, Madeline 1919- DLB-105

DeFrees, Madeline, The Poet's Kaleidoscope:
The Element of Surprise in the Making
of the Poem DLB-105

de Graff, Robert 1895-1981 . . . . Y-81

de Graft, Joe 1924-1978 . . . . DLB-117

De Heinrico circa 980? DLB-148

Deighton, Len 1929- DLB-87

DeJong, Meindert 1906-1991 . . . . . . DLB-52

Dekker, Thomas
circa 1572-1632 . . . . DLB-62, 172

Delacorte, Jr., George T.
1894-1991 . . . . DLB-91

Delafield, E. M. 1890-1943 . . . . DLB-34

Delahaye, Guy 1888-1969 . . . . DLB-92

de la Mare, Walter
1873-1956 . . . . DLB-19, 153, 162

Deland, Margaret 1857-1945 . . . . . . DLB-78

Delaney, Shelagh 1939- DLB-13

Delano, Amasa 1763-1823 . . . . DLB-183

Delany, Martin Robinson
1812-1885 . . . . DLB-50

Delany, Samuel R. 1942- DLB-8, 33

de la Roche, Mazo 1879-1961 . . . . . . DLB-68

Delbanco, Nicholas 1942- DLB-6

De León, Nephtal 1945- DLB-82

Delgado, Abelardo Barrientos
1931- DLB-82

De Libero, Libero 1906-1981 . . . . . . DLB-114

DeLillo, Don 1936- DLB-6, 173

de Lisser H. G. 1878-1944 . . . . DLB-117

Dell, Floyd 1887-1969 . . . . DLB-9

Dell Publishing Company DLB-46

delle Grazie, Marie Eugene
1864-1931 . . . . DLB-81

Deloney, Thomas died 1600 . . . . . DLB-167

Deloria, Ella C. 1889-1971 . . . . DLB-175

Deloria, Vine, Jr. 1933- DLB-175

del Rey, Lester 1915-1993 . . . . DLB-8

Del Vecchio, John M. 1947- DS-9

de Man, Paul 1919-1983 . . . . DLB-67

Demby, William 1922- DLB-33

Deming, Philander 1829-1915 . . . . . DLB-74

Demorest, William Jennings
1822-1895 . . . . DLB-79

De Morgan, William 1839-1917 . . . . DLB-153

Demosthenes 384 B.C.-322 B.C. DLB-176

Denham, Henry
[publishing house] DLB-170

Denham, Sir John
1615-1669 . . . . DLB-58, 126

Denison, Merrill 1893-1975 . . . . DLB-92

Denison, T. S., and Company DLB-49

Dennie, Joseph
1768-1812 . . . . DLB-37, 43, 59, 73

Dennis, John 1658-1734 . . . . DLB-101

Dennis, Nigel 1912-1989 . . . . . . DLB-13, 15

Dent, Tom 1932- DLB-38

Dent, J. M., and Sons DLB-112

Denton, Daniel circa 1626-1703 . . . . DLB-24

DePaola, Tomie 1934- DLB-61

De Quincey, Thomas
1785-1859. . . . . DLB-110, 144

Derby, George Horatio
1823-1861 . . . . DLB-11

Derby, J. C., and Company DLB-49

Derby and Miller DLB-49

Derleth, August 1909-1971. . . . . DLB-9

The Derrydale Press DLB-46

Derzhavin, Gavriil Romanovich
1743-1816 . . . . DLB-150

Desaulniers, Gonsalve
1863-1934 . . . . DLB-92

Desbiens, Jean-Paul 1927- DLB-53

des Forêts, Louis-Rene 1918- DLB-83

Desnica, Vladan 1905-1967 . . . . . . DLB-181

DesRochers, Alfred 1901-1978 . . . . . DLB-68

Desrosiers, Léo-Paul 1896-1967. . . . . DLB-68

Dessì, Giuseppe 1909-1977 . . . . . . DLB-177

Destouches, Louis-Ferdinand
(see Céline, Louis-Ferdinand)

De Tabley, Lord 1835-1895 . . . . . . DLB-35

Deutsch, Babette 1895-1982. . . . . . . DLB-45

Deutsch, Niklaus Manuel (see Manuel, Niklaus)

Deutsch, André, Limited DLB-112

Deveaux, Alexis 1948- DLB-38

The Development of the Author's Copyright
in Britain. DLB-154

The Development of Lighting in the Staging
of Drama, 1900-1945 . . . . DLB-10

The Development of Meiji Japan. . . . DLB-180

de Vere, Aubrey 1814-1902 . . . . . . DLB-35

Devereux, second Earl of Essex, Robert
1565-1601 . . . . DLB-136

The Devin-Adair Company DLB-46

De Voto, Bernard 1897-1955 . . . . . . DLB-9

De Vries, Peter 1910-1993 . . . . . DLB-6; Y-82

Dewdney, Christopher 1951- DLB-60

Dewdney, Selwyn 1909-1979 . . . . . DLB-68

DeWitt, Robert M., Publisher DLB-49

DeWolfe, Fiske and Company. DLB-49

Dexter, Colin 1930- DLB-87

de Young, M. H. 1849-1925. . . . . . DLB-25

Dhlomo, H. I. E. 1903-1956 . . . . . DLB-157

Dhuoda circa 803-after 843 . . . . . . DLB-148

The Dial Press DLB-46

Diamond, I. A. L. 1920-1988 . . . . . DLB-26

Di Cicco, Pier Giorgio 1949- DLB-60

Dick, Philip K. 1928-1982 . . . . DLB-8

Dick and Fitzgerald DLB-49

Dickens, Charles
1812-1870. . . . . DLB-21, 55, 70, 159, 166

Dickinson, Peter 1927- DLB-161

Dickey, James
1923-1997 . . . . . DLB-5; Y-82, 93; DS-7

James Dickey, American Poet Y-96

Dickey, William 1928-1994 . . . . DLB-5

Dickinson, Emily 1830-1886 . . . . DLB-1

Dickinson, John 1732-1808 . . . . . . DLB-31

Dickinson, Jonathan 1688-1747 . . . . DLB-24

Dickinson, Patric 1914- DLB-27

Dickinson, Peter 1927- DLB-87

Dicks, John [publishing house] DLB-106

Dickson, Gordon R. 1923- DLB-8

Dictionary of Literary Biography
Yearbook Awards Y-92, 93

The Dictionary of National Biography
. . . . DLB-144

Didion, Joan 1934- DLB-2, 173; Y-81, 86

Di Donato, Pietro 1911- DLB-9

Die Fürstliche Bibliothek Corvey Y-96

Diego, Gerardo 1896-1987 . . . . DLB-134

Digges, Thomas circa 1546-1595 . . . . DLB-136

Dillard, Annie 1945- Y-80

Dillard, R. H. W. 1937- DLB-5

Dillingham, Charles T.,
Company DLB-49

The Dillingham, G. W.,
Company DLB-49

Dilly, Edward and Charles
[publishing house] DLB-154

Dilthey, Wilhelm 1833-1911. . . . . . DLB-129

Dimitrova, Blaga 1922- DLB-181

Dimov, Dimitŭr 1909-1966 . . . . . . DLB-181

Dingelstedt, Franz von
1814-1881 . . . . DLB-133

Dintenfass, Mark 1941- Y-84

Diogenes, Jr. (see Brougham, John)

Diogenes Laertius circa 200 . . . . . . DLB-176

DiPrima, Diane 1934- DLB-5, 16

Disch, Thomas M. 1940- DLB-8

Disney, Walt 1901-1966 . . . . DLB-22

Disraeli, Benjamin 1804-1881 . . . . DLB-21, 55

D'Israeli, Isaac 1766-1848 . . . . DLB-107

Ditzen, Rudolf (see Fallada, Hans)

Dix, Dorothea Lynde 1802-1887 . . . . . DLB-1

Dix, Dorothy (see Gilmer,
Elizabeth Meriwether)

Dix, Edwards and Company. DLB-49

Dixie, Florence Douglas
1857-1905 . . . . DLB-174

Dixon, Paige (see Corcoran, Barbara)

Dixon, Richard Watson
1833-1900 . . . . DLB-19

Dixon, Stephen 1936- DLB-130

Dmitriev, Ivan Ivanovich
1760-1837 . . . . DLB-150

Dobell, Sydney 1824-1874 . . . . . . DLB-32

Döblin, Alfred 1878-1957 . . . . . . DLB-66

Dobson, Austin
1840-1921 . . . . DLB-35, 144

Doctorow, E. L.
1931- DLB-2, 28, 173; Y-80

Documents on Sixteenth-Century
Literature DLB-167, 172

Dodd, William E. 1869-1940. . . . . . DLB-17

Dodd, Anne [publishing house] DLB-154

Dodd, Mead and Company DLB-49

Doderer, Heimito von 1896-1968 . . . . DLB-85

Dodge, Mary Mapes
1831?-1905 . . . . DLB-42, 79; DS-13

Dodge, B. W., and Company DLB-46

Dodge Publishing Company DLB-49

Dodgson, Charles Lutwidge
(see Carroll, Lewis)

Dodsley, Robert 1703-1764. . . . . . . DLB-95

Dodsley, R. [publishing house] DLB-154

Dodson, Owen 1914-1983 . . . . DLB-76

Doesticks, Q. K. Philander, P. B.
(see Thomson, Mortimer)

Doheny, Carrie Estelle
1875-1958 . . . . DLB-140

Domínguez, Sylvia Maida
1935- DLB-122

Donahoe, Patrick
[publishing house]. DLB-49

Donald, David H. 1920- DLB-17

Donaldson, Scott 1928- DLB-111

Doni, Rodolfo 1919- DLB-177

Donleavy, J. P. 1926- DLB-6, 173

Donnadieu, Marguerite (see Duras,
Marguerite)

Donne, John 1572-1631 . . . . . . DLB-121, 151

Donnelley, R. R., and Sons
Company DLB-49

Donnelly, Ignatius 1831-1901. . . . . . DLB-12

Donohue and Henneberry DLB-49

Donoso, José 1924- DLB-113

Doolady, M. [publishing house] DLB-49

Dooley, Ebon (see Ebon)

Doolittle, Hilda 1886-1961. . . . . . DLB-4, 45

Doplicher, Fabio 1938- DLB-128

Dor, Milo 1923- DLB-85

Doran, George H., Company DLB-46

Dorgelès, Roland 1886-1973 . . . . . DLB-65

Dorn, Edward 1929- DLB-5

Dorr, Rheta Childe 1866-1948. . . . . DLB-25

Dorris, Michael 1945-1997 . . . . . . DLB-175

Dorset and Middlesex, Charles Sackville,
Lord Buckhurst,
Earl of 1643-1706 . . . . DLB-131

Dorst, Tankred 1925- DLB-75, 124

Dos Passos, John
1896-1970 . . . . DLB-4, 9; DS-1, 15

John Dos Passos: A Centennial
Commemoration Y-96

Doubleday and Company DLB-49

Dougall, Lily 1858-1923 . . . . DLB-92

Doughty, Charles M.
1843-1926 . . . . DLB-19, 57, 174

Douglas, Gavin 1476-1522 . . . . . . DLB-132

Douglas, Keith 1920-1944. . . . . . . DLB-27

Douglas, Norman 1868-1952 . . . . . DLB-34

Douglass, Frederick
1817?-1895 . . . . DLB-1, 43, 50, 79

Douglass, William circa
1691-1752 . . . . DLB-24

Dourado, Autran 1926- DLB-145

Dove, Rita 1952- DLB-120

Dover Publications DLB-46

Doves Press DLB-112

Dowden, Edward 1843-1913 . . . . DLB-35, 149

Dowell, Coleman 1925-1985 . . . . . DLB-130

Dowland, John 1563-1626. . . . . . . DLB-172

Downes, Gwladys 1915- DLB-88

Downing, J., Major (see Davis, Charles A.)

Downing, Major Jack (see Smith, Seba)

Dowriche, Anne
before 1560-after 1613 . . . . DLB-172

Dowson, Ernest 1867-1900 . . . . DLB-19, 135

Doxey, William
[publishing house]. DLB-49

Doyle, Sir Arthur Conan
1859-1930 . . . . . . DLB-18, 70, 156, 178

Doyle, Kirby 1932- DLB-16

Drabble, Margaret 1939- DLB-14, 155

Drach, Albert 1902- DLB-85

Dragojević, Danijel 1934- DLB-181

The Dramatic Publishing
Company DLB-49

Dramatists Play Service. DLB-46

Drant, Thomas
early 1540s?-1578 . . . . DLB-167

Draper, John W. 1811-1882 . . . . . . DLB-30

Draper, Lyman C. 1815-1891 . . . . . DLB-30

Drayton, Michael 1563-1631 . . . . . DLB-121

Dreiser, Theodore
1871-1945 . . . . DLB-9, 12, 102, 137; DS-1

Drewitz, Ingeborg 1923-1986 . . . . . DLB-75

Drieu La Rochelle, Pierre
1893-1945 . . . . DLB-72

Drinkwater, John 1882-1937
. . . . DLB-10, 19, 149

Droste-Hülshoff, Annette von
1797-1848 . . . . DLB-133

The Drue Heinz Literature Prize
Excerpt from "Excerpts from a Report
of the Commission," in David
Bosworth's *The Death of Descartes*
An Interview with David
Bosworth Y-82

Drummond, William Henry
1854-1907 . . . . DLB-92

Drummond, William, of Hawthornden
1585-1649 . . . . DLB-121

Dryden, Charles 1860?-1931 . . . . . DLB-171

Dryden, John 1631-1700 . . . DLB-80, 101, 131

Držić, Marin circa 1508-1567 . . . . . DLB-147

Duane, William 1760-1835 . . . . . . DLB-43

Dubé, Marcel 1930- DLB-53

Dubé, Rodolphe (see Hertel, François)

Dubie, Norman 1945- DLB-120

Du Bois, W. E. B.
1868-1963. . . . . DLB-47, 50, 91

Du Bois, William Pène 1916- DLB-61

Dubus, Andre 1936- DLB-130

Ducharme, Réjean 1941- DLB-60

Dučić, Jovan 1871-1943 . . . . DLB-147

Duck, Stephen 1705?-1756 . . . . DLB-95

Duckworth, Gerald, and
Company Limited DLB-112

Dudek, Louis 1918- DLB-88

Duell, Sloan and Pearce DLB-46

Duerer, Albrecht 1471-1528 . . . . . . DLB-179

Duff Gordon, Lucie 1821-1869 . . . . DLB-166

Duffield and Green DLB-46

Duffy, Maureen 1933- DLB-14

Dugan, Alan 1923- DLB-5

Dugard, William
[publishing house] DLB-170

Dugas, Marcel 1883-1947 . . . . DLB-92

Dugdale, William
[publishing house] DLB-106

Duhamel, Georges 1884-1966 . . . . . DLB-65

Dujardin, Edouard 1861-1949 . . . . . DLB-123

Dukes, Ashley 1885-1959 . . . . DLB-10

Du Maurier, George
1834-1896 . . . . DLB-153, 178

Dumas, Alexandre, père
1802-1870 . . . . DLB-119

Dumas, Henry 1934-1968 . . . . DLB-41

Dunbar, Paul Laurence
1872-1906 . . . . DLB-50, 54, 78

Dunbar, William
circa 1460-circa 1522 . . . . . DLB-132, 146

Duncan, Norman 1871-1916 . . . . . . DLB-92

Duncan, Quince 1940- DLB-145

Duncan, Robert 1919-1988 . . . . . . DLB-5, 16

Duncan, Ronald 1914-1982 . . . . DLB-13

Duncan, Sara Jeannette
1861-1922 . . . . DLB-92

Dunigan, Edward, and Brother DLB-49

Dunlap, John 1747-1812 . . . . DLB-43

Dunlap, William
1766-1839 . . . . DLB-30, 37, 59

Dunn, Douglas 1942- DLB-40

Dunn, Stephen 1939- DLB-105

Dunn, Stephen, The Good,
The Not So Good DLB-105

Dunne, Finley Peter
1867-1936 . . . . DLB-11, 23

Dunne, John Gregory 1932- Y-80

Dunne, Philip 1908-1992 . . . . DLB-26

Dunning, Ralph Cheever
1878-1930 . . . . DLB-4

Dunning, William A. 1857-1922 . . . . DLB-17

Duns Scotus, John
circa 1266-1308 . . . . DLB-115

Dunsany, Lord (Edward John Moreton
Drax Plunkett, Baron Dunsany)
1878-1957 . . . . DLB-10, 77, 153, 156

Dunton, John [publishing house] DLB-170

Dupin, Amantine-Aurore-Lucile (see Sand, George)

Durand, Lucile (see Bersianik, Louky)

Duranty, Walter 1884-1957 . . . . . . DLB-29

Duras, Marguerite 1914- DLB-83

Durfey, Thomas 1653-1723 . . . . DLB-80

Durrell, Lawrence
1912-1990 . . . . DLB-15, 27; Y-90

Durrell, William
[publishing house] DLB-49

Dürrenmatt, Friedrich
1921-1990 . . . . DLB-69, 124

Dutton, E. P., and Company DLB-49

Duvoisin, Roger 1904-1980 . . . . DLB-61

Duyckinck, Evert Augustus
1816-1878 . . . . DLB-3, 64

Duyckinck, George L. 1823-1863 . . . . DLB-3

Duyckinck and Company DLB-49

Dwight, John Sullivan 1813-1893 . . . . DLB-1

Dwight, Timothy 1752-1817 . . . . . . DLB-37

Dybek, Stuart 1942- DLB-130

Dyer, Charles 1928- DLB-13

Dyer, George 1755-1841 . . . . DLB-93

Dyer, John 1699-1757 . . . . DLB-95

Dyer, Sir Edward 1543-1607 . . . . . DLB-136

Dylan, Bob 1941- DLB-16

E

Eager, Edward 1911-1964 . . . . DLB-22

Eames, Wilberforce 1855-1937 . . . . . DLB-140

Earle, James H., and Company DLB-49

Earle, John 1600 or 1601-1665 . . . . . DLB-151

Early American Book Illustration,
by Sinclair Hamilton DLB-49

Eastlake, William 1917- DLB-6

Eastman, Carol ?- DLB-44

Eastman, Charles A. (Ohiyesa)
1858-1939 . . . . DLB-175

Eastman, Max 1883-1969 . . . . DLB-91

Eaton, Daniel Isaac 1753-1814 . . . . . DLB-158

Eberhart, Richard 1904- DLB-48

Ebner, Jeannie 1918- DLB-85

Ebner-Eschenbach, Marie von
1830-1916 . . . . DLB-81

Ebon 1942- DLB-41

Ecbasis Captivi circa 1045 . . . . DLB-148

Ecco Press DLB-46

Eckhart, Meister
circa 1260-circa 1328 . . . . DLB-115

The Eclectic Review 1805-1868 . . . . . DLB-110

Edel, Leon 1907- DLB-103

Edes, Benjamin 1732-1803 . . . . DLB-43

Edgar, David 1948- DLB-13

Edgeworth, Maria
1768-1849 . . . . DLB-116, 159, 163

The Edinburgh Review 1802-1929 . . . . DLB-110

Edinburgh University Press DLB-112

The Editor Publishing Company DLB-49

Editorial Statements DLB-137

Edmonds, Randolph 1900- DLB-51

Edmonds, Walter D. 1903- DLB-9

Edschmid, Kasimir 1890-1966 . . . . . DLB-56

Edwards, Amelia Anne Blandford
1831-1892 . . . . DLB-174

Edwards, Jonathan 1703-1758 . . . . . DLB-24

Edwards, Jonathan, Jr. 1745-1801 . . . DLB-37

Edwards, Junius 1929- DLB-33

Edwards, Matilda Barbara Betham-
1836-1919 . . . . DLB-174

Edwards, Richard 1524-1566 . . . . . . DLB-62

Edwards, James
[publishing house] DLB-154

Effinger, George Alec 1947- DLB-8

Egerton, George 1859-1945 . . . . . . DLB-135

Eggleston, Edward 1837-1902 . . . . . DLB-12

Eggleston, Wilfred 1901-1986 . . . . . DLB-92

Ehrenstein, Albert 1886-1950 . . . . . DLB-81

Ehrhart, W. D. 1948- DS-9

Eich, Günter 1907-1972 . . . . . . DLB-69, 124

Eichendorff, Joseph Freiherr von
1788-1857 . . . . DLB-90

1873 Publishers' Catalogues DLB-49

Eighteenth-Century Aesthetic
Theories DLB-31

Eighteenth-Century Philosophical
Background DLB-31

Eigner, Larry 1927- DLB-5

Eikon Basilike 1649 . . . . DLB-151

Eilhart von Oberge
circa 1140-circa 1195 . . . . DLB-148

Einhard circa 770-840 . . . . DLB-148

Eisenreich, Herbert 1925-1986 . . . . . DLB-85

Eisner, Kurt 1867-1919 . . . . DLB-66

Eklund, Gordon 1945- Y-83

Ekwensi, Cyprian 1921- DLB-117

Eld, George
[publishing house] DLB-170

Elder, Lonne III 1931- DLB-7, 38, 44

Elder, Paul, and Company DLB-49

Elements of Rhetoric (1828; revised, 1846),
by Richard Whately [excerpt] DLB-57

Elie, Robert 1915-1973 . . . . DLB-88

Elin Pelin 1877-1949 . . . . DLB-147

Eliot, George 1819-1880 . . . . . DLB-21, 35, 55

Eliot, John 1604-1690 . . . . DLB-24

Eliot, T. S. 1888-1965 . . . . DLB-7, 10, 45, 63

Eliot's Court Press DLB-170

Elizabeth I 1533-1603 . . . . DLB-136

Elizabeth of Nassau-Saarbrücken
    after 1393-1456 . . . . DLB-179

Elizondo, Salvador 1932- DLB-145

Elizondo, Sergio 1930- DLB-82

Elkin, Stanley 1930- DLB-2, 28; Y-80

Elles, Dora Amy (see Wentworth, Patricia)

Ellet, Elizabeth F. 1818?-1877 . . . . . DLB-30

Elliot, Ebenezer 1781-1849 . . . . DLB-96

Elliot, Frances Minto (Dickinson)
    1820-1898 . . . . DLB-166

Elliott, George 1923- DLB-68

Elliott, Janice 1931- DLB-14

Elliott, William 1788-1863 . . . . DLB-3

Elliott, Thomes and Talbot DLB-49

Ellis, Edward S. 1840-1916 . . . . DLB-42

Ellis, Frederick Staridge
    [publishing house] DLB-106

The George H. Ellis Company DLB-49

Ellison, Harlan 1934- DLB-8

Ellison, Ralph Waldo
    1914-1994 . . . . DLB-2, 76; Y-94

Ellmann, Richard
    1918-1987 . . . . DLB-103; Y-87

The Elmer Holmes Bobst Awards in Arts
    and Letters Y-87

Elyot, Thomas 1490?-1546 . . . . . . DLB-136

Emanuel, James Andrew 1921- DLB-41

Emecheta, Buchi 1944- DLB-117

The Emergence of Black Women
    Writers DS-8

Emerson, Ralph Waldo
    1803-1882 . . . . DLB-1, 59, 73, 183

Emerson, William 1769-1811 . . . . . . DLB-37

Emin, Fedor Aleksandrovich
    circa 1735-1770 . . . . DLB-150

Empedocles fifth century B.C. DLB-176

Empson, William 1906-1984 . . . . . . DLB-20

Enchi, Fumiko 1905-1986 . . . . DLB-182

Encounter with the West DLB-180

The End of English Stage Censorship,
    1945-1968 . . . . DLB-13

Ende, Michael 1929- DLB-75

Endō, Shūsaku 1923-1996 . . . . DLB-182

Engel, Marian 1933-1985 . . . . DLB-53

Engels, Friedrich 1820-1895 . . . . . . DLB-129

Engle, Paul 1908- DLB-48

English Composition and Rhetoric (1866),
    by Alexander Bain [excerpt] DLB-57

The English Language:
    410 to 1500 . . . . DLB-146

The English Renaissance of Art (1908),
    by Oscar Wilde DLB-35

Enright, D. J. 1920- DLB-27

Enright, Elizabeth 1909-1968 . . . . . . DLB-22

L'Envoi (1882), by Oscar Wilde DLB-35

Epictetus circa 55-circa 125-130 . . . . DLB-176

Epicurus 342/341 B.C.-271/270 B.C.
    . . . . DLB-176

Epps, Bernard 1936- DLB-53

Epstein, Julius 1909- and
    Epstein, Philip 1909-1952 . . . . . . DLB-26

Equiano, Olaudah
    circa 1745-1797 . . . . DLB-37, 50

Eragny Press DLB-112

Erasmus, Desiderius 1467-1536 . . . . DLB-136

Erba, Luciano 1922- DLB-128

Erdrich, Louise 1954- DLB-152, 178

Erichsen-Brown, Gwethalyn Graham
    (see Graham, Gwethalyn)

Eriugena, John Scottus
    circa 810-877 . . . . DLB-115

Ernest Hemingway's Toronto Journalism
    Revisited: With Three Previously
    Unrecorded Stories Y-92

Ernst, Paul 1866-1933 . . . . . . DLB-66, 118

Erskine, Albert 1911-1993 . . . . Y-93

Erskine, John 1879-1951 . . . . . . DLB-9, 102

Ervine, St. John Greer 1883-1971 . . . . DLB-10

Eschenburg, Johann Joachim
    1743-1820 . . . . DLB-97

Escoto, Julio 1944- DLB-145

Eshleman, Clayton 1935- DLB-5

Espriu, Salvador 1913-1985 . . . . . . DLB-134

Ess Ess Publishing Company DLB-49

Essay on Chatterton (1842), by
    Robert Browning DLB-32

Essex House Press DLB-112

Estes, Eleanor 1906-1988 . . . . DLB-22

Estes and Lauriat DLB-49

Etherege, George 1636-circa 1692 . . . DLB-80

Ethridge, Mark, Sr. 1896-1981 . . . . . DLB-127

Ets, Marie Hall 1893- DLB-22

Etter, David 1928- DLB-105

Ettner, Johann Christoph
    1654-1724 . . . . DLB-168

Eudora Welty: Eye of the Storyteller Y-87

Eugene O'Neill Memorial Theater
    Center DLB-7

Eugene O'Neill's Letters: A Review Y-88

Eupolemius
    flourished circa 1095 . . . . DLB-148

Euripides circa 484 B.C.-407/406 B.C.
    . . . . DLB-176

Evans, Caradoc 1878-1945 . . . . . . DLB-162

Evans, Donald 1884-1921 . . . . DLB-54

Evans, George Henry 1805-1856 . . . . DLB-43

Evans, Hubert 1892-1986 . . . . DLB-92

Evans, Mari 1923- DLB-41

Evans, Mary Ann (see Eliot, George)

Evans, Nathaniel 1742-1767 . . . . . . DLB-31

Evans, Sebastian 1830-1909 . . . . . . DLB-35

Evans, M., and Company DLB-46

Everett, Alexander Hill
    790-1847 . . . . DLB-59

Everett, Edward 1794-1865 . . . . . DLB-1, 59

Everson, R. G. 1903- DLB-88

Everson, William 1912-1994 . . . . . DLB-5, 16

Every Man His Own Poet; or, The
    Inspired Singer's Recipe Book (1877),
    by W. H. Mallock DLB-35

Ewart, Gavin 1916- DLB-40

Ewing, Juliana Horatia
    1841-1885 . . . . DLB-21, 163

The Examiner 1808-1881 . . . . DLB-110

Exley, Frederick
    1929-1992 . . . . DLB-143; Y-81

Experiment in the Novel (1929),
    by John D. Beresford DLB-36

von Eyb, Albrecht 1420-1475 . . . . . DLB-179

Eyre and Spottiswoode DLB-106

Ezzo ?-after 1065 . . . . DLB-148

F

"F. Scott Fitzgerald: St. Paul's Native Son
    and Distinguished American Writer":
    University of Minnesota Conference,
    29-31 October 1982 . . . . Y-82

Faber, Frederick William
    1814-1863 . . . . DLB-32

Faber and Faber Limited DLB-112

Faccio, Rena (see Aleramo, Sibilla)

Fagundo, Ana María 1938- DLB-134

Fair, Ronald L. 1932- DLB-33

Fairfax, Beatrice (see Manning, Marie)

Fairlie, Gerard 1899-1983 . . . . DLB-77

Fallada, Hans 1893-1947 . . . . DLB-56

Falsifying Hemingway Y-96

Fancher, Betsy 1928- Y-83

Fane, Violet 1843-1905 . . . . DLB-35

Fanfrolico Press DLB-112

Fanning, Katherine 1927- DLB-127

Fanshawe, Sir Richard
    1608-1666 . . . . DLB-126

Fantasy Press Publishers DLB-46

Fante, John 1909-1983 . . . . . DLB-130; Y-83

Al-Farabi circa 870-950 . . . . DLB-115

Farah, Nuruddin 1945- DLB-125

Farber, Norma 1909-1984 . . . . DLB-61

Farigoule, Louis (see Romains, Jules)

Farjeon, Eleanor 1881-1965 . . . . . . DLB-160

Farley, Walter 1920-1989 . . . . DLB-22

Farmer, Penelope 1939- DLB-161

Farmer, Philip José 1918- DLB-8

Farquhar, George circa 1677-1707 . . . . DLB-84

Farquharson, Martha (see Finley, Martha)

Farrar, Frederic William
1831-1903 . . . . DLB-163

Farrar and Rinehart. DLB-46

Farrar, Straus and Giroux DLB-46

Farrell, James T.
1904-1979 . . . . DLB-4, 9, 86; DS-2

Farrell, J. G. 1935-1979 . . . . DLB-14

Fast, Howard 1914- DLB-9

Faulkner, William 1897-1962
. . . . . . DLB-9, 11, 44, 102; DS-2; Y-86

Faulkner, George
[publishing house] DLB-154

Fauset, Jessie Redmon 1882-1961 . . . . DLB-51

Faust, Irvin 1924- DLB-2, 28; Y-80

Fawcett Books. DLB-46

Fearing, Kenneth 1902-1961 . . . . DLB-9

Federal Writers' Project. DLB-46

Federman, Raymond 1928- Y-80

Feiffer, Jules 1929- DLB-7, 44

Feinberg, Charles E. 1899-1988 . . . . . . Y-88

Feind, Barthold 1678-1721. . . . . . . DLB-168

Feinstein, Elaine 1930- DLB-14, 40

Feldman, Irving 1928- DLB-169

Felipe, Léon 1884-1968 . . . . DLB-108

Fell, Frederick, Publishers. DLB-46

Felltham, Owen 1602?-1668 . . . . DLB-126, 151

Fels, Ludwig 1946- DLB-75

Felton, Cornelius Conway
1807-1862. . . . . DLB-1

Fennario, David 1947- DLB-60

Fenno, John 1751-1798 . . . . DLB-43

Fenno, R. F., and Company DLB-49

Fenoglio, Beppe 1922-1963 . . . . . . DLB-177

Fenton, Geoffrey 1539?-1608 . . . . . DLB-136

Fenton, James 1949- DLB-40

Ferber, Edna 1885-1968 . . . . . DLB-9, 28, 86

Ferdinand, Vallery III (see Salaam, Kalamu ya)

Ferguson, Sir Samuel 1810-1886 . . . . . DLB-32

Ferguson, William Scott
1875-1954 . . . . DLB-47

Fergusson, Robert 1750-1774 . . . . . DLB-109

Ferland, Albert 1872-1943 . . . . DLB-92

Ferlinghetti, Lawrence 1919- DLB-5, 16

Fern, Fanny (see Parton, Sara Payson Willis)

Ferrars, Elizabeth 1907- DLB-87

Ferré, Rosario 1942- DLB-145

Ferret, E., and Company. DLB-49

Ferrier, Susan 1782-1854 . . . . DLB-116

Ferrini, Vincent 1913- DLB-48

Ferron, Jacques 1921-1985 . . . . DLB-60

Ferron, Madeleine 1922- DLB-53

Fetridge and Company DLB-49

Feuchtersleben, Ernst Freiherr von
1806-1849 . . . . DLB-133

Feuchtwanger, Lion 1884-1958 . . . . . DLB-66

Feuerbach, Ludwig 1804-1872. . . . . . DLB-133

Fichte, Johann Gottlieb
1762-1814 . . . . DLB-90

Ficke, Arthur Davison 1883-1945 . . . . DLB-54

Fiction Best-Sellers, 1910-1945 . . . . . . DLB-9

Fiction into Film, 1928-1975: A List of Movies
Based on the Works of Authors in
British Novelists, 1930-1959 . . . . . DLB-15

Fiedler, Leslie A. 1917- DLB-28, 67

Field, Edward 1924- DLB-105

Field, Edward, The Poetry File. DLB-105

Field, Eugene
1850-1895 . . . . . DLB-23, 42, 140; DS-13

Field, John 1545?-1588. . . . . DLB-167

Field, Marshall, III 1893-1956. . . . . DLB-127

Field, Marshall, IV 1916-1965 . . . . . DLB-127

Field, Marshall, V 1941- DLB-127

Field, Nathan 1587-1619 or 1620 . . . DLB-58

Field, Rachel 1894-1942 . . . . DLB-9, 22

A Field Guide to Recent Schools of American
Poetry. Y-86

Fielding, Henry
1707-1754 . . . . DLB-39, 84, 101

Fielding, Sarah 1710-1768. . . . . DLB-39

Fields, James Thomas 1817-1881 . . . . . DLB-1

Fields, Julia 1938- DLB-41

Fields, W. C. 1880-1946 . . . . DLB-44

Fields, Osgood and Company DLB-49

Fifty Penguin Years. Y-85

Figes, Eva 1932- DLB-14

Figuera, Angela 1902-1984 . . . . . . DLB-108

Filmer, Sir Robert 1586-1653 . . . . . DLB-151

Filson, John circa 1753-1788 . . . . . . DLB-37

Finch, Anne, Countess of Winchilsea
1661-1720 . . . . DLB-95

Finch, Robert 1900- DLB-88

Findley, Timothy 1930- DLB-53

Finlay, Ian Hamilton 1925- DLB-40

Finley, Martha 1828-1909. . . . . DLB-42

Finn, Elizabeth Anne (McCaul)
1825-1921 . . . . DLB-166

Finney, Jack 1911- DLB-8

Finney, Walter Braden (see Finney, Jack)

Firbank, Ronald 1886-1926. . . . . . . DLB-36

Firmin, Giles 1615-1697. . . . . DLB-24

Fischart, Johann
1546 or 1547-1590 or 1591 . . . . DLB-179

First Edition Library/Collectors'
Reprints, Inc. Y-91

First International F. Scott Fitzgerald
Conference Y-92

First Strauss "Livings" Awarded to Cynthia
Ozick and Raymond Carver
An Interview with Cynthia Ozick
An Interview with Raymond
Carver Y-83

Fischer, Karoline Auguste Fernandine
1764-1842 . . . . DLB-94

Fish, Stanley 1938- DLB-67

Fishacre, Richard 1205-1248. . . . . . DLB-115

Fisher, Clay (see Allen, Henry W.)

Fisher, Dorothy Canfield
1879-1958 . . . . DLB-9, 102

Fisher, Leonard Everett 1924- DLB-61

Fisher, Roy 1930- DLB-40

Fisher, Rudolph 1897-1934 . . . . . DLB-51, 102

Fisher, Sydney George 1856-1927 . . . . DLB-47

Fisher, Vardis 1895-1968. . . . . DLB-9

Fiske, John 1608-1677. . . . . DLB-24

Fiske, John 1842-1901 . . . . DLB-47, 64

Fitch, Thomas circa 1700-1774. . . . . . DLB-31

Fitch, William Clyde 1865-1909. . . . . . DLB-7

FitzGerald, Edward 1809-1883 . . . . . DLB-32

Fitzgerald, F. Scott 1896-1940
. . . . . DLB-4, 9, 86; Y-81; DS-1, 15, 16

F. Scott Fitzgerald Centenary
Celebrations. Y-96

Fitzgerald, Penelope 1916- DLB-14

Fitzgerald, Robert 1910-1985. . . . . . . Y-80

Fitzgerald, Thomas 1819-1891 . . . . . DLB-23

Fitzgerald, Zelda Sayre 1900-1948. . . . . Y-84

Fitzhugh, Louise 1928-1974 . . . . . . DLB-52

Fitzhugh, William
circa 1651-1701 . . . . DLB-24

Flanagan, Thomas 1923- Y-80

Flanner, Hildegarde 1899-1987 . . . . . DLB-48

Flanner, Janet 1892-1978 . . . . DLB-4

Flaubert, Gustave 1821-1880 . . . . . DLB-119

Flavin, Martin 1883-1967 . . . . DLB-9

Fleck, Konrad (flourished circa 1220)
. . . . DLB-138

Flecker, James Elroy 1884-1915 . . . DLB-10, 19

Fleeson, Doris 1901-1970 . . . . DLB-29

Fleißer, Marieluise 1901-1974 . . . . DLB-56, 124

Fleming, Ian 1908-1964 . . . . DLB-87

Fleming, Paul 1609-1640 . . . . DLB-164

The Fleshly School of Poetry and Other
Phenomena of the Day (1872), by Robert
Buchanan DLB-35

The Fleshly School of Poetry: Mr. D. G.
Rossetti (1871), by Thomas Maitland
(Robert Buchanan) DLB-35

Fletcher, Giles, the Elder
1546-1611 . . . . DLB-136

Fletcher, Giles, the Younger
1585 or 1586-1623 . . . . DLB-121

Fletcher, J. S. 1863-1935 . . . . DLB-70

Fletcher, John (see Beaumont, Francis)

Fletcher, John Gould 1886-1950 . . . DLB-4, 45

Fletcher, Phineas 1582-1650 . . . . . . DLB-121

Flieg, Helmut (see Heym, Stefan)

Flint, F. S. 1885-1960 . . . . DLB-19

Flint, Timothy 1780-1840 . . . . DLB-73

Florio, John 1553?-1625 . . . . DLB-172

Foix, J. V. 1893-1987 . . . . DLB-134

Foley, Martha (see Burnett, Whit, and
Martha Foley)

Folger, Henry Clay 1857-1930 . . . . DLB-140

Folio Society DLB-112

Follen, Eliza Lee (Cabot) 1787-1860 . . . DLB-1

Follett, Ken 1949- Y-81, DLB-87

Follett Publishing Company DLB-46

Folsom, John West
[publishing house] DLB-49

Folz, Hans
between 1435 and 1440-1513 . . . . DLB-179

Fontane, Theodor 1819-1898 . . . . . DLB-129

Fonvisin, Denis Ivanovich
1744 or 1745-1792 . . . . DLB-150

Foote, Horton 1916- DLB-26

Foote, Samuel 1721-1777 . . . . DLB-89

Foote, Shelby 1916- DLB-2, 17

Forbes, Calvin 1945- DLB-41

Forbes, Ester 1891-1967 . . . . DLB-22

Forbes and Company DLB-49

Force, Peter 1790-1868 . . . . DLB-30

Forché, Carolyn 1950- DLB-5

Ford, Charles Henri 1913- DLB-4, 48

Ford, Corey 1902-1969 . . . . DLB-11

Ford, Ford Madox
1873-1939 . . . . DLB-34, 98, 162

Ford, Jesse Hill 1928- DLB-6

Ford, John 1586-? DLB-58

Ford, R. A. D. 1915- DLB-88

Ford, Worthington C. 1858-1941 . . . DLB-47

Ford, J. B., and Company DLB-49

Fords, Howard, and Hulbert DLB-49

Foreman, Carl 1914-1984 . . . . DLB-26

Forester, Frank (see Herbert, Henry William)

Fornés, María Irene 1930- DLB-7

Forrest, Leon 1937- DLB-33

Forster, E. M.
1879-1970 . . . DLB-34, 98, 162, 178; DS-10

Forster, Georg 1754-1794 . . . . DLB-94

Forster, John 1812-1876 . . . . DLB-144

Forster, Margaret 1938- DLB-155

Forsyth, Frederick 1938- DLB-87

Forten, Charlotte L. 1837-1914 . . . . . DLB-50

Fortini, Franco 1917- DLB-128

Fortune, T. Thomas 1856-1928 . . . . DLB-23

Fosdick, Charles Austin
1842-1915 . . . . DLB-42

Foster, Genevieve 1893-1979 . . . . . . DLB-61

Foster, Hannah Webster
1758-1840 . . . . DLB-37

Foster, John 1648-1681 . . . . DLB-24

Foster, Michael 1904-1956 . . . . DLB-9

Foulis, Robert and Andrew / R. and A.
[publishing house] DLB-154

Fouqué, Caroline de la Motte
1774-1831 . . . . DLB-90

Fouqué, Friedrich de la Motte
1777-1843 . . . . DLB-90

Four Essays on the Beat Generation,
by John Clellon Holmes DLB-16

Four Seas Company DLB-46

Four Winds Press DLB-46

Fournier, Henri Alban (see Alain-Fournier)

Fowler and Wells Company DLB-49

Fowles, John 1926- DLB-14, 139

Fox, John, Jr. 1862 or
1863-1919 . . . . DLB-9; DS-13

Fox, Paula 1923- DLB-52

Fox, Richard Kyle 1846-1922 . . . . . DLB-79

Fox, William Price 1926- DLB-2; Y-81

Fox, Richard K.
[publishing house] DLB-49

Foxe, John 1517-1587 . . . . DLB-132

Fraenkel, Michael 1896-1957 . . . . . . DLB-4

France, Anatole 1844-1924 . . . . . . DLB-123

France, Richard 1938- DLB-7

Francis, Convers 1795-1863 . . . . DLB-1

Francis, Dick 1920- DLB-87

Francis, Jeffrey, Lord 1773-1850 . . . DLB-107

Francis, C. S. [publishing house] DLB-49

François 1863-1910 . . . . DLB-92

François, Louise von 1817-1893 . . . DLB-129

Franck, Sebastian 1499-1542 . . . . . DLB-179

Francke, Kuno 1855-1930 . . . . DLB-71

Frank, Bruno 1887-1945 . . . . DLB-118

Frank, Leonhard 1882-1961 . . . . . DLB-56, 118

Frank, Melvin (see Panama, Norman)

Frank, Waldo 1889-1967 . . . . . . DLB-9, 63

Franken, Rose 1895?-1988 . . . . Y-84

Franklin, Benjamin
1706-1790 . . . . DLB-24, 43, 73, 183

Franklin, James 1697-1735 . . . . DLB-43

Franklin Library DLB-46

Frantz, Ralph Jules 1902-1979 . . . . . DLB-4

Franzos, Karl Emil 1848-1904 . . . . DLB-129

Fraser, G. S. 1915-1980 . . . . DLB-27

Fraser, Kathleen 1935- DLB-169

Frattini, Alberto 1922- DLB-128

Frau Ava ?-1127 . . . . DLB-148

Frayn, Michael 1933- DLB-13, 14

Frederic, Harold
1856-1898 . . . . DLB-12, 23; DS-13

Freeling, Nicolas 1927- DLB-87

Freeman, Douglas Southall
1886-1953 . . . . DLB-17

Freeman, Legh Richmond
1842-1915 . . . . DLB-23

Freeman, Mary E. Wilkins
1852-1930 . . . . DLB-12, 78

Freeman, R. Austin 1862-1943 . . . . . DLB-70

Freidank circa 117?-circa 1233 . . . . DLB-138

Freiligrath, Ferdinand 1810-1876 . . . DLB-133

Frémont, John Charles 1813-1890
and Frémont, Jessie Benton
1834-1902 . . . . DLB-183

French, Alice 1850-1934 . . . . . DLB-74; DS-13

French, David 1939- DLB-53

French, James [publishing house] DLB-49

French, Samuel [publishing house] DLB-49

Samuel French, Limited DLB-106

Freneau, Philip 1752-1832 . . . . . DLB-37, 43

Freni, Melo 1934- DLB-128

Freshfield, Douglas W.
1845-1934 . . . . DLB-174

Freytag, Gustav 1816-1895 . . . . . . DLB-129

Fried, Erich 1921-1988 . . . . DLB-85

Friedman, Bruce Jay 1930- DLB-2, 28

Friedrich von Hausen
circa 1171-1190 . . . . DLB-138

Friel, Brian 1929- DLB-13

Friend, Krebs 1895?-1967? DLB-4

Fries, Fritz Rudolf 1935- DLB-75

Fringe and Alternative Theater
in Great Britain DLB-13

Frisch, Max 1911-1991 . . . . . . DLB-69, 124

Frischlin, Nicodemus 1547-1590 . . . . DLB-179

Frischmuth, Barbara 1941- DLB-85

Fritz, Jean 1915- DLB-52

Fromentin, Eugene 1820-1876 . . . . DLB-123

From *The Gay Science,* by
E. S. Dallas DLB-2č

Frost, A. B. 1851-1928 . . . . DS-13

Frost, Robert 1874-1963 . . . . . DLB-54; DS-7

Frothingham, Octavius Brooks
1822-1895 . . . . DLB-1

Froude, James Anthony
1818-1894 . . . . DLB-18, 57, 144

Fry, Christopher 1907- DLB-13

Fry, Roger 1866-1934 . . . . DS-10

Frye, Northrop 1912-1991 . . . . . DLB-67, 68

Fuchs, Daniel
1909-1993 . . . . DLB-9, 26, 28; Y-93

Fuentes, Carlos 1928- DLB-113

Fuertes, Gloria 1918- DLB-108

The Fugitives and the Agrarians:
The First Exhibition Y-85

Fulbecke, William 1560-1603? DLB-172

Fuller, Charles H., Jr. 1939- DLB-38

Fuller, Henry Blake 1857-1929 . . . . . DLB-12

Fuller, John 1937- DLB-40

Fuller, Margaret (see Fuller, Sarah Margaret,
Marchesa D'Ossoli)

Fuller, Roy 1912-1991 . . . . DLB-15, 20

Fuller, Samuel 1912- DLB-26

Fuller, Sarah Margaret, Marchesa
D'Ossoli 1810-1850 . . . DLB-1, 59, 73, 183

Fuller, Thomas 1608-1661 . . . . DLB-151

Fullerton, Hugh 1873-1945 . . . . . . DLB-171

Fulton, Len 1934- Y-86

Fulton, Robin 1937- DLB-40

Furbank, P. N. 1920- DLB-155

Furman, Laura 1945- Y-86

Furness, Horace Howard
1833-1912 . . . . DLB-64

Furness, William Henry 1802-1896 . . . . DLB-1

Furthman, Jules 1888-1966 . . . . . . DLB-26

Furui, Yoshikichi 1937- DLB-182

Futabatei, Shimei (Hasegawa Tatsunosuke)
1864-1909 . . . . DLB-180

The Future of the Novel (1899), by
Henry James DLB-18

Fyleman, Rose 1877-1957 . . . . DLB-160

G

The G. Ross Roy Scottish Poetry
Collection at the University of
South Carolina Y-89

Gadda, Carlo Emilio 1893-1973 . . . . DLB-177

Gaddis, William 1922- DLB-2

Gág, Wanda 1893-1946 . . . . DLB-22

Gagnon, Madeleine 1938- DLB-60

Gaine, Hugh 1726-1807 . . . . DLB-43

Gaine, Hugh [publishing house] DLB-49

Gaines, Ernest J.
1933- DLB-2, 33, 152; Y-80

Gaiser, Gerd 1908-1976 . . . . DLB-69

Galarza, Ernesto 1905-1984 . . . . . . DLB-122

Galaxy Science Fiction Novels DLB-46

Gale, Zona 1874-1938 . . . . DLB-9, 78

Galen of Pergamon 129-after 210 . . . DLB-176

Gall, Louise von 1815-1855 . . . . . . DLB-133

Gallagher, Tess 1943- DLB-120

Gallagher, Wes 1911- DLB-127

Gallagher, William Davis
1808-1894 . . . . DLB-73

Gallant, Mavis 1922- DLB-53

Gallico, Paul 1897-1976 . . . . . . DLB-9, 171

Galsworthy, John
1867-1933 . . . DLB-10, 34, 98, 162; DS-16

Galt, John 1779-1839 . . . . DLB-99, 116

Galton, Sir Francis 1822-1911 . . . . DLB-166

Galvin, Brendan 1938- DLB-5

Gambit DLB-46

Gamboa, Reymundo 1948- DLB-122

Gammer Gurton's Needle DLB-62

Gannett, Frank E. 1876-1957 . . . . . DLB-29

Gaos, Vicente 1919-1980 . . . . DLB-134

García, Lionel G. 1935- DLB-82

García Lorca, Federico
1898-1936 . . . . DLB-108

García Márquez, Gabriel
1928- DLB-113

Gardam, Jane 1928- DLB-14, 161

Garden, Alexander
circa 1685-1756 . . . . DLB-31

Gardiner, Margaret Power Farmer (see
Blessington, Marguerite, Countess of)

Gardner, John 1933-1982 . . . . . . DLB-2; Y-82

Garfield, Leon 1921- DLB-161

Garis, Howard R. 1873-1962 . . . . . . DLB-22

Garland, Hamlin
1860-1940 . . . . DLB-12, 71, 78

Garneau, Francis-Xavier
1809-1866 . . . . DLB-99

Garneau, Hector de Saint-Denys
1912-1943 . . . . DLB-88

Garneau, Michel 1939- DLB-53

Garner, Alan 1934- DLB-161

Garner, Hugh 1913-1979 . . . . DLB-68

Garnett, David 1892-1981 . . . . DLB-34

Garnett, Eve 1900-1991 . . . . DLB-160

Garraty, John A. 1920- DLB-17

Garrett, George
1929- DLB-2, 5, 130, 152; Y-83

Garrick, David 1717-1779 . . . . DLB-84

Garrison, William Lloyd
1805-1879 . . . . DLB-1, 43

Garro, Elena 1920- DLB-145

Garth, Samuel 1661-1719 . . . . DLB-95

Garve, Andrew 1908- DLB-87

Gary, Romain 1914-1980 . . . . DLB-83

Gascoigne, George 1539?-1577 . . . . DLB-136

Gascoyne, David 1916- DLB-20

Gaskell, Elizabeth Cleghorn
1810-1865 . . . . DLB-21, 144, 159

Gaspey, Thomas 1788-1871 . . . . . . DLB-116

Gass, William Howard 1924- DLB-2

Gates, Doris 1901- DLB-22

Gates, Henry Louis, Jr. 1950- DLB-67

Gates, Lewis E. 1860-1924 . . . . DLB-71

Gatto, Alfonso 1909-1976 . . . . DLB-114

Gaunt, Mary 1861-1942 . . . . DLB-174

Gautier, Théophile 1811-1872 . . . . . DLB-119

Gauvreau, Claude 1925-1971 . . . . . . DLB-88

The *Gawain*-Poet
flourished circa 1350-1400 . . . . . DLB-146

Gay, Ebenezer 1696-1787 . . . . DLB-24

Gay, John 1685-1732 . . . . DLB-84, 95

The Gay Science (1866), by E. S. Dallas [excerpt]
. . . . DLB-21

Gayarré, Charles E. A. 1805-1895 . . . . DLB-30

Gaylord, Edward King
1873-1974 . . . . DLB-127

Gaylord, Edward Lewis 1919- DLB-127

Gaylord, Charles
[publishing house] DLB-49

Geddes, Gary 1940- DLB-60

Geddes, Virgil 1897- DLB-4

Gedeon (Georgii Andreevich Krinovsky)
circa 1730-1763 . . . . DLB-150

Geibel, Emanuel 1815-1884 . . . . . . DLB-129

Geiogamah, Hanay 1945- DLB-175

Geis, Bernard, Associates DLB-46

Geisel, Theodor Seuss
1904-1991 . . . . DLB-61; Y-91

Gelb, Arthur 1924- DLB-103

Gelb, Barbara 1926- DLB-103

Gelber, Jack 1932- DLB-7

Gelinas, Gratien 1909- DLB-88

Gellert, Christian Füerchtegott
1715-1769 . . . . DLB-97

Gellhorn, Martha 1908- Y-82

Gems, Pam 1925- DLB-13

A General Idea of the College of Mirania (1753),
by William Smith [excerpts] DLB-31

Genet, Jean 1910-1986 . . . . . . DLB-72; Y-86

Genevoix, Maurice 1890-1980 . . . . . DLB-65

Genovese, Eugene D. 1930- DLB-17

Gent, Peter 1942- Y-82

Geoffrey of Monmouth
circa 1100-1155 . . . . DLB-146

George, Henry 1839-1897 . . . . DLB-23

George, Jean Craighead 1919- DLB-52

Georgslied 896? DLB-148

Gerhardie, William 1895-1977 . . . . . DLB-36

Gerhardt, Paul 1607-1676 . . . . DLB-164

Gérin, Winifred 1901-1981 . . . . DLB-155

Gérin-Lajoie, Antoine 1824-1882 . . . . . DLB-99

German Drama 800-1280 . . . . DLB-138

German Drama from Naturalism
to Fascism: 1889-1933. . . . . DLB-118

German Literature and Culture from
Charlemagne to the Early Courtly
Period DLB-148

German Radio Play, The DLB-124

German Transformation from the Baroque
to the Enlightenment, The. DLB-97

The Germanic Epic and Old English Heroic
Poetry: *Widseth, Waldere,* and *The
Fight at Finnsburg.* DLB-146

Germanophilism, by Hans Kohn. . . . DLB-66

Gernsback, Hugo 1884-1967 . . . . . DLB-8, 137

Gerould, Katharine Fullerton
1879-1944 . . . . DLB-78

Gerrish, Samuel [publishing house] . . . DLB-49

Gerrold, David 1944- DLB-8

The Ira Gershwin Centenary Y-96

Gersonides 1288-1344 . . . . DLB-115

Gerstäcker, Friedrich 1816-1872. . . . DLB-129

Gerstenberg, Heinrich Wilhelm von
1737-1823 . . . . DLB-97

Gervinus, Georg Gottfried
1805-1871 . . . . DLB-133

Geßner, Salomon 1730-1788 . . . . . . DLB-97

Geston, Mark S. 1946- DLB-8

Al-Ghazali 1058-1111. . . . . DLB-115

Gibbon, Edward 1737-1794 . . . . . . DLB-104

Gibbon, John Murray 1875-1952 . . . . DLB-92

Gibbon, Lewis Grassic (see Mitchell,
James Leslie)

Gibbons, Floyd 1887-1939 . . . . DLB-25

Gibbons, Reginald 1947- DLB-120

Gibbons, William ?-? DLB-73

Gibson, Charles Dana 1867-1944 . . . . . DS-13

Gibson, Charles Dana 1867-1944 . . . . . DS-13

Gibson, Graeme 1934- DLB-53

Gibson, Margaret 1944- DLB-120

Gibson, Margaret Dunlop
1843-1920 . . . . DLB-174

Gibson, Wilfrid 1878-1962 . . . . DLB-19

Gibson, William 1914- DLB-7

Gide, André 1869-1951 . . . . DLB-65

Giguère, Diane 1937- DLB-53

Giguère, Roland 1929- DLB-60

Gil de Biedma, Jaime 1929-1990 . . . . DLB-108

Gil-Albert, Juan 1906- DLB-134

Gilbert, Anthony 1899-1973 . . . . . . DLB-77

Gilbert, Michael 1912- DLB-87

Gilbert, Sandra M. 1936- DLB-120

Gilbert, Sir Humphrey
1537-1583 . . . . DLB-136

Gilchrist, Alexander
1828-1861 . . . . DLB-144

Gilchrist, Ellen 1935- DLB-130

Gilder, Jeannette L. 1849-1916 . . . . . DLB-79

Gilder, Richard Watson
1844-1909 . . . . DLB-64, 79

Gildersleeve, Basil 1831-1924 . . . . . . DLB-71

Giles, Henry 1809-1882 . . . . DLB-64

Giles of Rome circa 1243-1316 . . . . . DLB-115

Gilfillan, George 1813-1878 . . . . . . DLB-144

Gill, Eric 1882-1940 . . . . DLB-98

Gill, William F., Company DLB-49

Gillespie, A. Lincoln, Jr.
1895-1950 . . . . DLB-4

Gilliam, Florence ?-? DLB-4

Gilliatt, Penelope 1932-1993 . . . . . . DLB-14

Gillott, Jacky 1939-1980 . . . . DLB-14

Gilman, Caroline H. 1794-1888. . . . DLB-3, 73

Gilman, W. and J.
[publishing house]. DLB-49

Gilmer, Elizabeth Meriwether
1861-1951 . . . . DLB-29

Gilmer, Francis Walker
1790-1826 . . . . DLB-37

Gilroy, Frank D. 1925- DLB-7

Gimferrer, Pere (Pedro) 1945- DLB-134

Gingrich, Arnold 1903-1976 . . . . . . DLB-137

Ginsberg, Allen 1926- DLB-5, 16, 169

Ginzburg, Natalia 1916-1991 . . . . . . DLB-177

Ginzkey, Franz Karl 1871-1963 . . . . . DLB-81

Gioia, Dana 1950- DLB-120

Giono, Jean 1895-1970 . . . . DLB-72

Giotti, Virgilio 1885-1957 . . . . DLB-114

Giovanni, Nikki 1943- DLB-5, 41

Gipson, Lawrence Henry
1880-1971 . . . . DLB-17

Girard, Rodolphe 1879-1956 . . . . . . DLB-92

Giraudoux, Jean 1882-1944 . . . . . . DLB-65

Gissing, George 1857-1903 . . . . DLB-18, 135

Giudici, Giovanni 1924- DLB-128

Giuliani, Alfredo 1924- DLB-128

Gladstone, William Ewart
1809-1898 . . . . DLB-57

Glaeser, Ernst 1902-1963 . . . . DLB-69

Glancy, Diane 1941- DLB-175

Glanville, Brian 1931- DLB-15, 139

Glapthorne, Henry 1610-1643? DLB-58

Glasgow, Ellen 1873-1945 . . . . . . DLB-9, 12

Glaspell, Susan 1876-1948 . . . . . DLB-7, 9, 78

Glass, Montague 1877-1934 . . . . DLB-11

The Glass Key and Other Dashiell Hammett
Mysteries Y-96

Glassco, John 1909-1981 . . . . DLB-68

Glauser, Friedrich 1896-1938 . . . . . . DLB-56

F. Gleason's Publishing Hall DLB-49

Gleim, Johann Wilhelm Ludwig
1719-1803 . . . . DLB-97

Glendinning, Victoria 1937- DLB-155

Glover, Richard 1712-1785 . . . . DLB-95

Glück, Louise 1943- DLB-5

Glyn, Elinor 1864-1943 . . . . DLB-153

Gobineau, Joseph-Arthur de
1816-1882 . . . . DLB-123

Godbout, Jacques 1933- DLB-53

Goddard, Morrill 1865-1937 . . . . . . DLB-25

Goddard, William 1740-1817 . . . . . . DLB-43

Godden, Rumer 1907- DLB-161

Godey, Louis A. 1804-1878 . . . . DLB-73

Godey and McMichael DLB-49

Godfrey, Dave 1938- DLB-60

Godfrey, Thomas 1736-1763 . . . . . . DLB-31

Godine, David R., Publisher DLB-46

Godkin, E. L. 1831-1902 . . . . DLB-79

Godolphin, Sidney 1610-1643 . . . . . . DLB-126

Godwin, Gail 1937- DLB-6

Godwin, Mary Jane Clairmont
1766-1841 . . . . DLB-163

Godwin, Parke 1816-1904 . . . . . . DLB-3, 64

Godwin, William
1756-1836. . . . DLB-39, 104, 142, 158, 163

Godwin, M. J., and Company DLB-154

Goering, Reinhard 1887-1936 . . . . . . DLB-118

Goes, Albrecht 1908- DLB-69

Goethe, Johann Wolfgang von
1749-1832 . . . . DLB-94

Goetz, Curt 1888-1960 . . . . DLB-124

Goffe, Thomas circa 1592-1629 . . . . . DLB-58

Goffstein, M. B. 1940- DLB-61

Gogarty, Oliver St. John
1878-1957 . . . . DLB-15, 19

Goines, Donald 1937-1974 . . . . DLB-33

Gold, Herbert 1924- DLB-2; Y-81

Gold, Michael 1893-1967 . . . . . . DLB-9, 28

Goldbarth, Albert 1948- DLB-120

Goldberg, Dick 1947- DLB-7

Golden Cockerel Press DLB-112

Golding, Arthur 1536-1606 . . . . . . DLB-136

Golding, William 1911-1993 . . . . DLB-15, 100

Goldman, William 1931- DLB-44

Goldsmith, Oliver
1730?-1774. . . . DLB-39, 89, 104, 109, 142

Goldsmith, Oliver 1794-1861 . . . . DLB-99

Goldsmith Publishing Company DLB-46

Gollancz, Victor, Limited DLB-112

Gómez-Quiñones, Juan 1942- DLB-122

Gomme, Laurence James
[publishing house]. DLB-46

Goncourt, Edmond de 1822-1896 . . . DLB-123

Goncourt, Jules de 1830-1870 . . . . . DLB-123

Gonzales, Rodolfo "Corky"
1928- DLB-122

González, Angel 1925- DLB-108

Gonzalez, Genaro 1949- DLB-122

Gonzalez, Ray 1952- DLB-122

González de Mireles, Jovita
1899-1983 . . . . DLB-122

González-T., César A. 1931- DLB-82

Goodbye, Gutenberg? A Lecture at
the New York Public Library,
18 April 1995 . . . . Y-95

Goodison, Lorna 1947- DLB-157

Goodman, Paul 1911-1972 . . . . . . DLB-130

The Goodman Theatre DLB-7

Goodrich, Frances 1891-1984 and
Hackett, Albert 1900- DLB-26

Goodrich, Samuel Griswold
1793-1860 . . . . DLB-1, 42, 73

Goodrich, S. G. [publishing house] . . . DLB-49

Goodspeed, C. E., and Company DLB-49

Goodwin, Stephen 1943- Y-82

Googe, Barnabe 1540-1594 . . . . . . DLB-132

Gookin, Daniel 1612-1687 . . . . DLB-24

Gordon, Caroline
1895-1981 . . . . DLB-4, 9, 102; Y-81

Gordon, Giles 1940- DLB-14, 139

Gordon, Lyndall 1941- DLB-155

Gordon, Mary 1949- DLB-6; Y-81

Gordone, Charles 1925- DLB-7

Gore, Catherine 1800-1861 . . . . . . DLB-116

Gorey, Edward 1925- DLB-61

Gorgias of Leontini circa 485 B.C.-376 B.C.
. . . . DLB-176

Görres, Joseph 1776-1848 . . . . DLB-90

Gosse, Edmund 1849-1928 . . . . . DLB-57, 144

Gosson, Stephen 1554-1624 . . . . . . DLB-172

Gotlieb, Phyllis 1926- DLB-88

Gottfried von Straßburg
died before 1230 . . . . DLB-138

Gotthelf, Jeremias 1797-1854 . . . . . DLB-133

Gottschalk circa 804/808-869 . . . . . DLB-148

Gottsched, Johann Christoph
1700-1766 . . . . DLB-97

Götz, Johann Nikolaus
1721-1781 . . . . DLB-97

Gould, Wallace 1882-1940 . . . . DLB-54

Govoni, Corrado 1884-1965 . . . . . . DLB-114

Gower, John circa 1330-1408 . . . . . DLB-146

Goyen, William 1915-1983 . . . . DLB-2; Y-83

Goytisolo, José Augustín 1928- DLB-134

Gozzano, Guido 1883-1916 . . . . . . DLB-114

Grabbe, Christian Dietrich
1801-1836 . . . . DLB-133

Gracq, Julien 1910- DLB-83

Grady, Henry W. 1850-1889 . . . . . . DLB-23

Graf, Oskar Maria 1894-1967 . . . . . DLB-56

Graf Rudolf between circa 1170
and circa 1185 . . . . DLB-148

Grafton, Richard
[publishing house] DLB-170

Graham, George Rex
1813-1894 . . . . DLB-73

Graham, Gwethalyn 1913-1965 . . . . DLB-88

Graham, Jorie 1951- DLB-120

Graham, Katharine 1917- DLB-127

Graham, Lorenz 1902-1989 . . . . . . DLB-76

Graham, Philip 1915-1963 . . . . . . DLB-127

Graham, R. B. Cunninghame
1852-1936 . . . . DLB-98, 135, 174

Graham, Shirley 1896-1977 . . . . . . DLB-76

Graham, W. S. 1918- DLB-20

Graham, William H.
[publishing house] DLB-49

Graham, Winston 1910- DLB-77

Grahame, Kenneth
1859-1932 . . . . DLB-34, 141, 178

Grainger, Martin Allerdale
1874-1941 . . . . DLB-92

Gramatky, Hardie 1907-1979 . . . . . DLB-22

Grand, Sarah 1854-1943 . . . . DLB-135

Grandbois, Alain 1900-1975 . . . . . . DLB-92

Grange, John circa 1556-? DLB-136

Granich, Irwin (see Gold, Michael)

Grant, Duncan 1885-1978 . . . . DS-10

Grant, George 1918-1988 . . . . DLB-88

Grant, George Monro 1835-1902 . . . DLB-99

Grant, Harry J. 1881-1963 . . . . . . DLB-29

Grant, James Edward 1905-1966 . . . . DLB-26

Grass, Günter 1927- DLB-75, 124

Grasty, Charles H. 1863-1924 . . . . . DLB-25

Grau, Shirley Ann 1929- DLB-2

Graves, John 1920- Y-83

Graves, Richard 1715-1804 . . . . . . DLB-39

Graves, Robert
1895-1985 . . . . DLB-20, 100; Y-85

Gray, Asa 1810-1888 . . . . DLB-1

Gray, David 1838-1861 . . . . DLB-32

Gray, Simon 1936- DLB-13

Gray, Thomas 1716-1771 . . . . DLB-109

Grayson, William J. 1788-1863 . . . . DLB-3, 64

The Great Bibliographers Series Y-93

The Great War and the Theater, 1914-1918
[Great Britain]. DLB-10

Greeley, Horace 1811-1872 . . . . . . DLB-3, 43

Green, Adolph (see Comden, Betty)

Green, Duff 1791-1875 . . . . DLB-43

Green, Gerald 1922- DLB-28

Green, Henry 1905-1973 . . . . DLB-15

Green, Jonas 1712-1767 . . . . DLB-31

Green, Joseph 1706-1780 . . . . DLB-31

Green, Julien 1900- DLB-4, 72

Green, Paul 1894-1981 . . . . . . DLB-7, 9; Y-81

Green, T. and S.
[publishing house] DLB-49

Green, Timothy
[publishing house] DLB-49

Greenaway, Kate 1846-1901 . . . . . . DLB-141

Greenberg: Publisher DLB-46

Green Tiger Press DLB-46

Greene, Asa 1789-1838 . . . . DLB-11

Greene, Benjamin H.
[publishing house] DLB-49

Greene, Graham 1904-1991
. . . DLB-13, 15, 77, 100, 162; Y-85, Y-91

Greene, Robert 1558-1592 . . . . . DLB-62, 167

Greenhow, Robert 1800-1854 . . . . . DLB-30

Greenough, Horatio 1805-1852 . . . . . DLB-1

Greenwell, Dora 1821-1882 . . . . . . DLB-35

Greenwillow Books DLB-46

Greenwood, Grace (see Lippincott, Sara Jane
Clarke)

Greenwood, Walter 1903-1974 . . . . . DLB-10

Greer, Ben 1948- DLB-6

Greflinger, Georg 1620?-1677 . . . . . DLB-164

Greg, W. R. 1809-1881 . . . . DLB-55

Gregg, Josiah 1806-1850 . . . . DLB-183

Gregg Press DLB-46

Gregory, Isabella Augusta
Persse, Lady 1852-1932 . . . . . . DLB-10

Gregory, Horace 1898-1982 . . . . . . DLB-48

Gregory of Rimini
circa 1300-1358 . . . . DLB-115

Gregynog Press DLB-112

Greiffenberg, Catharina Regina von
1633-1694 . . . . DLB-168

Grenfell, Wilfred Thomason
1865-1940 . . . . DLB-92

Greve, Felix Paul (see Grove, Frederick Philip)

Greville, Fulke, First Lord Brooke
1554-1628 . . . . DLB-62, 172

Grey, Lady Jane 1537-1554 . . . . . . DLB-132

Grey Owl 1888-1938 . . . . DLB-92

Grey, Zane 1872-1939 . . . . DLB-9

Grey Walls Press DLB-112

Grier, Eldon 1917- DLB-88

Grieve, C. M. (see MacDiarmid, Hugh)

Griffin, Bartholomew
flourished 1596 . . . . DLB-172

Griffin, Gerald 1803-1840 . . . . DLB-159

Griffith, Elizabeth 1727?-1793 . . . . DLB-39, 89

Griffith, George 1857-1906 . . . . . . DLB-178

Griffiths, Trevor 1935- DLB-13

Griffiths, Ralph
[publishing house] DLB-154

Griggs, S. C., and Company DLB-49

Griggs, Sutton Elbert
1872-1930 . . . . DLB-50

Grignon, Claude-Henri 1894-1976 . . . . DLB-68

Grigson, Geoffrey 1905- DLB-27

Grillparzer, Franz 1791-1872 . . . . . DLB-133

Grimald, Nicholas
circa 1519-circa 1562 . . . . DLB-136

Grimké, Angelina Weld
1880-1958 . . . . DLB-50, 54

Grimm, Hans 1875-1959 . . . . DLB-66

Grimm, Jacob 1785-1863 . . . . DLB-90

Grimm, Wilhelm 1786-1859 . . . . DLB-90

Grimmelshausen, Johann Jacob Christoffel von
1621 or 1622-1676 . . . . DLB-168

Grimshaw, Beatrice Ethel
1871-1953 . . . . DLB-174

Grindal, Edmund
1519 or 1520-1583 . . . . DLB-132

Griswold, Rufus Wilmot
1815-1857 . . . . DLB-3, 59

Gross, Milt 1895-1953 . . . . DLB-11

Grosset and Dunlap DLB-49

Grossman Publishers DLB-46

Grosseteste, Robert
circa 1160-1253 . . . . DLB-115

Grosvenor, Gilbert H. 1875-1966 . . . . DLB-91

Groth, Klaus 1819-1899 . . . . DLB-129

Groulx, Lionel 1878-1967 . . . . DLB-68

Grove, Frederick Philip 1879-1949 . . . . DLB-92

Grove Press DLB-46

Grubb, Davis 1919-1980 . . . . DLB-6

Gruelle, Johnny 1880-1938 . . . . DLB-22

von Grumbach, Argula
1492-after 1563? DLB-179

Grymeston, Elizabeth
before 1563-before 1604 . . . . . . DLB-136

Gryphius, Andreas 1616-1664 . . . . . . DLB-164

Gryphius, Christian 1649-1706 . . . . . DLB-168

Guare, John 1938- DLB-7

Guerra, Tonino 1920- DLB-128

Guest, Barbara 1920- DLB-5

Guèvremont, Germaine
1893-1968 . . . . DLB-68

Guidacci, Margherita 1921-1992 . . . . DLB-128

Guide to the Archives of Publishers, Journals, and
Literary Agents in North American Libraries
. . . . Y-93

Guillén, Jorge 1893-1984 . . . . DLB-108

Guilloux, Louis 1899-1980 . . . . DLB-72

Guilpin, Everard
circa 1572-after 1608? DLB-136

Guiney, Louise Imogen 1861-1920 . . . . DLB-54

Guiterman, Arthur 1871-1943 . . . . . . DLB-11

Günderrode, Caroline von
1780-1806 . . . . DLB-90

Gundulić, Ivan 1589-1638 . . . . DLB-147

Gunn, Bill 1934-1989 . . . . DLB-38

Gunn, James E. 1923- DLB-8

Gunn, Neil M. 1891-1973 . . . . DLB-15

Gunn, Thom 1929- DLB-27

Gunnars, Kristjana 1948- DLB-60

Günther, Johann Christian
1695-1723 . . . . DLB-168

Gurik, Robert 1932- DLB-60

Gustafson, Ralph 1909- DLB-88

Gütersloh, Albert Paris 1887-1973 . . . . DLB-81

Guthrie, A. B., Jr. 1901- DLB-6

Guthrie, Ramon 1896-1973 . . . . DLB-4

The Guthrie Theater DLB-7

Guthrie, Thomas Anstey (see Anstey, FC)

Gutzkow, Karl 1811-1878 . . . . DLB-133

Guy, Ray 1939- DLB-60

Guy, Rosa 1925- DLB-33

Guyot, Arnold 1807-1884 . . . . DS-13

Gwynne, Erskine 1898-1948 . . . . DLB-4

Gyles, John 1680-1755 . . . . DLB-99

Gysin, Brion 1916- DLB-16

H

H. D. (see Doolittle, Hilda)

Habington, William 1605-1654 . . . . . DLB-126

Hacker, Marilyn 1942- DLB-120

Hackett, Albert (see Goodrich, Frances)

Hacks, Peter 1928- DLB-124

Hadas, Rachel 1948- DLB-120

Hadden, Briton 1898-1929 . . . . DLB-91

Hagedorn, Friedrich von
1708-1754 . . . . DLB-168

Hagelstange, Rudolf 1912-1984 . . . . . DLB-69

Haggard, H. Rider
1856-1925 . . . . . . DLB-70, 156, 174, 178

Haggard, William 1907-1993 . . . . Y-93

Hahn-Hahn, Ida Gräfin von
1805-1880 . . . . DLB-133

Haig-Brown, Roderick 1908-1976 . . . . DLB-88

Haight, Gordon S. 1901-1985 . . . . . . DLB-103

Hailey, Arthur 1920- DLB-88; Y-82

Haines, John 1924- DLB-5

Hake, Edward
flourished 1566-1604 . . . . DLB-136

Hake, Thomas Gordon 1809-1895 . . . . DLB-32

Hakluyt, Richard 1552?-1616 . . . . . . DLB-136

Halbe, Max 1865-1944 . . . . DLB-118

Haldane, J. B. S. 1892-1964 . . . . DLB-160

Haldeman, Joe 1943- DLB-8

Haldeman-Julius Company DLB-46

Hale, E. J., and Son DLB-49

Hale, Edward Everett
1822-1909 . . . . DLB-1, 42, 74

Hale, Janet Campbell 1946- DLB-175

Hale, Kathleen 1898- DLB-160

Hale, Leo Thomas (see Ebon)

Hale, Lucretia Peabody
1820-1900 . . . . DLB-42

Hale, Nancy 1908-1988 . . . . DLB-86; Y-80, 88

Hale, Sarah Josepha (Buell)
1788-1879 . . . . DLB-1, 42, 73

Hales, John 1584-1656 . . . . DLB-151

Haley, Alex 1921-1992 . . . . DLB-38

Haliburton, Thomas Chandler
1796-1865 . . . . DLB-11, 99

Hall, Anna Maria 1800-1881 . . . . . . DLB-159

Hall, Donald 1928- DLB-5

Hall, Edward 1497-1547 . . . . DLB-132

Hall, James 1793-1868 . . . . DLB-73, 74

Hall, Joseph 1574-1656 . . . . . . DLB-121, 151

Hall, Samuel [publishing house] DLB-49

Hallam, Arthur Henry 1811-1833 . . . . DLB-32

Halleck, Fitz-Greene 1790-1867 . . . . . DLB-3

Haller, Albrecht von 1708-1777 . . . . . DLB-168

Hallmann, Johann Christian
1640-1704 or 1716? DLB-168

Hallmark Editions DLB-46

Halper, Albert 1904-1984 . . . . DLB-9

Halperin, John William 1941- DLB-111

Halstead, Murat 1829-1908 . . . . DLB-23

Hamann, Johann Georg 1730-1788 . . . DLB-97

Hamburger, Michael 1924- DLB-27

Hamilton, Alexander 1712-1756 . . . . . DLB-31

Hamilton, Alexander 1755?-1804 . . . . DLB-37

Hamilton, Cicely 1872-1952 . . . . DLB-10

Hamilton, Edmond 1904-1977 . . . . DLB-8

Hamilton, Elizabeth 1758-1816 . . . . DLB-116, 158

Hamilton, Gail (see Corcoran, Barbara)

Hamilton, Ian 1938- DLB-40, 155

Hamilton, Patrick 1904-1962 . . . . DLB-10

Hamilton, Virginia 1936- DLB-33, 52

Hamilton, Hamish, Limited DLB-112

Hammett, Dashiell 1894-1961 . . . . DS-6

Dashiell Hammett:
An Appeal in *TAC* Y-91

Hammon, Jupiter 1711-died between
1790 and 1806 . . . . DLB-31, 50

Hammond, John ?-1663 . . . . DLB-24

Hamner, Earl 1923- DLB-6

Hampton, Christopher 1946- DLB-13

Handel-Mazzetti, Enrica von
1871-1955 . . . . DLB-81

Handke, Peter 1942- DLB-85, 124

Handlin, Oscar 1915- DLB-17

Hankin, St. John 1869-1909 . . . . . . DLB-10

Hanley, Clifford 1922- DLB-14

Hannah, Barry 1942- DLB-6

Hannay, James 1827-1873 . . . . DLB-21

Hansberry, Lorraine 1930-1965 . . . . DLB-7, 38

Hapgood, Norman 1868-1937 . . . . . DLB-91

Happel, Eberhard Werner
1647-1690 . . . . DLB-168

Harcourt Brace Jovanovich DLB-46

Hardenberg, Friedrich von (see Novalis)

Harding, Walter 1917- DLB-111

Hardwick, Elizabeth 1916- DLB-6

Hardy, Thomas 1840-1928 . . . . DLB-18, 19, 135

Hare, Cyril 1900-1958 . . . . DLB-77

Hare, David 1947- DLB-13

Hargrove, Marion 1919- DLB-11

Häring, Georg Wilhelm Heinrich (see Alexis, Willibald)

Harington, Donald 1935- DLB-152

Harington, Sir John 1560-1612 . . . . . DLB-136

Harjo, Joy 1951- DLB-120, 175

Harlow, Robert 1923- DLB-60

Harman, Thomas
flourished 1566-1573 . . . . DLB-136

Harness, Charles L. 1915- DLB-8

Harnett, Cynthia 1893-1981 . . . . DLB-161

Harper, Fletcher 1806-1877 . . . . DLB-79

Harper, Frances Ellen Watkins
1825-1911 . . . . DLB-50

Harper, Michael S. 1938- DLB-41

Harper and Brothers DLB-49

Harraden, Beatrice 1864-1943 . . . . . . DLB-153

Harrap, George G., and Company
Limited DLB-112

Harriot, Thomas 1560-1621 . . . . DLB-136

Harris, Benjamin ?-circa 1720 . . . . DLB-42, 43

Harris, Christie 1907- DLB-88

Harris, Frank 1856-1931 . . . . DLB-156

Harris, George Washington
1814-1869 . . . . DLB-3, 11

Harris, Joel Chandler
1848-1908 . . . . . DLB-11, 23, 42, 78, 91

Harris, Mark 1922- DLB-2; Y-80

Harris, Wilson 1921- DLB-117

Harrison, Charles Yale
1898-1954 . . . . DLB-68

Harrison, Frederic 1831-1923 . . . . . . DLB-57

Harrison, Harry 1925- DLB-8

Harrison, Jim 1937- Y-82

Harrison, Mary St. Leger Kingsley (see Malet, Lucas)

Harrison, Paul Carter 1936- DLB-38

Harrison, Susan Frances
1859-1935 . . . . DLB-99

Harrison, Tony 1937- DLB-40

Harrison, William 1535-1593 . . . . . DLB-136

Harrison, James P., Company DLB-49

Harrisse, Henry 1829-1910 . . . . DLB-47

Harsdörffer, Georg Philipp
1607-1658 . . . . DLB-164

Harsent, David 1942- DLB-40

Hart, Albert Bushnell 1854-1943 . . . . DLB-17

Hart, Julia Catherine 1796-1867 . . . . DLB-99

The Lorenz Hart Centenary Y-95

Hart, Moss 1904-1961 . . . . DLB-7

Hart, Oliver 1723-1795 . . . . DLB-31

Hart-Davis, Rupert, Limited DLB-112

Harte, Bret 1836-1902 . . . . DLB-12, 64, 74, 79

Harte, Edward Holmead 1922- DLB-127

Harte, Houston Harriman 1927- DLB-127

Hartlaub, Felix 1913-1945 . . . . DLB-56

Hartlebon, Otto Erich
1864-1905 . . . . DLB-118

Hartley, L. P. 1895-1972 . . . . . . DLB-15, 139

Hartley, Marsden 1877-1943 . . . . . . DLB-54

Hartling, Peter 1933- DLB-75

Hartman, Geoffrey H. 1929- DLB-67

Hartmann, Sadakichi 1867-1944 . . . . DLB-54

Hartmann von Aue
circa 1160-circa 1205 . . . . DLB-138

Harvey, Gabriel 1550?-1631 . . . . . . DLB-167

Harvey, Jean-Charles 1891-1967 . . . . DLB-88

Harvill Press Limited DLB-112

Harwood, Lee 1939- DLB-40

Harwood, Ronald 1934- DLB-13

Haskins, Charles Homer
1870-1937 . . . . DLB-47

Hass, Robert 1941- DLB-105

The Hatch-Billops Collection DLB-76

Hathaway, William 1944- DLB-120

Hauff, Wilhelm 1802-1827 . . . . DLB-90

A Haughty and Proud Generation (1922),
by Ford Madox Hueffer DLB-36

Haugwitz, August Adolph von
1647-1706 . . . . DLB-168

Hauptmann, Carl
1858-1921 . . . . DLB-66, 118

Hauptmann, Gerhart
1862-1946 . . . . DLB-66, 118

Hauser, Marianne 1910- Y-83

Hawes, Stephen
1475?-before 1529 . . . . DLB-132

Hawker, Robert Stephen
1803-1875 . . . . DLB-32

Hawkes, John 1925- DLB-2, 7; Y-80

Hawkesworth, John 1720-1773 . . . . DLB-142

Hawkins, Sir Anthony Hope (see Hope, Anthony)

Hawkins, Sir John
1719-1789 . . . . DLB-104, 142

Hawkins, Walter Everette 1883-? DLB-50

Hawthorne, Nathaniel
1804-1864 . . . . DLB-1, 74, 183

Hawthorne, Nathaniel 1804-1864 and
Hawthorne, Sophia Peabody
1809-1871 . . . . DLB-183

Hay, John 1838-1905 . . . . DLB-12, 47

Hayashi, Fumiko 1903-1951 . . . . . . DLB-180

Hayden, Robert 1913-1980 . . . . DLB-5, 76

Haydon, Benjamin Robert
1786-1846 . . . . DLB-110

Hayes, John Michael 1919- DLB-26

Hayley, William 1745-1820 . . . . DLB-93, 142

Haym, Rudolf 1821-1901 . . . . DLB-129

Hayman, Robert 1575-1629 . . . . . . DLB-99

Hayman, Ronald 1932- DLB-155

Hayne, Paul Hamilton
1830-1886 . . . . DLB-3, 64, 79

Hays, Mary 1760-1843 . . . . . DLB-142, 158

Haywood, Eliza 1693?-1756 . . . . . . DLB-39

Hazard, Willis P. [publishing house] DLB-49

Hazlitt, William 1778-1830 . . . . DLB-110, 158

Hazzard, Shirley 1931- Y-82

Head, Bessie 1937-1986 . . . . DLB-117

Headley, Joel T.
1813-1897 . . . . DLB-30, 183; DS-13

Heaney, Seamus 1939- DLB-40

Heard, Nathan C. 1936- DLB-33

Hearn, Lafcadio 1850-1904 . . . . . . DLB-12, 78

Hearne, John 1926- DLB-117

Hearne, Samuel 1745-1792 . . . . . . DLB-99

Hearst, William Randolph
1863-1951 . . . . DLB-25

Hearst, William Randolph, Jr
　1908-1993 . . . . DLB-127

Heath, Catherine 1924- DLB-14

Heath, Roy A. K. 1926- DLB-117

Heath-Stubbs, John 1918- DLB-27

Heavysege, Charles 1816-1876 . . . . . DLB-99

Hebbel, Friedrich 1813-1863. . . . . . DLB-129

Hebel, Johann Peter 1760-1826. . . . . DLB-90

Hébert, Anne 1916- DLB-68

Hébert, Jacques 1923- DLB-53

Hecht, Anthony 1923- DLB-5, 169

Hecht, Ben 1894-1964
　. . . . . DLB-7, 9, 25, 26, 28, 86

Hecker, Isaac Thomas 1819-1888 . . . . DLB-1

Hedge, Frederic Henry
　1805-1890 . . . . DLB-1, 59

Hefner, Hugh M. 1926- DLB-137

Hegel, Georg Wilhelm Friedrich
　1770-1831 . . . . DLB-90

Heidish, Marcy 1947- Y-82

Heißenbüttel 1921- DLB-75

Hein, Christoph 1944- DLB-124

Heine, Heinrich 1797-1856 . . . . . . DLB-90

Heinemann, Larry 1944- DS-9

Heinemann, William, Limited. DLB-112

Heinlein, Robert A. 1907-1988 . . . . DLB-8

Heinrich Julius of Brunswick
　1564-1613 . . . . DLB-164

Heinrich von dem Türlin
　flourished circa 1230 . . . . DLB-138

Heinrich von Melk
　flourished after 1160 . . . . DLB-148

Heinrich von Veldeke
　circa 1145-circa 1190 . . . . DLB-138

Heinrich, Willi 1920- DLB-75

Heiskell, John 1872-1972 . . . . DLB-127

Heinse, Wilhelm 1746-1803 . . . . . . DLB-94

Heinz, W. C. 1915- DLB-171

Hejinian, Lyn 1941- DLB-165

Heliand circa 850 . . . . DLB-148

Heller, Joseph 1923- DLB-2, 28; Y-80

Heller, Michael 1937- DLB-165

Hellman, Lillian 1906-1984 . . . . DLB-7; Y-84

Hellwig, Johann 1609-1674 . . . . . . DLB-164

Helprin, Mark 1947- Y-85

Helwig, David 1938- DLB-60

Hemans, Felicia 1793-1835 . . . . . . DLB-96

Hemingway, Ernest 1899-1961
　. . . DLB-4, 9, 102; Y-81, 87; DS-1, 15, 16

Hemingway: Twenty-Five Years
　Later Y-85

Hémon, Louis 1880-1913 . . . . DLB-92

Hemphill, Paul 1936- Y-87

Hénault, Gilles 1920- DLB-88

Henchman, Daniel 1689-1761 . . . . . DLB-24

Henderson, Alice Corbin
　1881-1949 . . . . DLB-54

Henderson, Archibald
　1877-1963 . . . . DLB-103

Henderson, David 1942- DLB-41

Henderson, George Wylie
　1904- DLB-51

Henderson, Zenna 1917-1983 . . . . . . DLB-8

Henisch, Peter 1943- DLB-85

Henley, Beth 1952- Y-86

Henley, William Ernest
　1849-1903 . . . . DLB-19

Henniker, Florence 1855-1923 . . . . . DLB-135

Henry, Alexander 1739-1824 . . . . . . DLB-99

Henry, Buck 1930- DLB-26

Henry VIII of England
　1491-1547 . . . . DLB-132

Henry, Marguerite 1902- DLB-22

Henry, O. (see Porter, William Sydney)

Henry of Ghent
　circa 1217-1229 - 1293 . . . . . . DLB-115

Henry, Robert Selph 1889-1970 . . . . DLB-17

Henry, Will (see Allen, Henry W.)

Henryson, Robert
　1420s or 1430s-circa 1505 . . . . DLB-146

Henschke, Alfred (see Klabund)

Hensley, Sophie Almon 1866-1946. . . . DLB-99

Henson, Lance 1944- DLB-175

Henty, G. A. 1832?-1902 . . . . . DLB-18, 141

Hentz, Caroline Lee 1800-1856 . . . . . DLB-3

Heraclitus flourished circa 500 B.C.
　. . . . . DLB-176

Herbert, Agnes circa 1880-1960. . . . . DLB-174

Herbert, Alan Patrick 1890-1971 . . . . DLB-10

Herbert, Edward, Lord, of Cherbury
　1582-1648. . . . . DLB-121, 151

Herbert, Frank 1920-1986 . . . . DLB-8

Herbert, George 1593-1633 . . . . . . DLB-126

Herbert, Henry William
　1807-1858 . . . . DLB-3, 73

Herbert, John 1926- DLB-53

Herbert, Mary Sidney, Countess of Pembroke
　(see Sidney, Mary)

Herbst, Josephine 1892-1969 . . . . . . DLB-9

Herburger, Gunter 1932- DLB-75, 124

Hercules, Frank E. M. 1917- DLB-33

Herder, Johann Gottfried
　1744-1803 . . . . DLB-97

Herder, B., Book Company DLB-49

Herford, Charles Harold
　1853-1931 . . . . DLB-149

Hergesheimer, Joseph
　1880-1954 . . . . DLB-9, 102

Heritage Press DLB-46

Hermann the Lame 1013-1054 . . . . DLB-148

Hermes, Johann Timotheus
　1738-1821 . . . . DLB-97

Hermlin, Stephan 1915- DLB-69

Hernández, Alfonso C. 1938- DLB-122

Hernández, Inés 1947- DLB-122

Hernández, Miguel 1910-1942. . . . . DLB-134

Hernton, Calvin C. 1932- DLB-38

"The Hero as Man of Letters: Johnson,
　Rousseau, Burns" (1841), by Thomas
　Carlyle [excerpt] DLB-57

The Hero as Poet. Dante; Shakspeare (1841),
　by Thomas Carlyle. DLB-32

Herodotus circa 484 B.C.-circa 420 B.C.
　. . . . . DLB-176

Heron, Robert 1764-1807 . . . . DLB-142

Herrera, Juan Felipe 1948- DLB-122

Herrick, Robert 1591-1674 . . . . . . DLB-126

Herrick, Robert 1868-1938 . . . . DLB-9, 12, 78

Herrick, William 1915- Y-83

Herrick, E. R., and Company DLB-49

Herrmann, John 1900-1959 . . . . . . DLB-4

Hersey, John 1914-1993 . . . . DLB-6

Hertel, François 1905-1985 . . . . . . DLB-68

Hervé-Bazin, Jean Pierre Marie (see Bazin, Hervé)

Hervey, John, Lord 1696-1743 . . . . . DLB-101

Herwig, Georg 1817-1875 . . . . DLB-133

Herzog, Emile Salomon Wilhelm (see Maurois, An-
　dré)

Hesiod eighth century B.C. DLB-176

Hesse, Hermann 1877-1962 . . . . . . DLB-66

Hessus, Helius Eobanus
　1488-1540 . . . . DLB-179

Hewat, Alexander
　circa 1743-circa 1824 . . . . DLB-30

Hewitt, John 1907- DLB-27

Hewlett, Maurice 1861-1923 . . . . DLB-34, 156

Heyen, William 1940- DLB-5

Heyer, Georgette 1902-1974 . . . . . . DLB-77

Heym, Stefan 1913- DLB-69

Heyse, Paul 1830-1914 . . . . DLB-129

Heytesbury, William
　circa 1310-1372 or 1373 . . . . . . DLB-115

Heyward, Dorothy 1890-1961 . . . . . . DLB-7

Heyward, DuBose
　1885-1940 . . . . DLB-7, 9, 45

Heywood, John 1497?-1580? DLB-136

Heywood, Thomas
　1573 or 1574-1641 . . . . DLB-62

Hibbs, Ben 1901-1975 . . . . DLB-137

Hichens, Robert S. 1864-1950. . . . . DLB-153

Hickman, William Albert
　1877-1957 . . . . DLB-92

Hidalgo, José Luis 1919-1947 . . . . . . DLB-108

Hiebert, Paul 1892-1987 . . . . DLB-68

Hieng, Andrej 1925- DLB-181

Hierro, José 1922- DLB-108

Higgins, Aidan 1927- DLB-14

Higgins, Colin 1941-1988 . . . . DLB-26

Higgins, George V. 1939- . . . DLB-2; Y-81

Higginson, Thomas Wentworth
    1823-1911 . . . . DLB-1, 64

Highwater, Jamake 1942?- DLB-52; Y-85

Hijuelos, Oscar 1951- DLB-145

Hildegard von Bingen
    1098-1179 . . . . DLB-148

Das Hildesbrandslied circa 820 . . . . . . DLB-148

Hildesheimer, Wolfgang
    1916-1991 . . . . DLB-69, 124

Hildreth, Richard
    1807-1865 . . . . DLB-1, 30, 59

Hill, Aaron 1685-1750 . . . . DLB-84

Hill, Geoffrey 1932- DLB-40

Hill, "Sir" John 1714?-1775 . . . . . . DLB-39

Hill, Leslie 1880-1960 . . . . DLB-51

Hill, Susan 1942- DLB-14, 139

Hill, Walter 1942- DLB-44

Hill and Wang DLB-46

Hill, George M., Company DLB-49

Hill, Lawrence, and Company,
    Publishers DLB-46

Hillberry, Conrad 1928- DLB-120

Hilliard, Gray and Company DLB-49

Hills, Lee 1906- DLB-127

Hillyer, Robert 1895-1961 . . . . DLB-54

Hilton, James 1900-1954 . . . . DLB-34, 77

Hilton, Walter died 1396 . . . . DLB-146

Hilton and Company DLB-49

Himes, Chester
    1909-1984 . . . . DLB-2, 76, 143

Hindmarsh, Joseph
    [publishing house] DLB-170

Hine, Daryl 1936- DLB-60

Hingley, Ronald 1920- DLB-155

Hinojosa-Smith, Rolando
    1929- DLB-82

Hippel, Theodor Gottlieb von
    1741-1796 . . . . DLB-97

Hippocrates of Cos flourished circa 425 B.C.
    . . . . DLB-176

Hirabayashi, Taiko 1905-1972 . . . . . DLB-180

Hirsch, E. D., Jr. 1928- DLB-67

Hirsch, Edward 1950- DLB-120

The History of the Adventures of Joseph Andrews
    (1742), by Henry Fielding
    [excerpt] DLB-39

Hoagland, Edward 1932- DLB-6

Hoagland, Everett H., III 1942- . . . DLB-41

Hoban, Russell 1925- DLB-52

Hobbes, Thomas 1588-1679 . . . . . . DLB-151

Hobby, Oveta 1905- DLB-127

Hobby, William 1878-1964 . . . . . . DLB-127

Hobsbaum, Philip 1932- DLB-40

Hobson, Laura Z. 1900- DLB-28

Hoby, Thomas 1530-1566 . . . . DLB-132

Hoccleve, Thomas
    circa 1368-circa 1437 . . . . DLB-146

Hochhuth, Rolf 1931- DLB-124

Hochman, Sandra 1936- DLB-5

Hodder and Stoughton, Limited DLB-106

Hodgins, Jack 1938- DLB-60

Hodgman, Helen 1945- DLB-14

Hodgskin, Thomas 1787-1869 . . . . . DLB-158

Hodgson, Ralph 1871-1962 . . . . . . DLB-19

Hodgson, William Hope
    1877-1918 . . . . . DLB-70, 153, 156, 178

Hoffenstein, Samuel 1890-1947 . . . . . DLB-11

Hoffman, Charles Fenno
    1806-1884 . . . . DLB-3

Hoffman, Daniel 1923- DLB-5

Hoffmann, E. T. A. 1776-1822 . . . . DLB-90

Hoffmanswaldau, Christian Hoffman von
    1616-1679 . . . . DLB-168

Hofmann, Michael 1957- DLB-40

Hofmannsthal, Hugo von
    1874-1929 . . . . DLB-81, 118

Hofstadter, Richard 1916-1970 . . . . . DLB-17

Hogan, Desmond 1950- DLB-14

Hogan, Linda 1947- DLB-175

Hogan and Thompson DLB-49

Hogarth Press DLB-112

Hogg, James 1770-1835 . . . . DLB-93, 116, 159

Hohberg, Wolfgang Helmhard Freiherr von
    1612-1688 . . . . DLB-168

von Hohenheim, Philippus Aureolus
    Theophrastus Bombastus (see Paracelsus)

Hohl, Ludwig 1904-1980 . . . . DLB-56

Holbrook, David 1923- DLB-14, 40

Holcroft, Thomas
    1745-1809 . . . . DLB-39, 89, 158

Holden, Jonathan 1941- DLB-105

Holden, Jonathan, Contemporary
    Verse Story-telling DLB-105

Holden, Molly 1927-1981 . . . . DLB-40

Hölderlin, Friedrich 1770-1843 . . . . . DLB-90

Holiday House DLB-46

Holinshed, Raphael died 1580 . . . . . DLB-167

Holland, J. G. 1819-1881 . . . . DS-13

Holland, Norman N. 1927- DLB-67

Hollander, John 1929- DLB-5

Holley, Marietta 1836-1926 . . . . DLB-11

Hollingsworth, Margaret 1940- DLB-60

Hollo, Anselm 1934- DLB-40

Holloway, Emory 1885-1977 . . . . . DLB-103

Holloway, John 1920- DLB-27

Holloway House Publishing
    Company DLB-46

Holme, Constance 1880-1955 . . . . . DLB-34

Holmes, Abraham S. 1821?-1908 . . . . DLB-99

Holmes, John Clellon 1926-1988 . . . . . DLB-16

Holmes, Oliver Wendell
    1809-1894 . . . . DLB-1

Holmes, Richard 1945- DLB-155

Holroyd, Michael 1935- DLB-155

Holst, Hermann E. von
    1841-1904 . . . . DLB-47

Holt, John 1721-1784 . . . . DLB-43

Holt, Henry, and Company DLB-49

Holt, Rinehart and Winston DLB-46

Holthusen, Hans Egon 1913- DLB-69

Hölty, Ludwig Christoph Heinrich
    1748-1776 . . . . DLB-94

Holz, Arno 1863-1929 . . . . DLB-118

Home, Henry, Lord Kames (see Kames, Henry
    Home, Lord)

Home, John 1722-1808 . . . . DLB-84

Home, William Douglas 1912- DLB-13

Home Publishing Company DLB-49

Homer circa eighth-seventh centuries B.C.
    . . . . DLB-176

Homes, Geoffrey (see Mainwaring, Daniel)

Honan, Park 1928- DLB-111

Hone, William 1780-1842 . . . . . DLB-110, 158

Hongo, Garrett Kaoru 1951- DLB-120

Honig, Edwin 1919- DLB-5

Hood, Hugh 1928- DLB-53

Hood, Thomas 1799-1845 . . . . DLB-96

Hook, Theodore 1788-1841 . . . . . . DLB-116

Hooker, Jeremy 1941- DLB-40

Hooker, Richard 1554-1600 . . . . . . DLB-132

Hooker, Thomas 1586-1647 . . . . . . DLB-24

Hooper, Johnson Jones
    1815-1862 . . . . DLB-3, 11

Hope, Anthony 1863-1933 . . . . DLB-153, 156

Hopkins, Gerard Manley
    1844-1889 . . . . DLB-35, 57

Hopkins, John (see Sternhold, Thomas)

Hopkins, Lemuel 1750-1801 . . . . . . DLB-37

Hopkins, Pauline Elizabeth
    1859-1930 . . . . DLB-50

Hopkins, Samuel 1721-1803 . . . . . . DLB-31

Hopkins, John H., and Son DLB-46

Hopkinson, Francis 1737-1791 . . . . . DLB-31

Horgan, Paul 1903- DLB-102; Y-85

Horizon Press DLB-46

Horne, Frank 1899-1974 . . . . DLB-51

Horne, Richard Henry (Hengist)
1802 or 1803-1884 . . . . DLB-32

Hornung, E. W. 1866-1921 . . . . DLB-70

Horovitz, Israel 1939- DLB-7

Horton, George Moses
1797?-1883? DLB-50

Horváth, Ödön von
1901-1938 . . . . DLB-85, 124

Horwood, Harold 1923- DLB-60

Hosford, E. and E.
[publishing house]. DLB-49

Hoskyns, John 1566-1638 . . . . DLB-121

Hotchkiss and Company DLB-49

Hough, Emerson 1857-1923 . . . . DLB-9

Houghton Mifflin Company DLB-49

Houghton, Stanley 1881-1913 . . . . . DLB-10

Household, Geoffrey 1900-1988 . . . . DLB-87

Housman, A. E. 1859-1936. . . . . . . DLB-19

Housman, Laurence 1865-1959. . . . . DLB-10

Houwald, Ernst von 1778-1845 . . . . DLB-90

Hovey, Richard 1864-1900 . . . . DLB-54

Howard, Donald R. 1927-1987 . . . . . DLB-111

Howard, Maureen 1930- Y-83

Howard, Richard 1929- DLB-5

Howard, Roy W. 1883-1964 . . . . . . DLB-29

Howard, Sidney 1891-1939 . . . . . DLB-7, 26

Howe, E. W. 1853-1937 . . . . . . DLB-12, 25

Howe, Henry 1816-1893 . . . . DLB-30

Howe, Irving 1920-1993 . . . . DLB-67

Howe, Joseph 1804-1873 . . . . DLB-99

Howe, Julia Ward 1819-1910 . . . . . . DLB-1

Howe, Percival Presland
1886-1944 . . . . DLB-149

Howe, Susan 1937- DLB-120

Howell, Clark, Sr. 1863-1936. . . . . . DLB-25

Howell, Evan P. 1839-1905 . . . . . . DLB-23

Howell, James 1594?-1666. . . . . . . DLB-151

Howell, Warren Richardson
1912-1984 . . . . DLB-140

Howell, Soskin and Company DLB-46

Howells, William Dean
1837-1920 . . . . DLB-12, 64, 74, 79

Howitt, William 1792-1879 and
Howitt, Mary 1799-1888 . . . . . . DLB-110

Hoyem, Andrew 1935- DLB-5

Hoyers, Anna Ovena 1584-1655 . . . . DLB-164

Hoyos, Angela de 1940- DLB-82

Hoyt, Palmer 1897-1979. . . . . DLB-127

Hoyt, Henry [publishing house] DLB-49

Hrabanus Maurus 776?-856. . . . . . DLB-148

Hrotsvit of Gandersheim
circa 935-circa 1000 . . . . DLB-148

Hubbard, Elbert 1856-1915. . . . . . . DLB-91

Hubbard, Kin 1868-1930 . . . . DLB-11

Hubbard, William circa 1621-1704. . . . DLB-24

Huber, Therese 1764-1829 . . . . DLB-90

Huch, Friedrich 1873-1913 . . . . DLB-66

Huch, Ricarda 1864-1947. . . . . DLB-66

Huck at 100: How Old Is
Huckleberry Finn? Y-85

Huddle, David 1942- DLB-130

Hudgins, Andrew 1951- DLB-120

Hudson, Henry Norman
1814-1886 . . . . DLB-64

Hudson, W. H.
1841-1922 . . . . DLB-98, 153, 174

Hudson and Goodwin DLB-49

Huebsch, B. W.
[publishing house]. DLB-46

Hughes, David 1930- DLB-14

Hughes, John 1677-1720 . . . . DLB-84

Hughes, Langston
1902-1967 . . . . . . DLB-4, 7, 48, 51, 86

Hughes, Richard 1900-1976. . . . . DLB-15, 161

Hughes, Ted 1930- DLB-40, 161

Hughes, Thomas 1822-1896 . . . . DLB-18, 163

Hugo, Richard 1923-1982 . . . . DLB-5

Hugo, Victor 1802-1885. . . . . DLB-119

Hugo Awards and Nebula Awards DLB-8

Hull, Richard 1896-1973 . . . . DLB-77

Hulme, T. E. 1883-1917 . . . . DLB-19

Humboldt, Alexander von
1769-1859 . . . . DLB-90

Humboldt, Wilhelm von
1767-1835 . . . . DLB-90

Hume, David 1711-1776 . . . . DLB-104

Hume, Fergus 1859-1932 . . . . DLB-70

Hummer, T. R. 1950- DLB-120

Humorous Book Illustration DLB-11

Humphrey, William 1924- DLB-6

Humphreys, David 1752-1818 . . . . . DLB-37

Humphreys, Emyr 1919- DLB-15

Huncke, Herbert 1915- DLB-16

Huneker, James Gibbons
1857-1921 . . . . DLB-71

Hunold, Christian Friedrich
1681-1721 . . . . DLB-168

Hunt, Irene 1907- DLB-52

Hunt, Leigh 1784-1859 . . . . DLB-96, 110, 144

Hunt, Violet 1862-1942 . . . . DLB-162

Hunt, William Gibbes 1791-1833 . . . . DLB-73

Hunter, Evan 1926- Y-82

Hunter, Jim 1939- DLB-14

Hunter, Kristin 1931- DLB-33

Hunter, Mollie 1922- DLB-161

Hunter, N. C. 1908-1971. . . . . DLB-10

Hunter-Duvar, John 1821-1899 . . . . . DLB-99

Huntington, Henry E.
1850-1927 . . . . DLB-140

Hurd and Houghton DLB-49

Hurst, Fannie 1889-1968 . . . . DLB-86

Hurst and Blackett. DLB-106

Hurst and Company DLB-49

Hurston, Zora Neale
1901?-1960 . . . . DLB-51, 86

Husson, Jules-François-Félix (see Champfleury)

Huston, John 1906-1987 . . . . DLB-26

Hutcheson, Francis 1694-1746 . . . . . DLB-31

Hutchinson, Thomas
1711-1780 . . . . DLB-30, 31

Hutchinson and Company
(Publishers) Limited DLB-112

von Hutton, Ulrich 1488-1523 . . . . . DLB-179

Hutton, Richard Holt 1826-1897. . . . . DLB-57

Huxley, Aldous
1894-1963 . . . . DLB-36, 100, 162

Huxley, Elspeth Josceline 1907- DLB-77

Huxley, T. H. 1825-1895. . . . . DLB-57

Huyghue, Douglas Smith
1816-1891 . . . . DLB-99

Huysmans, Joris-Karl 1848-1907 . . . . DLB-123

Hyman, Trina Schart 1939- DLB-61

I

Iavorsky, Stefan 1658-1722 . . . . DLB-150

Ibn Bajja circa 1077-1138 . . . . DLB-115

Ibn Gabirol, Solomon
circa 1021-circa 1058 . . . . DLB-115

Ibuse, Masuji 1898-1993 . . . . DLB-180

The Iconography of Science-Fiction
Art DLB-8

Iffland, August Wilhelm
1759-1814 . . . . DLB-94

Ignatow, David 1914- DLB-5

Ike, Chukwuemeka 1931- DLB-157

Iles, Francis (see Berkeley, Anthony)

The Illustration of Early German
Literary Manuscripts,
circa 1150-circa 1300 . . . . DLB-148

Imbs, Bravig 1904-1946 . . . . DLB-4

Imbuga, Francis D. 1947- DLB-157

Immermann, Karl 1796-1840 . . . . . DLB-133

Inchbald, Elizabeth 1753-1821 . . . DLB-39, 89

Inge, William 1913-1973 . . . . DLB-7

Ingelow, Jean 1820-1897 . . . . . . DLB-35, 163

Ingersoll, Ralph 1900-1985 . . . . DLB-127

The Ingersoll Prizes Y-84

Ingoldsby, Thomas (see Barham, Richard Harris)

Ingraham, Joseph Holt 1809-1860 . . . . . DLB-3

Inman, John 1805-1850 . . . . DLB-73

Innerhofer, Franz 1944- DLB-85

Innis, Harold Adams 1894-1952 . . . . . DLB-88

Innis, Mary Quayle 1899-1972 . . . . . . DLB-88

Inoue, Yasushi 1907-1991 . . . . DLB-181

International Publishers Company DLB-46

An Interview with David Rabe Y-91

An Interview with George Greenfield, Literary Agent Y-91

An Interview with James Ellroy Y-91

An Interview with Peter S. Prescott Y-86

An Interview with Russell Hoban Y-90

An Interview with Tom Jenks Y-86

Introduction to Paul Laurence Dunbar, Lyrics of Lowly Life (1896), by William Dean Howells DLB-50

Introductory Essay: Letters of Percy Bysshe Shelley (1852), by Robert Browning DLB-32

Introductory Letters from the Second Edition of Pamela (1741), by Samuel Richardson DLB-39

Irving, John 1942- DLB-6; Y-82

Irving, Washington 1783-1859 . . . . . . DLB-3, 11, 30, 59, 73, 74, 183

Irwin, Grace 1907- DLB-68

Irwin, Will 1873-1948 . . . . DLB-25

Isherwood, Christopher 1904-1986 . . . . DLB-15; Y-86

Ishikawa, Jun 1899-1987 . . . . DLB-182

The Island Trees Case: A Symposium on School Library Censorship
An Interview with Judith Krug
An Interview with Phyllis Schlafly
An Interview with Edward B. Jenkinson
An Interview with Lamarr Mooneyham
An Interview with Harriet Bernstein Y-82

Islas, Arturo 1938-1991 . . . . DLB-122

Ivanišević, Drago 1907-1981 . . . . . . DLB-181

Ivers, M. J., and Company DLB-49

Iwano, Hōmei 1873-1920 . . . . DLB-180

Iyayi, Festus 1947- DLB-157

Izumi, Kyōka 1873-1939 . . . . DLB-180

J

Jackmon, Marvin E. (see Marvin X)

Jacks, L. P. 1860-1955 . . . . DLB-135

Jackson, Angela 1951- DLB-41

Jackson, Helen Hunt 1830-1885 . . . . DLB-42, 47

Jackson, Holbrook 1874-1948 . . . . . . DLB-98

Jackson, Laura Riding 1901-1991 . . . . DLB-48

Jackson, Shirley 1919-1965 . . . . DLB-6

Jacob, Piers Anthony Dillingham (see Anthony, Piers)

Jacobi, Friedrich Heinrich 1743-1819 . . . . DLB-94

Jacobi, Johann Georg 1740-1841 . . . . . DLB-97

Jacobs, Joseph 1854-1916 . . . . DLB-141

Jacobs, W. W. 1863-1943 . . . . DLB-135

Jacobs, George W., and Company . . . DLB-49

Jacobson, Dan 1929- DLB-14

Jaggard, William [publishing house] DLB-170

Jahier, Piero 1884-1966 . . . . DLB-114

Jahnn, Hans Henny 1894-1959 . . . . DLB-56, 124

Jakes, John 1932- Y-83

James, C. L. R. 1901-1989 . . . . DLB-125

James, George P. R. 1801-1860 . . . . . DLB-116

James, Henry 1843-1916 . . . . . . DLB-12, 71, 74; DS-13

James, John circa 1633-1729 . . . . . . DLB-24

The James Jones Society Y-92

James, M. R. 1862-1936 . . . . DLB-156

James, P. D. 1920- DLB-87

James, Will 1892-1942 . . . . DS-16

James Joyce Centenary: Dublin, 1982 . . . . Y-82

James Joyce Conference Y-85

James VI of Scotland, I of England 1566-1625 . . . . DLB-151, 172

James, U. P. [publishing house] DLB-49

Jameson, Anna 1794-1860 . . . . . . DLB-99, 166

Jameson, Fredric 1934- DLB-67

Jameson, J. Franklin 1859-1937 . . . . . DLB-17

Jameson, Storm 1891-1986 . . . . DLB-36

Jančar, Drago 1948- DLB-181

Janés, Clara 1940- DLB-134

Janevski, Slavko 1920- DLB-181

Jaramillo, Cleofas M. 1878-1956 . . . DLB-122

Jarman, Mark 1952- DLB-120

Jarrell, Randall 1914-1965 . . . . . DLB-48, 52

Jarrold and Sons DLB-106

Jasmin, Claude 1930- DLB-60

Jay, John 1745-1829 . . . . DLB-31

Jefferies, Richard 1848-1887 . . . . DLB-98, 141

Jeffers, Lance 1919-1985 . . . . DLB-41

Jeffers, Robinson 1887-1962 . . . . DLB-45

Jefferson, Thomas 1743-1826 . . . . DLB-31, 183

Jelinek, Elfriede 1946- DLB-85

Jellicoe, Ann 1927- DLB-13

Jenkins, Elizabeth 1905- DLB-155

Jenkins, Robin 1912- DLB-14

Jenkins, William Fitzgerald (see Leinster, Murray)

Jenkins, Herbert, Limited DLB-112

Jennings, Elizabeth 1926- DLB-27

Jens, Walter 1923- DLB-69

Jensen, Merrill 1905-1980 . . . . DLB-17

Jephson, Robert 1736-1803 . . . . DLB-89

Jerome, Jerome K. 1859-1927 . . . . DLB-10, 34, 135

Jerome, Judson 1927-1991 . . . . DLB-105

Jerome, Judson, Reflections: After a Tornado DLB-105

Jerrold, Douglas 1803-1857 . . . . DLB-158, 159

Jesse, F. Tennyson 1888-1958 . . . . . . DLB-77

Jewett, Sarah Orne 1849-1909 . . . . DLB-12, 74

Jewett, John P., and Company DLB-49

The Jewish Publication Society DLB-49

Jewitt, John Rodgers 1783-1821 . . . . . DLB-99

Jewsbury, Geraldine 1812-1880 . . . . . DLB-21

Jhabvala, Ruth Prawer 1927- DLB-139

Jiménez, Juan Ramón 1881-1958 . . . . DLB-134

Joans, Ted 1928- DLB-16, 41

John, Eugenie (see Marlitt, E.)

John of Dumbleton circa 1310-circa 1349 . . . . DLB-115

John Edward Bruce: Three Documents DLB-50

John O'Hara's Pottsville Journalism Y-88

John Steinbeck Research Center Y-85

John Webster: The Melbourne Manuscript Y-86

Johns, Captain W. E. 1893-1968 . . . . DLB-160

Johnson, B. S. 1933-1973 . . . . . DLB-14, 40

Johnson, Charles 1679-1748 . . . . . . DLB-84

Johnson, Charles R. 1948- DLB-33

Johnson, Charles S. 1893-1956 . . . DLB-51, 91

Johnson, Denis 1949- DLB-120

Johnson, Diane 1934- Y-80

Johnson, Edgar 1901- DLB-103

Johnson, Edward 1598-1672 . . . . DLB-24

Johnson E. Pauline (Tekahionwake) 1861-1913 . . . . DLB-175

Johnson, Fenton 1888-1958 . . . . . DLB-45, 50

Johnson, Georgia Douglas 1886-1966 . . . . DLB-51

Johnson, Gerald W. 1890-1980 . . . . . DLB-29

Johnson, Helene 1907- DLB-51

Johnson, James Weldon 1871-1938 . . . . DLB-51

Johnson, John H. 1918- DLB-137

Johnson, Linton Kwesi 1952- DLB-157

Johnson, Lionel 1867-1902 . . . . DLB-19

Johnson, Nunnally 1897-1977 . . . . . DLB-26

Johnson, Owen 1878-1952 . . . . Y-87

Johnson, Pamela Hansford
1912- DLB-15

Johnson, Pauline 1861-1913. . . . . . . DLB-92

Johnson, Ronald 1935- DLB-169

Johnson, Samuel 1696-1772. . . . . . . DLB-24

Johnson, Samuel
1709-1784 . . . . . . DLB-39, 95, 104, 142

Johnson, Samuel 1822-1882 . . . . DLB-1

Johnson, Uwe 1934-1984 . . . . DLB-75

Johnson, Benjamin
[publishing house]. DLB-49

Johnson, Benjamin, Jacob, and
Robert [publishing house] DLB-49

Johnson, Jacob, and Company. DLB-49

Johnson, Joseph [publishing house] DLB-154

Johnston, Annie Fellows 1863-1931 . . . DLB-42

Johnston, Basil H. 1929- DLB-60

Johnston, Denis 1901-1984 . . . . DLB-10

Johnston, George 1913- DLB-88

Johnston, Sir Harry 1858-1927 . . . . . DLB-174

Johnston, Jennifer 1930- DLB-14

Johnston, Mary 1870-1936 . . . . DLB-9

Johnston, Richard Malcolm
1822-1898 . . . . DLB-74

Johnstone, Charles 1719?-1800? DLB-39

Johst, Hanns 1890-1978 . . . . DLB-124

Jolas, Eugene 1894-1952 . . . . DLB-4, 45

Jones, Alice C. 1853-1933 . . . . DLB-92

Jones, Charles C., Jr. 1831-1893 . . . . . DLB-30

Jones, D. G. 1929- DLB-53

Jones, David 1895-1974 . . . . DLB-20, 100

Jones, Diana Wynne 1934- DLB-161

Jones, Ebenezer 1820-1860 . . . . . . DLB-32

Jones, Ernest 1819-1868. . . . . DLB-32

Jones, Gayl 1949- DLB-33

Jones, George 1800-1870 . . . . DLB-183

Jones, Glyn 1905- DLB-15

Jones, Gwyn 1907- DLB-15, 139

Jones, Henry Arthur 1851-1929 . . . . . DLB-10

Jones, Hugh circa 1692-1760 . . . . . . DLB-24

Jones, James 1921-1977. . . . . . . DLB-2, 143

Jones, Jenkin Lloyd 1911- DLB-127

Jones, LeRoi (see Baraka, Amiri)

Jones, Lewis 1897-1939 . . . . DLB-15

Jones, Madison 1925- DLB-152

Jones, Major Joseph (see Thompson, William Tappan)

Jones, Preston 1936-1979 . . . . DLB-7

Jones, Rodney 1950- DLB-120

Jones, Sir William 1746-1794 . . . . . DLB-109

Jones, William Alfred 1817-1900 . . . . DLB-59

Jones's Publishing House DLB-49

Jong, Erica 1942- DLB-2, 5, 28, 152

Jonke, Gert F. 1946- DLB-85

Jonson, Ben 1572?-1637 . . . . . . DLB-62, 121

Jordan, June 1936- DLB-38

Joseph, Jenny 1932- DLB-40

Joseph, Michael, Limited DLB-112

Josephson, Matthew 1899-1978 . . . . . DLB-4

Josephus, Flavius 37-100. . . . . . . DLB-176

Josiah Allen's Wife (see Holley, Marietta)

Josipovici, Gabriel 1940- DLB-14

Josselyn, John ?-1675 . . . . DLB-24

Joudry, Patricia 1921- DLB-88

Jovine, Giuseppe 1922- DLB-128

Joyaux, Philippe (see Sollers, Philippe)

Joyce, Adrien (see Eastman, Carol)

Joyce, James
1882-1941 . . . . DLB-10, 19, 36, 162

Judd, Sylvester 1813-1853 . . . . DLB-1

Judd, Orange, Publishing
Company DLB-49

Judith circa 930 . . . . DLB-146

Julian of Norwich
1342-circa 1420. . . . . DLB-1146

Julian Symons at Eighty Y-92

June, Jennie (see Croly, Jane Cunningham)

Jung, Franz 1888-1963. . . . . DLB-118

Jünger, Ernst 1895- DLB-56

Der jüngere Titurel circa 1275 . . . . . DLB-138

Jung-Stilling, Johann Heinrich
1740-1817 . . . . DLB-94

Justice, Donald 1925- Y-83

The Juvenile Library (see Godwin, M. J., and
Company)

K

Kacew, Romain (see Gary, Romain)

Kafka, Franz 1883-1924. . . . . DLB-81

Kahn, Roger 1927. . . . . DLB-171

Kaikō, Takeshi 1939-1989. . . . . . . DLB-182

Kaiser, Georg 1878-1945 . . . . DLB-124

Kaiserchronik circca 1147 . . . . DLB-148

Kaleb, Vjekoslav 1905- DLB-181

Kalechofsky, Roberta 1931- DLB-28

Kaler, James Otis 1848-1912 . . . . . . DLB-12

Kames, Henry Home, Lord
1696-1782 . . . . DLB-31, 104

Kandel, Lenore 1932- DLB-16

Kanin, Garson 1912- DLB-7

Kant, Hermann 1926- DLB-75

Kant, Immanuel 1724-1804. . . . . . . DLB-94

Kantemir, Antiokh Dmitrievich
1708-1744 . . . . DLB-150

Kantor, Mackinlay 1904-1977 . . . . DLB-9, 102

Kaplan, Fred 1937- DLB-111

Kaplan, Johanna 1942- DLB-28

Kaplan, Justin 1925- DLB-111

Kapnist, Vasilii Vasilevich
1758?-1823 . . . . DLB-150

Karadžić, Vuk Stefanović
1787-1864 . . . . DLB-147

Karamzin, Nikolai Mikhailovich
1766-1826 . . . . DLB-150

Karsch, Anna Louisa 1722-1791 . . . . . DLB-97

Kasack, Hermann 1896-1966 . . . . . . DLB-69

Kasai, Zenzō 1887-1927 . . . . DLB-180

Kaschnitz, Marie Luise 1901-1974 . . . . DLB-69

Kaštelan, Jure 1919-1990 . . . . DLB-147

Kästner, Erich 1899-1974 . . . . DLB-56

Kattan, Naim 1928- DLB-53

Katz, Steve 1935- Y-83

Kauffman, Janet 1945- Y-86

Kauffmann, Samuel 1898-1971 . . . . . DLB-127

Kaufman, Bob 1925- DLB-16, 41

Kaufman, George S. 1889-1961 . . . . . DLB-7

Kavanagh, P. J. 1931- DLB-40

Kavanagh, Patrick 1904-1967 . . . . DLB-15, 20

Kawabata, Yasunari 1899-1972 . . . . . DLB-180

Kaye-Smith, Sheila 1887-1956. . . . . . DLB-36

Kazin, Alfred 1915- DLB-67

Keane, John B. 1928- DLB-13

Keary, Annie 1825-1879. . . . . DLB-163

Keating, H. R. F. 1926- DLB-87

Keats, Ezra Jack 1916-1983. . . . . . . DLB-61

Keats, John 1795-1821 . . . . . . DLB-96, 110

Keble, John 1792-1866 . . . . DLB-32, 55

Keeble, John 1944- Y-83

Keeffe, Barrie 1945- DLB-13

Keeley, James 1867-1934 . . . . DLB-25

W. B. Keen, Cooke
and Company. DLB-49

Keillor, Garrison 1942- Y-87

Keith, Marian 1874?-1961 . . . . DLB-92

Keller, Gary D. 1943- DLB-82

Keller, Gottfried 1819-1890 . . . . . . DLB-129

Kelley, Edith Summers 1884-1956. . . . . DLB-9

Kelley, William Melvin 1937- DLB-33

Kellogg, Ansel Nash 1832-1886 . . . . . DLB-23

Kellogg, Steven 1941- DLB-61

Kelly, George 1887-1974. . . . . DLB-7

Kelly, Hugh 1739-1777 . . . . DLB-89

Kelly, Robert 1935- DLB-5, 130, 165

Kelly, Piet and Company DLB-49

Kelmscott Press DLB-112

Kemble, Fanny 1809-1893 . . . . DLB-32

Kemelman, Harry 1908- DLB-28

Kempe, Margery circa 1373-1438. . . . DLB-146

Kempner, Friederike 1836-1904 . . . . . DLB-129

Kempowski, Walter 1929- DLB-75

Kendall, Claude [publishing company]. . DLB-46

Kendell, George 1809-1867 . . . . DLB-43

Kenedy, P. J., and Sons DLB-49

Kennedy, Adrienne 1931- DLB-38

Kennedy, John Pendleton 1795-1870 . . . . DLB-3

Kennedy, Leo 1907- DLB-88

Kennedy, Margaret 1896-1967 . . . . . . DLB-36

Kennedy, Patrick 1801-1873. . . . . . . DLB-159

Kennedy, Richard S. 1920- DLB-111

Kennedy, William 1928- DLB-143; Y-85

Kennedy, X. J. 1929- DLB-5

Kennelly, Brendan 1936- DLB-40

Kenner, Hugh 1923- DLB-67

Kennerley, Mitchell
[publishing house]. DLB-46

Kenny, Maurice 1929- DLB-175

Kent, Frank R. 1877-1958 . . . . DLB-29

Kenyon, Jane 1947- DLB-120

Keough, Hugh Edmund 1864-1912. . . DLB-171

Keppler and Schwartzmann. DLB-49

Kerner, Justinus 1776-1862 . . . . DLB-90

Kerouac, Jack 1922-1969 . . . . DLB-2, 16; DS-3

The Jack Kerouac Revival. Y-95

Kerouac, Jan 1952- DLB-16

Kerr, Orpheus C. (see Newell, Robert Henry)

Kerr, Charles H., and Company DLB-49

Kesey, Ken 1935- DLB-2, 16

Kessel, Joseph 1898-1979 . . . . DLB-72

Kessel, Martin 1901- DLB-56

Kesten, Hermann 1900- DLB-56

Keun, Irmgard 1905-1982. . . . . DLB-69

Key and Biddle DLB-49

Keynes, John Maynard 1883-1946. . . . . DS-10

Keyserling, Eduard von 1855-1918 . . . DLB-66

Khan, Ismith 1925- DLB-125

Khaytov, Nikolay 1919- DLB-181

Khemnitser, Ivan Ivanovich
1745-1784 . . . . DLB-150

Kheraskov, Mikhail Matveevich
1733-1807 . . . . DLB-150

Khristov, Boris 1945- DLB-181

Khvostov, Dmitrii Ivanovich
1757-1835 . . . . DLB-150

Kidd, Adam 1802?-1831 . . . . DLB-99

Kidd, William
[publishing house] DLB-106

Kiely, Benedict 1919- DLB-15

Kieran, John 1892-1981 . . . . DLB-171

Kiggins and Kellogg. DLB-49

Kiley, Jed 1889-1962 . . . . DLB-4

Kilgore, Bernard 1908-1967 . . . . . . DLB-127

Killens, John Oliver 1916- DLB-33

Killigrew, Anne 1660-1685 . . . . . . DLB-131

Killigrew, Thomas 1612-1683. . . . . . DLB-58

Kilmer, Joyce 1886-1918 . . . . DLB-45

Kilwardby, Robert
circa 1215-1279 . . . . DLB-115

Kincaid, Jamaica 1949- DLB-157

King, Clarence 1842-1901 . . . . DLB-12

King, Florence 1936 . . . . Y-85

King, Francis 1923- DLB-15, 139

King, Grace 1852-1932 . . . . DLB-12, 78

King, Henry 1592-1669 . . . . DLB-126

King, Stephen 1947- DLB-143; Y-80

King, Thomas 1943- DLB-175

King, Woodie, Jr. 1937- DLB-38

King, Solomon [publishing house] DLB-49

Kinglake, Alexander William
1809-1891 . . . . DLB-55, 166

Kingsley, Charles
1819-1875 . . . . . . DLB-21, 32, 163, 178

Kingsley, Mary Henrietta
1862-1900 . . . . DLB-174

Kingsley, Henry 1830-1876 . . . . . . DLB-21

Kingsley, Sidney 1906- DLB-7

Kingsmill, Hugh 1889-1949 . . . . . . DLB-149

Kingston, Maxine Hong
1940- DLB-173; Y-80

Kingston, William Henry Giles
1814-1880 . . . . DLB-163

Kinnell, Galway 1927- DLB-5; Y-87

Kinsella, Thomas 1928- DLB-27

Kipling, Rudyard
1865-1936 . . . . . . DLB-19, 34, 141, 156

Kipphardt, Heinar 1922-1982 . . . . . DLB-124

Kirby, William 1817-1906 . . . . DLB-99

Kircher, Athanasius 1602-1680 . . . . DLB-164

Kirk, John Foster 1824-1904 . . . . . . DLB-79

Kirkconnell, Watson 1895-1977 . . . . . DLB-68

Kirkland, Caroline M.
1801-1864 . . . . . . DLB-3, 73, 74; DS-13

Kirkland, Joseph 1830-1893 . . . . . . DLB-12

Kirkman, Francis
[publishing house] DLB-170

Kirkpatrick, Clayton 1915- DLB-127

Kirkup, James 1918- DLB-27

Kirouac, Conrad (see Marie-Victorin, Frère)

Kirsch, Sarah 1935- DLB-75

Kirst, Hans Hellmut 1914-1989 . . . . DLB-69

Kiš, Danilo 1935-1989 . . . . DLB-181

Kita, Morio 1927- DLB-182

Kitcat, Mabel Greenhow
1859-1922 . . . . DLB-135

Kitchin, C. H. B. 1895-1967 . . . . . . DLB-77

Kizer, Carolyn 1925- DLB-5, 169

Klabund 1890-1928 . . . . DLB-66

Klaj, Johann 1616-1656 . . . . DLB-164

Klappert, Peter 1942- DLB-5

Klass, Philip (see Tenn, William)

Klein, A. M. 1909-1972. . . . . DLB-68

Kleist, Ewald von 1715-1759 . . . . . . DLB-97

Kleist, Heinrich von 1777-1811 . . . . . DLB-90

Klinger, Friedrich Maximilian
1752-1831 . . . . DLB-94

Klopstock, Friedrich Gottlieb
1724-1803 . . . . DLB-97

Klopstock, Meta 1728-1758 . . . . DLB-97

Kluge, Alexander 1932- DLB-75

Knapp, Joseph Palmer 1864-1951 . . . . DLB-91

Knapp, Samuel Lorenzo
1783-1838 . . . . DLB-59

Knapton, J. J. and P.
[publishing house] DLB-154

Kniazhnin, Iakov Borisovich
1740-1791 . . . . DLB-150

Knickerbocker, Diedrich (see Irving,
Washington)

Knigge, Adolph Franz Friedrich Ludwig,
Freiherr von 1752-1796 . . . . . . DLB-94

Knight, Damon 1922- DLB-8

Knight, Etheridge 1931-1992 . . . . . . DLB-41

Knight, John S. 1894-1981 . . . . DLB-29

Knight, Sarah Kemble 1666-1727 . . . . DLB-24

Knight, Charles, and Company. DLB-106

Knight-Bruce, G. W. H.
1852-1896 . . . . DLB-174

Knister, Raymond 1899-1932. . . . . . DLB-68

Knoblock, Edward 1874-1945 . . . . . DLB-10

Knopf, Alfred A. 1892-1984 . . . . Y-84

Knopf, Alfred A.
[publishing house]. DLB-46

Knorr von Rosenroth, Christian
1636-1689 . . . . DLB-168

Knowles, John 1926- DLB-6

Knox, Frank 1874-1944 . . . . DLB-29

Knox, John circa 1514-1572 . . . . . . DLB-132

Knox, John Armoy 1850-1906 . . . . . DLB-23

Knox, Ronald Arbuthnott
1888-1957 . . . . DLB-77

Kobayashi, Takiji 1903-1933 . . . . . DLB-180

Kober, Arthur 1900-1975 . . . . DLB-11

Kocbek, Edvard 1904-1981 . . . . DLB-147

Koch, Howard 1902- DLB-26

Koch, Kenneth 1925- DLB-5

Kōda, Rohan 1867-1947. . . . . DLB-180

Koenigsberg, Moses 1879-1945. . . . . . DLB-25

Koeppen, Wolfgang 1906- DLB-69

Koertge, Ronald 1940- DLB-105

Koestler, Arthur 1905-1983. . . . . Y-83

Kokoschka, Oskar 1886-1980 . . . . . . DLB-124

Kolb, Annette 1870-1967 . . . . DLB-66

Kolbenheyer, Erwin Guido
   1878-1962 . . . . DLB-66, 124

Kolleritsch, Alfred 1931- DLB-85

Kolodny, Annette 1941- DLB-67

Komarov, Matvei
   circa 1730-1812 . . . . DLB-150

Komroff, Manuel 1890-1974 . . . . DLB-4

Komunyakaa, Yusef 1947- DLB-120

Koneski, Blaže 1921-1993 . . . . DLB-181

Konigsburg, E. L. 1930- DLB-52

Konrad von Würzburg
   circa 1230-1287 . . . . DLB-138

Konstantinov, Aleko 1863-1897 . . . . . DLB-147

Kooser, Ted 1939- DLB-105

Kopit, Arthur 1937- DLB-7

Kops, Bernard 1926?- DLB-13

Kornbluth, C. M. 1923-1958 . . . . DLB-8

Körner, Theodor 1791-1813 . . . . . . DLB-90

Kornfeld, Paul 1889-1942 . . . . DLB-118

Kosinski, Jerzy 1933-1991 . . . . . DLB-2; Y-82

Kosmač, Ciril 1910-1980 . . . . DLB-181

Kosovel, Srečko 1904-1926 . . . . . . DLB-147

Kostrov, Ermil Ivanovich
   1755-1796 . . . . DLB-150

Kotzebue, August von 1761-1819 . . . . DLB-94

Kotzwinkle, William 1938- DLB-173

Kovačić, Ante 1854-1889 . . . . DLB-147

Kovič, Kajetan 1931- DLB-181

Kraf, Elaine 1946- Y-81

Kranjčević, Silvije Strahimir
   1865-1908. . . . . DLB-147

Krasna, Norman 1909-1984 . . . . . . DLB-26

Kraus, Karl 1874-1936. . . . . DLB-118

Krauss, Ruth 1911-1993 . . . . DLB-52

Kreisel, Henry 1922- DLB-88

Kreuder, Ernst 1903-1972. . . . . DLB-69

Kreymborg, Alfred 1883-1966. . . . . DLB-4, 54

Krieger, Murray 1923- DLB-67

Krim, Seymour 1922-1989 . . . . DLB-16

Krleža, Miroslav 1893-1981 . . . . . . DLB-147

Krock, Arthur 1886-1974 . . . . DLB-29

Kroetsch, Robert 1927- DLB-53

Krutch, Joseph Wood 1893-1970 . . . . DLB-63

Krylov, Ivan Andreevich
   1769-1844 . . . . DLB-150

Kubin, Alfred 1877-1959 . . . . DLB-81

Kubrick, Stanley 1928- DLB-26

Kudrun circa 1230-1240 . . . . DLB-138

Kuffstein, Hans Ludwig von
   1582-1656 . . . . DLB-164

Kuhlmann, Quirinus 1651-1689 . . . . DLB-168

Kuhnau, Johann 1660-1722 . . . . . . DLB-168

Kumin, Maxine 1925- DLB-5

Kunene, Mazisi 1930- DLB-117

Kunikida, Doppo 1869-1908. . . . . . DLB-180

Kunitz, Stanley 1905- DLB-48

Kunjufu, Johari M. (see Amini, Johari M.)

Kunnert, Gunter 1929- DLB-75

Kunze, Reiner 1933- DLB-75

Kupferberg, Tuli 1923- DLB-16

Kurahashi, Yumiko 1935- DLB-182

Kürnberger, Ferdinand
   1821-1879 . . . . DLB-129

Kurz, Isolde 1853-1944 . . . . DLB-66

Kusenberg, Kurt 1904-1983 . . . . . . DLB-69

Kuttner, Henry 1915-1958 . . . . DLB-8

Kyd, Thomas 1558-1594 . . . . DLB-62

Kyffin, Maurice
   circa 1560?-1598 . . . . DLB-136

Kyger, Joanne 1934- DLB-16

Kyne, Peter B. 1880-1957 . . . . DLB-78

L

L. E. L. (see Landon, Letitia Elizabeth)

Laberge, Albert 1871-1960 . . . . DLB-68

Laberge, Marie 1950- DLB-60

Lacombe, Patrice (see Trullier-Lacombe,
   Joseph Patrice)

Lacretelle, Jacques de 1888-1985 . . . . . DLB-65

Lacy, Sam 1903- DLB-171

Ladd, Joseph Brown 1764-1786 . . . . . DLB-37

La Farge, Oliver 1901-1963 . . . . DLB-9

Lafferty, R. A. 1914- DLB-8

La Flesche, Francis 1857-1932 . . . . . DLB-175

La Guma, Alex 1925-1985 . . . . DLB-117

Lahaise, Guillaume (see Delahaye, Guy)

Lahontan, Louis-Armand de Lom d'Arce,
   Baron de 1666-1715? DLB-99

Laing, Kojo 1946- DLB-157

Laird, Carobeth 1895- Y-82

Laird and Lee. DLB-49

Lalić, Ivan V. 1931-1996 . . . . DLB-181

Lalić, Mihailo 1914-1992 . . . . DLB-181

Lalonde, Michèle 1937- DLB-60

Lamantia, Philip 1927- DLB-16

Lamb, Charles
   1775-1834 . . . . DLB-93, 107, 163

Lamb, Lady Caroline 1785-1828 . . . . DLB-116

Lamb, Mary 1764-1874 . . . . DLB-163

Lambert, Betty 1933-1983 . . . . DLB-60

Lamming, George 1927- DLB-125

L'Amour, Louis 1908?- Y-80

Lampman, Archibald 1861-1899 . . . . DLB-92

Lamson, Wolffe and Company DLB-49

Lancer Books DLB-46

Landesman, Jay 1919- and
   Landesman, Fran 1927- DLB-16

Landolfi, Tommaso 1908-1979 . . . . . DLB-177

Landon, Letitia Elizabeth 1802-1838 . . . DLB-96

Landor, Walter Savage
   1775-1864 . . . . DLB-93, 107

Landry, Napoléon-P. 1884-1956 . . . . . DLB-92

Lane, Charles 1800-1870. . . . . DLB-1

Lane, Laurence W. 1890-1967 . . . . . DLB-91

Lane, M. Travis 1934- DLB-60

Lane, Patrick 1939- DLB-53

Lane, Pinkie Gordon 1923- DLB-41

Lane, John, Company DLB-49

Laney, Al 1896-1988 . . . . DLB-4, 171

Lang, Andrew 1844-1912 . . . . . DLB-98, 141

Langevin, André 1927- DLB-60

Langgässer, Elisabeth 1899-1950 . . . . DLB-69

Langhorne, John 1735-1779 . . . . . . DLB-109

Langland, William
   circa 1330-circa 1400 . . . . DLB-146

Langton, Anna 1804-1893 . . . . DLB-99

Lanham, Edwin 1904-1979 . . . . DLB-4

Lanier, Sidney 1842-1881 . . . DLB-64; DS-13

Lanyer, Aemilia 1569-1645 . . . . . . DLB-121

Lapointe, Gatien 1931-1983. . . . . . . DLB-88

Lapointe, Paul-Marie 1929- DLB-88

Lardner, John 1912-1960 . . . . DLB-171

Lardner, Ring
   1885-1933 . . . DLB-11, 25, 86, 171; DS-16

Lardner, Ring, Jr. 1915- DLB-26

Lardner 100: Ring Lardner
   Centennial Symposium. Y-85

Larkin, Philip 1922-1985 . . . . DLB-27

La Roche, Sophie von 1730-1807 . . . . DLB-94

La Rocque, Gilbert 1943-1984 . . . . . DLB-60

Laroque de Roquebrune, Robert (see Roquebrune,
   Robert de)

Larrick, Nancy 1910- DLB-61

Larsen, Nella 1893-1964 . . . . DLB-51

Lasker-Schüler, Else
   1869-1945 . . . . DLB-66, 124

Lasnier, Rina 1915- DLB-88

Lassalle, Ferdinand 1825-1864. . . . . . DLB-129

Lathrop, Dorothy P. 1891-1980 . . . . . DLB-22

Lathrop, George Parsons
1851-1898 . . . . DLB-71

Lathrop, John, Jr. 1772-1820 . . . . . . DLB-37

Latimer, Hugh 1492?-1555 . . . . DLB-136

Latimore, Jewel Christine McLawler
(see Amini, Johari M.)

Latymer, William 1498-1583 . . . . . . DLB-132

Laube, Heinrich 1806-1884 . . . . DLB-133

Laughlin, James 1914- DLB-48

Laumer, Keith 1925- DLB-8

Lauremberg, Johann 1590-1658 . . . . . DLB-164

Laurence, Margaret 1926-1987 . . . . . DLB-53

Laurentius von Schnüffis
1633-1702 . . . . DLB-168

Laurents, Arthur 1918- DLB-26

Laurie, Annie (see Black, Winifred)

Laut, Agnes Christiana 1871-1936 . . . . DLB-92

Lavater, Johann Kaspar 1741-1801. . . . DLB-97

Lavin, Mary 1912- DLB-15

Lawes, Henry 1596-1662 . . . . DLB-126

Lawless, Anthony (see MacDonald, Philip)

Lawrence, D. H.
1885-1930 . . . . . DLB-10, 19, 36, 98, 162

Lawrence, David 1888-1973 . . . . DLB-29

Lawrence, Seymour 1926-1994. . . . . . . Y-94

Lawson, John ?-1711 . . . . DLB-24

Lawson, Robert 1892-1957 . . . . DLB-22

Lawson, Victor F. 1850-1925. . . . . . . DLB-25

Layard, Sir Austen Henry
1817-1894 . . . . DLB-166

Layton, Irving 1912- DLB-88

LaZamon flourished circa 1200. . . . . . DLB-146

Lazarević, Laza K. 1851-1890. . . . . . DLB-147

Lea, Henry Charles 1825-1909 . . . . . . DLB-47

Lea, Sydney 1942- DLB-120

Lea, Tom 1907- DLB-6

Leacock, John 1729-1802 . . . . DLB-31

Leacock, Stephen 1869-1944 . . . . DLB-92

Lead, Jane Ward 1623-1704 . . . . DLB-131

Leadenhall Press DLB-106

Leapor, Mary 1722-1746 . . . . DLB-109

Lear, Edward 1812-1888 . . . DLB-32, 163, 166

Leary, Timothy 1920-1996 . . . . DLB-16

Leary, W. A., and Company DLB-49

Léautaud, Paul 1872-1956 . . . . DLB-65

Leavitt, David 1961- DLB-130

Leavitt and Allen DLB-49

Le Blond, Mrs. Aubrey
1861-1934 . . . . DLB-174

le Carré, John 1931- DLB-87

Lécavelé, Roland (see Dorgeles, Roland)

Lechlitner, Ruth 1901- DLB-48

Leclerc, Félix 1914- DLB-60

Le Clézio, J. M. G. 1940- DLB-83

Lectures on Rhetoric and Belles Lettres (1783),
by Hugh Blair [excerpts] DLB-31

Leder, Rudolf (see Hermlin, Stephan)

Lederer, Charles 1910-1976. . . . . . . DLB-26

Ledwidge, Francis 1887-1917. . . . . . . DLB-20

Lee, Dennis 1939- DLB-53

Lee, Don L. (see Madhubuti, Haki R.)

Lee, George W. 1894-1976. . . . . DLB-51

Lee, Harper 1926- DLB-6

Lee, Harriet (1757-1851) and
Lee, Sophia (1750-1824) DLB-39

Lee, Laurie 1914- DLB-27

Lee, Li-Young 1957- DLB-165

Lee, Manfred B. (see Dannay, Frederic, and
Manfred B. Lee)

Lee, Nathaniel circa 1645 - 1692 . . . . DLB-80

Lee, Sir Sidney 1859-1926. . . . . DLB-149

Lee, Sir Sidney, "Principles of Biography," in
Elizabethan and Other Essays. DLB-149

Lee, Vernon
1856-1935. . . . DLB-57, 153, 156, 174, 178

Lee and Shepard DLB-49

Le Fanu, Joseph Sheridan
1814-1873 . . . . . . DLB-21, 70, 159, 178

Leffland, Ella 1931- Y-84

le Fort, Gertrud von 1876-1971 . . . . . DLB-66

Le Gallienne, Richard 1866-1947 . . . . . DLB-4

Legaré, Hugh Swinton
1797-1843 . . . . DLB-3, 59, 73

Legaré, James M. 1823-1859 . . . . . . DLB-3

The Legends of the Saints and a Medieval
Christian Worldview DLB-148

Léger, Antoine-J. 1880-1950. . . . . . . DLB-88

Le Guin, Ursula K. 1929- DLB-8, 52

Lehman, Ernest 1920- DLB-44

Lehmann, John 1907- DLB-27, 100

Lehmann, Rosamond 1901-1990 . . . . . DLB-15

Lehmann, Wilhelm 1882-1968 . . . . . . DLB-56

Lehmann, John, Limited. DLB-112

Leiber, Fritz 1910-1992 . . . . DLB-8

Leibniz, Gottfried Wilhelm
1646-1716 . . . . DLB-168

Leicester University Press DLB-112

Leinster, Murray 1896-1975 . . . . DLB-8

Leisewitz, Johann Anton
1752-1806 . . . . DLB-94

Leitch, Maurice 1933- DLB-14

Leithauser, Brad 1943- DLB-120

Leland, Charles G. 1824-1903 . . . . . DLB-11

Leland, John 1503?-1552 . . . . DLB-136

Lemay, Pamphile 1837-1918 . . . . . . DLB-99

Lemelin, Roger 1919- DLB-88

Lemon, Mark 1809-1870 . . . . DLB-163

Le Moine, James MacPherson
1825-1912 . . . . DLB-99

Le Moyne, Jean 1913- DLB-88

L'Engle, Madeleine 1918- DLB-52

Lennart, Isobel 1915-1971 . . . . DLB-44

Lennox, Charlotte
1729 or 1730-1804 . . . . DLB-39

Lenox, James 1800-1880. . . . . DLB-140

Lenski, Lois 1893-1974 . . . . DLB-22

Lenz, Hermann 1913- DLB-69

Lenz, J. M. R. 1751-1792 . . . . DLB-94

Lenz, Siegfried 1926- DLB-75

Leonard, Elmore 1925- DLB-173

Leonard, Hugh 1926- DLB-13

Leonard, William Ellery
1876-1944 . . . . DLB-54

Leonowens, Anna 1834-1914 . . . . DLB-99, 166

LePan, Douglas 1914- DLB-88

Leprohon, Rosanna Eleanor
1829-1879 . . . . DLB-99

Le Queux, William 1864-1927 . . . . . DLB-70

Lerner, Max 1902-1992. . . . . DLB-29

Lernet-Holenia, Alexander
1897-1976 . . . . DLB-85

Le Rossignol, James 1866-1969. . . . . DLB-92

Lescarbot, Marc circa 1570-1642 . . . . DLB-99

LeSeur, William Dawson
1840-1917 . . . . DLB-92

LeSieg, Theo. (see Geisel, Theodor Seuss)

Leslie, Frank 1821-1880 . . . . . . DLB-43, 79

Leslie, Frank, Publishing House DLB-49

Lesperance, John 1835?-1891 . . . . . . DLB-99

Lessing, Bruno 1870-1940 . . . . DLB-28

Lessing, Doris 1919- DLB-15, 139; Y-85

Lessing, Gotthold Ephraim
1729-1781 . . . . DLB-97

Lettau, Reinhard 1929- DLB-75

Letter from Japan. Y-94

Letter from London Y-96

Letter to [Samuel] Richardson on *Clarissa*
(1748), by Henry Fielding DLB-39

Lever, Charles 1806-1872. . . . . DLB-21

Leverson, Ada 1862-1933 . . . . DLB-153

Levertov, Denise 1923- DLB-5, 165

Levi, Peter 1931- DLB-40

Levi, Primo 1919-1987 . . . . DLB-177

Levien, Sonya 1888-1960 . . . . DLB-44

Levin, Meyer 1905-1981 . . . . DLB-9, 28; Y-81

Levine, Norman 1923- DLB-88

Levine, Philip 1928- DLB-5

Levis, Larry 1946- DLB-120

Levy, Amy 1861-1889 . . . . DLB-156

Levy, Benn Wolfe
 1900-1973 . . . . DLB-13; Y-81

Lewald, Fanny 1811-1889 . . . . DLB-129

Lewes, George Henry
 1817-1878 . . . . DLB-55, 144

Lewis, Agnes Smith 1843-1926 . . . . . DLB-174

Lewis, Alfred H. 1857-1914 . . . . . . DLB-25

Lewis, Alun 1915-1944 . . . . DLB-20, 162

Lewis, C. Day (see Day Lewis, C.)

Lewis, C. S. 1898-1963 . . . . DLB-15, 100, 160

Lewis, Charles B. 1842-1924 . . . . . . DLB-11

Lewis, Henry Clay 1825-1850 . . . . . . DLB-3

Lewis, Janet 1899- Y-87

Lewis, Matthew Gregory
 1775-1818 . . . . DLB-39, 158, 178

Lewis, Meriwether 1774-1809 and
 Clark, William 1770-1838 . . . . . DLB-183

Lewis, R. W. B. 1917- DLB-111

Lewis, Richard circa 1700-1734 . . . . DLB-24

Lewis, Sinclair
 1885-1951 . . . . DLB-9, 102; DS-1

Lewis, Wilmarth Sheldon
 1895-1979 . . . . DLB-140

Lewis, Wyndham 1882-1957 . . . . . . DLB-15

Lewisohn, Ludwig
 1882-1955 . . . . DLB-4, 9, 28, 102

Lezama Lima, José 1910-1976 . . . . . DLB-113

The Library of America DLB-46

The Licensing Act of 1737 . . . . DLB-84

Lichfield, Leonard I
 [publishing house] DLB-170

Lichtenberg, Georg Christoph
 1742-1799 . . . . DLB-94

Lieb, Fred 1888-1980 . . . . DLB-171

Liebling, A. J. 1904-1963 . . . . . . DLB-4, 171

Lieutenant Murray (see Ballou, Maturin
 Murray)

Lighthall, William Douw
 1857-1954 . . . . DLB-92

Lilar, Françoise (see Mallet-Joris, Françoise)

Lillo, George 1691-1739 . . . . DLB-84

Lilly, J. K., Jr. 1893-1966 . . . . DLB-140

Lilly, Wait and Company DLB-49

Lily, William circa 1468-1522 . . . . . DLB-132

Limited Editions Club DLB-46

Lincoln and Edmands DLB-49

Lindsay, Jack 1900- Y-84

Lindsay, Sir David
 circa 1485-1555 . . . . DLB-132

Lindsay, Vachel 1879-1931 . . . . DLB-54

Linebarger, Paul Myron Anthony (see Smith,
 Cordwainer)

Link, Arthur S. 1920- DLB-17

Linn, John Blair 1777-1804 . . . . . . DLB-37

Lins, Osman 1924-1978 . . . . DLB-145

Linton, Eliza Lynn 1822-1898 . . . . . DLB-18

Linton, William James 1812-1897 . . . DLB-32

Lintot, Barnaby Bernard
 [publishing house] DLB-170

Lion Books DLB-46

Lionni, Leo 1910- DLB-61

Lippincott, Sara Jane Clarke
 1823-1904 . . . . DLB-43

Lippincott, J. B., Company DLB-49

Lippmann, Walter 1889-1974 . . . . . . DLB-29

Lipton, Lawrence 1898-1975 . . . . . . DLB-16

Liscow, Christian Ludwig
 1701-1760 . . . . DLB-97

Lish, Gordon 1934- DLB-130

Lispector, Clarice 1925-1977 . . . . . DLB-113

The Literary Chronicle and Weekly Review
 1819-1828 . . . . DLB-110

Literary Documents: William Faulkner
 and the People-to-People
 Program Y-86

Literary Documents II: *Library Journal*
 Statements and Questionnaires from
 First Novelists Y-87

Literary Effects of World War II
 [British novel] DLB-15

Literary Prizes [British] DLB-15

Literary Research Archives: The Humanities
 Research Center, University of
 Texas Y-82

Literary Research Archives II: Berg
 Collection of English and American
 Literature of the New York Public
 Library Y-83

Literary Research Archives III:
 The Lilly Library Y-84

Literary Research Archives IV:
 The John Carter Brown Library Y-85

Literary Research Archives V:
 Kent State Special Collections Y-86

Literary Research Archives VI: The Modern
 Literary Manuscripts Collection in the
 Special Collections of the Washington
 University Libraries Y-87

Literary Research Archives VII:
 The University of Virginia
 Libraries Y-91

Literary Research Archives VIII:
 The Henry E. Huntington
 Library Y-92

"Literary Style" (1857), by William
 Forsyth [excerpt] DLB-57

Literatura Chicanesca: The View From Without
 . . . . DLB-82

Literature at Nurse, or Circulating Morals (1885),
 by George Moore DLB-18

Littell, Eliakim 1797-1870 . . . . DLB-79

Littell, Robert S. 1831-1896 . . . . . . DLB-79

Little, Brown and Company DLB-49

Little Magazines and Newspapers DS-15

The Little Review 1914-1929 . . . . . . DS-15

Littlewood, Joan 1914- DLB-13

Lively, Penelope 1933- DLB-14, 161

Liverpool University Press DLB-112

The Lives of the Poets DLB-142

Livesay, Dorothy 1909- DLB-68

Livesay, Florence Randal
 1874-1953 . . . . DLB-92

Livings, Henry 1929- DLB-13

Livingston, Anne Howe
 1763-1841 . . . . DLB-37

Livingston, Myra Cohn 1926- DLB-61

Livingston, William 1723-1790 . . . . . DLB-31

Livingstone, David 1813-1873 . . . . . DLB-166

Liyong, Taban lo (see Taban lo Liyong)

Lizárraga, Sylvia S. 1925- DLB-82

Llewellyn, Richard 1906-1983 . . . . . DLB-15

Lloyd, Edward
 [publishing house] DLB-106

Lobel, Arnold 1933- DLB-61

Lochridge, Betsy Hopkins (see Fancher, Betsy)

Locke, David Ross 1833-1888 . . . . DLB-11, 23

Locke, John 1632-1704 . . . . . DLB-31, 101

Locke, Richard Adams 1800-1871 . . . . DLB-43

Locker-Lampson, Frederick
 1821-1895 . . . . DLB-35

Lockhart, John Gibson
 1794-1854 . . . . DLB-110, 116 144

Lockridge, Ross, Jr.
 1914-1948 . . . . DLB-143; Y-80

Locrine and *Selimus* DLB-62

Lodge, David 1935- DLB-14

Lodge, George Cabot 1873-1909 . . . . DLB-54

Lodge, Henry Cabot 1850-1924 . . . . . DLB-47

Lodge, Thomas 1558-1625 . . . . DLB-172

Loeb, Harold 1891-1974 . . . . DLB-4

Loeb, William 1905-1981 . . . . DLB-127

Lofting, Hugh 1886-1947 . . . . DLB-160

Logan, James 1674-1751 . . . . . DLB-24, 140

Logan, John 1923- DLB-5

Logan, William 1950- DLB-120

Logau, Friedrich von 1605-1655 . . . . DLB-164

Logue, Christopher 1926- DLB-27

Lohenstein, Daniel Casper von
 1635-1683 . . . . DLB-168

Lomonosov, Mikhail Vasil'evich
 1711-1765 . . . . DLB-150

London, Jack 1876-1916 . . . . . DLB-8, 12, 78

The London Magazine 1820-1829 . . . . . DLB-110

Long, Haniel 1888-1956 . . . . DLB-45

Long, Ray 1878-1935 . . . . DLB-137

Long, H., and Brother DLB-49

Longfellow, Henry Wadsworth 1807-1882 . . . . DLB-1, 59

Longfellow, Samuel 1819-1892 . . . . . . DLB-1

Longford, Elizabeth 1906- DLB-155

Longinus circa first century DLB-176

Longley, Michael 1939- DLB-40

Longman, T. [publishing house] DLB-154

Longmans, Green and Company DLB-49

Longmore, George 1793?-1867 . . . . . . DLB-99

Longstreet, Augustus Baldwin 1790-1870 . . . . DLB-3, 11, 74

Longworth, D. [publishing house] DLB-49

Lonsdale, Frederick 1881-1954 . . . . . . DLB-10

A Look at the Contemporary Black Theatre Movement DLB-38

Loos, Anita 1893-1981 . . . . DLB-11, 26; Y-81

Lopate, Phillip 1943- Y-80

López, Diana (see Isabella, Ríos)

Loranger, Jean-Aubert 1896-1942 . . . . . DLB-92

Lorca, Federico García 1898-1936 . . . DLB-108

Lord, John Keast 1818-1872 . . . . . . DLB-99

The Lord Chamberlain's Office and Stage Censorship in England DLB-10

Lorde, Audre 1934-1992 . . . . DLB-41

Lorimer, George Horace 1867-1939 . . . . DLB-91

Loring, A. K. [publishing house] DLB-49

Loring and Mussey DLB-46

Lossing, Benson J. 1813-1891 . . . . . DLB-30

Lothar, Ernst 1890-1974 . . . . DLB-81

Lothrop, Harriet M. 1844-1924 . . . . DLB-42

Lothrop, D., and Company DLB-49

Loti, Pierre 1850-1923 . . . . DLB-123

Lotichius Secundus, Petrus 1528-1560 . . . . DLB-179

Lott, Emeline ?-? DLB-166

The Lounger, no. 20 (1785), by Henry Mackenzie DLB-39

Lounsbury, Thomas R. 1838-1915 . . . . DLB-71

Loüys, Pierre 1870-1925 . . . . DLB-123

Lovelace, Earl 1935- DLB-125

Lovelace, Richard 1618-1657 . . . . . . DLB-131

Lovell, Coryell and Company DLB-49

Lovell, John W., Company DLB-49

Lover, Samuel 1797-1868 . . . . DLB-159

Lovesey, Peter 1936- DLB-87

Lovingood, Sut (see Harris, George Washington)

Low, Samuel 1765-? DLB-37

Lowell, Amy 1874-1925 . . . . . . DLB-54, 140

Lowell, James Russell 1819-1891 . . . . DLB-1, 11, 64, 79

Lowell, Robert 1917-1977 . . . . . DLB-5, 169

Lowenfels, Walter 1897-1976 . . . . . . DLB-4

Lowndes, Marie Belloc 1868-1947 . . . . DLB-70

Lownes, Humphrey [publishing house] DLB-170

Lowry, Lois 1937- DLB-52

Lowry, Malcolm 1909-1957 . . . . . . DLB-15

Lowther, Pat 1935-1975 . . . . DLB-53

Loy, Mina 1882-1966 . . . . DLB-4, 54

Lozeau, Albert 1878-1924 . . . . DLB-92

Lubbock, Percy 1879-1965 . . . . . . DLB-149

Lucas, E. V. 1868-1938 . . . . DLB-98, 149, 153

Lucas, Fielding, Jr. [publishing house] DLB-49

Luce, Henry R. 1898-1967 . . . . DLB-91

Luce, John W., and Company DLB-46

Lucian circa 120-180 . . . . DLB-176

Lucie-Smith, Edward 1933- DLB-40

Lucini, Gian Pietro 1867-1914 . . . . . DLB-114

Luder, Peter circa 1415-1472 . . . . . . DLB-179

Ludlum, Robert 1927- Y-82

Ludus de Antichristo circa 1160 . . . . . DLB-148

Ludvigson, Susan 1942- DLB-120

Ludwig, Jack 1922- DLB-60

Ludwig, Otto 1813-1865 . . . . DLB-129

Ludwigslied 881 or 882 . . . . DLB-148

Luera, Yolanda 1953- DLB-122

Luft, Lya 1938- DLB-145

Luke, Peter 1919- DLB-13

Lupton, F. M., Company DLB-49

Lupus of Ferrières circa 805-circa 862 . . . . DLB-148

Lurie, Alison 1926- DLB-2

Luther, Martin 1483-1546 . . . . DLB-179

Luzi, Mario 1914- DLB-128

L'vov, Nikolai Aleksandrovich 1751-1803 . . . . DLB-150

Lyall, Gavin 1932- DLB-87

Lydgate, John circa 1370-1450 . . . . . DLB-146

Lyly, John circa 1554-1606 . . . . . DLB-62, 167

Lynch, Patricia 1898-1972 . . . . DLB-160

Lynch, Richard flourished 1596-1601 . . . . DLB-172

Lynd, Robert 1879-1949 . . . . DLB-98

Lyon, Matthew 1749-1822 . . . . DLB-43

Lysias circa 459 B.C.-circa 380 B.C. DLB-176

Lytle, Andrew 1902-1995 . . . . . DLB-6; Y-95

Lytton, Edward (see Bulwer-Lytton, Edward)

Lytton, Edward Robert Bulwer 1831-1891 . . . . DLB-32

M

Maass, Joachim 1901-1972 . . . . DLB-69

Mabie, Hamilton Wright 1845-1916 . . . . DLB-71

Mac A'Ghobhainn, Iain (see Smith, Iain Crichton)

MacArthur, Charles 1895-1956 . . . . DLB-7, 25, 44

Macaulay, Catherine 1731-1791 . . . . DLB-104

Macaulay, David 1945- DLB-61

Macaulay, Rose 1881-1958 . . . . DLB-36

Macaulay, Thomas Babington 1800-1859 . . . . DLB-32, 55

Macaulay Company DLB-46

MacBeth, George 1932- DLB-40

Macbeth, Madge 1880-1965 . . . . . . DLB-92

MacCaig, Norman 1910- DLB-27

MacDiarmid, Hugh 1892-1978 . . . . . DLB-20

MacDonald, Cynthia 1928- DLB-105

MacDonald, George 1824-1905 . . . . DLB-18, 163, 178

MacDonald, John D. 1916-1986 . . . . DLB-8; Y-86

MacDonald, Philip 1899?-1980 . . . . . DLB-77

Macdonald, Ross (see Millar, Kenneth)

MacDonald, Wilson 1880-1967 . . . . . DLB-92

Macdonald and Company (Publishers) DLB-112

MacEwen, Gwendolyn 1941- DLB-53

Macfadden, Bernarr 1868-1955 . . . . DLB-25, 91

MacGregor, John 1825-1892 . . . . . . DLB-166

MacGregor, Mary Esther (see Keith, Marian)

Machado, Antonio 1875-1939 . . . . . DLB-108

Machado, Manuel 1874-1947 . . . . . DLB-108

Machar, Agnes Maule 1837-1927 . . . . DLB-92

Machen, Arthur Llewelyn Jones 1863-1947 . . . . DLB-36, 156, 178

MacInnes, Colin 1914-1976 . . . . . . DLB-14

MacInnes, Helen 1907-1985 . . . . . . DLB-87

Mack, Maynard 1909- DLB-111

Mackall, Leonard L. 1879-1937 . . . . . DLB-140

MacKaye, Percy 1875-1956 . . . . . . DLB-54

Macken, Walter 1915-1967 . . . . . . DLB-13

Mackenzie, Alexander 1763-1820 . . . . DLB-99

Mackenzie, Alexander Slidell 1803-1848 . . . . DLB-183

Mackenzie, Compton 1883-1972 . . . . DLB-34, 100

Mackenzie, Henry 1745-1831. . . . . . . DLB-39

Mackey, Nathaniel 1947- DLB-169

Mackey, William Wellington
1937- DLB-38

Mackintosh, Elizabeth (see Tey, Josephine)

Mackintosh, Sir James
1765-1832 . . . . DLB-158

Maclaren, Ian (see Watson, John)

Macklin, Charles 1699-1797 . . . . . . DLB-89

MacLean, Katherine Anne 1925- DLB-8

MacLeish, Archibald
1892-1982 . . . . DLB-4, 7, 45; Y-82

MacLennan, Hugh 1907-1990 . . . . . . DLB-68

Macleod, Fiona (see Sharp, William)

MacLeod, Alistair 1936- DLB-60

Macleod, Norman 1906-1985 . . . . . . DLB-4

Macmillan and Company DLB-106

The Macmillan Company DLB-49

Macmillan's English Men of Letters,
First Series (1878-1892) DLB-144

MacNamara, Brinsley 1890-1963 . . . . DLB-10

MacNeice, Louis 1907-1963 . . . . DLB-10, 20

MacPhail, Andrew 1864-1938 . . . . . . DLB-92

Macpherson, James 1736-1796 . . . . . DLB-109

Macpherson, Jay 1931- DLB-53

Macpherson, Jeanie 1884-1946 . . . . . DLB-44

Macrae Smith Company DLB-46

Macrone, John
[publishing house] DLB-106

MacShane, Frank 1927- DLB-111

Macy-Masius. DLB-46

Madden, David 1933- DLB-6

Maddow, Ben 1909-1992 . . . . DLB-44

Maddux, Rachel 1912-1983 . . . . Y-93

Madgett, Naomi Long 1923- DLB-76

Madhubuti, Haki R.
1942- DLB-5, 41; DS-8

Madison, James 1751-1836 . . . . DLB-37

Maginn, William 1794-1842 . . . . DLB-110, 159

Mahan, Alfred Thayer 1840-1914 . . . . DLB-47

Maheux-Forcier, Louise 1929- DLB-60

Mahin, John Lee 1902-1984 . . . . . . DLB-44

Mahon, Derek 1941- DLB-40

Maikov, Vasilii Ivanovich
1728-1778 . . . . DLB-150

Mailer, Norman
1923- DLB-2, 16, 28; Y-80, 83; DS-3

Maillet, Adrienne 1885-1963 . . . . . . DLB-68

Maimonides, Moses 1138-1204 . . . . . DLB-115

Maillet, Antonine 1929- DLB-60

Maillu, David G. 1939- DLB-157

Main Selections of the Book-of-the-Month
Club, 1926-1945 . . . . DLB-9

Main Trends in Twentieth-Century Book Clubs
. . . . DLB-46

Mainwaring, Daniel 1902-1977 . . . . . DLB-44

Mair, Charles 1838-1927 . . . . DLB-99

Mais, Roger 1905-1955 . . . . DLB-125

Major, Andre 1942- DLB-60

Major, Clarence 1936- DLB-33

Major, Kevin 1949- DLB-60

Major Books. DLB-46

Makemie, Francis circa 1658-1708 . . . . DLB-24

The Making of a People, by
J. M. Ritchie DLB-66

Maksimović, Desanka 1898-1993 . . . . DLB-147

Malamud, Bernard
1914-1986 . . . . . DLB-2, 28, 152; Y-80, 86

Malet, Lucas 1852-1931 . . . . DLB-153

Malleson, Lucy Beatrice (see Gilbert, Anthony)

Mallet-Joris, Françoise 1930- DLB-83

Mallock, W. H. 1849-1923. . . . . DLB-18, 57

Malone, Dumas 1892-1986 . . . . DLB-17

Malone, Edmond 1741-1812 . . . . . . DLB-142

Malory, Sir Thomas
circa 1400-1410 - 1471 . . . . DLB-146

Malraux, André 1901-1976 . . . . DLB-72

Malthus, Thomas Robert
1766-1834. . . . . DLB-107, 158

Maltz, Albert 1908-1985 . . . . DLB-102

Malzberg, Barry N. 1939- DLB-8

Mamet, David 1947- DLB-7

Manaka, Matsemela 1956- DLB-157

Manchester University Press DLB-112

Mandel, Eli 1922- DLB-53

Mandeville, Bernard 1670-1733 . . . . . DLB-101

Mandeville, Sir John
mid fourteenth century DLB-146

Mandiargues, André Pieyre de
1909- DLB-83

Manfred, Frederick 1912-1994 . . . . . . DLB-6

Mangan, Sherry 1904-1961 . . . . DLB-4

Mankiewicz, Herman 1897-1953 . . . . . DLB-26

Mankiewicz, Joseph L. 1909-1993 . . . . DLB-44

Mankowitz, Wolf 1924- DLB-15

Manley, Delarivière
1672?-1724 . . . . DLB-39, 80

Mann, Abby 1927- DLB-44

Mann, Heinrich 1871-1950 . . . . DLB-66, 118

Mann, Horace 1796-1859 . . . . DLB-1

Mann, Klaus 1906-1949. . . . . DLB-56

Mann, Thomas 1875-1955 . . . . DLB-66

Mann, William D'Alton
1839-1920 . . . . DLB-137

Manning, Marie 1873?-1945 . . . . DLB-29

Manning and Loring DLB-49

Mannyng, Robert
flourished 1303-1338 . . . . DLB-146

Mano, D. Keith 1942- DLB-6

Manor Books DLB-46

Mansfield, Katherine 1888-1923. . . . . DLB-162

Manuel, Niklaus circa 1484-1530 . . . . DLB-179

Manzini, Gianna 1896-1974 . . . . DLB-177

Mapanje, Jack 1944- DLB-157

March, William 1893-1954 . . . . . DLB-9, 86

Marchand, Leslie A. 1900- DLB-103

Marchant, Bessie 1862-1941. . . . . . . DLB-160

Marchessault, Jovette 1938- DLB-60

Marcus, Frank 1928- DLB-13

Marden, Orison Swett
1850-1924 . . . . DLB-137

Marechera, Dambudzo
1952-1987 . . . . DLB-157

Marek, Richard, Books DLB-46

Mares, E. A. 1938- DLB-122

Mariani, Paul 1940- DLB-111

Marie-Victorin, Frère 1885-1944 . . . . DLB-92

Marin, Biagio 1891-1985. . . . . DLB-128

Marincoviœ, Ranko 1913- DLB-147

Marinetti, Filippo Tommaso
1876-1944 . . . . DLB-114

Marion, Frances 1886-1973 . . . . DLB-44

Marius, Richard C. 1933- Y-85

The Mark Taper Forum DLB-7

Mark Twain on Perpetual Copyright Y-92

Markfield, Wallace 1926- DLB-2, 28

Markham, Edwin 1852-1940 . . . . . . DLB-54

Markle, Fletcher 1921-1991 . . . . DLB-68; Y-91

Marlatt, Daphne 1942- DLB-60

Marlitt, E. 1825-1887 . . . . DLB-129

Marlowe, Christopher 1564-1593. . . . . DLB-62

Marlyn, John 1912- DLB-88

Marmion, Shakerley 1603-1639. . . . . . DLB-58

Der Marner
before 1230-circa 1287 . . . . DLB-138

The *Marprelate Tracts* 1588-1589. . . . . DLB-132

Marquand, John P. 1893-1960 . . . . DLB-9, 102

Marqués, René 1919-1979. . . . . . . DLB-113

Marquis, Don 1878-1937. . . . . . . DLB-11, 25

Marriott, Anne 1913- DLB-68

Marryat, Frederick 1792-1848. . . . DLB-21, 163

Marsh, George Perkins
1801-1882 . . . . DLB-1, 64

Marsh, James 1794-1842. . . . . . . DLB-1, 59

Marsh, Capen, Lyon and Webb. DLB-49

Marsh, Ngaio 1899-1982 . . . . DLB-77

Marshall, Edison 1894-1967 . . . . . . DLB-102

Marshall, Edward 1932- DLB-16

Marshall, Emma 1828-1899 . . . . . . DLB-163

Marshall, James 1942-1992 . . . . DLB-61

Marshall, Joyce 1913- DLB-88

Marshall, Paule 1929- DLB-33, 157

Marshall, Tom 1938- DLB-60

Marsilius of Padua
    circa 1275-circa 1342 . . . . DLB-115

Marson, Una 1905-1965. . . . . DLB-157

Marston, John 1576-1634 . . . . . DLB-58, 172

Marston, Philip Bourke 1850-1887. . . . DLB-35

Martens, Kurt 1870-1945 . . . . DLB-66

Martien, William S.
    [publishing house]. DLB-49

Martin, Abe (see Hubbard, Kin)

Martin, Charles 1942- DLB-120

Martin, Claire 1914- DLB-60

Martin, Jay 1935- DLB-111

Martin, Johann (see Laurentius von Schnüffis)

Martin, Violet Florence (see Ross, Martin)

Martin du Gard, Roger 1881-1958 . . . DLB-65

Martineau, Harriet
    1802-1876 . . . . DLB-21, 55, 159, 163, 166

Martínez, Eliud 1935- DLB-122

Martínez, Max 1943- DLB-82

Martyn, Edward 1859-1923. . . . . . . DLB-10

Marvell, Andrew 1621-1678. . . . . . DLB-131

Marvin X 1944- DLB-38

Marx, Karl 1818-1883. . . . . DLB-129

Marzials, Theo 1850-1920 . . . . DLB-35

Masefield, John
    1878-1967 . . . . . . DLB-10, 19, 153, 160

Mason, A. E. W. 1865-1948. . . . . . . DLB-70

Mason, Bobbie Ann
    1940- DLB-173; Y-87

Mason, William 1725-1797 . . . . . . DLB-142

Mason Brothers DLB-49

Massey, Gerald 1828-1907 . . . . DLB-32

Massinger, Philip 1583-1640 . . . . . . DLB-58

Masson, David 1822-1907. . . . . . . DLB-144

Masters, Edgar Lee 1868-1950 . . . . . DLB-54

Mastronardi, Lucio 1930-1979. . . . . DLB-177

Matevski, Mateja 1929- DLB-181

Mather, Cotton
    1663-1728 . . . . DLB-24, 30, 140

Mather, Increase 1639-1723. . . . . . . DLB-24

Mather, Richard 1596-1669. . . . . . . DLB-24

Matheson, Richard 1926- DLB-8, 44

Matheus, John F. 1887- DLB-51

Mathews, Cornelius
    1817?-1889 . . . . DLB-3, 64

Mathews, John Joseph
    1894-1979 . . . . DLB-175

Mathews, Elkin
    [publishing house] DLB-112

Mathias, Roland 1915- DLB-27

Mathis, June 1892-1927 . . . . DLB-44

Mathis, Sharon Bell 1937- DLB-33

Matković, Marijan 1915-1985 . . . . . DLB-181

Matoš, Antun Gustav 1873-1914 . . . . DLB-147

Matsumoto, Seichō 1909-1992. . . . . DLB-182

The Matter of England
    1240-1400 . . . . DLB-146

The Matter of Rome
    early twelfth to late fifteenth
    century. DLB-146

Matthews, Brander
    1852-1929. . . . . DLB-71, 78; DS-13

Matthews, Jack 1925- DLB-6

Matthews, William 1942- DLB-5

Matthiessen, F. O. 1902-1950 . . . . . DLB-63

Maturin, Charles Robert
    1780-1824 . . . . DLB-178

Matthiessen, Peter 1927- DLB-6, 173

Maugham, W. Somerset
    1874-1965 . . . . . DLB-10, 36, 77, 100, 162

Maupassant, Guy de 1850-1893 . . . . DLB-123

Mauriac, Claude 1914- DLB-83

Mauriac, François 1885-1970 . . . . . . DLB-65

Maurice, Frederick Denison
    1805-1872 . . . . DLB-55

Maurois, André 1885-1967 . . . . DLB-65

Maury, James 1718-1769 . . . . DLB-31

Mavor, Elizabeth 1927- DLB-14

Mavor, Osborne Henry (see Bridie, James)

Maxwell, William 1908- Y-80

Maxwell, H. [publishing house] DLB-49

Maxwell, John [publishing house]. . . . DLB-106

May, Elaine 1932- DLB-44

May, Karl 1842-1912 . . . . DLB-129

May, Thomas 1595 or 1596-1650 . . . . DLB-58

Mayer, Bernadette 1945- DLB-165

Mayer, Mercer 1943- DLB-61

Mayer, O. B. 1818-1891 . . . . DLB-3

Mayes, Herbert R. 1900-1987. . . . . . DLB-137

Mayes, Wendell 1919-1992 . . . . DLB-26

Mayfield, Julian 1928-1984. . . . . DLB-33; Y-84

Mayhew, Henry 1812-1887 . . . . . DLB-18, 55

Mayhew, Jonathan 1720-1766 . . . . . DLB-31

Mayne, Jasper 1604-1672 . . . . DLB-126

Mayne, Seymour 1944- DLB-60

Mayor, Flora Macdonald
    1872-1932 . . . . DLB-36

Mayröcker, Friederike 1924- DLB-85

Mazrui, Ali A. 1933- DLB-125

Mažuranić, Ivan 1814-1890 . . . . . . DLB-147

Mazursky, Paul 1930- DLB-44

McAlmon, Robert
    1896-1956 . . . . DLB-4, 45; DS-15

McArthur, Peter 1866-1924. . . . . . . DLB-92

McBride, Robert M., and
    Company DLB-46

McCaffrey, Anne 1926- DLB-8

McCarthy, Cormac 1933- DLB-6, 143

McCarthy, Mary 1912-1989 . . . . DLB-2; Y-81

McCay, Winsor 1871-1934. . . . . . . DLB-22

McClane, Albert Jules 1922-1991 . . . . DLB-171

McClatchy, C. K. 1858-1936. . . . . . DLB-25

McClellan, George Marion
    1860-1934 . . . . DLB-50

McCloskey, Robert 1914- DLB-22

McClung, Nellie Letitia 1873-1951. . . . DLB-92

McClure, Joanna 1930- DLB-16

McClure, Michael 1932- DLB-16

McClure, Phillips and Company. DLB-46

McClure, S. S. 1857-1949 . . . . DLB-91

McClurg, A. C., and Company DLB-49

McCluskey, John A., Jr. 1944- DLB-33

McCollum, Michael A. 1946. . . . . . . Y-87

McConnell, William C. 1917- DLB-88

McCord, David 1897- DLB-61

McCorkle, Jill 1958- Y-87

McCorkle, Samuel Eusebius
    1746-1811 . . . . DLB-37

McCormick, Anne O'Hare
    1880-1954 . . . . DLB-29

McCormick, Robert R. 1880-1955 . . . . DLB-29

McCourt, Edward 1907-1972. . . . . . DLB-88

McCoy, Horace 1897-1955 . . . . DLB-9

McCrae, John 1872-1918 . . . . DLB-92

McCullagh, Joseph B. 1842-1896. . . . . DLB-23

McCullers, Carson
    1917-1967 . . . . DLB-2, 7, 173

McCulloch, Thomas 1776-1843 . . . . . DLB-99

McDonald, Forrest 1927- DLB-17

McDonald, Walter
    1934- DLB-105, DS-9

McDonald, Walter, Getting Started:
    Accepting the Regions You Own—
    or Which Own You DLB-105

McDougall, Colin 1917-1984 . . . . . . DLB-68

McDowell, Obolensky DLB-46

McEwan, Ian 1948- DLB-14

McFadden, David 1940- DLB-60

McFall, Frances Elizabeth Clarke
    (see Grand, Sarah)

McFarlane, Leslie 1902-1977 . . . . . . DLB-88

McFee, William 1881-1966 . . . . DLB-153

McGahern, John 1934- DLB-14

McGee, Thomas D'Arcy
   1825-1868 . . . . DLB-99

McGeehan, W. O. 1879-1933 . . . DLB-25, 171

McGill, Ralph 1898-1969 . . . . DLB-29

McGinley, Phyllis 1905-1978 . . . . . DLB-11, 48

McGirt, James E. 1874-1930 . . . . . . DLB-50

McGlashan and Gill DLB-106

McGough, Roger 1937- DLB-40

McGraw-Hill DLB-46

McGuane, Thomas 1939- DLB-2; Y-80

McGuckian, Medbh 1950- DLB-40

McGuffey, William Holmes
   1800-1873 . . . . DLB-42

McIlvanney, William 1936- DLB-14

McIlwraith, Jean Newton
   1859-1938 . . . . DLB-92

McIntyre, James 1827-1906 . . . . DLB-99

McIntyre, O. O. 1884-1938 . . . . DLB-25

McKay, Claude
   1889-1948 . . . . DLB-4, 45, 51, 117

The David McKay Company DLB-49

McKean, William V. 1820-1903 . . . . . DLB-23

The McKenzie Trust Y-96

McKinley, Robin 1952- DLB-52

McLachlan, Alexander 1818-1896 . . . DLB-99

McLaren, Floris Clark 1904-1978 . . . DLB-68

McLaverty, Michael 1907- DLB-15

McLean, John R. 1848-1916 . . . . . . DLB-23

McLean, William L. 1852-1931 . . . . . DLB-25

McLennan, William 1856-1904 . . . . . DLB-92

McLoughlin Brothers DLB-49

McLuhan, Marshall 1911-1980 . . . . . DLB-88

McMaster, John Bach 1852-1932 . . . . DLB-47

McMurtry, Larry
   1936- DLB-2, 143; Y-80, 87

McNally, Terrence 1939- DLB-7

McNeil, Florence 1937- DLB-60

McNeile, Herman Cyril
   1888-1937 . . . . DLB-77

McNickle, D'Arcy 1904-1977 . . . . . DLB-175

McPherson, James Alan 1943- DLB-38

McPherson, Sandra 1943- Y-86

McWhirter, George 1939- DLB-60

McWilliams, Carey 1905-1980 . . . . DLB-137

Mead, L. T. 1844-1914 . . . . DLB-141

Mead, Matthew 1924- DLB-40

Mead, Taylor ?- DLB-16

Meany, Tom 1903-1964 . . . . DLB-171

Mechthild von Magdeburg
   circa 1207-circa 1282 . . . . DLB-138

Medill, Joseph 1823-1899 . . . . DLB-43

Medoff, Mark 1940- DLB-7

Meek, Alexander Beaufort
   1814-1865 . . . . DLB-3

Meeke, Mary ?-1816? DLB-116

Meinke, Peter 1932- DLB-5

Mejia Vallejo, Manuel 1923- DLB-113

Melanchton, Philipp 1497-1560 . . . . DLB-179

Melançon, Robert 1947- DLB-60

Mell, Max 1882-1971 . . . . DLB-81, 124

Mellow, James R. 1926- DLB-111

Meltzer, David 1937- DLB-16

Meltzer, Milton 1915- DLB-61

Melville, Elizabeth, Lady Culross
   circa 1585-1640 . . . . DLB-172

Melville, Herman 1819-1891 . . . . . DLB-3, 74

Memoirs of Life and Literature (1920),
   by W. H. Mallock [excerpt] DLB-57

Menander 342-341 B.C.-circa 292-291 B.C.
   . . . . DLB-176

Menantes (see Hunold, Christian Friedrich)

Mencke, Johann Burckhard
   1674-1732 . . . . DLB-168

Mencken, H. L.
   1880-1956 . . . . DLB-11, 29, 63, 137

Mencken and Nietzsche: An Unpublished Excerpt
   from H. L. Mencken's *My Life
   as Author and Editor*. Y-93

Mendelssohn, Moses 1729-1786 . . . . DLB-97

Méndez M., Miguel 1930- DLB-82

The Mercantile Library of
   New York Y-96

Mercer, Cecil William (see Yates, Dornford)

Mercer, David 1928-1980 . . . . DLB-13

Mercer, John 1704-1768 . . . . DLB-31

Meredith, George
   1828-1909 . . . . DLB-18, 35, 57, 159

Meredith, Louisa Anne
   1812-1895 . . . . DLB-166

Meredith, Owen (see Lytton, Edward Robert Bulwer)

Meredith, William 1919- DLB-5

Mergerle, Johann Ulrich
   (see Abraham ä Sancta Clara)

Mérimée, Prosper 1803-1870 . . . . . DLB-119

Merivale, John Herman
   1779-1844 . . . . DLB-96

Meriwether, Louise 1923- DLB-33

Merlin Press DLB-112

Merriam, Eve 1916-1992 . . . . DLB-61

The Merriam Company DLB-49

Merrill, James
   1926-1995 . . . . DLB-5, 165; Y-85

Merrill and Baker DLB-49

The Mershon Company DLB-49

Merton, Thomas 1915-1968 . . . . DLB-48; Y-81

Merwin, W. S. 1927- DLB-5, 169

Messner, Julian [publishing house] DLB-46

Metcalf, J. [publishing house] DLB-49

Metcalf, John 1938- DLB-60

The Methodist Book Concern DLB-49

Methuen and Company DLB-112

Mew, Charlotte 1869-1928 . . . . . DLB-19, 135

Mewshaw, Michael 1943- Y-80

Meyer, Conrad Ferdinand 1825-1898 . . . DLB-129

Meyer, E. Y. 1946- DLB-75

Meyer, Eugene 1875-1959 . . . . DLB-29

Meyer, Michael 1921- DLB-155

Meyers, Jeffrey 1939- DLB-111

Meynell, Alice
   1847-1922 . . . . DLB-19, 98

Meynell, Viola 1885-1956 . . . . DLB-153

Meyrink, Gustav 1868-1932 . . . . . . DLB-81

Michaels, Leonard 1933- DLB-130

Micheaux, Oscar 1884-1951 . . . . . . DLB-50

Michel of Northgate, Dan
   circa 1265-circa 1340 . . . . DLB-146

Micheline, Jack 1929- DLB-16

Michener, James A. 1907?- DLB-6

Micklejohn, George
   circa 1717-1818 . . . . DLB-31

Middle English Literature:
   An Introduction DLB-146

The Middle English Lyric DLB-146

Middle Hill Press DLB-106

Middleton, Christopher 1926- DLB-40

Middleton, Richard 1882-1911 . . . . DLB-156

Middleton, Stanley 1919- DLB-14

Middleton, Thomas 1580-1627 . . . . . DLB-58

Miegel, Agnes 1879-1964 . . . . DLB-56

Mihailović, Dragoslav 1930- DLB-181

Mihalić, Slavko 1928- DLB-181

Miles, Josephine 1911-1985 . . . . . . DLB-48

Miliković, Branko 1934-1961 . . . . . DLB-181

Milius, John 1944- DLB-44

Mill, James 1773-1836 . . . . . . DLB-107, 158

Mill, John Stuart 1806-1873 . . . . . . DLB-55

Millar, Kenneth
   1915-1983 . . . . DLB-2; Y-83; DS-6

Millar, Andrew
   [publishing house] DLB-154

Millay, Edna St. Vincent
   1892-1950 . . . . DLB-45

Miller, Arthur 1915- DLB-7

Miller, Caroline 1903-1992 . . . . DLB-9

Miller, Eugene Ethelbert 1950- DLB-41

Miller, Heather Ross 1939- DLB-120

Miller, Henry 1891-1980 . . . . DLB-4, 9; Y-80

Miller, J. Hillis 1928- DLB-67

Miller, James [publishing house] DLB-49

Miller, Jason 1939- DLB-7

Miller, May 1899- DLB-41

Miller, Paul 1906-1991 . . . . DLB-127

Miller, Perry 1905-1963 . . . . DLB-17, 63

Miller, Sue 1943- DLB-143

Miller, Vassar 1924- DLB-105

Miller, Walter M., Jr. 1923- DLB-8

Miller, Webb 1892-1940 . . . . DLB-29

Millhauser, Steven 1943- DLB-2

Millican, Arthenia J. Bates
1920- DLB-38

Mills and Boon DLB-112

Milman, Henry Hart 1796-1868 . . . . DLB-96

Milne, A. A.
1882-1956 . . . . . . DLB-10, 77, 100, 160

Milner, Ron 1938- DLB-38

Milner, William
[publishing house] DLB-106

Milnes, Richard Monckton (Lord Houghton)
1809-1885 . . . . DLB-32

Milton, John 1608-1674 . . . . . DLB-131, 151

Minakami, Tsutomu 1919- DLB-182

The Minerva Press DLB-154

Minnesang circa 1150-1280 . . . . DLB-138

Minns, Susan 1839-1938 . . . . DLB-140

Minor Illustrators, 1880-1914 . . . . . . DLB-141

Minor Poets of the Earlier Seventeenth
Century DLB-121

Minton, Balch and Company DLB-46

Mirbeau, Octave 1848-1917 . . . . DLB-123

Mirk, John died after 1414? DLB-146

Miron, Gaston 1928- DLB-60

A Mirror for Magistrates DLB-167

Mishima, Yukio 1925-1970 . . . . DLB-182

Mitchel, Jonathan 1624-1668 . . . . . . DLB-24

Mitchell, Adrian 1932- DLB-40

Mitchell, Donald Grant
1822-1908 . . . . DLB-1; DS-13

Mitchell, Gladys 1901-1983 . . . . DLB-77

Mitchell, James Leslie 1901-1935 . . . . DLB-15

Mitchell, John (see Slater, Patrick)

Mitchell, John Ames 1845-1918 . . . . DLB-79

Mitchell, Joseph 1908-1996 . . . . Y-96

Mitchell, Julian 1935- DLB-14

Mitchell, Ken 1940- DLB-60

Mitchell, Langdon 1862-1935 . . . . . . DLB-7

Mitchell, Loften 1919- DLB-38

Mitchell, Margaret 1900-1949 . . . . . . DLB-9

Mitchell, W. O. 1914- DLB-88

Mitchison, Naomi Margaret (Haldane)
1897- DLB-160

Mitford, Mary Russell
1787-1855 . . . . DLB-110, 116

Mittelholzer, Edgar 1909-1965 . . . . . . DLB-117

Mitterer, Erika 1906- DLB-85

Mitterer, Felix 1948- DLB-124

Mitternacht, Johann Sebastian
1613-1679 . . . . DLB-168

Miyamoto, Yuriko 1899-1951 . . . . . DLB-180

Mizener, Arthur 1907-1988 . . . . . . DLB-103

Modern Age Books DLB-46

"Modern English Prose" (1876),
by George Saintsbury DLB-57

The Modern Language Association of America
Celebrates Its Centennial Y-84

The Modern Library DLB-46

"Modern Novelists – Great and Small" (1855), by
Margaret Oliphant DLB-21

"Modern Style" (1857), by Cockburn
Thomson [excerpt] DLB-57

The Modernists (1932), by Joseph Warren Beach
DLB-36

Modiano, Patrick 1945- DLB-83

Moffat, Yard and Company DLB-46

Moffet, Thomas 1553-1604 . . . . DLB-136

Mohr, Nicholasa 1938- DLB-145

Moix, Ana María 1947- DLB-134

Molesworth, Louisa 1839-1921 . . . . . DLB-135

Möllhausen, Balduin 1825-1905 . . . . . DLB-129

Momaday, N. Scott 1934- DLB-143, 175

Monkhouse, Allan 1858-1936 . . . . . . DLB-10

Monro, Harold 1879-1932 . . . . DLB-19

Monroe, Harriet 1860-1936 . . . . . DLB-54, 91

Monsarrat, Nicholas 1910-1979 . . . . . DLB-15

Montagu, Lady Mary Wortley
1689-1762 . . . . DLB-95, 101

Montague, John 1929- DLB-40

Montale, Eugenio 1896-1981 . . . . . . DLB-114

Monterroso, Augusto 1921- DLB-145

Montgomerie, Alexander
circa 1550?-1598 . . . . DLB-167

Montgomery, James
1771-1854 . . . . DLB-93, 158

Montgomery, John 1919- DLB-16

Montgomery, Lucy Maud
1874-1942 . . . . DLB-92; DS-14

Montgomery, Marion 1925- DLB-6

Montgomery, Robert Bruce (see Crispin, Edmund)

Montherlant, Henry de 1896-1972 . . . . DLB-72

The Monthly Review 1749-1844 . . . . . . DLB-110

Montigny, Louvigny de 1876-1955 . . . DLB-92

Montoya, José 1932- DLB-122

Moodie, John Wedderburn Dunbar
1797-1869 . . . . DLB-99

Moodie, Susanna 1803-1885 . . . . . . DLB-99

Moody, Joshua circa 1633-1697 . . . . . DLB-24

Moody, William Vaughn
1869-1910 . . . . DLB-7, 54

Moorcock, Michael 1939- DLB-14

Moore, Catherine L. 1911- DLB-8

Moore, Clement Clarke 1779-1863 . . . DLB-42

Moore, Dora Mavor 1888-1979 . . . . . DLB-92

Moore, George
1852-1933 . . . . DLB-10, 18, 57, 135

Moore, Marianne
1887-1972 . . . . DLB-45; DS-7

Moore, Mavor 1919- DLB-88

Moore, Richard 1927- DLB-105

Moore, Richard, The No Self, the Little Self,
and the Poets DLB-105

Moore, T. Sturge 1870-1944 . . . . . . DLB-19

Moore, Thomas 1779-1852 . . . . . DLB-96, 144

Moore, Ward 1903-1978 . . . . DLB-8

Moore, Wilstach, Keys and
Company DLB-49

The Moorland-Spingarn Research
Center DLB-76

Moorman, Mary C. 1905-1994 . . . . . DLB-155

Moraga, Cherríe 1952- DLB-82

Morales, Alejandro 1944- DLB-82

Morales, Mario Roberto 1947- DLB-145

Morales, Rafael 1919- DLB-108

Morality Plays: *Mankind* circa 1450-1500 and
Everyman circa 1500 . . . . DLB-146

Morante, Elsa 1912-1985 . . . . DLB-177

Morata, Olympia Fulvia
1526-1555 . . . . DLB-179

Moravia, Alberto 1907-1990 . . . . . . DLB-177

Mordaunt, Elinor 1872-1942 . . . . . . DLB-174

More, Hannah
1745-1833 . . . . . DLB-107, 109, 116, 158

More, Henry 1614-1687 . . . . DLB-126

More, Sir Thomas
1477 or 1478-1535 . . . . DLB-136

Moreno, Dorinda 1939- DLB-122

Morency, Pierre 1942- DLB-60

Moretti, Marino 1885-1979 . . . . . . DLB-114

Morgan, Berry 1919- DLB-6

Morgan, Charles 1894-1958 . . . . . DLB-34, 100

Morgan, Edmund S. 1916- DLB-17

Morgan, Edwin 1920- DLB-27

Morgan, John Pierpont
1837-1913 . . . . DLB-140

Morgan, John Pierpont, Jr.
1867-1943 . . . . DLB-140

Morgan, Robert 1944- DLB-120

Morgan, Sydney Owenson, Lady
1776?-1859 . . . . DLB-116, 158

Morgner, Irmtraud 1933- DLB-75

Morhof, Daniel Georg
1639-1691 . . . . DLB-164

Mori, Ōgai 1862-1922 . . . . DLB-180

Morier, James Justinian
1782 or 1783?-1849 . . . . DLB-116

Mörike, Eduard 1804-1875 . . . . . . DLB-133

Morin, Paul 1889-1963 . . . . DLB-92

Morison, Richard 1514?-1556 . . . . . DLB-136

Morison, Samuel Eliot 1887-1976 . . . . DLB-17

Moritz, Karl Philipp 1756-1793 . . . . . DLB-94

Moriz von Craûn
circa 1220-1230 . . . . DLB-138

Morley, Christopher 1890-1957 . . . . . DLB-9

Morley, John 1838-1923 . . . . . . DLB-57, 144

Morris, George Pope 1802-1864 . . . . DLB-73

Morris, Lewis 1833-1907 . . . . DLB-35

Morris, Richard B. 1904-1989 . . . . . DLB-17

Morris, William
1834-1896 . . . . . DLB-18, 35, 57, 156, 178

Morris, Willie 1934- Y-80

Morris, Wright 1910- DLB-2; Y-81

Morrison, Arthur 1863-1945 . . . DLB-70, 135

Morrison, Charles Clayton
1874-1966 . . . . DLB-91

Morrison, Toni
1931- DLB-6, 33, 143; Y-81

Morrow, William, and Company DLB-46

Morse, James Herbert 1841-1923 . . . . DLB-71

Morse, Jedidiah 1761-1826 . . . . . . DLB-37

Morse, John T., Jr. 1840-1937 . . . . . DLB-47

Morselli, Guido 1912-1973 . . . . . . DLB-177

Mortimer, Favell Lee 1802-1878 . . . . DLB-163

Mortimer, John 1923- DLB-13

Morton, Carlos 1942- DLB-122

Morton, John P., and Company DLB-49

Morton, Nathaniel 1613-1685 . . . . . DLB-24

Morton, Sarah Wentworth
1759-1846 . . . . DLB-37

Morton, Thomas
circa 1579-circa 1647 . . . . DLB-24

Moscherosch, Johann Michael
1601-1669 . . . . DLB-164

Moseley, Humphrey
[publishing house] DLB-170

Möser, Justus 1720-1794 . . . . DLB-97

Mosley, Nicholas 1923- DLB-14

Moss, Arthur 1889-1969 . . . . DLB-4

Moss, Howard 1922-1987 . . . . DLB-5

Moss, Thylias 1954- DLB-120

The Most Powerful Book Review in America
[*New York Times Book Review*] Y-82

Motion, Andrew 1952- DLB-40

Motley, John Lothrop
1814-1877 . . . . DLB-1, 30, 59

Motley, Willard 1909-1965 . . . . DLB-76, 143

Motte, Benjamin Jr.
[publishing house] DLB-154

Motteux, Peter Anthony
1663-1718 . . . . DLB-80

Mottram, R. H. 1883-1971 . . . . . . DLB-36

Mouré, Erin 1955- DLB-60

Mourning Dove (Humishuma)
between 1882 and 1888?-1936 . . . . DLB-175

Movies from Books, 1920-1974 . . . . . DLB-9

Mowat, Farley 1921- DLB-68

Mowbray, A. R., and Company,
Limited DLB-106

Mowrer, Edgar Ansel 1892-1977 . . . . DLB-29

Mowrer, Paul Scott 1887-1971 . . . . . DLB-29

Moxon, Edward
[publishing house] DLB-106

Moxon, Joseph
[publishing house] DLB-170

Mphahlele, Es'kia (Ezekiel)
1919- DLB-125

Mtshali, Oswald Mbuyiseni
1940- DLB-125

Mucedorus DLB-62

Mudford, William 1782-1848 . . . . . DLB-159

Mueller, Lisel 1924- DLB-105

Muhajir, El (see Marvin X)

Muhajir, Nazzam Al Fitnah (see Marvin X)

Mühlbach, Luise 1814-1873 . . . . . . DLB-133

Muir, Edwin 1887-1959 . . . . . . DLB-20, 100

Muir, Helen 1937- DLB-14

Mukherjee, Bharati 1940- DLB-60

Mulcaster, Richard
1531 or 1532-1611 . . . . DLB-167

Muldoon, Paul 1951- DLB-40

Müller, Friedrich (see Müller, Maler)

Müller, Heiner 1929- DLB-124

Müller, Maler 1749-1825 . . . . DLB-94

Müller, Wilhelm 1794-1827 . . . . . . DLB-90

Mumford, Lewis 1895-1990 . . . . . . DLB-63

Munby, Arthur Joseph 1828-1910 . . . . DLB-35

Munday, Anthony 1560-1633 . . . . DLB-62, 172

Mundt, Clara (see Mühlbach, Luise)

Mundt, Theodore 1808-1861 . . . . . DLB-133

Munford, Robert circa 1737-1783 . . . . DLB-31

Mungoshi, Charles 1947- DLB-157

Munonye, John 1929- DLB-117

Munro, Alice 1931- DLB-53

Munro, H. H. 1870-1916 . . . . . DLB-34, 162

Munro, Neil 1864-1930 . . . . DLB-156

N

Nabl, Franz 1883-1974 . . . . DLB-81

Nabokov, Vladimir
1899-1977 . . . . DLB-2; Y-80, Y-91; DS-3

Nabokov Festival at Cornell Y-83

The Vladimir Nabokov Archive
in the Berg Collection Y-91

Nafis and Cornish DLB-49

Nagai, Kafū 1879-1959 . . . . DLB-180

Naipaul, Shiva 1945-1985 . . . . . DLB-157; Y-85

Naipaul, V. S. 1932- DLB-125; Y-85

Nakagami, Kenji 1946-1992 . . . . . . DLB-182

Nancrede, Joseph
[publishing house] DLB-49

Naranjo, Carmen 1930- DLB-145

Narrache, Jean 1893-1970 . . . . . . DLB-92

Nasby, Petroleum Vesuvius (see Locke, David
Ross)

Nash, Ogden 1902-1971 . . . . DLB-11

Nash, Eveleigh
[publishing house] DLB-112

Nashe, Thomas 1567-1601? DLB-167

Nast, Conde 1873-1942 . . . . DLB-91

Nastasijević, Momčilo 1894-1938 . . . . DLB-147

Nathan, George Jean 1882-1958 . . . . DLB-137

Nathan, Robert 1894-1985 . . . . DLB-9

The National Jewish Book Awards Y-85

The National Theatre and the Royal
Shakespeare Company: The
National Companies DLB-13

Natsume, Sōseki 1867-1916 . . . . . . DLB-180

Naughton, Bill 1910- DLB-13

Naylor, Gloria 1950- DLB-173

Nazor, Vladimir 1876-1949 . . . . . . DLB-147

Ndebele, Njabulo 1948- DLB-157

Neagoe, Peter 1881-1960 . . . . DLB-4

Neal, John 1793-1876 . . . . DLB-1, 59

Neal, Joseph C. 1807-1847 . . . . DLB-11

Neal, Larry 1937-1981 . . . . DLB-38

The Neale Publishing Company DLB-49

Neely, F. Tennyson
[publishing house] DLB-49

Negri, Ada 1870-1945 . . . . DLB-114

"The Negro as a Writer," by
G. M. McClellan DLB-50

"Negro Poets and Their Poetry," by
Wallace Thurman DLB-50

Neidhart von Reuental
circa 1185-circa 1240 . . . . DLB-138

Neihardt, John G. 1881-1973 . . . . . DLB-9, 54

Neledinsky-Meletsky, Iurii Aleksandrovich
1752-1828 . . . . DLB-150

Nelligan, Emile 1879-1941 . . . . . . DLB-92

Nelson, Alice Moore Dunbar
1875-1935 . . . . DLB-50

Nelson, Thomas, and Sons [U.S.] DLB-49

Nelson, Thomas, and Sons [U.K.] . . . DLB-106

Nelson, William 1908-1978 . . . . DLB-103

Nelson, William Rockhill
1841-1915 . . . . DLB-23

Nemerov, Howard 1920-1991 . . . DLB-5, 6; Y-83

Nesbit, E. 1858-1924 . . . . . DLB-141, 153, 178

Ness, Evaline 1911-1986 . . . . DLB-61

Nestroy, Johann 1801-1862 . . . . DLB-133

Neukirch, Benjamin 1655-1729 . . . . . DLB-168

Neugeboren, Jay 1938- DLB-28

Neumann, Alfred 1895-1952 . . . . DLB-56

Neumark, Georg 1621-1681 . . . . DLB-164

Neumeister, Erdmann 1671-1756 . . . . DLB-168

Nevins, Allan 1890-1971 . . . . DLB-17

Nevinson, Henry Woodd
1856-1941 . . . . DLB-135

The New American Library DLB-46

New Approaches to Biography: Challenges
from Critical Theory, USC Conference
on Literary Studies, 1990 . . . . Y-90

New Directions Publishing
Corporation DLB-46

A New Edition of *Huck Finn* Y-85

New Forces at Work in the American Theatre:
1915-1925. . . . . DLB-7

New Literary Periodicals:
A Report for 1987 . . . . Y-87

New Literary Periodicals:
A Report for 1988 . . . . Y-88

New Literary Periodicals:
A Report for 1989 . . . . Y-89

New Literary Periodicals:
A Report for 1990 . . . . Y-90

New Literary Periodicals:
A Report for 1991 . . . . Y-91

New Literary Periodicals:
A Report for 1992 . . . . Y-92

New Literary Periodicals:
A Report for 1993 . . . . Y-93

The New Monthly Magazine
1814-1884 . . . . DLB-110

The New *Ulysses* Y-84

The New Variorum Shakespeare Y-85

A New Voice: The Center for the Book's First
Five Years Y-83

The New Wave [Science Fiction] DLB-8

New York City Bookshops in the 1930s and
1940s: The Recollections of Walter
Goldwater Y-93

Newbery, John
[publishing house] DLB-154

Newbolt, Henry 1862-1938 . . . . DLB-19

Newbound, Bernard Slade (see Slade, Bernard)

Newby, P. H. 1918- DLB-15

Newby, Thomas Cautley
[publishing house] DLB-106

Newcomb, Charles King 1820-1894 . . . . DLB-1

Newell, Peter 1862-1924 . . . . DLB-42

Newell, Robert Henry 1836-1901 . . . . DLB-11

Newhouse, Samuel I. 1895-1979 . . . . DLB-127

Newman, Cecil Earl 1903-1976 . . . . . DLB-127

Newman, David (see Benton, Robert)

Newman, Frances 1883-1928 . . . . Y-80

Newman, John Henry
1801-1890 . . . . DLB-18, 32, 55

Newman, Mark [publishing house] DLB-49

Newnes, George, Limited DLB-112

Newsome, Effie Lee 1885-1979 . . . . . DLB-76

Newspaper Syndication of American
Humor DLB-11

Newton, A. Edward 1864-1940 . . . . . DLB-140

Ngugi wa Thiong'o 1938- DLB-125

Niatum, Duane 1938- DLB-175

The *Nibelungenlied* and the *Klage*
circa 1200 . . . . DLB-138

Nichol, B. P. 1944- DLB-53

Nicholas of Cusa 1401-1464 . . . . . . DLB-115

Nichols, Dudley 1895-1960 . . . . DLB-26

Nichols, Grace 1950- DLB-157

Nichols, John 1940- Y-82

Nichols, Mary Sargeant (Neal) Gove 1810-11884
. . . . DLB-1

Nichols, Peter 1927- DLB-13

Nichols, Roy F. 1896-1973 . . . . DLB-17

Nichols, Ruth 1948- DLB-60

Nicholson, Norman 1914- DLB-27

Nicholson, William 1872-1949 . . . . . DLB-141

Ní Chuilleanáin, Eiléan 1942- DLB-40

Nicol, Eric 1919- DLB-68

Nicolai, Friedrich 1733-1811 . . . . . . DLB-97

Nicolay, John G. 1832-1901 and
Hay, John 1838-1905 . . . . DLB-47

Nicolson, Harold 1886-1968 . . . . DLB-100, 149

Nicolson, Nigel 1917- DLB-155

Niebuhr, Reinhold 1892-1971 . . . . . DLB-17

Niedecker, Lorine 1903-1970 . . . . . . DLB-48

Nieman, Lucius W. 1857-1935 . . . . . DLB-25

Nietzsche, Friedrich 1844-1900 . . . . . DLB-129

Niggli, Josefina 1910- Y-80

Nightingale, Florence 1820-1910 . . . . . DLB-166

Nikolev, Nikolai Petrovich
1758-1815 . . . . DLB-150

Niles, Hezekiah 1777-1839 . . . . DLB-43

Nims, John Frederick 1913- DLB-5

Nin, Anaïs 1903-1977 . . . . . DLB-2, 4, 152

1985: The Year of the Mystery:
A Symposium Y-85

Nissenson, Hugh 1933- DLB-28

Niven, Frederick John 1878-1944 . . . . DLB-92

Niven, Larry 1938- DLB-8

Nizan, Paul 1905-1940 . . . . DLB-72

Njegoš, Petar II Petrović
1813-1851 . . . . DLB-147

Nkosi, Lewis 1936- DLB-157

Nobel Peace Prize

The 1986 Nobel Peace Prize
Nobel Lecture 1986: Hope, Despair and Memory
Tributes from Abraham Bernstein,
Norman Lamm, and
John R. Silber Y-86

The Nobel Prize and Literary Politics . . . Y-86

Nobel Prize in Literature

The 1982 Nobel Prize in Literature
Announcement by the Swedish Academy
of the Nobel Prize Nobel Lecture 1982:
The Solitude of Latin America Excerpt
from *One Hundred Years of Solitude* The
Magical World of Macondo A Tribute
to Gabriel García Márquez. Y-82

The 1983 Nobel Prize in Literature
Announcement by the Swedish Academy No-
bel Lecture 1983 The Stature of
William Golding Y-83

The 1984 Nobel Prize in Literature
Announcement by the Swedish Academy
Jaroslav Seifert Through the Eyes of the
English-Speaking Reader
Three Poems by Jaroslav Seifert Y-84

The 1985 Nobel Prize in Literature
Announcement by the Swedish Academy
Nobel Lecture 1985 . . . . Y-85

The 1986 Nobel Prize in Literature
Nobel Lecture 1986: This Past Must Address
Its Present Y-86

The 1987 Nobel Prize in Literature
Nobel Lecture 1987 . . . . Y-87

The 1988 Nobel Prize in Literature
Nobel Lecture 1988 . . . . Y-88

The 1989 Nobel Prize in Literature
Nobel Lecture 1989 . . . . Y-89

The 1990 Nobel Prize in Literature
Nobel Lecture 1990 . . . . Y-90

The 1991 Nobel Prize in Literature
Nobel Lecture 1991 . . . . Y-91

The 1992 Nobel Prize in Literature
Nobel Lecture 1992 . . . . Y-92

The 1993 Nobel Prize in Literature
Nobel Lecture 1993 . . . . Y-93

The 1994 Nobel Prize in Literature
Nobel Lecture 1994 . . . . Y-94

The 1995 Nobel Prize in Literature
Nobel Lecture 1995 . . . . Y-95

Nodier, Charles 1780-1844 . . . . DLB-119

Noel, Roden 1834-1894 . . . . DLB-35

Nogami, Yaeko 1885-1985 . . . . DLB-180

Nogo, Rajko Petrov 1945- DLB-181

Nolan, William F. 1928- DLB-8

Noland, C. F. M. 1810?-1858 . . . . . . DLB-11

Noma, Hiroshi 1915-1991 . . . . DLB-182

Nonesuch Press DLB-112

Noonday Press DLB-46

Noone, John 1936- DLB-14

Nora, Eugenio de 1923- DLB-134

Nordhoff, Charles 1887-1947 . . . . . . DLB-9

Norman, Charles 1904- DLB-111

Norman, Marsha 1947- Y-84

Norris, Charles G. 1881-1945 . . . . DLB-9

Norris, Frank 1870-1902 . . . . . . DLB-12, 71

Norris, Leslie 1921- DLB-27

Norse, Harold 1916- DLB-16

North, Marianne 1830-1890 . . . . . . DLB-174

North Point Press DLB-46

Nortje, Arthur 1942-1970 . . . . DLB-125

Norton, Alice Mary (see Norton, Andre)

Norton, Andre 1912- DLB-8, 52

Norton, Andrews 1786-1853 . . . . DLB-1

Norton, Caroline 1808-1877 . . . . DLB-21, 159

Norton, Charles Eliot 1827-1908 . . . DLB-1, 64

Norton, John 1606-1663 . . . . DLB-24

Norton, Mary 1903-1992 . . . . DLB-160

Norton, Thomas (see Sackville, Thomas)

Norton, W. W., and Company DLB-46

Norwood, Robert 1874-1932 . . . . . . DLB-92

Nosaka, Akiyuki 1930- DLB-182

Nossack, Hans Erich 1901-1977 . . . . DLB-69

Notker Balbulus circa 840-912 . . . . . DLB-148

Notker III of Saint Gall
circa 950-1022 . . . . DLB-148

Notker von Zweifalten ?-1095 . . . . . DLB-148

A Note on Technique (1926), by
Elizabeth A. Drew [excerpts] DLB-36

Nourse, Alan E. 1928- DLB-8

Novak, Slobodan 1924- DLB-181

Novak, Vjenceslav 1859-1905 . . . . . DLB-147

Novalis 1772-1801 . . . . DLB-90

Novaro, Mario 1868-1944 . . . . DLB-114

Novás Calvo, Lino 1903-1983 . . . . . DLB-145

"The Novel in [Robert Browning's] 'The Ring
and the Book' " (1912), by
Henry James DLB-32

The Novel of Impressionism,
by Jethro Bithell DLB-66

Novel-Reading: The Works of Charles Dickens,
The Works of W. Makepeace Thackeray
(1879), by Anthony Trollope DLB-21

The Novels of Dorothy Richardson (1918),
by May Sinclair DLB-36

Novels with a Purpose (1864), by
Justin M'Carthy DLB-21

Noventa, Giacomo 1898-1960 . . . . . DLB-114

Novikov, Nikolai Ivanovich
1744-1818 . . . . DLB-150

Nowlan, Alden 1933-1983 . . . . DLB-53

Noyes, Alfred 1880-1958 . . . . DLB-20

Noyes, Crosby S. 1825-1908 . . . . . . DLB-23

Noyes, Nicholas 1647-1717 . . . . DLB-24

Noyes, Theodore W. 1858-1946 . . . . DLB-29

N-Town Plays circa 1468 to early
sixteenth century DLB-146

Nugent, Frank 1908-1965 . . . . DLB-44

Nugent, Richard Bruce 1906- DLB-151

Nušić, Branislav 1864-1938 . . . . . . DLB-147

Nutt, David [publishing house] DLB-106

Nwapa, Flora 1931- DLB-125

Nye, Edgar Wilson (Bill)
1850-1896 . . . . DLB-11, 23

Nye, Naomi Shihab 1952- DLB-120

Nye, Robert 1939- DLB-14

O

Oakes, Urian circa 1631-1681 . . . . . DLB-24

Oates, Joyce Carol
1938- DLB-2, 5, 130; Y-81

Ōba, Minako 1930- DLB-182

Ober, William 1920-1993 . . . . Y-93

Oberholtzer, Ellis Paxson
1868-1936 . . . . DLB-47

Obradović, Dositej 1740?-1811 . . . . . DLB-147

O'Brien, Edna 1932- DLB-14

O'Brien, Fitz-James 1828-1862 . . . . . DLB-74

O'Brien, Kate 1897-1974 . . . . DLB-15

O'Brien, Tim
1946- DLB-152; Y-80; DS-9

O'Casey, Sean 1880-1964 . . . . DLB-10

Occom, Samson 1723-1792 . . . . . . DLB-175

Ochs, Adolph S. 1858-1935 . . . . . . DLB-25

Ochs-Oakes, George Washington
1861-1931 . . . . DLB-137

O'Connor, Flannery
1925-1964 . . . . . DLB-2, 152; Y-80; DS-12

O'Connor, Frank 1903-1966 . . . . . . DLB-162

Octopus Publishing Group DLB-112

Oda, Sakunosuke 1913-1947 . . . . . . DLB-182

Odell, Jonathan 1737-1818 . . . . . . DLB-31, 99

O'Dell, Scott 1903-1989 . . . . DLB-52

Odets, Clifford 1906-1963 . . . . DLB-7, 26

Odhams Press Limited DLB-112

O'Donnell, Peter 1920- DLB-87

O'Donovan, Michael (see O'Connor, Frank)

Ōe, Kenzaburō 1935- DLB-182

O'Faolain, Julia 1932- DLB-14

O'Faolain, Sean 1900- DLB-15, 162

Off Broadway and Off-Off Broadway . . DLB-7

Off-Loop Theatres DLB-7

Offord, Carl Ruthven 1910- DLB-76

O'Flaherty, Liam
1896-1984 . . . . DLB-36, 162; Y-84

Ogilvie, J. S., and Company DLB-49

Ogot, Grace 1930- DLB-125

O'Grady, Desmond 1935- DLB-40

Ogunyemi, Wale 1939- DLB-157

O'Hagan, Howard 1902-1982 . . . . . DLB-68

O'Hara, Frank 1926-1966 . . . . DLB-5, 16

O'Hara, John 1905-1970 . . . . DLB-9, 86; DS-2

Okara, Gabriel 1921- DLB-125

O'Keeffe, John 1747-1833 . . . . DLB-89

Okes, Nicholas
[publishing house] DLB-170

Okigbo, Christopher 1930-1967 . . . . DLB-125

Okot p'Bitek 1931-1982 . . . . DLB-125

Okpewho, Isidore 1941- DLB-157

Okri, Ben 1959- DLB-157

Olaudah Equiano and Unfinished Journeys:
The Slave-Narrative Tradition and
Twentieth-Century Continuities, by
Paul Edwards and Pauline T.
Wangman DLB-117

Old English Literature:
An Introduction DLB-146

Old English Riddles
eighth to tenth centuries DLB-146

Old Franklin Publishing House DLB-49

Old German Genesis and Old German Exodus
circa 1050-circa 1130 . . . . DLB-148

Old High German Charms and
Blessings DLB-148

The Old High German Isidor
circa 790-800 . . . . DLB-148

Older, Fremont 1856-1935 . . . . DLB-25

Oldham, John 1653-1683 . . . . DLB-131

Olds, Sharon 1942- DLB-120

Olearius, Adam 1599-1671 . . . . DLB-164

Oliphant, Laurence
1829?-1888 . . . . DLB-18, 166

Oliphant, Margaret 1828-1897 . . . . . DLB-18

Oliver, Chad 1928- DLB-8

Oliver, Mary 1935- DLB-5

Ollier, Claude 1922- DLB-83

Olsen, Tillie 1913?- DLB-28; Y-80

Olson, Charles 1910-1970 . . . . DLB-5, 16

Olson, Elder 1909- DLB-48, 63

Omotoso, Kole 1943- DLB-125

"On Art in Fiction " (1838),
by Edward Bulwer DLB-21

On Learning to Write Y-88

On Some of the Characteristics of Modern
Poetry and On the Lyrical Poems of
Alfred Tennyson (1831), by Arthur
Henry Hallam DLB-32

"On Style in English Prose" (1898), by
Frederic Harrison DLB-57

"On Style in Literature: Its Technical
Elements" (1885), by Robert Louis
Stevenson DLB-57

"On the Writing of Essays" (1862),
by Alexander Smith DLB-57

Ondaatje, Michael 1943- DLB-60

O'Neill, Eugene 1888-1953 . . . . DLB-7

Onetti, Juan Carlos 1909-1994 . . . . . DLB-113

Onions, George Oliver
1872-1961 . . . . DLB-153

Onofri, Arturo 1885-1928 . . . . DLB-114

Opie, Amelia 1769-1853 . . . . . DLB-116, 159

Opitz, Martin 1597-1639 . . . . DLB-164

Oppen, George 1908-1984 . . . . . DLB-5, 165

Oppenheim, E. Phillips 1866-1946 . . . . DLB-70

Oppenheim, James 1882-1932 . . . . . . DLB-28

Oppenheimer, Joel 1930- DLB-5

Optic, Oliver (see Adams, William Taylor)

Orczy, Emma, Baroness
1865-1947 . . . . DLB-70

Origo, Iris 1902-1988 . . . . DLB-155

Orlovitz, Gil 1918-1973 . . . . DLB-2, 5

Orlovsky, Peter 1933- DLB-16

Ormond, John 1923- DLB-27

Ornitz, Samuel 1890-1957 . . . . . DLB-28, 44

Ortese, Anna Maria 1914- DLB-177

Ortiz, Simon J. 1941- DLB-120, 175

Ortnit and *Wolfdietrich*
circa 1225-1250 . . . . DLB-138

Orton, Joe 1933-1967 . . . . DLB-13

Orwell, George 1903-1950 . . . . . DLB-15, 98

The Orwell Year Y-84

Ory, Carlos Edmundo de 1923- . . . DLB-134

Osbey, Brenda Marie 1957- DLB-120

Osbon, B. S. 1827-1912 . . . . DLB-43

Osborne, John 1929-1994 . . . . DLB-13

Osgood, Herbert L. 1855-1918 . . . . . DLB-47

Osgood, James R., and
Company DLB-49

Osgood, McIlvaine and
Company DLB-112

O'Shaughnessy, Arthur
1844-1881 . . . . DLB-35

O'Shea, Patrick
[publishing house] DLB-49

Osipov, Nikolai Petrovich
1751-1799 . . . . DLB-150

Oskison, John Milton 1879-1947 . . . . DLB-175

Osofisan, Femi 1946- DLB-125

Ostenso, Martha 1900-1963 . . . . DLB-92

Ostriker, Alicia 1937- DLB-120

Osundare, Niyi 1947- DLB-157

Oswald, Eleazer 1755-1795 . . . . DLB-43

Oswald von Wolkenstein
1376 or 1377-1445 . . . . DLB-179

Otero, Blas de 1916-1979 . . . . DLB-134

Otero, Miguel Antonio
1859-1944 . . . . DLB-82

Otero Silva, Miguel 1908-1985 . . . . . DLB-145

Otfried von Weißenburg
circa 800-circa 875? DLB-148

Otis, James (see Kaler, James Otis)

Otis, James, Jr. 1725-1783 . . . . DLB-31

Otis, Broaders and Company DLB-49

Ottaway, James 1911- DLB-127

Ottendorfer, Oswald 1826-1900 . . . . . DLB-23

Ottieri, Ottiero 1924- DLB-177

Otto-Peters, Louise 1819-1895 . . . . . DLB-129

Otway, Thomas 1652-1685 . . . . DLB-80

Ouellette, Fernand 1930- DLB-60

Ouida 1839-1908 . . . . DLB-18, 156

Outing Publishing Company DLB-46

Outlaw Days, by Joyce Johnson DLB-16

Overbury, Sir Thomas
circa 1581-1613 . . . . DLB-151

The Overlook Press DLB-46

Overview of U.S. Book Publishing,
1910-1945 . . . . DLB-9

Owen, Guy 1925- DLB-5

Owen, John 1564-1622 . . . . DLB-121

Owen, John [publishing house] DLB-49

Owen, Robert 1771-1858 . . . . . DLB-107, 158

Owen, Wilfred 1893-1918 . . . . DLB-20

Owen, Peter, Limited DLB-112

The Owl and the Nightingale
circa 1189-1199 . . . . DLB-146

Owsley, Frank L. 1890-1956 . . . . . . DLB-17

Oxford, Seventeenth Earl of, Edward de Vere
1550-1604 . . . . DLB-172

Ozerov, Vladislav Aleksandrovich
1769-1816 . . . . DLB-150

Ozick, Cynthia 1928- DLB-28, 152; Y-82

P

Pace, Richard 1482?-1536 . . . . DLB-167

Pacey, Desmond 1917-1975 . . . . . . DLB-88

Pack, Robert 1929- DLB-5

Packaging Papa: *The Garden of Eden* Y-86

Padell Publishing Company DLB-46

Padgett, Ron 1942- DLB-5

Padilla, Ernesto Chávez 1944- DLB-122

Page, L. C., and Company DLB-49

Page, P. K. 1916- DLB-68

Page, Thomas Nelson
1853-1922 . . . . DLB-12, 78; DS-13

Page, Walter Hines 1855-1918 . . . . DLB-71, 91

Paget, Francis Edward
1806-1882 . . . . DLB-163

Paget, Violet (see Lee, Vernon)

Pagliarani, Elio 1927- DLB-128

Pain, Barry 1864-1928 . . . . DLB-135

Pain, Philip ?-circa 1666 . . . . DLB-24

Paine, Robert Treat, Jr. 1773-1811 . . . DLB-37

Paine, Thomas
1737-1809 . . . . DLB-31, 43, 73, 158

Painter, George D. 1914- DLB-155

Painter, William 1540?-1594 . . . . . . DLB-136

Palazzeschi, Aldo 1885-1974 . . . . . . DLB-114

Paley, Grace 1922- DLB-28

Palfrey, John Gorham
1796-1881 . . . . DLB-1, 30

Palgrave, Francis Turner
1824-1897 . . . . DLB-35

Palmer, Joe H. 1904-1952 . . . . DLB-171

Palmer, Michael 1943- DLB-169

Paltock, Robert 1697-1767 . . . . DLB-39

Pan Books Limited DLB-112

Panama, Norman 1914- and
Frank, Melvin 1913-1988 . . . . . . DLB-26

Pancake, Breece D'J 1952-1979 . . . . . DLB-130

Panero, Leopoldo 1909-1962 . . . . . . DLB-108

Pangborn, Edgar 1909-1976 . . . . . . DLB-8

"Panic Among the Philistines": A Postscript,
An Interview with Bryan Griffin Y-81

Panneton, Philippe (see Ringuet)

Panshin, Alexei 1940- DLB-8

Pansy (see Alden, Isabella)

Pantheon Books DLB-46

Paperback Library DLB-46

Paperback Science Fiction DLB-8

Paquet, Alfons 1881-1944 . . . . DLB-66

Paracelsus 1493-1541 . . . . DLB-179

Paradis, Suzanne 1936- DLB-53

Pareja Diezcanseco, Alfredo
1908-1993 . . . . DLB-145

Pardoe, Julia 1804-1862 . . . . DLB-166

Parents' Magazine Press DLB-46

Parise, Goffredo 1929-1986 . . . . . . DLB-177

Parisian Theater, Fall 1984: Toward
A New Baroque Y-85

Parizeau, Alice 1930- DLB-60

Parke, John 1754-1789 . . . . DLB-31

Parker, Dorothy
1893-1967 . . . . DLB-11, 45, 86

Parker, Gilbert 1860-1932 . . . . DLB-99

Parker, James 1714-1770 . . . . DLB-43

Parker, Theodore 1810-1860 . . . . DLB-1

Parker, William Riley 1906-1968 . . . . DLB-103

Parker, J. H. [publishing house] DLB-106

Parker, John [publishing house] DLB-106

Parkman, Francis, Jr.
1823-1893 . . . . DLB-1, 30, 183

Parks, Gordon 1912- DLB-33

Parks, William 1698-1750 . . . . DLB-43

Parks, William [publishing house] DLB-49

Parley, Peter (see Goodrich, Samuel Griswold)

Parmenides late sixth-fifth century B.C.
. . . . DLB-176

Parnell, Thomas 1679-1718 . . . . DLB-95

Parr, Catherine 1513?-1548 . . . . DLB-136

Parrington, Vernon L.
1871-1929 . . . . DLB-17, 63

Parronchi, Alessandro 1914- DLB-128

Partridge, S. W., and Company DLB-106

Parton, James 1822-1891 . . . . DLB-30

Parton, Sara Payson Willis
1811-1872 . . . . DLB-43, 74

Parun, Vesna 1922- DLB-181

Pasinetti, Pier Maria 1913- DLB-177

Pasolini, Pier Paolo 1922- DLB-128, 177

Pastan, Linda 1932- DLB-5

Paston, George 1860-1936 . . . . DLB-149

The Paston Letters 1422-1509 . . . . . . DLB-146

Pastorius, Francis Daniel
1651-circa 1720 . . . . DLB-24

Patchen, Kenneth 1911-1972 . . . . DLB-16, 48

Pater, Walter 1839-1894 . . . . . DLB-57, 156

Paterson, Katherine 1932- DLB-52

Patmore, Coventry 1823-1896 . . . . DLB-35, 98

Paton, Joseph Noel 1821-1901 . . . . . DLB-35

Paton Walsh, Jill 1937- DLB-161

Patrick, Edwin Hill ("Ted")
1901-1964 . . . . DLB-137

Patrick, John 1906- DLB-7

Pattee, Fred Lewis 1863-1950 . . . . . DLB-71

Pattern and Paradigm: History as
Design, by Judith Ryan DLB-75

Patterson, Alicia 1906-1963 . . . . . . DLB-127

Patterson, Eleanor Medill
1881-1948 . . . . DLB-29

Patterson, Eugene 1923- DLB-127

Patterson, Joseph Medill
1879-1946 . . . . DLB-29

Pattillo, Henry 1726-1801 . . . . DLB-37

Paul, Elliot 1891-1958 . . . . DLB-4

Paul, Jean (see Richter, Johann Paul Friedrich)

Paul, Kegan, Trench, Trubner and Company
Limited DLB-106

Paul, Peter, Book Company DLB-49

Paul, Stanley, and Company
Limited DLB-112

Paulding, James Kirke
1778-1860 . . . . DLB-3, 59, 74

Paulin, Tom 1949- DLB-40

Pauper, Peter, Press DLB-46

Pavese, Cesare 1908-1950 . . . . DLB-128, 177

Pavić, Milorad 1929- DLB-181

Pavlov, Konstantin 1933- DLB-181

Pavlović, Miodrag 1928- DLB-181

Paxton, John 1911-1985 . . . . DLB-44

Payn, James 1830-1898 . . . . DLB-18

Payne, John 1842-1916 . . . . DLB-35

Payne, John Howard 1791-1852 . . . . DLB-37

Payson and Clarke DLB-46

Peabody, Elizabeth Palmer
1804-1894 . . . . DLB-1

Peabody, Elizabeth Palmer
[publishing house] DLB-49

Peabody, Oliver William Bourn
1799-1848 . . . . DLB-59

Peace, Roger 1899-1968 . . . . DLB-127

Peacham, Henry 1578-1644? DLB-151

Peacham, Henry, the Elder
1547-1634 . . . . DLB-172

Peachtree Publishers, Limited DLB-46

Peacock, Molly 1947- DLB-120

Peacock, Thomas Love
1785-1866 . . . . DLB-96, 116

Pead, Deuel ?-1727 . . . . DLB-24

Peake, Mervyn 1911-1968 . . . . . DLB-15, 160

Peale, Rembrandt 1778-1860 . . . . . DLB-183

Pear Tree Press DLB-112

Pearce, Philippa 1920- DLB-161

Pearson, H. B. [publishing house] DLB-49

Pearson, Hesketh 1887-1964 . . . . . . DLB-149

Peck, George W. 1840-1916 . . . . DLB-23, 42

Peck, H. C., and Theo. Bliss
[publishing house] DLB-49

Peck, Harry Thurston
1856-1914 . . . . DLB-71, 91

Peele, George 1556-1596 . . . . . DLB-62, 167

Pegler, Westbrook 1894-1969 . . . . . DLB-171

Pekić, Borislav 1930-1992 . . . . DLB-181

Pellegrini and Cudahy DLB-46

Pelletier, Aimé (see Vac, Bertrand)

Pemberton, Sir Max 1863-1950 . . . . DLB-70

Penguin Books [U.S.] DLB-46

Penguin Books [U.K.] DLB-112

Penn Publishing Company DLB-49

Penn, William 1644-1718 . . . . DLB-24

Penna, Sandro 1906-1977 . . . . DLB-114

Penner, Jonathan 1940- Y-83

Pennington, Lee 1939- Y-82

Pepys, Samuel 1633-1703 . . . . DLB-101

Percy, Thomas 1729-1811 . . . . DLB-104

Percy, Walker 1916-1990 . . . . DLB-2; Y-80, 90

Percy, William 1575-1648 . . . . DLB-172

Perec, Georges 1936-1982 . . . . DLB-83

Perelman, S. J. 1904-1979 . . . . . DLB-11, 44

Perez, Raymundo "Tigre"
1946- DLB-122

Peri Rossi, Cristina 1941- DLB-145

Periodicals of the Beat Generation DLB-16

Perkins, Eugene 1932- DLB-41

Perkoff, Stuart Z. 1930-1974 . . . . . . DLB-16

Perley, Moses Henry 1804-1862 . . . . DLB-99

Permabooks DLB-46

Perrin, Alice 1867-1934 . . . . DLB-156

Perry, Bliss 1860-1954 . . . . DLB-71

Perry, Eleanor 1915-1981 . . . . DLB-44

Perry, Matthew 1794-1858 . . . . DLB-183

Perry, Sampson 1747-1823 . . . . DLB-158

"Personal Style" (1890), by John Addington
Symonds DLB-57

Perutz, Leo 1882-1957 . . . . DLB-81

Pesetsky, Bette 1932- DLB-130

Pestalozzi, Johann Heinrich
1746-1827 . . . . DLB-94

Peter, Laurence J. 1919-1990 . . . . . . DLB-53

Peter of Spain circa 1205-1277 . . . . . DLB-115

Peterkin, Julia 1880-1961 . . . . DLB-9

Peters, Lenrie 1932- DLB-117

Peters, Robert 1924- DLB-105

Peters, Robert, Foreword to
Ludwig of Bavaria DLB-105

Petersham, Maud 1889-1971 and
Petersham, Miska 1888-1960 . . . . . DLB-22

Peterson, Charles Jacobs
1819-1887 . . . . DLB-79

Peterson, Len 1917- DLB-88

Peterson, Louis 1922- DLB-76

Peterson, T. B., and Brothers DLB-49

Petitclair, Pierre 1813-1860 . . . . . . DLB-99

Petrov, Aleksandar 1938- DLB-181

Petrov, Gavriil 1730-1801 . . . . DLB-150

Petrov, Vasilii Petrovich
1736-1799 . . . . DLB-150

Petrov, Valeri 1920- DLB-181

Petrović, Rastko 1898-1949 . . . . . . DLB-147

Petruslied circa 854? DLB-148

Petry, Ann 1908- DLB-76

Pettie, George circa 1548-1589 . . . . . DLB-136

Peyton, K. M. 1929- DLB-161

Pfaffe Konrad
  flourished circa 1172 . . . . DLB-148

Pfaffe Lamprecht
  flourished circa 1150 . . . . DLB-148

Pforzheimer, Carl H. 1879-1957 . . . . DLB-140

Phaer, Thomas 1510?-1560 . . . . . . DLB-167

Phaidon Press Limited. DLB-112

Pharr, Robert Deane 1916-1992 . . . . . DLB-33

Phelps, Elizabeth Stuart
  1844-1911 . . . . DLB-74

Philander von der Linde
  (see Mencke, Johann Burckhard)

Philip, Marlene Nourbese
  1947- DLB-157

Philippe, Charles-Louis
  1874-1909 . . . . DLB-65

Philips, John 1676-1708 . . . . DLB-95

Philips, Katherine 1632-1664 . . . . . DLB-131

Phillips, Caryl 1958- DLB-157

Phillips, David Graham
  1867-1911 . . . . DLB-9, 12

Phillips, Jayne Anne 1952- Y-80

Phillips, Robert 1938- DLB-105

Phillips, Robert, Finding, Losing,
  Reclaiming: A Note on My
  Poems DLB-105

Phillips, Stephen 1864-1915 . . . . DLB-10

Phillips, Ulrich B. 1877-1934 . . . . . . DLB-17

Phillips, Willard 1784-1873 . . . . DLB-59

Phillips, William 1907- DLB-137

Phillips, Sampson and Company. DLB-49

Phillpotts, Eden
  1862-1960 . . . . . . DLB-10, 70, 135, 153

Philo circa 20-15 B.C.-circa A.D. 50
  . . . . DLB-176

Philosophical Library DLB-46

"The Philosophy of Style" (1852), by
  Herbert Spencer. DLB-57

Phinney, Elihu [publishing house] DLB-49

Phoenix, John (see Derby, George Horatio)

PHYLON (Fourth Quarter, 1950),
  The Negro in Literature:
  The Current Scene DLB-76

Physiologus
  circa 1070-circa 1150 . . . . DLB-148

Piccolo, Lucio 1903-1969 . . . . DLB-114

Pickard, Tom 1946- DLB-40

Pickering, William
  [publishing house] DLB-106

Pickthall, Marjorie 1883-1922 . . . . . . DLB-92

Pictorial Printing Company. DLB-49

Piel, Gerard 1915- DLB-137

Piercy, Marge 1936- DLB-120

Pierro, Albino 1916- DLB-128

Pignotti, Lamberto 1926- DLB-128

Pike, Albert 1809-1891 . . . . DLB-74

Pike, Zebulon Montgomery 1779-1813 . . DLB-183

Pilon, Jean-Guy 1930- DLB-60

Pinckney, Josephine 1895-1957 . . . . . DLB-6

Pindar circa 518 B.C.-circa 438 B.C.
  . . . . DLB-176

Pindar, Peter (see Wolcot, John)

Pinero, Arthur Wing 1855-1934 . . . . . DLB-10

Pinget, Robert 1919- DLB-83

Pinnacle Books DLB-46

Piñon, Nélida 1935- DLB-145

Pinsky, Robert 1940- Y-82

Pinter, Harold 1930- DLB-13

Piontek, Heinz 1925- DLB-75

Piozzi, Hester Lynch [Thrale]
  1741-1821. . . . . DLB-104, 142

Piper, H. Beam 1904-1964. . . . . . . DLB-8

Piper, Watty. DLB-22

Pirckheimer, Caritas 1467-1532 . . . . . DLB-179

Pirckheimer, Willibald
  1470-1530 . . . . DLB-179

Pisar, Samuel 1929- Y-83

Pitkin, Timothy 1766-1847 . . . . DLB-30

The Pitt Poetry Series: Poetry Publishing Today
  . . . . Y-85

Pitter, Ruth 1897- DLB-20

Pix, Mary 1666-1709 . . . . DLB-80

Plaatje, Sol T. 1876-1932 . . . . DLB-125

The Place of Realism in Fiction (1895), by
  George Gissing DLB-18

Plante, David 1940- Y-83

Platen, August von 1796-1835 . . . . . DLB-90

Plath, Sylvia 1932-1963 . . . . . DLB-5, 6, 152

Plato circa 428 B.C.-348-347 B.C.
  . . . . DLB-176

Platon 1737-1812. . . . . DLB-150

Platt and Munk Company DLB-46

Playboy Press DLB-46

Playford, John
  [publishing house] DLB-170

Plays, Playwrights, and Playgoers DLB-84

Playwrights and Professors, by
  Tom Stoppard DLB-13

Playwrights on the Theater DLB-80

Der Pleier flourished circa 1250 . . . . DLB-138

Plenzdorf, Ulrich 1934- DLB-75

Plessen, Elizabeth 1944- DLB-75

Plievier, Theodor 1892-1955 . . . . . . DLB-69

Plomer, William 1903-1973 . . . . DLB-20, 162

Plotinus 204-270 . . . . DLB-176

Plumly, Stanley 1939- DLB-5

Plumpp, Sterling D. 1940- DLB-41

Plunkett, James 1920- DLB-14

Plutarch circa 46-circa 120 . . . . . . DLB-176

Plymell, Charles 1935- DLB-16

Pocket Books DLB-46

Poe, Edgar Allan
  1809-1849 . . . . DLB-3, 59, 73, 74

Poe, James 1921-1980. . . . . DLB-44

The Poet Laureate of the United States
  Statements from Former Consultants
  in Poetry Y-86

Pohl, Frederik 1919- DLB-8

Poirier, Louis (see Gracq, Julien)

Polanyi, Michael 1891-1976 . . . . . . DLB-100

Pole, Reginald 1500-1558 . . . . DLB-132

Poliakoff, Stephen 1952- DLB-13

Polidori, John William
  1795-1821 . . . . DLB-116

Polite, Carlene Hatcher 1932- DLB-33

Pollard, Edward A. 1832-1872 . . . . . DLB-30

Pollard, Percival 1869-1911 . . . . . . DLB-71

Pollard and Moss. DLB-49

Pollock, Sharon 1936- DLB-60

Polonsky, Abraham 1910- DLB-26

Polotsky, Simeon 1629-1680. . . . . . DLB-150

Polybius circa 200 B.C.-118 B.C.. . . . DLB-176

Pomilio, Mario 1921-1990. . . . . . . DLB-177

Ponce, Mary Helen 1938- DLB-122

Ponce-Montoya, Juanita 1949- DLB-122

Ponet, John 1516?-1556 . . . . DLB-132

Poniatowski, Elena 1933- DLB-113

Ponsonby, William
  [publishing house] DLB-170

Pony Stories DLB-160

Poole, Ernest 1880-1950 . . . . DLB-9

Poole, Sophia 1804-1891. . . . . DLB-166

Poore, Benjamin Perley
  1820-1887 . . . . DLB-23

Popa, Vasko 1922-1991 . . . . DLB-181

Pope, Abbie Hanscom
  1858-1894 . . . . DLB-140

Pope, Alexander 1688-1744 . . . . . DLB-95, 101

Popov, Mikhail Ivanovich
  1742-circa 1790 . . . . DLB-150

Popović, Aleksandar 1929-1996 . . . . DLB-181

Popular Library DLB-46

Porlock, Martin (see MacDonald, Philip)

Porpoise Press DLB-112

Porta, Antonio 1935-1989 . . . . DLB-128

Porter, Anna Maria
  1780-1832. . . . . DLB-116, 159

Porter, David 1780-1843. . . . . DLB-183

Porter, Eleanor H. 1868-1920 . . . . . . DLB-9

Porter, Gene Stratton (see Stratton-Porter, Gene)

Porter, Henry ?-? DLB-62

Porter, Jane 1776-1850 . . . . . . DLB-116, 159

Porter, Katherine Anne
1890-1980. . . . DLB-4, 9, 102; Y-80; DS-12

Porter, Peter 1929- DLB-40

Porter, William Sydney
1862-1910. . . . . DLB-12, 78, 79

Porter, William T. 1809-1858 . . . . . DLB-3, 43

Porter and Coates DLB-49

Portis, Charles 1933- DLB-6

Posey, Alexander 1873-1908 . . . . . . DLB-175

Postans, Marianne
circa 1810-1865 . . . . DLB-166

Postl, Carl (see Sealsfield, Carl)

Poston, Ted 1906-1974 . . . . DLB-51

Postscript to [the Third Edition of] *Clarissa*
(1751), by Samuel Richardson . . . DLB-39

Potok, Chaim 1929- DLB-28, 152; Y-84

Potter, Beatrix 1866-1943 . . . . DLB-141

Potter, David M. 1910-1971 . . . . . . DLB-17

Potter, John E., and Company DLB-49

Pottle, Frederick A.
1897-1987 . . . . DLB-103; Y-87

Poulin, Jacques 1937- DLB-60

Pound, Ezra 1885-1972 . . DLB-4, 45, 63; DS-15

Povich, Shirley 1905- DLB-171

Powell, Anthony 1905- DLB-15

Powers, J. F. 1917- DLB-130

Pownall, David 1938- DLB-14

Powys, John Cowper 1872-1963 . . . . DLB-15

Powys, Llewelyn 1884-1939 . . . . . . DLB-98

Powys, T. F. 1875-1953 . . . . . DLB-36, 162

Poynter, Nelson 1903-1978 . . . . . . DLB-127

The Practice of Biography: An Interview
with Stanley Weintraub Y-82

The Practice of Biography II: An Interview
with B. L. Reid Y-83

The Practice of Biography III: An Interview
with Humphrey Carpenter Y-84

The Practice of Biography IV: An Interview with
William Manchester Y-85

The Practice of Biography V: An Interview
with Justin Kaplan Y-86

The Practice of Biography VI: An Interview with
David Herbert Donald Y-87

The Practice of Biography VII: An Interview with
John Caldwell Guilds Y-92

The Practice of Biography VIII: An Interview
with Joan Mellen Y-94

The Practice of Biography IX: An Interview
with Michael Reynolds Y-95

Prados, Emilio 1899-1962 . . . . DLB-134

Praed, Winthrop Mackworth
1802-1839 . . . . DLB-96

Praeger Publishers DLB-46

Praetorius, Johannes 1630-1680 . . . . DLB-168

Pratolini, Vasco 1913—1991 . . . . . . DLB-177

Pratt, E. J. 1882-1964 . . . . DLB-92

Pratt, Samuel Jackson 1749-1814 . . . . DLB-39

Preface to *Alwyn* (1780), by
Thomas Holcroft DLB-39

Preface to *Colonel Jack* (1722), by
Daniel Defoe DLB-39

Preface to *Evelina* (1778), by
Fanny Burney DLB-39

Preface to *Ferdinand Count Fathom* (1753), by
Tobias Smollett DLB-39

Preface to *Incognita* (1692), by
William Congreve DLB-39

Preface to *Joseph Andrews* (1742), by
Henry Fielding DLB-39

Preface to *Moll Flanders* (1722), by
Daniel Defoe DLB-39

Preface to *Poems* (1853), by
Matthew Arnold DLB-32

Preface to *Robinson Crusoe* (1719), by
Daniel Defoe DLB-39

Preface to *Roderick Random* (1748), by
Tobias Smollett DLB-39

Preface to *Roxana* (1724), by
Daniel Defoe DLB-39

Preface to *St. Leon* (1799), by
William Godwin DLB-39

Preface to Sarah Fielding's *Familiar Letters*
(1747), by Henry Fielding
[excerpt] DLB-39

Preface to Sarah Fielding's *The Adventures of
David Simple* (1744), by
Henry Fielding DLB-39

Preface to *The Cry* (1754), by
Sarah Fielding DLB-39

Preface to *The Delicate Distress* (1769), by
Elizabeth Griffin DLB-39

Preface to *The Disguis'd Prince* (1733), by
Eliza Haywood [excerpt] DLB-39

Preface to *The Farther Adventures of Robinson
Crusoe* (1719), by Daniel Defoe . . . DLB-39

Preface to the First Edition of *Pamela* (1740), by
Samuel Richardson DLB-39

Preface to the First Edition of *The Castle of
Otranto* (1764), by
Horace Walpole DLB-39

Preface to *The History of Romances* (1715), by
Pierre Daniel Huet [excerpts] DLB-39

Preface to *The Life of Charlotta du Pont* (1723),
by Penelope Aubin DLB-39

Preface to *The Old English Baron* (1778), by
Clara Reeve DLB-39

Preface to the Second Edition of *The Castle of
Otranto* (1765), by Horace
Walpole DLB-39

Preface to *The Secret History, of Queen Zarah,
and the Zarazians* (1705), by Delariviere
Manley DLB-39

Preface to the Third Edition of *Clarissa* (1751),
by Samuel Richardson
[excerpt] DLB-39

Preface to *The Works of Mrs. Davys* (1725), by
Mary Davys DLB-39

Preface to Volume 1 of *Clarissa* (1747), by
Samuel Richardson DLB-39

Preface to Volume 3 of *Clarissa* (1748), by
Samuel Richardson DLB-39

Préfontaine, Yves 1937- DLB-53

Prelutsky, Jack 1940- DLB-61

Premisses, by Michael Hamburger DLB-66

Prentice, George D. 1802-1870 . . . . . DLB-43

Prentice-Hall DLB-46

Prescott, Orville 1906-1996 . . . . Y-96

Prescott, William Hickling
1796-1859 . . . . DLB-1, 30, 59

The Present State of the English Novel (1892),
by George Saintsbury DLB-18

Prešeren, Francè 1800-1849 . . . . . . DLB-147

Preston, Thomas 1537-1598 . . . . . . DLB-62

Price, Reynolds 1933- DLB-2

Price, Richard 1723-1791 . . . . DLB-158

Price, Richard 1949- Y-81

Priest, Christopher 1943- DLB-14

Priestley, J. B. 1894-1984
. . . . . . DLB-10, 34, 77, 100, 139; Y-84

Primary Bibliography: A
Retrospective Y-95

Prime, Benjamin Young 1733-1791 . . . DLB-31

Primrose, Diana
floruit circa 1630 . . . . DLB-126

Prince, F. T. 1912- DLB-20

Prince, Thomas 1687-1758 . . . . . DLB-24, 140

The Principles of Success in Literature (1865), by
George Henry Lewes [excerpt] . . . DLB-57

Printz, Wolfgang Casper
1641-1717 . . . . DLB-168

Prior, Matthew 1664-1721 . . . . DLB-95

Prisco, Michele 1920- DLB-177

Pritchard, William H. 1932- DLB-111

Pritchett, V. S. 1900- DLB-15, 139

Procter, Adelaide Anne 1825-1864 . . . . DLB-32

Procter, Bryan Waller
1787-1874 . . . . DLB-96, 144

The Profession of Authorship:
Scribblers for Bread Y-89

The Progress of Romance (1785), by Clara Reeve
[excerpt] DLB-39

Prokopovich, Feofan 1681?-1736 . . . . DLB-150

Prokosch, Frederic 1906-1989 . . . . . DLB-48

The Proletarian Novel DLB-9

Propper, Dan 1937- DLB-16

The Prospect of Peace (1778), by
Joel Barlow DLB-37

Protagoras circa 490 B.C.-420 B.C.
. . . . DLB-176

Proud, Robert 1728-1813. . . . . DLB-30

Proust, Marcel 1871-1922. . . . . DLB-65

Prynne, J. H. 1936- DLB-40

Przybyszewski, Stanislaw
1868-1927 . . . . DLB-66

Pseudo-Dionysius the Areopagite floruit
circa 500 . . . . DLB-115

The Public Lending Right in America
Statement by Sen. Charles McC.
Mathias, Jr. PLR and the Meaning
of Literary Property Statements on
PLR by American Writers Y-83

The Public Lending Right in the United Kingdom
Public Lending Right: The First Year in the
United Kingdom Y-83

The Publication of English
Renaissance Plays. DLB-62

Publications and Social Movements
[Transcendentalism] DLB-1

Publishers and Agents: The Columbia
Connection Y-87

A Publisher's Archives: G. P. Putnam . . . Y-92

Publishing Fiction at LSU Press. Y-87

Pückler-Muskau, Hermann von
1785-1871 . . . . DLB-133

Pufendorf, Samuel von
1632-1694 . . . . DLB-168

Pugh, Edwin William 1874-1930 . . . . DLB-135

Pugin, A. Welby 1812-1852 . . . . DLB-55

Puig, Manuel 1932-1990. . . . . DLB-113

Pulitzer, Joseph 1847-1911 . . . . DLB-23

Pulitzer, Joseph, Jr. 1885-1955 . . . . . DLB-29

Pulitzer Prizes for the Novel,
1917-1945. . . . . DLB-9

Pulliam, Eugene 1889-1975 . . . . . . DLB-127

Purchas, Samuel 1577?-1626 . . . . . DLB-151

Purdy, Al 1918- DLB-88

Purdy, James 1923- DLB-2

Purdy, Ken W. 1913-1972 . . . . . . DLB-137

Pusey, Edward Bouverie
1800-1882 . . . . DLB-55

Putnam, George Palmer
1814-1872 . . . . DLB-3, 79

Putnam, Samuel 1892-1950 . . . . DLB-4

G. P. Putnam's Sons [U.S.] DLB-49

G. P. Putnam's Sons [U.K.] DLB-106

Puzo, Mario 1920- DLB-6

Pyle, Ernie 1900-1945. . . . . DLB-29

Pyle, Howard 1853-1911 . . . . DLB-42; DS-13

Pym, Barbara 1913-1980. . . . . DLB-14; Y-87

Pynchon, Thomas 1937- DLB-2, 173

Pyramid Books DLB-46

Pyrnelle, Louise-Clarke 1850-1907 . . . DLB-42

Pythagoras circa 570 B.C.-? DLB-176

Q

Quad, M. (see Lewis, Charles B.)

Quarles, Francis 1592-1644 . . . . . . DLB-126

The Quarterly Review
1809-1967 . . . . DLB-110

Quasimodo, Salvatore 1901-1968 . . . . DLB-114

Queen, Ellery (see Dannay, Frederic, and
Manfred B. Lee)

The Queen City Publishing House . . . DLB-49

Queneau, Raymond 1903-1976. . . . . DLB-72

Quennell, Sir Peter 1905-1993 . . . . DLB-155

Quesnel, Joseph 1746-1809 . . . . . . DLB-99

The Question of American Copyright
in the Nineteenth Century
Headnote
Preface, by George Haven Putnam
The Evolution of Copyright, by Brander
Matthews
Summary of Copyright Legislation in
the United States, by R. R. Bowker
Analysis of the Provisions of the
Copyright Law of 1891, by
George Haven Putnam
The Contest for International Copyright,
by George Haven Putnam
Cheap Books and Good Books,
by Brander Matthews. DLB-49

Quiller-Couch, Sir Arthur Thomas
1863-1944. . . . . DLB-135, 153

Quin, Ann 1936-1973. . . . . DLB-14

Quincy, Samuel, of Georgia ?-? DLB-31

Quincy, Samuel, of Massachusetts
1734-1789 . . . . DLB-31

Quinn, Anthony 1915- DLB-122

Quintana, Leroy V. 1944- DLB-82

Quintana, Miguel de 1671-1748
A Forerunner of Chicano
Literature. DLB-122

Quist, Harlin, Books DLB-46

Quoirez, Françoise (see Sagan, Françoise)

R

Raabe, Wilhelm 1831-1910 . . . . . . DLB-129

Rabe, David 1940- DLB-7

Raboni, Giovanni 1932-. DLB-128

Rachilde 1860-1953 . . . . DLB-123

Racin, Kočo 1908-1943 . . . . DLB-147

Rackham, Arthur 1867-1939 . . . . . DLB-141

Radcliffe, Ann 1764-1823 . . . . . DLB-39, 178

Raddall, Thomas 1903- DLB-68

Radichkov, Yordan 1929- DLB-181

Radiguet, Raymond 1903-1923. . . . . DLB-65

Radishchev, Aleksandr Nikolaevich
1749-1802 . . . . DLB-150

Radványi, Netty Reiling (see Seghers, Anna)

Rahv, Philip 1908-1973 . . . . DLB-137

Raičković, Stevan 1928- DLB-181

Raimund, Ferdinand Jakob
1790-1836 . . . . DLB-90

Raine, Craig 1944- DLB-40

Raine, Kathleen 1908- DLB-20

Rainolde, Richard
circa 1530-1606 . . . . DLB-136

Rakić, Milan 1876-1938 . . . . DLB-147

Ralegh, Sir Walter 1554?-1618 . . . . DLB-172

Ralin, Radoy 1923- DLB-181

Ralph, Julian 1853-1903. . . . . DLB-23

Ralph Waldo Emerson in 1982 . . . . . . Y-82

Ramat, Silvio 1939- DLB-128

Rambler, no. 4 (1750), by Samuel Johnson
[excerpt] DLB-39

Ramée, Marie Louise de la (see Ouida)

Ramírez, Sergío 1942- DLB-145

Ramke, Bin 1947- DLB-120

Ramler, Karl Wilhelm 1725-1798 . . . DLB-97

Ramon Ribeyro, Julio 1929- DLB-145

Ramous, Mario 1924-. DLB-128

Rampersad, Arnold 1941- DLB-111

Ramsay, Allan 1684 or 1685-1758. . . DLB-95

Ramsay, David 1749-1815 . . . . . . DLB-30

Ranck, Katherine Quintana
1942- DLB-122

Rand, Avery and Company DLB-49

Rand McNally and Company DLB-49

Randall, David Anton
1905-1975 . . . . DLB-140

Randall, Dudley 1914- DLB-41

Randall, Henry S. 1811-1876. . . . . DLB-30

Randall, James G. 1881-1953. . . . . DLB-17

The Randall Jarrell Symposium: A Small
Collection of Randall Jarrells
Excerpts From Papers Delivered at
the Randall Jarrell
Symposium. Y-86

Randolph, A. Philip 1889-1979. . . . . DLB-91

Randolph, Anson D. F.
[publishing house]. DLB-49

Randolph, Thomas 1605-1635 . . . DLB-58, 126

Random House DLB-46

Ranlet, Henry [publishing house] DLB-49

Ransom, John Crowe
1888-1974. . . . . DLB-45, 63

Ransome, Arthur 1884-1967. . . . . . DLB-160

Raphael, Frederic 1931- DLB-14

Raphaelson, Samson 1896-1983 . . . . DLB-44

Raskin, Ellen 1928-1984 . . . . DLB-52

Rastell, John 1475?-1536. . . . . . DLB-136, 170

Rattigan, Terence 1911-1977 . . . . . . DLB-13

Rawlings, Marjorie Kinnan
1896-1953 . . . . DLB-9, 22, 102

Raworth, Tom 1938- DLB-40

Ray, David 1932- DLB-5

Ray, Gordon Norton
1915-1986 . . . . DLB-103, 140

Ray, Henrietta Cordelia
1849-1916 . . . . DLB-50

Raymond, Henry J. 1820-1869 . . . DLB-43, 79

Raymond Chandler Centenary Tributes
from Michael Avallone, James Elroy, Joe
Gores,
and William F. Nolan Y-88

Reach, Angus 1821-1856 . . . . DLB-70

Read, Herbert 1893-1968 . . . . . DLB-20, 149

Read, Herbert, "The Practice of Biography," in
*The English Sense of Humour and Other
Essays* DLB-149

Read, Opie 1852-1939 . . . . DLB-23

Read, Piers Paul 1941- DLB-14

Reade, Charles 1814-1884 . . . . DLB-21

Reader's Digest Condensed
Books DLB-46

Reading, Peter 1946- DLB-40

Reading Series in New York City Y-96

Reaney, James 1926- DLB-68

Rebhun, Paul 1500?-1546 . . . . DLB-179

Rèbora, Clemente 1885-1957 . . . . . . DLB-114

Rechy, John 1934- DLB-122; Y-82

The Recovery of Literature: Criticism in the
1990s: A Symposium Y-91

Redding, J. Saunders
1906-1988 . . . . DLB-63, 76

Redfield, J. S. [publishing house] DLB-49

Redgrove, Peter 1932- DLB-40

Redmon, Anne 1943- Y-86

Redmond, Eugene B. 1937- DLB-41

Redpath, James [publishing house] . . . DLB-49

Reed, Henry 1808-1854 . . . . DLB-59

Reed, Henry 1914- DLB-27

Reed, Ishmael
1938- DLB-2, 5, 33, 169; DS-8

Reed, Sampson 1800-1880 . . . . DLB-1

Reed, Talbot Baines 1852-1893 . . . . DLB-141

Reedy, William Marion 1862-1920 . . . DLB-91

Reese, Lizette Woodworth
1856-1935 . . . . DLB-54

Reese, Thomas 1742-1796 . . . . DLB-37

Reeve, Clara 1729-1807 . . . . DLB-39

Reeves, James 1909-1978 . . . . DLB-161

Reeves, John 1926- DLB-88

Regnery, Henry, Company DLB-46

Rehberg, Hans 1901-1963 . . . . DLB-124

Rehfisch, Hans José 1891-1960 . . . . DLB-124

Reid, Alastair 1926- DLB-27

Reid, B. L. 1918-1990 . . . . DLB-111

Reid, Christopher 1949- DLB-40

Reid, Forrest 1875-1947 . . . . DLB-153

Reid, Helen Rogers 1882-1970 . . . . . DLB-29

Reid, James ?-? DLB-31

Reid, Mayne 1818-1883 . . . . . . DLB-21, 163

Reid, Thomas 1710-1796 . . . . DLB-31

Reid, V. S. (Vic) 1913-1987 . . . . . DLB-125

Reid, Whitelaw 1837-1912 . . . . DLB-23

Reilly and Lee Publishing
Company DLB-46

Reimann, Brigitte 1933-1973 . . . . . . DLB-75

Reinmar der Alte
circa 1165-circa 1205 . . . . DLB-138

Reinmar von Zweter
circa 1200-circa 1250 . . . . DLB-138

Reisch, Walter 1903-1983 . . . . DLB-44

Remarque, Erich Maria 1898-1970 . . . DLB-56

"Re-meeting of Old Friends": The Jack
Kerouac Conference Y-82

Remington, Frederic 1861-1909 . . . . . DLB-12

Renaud, Jacques 1943- DLB-60

Renault, Mary 1905-1983 . . . . Y-83

Rendell, Ruth 1930- DLB-87

Representative Men and Women: A Historical
Perspective on the British Novel,
1930-1960 . . . . DLB-15

(Re-)Publishing Orwell Y-86

Rettenbacher, Simon 1634-1706 . . . . DLB-168

Reuchlin, Johannes 1455-1522 . . . . . DLB-179

Reuter, Christian 1665-after 1712 . . . DLB-168

Reuter, Fritz 1810-1874 . . . . DLB-129

Reuter, Gabriele 1859-1941 . . . . . . DLB-66

Revell, Fleming H., Company DLB-49

Reventlow, Franziska Gräfin zu
1871-1918 . . . . DLB-66

Review of Reviews Office DLB-112

Review of [Samuel Richardson's] *Clarissa* (1748),
by Henry Fielding DLB-39

The Revolt (1937), by Mary Colum
[excerpts] DLB-36

Rexroth, Kenneth
1905-1982 . . . . . DLB-16, 48, 165; Y-82

Rey, H. A. 1898-1977 . . . . DLB-22

Reynal and Hitchcock DLB-46

Reynolds, G. W. M. 1814-1879 . . . . DLB-21

Reynolds, John Hamilton
1794-1852 . . . . DLB-96

Reynolds, Mack 1917- DLB-8

Reynolds, Sir Joshua 1723-1792 . . . . DLB-104

Reznikoff, Charles 1894-1976 . . . . DLB-28, 45

"Rhetoric" (1828; revised, 1859), by
Thomas de Quincey [excerpt] . . . DLB-57

Rhett, Robert Barnwell 1800-1876 . . . . DLB-43

Rhode, John 1884-1964 . . . . DLB-77

Rhodes, James Ford 1848-1927 . . . . . DLB-47

Rhys, Jean 1890-1979 . . . . DLB-36, 117, 162

Ricardo, David 1772-1823 . . . . DLB-107, 158

Ricardou, Jean 1932- DLB-83

Rice, Elmer 1892-1967 . . . . DLB-4, 7

Rice, Grantland 1880-1954 . . . . . DLB-29, 171

Rich, Adrienne 1929- DLB-5, 67

Richards, David Adams 1950- DLB-53

Richards, George circa 1760-1814 . . . DLB-37

Richards, I. A. 1893-1979 . . . . DLB-27

Richards, Laura E. 1850-1943 . . . . . DLB-42

Richards, William Carey
1818-1892 . . . . DLB-73

Richards, Grant
[publishing house] DLB-112

Richardson, Charles F. 1851-1913 . . . DLB-71

Richardson, Dorothy M.
1873-1957 . . . . DLB-36

Richardson, Jack 1935- DLB-7

Richardson, John 1796-1852 . . . . . . DLB-99

Richardson, Samuel
1689-1761 . . . . DLB-39, 154

Richardson, Willis 1889-1977 . . . . . DLB-51

Riche, Barnabe 1542-1617 . . . . . . DLB-136

Richler, Mordecai 1931- DLB-53

Richter, Conrad 1890-1968 . . . . DLB-9

Richter, Hans Werner 1908- DLB-69

Richter, Johann Paul Friedrich
1763-1825 . . . . DLB-94

Rickerby, Joseph
[publishing house] DLB-106

Rickword, Edgell 1898-1982 . . . . . . DLB-20

Riddell, Charlotte 1832-1906 . . . . . DLB-156

Riddell, John (see Ford, Corey)

Ridge, John Rollin 1827-1867 . . . . . DLB-175

Ridge, Lola 1873-1941 . . . . DLB-54

Ridge, William Pett 1859-1930 . . . . DLB-135

Riding, Laura (see Jackson, Laura Riding)

Ridler, Anne 1912- DLB-27

Ridruego, Dionisio 1912-1975 . . . . . DLB-108

Riel, Louis 1844-1885 . . . . DLB-99

Riemer, Johannes 1648-1714 . . . . . DLB-168

Riffaterre, Michael 1924- DLB-67

Riggs, Lynn 1899-1954 . . . . DLB-175

Riis, Jacob 1849-1914 . . . . DLB-23

Riker, John C. [publishing house] . . . DLB-49

Riley, James 1777-1840 . . . . DLB-183

Riley, John 1938-1978 . . . . DLB-40

Rilke, Rainer Maria 1875-1926 . . . . . DLB-81

Rimanelli, Giose 1926- DLB-177

Rinehart and Company. DLB-46

Ringuet 1895-1960. . . . . DLB-68

Ringwood, Gwen Pharis
1910-1984 . . . . DLB-88

Rinser, Luise 1911- DLB-69

Ríos, Alberto 1952- DLB-122

Ríos, Isabella 1948- DLB-82

Ripley, Arthur 1895-1961. . . . . DLB-44

Ripley, George 1802-1880. . . . . DLB-1, 64, 73

The Rising Glory of America:
Three Poems DLB-37

The Rising Glory of America: Written in 1771
(1786), by Hugh Henry Brackenridge and
Philip Freneau. DLB-37

Riskin, Robert 1897-1955. . . . . DLB-26

Risse, Heinz 1898- DLB-69

Rist, Johann 1607-1667 . . . . DLB-164

Ritchie, Anna Mowatt 1819-1870 . . . . DLB-3

Ritchie, Anne Thackeray
1837-1919 . . . . DLB-18

Ritchie, Thomas 1778-1854. . . . . . . DLB-43

Rites of Passage
[on William Saroyan] Y-83

The Ritz Paris Hemingway Award Y-85

Rivard, Adjutor 1868-1945 . . . . DLB-92

Rive, Richard 1931-1989 . . . . DLB-125

Rivera, Marina 1942- DLB-122

Rivera, Tomás 1935-1984 . . . . DLB-82

Rivers, Conrad Kent 1933-1968 . . . . DLB-41

Riverside Press DLB-49

Rivington, James circa 1724-1802 . . . . DLB-43

Rivington, Charles
[publishing house] DLB-154

Rivkin, Allen 1903-1990 . . . . DLB-26

Roa Bastos, Augusto 1917- DLB-113

Robbe-Grillet, Alain 1922- DLB-83

Robbins, Tom 1936- Y-80

Roberts, Charles G. D. 1860-1943. . . . DLB-92

Roberts, Dorothy 1906-1993 . . . . . . DLB-88

Roberts, Elizabeth Madox
1881-1941. . . . . DLB-9, 54, 102

Roberts, Kenneth 1885-1957. . . . . . . DLB-9

Roberts, William 1767-1849 . . . . . . DLB-142

Roberts Brothers DLB-49

Roberts, James [publishing house] . . . DLB-154

Robertson, A. M., and Company DLB-49

Robertson, William 1721-1793 . . . . . DLB-104

Robinson, Casey 1903-1979 . . . . . . DLB-44

Robinson, Edwin Arlington
1869-1935 . . . . DLB-54

Robinson, Henry Crabb
1775-1867 . . . . DLB-107

Robinson, James Harvey
1863-1936 . . . . DLB-47

Robinson, Lennox 1886-1958. . . . . . DLB-10

Robinson, Mabel Louise
1874-1962 . . . . DLB-22

Robinson, Mary 1758-1800 . . . . . . DLB-158

Robinson, Richard
circa 1545-1607 . . . . DLB-167

Robinson, Therese
1797-1870 . . . . DLB-59, 133

Robison, Mary 1949- DLB-130

Roblès, Emmanuel 1914- DLB-83

Roccatagliata Ceccardi, Ceccardo
1871-1919 . . . . DLB-114

Rochester, John Wilmot, Earl of
1647-1680 . . . . DLB-131

Rock, Howard 1911-1976 . . . . DLB-127

Rodgers, Carolyn M. 1945- DLB-41

Rodgers, W. R. 1909-1969. . . . . . . DLB-20

Rodríguez, Claudio 1934- DLB-134

Rodriguez, Richard 1944- DLB-82

Rodríguez Julia, Edgardo
1946- DLB-145

Roethke, Theodore 1908-1963 . . . . . DLB-5

Rogers, Pattiann 1940- DLB-105

Rogers, Samuel 1763-1855 . . . . . . DLB-93

Rogers, Will 1879-1935. . . . . DLB-11

Rohmer, Sax 1883-1959 . . . . DLB-70

Roiphe, Anne 1935- Y-80

Rojas, Arnold R. 1896-1988 . . . . . . DLB-82

Rolfe, Frederick William
1860-1913 . . . . DLB-34, 156

Rolland, Romain 1866-1944 . . . . . . DLB-65

Rolle, Richard
circa 1290-1300 - 1340 . . . . . . DLB-146

Rölvaag, O. E. 1876-1931. . . . . DLB-9

Romains, Jules 1885-1972. . . . . DLB-65

Roman, A., and Company DLB-49

Romano, Lalla 1906- DLB-177

Romano, Octavio 1923- DLB-122

Romero, Leo 1950- DLB-122

Romero, Lin 1947- DLB-122

Romero, Orlando 1945- DLB-82

Rook, Clarence 1863-1915 . . . . DLB-135

Roosevelt, Theodore 1858-1919 . . . . DLB-47

Root, Waverley 1903-1982. . . . . DLB-4

Root, William Pitt 1941- DLB-120

Roquebrune, Robert de 1889-1978. . . . DLB-68

Rosa, João Guimarães
1908-1967 . . . . DLB-113

Rosales, Luis 1910-1992. . . . . DLB-134

Roscoe, William 1753-1831 . . . . . . DLB-163

Rose, Reginald 1920- DLB-26

Rose, Wendy 1948- DLB-175

Rosegger, Peter 1843-1918. . . . . . . DLB-129

Rosei, Peter 1946- DLB-85

Rosen, Norma 1925- DLB-28

Rosenbach, A. S. W. 1876-1952 . . . . DLB-140

Rosenberg, Isaac 1890-1918. . . . . . . DLB-20

Rosenfeld, Isaac 1918-1956 . . . . . . DLB-28

Rosenthal, M. L. 1917- DLB-5

Ross, Alexander 1591-1654 . . . . . . DLB-151

Ross, Harold 1892-1951. . . . . DLB-137

Ross, Leonard Q. (see Rosten, Leo)

Ross, Martin 1862-1915 . . . . DLB-135

Ross, Sinclair 1908- DLB-88

Ross, W. W. E. 1894-1966 . . . . . . DLB-88

Rosselli, Amelia 1930- DLB-128

Rossen, Robert 1908-1966 . . . . . . DLB-26

Rossetti, Christina Georgina
1830-1894 . . . . DLB-35, 163

Rossetti, Dante Gabriel 1828-1882 . . . DLB-35

Rossner, Judith 1935- DLB-6

Rosten, Leo 1908- DLB-11

Rostenberg, Leona 1908- DLB-140

Rostovsky, Dimitrii 1651-1709 . . . . . DLB-150

Bertram Rota and His Bookshop Y-91

Roth, Gerhard 1942- DLB-85, 124

Roth, Henry 1906?- DLB-28

Roth, Joseph 1894-1939. . . . . DLB-85

Roth, Philip 1933- DLB-2, 28, 173; Y-82

Rothenberg, Jerome 1931- DLB-5

Rotimi, Ola 1938- DLB-125

Routhier, Adolphe-Basile
1839-1920 . . . . DLB-99

Routier, Simone 1901-1987. . . . . . . DLB-88

Routledge, George, and Sons DLB-106

Roversi, Roberto 1923- DLB-128

Rowe, Elizabeth Singer
1674-1737 . . . . DLB-39, 95

Rowe, Nicholas 1674-1718 . . . . DLB-84

Rowlands, Samuel
circa 1570-1630 . . . . DLB-121

Rowlandson, Mary
circa 1635-circa 1678 . . . . DLB-24

Rowley, William circa 1585-1626 . . . . DLB-58

Rowse, A. L. 1903- DLB-155

Rowson, Susanna Haswell
circa 1762-1824 . . . . DLB-37

Roy, Camille 1870-1943 . . . . DLB-92

Roy, Gabrielle 1909-1983. . . . . DLB-68

Roy, Jules 1907- DLB-83

The Royal Court Theatre and the English
Stage Company. DLB-13

The Royal Court Theatre and the New Drama
. . . . DLB-10

The Royal Shakespeare Company
at the Swan Y-88

Royall, Anne 1769-1854 . . . . DLB-43

The Roycroft Printing Shop DLB-49

Royster, Vermont 1914- DLB-127

Royston, Richard
[publishing house] DLB-170

Ruark, Gibbons 1941- DLB-120

Ruban, Vasilii Grigorevich
1742-1795 . . . . DLB-150

Rubens, Bernice 1928- DLB-14

Rudd and Carleton DLB-49

Rudkin, David 1936- DLB-13

Rudolf von Ems
circa 1200-circa 1254 . . . . DLB-138

Ruffin, Josephine St. Pierre
1842-1924 . . . . DLB-79

Ruganda, John 1941- DLB-157

Ruggles, Henry Joseph 1813-1906 . . . . DLB-64

Rukeyser, Muriel 1913-1980 . . . . . . DLB-48

Rule, Jane 1931- DLB-60

Rulfo, Juan 1918-1986 . . . . DLB-113

Rumaker, Michael 1932- DLB-16

Rumens, Carol 1944- DLB-40

Runyon, Damon 1880-1946 . . DLB-11, 86, 171

Ruodlieb circa 1050-1075 . . . . DLB-148

Rush, Benjamin 1746-1813 . . . . . . DLB-37

Rusk, Ralph L. 1888-1962 . . . . . . DLB-103

Ruskin, John 1819-1900 . . . . . . DLB-55, 163

Russ, Joanna 1937- DLB-8

Russell, B. B., and Company DLB-49

Russell, Benjamin 1761-1845 . . . . . DLB-43

Russell, Bertrand 1872-1970 . . . . . DLB-100

Russell, Charles Edward
1860-1941 . . . . DLB-25

Russell, George William (see AE)

Russell, R. H., and Son DLB-49

Rutherford, Mark 1831-1913 . . . . . DLB-18

Ryan, Michael 1946- Y-82

Ryan, Oscar 1904- DLB-68

Ryga, George 1932- DLB-60

Rymer, Thomas 1643?-1713 . . . . . DLB-101

Ryskind, Morrie 1895-1985 . . . . . . DLB-26

Rzhevsky, Aleksei Andreevich
1737-1804 . . . . DLB-150

S

The Saalfield Publishing
Company DLB-46

Saba, Umberto 1883-1957 . . . . . . DLB-114

Sábato, Ernesto 1911- DLB-145

Saberhagen, Fred 1930- DLB-8

Sacer, Gottfried Wilhelm
1635-1699 . . . . DLB-168

Sachs, Hans 1494-1576 . . . . DLB-179

Sackler, Howard 1929-1982 . . . . . . DLB-7

Sackville, Thomas 1536-1608 . . . . . DLB-132

Sackville, Thomas 1536-1608
and Norton, Thomas
1532-1584 . . . . DLB-62

Sackville-West, V. 1892-1962 . . . . . DLB-34

Sadlier, D. and J., and Company DLB-49

Sadlier, Mary Anne 1820-1903 . . . . . DLB-99

Sadoff, Ira 1945- DLB-120

Saenz, Jaime 1921-1986 . . . . DLB-145

Saffin, John circa 1626-1710 . . . . . DLB-24

Sagan, Françoise 1935- DLB-83

Sage, Robert 1899-1962 . . . . DLB-4

Sagel, Jim 1947- DLB-82

Sagendorph, Robb Hansell
1900-1970 . . . . DLB-137

Sahagún, Carlos 1938- DLB-108

Sahkomaapii, Piitai (see Highwater, Jamake)

Sahl, Hans 1902- DLB-69

Said, Edward W. 1935- DLB-67

Saiko, George 1892-1962 . . . . DLB-85

St. Dominic's Press DLB-112

Saint-Exupéry, Antoine de
1900-1944 . . . . DLB-72

St. Johns, Adela Rogers 1894-1988 . . . DLB-29

St. Martin's Press DLB-46

St. Omer, Garth 1931- DLB-117

Saint Pierre, Michel de 1916-1987 . . . DLB-83

Saintsbury, George
1845-1933 . . . . DLB-57, 149

Saki (see Munro, H. H.)

Salaam, Kalamu ya 1947- DLB-38

Šalamun, Tomaž 1941- DLB-181

Salas, Floyd 1931- DLB-82

Sálaz-Marquez, Rubén 1935- DLB-122

Salemson, Harold J. 1910-1988 . . . . . DLB-4

Salinas, Luis Omar 1937- DLB-82

Salinas, Pedro 1891-1951 . . . . . . DLB-134

Salinger, J. D. 1919- DLB-2, 102, 173

Salkey, Andrew 1928- DLB-125

Salt, Waldo 1914- DLB-44

Salter, James 1925- DLB-130

Salter, Mary Jo 1954- DLB-120

Salustri, Carlo Alberto (see Trilussa)

Salverson, Laura Goodman
1890-1970 . . . . DLB-92

Sampson, Richard Henry (see Hull, Richard)

Samuels, Ernest 1903- DLB-111

Sanborn, Franklin Benjamin
1831-1917 . . . . DLB-1

Sánchez, Luis Rafael 1936- DLB-145

Sánchez, Philomeno "Phil"
1917- DLB-122

Sánchez, Ricardo 1941- DLB-82

Sanchez, Sonia 1934- DLB-41; DS-8

Sand, George 1804-1876 . . . . DLB-119

Sandburg, Carl 1878-1967 . . . . . DLB-17, 54

Sanders, Ed 1939- DLB-16

Sandoz, Mari 1896-1966 . . . . DLB-9

Sandwell, B. K. 1876-1954 . . . . . . DLB-92

Sandy, Stephen 1934- DLB-165

Sandys, George 1578-1644 . . . . DLB-24, 121

Sangster, Charles 1822-1893 . . . . . DLB-99

Sanguineti, Edoardo 1930- DLB-128

Sansom, William 1912-1976 . . . . . DLB-139

Santayana, George
1863-1952 . . . . DLB-54, 71; DS-13

Santiago, Danny 1911-1988 . . . . . DLB-122

Santmyer, Helen Hooven 1895-1986 . . . Y-84

Sapidus, Joannes 1490-1561 . . . . . DLB-179

Sapir, Edward 1884-1939 . . . . . . DLB-92

Sapper (see McNeile, Herman Cyril)

Sappho circa 620 B.C.-circa 550 B.C.
. . . . DLB-176

Sarduy, Severo 1937- DLB-113

Sargent, Pamela 1948- DLB-8

Saro-Wiwa, Ken 1941- DLB-157

Saroyan, William
1908-1981 . . . . DLB-7, 9, 86; Y-81

Sarraute, Nathalie 1900- DLB-83

Sarrazin, Albertine 1937-1967 . . . . . DLB-83

Sarris, Greg 1952- DLB-175

Sarton, May 1912- DLB-48; Y-81

Sartre, Jean-Paul 1905-1980 . . . . . DLB-72

Sassoon, Siegfried 1886-1967 . . . . . DLB-20

Sata, Ineko 1904- DLB-180

Saturday Review Press DLB-46

Saunders, James 1925- DLB-13

Saunders, John Monk 1897-1940 . . . . DLB-26

Saunders, Margaret Marshall
1861-1947 . . . . DLB-92

Saunders and Otley DLB-106

Savage, James 1784-1873 . . . . . . DLB-30

Savage, Marmion W. 1803?-1872 . . . . DLB-21

Savage, Richard 1697?-1743 . . . . . DLB-95

Savard, Félix-Antoine 1896-1982 . . . . DLB-68

Saville, (Leonard) Malcolm
1901-1982 . . . . DLB-160

Sawyer, Ruth 1880-1970 . . . . DLB-22

Sayers, Dorothy L.
1893-1957 . . . . DLB-10, 36, 77, 100

Sayles, John Thomas 1950- DLB-44

Sbarbaro, Camillo 1888-1967 . . . . . DLB-114

Scannell, Vernon 1922- DLB-27

Scarry, Richard 1919-1994 . . . . DLB-61

Schaeffer, Albrecht 1885-1950 . . . . . DLB-66

Schaeffer, Susan Fromberg 1941- DLB-28

Schaff, Philip 1819-1893 . . . . DS-13

Schaper, Edzard 1908-1984 . . . . DLB-69

Scharf, J. Thomas 1843-1898 . . . . . . DLB-47

Schede, Paul Melissus 1539-1602 . . . . DLB-179

Scheffel, Joseph Viktor von
1826-1886 . . . . DLB-129

Scheffler, Johann 1624-1677 . . . . . . DLB-164

Schelling, Friedrich Wilhelm Joseph von
1775-1854 . . . . DLB-90

Scherer, Wilhelm 1841-1886 . . . . . . DLB-129

Schickele, René 1883-1940 . . . . DLB-66

Schiff, Dorothy 1903-1989 . . . . DLB-127

Schiller, Friedrich 1759-1805 . . . . . . DLB-94

Schirmer, David 1623-1687 . . . . . . DLB-164

Schlaf, Johannes 1862-1941 . . . . . . DLB-118

Schlegel, August Wilhelm
1767-1845 . . . . DLB-94

Schlegel, Dorothea 1763-1839 . . . . . . DLB-90

Schlegel, Friedrich 1772-1829 . . . . . . DLB-90

Schleiermacher, Friedrich
1768-1834 . . . . DLB-90

Schlesinger, Arthur M., Jr. 1917- DLB-17

Schlumberger, Jean 1877-1968 . . . . . DLB-65

Schmid, Eduard Hermann Wilhelm (see Edschmid, Kasimir)

Schmidt, Arno 1914-1979 . . . . DLB-69

Schmidt, Johann Kaspar (see Stirner, Max)

Schmidt, Michael 1947- DLB-40

Schmidtbonn, Wilhelm August
1876-1952 . . . . DLB-118

Schmitz, James H. 1911- DLB-8

Schnabel, Johann Gottfried
1692-1760 . . . . DLB-168

Schnackenberg, Gjertrud 1953- DLB-120

Schnitzler, Arthur 1862-1931 . . . . DLB-81, 118

Schnurre, Wolfdietrich 1920- DLB-69

Schocken Books DLB-46

Scholartis Press DLB-112

The Schomburg Center for Research
in Black Culture DLB-76

Schönbeck, Virgilio (see Giotti, Virgilio)

Schönherr, Karl 1867-1943 . . . . DLB-118

Schoolcraft, Jane Johnston
1800-1841 . . . . DLB-175

School Stories, 1914-1960 . . . . DLB-160

Schopenhauer, Arthur 1788-1860 . . . . DLB-90

Schopenhauer, Johanna 1766-1838 . . . . DLB-90

Schorer, Mark 1908-1977 . . . . DLB-103

Schottelius, Justus Georg
1612-1676 . . . . DLB-164

Schouler, James 1839-1920 . . . . DLB-47

Schrader, Paul 1946- DLB-44

Schreiner, Olive 1855-1920 . . . . DLB-18, 156

Schroeder, Andreas 1946- DLB-53

Schubart, Christian Friedrich Daniel
1739-1791 . . . . DLB-97

Schubert, Gotthilf Heinrich
1780-1860 . . . . DLB-90

Schücking, Levin 1814-1883 . . . . . . DLB-133

Schulberg, Budd
1914- DLB-6, 26, 28; Y-81

Schulte, F. J., and Company DLB-49

Schulze, Hans (see Praetorius, Johannes)

Schupp, Johann Balthasar
1610-1661 . . . . DLB-164

Schurz, Carl 1829-1906 . . . . DLB-23

Schuyler, George S. 1895-1977 . . . DLB-29, 51

Schuyler, James 1923-1991 . . . . . DLB-5, 169

Schwartz, Delmore 1913-1966 . . . . DLB-28, 48

Schwartz, Jonathan 1938- Y-82

Schwarz, Sibylle 1621-1638 . . . . . . DLB-164

Schwerner, Armand 1927- DLB-165

Schwob, Marcel 1867-1905 . . . . . . DLB-123

Sciascia, Leonardo 1921-1989 . . . . . DLB-177

Science Fantasy DLB-8

Science-Fiction Fandom and
Conventions DLB-8

Science-Fiction Fanzines: The Time
Binders DLB-8

Science-Fiction Films DLB-8

Science Fiction Writers of America and the
Nebula Awards DLB-8

Scot, Reginald circa 1538-1599 . . . . DLB-136

Scotellaro, Rocco 1923-1953 . . . . . . DLB-128

Scott, Dennis 1939-1991 . . . . DLB-125

Scott, Dixon 1881-1915 . . . . DLB-98

Scott, Duncan Campbell
1862-1947 . . . . DLB-92

Scott, Evelyn 1893-1963 . . . . . . DLB-9, 48

Scott, F. R. 1899-1985 . . . . DLB-88

Scott, Frederick George
1861-1944 . . . . DLB-92

Scott, Geoffrey 1884-1929 . . . . DLB-149

Scott, Harvey W. 1838-1910 . . . . . . DLB-23

Scott, Paul 1920-1978 . . . . DLB-14

Scott, Sarah 1723-1795 . . . . DLB-39

Scott, Tom 1918- DLB-27

Scott, Sir Walter
1771-1832 . . . . DLB-93, 107, 116, 144, 159

Scott, William Bell 1811-1890 . . . . . DLB-32

Scott, Walter, Publishing
Company Limited DLB-112

Scott, William R.
[publishing house] DLB-46

Scott-Heron, Gil 1949- DLB-41

Scribner, Charles, Jr. 1921-1995 . . . . . . Y-95

Charles Scribner's Sons DLB-49; DS-13

Charles Scribner's Sons:
Charles and Arthur DS-16

Scripps, E. W. 1854-1926 . . . . DLB-25

Scudder, Horace Elisha
1838-1902 . . . . DLB-42, 71

Scudder, Vida Dutton 1861-1954 . . . . DLB-71

Scupham, Peter 1933- DLB-40

Seabrook, William 1886-1945 . . . . . . DLB-4

Seabury, Samuel 1729-1796 . . . . DLB-31

Seacole, Mary Jane Grant
1805-1881 . . . . DLB-166

The Seafarer circa 970 . . . . DLB-146

Sealsfield, Charles 1793-1864 . . . . . . DLB-133

Sears, Edward I. 1819?-1876 . . . . . . DLB-79

Sears Publishing Company DLB-46

Seaton, George 1911-1979 . . . . DLB-44

Seaton, William Winston
1785-1866 . . . . DLB-43

Secker, Martin, and Warburg
Limited DLB-112

Secker, Martin [publishing house] DLB-112

Second-Generation Minor Poets of the
Seventeenth Century DLB-126

Sedgwick, Arthur George
1844-1915 . . . . DLB-64

Sedgwick, Catharine Maria
1789-1867 . . . . DLB-1, 74, 183

Sedgwick, Ellery 1872-1930 . . . . . . DLB-91

Sedley, Sir Charles 1639-1701 . . . . . DLB-131

Seeger, Alan 1888-1916 . . . . DLB-45

Seers, Eugene (see Dantin, Louis)

Segal, Erich 1937- Y-86

Šegedin, Petar 1909- DLB-181

Seghers, Anna 1900-1983 . . . . DLB-69

Seid, Ruth (see Sinclair, Jo)

Seidel, Frederick Lewis 1936- Y-84

Seidel, Ina 1885-1974 . . . . DLB-56

Seigenthaler, John 1927- DLB-127

Seizin Press DLB-112

Séjour, Victor 1817-1874 . . . . DLB-50

Séjour Marcou et Ferrand, Juan Victor (see Séjour, Victor)

Selby, Hubert, Jr. 1928- DLB-2

Selden, George 1929-1989 . . . . DLB-52

Selected English-Language Little Magazines
and Newspapers [France,
1920-1939] DLB-4

Selected Humorous Magazines
(1820-1950) DLB-11

Selected Science-Fiction Magazines and Anthologies DLB-8

Selenić, Slobodan 1933-1995 . . . . . . DLB-181

Self, Edwin F. 1920- DLB-137

Seligman, Edwin R. A. 1861-1939 . . . . DLB-47

Selimović, Meša 1910-1982 . . . . . . DLB-181

Selous, Frederick Courteney 1851-1917 . . . . DLB-174

Seltzer, Chester E. (see Muro, Amado)

Seltzer, Thomas [publishing house]. DLB-46

Selvon, Sam 1923-1994 . . . . DLB-125

Senancour, Etienne de 1770-1846. . . . DLB-119

Sendak, Maurice 1928- DLB-61

Senécal, Eva 1905- DLB-92

Sengstacke, John 1912- DLB-127

Senior, Olive 1941- DLB-157

Šenoa, August 1838-1881 . . . . DLB-147

"Sensation Novels" (1863), by H. L. Manse DLB-21

Sepamla, Sipho 1932- DLB-157

Seredy, Kate 1899-1975 . . . . DLB-22

Sereni, Vittorio 1913-1983 . . . . DLB-128

Seres, William [publishing house] DLB-170

Serling, Rod 1924-1975 . . . . DLB-26

Serote, Mongane Wally 1944- DLB-125

Serraillier, Ian 1912-1994 . . . . DLB-161

Serrano, Nina 1934- DLB-122

Service, Robert 1874-1958 . . . . DLB-92

Seth, Vikram 1952- DLB-120

Seton, Ernest Thompson 1860-1942 . . . . DLB-92; DS-13

Setouchi, Harumi 1922- DLB-182

Settle, Mary Lee 1918- DLB-6

Seume, Johann Gottfried 1763-1810 . . . . DLB-94

Seuse, Heinrich 1295?-1366 . . . . . . DLB-179

Seuss, Dr. (see Geisel, Theodor Seuss)

The Seventy-fifth Anniversary of the Armistice: The Wilfred Owen Centenary and the Great War Exhibit at the University of Virginia Y-93

Sewall, Joseph 1688-1769 . . . . DLB-24

Sewall, Richard B. 1908- DLB-111

Sewell, Anna 1820-1878 . . . . DLB-163

Sewell, Samuel 1652-1730 . . . . DLB-24

Sex, Class, Politics, and Religion [in the British Novel, 1930-1959] DLB-15

Sexton, Anne 1928-1974 . . . . . . DLB-5, 169

Seymour-Smith, Martin 1928- DLB-155

Shaara, Michael 1929-1988 . . . . Y-83

Shadwell, Thomas 1641?-1692 . . . . . DLB-80

Shaffer, Anthony 1926- DLB-13

Shaffer, Peter 1926- DLB-13

Shaftesbury, Anthony Ashley Cooper, Third Earl of 1671-1713 . . . . . DLB-101

Shairp, Mordaunt 1887-1939 . . . . . . DLB-10

Shakespeare, William 1564-1616 . . . . DLB-62, 172

The Shakespeare Globe Trust Y-93

Shakespeare Head Press DLB-112

Shakhovskoi, Aleksandr Aleksandrovich 1777-1846 . . . . DLB-150

Shange, Ntozake 1948- DLB-38

Shapiro, Karl 1913- DLB-48

Sharon Publications DLB-46

Sharp, Margery 1905-1991 . . . . DLB-161

Sharp, William 1855-1905 . . . . DLB-156

Sharpe, Tom 1928- DLB-14

Shaw, Albert 1857-1947 . . . . DLB-91

Shaw, Bernard 1856-1950 . . . . . DLB-10, 57

Shaw, Henry Wheeler 1818-1885 . . . . DLB-11

Shaw, Joseph T. 1874-1952 . . . . . . DLB-137

Shaw, Irwin 1913-1984 . . . . DLB-6, 102; Y-84

Shaw, Robert 1927-1978 . . . . . . DLB-13, 14

Shaw, Robert B. 1947- DLB-120

Shawn, William 1907-1992 . . . . . . DLB-137

Shay, Frank [publishing house] DLB-46

Shea, John Gilmary 1824-1892 . . . . . DLB-30

Sheaffer, Louis 1912-1993 . . . . DLB-103

Shearing, Joseph 1886-1952 . . . . . . DLB-70

Shebbeare, John 1709-1788 . . . . . . DLB-39

Sheckley, Robert 1928- DLB-8

Shedd, William G. T. 1820-1894 . . . . DLB-64

Sheed, Wilfred 1930- DLB-6

Sheed and Ward [U.S.] DLB-46

Sheed and Ward Limited [U.K.] DLB-112

Sheldon, Alice B. (see Tiptree, James, Jr.)

Sheldon, Edward 1886-1946 . . . . . . DLB-7

Sheldon and Company DLB-49

Shelley, Mary Wollstonecraft 1797-1851 . . . . . . DLB-110, 116, 159, 178

Shelley, Percy Bysshe 1792-1822 . . . . DLB-96, 110, 158

Shelnutt, Eve 1941- DLB-130

Shenstone, William 1714-1763 . . . . . DLB-95

Shepard, Ernest Howard 1879-1976 . . . . DLB-160

Shepard, Sam 1943- DLB-7

Shepard, Thomas I, 1604 or 1605-1649 . . . . DLB-24

Shepard, Thomas II, 1635-1677 . . . . DLB-24

Shepard, Clark and Brown DLB-49

Shepherd, Luke flourished 1547-1554 . . . . DLB-136

Sherburne, Edward 1616-1702 . . . . . DLB-131

Sheridan, Frances 1724-1766 . . . . . DLB-39, 84

Sheridan, Richard Brinsley 1751-1816 . . . . DLB-89

Sherman, Francis 1871-1926 . . . . . . DLB-92

Sherriff, R. C. 1896-1975 . . . . DLB-10

Sherry, Norman 1935- DLB-155

Sherwood, Mary Martha 1775-1851 . . . . DLB-163

Sherwood, Robert 1896-1955 . . . . . DLB-7, 26

Shiel, M. P. 1865-1947 . . . . DLB-153

Shiels, George 1886-1949 . . . . DLB-10

Shiga, Naoya 1883-1971 . . . . DLB-180

Shiina, Rinzō 1911-1973 . . . . DLB-182

Shillaber, B.[enjamin] P.[enhallow] 1814-1890 . . . . DLB-1, 11

Shimao, Toshio 1917-1986 . . . . . . DLB-182

Shimazaki, Tōson 1872-1943 . . . . . DLB-180

Shine, Ted 1931- DLB-38

Ship, Reuben 1915-1975 . . . . DLB-88

Shirer, William L. 1904-1993 . . . . . . DLB-4

Shirinsky-Shikhmatov, Sergii Aleksandrovich 1783-1837 . . . . DLB-150

Shirley, James 1596-1666 . . . . DLB-58

Shishkov, Aleksandr Semenovich 1753-1841 . . . . DLB-150

Shockley, Ann Allen 1927- DLB-33

Shōno, Junzō 1921- DLB-182

Short, Peter [publishing house] DLB-170

Shorthouse, Joseph Henry 1834-1903 . . . . DLB-18

Showalter, Elaine 1941- DLB-67

Shulevitz, Uri 1935- DLB-61

Shulman, Max 1919-1988 . . . . DLB-11

Shute, Henry A. 1856-1943 . . . . DLB-9

Shuttle, Penelope 1947- DLB-14, 40

Sibbes, Richard 1577-1635 . . . . . . DLB-151

Sidgwick and Jackson Limited DLB-112

Sidney, Margaret (see Lothrop, Harriet M.)

Sidney, Mary 1561-1621 . . . . DLB-167

Sidney, Sir Philip 1554-1586 . . . . . DLB-167

Sidney's Press DLB-49

Siegfried Loraine Sassoon: A Centenary Essay Tributes from Vivien F. Clarke and Michael Thorpe Y-86

Sierra, Rubén 1946- DLB-122

Sierra Club Books DLB-49

Siger of Brabant circa 1240-circa 1284 . . . . DLB-115

Sigourney, Lydia Howard (Huntley) 1791-1865 . . . . DLB-1, 42, 73, 183

Silkin, Jon 1930- DLB-27

Silko, Leslie Marmon 1948- DLB-143, 175

Silliman, Benjamin 1779-1864 . . . . . . DLB-183

Silliman, Ron 1946- DLB-169

Silliphant, Stirling 1918- DLB-26

Sillitoe, Alan 1928- DLB-14, 139

Silman, Roberta 1934- DLB-28

Silva, Beverly 1930- DLB-122

Silverberg, Robert 1935- DLB-8

Silverman, Kenneth 1936- DLB-111

Simak, Clifford D. 1904-1988 . . . . . . DLB-8

Simcoe, Elizabeth 1762-1850 . . . . . . DLB-99

Simcox, George Augustus
1841-1905 . . . . DLB-35

Sime, Jessie Georgina 1868-1958 . . . . . DLB-92

Simenon, Georges
1903-1989 . . . . DLB-72; Y-89

Simic, Charles 1938- DLB-105

Simic, Charles,
Images and "Images" DLB-105

Simmel, Johannes Mario 1924- DLB-69

Simmes, Valentine
[publishing house] DLB-170

Simmons, Ernest J. 1903-1972 . . . . . DLB-103

Simmons, Herbert Alfred 1930- DLB-33

Simmons, James 1933- DLB-40

Simms, William Gilmore
1806-1870 . . . . DLB-3, 30, 59, 73

Simms and M'Intyre DLB-106

Simon, Claude 1913- DLB-83

Simon, Neil 1927- DLB-7

Simon and Schuster DLB-46

Simons, Katherine Drayton Mayrant
1890-1969 . . . . Y-83

Simović, Ljubomir 1935- DLB-181

Simpkin and Marshall
[publishing house] DLB-154

Simpson, Helen 1897-1940 . . . . DLB-77

Simpson, Louis 1923- DLB-5

Simpson, N. F. 1919- DLB-13

Sims, George 1923- DLB-87

Sims, George Robert
1847-1922 . . . . DLB-35, 70, 135

Sinán, Rogelio 1904- DLB-145

Sinclair, Andrew 1935- DLB-14

Sinclair, Bertrand William
1881-1972 . . . . DLB-92

Sinclair, Catherine
1800-1864 . . . . DLB-163

Sinclair, Jo 1913- DLB-28

Sinclair Lewis Centennial
Conference Y-85

Sinclair, Lister 1921- DLB-88

Sinclair, May 1863-1946 . . . . . . DLB-36, 135

Sinclair, Upton 1878-1968 . . . . DLB-9

Sinclair, Upton [publishing house] DLB-46

Singer, Isaac Bashevis
1904-1991 . . . . DLB-6, 28, 52; Y-91

Singmaster, Elsie 1879-1958 . . . . DLB-9

Sinisgalli, Leonardo 1908-1981 . . . . . DLB-114

Siodmak, Curt 1902- DLB-44

Sissman, L. E. 1928-1976 . . . . DLB-5

Sisson, C. H. 1914- DLB-27

Sitwell, Edith 1887-1964 . . . . DLB-20

Sitwell, Osbert 1892-1969 . . . . DLB-100

Skármeta, Antonio 1940- DLB-145

Skeffington, William
[publishing house] DLB-106

Skelton, John 1463-1529 . . . . DLB-136

Skelton, Robin 1925- DLB-27, 53

Skinner, Constance Lindsay
1877-1939 . . . . DLB-92

Skinner, John Stuart 1788-1851 . . . . . DLB-73

Skipsey, Joseph 1832-1903 . . . . DLB-35

Slade, Bernard 1930- DLB-53

Slamnig, Ivan 1930- DLB-181

Slater, Patrick 1880-1951 . . . . DLB-68

Slaveykov, Pencho 1866-1912 . . . . . . DLB-147

Slaviček, Milivoj 1929- DLB-181

Slavitt, David 1935- DLB-5, 6

Sleigh, Burrows Willcocks Arthur
1821-1869 . . . . DLB-99

A Slender Thread of Hope: The Kennedy
Center Black Theatre Project DLB-38

Slesinger, Tess 1905-1945 . . . . DLB-102

Slick, Sam (see Haliburton, Thomas Chandler)

Sloane, William, Associates DLB-46

Small, Maynard and Company DLB-49

Small Presses in Great Britain and Ireland,
1960-1985 . . . . DLB-40

Small Presses I: Jargon Society Y-84

Small Presses II: The Spirit That Moves
Us Press Y-85

Small Presses III: Pushcart Press Y-87

Smart, Christopher 1722-1771 . . . . . . DLB-109

Smart, David A. 1892-1957 . . . . DLB-137

Smart, Elizabeth 1913-1986 . . . . DLB-88

Smellie, William
[publishing house] DLB-154

Smiles, Samuel 1812-1904 . . . . DLB-55

Smith, A. J. M. 1902-1980 . . . . DLB-88

Smith, Adam 1723-1790 . . . . DLB-104

Smith, Alexander 1829-1867 . . . . DLB-32, 55

Smith, Betty 1896-1972 . . . . Y-82

Smith, Carol Sturm 1938- Y-81

Smith, Charles Henry 1826-1903 . . . . DLB-11

Smith, Charlotte 1749-1806 . . . . DLB-39, 109

Smith, Chet 1899-1973 . . . . DLB-171

Smith, Cordwainer 1913-1966 . . . . . . DLB-8

Smith, Dave 1942- DLB-5

Smith, Dodie 1896- DLB-10

Smith, Doris Buchanan 1934- DLB-52

Smith, E. E. 1890-1965 . . . . DLB-8

Smith, Elihu Hubbard 1771-1798 . . . . DLB-37

Smith, Elizabeth Oakes (Prince)
1806-1893 . . . . DLB-1

Smith, F. Hopkinson 1838-1915 . . . . . DS-13

Smith, George D. 1870-1920 . . . . . . DLB-140

Smith, George O. 1911-1981 . . . . . . DLB-8

Smith, Goldwin 1823-1910 . . . . DLB-99

Smith, H. Allen 1907-1976 . . . . . DLB-11, 29

Smith, Hazel Brannon 1914- DLB-127

Smith, Henry
circa 1560-circa 1591 . . . . DLB-136

Smith, Horatio (Horace)
1779-1849 . . . . DLB-116

Smith, Horatio (Horace) 1779-1849 and
James Smith 1775-1839 . . . . DLB-96

Smith, Iain Crichton
1928- DLB-40, 139

Smith, J. Allen 1860-1924 . . . . DLB-47

Smith, John 1580-1631 . . . . DLB-24, 30

Smith, Josiah 1704-1781 . . . . DLB-24

Smith, Ken 1938- DLB-40

Smith, Lee 1944- DLB-143; Y-83

Smith, Logan Pearsall 1865-1946 . . . . . DLB-98

Smith, Mark 1935- Y-82

Smith, Michael 1698-circa 1771 . . . . . DLB-31

Smith, Red 1905-1982 . . . . DLB-29, 171

Smith, Roswell 1829-1892 . . . . DLB-79

Smith, Samuel Harrison
1772-1845 . . . . DLB-43

Smith, Samuel Stanhope
1751-1819 . . . . DLB-37

Smith, Sarah (see Stretton, Hesba)

Smith, Seba 1792-1868 . . . . DLB-1, 11

Smith, Sir Thomas 1513-1577 . . . . . . DLB-132

Smith, Stevie 1902-1971 . . . . DLB-20

Smith, Sydney 1771-1845 . . . . DLB-107

Smith, Sydney Goodsir 1915-1975 . . . . DLB-27

Smith, Wendell 1914-1972 . . . . DLB-171

Smith, William
flourished 1595-1597 . . . . DLB-136

Smith, William 1727-1803 . . . . DLB-31

Smith, William 1728-1793 . . . . DLB-30

Smith, William Gardner
1927-1974 . . . . DLB-76

Smith, William Henry
1808-1872 . . . . DLB-159

Smith, William Jay 1918- DLB-5

Smith, Elder and Company DLB-154

Smith, Harrison, and Robert Haas
[publishing house] DLB-46

Smith, J. Stilman, and Company DLB-49

Smith, W. B., and Company DLB-49

Smith, W. H., and Son DLB-106

Smithers, Leonard
[publishing house] DLB-112

Smollett, Tobias 1721-1771 . . . . . DLB-39, 104

Snellings, Rolland (see Touré, Askia
Muhammad)

Snodgrass, W. D. 1926- DLB-5

Snow, C. P. 1905-1980 . . . . DLB-15, 77

Snyder, Gary 1930- DLB-5, 16, 165

Sobiloff, Hy 1912-1970 . . . . DLB-48

The Society for Textual Scholarship and
TEXT Y-87

The Society for the History of Authorship, Reading and Publishing Y-92

Soffici, Ardengo 1879-1964 . . . . DLB-114

Sofola, 'Zulu 1938- DLB-157

Solano, Solita 1888-1975 . . . . DLB-4

Soldati, Mario 1906- DLB-177

Šoljan, Antun 1932-1993 . . . . DLB-181

Sollers, Philippe 1936- DLB-83

Solmi, Sergio 1899-1981 . . . . DLB-114

Solomon, Carl 1928- DLB-16

Solway, David 1941- DLB-53

Solzhenitsyn and America Y-85

Somerville, Edith Œnone
1858-1949 . . . . DLB-135

Song, Cathy 1955- DLB-169

Sono, Ayako 1931- DLB-182

Sontag, Susan 1933- DLB-2, 67

Sophocles 497/496 B.C.-406/405 B.C.
. . . . DLB-176

Šopov, Aco 1923-1982 . . . . DLB-181

Sorge, Reinhard Johannes
1892-1916 . . . . DLB-118

Sorrentino, Gilbert
1929- DLB-5, 173; Y-80

Sotheby, William 1757-1833 . . . . DLB-93

Soto, Gary 1952- DLB-82

Sources for the Study of Tudor and Stuart Drama
DLB-62

Souster, Raymond 1921- DLB-88

The *South English Legendary*
circa thirteenth-fifteenth
centuries DLB-146

Southerland, Ellease 1943- DLB-33

Southern Illinois University Press Y-95

Southern, Terry 1924- DLB-2

Southern Writers Between the
Wars DLB-9

Southerne, Thomas 1659-1746 . . . . . DLB-80

Southey, Caroline Anne Bowles
1786-1854 . . . . DLB-116

Southey, Robert
1774-1843 . . . . DLB-93, 107, 142

Southwell, Robert 1561?-1595 . . . . . DLB-167

Sowande, Bode 1948- DLB-157

Sowle, Tace
[publishing house] DLB-170

Soyfer, Jura 1912-1939 . . . . DLB-124

Soyinka, Wole 1934- DLB-125; Y-86, 87

Spacks, Barry 1931- DLB-105

Spalding, Frances 1950- DLB-155

Spark, Muriel 1918- DLB-15, 139

Sparke, Michael
[publishing house] DLB-170

Sparks, Jared 1789-1866 . . . . DLB-1, 30

Sparshott, Francis 1926- DLB-60

Späth, Gerold 1939- DLB-75

Spatola, Adriano 1941-1988 . . . . . . DLB-128

Spaziani, Maria Luisa 1924- DLB-128

The Spectator 1828- DLB-110

Spedding, James 1808-1881 . . . . . . DLB-144

Spee von Langenfeld, Friedrich
1591-1635 . . . . DLB-164

Speght, Rachel 1597-after 1630 . . . . DLB-126

Speke, John Hanning 1827-1864 . . . . DLB-166

Spellman, A. B. 1935- DLB-41

Spence, Thomas 1750-1814 . . . . . . DLB-158

Spencer, Anne 1882-1975 . . . . . . DLB-51, 54

Spencer, Elizabeth 1921- DLB-6

Spencer, Herbert 1820-1903 . . . . . . DLB-57

Spencer, Scott 1945- Y-86

Spender, J. A. 1862-1942 . . . . DLB-98

Spender, Stephen 1909- DLB-20

Spener, Philipp Jakob 1635-1705 . . . . DLB-164

Spenser, Edmund circa 1552-1599 . . . DLB-167

Sperr, Martin 1944- DLB-124

Spicer, Jack 1925-1965 . . . . DLB-5, 16

Spielberg, Peter 1929- Y-81

Spielhagen, Friedrich 1829-1911 . . . . . DLB-129

"*Spielmannsepen*"
(circa 1152-circa 1500) DLB-148

Spier, Peter 1927- DLB-61

Spinrad, Norman 1940- DLB-8

Spires, Elizabeth 1952- DLB-120

Spitteler, Carl 1845-1924 . . . . DLB-129

Spivak, Lawrence E. 1900- DLB-137

Spofford, Harriet Prescott
1835-1921 . . . . DLB-74

Squibob (see Derby, George Horatio)

The St. John's College Robert Graves Trust
. . . . Y-96

Stacpoole, H. de Vere
1863-1951 . . . . DLB-153

Staël, Germaine de 1766-1817 . . . . . DLB-119

Staël-Holstein, Anne-Louise Germaine de
(see Staël, Germaine de)

Stafford, Jean 1915-1979 . . . . . DLB-2, 173

Stafford, William 1914- DLB-5

Stage Censorship: "The Rejected Statement"
(1911), by Bernard Shaw
[excerpts] DLB-10

Stallings, Laurence 1894-1968 . . . . . DLB-7, 44

Stallworthy, Jon 1935- DLB-40

Stampp, Kenneth M. 1912- DLB-17

Stanev, Emiliyan 1907-1979 . . . . . . DLB-181

Stanford, Ann 1916- DLB-5

Stanković, Borisav ("Bora")
1876-1927 . . . . DLB-147

Stanley, Henry M. 1841-1904 . . . . . . DS-13

Stanley, Thomas 1625-1678 . . . . . . DLB-131

Stannard, Martin 1947- DLB-155

Stansby, William
[publishing house] DLB-170

Stanton, Elizabeth Cady 1815-1902 . . . DLB-79

Stanton, Frank L. 1857-1927 . . . . . . DLB-25

Stanton, Maura 1946- DLB-120

Stapledon, Olaf 1886-1950 . . . . DLB-15

Star Spangled Banner Office DLB-49

Starkey, Thomas circa 1499-1538 . . . . DLB-132

Starkweather, David 1935- DLB-7

Statements on the Art of Poetry DLB-54

Stationers' Company of
London, The DLB-170

Stead, Robert J. C. 1880-1959 . . . . . DLB-92

Steadman, Mark 1930- DLB-6

The Stealthy School of Criticism (1871), by
Dante Gabriel Rossetti DLB-35

Stearns, Harold E. 1891-1943 . . . . . . DLB-4

Stedman, Edmund Clarence
1833-1908 . . . . DLB-64

Steegmuller, Francis 1906-1994 . . . . . DLB-111

Steel, Flora Annie
1847-1929 . . . . DLB-153, 156

Steele, Max 1922- Y-80

Steele, Richard 1672-1729 . . . . . DLB-84, 101

Steele, Timothy 1948- DLB-120

Steele, Wilbur Daniel 1886-1970 . . . . DLB-86

Steere, Richard circa 1643-1721 . . . . DLB-24

Stefanovski, Goran 1952- DLB-181

Stegner, Wallace 1909-1993 . . . . DLB-9; Y-93

Stehr, Hermann 1864-1940 . . . . . . DLB-66

Steig, William 1907- DLB-61

Stein, Gertrude 1874-1946 DLB-4, 54, 86; DS-15

Stein, Leo 1872-1947 . . . . DLB-4

Stein and Day Publishers DLB-46

Steinbeck, John 1902-1968 . . . . DLB-7, 9; DS-2

Steiner, George 1929- DLB-67

Steinhoewel, Heinrich
    1411/1412-1479 . . . . DLB-179

Stendhal 1783-1842 . . . . DLB-119

Stephen Crane: A Revaluation Virginia
    Tech Conference, 1989 . . . . Y-89

Stephen, Leslie 1832-1904 . . . . . DLB-57, 144

Stephens, Alexander H. 1812-1883 . . . . DLB-47

Stephens, Ann 1810-1886 . . . . . . DLB-3, 73

Stephens, Charles Asbury
    1844?-1931 . . . . DLB-42

Stephens, James
    1882?-1950 . . . . DLB-19, 153, 162

Stephens, John Lloyd 1805-1852 . . . . DLB-183

Sterling, George 1869-1926 . . . . DLB-54

Sterling, James 1701-1763 . . . . DLB-24

Sterling, John 1806-1844 . . . . DLB-116

Stern, Gerald 1925- DLB-105

Stern, Madeleine B. 1912- DLB-111, 140

Stern, Gerald, Living in Ruin DLB-105

Stern, Richard 1928- Y-87

Stern, Stewart 1922- DLB-26

Sterne, Laurence 1713-1768 . . . . DLB-39

Sternheim, Carl 1878-1942 . . . . DLB-56, 118

Sternhold, Thomas ?-1549 and
    John Hopkins ?-1570 . . . . DLB-132

Stevens, Henry 1819-1886 . . . . DLB-140

Stevens, Wallace 1879-1955 . . . . DLB-54

Stevenson, Anne 1933- DLB-40

Stevenson, Lionel 1902-1973 . . . . . DLB-155

Stevenson, Robert Louis 1850-1894
    . . . . . DLB-18, 57, 141, 156, 174; DS-13

Stewart, Donald Ogden
    1894-1980 . . . . DLB-4, 11, 26

Stewart, Dugald 1753-1828 . . . . DLB-31

Stewart, George, Jr. 1848-1906 . . . . . DLB-99

Stewart, George R. 1895-1980 . . . . . . DLB-8

Stewart and Kidd Company DLB-46

Stewart, Randall 1896-1964 . . . . . . DLB-103

Stickney, Trumbull 1874-1904 . . . . . DLB-54

Stieler, Caspar 1632-1707 . . . . DLB-164

Stifter, Adalbert 1805-1868 . . . . . . DLB-133

Stiles, Ezra 1727-1795 . . . . DLB-31

Still, James 1906- DLB-9

Stirner, Max 1806-1856 . . . . DLB-129

Stith, William 1707-1755 . . . . DLB-31

Stock, Elliot [publishing house] DLB-106

Stockton, Frank R.
    1834-1902 . . . . DLB-42, 74; DS-13

Stoddard, Ashbel
    [publishing house] DLB-49

Stoddard, Richard Henry
    1825-1903 . . . . DLB-3, 64; DS-13

Stoddard, Solomon 1643-1729 . . . . . DLB-24

Stoker, Bram 1847-1912 . . . . DLB-36, 70, 178

Stokes, Frederick A., Company DLB-49

Stokes, Thomas L. 1898-1958 . . . . . DLB-29

Stokesbury, Leon 1945- DLB-120

Stolberg, Christian Graf zu
    1748-1821 . . . . DLB-94

Stolberg, Friedrich Leopold Graf zu
    1750-1819 . . . . DLB-94

Stone, Herbert S., and Company . . . DLB-49

Stone, Lucy 1818-1893 . . . . DLB-79

Stone, Melville 1848-1929 . . . . DLB-25

Stone, Robert 1937- DLB-152

Stone, Ruth 1915- DLB-105

Stone, Samuel 1602-1663 . . . . DLB-24

Stone and Kimball DLB-49

Stoppard, Tom 1937- DLB-13; Y-85

Storey, Anthony 1928- DLB-14

Storey, David 1933- DLB-13, 14

Storm, Theodor 1817-1888 . . . . . . DLB-129

Story, Thomas circa 1670-1742 . . . . DLB-31

Story, William Wetmore 1819-1895 . . . . DLB-1

Storytelling: A Contemporary
    Renaissance Y-84

Stoughton, William 1631-1701 . . . . . DLB-24

Stow, John 1525-1605 . . . . DLB-132

Stowe, Harriet Beecher
    1811-1896 . . . . DLB-1, 12, 42, 74

Stowe, Leland 1899- DLB-29

Stoyanov, Dimitŭr Ivanov (see Elin Pelin)

Strabo 64 or 63 B.C.-circa A.D. 25
    . . . . DLB-176

Strachey, Lytton
    1880-1932 . . . . DLB-149; DS-10

Strachey, Lytton, Preface to Eminent
    Victorians DLB-149

Strahan and Company DLB-106

Strahan, William
    [publishing house] DLB-154

Strand, Mark 1934- DLB-5

The Strasbourg Oaths 842 . . . . DLB-148

Stratemeyer, Edward 1862-1930 . . . . DLB-42

Strati, Saverio 1924- DLB-177

Stratton and Barnard DLB-49

Stratton-Porter, Gene 1863-1924 . . . . DS-14

Straub, Peter 1943- Y-84

Strauß, Botho 1944- DLB-124

Strauß, David Friedrich
    1808-1874 . . . . DLB-133

The Strawberry Hill Press DLB-154

Streatfeild, Noel 1895-1986 . . . . . . DLB-160

Street, Cecil John Charles (see Rhode, John)

Street, G. S. 1867-1936 . . . . DLB-135

Street and Smith DLB-49

Streeter, Edward 1891-1976 . . . . . . DLB-11

Streeter, Thomas Winthrop
    1883-1965 . . . . DLB-140

Stretton, Hesba 1832-1911 . . . . . . DLB-163

Stribling, T. S. 1881-1965 . . . . DLB-9

Der Stricker circa 1190-circa 1250 . . . DLB-138

Strickland, Samuel 1804-1867 . . . . . DLB-99

Stringer and Townsend DLB-49

Stringer, Arthur 1874-1950 . . . . . . DLB-92

Strittmatter, Erwin 1912- DLB-69

Strniša, Gregor 1930-1987 . . . . . . DLB-181

Strode, William 1630-1645 . . . . . . DLB-126

Strother, David Hunter 1816-1888 . . . DLB-3

Strouse, Jean 1945- DLB-111

Stuart, Dabney 1937- DLB-105

Stuart, Dabney, Knots into Webs: Some Autobio-
    graphical Sources DLB-105

Stuart, Jesse
    1906-1984 . . . . . . DLB-9, 48, 102; Y-84

Stuart, Lyle [publishing house] DLB-46

Stubbs, Harry Clement (see Clement, Hal)

Stubenberg, Johann Wilhelm von
    1619-1663 . . . . DLB-164

Studio DLB-112

The Study of Poetry (1880), by
    Matthew Arnold DLB-35

Sturgeon, Theodore
    1918-1985 . . . . DLB-8; Y-85

Sturges, Preston 1898-1959 . . . . . . DLB-26

"Style" (1840; revised, 1859), by
    Thomas de Quincey [excerpt] DLB-57

"Style" (1888), by Walter Pater DLB-57

Style (1897), by Walter Raleigh
    [excerpt] DLB-57

"Style" (1877), by T. H. Wright
    [excerpt] DLB-57

"Le Style c'est l'homme" (1892), by
    W. H. Mallock DLB-57

Styron, William 1925- DLB-2, 143; Y-80

Suárez, Mario 1925- DLB-82

Such, Peter 1939- DLB-60

Suckling, Sir John 1609-1641? . . . DLB-58, 126

Suckow, Ruth 1892-1960 . . . . . . DLB-9, 102

Sudermann, Hermann 1857-1928 . . . . DLB-118

Sue, Eugène 1804-1857 . . . . DLB-119

Sue, Marie-Joseph (see Sue, Eugène)

Suggs, Simon (see Hooper, Johnson Jones)

Sukenick, Ronald 1932- DLB-173; Y-81

Suknaski, Andrew 1942- DLB-53

Sullivan, Alan 1868-1947 . . . . DLB-92

Sullivan, C. Gardner 1886-1965 . . . . DLB-26

Sullivan, Frank 1892-1976 . . . . . . DLB-11

Sulte, Benjamin 1841-1923 . . . . . . DLB-99

Sulzberger, Arthur Hays
    1891-1968 . . . . DLB-127

Sulzberger, Arthur Ochs 1926- DLB-127

Sulzer, Johann Georg 1720-1779 . . . . . DLB-97

Sumarokov, Aleksandr Petrovich
    1717-1777 . . . . DLB-150

Summers, Hollis 1916- DLB-6

Sumner, Henry A.
    [publishing house]. DLB-49

Surtees, Robert Smith 1803-1864. . . . . DLB-21

Surveys: Japanese Literature,
    1987-1995 . . . . DLB-182

A Survey of Poetry Anthologies,
    1879-1960 . . . . DLB-54

Surveys of the Year's Biographies

A Transit of Poets and Others: American
    Biography in 1982 . . . . Y-82

The Year in Literary Biography . . . Y-83–Y-96

Survey of the Year's Book Publishing

The Year in Book Publishing Y-86

Survey of the Year's Children's Books

The Year in Children's Books Y-92–Y-96

Surveys of the Year's Drama

The Year in Drama
    . . . . Y-82–Y-85, Y-87–Y-96

The Year in London Theatre Y-92

Surveys of the Year's Fiction

The Year's Work in Fiction:
    A Survey Y-82

The Year in Fiction: A Biased View Y-83

The Year in
    Fiction Y-84–Y-86, Y-89, Y-94–Y-96

The Year in the
    Novel Y-87, Y-88, Y-90–Y-93

The Year in Short Stories Y-87

The Year in the
    Short Story Y-88, Y-90–Y-93

Survey of the Year's Literary Theory

The Year in Literary Theory Y-92–Y-93

Surveys of the Year's Poetry

The Year's Work in American
    Poetry. Y-82

The Year in Poetry Y-83–Y-92, Y-94–Y-96

Sutherland, Efua Theodora
    1924- DLB-117

Sutherland, John 1919-1956. . . . . . . DLB-68

Sutro, Alfred 1863-1933. . . . . DLB-10

Swados, Harvey 1920-1972 . . . . DLB-2

Swain, Charles 1801-1874 . . . . DLB-32

Swallow Press DLB-46

Swan Sonnenschein Limited. DLB-106

Swanberg, W. A. 1907- DLB-103

Swenson, May 1919-1989 . . . . DLB-5

Swerling, Jo 1897- DLB-44

Swift, Jonathan
    1667-1745 . . . . DLB-39, 95, 101

Swinburne, A. C. 1837-1909. . . . . DLB-35, 57

Swineshead, Richard floruit
    circa 1350 . . . . DLB-115

Swinnerton, Frank 1884-1982. . . . . . DLB-34

Swisshelm, Jane Grey 1815-1884. . . . . DLB-43

Swope, Herbert Bayard 1882-1958. . . . DLB-25

Swords, T. and J., and Company DLB-49

Swords, Thomas 1763-1843 and
    Swords, James ?-1844 . . . . DLB-73

Sykes, Ella C. ?-1939 . . . . DLB-174

Sylvester, Josuah
    1562 or 1563 - 1618 . . . . DLB-121

Symonds, Emily Morse (see Paston, George)

Symonds, John Addington
    1840-1893 . . . . DLB-57, 144

Symons, A. J. A. 1900-1941 . . . . . . DLB-149

Symons, Arthur
    1865-1945 . . . . DLB-19, 57, 149

Symons, Julian
    1912-1994. . . . . DLB-87, 155; Y-92

Symons, Scott 1933- DLB-53

A Symposium on *The Columbia History of
    the Novel*. Y-92

Synge, John Millington
    1871-1909 . . . . DLB-10, 19

Synge Summer School: J. M. Synge and the Irish
    Theater, Rathdrum, County Wiclow, Ireland
    . . . . Y-93

Syrett, Netta 1865-1943 . . . . DLB-135

Szymborska, Wisława 1923- Y-96

T

Taban lo Liyong 1939?- DLB-125

Taché, Joseph-Charles 1820-1894. . . . . DLB-99

Tachihara, Masaaki 1926-1980 . . . . . DLB-182

Tadijanović, Dragutin 1905- DLB-181

Tafolla, Carmen 1951- DLB-82

Taggard, Genevieve 1894-1948. . . . . . DLB-45

Tagger, Theodor (see Bruckner, Ferdinand)

Tait, J. Selwin, and Sons DLB-49

Tait's Edinburgh Magazine
    1832-1861 . . . . DLB-110

The Takarazaka Revue Company Y-91

Talander (see Bohse, August)

Talev, Dimitŭr 1898-1966. . . . . . . DLB-181

Tallent, Elizabeth 1954- DLB-130

Talvj 1797-1870 . . . . DLB-59, 133

Tan, Amy 1952- DLB-173

Tanizaki, Jun'ichirō 1886-1965 . . . . . DLB-180

Tapahonso, Luci 1953- DLB-175

Taradash, Daniel 1913- DLB-44

Tarbell, Ida M. 1857-1944 . . . . DLB-47

Tardivel, Jules-Paul 1851-1905 . . . . . . DLB-99

Targan, Barry 1932- DLB-130

Tarkington, Booth 1869-1946 . . . . DLB-9, 102

Tashlin, Frank 1913-1972. . . . . DLB-44

Tate, Allen 1899-1979. . . . . . DLB-4, 45, 63

Tate, James 1943- DLB-5, 169

Tate, Nahum circa 1652-1715 . . . . . . DLB-80

Tatian circa 830 . . . . DLB-148

Taufer, Veno 1933- DLB-181

Tauler, Johannes circa 1300-1361. . . . DLB-179

Tavčar, Ivan 1851-1923 . . . . DLB-147

Taylor, Ann 1782-1866 . . . . DLB-163

Taylor, Bayard 1825-1878 . . . . DLB-3

Taylor, Bert Leston 1866-1921 . . . . . DLB-25

Taylor, Charles H. 1846-1921 . . . . . . DLB-25

Taylor, Edward circa 1642-1729 . . . . . DLB-24

Taylor, Elizabeth 1912-1975. . . . . . DLB-139

Taylor, Henry 1942- DLB-5

Taylor, Sir Henry 1800-1886. . . . . . DLB-32

Taylor, Jane 1783-1824 . . . . DLB-163

Taylor, Jeremy circa 1613-1667 . . . . . DLB-151

Taylor, John 1577 or 1578 - 1653. . . DLB-121

Taylor, Mildred D. ?- DLB-52

Taylor, Peter 1917-1994. . . . . . . Y-81, Y-94

Taylor, William, and Company DLB-49

Taylor-Made Shakespeare? Or Is
    "Shall I Die?" the Long-Lost Text
    of Bottom's Dream?. Y-85

Teasdale, Sara 1884-1933 . . . . DLB-45

The Tea-Table (1725), by Eliza Haywood [excerpt]
    DLB-39

Telles, Lygia Fagundes 1924- DLB-113

Temple, Sir William 1628-1699. . . . . DLB-101

Tenn, William 1919- DLB-8

Tennant, Emma 1937- DLB-14

Tenney, Tabitha Gilman 1762-1837 . . . DLB-37

Tennyson, Alfred 1809-1892 . . . . . . DLB-32

Tennyson, Frederick 1807-1898 . . . . . DLB-32

Terhune, Albert Payson 1872-1942 . . . . DLB-9

Terhune, Mary Virginia 1830-1922 . . . . DS-13

Terry, Megan 1932- DLB-7

Terson, Peter 1932- DLB-13

Tesich, Steve 1943- Y-83

Tessa, Delio 1886-1939 . . . . DLB-114

Testori, Giovanni 1923-1993 . . . . DLB-128, 177

Tey, Josephine 1896?-1952 . . . . DLB-77

Thacher, James 1754-1844 . . . . DLB-37

Thackeray, William Makepeace
    1811-1863 . . . . . . DLB-21, 55, 159, 163

Thames and Hudson Limited. DLB-112

Thanet, Octave (see French, Alice)

The Theater in Shakespeare's Time . . . DLB-62

The Theatre Guild DLB-7

Thegan and the Astronomer
  flourished circa 850 . . . . DLB-148

Thelwall, John 1764-1834 . . . . . DLB-93, 158

Theocritus circa 300 B.C.-260 B.C.
  . . . . DLB-176

Theodulf circa 760-circa 821 . . . . . DLB-148

Theophrastus circa 371 B.C.-287 B.C.
  . . . . DLB-176

Theriault, Yves 1915-1983 . . . . DLB-88

Thério, Adrien 1925- DLB-53

Theroux, Paul 1941- DLB-2

They All Came to Paris DS-16

Thibaudeau, Colleen 1925- DLB-88

Thielen, Benedict 1903-1965 . . . . . . DLB-102

Thiong'o Ngugi wa (see Ngugi wa Thiong'o)

Third-Generation Minor Poets of the
  Seventeenth Century DLB-131

This Quarter 1925-1927, 1929-1932 . . . . . DS-15

Thoma, Ludwig 1867-1921 . . . . DLB-66

Thoma, Richard 1902- DLB-4

Thomas, Audrey 1935- DLB-60

Thomas, D. M. 1935- DLB-40

Thomas, Dylan
  1914-1953 . . . . DLB-13, 20, 139

Thomas, Edward
  1878-1917 . . . . DLB-19, 98, 156

Thomas, Gwyn 1913-1981 . . . . DLB-15

Thomas, Isaiah 1750-1831 . . . . . DLB-43, 73

Thomas, Isaiah [publishing house] DLB-49

Thomas, Johann 1624-1679 . . . . . . DLB-168

Thomas, John 1900-1932 . . . . DLB-4

Thomas, Joyce Carol 1938- DLB-33

Thomas, Lorenzo 1944- DLB-41

Thomas, R. S. 1915- DLB-27

Thomasîn von Zerclære
  circa 1186-circa 1259 . . . . DLB-138

Thomasius, Christian 1655-1728 . . . . DLB-168

Thompson, David 1770-1857 . . . . . . DLB-99

Thompson, Dorothy 1893-1961 . . . . . DLB-29

Thompson, Francis 1859-1907 . . . . . DLB-19

Thompson, George Selden (see Selden, George)

Thompson, John 1938-1976 . . . . . . DLB-60

Thompson, John R. 1823-1873 . . . . DLB-3, 73

Thompson, Lawrance 1906-1973 . . . . DLB-103

Thompson, Maurice
  1844-1901 . . . . DLB-71, 74

Thompson, Ruth Plumly
  1891-1976 . . . . DLB-22

Thompson, Thomas Phillips
  1843-1933 . . . . DLB-99

Thompson, William 1775-1833 . . . . . DLB-158

Thompson, William Tappan
  1812-1882 . . . . DLB-3, 11

Thomson, Edward William
  1849-1924 . . . . DLB-92

Thomson, James 1700-1748 . . . . . . DLB-95

Thomson, James 1834-1882 . . . . . . DLB-35

Thomson, Joseph 1858-1895 . . . . . DLB-174

Thomson, Mortimer 1831-1875 . . . . DLB-11

Thoreau, Henry David
  1817-1862 . . . . DLB-1, 183

Thorpe, Thomas Bangs
  1815-1878 . . . . DLB-3, 11

Thoughts on Poetry and Its Varieties (1833),
  by John Stuart Mill DLB-32

Thrale, Hester Lynch (see Piozzi, Hester
  Lynch [Thrale])

Thucydides circa 455 B.C.-circa 395 B.C.
  . . . . DLB-176

Thümmel, Moritz August von
  1738-1817 . . . . DLB-97

Thurber, James
  1894-1961 . . . . DLB-4, 11, 22, 102

Thurman, Wallace 1902-1934 . . . . . DLB-51

Thwaite, Anthony 1930- DLB-40

Thwaites, Reuben Gold
  1853-1913 . . . . DLB-47

Ticknor, George
  1791-1871 . . . . DLB-1, 59, 140

Ticknor and Fields DLB-49

Ticknor and Fields (revived) DLB-46

Tieck, Ludwig 1773-1853 . . . . DLB-90

Tietjens, Eunice 1884-1944 . . . . . . DLB-54

Tilney, Edmund circa 1536-1610 . . . . DLB-136

Tilt, Charles [publishing house] DLB-106

Tilton, J. E., and Company DLB-49

Time and Western Man (1927), by Wyndham
  Lewis [excerpts] DLB-36

Time-Life Books DLB-46

Times Books DLB-46

Timothy, Peter circa 1725-1782 . . . . DLB-43

Timrod, Henry 1828-1867 . . . . DLB-3

Tinker, Chauncey Brewster
  1876-1963 . . . . DLB-140

Tinsley Brothers DLB-106

Tiptree, James, Jr. 1915-1987 . . . . . . DLB-8

Tišma, Aleksandar 1924- DLB-181

Titus, Edward William
  1870-1952 . . . . DLB-4; DS-15

Tlali, Miriam 1933- DLB-157

Todd, Barbara Euphan
  1890-1976 . . . . DLB-160

Tofte, Robert
  1561 or 1562-1619 or 1620 . . . . DLB-172

Toklas, Alice B. 1877-1967 . . . . DLB-4

Tokuda, Shūsei 1872-1943 . . . . DLB-180

Tolkien, J. R. R. 1892-1973 . . . . DLB-15, 160

Toller, Ernst 1893-1939 . . . . DLB-124

Tollet, Elizabeth 1694-1754 . . . . DLB-95

Tolson, Melvin B. 1898-1966 . . . . DLB-48, 76

Tom Jones (1749), by Henry Fielding
  [excerpt] DLB-39

Tomalin, Claire 1933- DLB-155

Tomasi di Lampedusa,
  Giuseppe 1896-1957 . . . . DLB-177

Tomlinson, Charles 1927- DLB-40

Tomlinson, H. M. 1873-1958 . . . DLB-36, 100

Tompkins, Abel [publishing house] . . . DLB-49

Tompson, Benjamin 1642-1714 . . . . . DLB-24

Tonks, Rosemary 1932- DLB-14

Tonna, Charlotte Elizabeth
  1790-1846 . . . . DLB-163

Tonson, Jacob the Elder
  [publishing house] DLB-170

Toole, John Kennedy 1937-1969 . . . . . Y-81

Toomer, Jean 1894-1967 . . . . . . DLB-45, 51

Tor Books DLB-46

Torberg, Friedrich 1908-1979 . . . . . . DLB-85

Torrence, Ridgely 1874-1950 . . . . . . DLB-54

Torres-Metzger, Joseph V.
  1933- DLB-122

Toth, Susan Allen 1940- Y-86

Tottell, Richard
  [publishing house] DLB-170

Tough-Guy Literature DLB-9

Touré, Askia Muhammad 1938- DLB-41

Tourgée, Albion W. 1838-1905 . . . . . DLB-79

Tourneur, Cyril circa 1580-1626 . . . . . DLB-58

Tournier, Michel 1924- DLB-83

Tousey, Frank [publishing house] DLB-49

Tower Publications DLB-46

Towne, Benjamin circa 1740-1793 . . . . DLB-43

Towne, Robert 1936- DLB-44

The Townely Plays
  fifteenth and sixteenth
  centuries DLB-146

Townshend, Aurelian
  by 1583 - circa 1651 . . . . DLB-121

Tracy, Honor 1913- DLB-15

Traherne, Thomas 1637?-1674 . . . . . DLB-131

Traill, Catharine Parr 1802-1899 . . . . DLB-99

Train, Arthur 1875-1945 . . . . . DLB-86; DS-16

The Transatlantic Publishing
  Company DLB-49

The Transatlantic Review 1924-1925 . . . . . DS-15

Transcendentalists, American DS-5

transition 1927-1938 . . . . DS-15

Translators of the Twelfth Century:
Literary Issues Raised and Impact
Created. DLB-115

Travel Writing, 1837-1875 . . . . . . DLB-166

Travel Writing, 1876-1909 . . . . . . DLB-174

Traven, B.
1882? or 1890?-1969? DLB-9, 56

Travers, Ben 1886-1980 . . . . DLB-10

Travers, P. L. (Pamela Lyndon)
1899- DLB-160

Trediakovsky, Vasilii Kirillovich
1703-1769 . . . . DLB-150

Treece, Henry 1911-1966 . . . . DLB-160

Trejo, Ernesto 1950- DLB-122

Trelawny, Edward John
1792-1881 . . . . DLB-110, 116, 144

Tremain, Rose 1943- DLB-14

Tremblay, Michel 1942- DLB-60

Trends in Twentieth-Century
Mass Market Publishing DLB-46

Trent, William P. 1862-1939 . . . . . . DLB-47

Trescot, William Henry
1822-1898 . . . . DLB-30

Trevelyan, Sir George Otto
1838-1928 . . . . DLB-144

Trevisa, John
circa 1342-circa 1402 . . . . DLB-146

Trevor, William 1928- DLB-14, 139

Trierer Floyris circa 1170-1180 . . . . . DLB-138

Trilling, Lionel 1905-1975 . . . . . DLB-28, 63

Trilussa 1871-1950 . . . . DLB-114

Trimmer, Sarah 1741-1810 . . . . . . DLB-158

Triolet, Elsa 1896-1970 . . . . DLB-72

Tripp, John 1927- DLB-40

Trocchi, Alexander 1925- DLB-15

Trollope, Anthony
1815-1882 . . . . DLB-21, 57, 159

Trollope, Frances 1779-1863 . . . . DLB-21, 166

Troop, Elizabeth 1931- DLB-14

Trotter, Catharine 1679-1749 . . . . . . DLB-84

Trotti, Lamar 1898-1952 . . . . DLB-44

Trottier, Pierre 1925- DLB-60

Troupe, Quincy Thomas, Jr.
1943- DLB-41

Trow, John F., and Company DLB-49

Truillier-Lacombe, Joseph-Patrice
1807-1863 . . . . DLB-99

Trumbo, Dalton 1905-1976 . . . . DLB-26

Trumbull, Benjamin 1735-1820 . . . . . DLB-30

Trumbull, John 1750-1831 . . . . DLB-31

Trumbull, John 1756-1843 . . . . DLB-183

Tscherning, Andreas 1611-1659 . . . . . DLB-164

T. S. Eliot Centennial Y-88

Tsubouchi, Shōyō 1859-1935 . . . . . DLB-180

Tucholsky, Kurt 1890-1935 . . . . DLB-56

Tucker, Charlotte Maria
1821-1893 . . . . DLB-163

Tucker, George 1775-1861 . . . . . DLB-3, 30

Tucker, Nathaniel Beverley
1784-1851 . . . . DLB-3

Tucker, St. George 1752-1827 . . . . . DLB-37

Tuckerman, Henry Theodore
1813-1871 . . . . DLB-64

Tunis, John R. 1889-1975 . . . . DLB-22, 171

Tunstall, Cuthbert 1474-1559 . . . . . DLB-132

Tuohy, Frank 1925- DLB-14, 139

Tupper, Martin F. 1810-1889 . . . . DLB-32

Turbyfill, Mark 1896- DLB-45

Turco, Lewis 1934- Y-84

Turnbull, Andrew 1921-1970 . . . . . DLB-103

Turnbull, Gael 1928- DLB-40

Turner, Arlin 1909-1980 . . . . DLB-103

Turner, Charles (Tennyson)
1808-1879 . . . . DLB-32

Turner, Frederick 1943- DLB-40

Turner, Frederick Jackson
1861-1932 . . . . DLB-17

Turner, Joseph Addison
1826-1868 . . . . DLB-79

Turpin, Waters Edward
1910-1968 . . . . DLB-51

Turrini, Peter 1944- DLB-124

Tutuola, Amos 1920- DLB-125

Twain, Mark (see Clemens,
Samuel Langhorne)

Tweedie, Ethel Brilliana
circa 1860-1940 . . . . DLB-174

The 'Twenties and Berlin, by
Alex Natan DLB-66

Tyler, Anne 1941- DLB-6, 143; Y-82

Tyler, Moses Coit 1835-1900 . . . . DLB-47, 64

Tyler, Royall 1757-1826 . . . . DLB-37

Tylor, Edward Burnett 1832-1917 . . . . DLB-57

Tynan, Katharine 1861-1931 . . . . . . DLB-153

Tyndale, William
circa 1494-1536 . . . . DLB-132

Ulica, Jorge 1870-1926 . . . . DLB-82

Ulizio, B. George 1889-1969 . . . . . DLB-140

Ulrich von Liechtenstein
circa 1200-circa 1275 . . . . DLB-138

Ulrich von Zatzikhoven
before 1194-after 1214 . . . . . . DLB-138

Unamuno, Miguel de 1864-1936 . . . . DLB-108

Under the Microscope (1872), by
A. C. Swinburne DLB-35

Unger, Friederike Helene
1741-1813 . . . . DLB-94

Ungaretti, Giuseppe 1888-1970 . . . . DLB-114

United States Book Company DLB-49

Universal Publishing and Distributing
Corporation DLB-46

The University of Iowa Writers' Workshop
Golden Jubilee Y-86

The University of South Carolina
Press Y-94

University of Wales Press DLB-112

"The Unknown Public" (1858), by
Wilkie Collins [excerpt] DLB-57

Uno, Chiyo 1897-1996 . . . . DLB-180

Unruh, Fritz von 1885-1970 . . . . DLB-56, 118

Unspeakable Practices II: The Festival of
Vanguard Narrative at Brown
University Y-93

Unwin, T. Fisher
[publishing house] DLB-106

Upchurch, Boyd B. (see Boyd, John)

Updike, John
1932- DLB-2, 5, 143; Y-80, 82; DS-3

Upton, Bertha 1849-1912 . . . . DLB-141

Upton, Charles 1948- DLB-16

Upton, Florence K. 1873-1922 . . . . . DLB-141

Upward, Allen 1863-1926 . . . . DLB-36

Urista, Alberto Baltazar (see Alurista)

Urzidil, Johannes 1896-1976 . . . . . . DLB-85

Urquhart, Fred 1912- DLB-139

The Uses of Facsimile Y-90

Usk, Thomas died 1388 . . . . DLB-146

Uslar Pietri, Arturo 1906- DLB-113

Ustinov, Peter 1921- DLB-13

Uttley, Alison 1884-1976 . . . . DLB-160

Uz, Johann Peter 1720-1796 . . . . . . DLB-97

U

Udall, Nicholas 1504-1556 . . . . DLB-62

Ugrěsić, Dubravka 1949- DLB-181

Uhland, Ludwig 1787-1862 . . . . . . DLB-90

Uhse, Bodo 1904-1963 . . . . DLB-69

Ujević, Augustin ("Tin")
1891-1955 . . . . DLB-147

Ulenhart, Niclas
flourished circa 1600 . . . . DLB-164

Ulibarrí, Sabine R. 1919- DLB-82

V

Vac, Bertrand 1914- DLB-88

Vail, Laurence 1891-1968 . . . . DLB-4

Vailland, Roger 1907-1965 . . . . DLB-83

Vajda, Ernest 1887-1954 . . . . DLB-44

Valdés, Gina 1943- DLB-122

Valdez, Luis Miguel 1940- DLB-122

Valduga, Patrizia 1953- DLB-128

Valente, José Angel 1929- DLB-108

Valenzuela, Luisa 1938- DLB-113

Valeri, Diego 1887-1976 . . . . DLB-128

Valgardson, W. D. 1939- DLB-60

Valle, Víctor Manuel 1950- DLB-122

Valle-Inclán, Ramón del
1866-1936 . . . . DLB-134

Vallejo, Armando 1949- DLB-122

Vallès, Jules 1832-1885 . . . . DLB-123

Vallette, Marguerite Eymery (see Rachilde)

Valverde, José María 1926- DLB-108

Van Allsburg, Chris 1949- DLB-61

Van Anda, Carr 1864-1945 . . . . . . DLB-25

Van Doren, Mark 1894-1972 . . . . . DLB-45

van Druten, John 1901-1957 . . . . . DLB-10

Van Duyn, Mona 1921- DLB-5

Van Dyke, Henry
1852-1933 . . . . DLB-71; DS-13

Van Dyke, Henry 1928- DLB-33

van Itallie, Jean-Claude 1936- DLB-7

Van Loan, Charles E. 1876-1919 . . . . DLB-171

Van Rensselaer, Mariana Griswold
1851-1934 . . . . DLB-47

Van Rensselaer, Mrs. Schuyler (see Van
Rensselaer, Mariana Griswold)

Van Vechten, Carl 1880-1964 . . . . DLB-4, 9

van Vogt, A. E. 1912- DLB-8

Vanbrugh, Sir John 1664-1726 . . . . . DLB-80

Vance, Jack 1916?- DLB-8

Vane, Sutton 1888-1963 . . . . DLB-10

Vanguard Press DLB-46

Vann, Robert L. 1879-1940 . . . . . . DLB-29

Vargas, Llosa, Mario 1936- DLB-145

Varley, John 1947- Y-81

Varnhagen von Ense, Karl August
1785-1858 . . . . DLB-90

Varnhagen von Ense, Rahel
1771-1833 . . . . DLB-90

Vásquez Montalbán, Manuel
1939- DLB-134

Vassa, Gustavus (see Equiano, Olaudah)

Vassalli, Sebastiano 1941- DLB-128

Vaughan, Henry 1621-1695 . . . . . . DLB-131

Vaughan, Thomas 1621-1666 . . . . . DLB-131

Vaux, Thomas, Lord 1509-1556 . . . . DLB-132

Vazov, Ivan 1850-1921 . . . . DLB-147

Vega, Janine Pommy 1942- DLB-16

Veiller, Anthony 1903-1965 . . . . . . DLB-44

Velásquez-Trevino, Gloria
1949- DLB-122

Veloz Maggiolo, Marcio 1936- DLB-145

Venegas, Daniel ?-? DLB-82

Vergil, Polydore circa 1470-1555 . . . . DLB-132

Veríssimo, Erico 1905-1975 . . . . . . DLB-145

Verne, Jules 1828-1905 . . . . DLB-123

Verplanck, Gulian C. 1786-1870 . . . . DLB-59

Very, Jones 1813-1880 . . . . DLB-1

Vian, Boris 1920-1959 . . . . DLB-72

Vickers, Roy 1888?-1965 . . . . DLB-77

Victoria 1819-1901 . . . . DLB-55

Victoria Press DLB-106

Vidal, Gore 1925- DLB-6, 152

Viebig, Clara 1860-1952 . . . . DLB-66

Viereck, George Sylvester
1884-1962 . . . . DLB-54

Viereck, Peter 1916- DLB-5

Viets, Roger 1738-1811 . . . . DLB-99

Viewpoint: Politics and Performance, by
David Edgar DLB-13

Vigil-Piñon, Evangelina 1949- DLB-122

Vigneault, Gilles 1928- DLB-60

Vigny, Alfred de 1797-1863 . . . . . . DLB-119

Vigolo, Giorgio 1894-1983 . . . . . . DLB-114

The Viking Press DLB-46

Villanueva, Alma Luz 1944- DLB-122

Villanueva, Tino 1941- DLB-82

Villard, Henry 1835-1900 . . . . DLB-23

Villard, Oswald Garrison
1872-1949 . . . . DLB-25, 91

Villarreal, José Antonio 1924- DLB-82

Villegas de Magnón, Leonor
1876-1955 . . . . DLB-122

Villemaire, Yolande 1949- DLB-60

Villena, Luis Antonio de 1951- DLB-134

Villiers de l'Isle-Adam, Jean-Marie
Mathias Philippe-Auguste, Comte de
1838-1889 . . . . DLB-123

Villiers, George, Second Duke
of Buckingham 1628-1687 . . . . . . DLB-80

Vine Press DLB-112

Viorst, Judith ?- DLB-52

Vipont, Elfrida (Elfrida Vipont Foulds,
Charles Vipont) 1902-1992 . . . . DLB-160

Viramontes, Helena María
1954- DLB-122

Vischer, Friedrich Theodor
1807-1887 . . . . DLB-133

Vivanco, Luis Felipe 1907-1975 . . . . DLB-108

Viviani, Cesare 1947- DLB-128

Vizenor, Gerald 1934- DLB-175

Vizetelly and Company DLB-106

Voaden, Herman 1903- DLB-88

Voigt, Ellen Bryant 1943- DLB-120

Vojnović, Ivo 1857-1929 . . . . DLB-147

Volkoff, Vladimir 1932- DLB-83

Volland, P. F., Company DLB-46

Volponi, Paolo 1924- DLB-177

von der Grün, Max 1926- DLB-75

Vonnegut, Kurt
1922- DLB-2, 8, 152; Y-80; DS-3

Voranc, Prežihov 1893-1950 . . . . . . DLB-147

Voß, Johann Heinrich 1751-1826 . . . . DLB-90

Vroman, Mary Elizabeth
circa 1924-1967 . . . . DLB-33

W

Wace, Robert ("Maistre")
circa 1100-circa 1175 . . . . DLB-146

Wackenroder, Wilhelm Heinrich
1773-1798 . . . . DLB-90

Wackernagel, Wilhelm
1806-1869 . . . . DLB-133

Waddington, Miriam 1917- DLB-68

Wade, Henry 1887-1969 . . . . DLB-77

Wagenknecht, Edward 1900- DLB-103

Wagner, Heinrich Leopold
1747-1779 . . . . DLB-94

Wagner, Henry R. 1862-1957 . . . . . DLB-140

Wagner, Richard 1813-1883 . . . . . . DLB-129

Wagoner, David 1926- DLB-5

Wah, Fred 1939- DLB-60

Waiblinger, Wilhelm 1804-1830 . . . . DLB-90

Wain, John
1925-1994 . . . . . . DLB-15, 27, 139, 155

Wainwright, Jeffrey 1944- DLB-40

Waite, Peirce and Company DLB-49

Wakoski, Diane 1937- DLB-5

Walahfrid Strabo circa 808-849 . . . . DLB-148

Walck, Henry Z. DLB-46

Walcott, Derek
1930- DLB-117; Y-81, 92

Waldegrave, Robert
[publishing house] DLB-170

Waldman, Anne 1945- DLB-16

Waldrop, Rosmarie 1935- DLB-169

Walker, Alice 1944- DLB-6, 33, 143

Walker, George F. 1947- DLB-60

Walker, Joseph A. 1935- DLB-38

Walker, Margaret 1915- DLB-76, 152

Walker, Ted 1934- DLB-40

Walker and Company DLB-49

Walker, Evans and Cogswell
Company DLB-49

Walker, John Brisben 1847-1931 . . . . DLB-79

Wallace, Dewitt 1889-1981 and
Lila Acheson Wallace
1889-1984 . . . . DLB-137

Wallace, Edgar 1875-1932 . . . . DLB-70

Wallace, Lila Acheson (see Wallace, Dewitt,
and Lila Acheson Wallace)

Wallant, Edward Lewis
1926-1962. . . . . DLB-2, 28, 143

Waller, Edmund 1606-1687 . . . . DLB-126

Walpole, Horace 1717-1797 . . . . . DLB-39, 104

Walpole, Hugh 1884-1941 . . . . DLB-34

Walrond, Eric 1898-1966 . . . . DLB-51

Walser, Martin 1927- DLB-75, 124

Walser, Robert 1878-1956 . . . . DLB-66

Walsh, Ernest 1895-1926 . . . . . . DLB-4, 45

Walsh, Robert 1784-1859 . . . . DLB-59

Waltharius circa 825 . . . . DLB-148

Walters, Henry 1848-1931 . . . . DLB-140

Walther von der Vogelweide
circa 1170-circa 1230 . . . . DLB-138

Walton, Izaak 1593-1683 . . . . DLB-151

Wambaugh, Joseph 1937- DLB-6; Y-83

Waniek, Marilyn Nelson 1946- DLB-120

Warburton, William 1698-1779 . . . . DLB-104

Ward, Aileen 1919- DLB-111

Ward, Artemus (see Browne, Charles Farrar)

Ward, Arthur Henry Sarsfield
(see Rohmer, Sax)

Ward, Douglas Turner 1930- DLB-7, 38

Ward, Lynd 1905-1985 . . . . DLB-22

Ward, Lock and Company DLB-106

Ward, Mrs. Humphry 1851-1920 . . . . DLB-18

Ward, Nathaniel circa 1578-1652 . . . . DLB-24

Ward, Theodore 1902-1983 . . . . . . DLB-76

Wardle, Ralph 1909-1988 . . . . DLB-103

Ware, William 1797-1852 . . . . DLB-1

Warne, Frederick, and
Company [U.S.] DLB-49

Warne, Frederick, and
Company [U.K.] DLB-106

Warner, Charles Dudley
1829-1900 . . . . DLB-64

Warner, Rex 1905- DLB-15

Warner, Susan Bogert
1819-1885 . . . . DLB-3, 42

Warner, Sylvia Townsend
1893-1978 . . . . DLB-34, 139

Warner, William 1558-1609 . . . . . . DLB-172

Warner Books DLB-46

Warr, Bertram 1917-1943 . . . . DLB-88

Warren, John Byrne Leicester (see De Tabley,
Lord)

Warren, Lella 1899-1982 . . . . Y-83

Warren, Mercy Otis 1728-1814 . . . . . DLB-31

Warren, Robert Penn
1905-1989 . . . . . DLB-2, 48, 152; Y-80, 89

Die Wartburgkrieg
circa 1230-circa 1280 . . . . DLB-138

Warton, Joseph 1722-1800 . . . . DLB-104, 109

Warton, Thomas 1728-1790 . . . . DLB-104, 109

Washington, George 1732-1799 . . . . . DLB-31

Wassermann, Jakob 1873-1934 . . . . . DLB-66

Wasson, David Atwood 1823-1887 . . . . DLB-1

Waterhouse, Keith 1929- DLB-13, 15

Waterman, Andrew 1940- DLB-40

Waters, Frank 1902- Y-86

Waters, Michael 1949- DLB-120

Watkins, Tobias 1780-1855 . . . . DLB-73

Watkins, Vernon 1906-1967 . . . . . . DLB-20

Watmough, David 1926- DLB-53

Watson, James Wreford (see Wreford, James)

Watson, John 1850-1907 . . . . DLB-156

Watson, Sheila 1909- DLB-60

Watson, Thomas 1545?-1592 . . . . . DLB-132

Watson, Wilfred 1911- DLB-60

Watt, W. J., and Company DLB-46

Watterson, Henry 1840-1921 . . . . . . DLB-25

Watts, Alan 1915-1973 . . . . DLB-16

Watts, Franklin [publishing house] . . . DLB-46

Watts, Isaac 1674-1748 . . . . DLB-95

Waugh, Auberon 1939- DLB-14

Waugh, Evelyn 1903-1966 . . . . DLB-15, 162

Way and Williams DLB-49

Wayman, Tom 1945- DLB-53

Weatherly, Tom 1942- DLB-41

Weaver, Gordon 1937- DLB-130

Weaver, Robert 1921- DLB-88

Webb, Frank J. ?-? DLB-50

Webb, James Watson 1802-1884 . . . . DLB-43

Webb, Mary 1881-1927 . . . . DLB-34

Webb, Phyllis 1927- DLB-53

Webb, Walter Prescott 1888-1963 . . . . DLB-17

Webbe, William ?-1591 . . . . DLB-132

Webster, Augusta 1837-1894 . . . . . . DLB-35

Webster, Charles L.,
and Company DLB-49

Webster, John
1579 or 1580-1634? DLB-58

Webster, Noah
1758-1843 . . . . . . DLB-1, 37, 42, 43, 73

Weckherlin, Georg Rodolf
1584-1653 . . . . DLB-164

Wedekind, Frank 1864-1918 . . . . . DLB-118

Weeks, Edward Augustus, Jr.
1898-1989 . . . . DLB-137

Weems, Mason Locke
1759-1825 . . . . DLB-30, 37, 42

Weerth, Georg 1822-1856 . . . . DLB-129

Weidenfeld and Nicolson DLB-112

Weidman, Jerome 1913- DLB-28

Weigl, Bruce 1949- DLB-120

Weinbaum, Stanley Grauman
1902-1935 . . . . DLB-8

Weintraub, Stanley 1929- DLB-111

Weise, Christian 1642-1708 . . . . . . DLB-168

Weisenborn, Gunther
1902-1969 . . . . DLB-69, 124

Weiß, Ernst 1882-1940 . . . . DLB-81

Weiss, John 1818-1879 . . . . DLB-1

Weiss, Peter 1916-1982 . . . . . . DLB-69, 124

Weiss, Theodore 1916- DLB-5

Weisse, Christian Felix 1726-1804 . . . . DLB-97

Weitling, Wilhelm 1808-1871 . . . . . DLB-129

Welch, James 1940- DLB-175

Welch, Lew 1926-1971? DLB-16

Weldon, Fay 1931- DLB-14

Wellek, René 1903- DLB-63

Wells, Carolyn 1862-1942 . . . . DLB-11

Wells, Charles Jeremiah
circa 1800-1879 . . . . DLB-32

Wells, Gabriel 1862-1946 . . . . DLB-140

Wells, H. G.
1866-1946 . . . . . . DLB-34, 70, 156, 178

Wells, Robert 1947- DLB-40

Wells-Barnett, Ida B. 1862-1931 . . . . DLB-23

Welty, Eudora
1909- DLB-2, 102, 143; Y-87; DS-12

Wendell, Barrett 1855-1921 . . . . . . DLB-71

Wentworth, Patricia 1878-1961 . . . . DLB-77

Werder, Diederich von dem
1584-1657 . . . . DLB-164

Werfel, Franz 1890-1945 . . . . . DLB-81, 124

The Werner Company DLB-49

Werner, Zacharias 1768-1823 . . . . . DLB-94

Wersba, Barbara 1932- DLB-52

Wescott, Glenway 1901- DLB-4, 9, 102

Wesker, Arnold 1932- DLB-13

Wesley, Charles 1707-1788 . . . . DLB-95

Wesley, John 1703-1791 . . . . DLB-104

Wesley, Richard 1945- DLB-38

Wessels, A., and Company DLB-46

Wessobrunner Gebet
circa 787-815 . . . . DLB-148

West, Anthony 1914-1988 . . . . DLB-15

West, Dorothy 1907- DLB-76

West, Jessamyn 1902-1984 . . . . . DLB-6; Y-84

West, Mae 1892-1980 . . . . DLB-44

West, Nathanael 1903-1940 . . . . DLB-4, 9, 28

West, Paul 1930- DLB-14

West, Rebecca 1892-1983 . . . . . DLB-36; Y-83

West and Johnson DLB-49

Western Publishing Company DLB-46

The Westminster Review 1824-1914 . . . . DLB-110

Weston, Elizabeth Jane
circa 1582-1612 . . . . DLB-172

Wetherald, Agnes Ethelwyn
1857-1940 . . . . DLB-99

Wetherell, Elizabeth
(see Warner, Susan Bogert)

Wetzel, Friedrich Gottlob
1779-1819 . . . . DLB-90

Weyman, Stanley J.
1855-1928. . . . . DLB-141, 156

Wezel, Johann Karl 1747-1819 . . . . . DLB-94

Whalen, Philip 1923- DLB-16

Whalley, George 1915-1983 . . . . . . DLB-88

Wharton, Edith
1862-1937 . . . . DLB-4, 9, 12, 78; DS-13

Wharton, William 1920s?- Y-80

Whately, Mary Louisa
1824-1889 . . . . DLB-166

What's Really Wrong With Bestseller
Lists Y-84

Wheatley, Dennis Yates
1897-1977 . . . . DLB-77

Wheatley, Phillis
circa 1754-1784 . . . . DLB-31, 50

Wheeler, Anna Doyle
1785-1848? DLB-158

Wheeler, Charles Stearns
1816-1843. . . . . DLB-1

Wheeler, Monroe 1900-1988. . . . . . DLB-4

Wheelock, John Hall 1886-1978 . . . . DLB-45

Wheelwright, John
circa 1592-1679 . . . . DLB-24

Wheelwright, J. B. 1897-1940 . . . . . DLB-45

Whetstone, Colonel Pete
(see Noland, C. F. M.)

Whetstone, George 1550-1587 . . . . . DLB-136

Whicher, Stephen E. 1915-1961 . . . . DLB-111

Whipple, Edwin Percy
1819-1886 . . . . DLB-1, 64

Whitaker, Alexander 1585-1617 . . . . DLB-24

Whitaker, Daniel K. 1801-1881 . . . . DLB-73

Whitcher, Frances Miriam
1814-1852 . . . . DLB-11

White, Andrew 1579-1656 . . . . DLB-24

White, Andrew Dickson
1832-1918 . . . . DLB-47

White, E. B. 1899-1985 . . . . . . DLB-11, 22

White, Edgar B. 1947- DLB-38

White, Ethel Lina 1887-1944. . . . . . DLB-77

White, Henry Kirke 1785-1806 . . . . DLB-96

White, Horace 1834-1916. . . . . . . DLB-23

White, Phyllis Dorothy James
(see James, P. D.)

White, Richard Grant 1821-1885 . . . . DLB-64

White, T. H. 1906-1964. . . . . DLB-160

White, Walter 1893-1955 . . . . DLB-51

White, William, and Company DLB-49

White, William Allen
1868-1944 . . . . DLB-9, 25

White, William Anthony Parker (see Boucher, Anthony)

White, William Hale (see Rutherford, Mark)

Whitechurch, Victor L.
1868-1933 . . . . DLB-70

Whitehead, Alfred North
1861-1947 . . . . DLB-100

Whitehead, James 1936- Y-81

Whitehead, William
1715-1785 . . . . DLB-84, 109

Whitfield, James Monroe
1822-1871 . . . . DLB-50

Whitgift, John circa 1533-1604 . . . . . DLB-132

Whiting, John 1917-1963 . . . . DLB-13

Whiting, Samuel 1597-1679 . . . . . . DLB-24

Whitlock, Brand 1869-1934. . . . . . . DLB-12

Whitman, Albert, and Company. DLB-46

Whitman, Albery Allson
1851-1901 . . . . DLB-50

Whitman, Alden 1913-1990 . . . . Y-91

Whitman, Sarah Helen (Power)
1803-1878 . . . . DLB-1

Whitman, Walt 1819-1892 . . . . . DLB-3, 64

Whitman Publishing Company. DLB-46

Whitney, Geoffrey
1548 or 1552?-1601 . . . . DLB-136

Whitney, Isabella
flourished 1566-1573 . . . . DLB-136

Whitney, John Hay 1904-1982 . . . . . DLB-127

Whittemore, Reed 1919- DLB-5

Whittier, John Greenleaf 1807-1892. . . . DLB-1

Whittlesey House DLB-46

Who Runs American Literature? Y-94

Wideman, John Edgar 1941- DLB-33, 143

Widener, Harry Elkins 1885-1912 . . . DLB-140

Wiebe, Rudy 1934- DLB-60

Wiechert, Ernst 1887-1950 . . . . . . DLB-56

Wied, Martina 1882-1957. . . . . DLB-85

Wiehe, Evelyn May Clowes (see Mordaunt,
Elinor)

Wieland, Christoph Martin
1733-1813 . . . . DLB-97

Wienbarg, Ludolf 1802-1872 . . . . . . DLB-133

Wieners, John 1934- DLB-16

Wier, Ester 1910- DLB-52

Wiesel, Elie 1928- DLB-83; Y-87

Wiggin, Kate Douglas 1856-1923 . . . . DLB-42

Wigglesworth, Michael 1631-1705 . . . . DLB-24

Wilberforce, William 1759-1833. . . . . DLB-158

Wilbrandt, Adolf 1837-1911. . . . . . . DLB-129

Wilbur, Richard 1921- DLB-5, 169

Wild, Peter 1940- DLB-5

Wilde, Oscar
1854-1900. . . . DLB-10, 19, 34, 57, 141, 156

Wilde, Richard Henry
1789-1847 . . . . DLB-3, 59

Wilde, W. A., Company. DLB-49

Wilder, Billy 1906- DLB-26

Wilder, Laura Ingalls 1867-1957 . . . . DLB-22

Wilder, Thornton 1897-1975 . . . . DLB-4, 7, 9

Wildgans, Anton 1881-1932. . . . . . . DLB-118

Wiley, Bell Irvin 1906-1980 . . . . . . DLB-17

Wiley, John, and Sons DLB-49

Wilhelm, Kate 1928- DLB-8

Wilkes, Charles 1798-1877 . . . . . . DLB-183

Wilkes, George 1817-1885 . . . . DLB-79

Wilkinson, Anne 1910-1961 . . . . . . DLB-88

Wilkinson, Sylvia 1940- Y-86

Wilkinson, William Cleaver
1833-1920 . . . . DLB-71

Willard, Barbara 1909-1994 . . . . . . DLB-161

Willard, L. [publishing house] DLB-49

Willard, Nancy 1936- DLB-5, 52

Willard, Samuel 1640-1707 . . . . . . DLB-24

William of Auvergne 1190-1249 . . . . DLB-115

William of Conches
circa 1090-circa 1154 . . . . DLB-115

William of Ockham
circa 1285-1347 . . . . DLB-115

William of Sherwood
1200/1205 - 1266/1271 . . . . DLB-115

The William Chavrat American Fiction
Collection at the Ohio State University Libraries Y-92

Williams, A., and Company DLB-49

Williams, Ben Ames 1889-1953. . . . . DLB-102

Williams, C. K. 1936- DLB-5

Williams, Chancellor 1905- DLB-76

Williams, Charles
1886-1945. . . . . DLB-100, 153

Williams, Denis 1923- DLB-117

Williams, Emlyn 1905- DLB-10, 77

Williams, Garth 1912- DLB-22

Williams, George Washington
1849-1891 . . . . DLB-47

Williams, Heathcote 1941- DLB-13

Williams, Helen Maria
1761-1827 . . . . DLB-158

Williams, Hugo 1942- DLB-40

Williams, Isaac 1802-1865 . . . . DLB-32

Williams, Joan 1928- DLB-6

Williams, John A. 1925- DLB-2, 33

Williams, John E. 1922-1994 . . . . . . DLB-6

Williams, Jonathan 1929- DLB-5

Williams, Miller 1930- DLB-105

Williams, Raymond 1921- DLB-14

Williams, Roger circa 1603-1683 . . . . . DLB-24

Williams, Samm-Art 1946- DLB-38

Williams, Sherley Anne 1944- DLB-41

Williams, T. Harry 1909-1979 . . . . . DLB-17

Williams, Tennessee
1911-1983 . . . . DLB-7; Y-83; DS-4

Williams, Ursula Moray 1911- . . . DLB-160

Williams, Valentine 1883-1946 . . . . . DLB-77

Williams, William Appleman
1921- DLB-17

Williams, William Carlos
1883-1963 . . . . DLB-4, 16, 54, 86

Williams, Wirt 1921- DLB-6

Williams Brothers DLB-49

Williamson, Jack 1908- DLB-8

Willingham, Calder Baynard, Jr.
1922- DLB-2, 44

Williram of Ebersberg
circa 1020-1085 . . . . DLB-148

Willis, Nathaniel Parker
1806-1867 . . . DLB-3, 59, 73, 74, 183; DS-13

Willkomm, Ernst 1810-1886 . . . . . . DLB-133

Wilmer, Clive 1945- DLB-40

Wilson, A. N. 1950- DLB-14, 155

Wilson, Angus
1913-1991 . . . . DLB-15, 139, 155

Wilson, Arthur 1595-1652 . . . . DLB-58

Wilson, Augusta Jane Evans
1835-1909 . . . . DLB-42

Wilson, Colin 1931- DLB-14

Wilson, Edmund 1895-1972 . . . . . . DLB-63

Wilson, Ethel 1888-1980 . . . . DLB-68

Wilson, Harriet E. Adams
1828?-1863? DLB-50

Wilson, Harry Leon 1867-1939 . . . . . DLB-9

Wilson, John 1588-1667 . . . . DLB-24

Wilson, John 1785-1854 . . . . DLB-110

Wilson, Lanford 1937- DLB-7

Wilson, Margaret 1882-1973 . . . . . . DLB-9

Wilson, Michael 1914-1978 . . . . DLB-44

Wilson, Mona 1872-1954 . . . . DLB-149

Wilson, Thomas
1523 or 1524-1581 . . . . DLB-132

Wilson, Woodrow 1856-1924 . . . . . . DLB-47

Wilson, Effingham
[publishing house] DLB-154

Wimsatt, William K., Jr.
1907-1975 . . . . DLB-63

Winchell, Walter 1897-1972 . . . . . . DLB-29

Winchester, J. [publishing house] DLB-49

Winckelmann, Johann Joachim
1717-1768 . . . . DLB-97

Winckler, Paul 1630-1686 . . . . DLB-164

Wind, Herbert Warren 1916- DLB-171

Windet, John [publishing house] DLB-170

Windham, Donald 1920- DLB-6

Wingate, Allan [publishing house] . . . DLB-112

Winnemucca, Sarah 1844-1921 . . . . . DLB-175

Winnifrith, Tom 1938- DLB-155

Winsloe, Christa 1888-1944 . . . . . . DLB-124

Winsor, Justin 1831-1897 . . . . DLB-47

John C. Winston Company DLB-49

Winters, Yvor 1900-1968 . . . . DLB-48

Winthrop, John 1588-1649 . . . . . DLB-24, 30

Winthrop, John, Jr. 1606-1676 . . . . . DLB-24

Wirt, William 1772-1834 . . . . DLB-37

Wise, John 1652-1725 . . . . DLB-24

Wiseman, Adele 1928- DLB-88

Wishart and Company DLB-112

Wisner, George 1812-1849 . . . . DLB-43

Wister, Owen 1860-1938 . . . . DLB-9, 78

Wither, George 1588-1667 . . . . DLB-121

Witherspoon, John 1723-1794 . . . . . . DLB-31

Withrow, William Henry 1839-1908 . . . . DLB-99

Wittig, Monique 1935- DLB-83

Wodehouse, P. G.
1881-1975 . . . . DLB-34, 162

Wohmann, Gabriele 1932- DLB-75

Woiwode, Larry 1941- DLB-6

Wolcot, John 1738-1819 . . . . DLB-109

Wolcott, Roger 1679-1767 . . . . DLB-24

Wolf, Christa 1929- DLB-75

Wolf, Friedrich 1888-1953 . . . . DLB-124

Wolfe, Gene 1931- DLB-8

Wolfe, John [publishing house] DLB-170

Wolfe, Reyner (Reginald)
[publishing house] DLB-170

Wolfe, Thomas
1900-1938 . . . . DLB-9, 102; Y-85; DS-2, 16

Wolfe, Tom 1931- DLB-152

Wolff, Helen 1906-1994 . . . . Y-94

Wolff, Tobias 1945- DLB-130

Wolfram von Eschenbach
circa 1170-after 1220 . . . . DLB-138

Wolfram von Eschenbach's *Parzival*:
Prologue and Book 3 . . . . DLB-138

Wollstonecraft, Mary
1759-1797 . . . . DLB-39, 104, 158

Wondratschek, Wolf 1943- DLB-75

Wood, Benjamin 1820-1900 . . . . . . DLB-23

Wood, Charles 1932- DLB-13

Wood, Mrs. Henry 1814-1887 . . . . . DLB-18

Wood, Joanna E. 1867-1927 . . . . . . DLB-92

Wood, Samuel [publishing house] DLB-49

Wood, William ?-? DLB-24

Woodberry, George Edward
1855-1930 . . . . DLB-71, 103

Woodbridge, Benjamin 1622-1684 . . . . DLB-24

Woodcock, George 1912- DLB-88

Woodhull, Victoria C. 1838-1927 . . . . DLB-79

Woodmason, Charles circa 1720-? DLB-31

Woodress, Jr., James Leslie
1916- DLB-111

Woodson, Carter G. 1875-1950 . . . . . DLB-17

Woodward, C. Vann 1908- DLB-17

Woodward, Stanley 1895-1965 . . . . . DLB-171

Wooler, Thomas
1785 or 1786-1853 . . . . DLB-158

Woolf, David (see Maddow, Ben)

Woolf, Leonard 1880-1969 . . . . DLB-100; DS-10

Woolf, Virginia
1882-1941 . . . . . DLB-36, 100, 162; DS-10

Woolf, Virginia, "The New Biography," *New York
Herald Tribune,* 30 October 1927
. . . . DLB-149

Woollcott, Alexander 1887-1943 . . . . . DLB-29

Woolman, John 1720-1772 . . . . DLB-31

Woolner, Thomas 1825-1892 . . . . . . DLB-35

Woolsey, Sarah Chauncy
1835-1905 . . . . DLB-42

Woolson, Constance Fenimore
1840-1894 . . . . DLB-12, 74

Worcester, Joseph Emerson
1784-1865 . . . . DLB-1

Worde, Wynkyn de
[publishing house] DLB-170

Wordsworth, Christopher
1807-1885 . . . . DLB-166

Wordsworth, Dorothy
1771-1855 . . . . DLB-107

Wordsworth, Elizabeth
1840-1932 . . . . DLB-98

Wordsworth, William
1770-1850 . . . . DLB-93, 107

The Works of the Rev. John Witherspoon
(1800-1801) [excerpts] DLB-31

A World Chronology of Important Science
Fiction Works (1818-1979) DLB-8

World Publishing Company DLB-46

World War II Writers Symposium at the
University of South Carolina,
12–14 April 1995 . . . . Y-95

Worthington, R., and Company DLB-49

Wotton, Sir Henry 1568-1639 . . . . . DLB-121

Wouk, Herman 1915- Y-82

Wreford, James 1915- DLB-88

Wren, Percival Christopher
1885-1941 . . . . DLB-153

Wrenn, John Henry 1841-1911 . . . . . DLB-140

Cumulative Index

Wright, C. D. 1949- DLB-120

Wright, Charles 1935- DLB-165; Y-82

Wright, Charles Stevenson 1932- DLB-33

Wright, Frances 1795-1852 . . . . DLB-73

Wright, Harold Bell 1872-1944 . . . . . DLB-9

Wright, James 1927-1980 . . . . DLB-5, 169

Wright, Jay 1935- DLB-41

Wright, Louis B. 1899-1984 . . . . . . DLB-17

Wright, Richard
  1908-1960 . . . . DLB-76, 102; DS-2

Wright, Richard B. 1937- DLB-53

Wright, Sarah Elizabeth 1928- DLB-33

Wright, Willard Huntington ("S. S. Van Dine")
  1888-1939 . . . . DS-16

Writers and Politics: 1871-1918,
  by Ronald Gray DLB-66

Writers and their Copyright Holders:
  the WATCH Project Y-94

Writers' Forum Y-85

Writing for the Theatre, by
  Harold Pinter DLB-13

Wroth, Lady Mary 1587-1653 . . . . DLB-121

Wurlitzer, Rudolph 1937- DLB-173

Wyatt, Sir Thomas
  circa 1503-1542 . . . . DLB-132

Wycherley, William 1641-1715 . . . . . DLB-80

Wyclif, John
  circa 1335-31 December 1384 . . . DLB-146

Wyeth, N. C. 1882-1945 . . . . DS-16

Wylie, Elinor 1885-1928 . . . . DLB-9, 45

Wylie, Philip 1902-1971 . . . . DLB-9

Wyllie, John Cook
  1908-1968 . . . . DLB-140

X

Xenophon circa 430 B.C.-circa 356 B.C.
  . . . . DLB-176

Y

Yasuoka, Shōtarō 1920- DLB-182

Yates, Dornford 1885-1960 . . . . DLB-77, 153

Yates, J. Michael 1938- DLB-60

Yates, Richard
  1926-1992 . . . . DLB-2; Y-81, 92

Yavorov, Peyo 1878-1914 . . . . DLB-147

Yearsley, Ann 1753-1806 . . . . DLB-109

Yeats, William Butler
  1865-1939 . . . . DLB-10, 19, 98, 156

Yep, Laurence 1948- DLB-52

Yerby, Frank 1916-1991 . . . . DLB-76

Yezierska, Anzia 1885-1970 . . . . . . DLB-28

Yolen, Jane 1939- DLB-52

Yonge, Charlotte Mary
  1823-1901 . . . . DLB-18, 163

The York Cycle
  circa 1376-circa 1569 . . . . DLB-146

A Yorkshire Tragedy DLB-58

Yoseloff, Thomas
  [publishing house] DLB-46

Young, Al 1939- DLB-33

Young, Arthur
  1741-1820 . . . . DLB-158

Young, Dick
  1917 or 1918 - 1987 . . . . DLB-171

Young, Edward 1683-1765 . . . . DLB-95

Young, Stark
  1881-1963 . . . . DLB-9, 102; DS-16

Young, Waldeman
  1880-1938 . . . . DLB-26

Young, William [publishing house] DLB-49

Young Bear, Ray A.
  1950- DLB-175

Yourcenar, Marguerite
  1903-1987 . . . . DLB-72; Y-88

"You've Never Had It So Good," Gusted by
  "Winds of Change": British Fiction in the
  1950s, 1960s, and After DLB-14

Yovkov, Yordan
  1880-1937 . . . . DLB-147

Z

Zachariä, Friedrich Wilhelm
  1726-1777 . . . . DLB-97

Zajc, Dane 1929- DLB-181

Zamora, Bernice 1938- DLB-82

Zand, Herbert 1923-1970 . . . . DLB-85

Zangwill, Israel 1864-1926 . . . . . DLB-10, 135

Zanzotto, Andrea 1921- DLB-128

Zapata Olivella, Manuel 1920- DLB-113

Zebra Books DLB-46

Zebrowski, George 1945- DLB-8

Zech, Paul 1881-1946 . . . . DLB-56

Zepheria DLB-172

Zeidner, Lisa 1955- DLB-120

Zelazny, Roger 1937-1995 . . . . DLB-8

Zenger, John Peter 1697-1746 . . . . DLB-24, 43

Zesen, Philipp von 1619-1689 . . . . . DLB-164

Zieber, G. B., and Company DLB-49

Zieroth, Dale 1946- DLB-60

Zigler und Kliphausen, Heinrich Anshelm von
  1663-1697 . . . . DLB-168

Zimmer, Paul 1934- DLB-5

Zingref, Julius Wilhelm
  1591-1635 . . . . DLB-164

Zindel, Paul 1936- DLB-7, 52

Zinzendorf, Nikolaus Ludwig von
  1700-1760 . . . . DLB-168

Zitkala-Ša 1876-1938 . . . . DLB-175

Zola, Emile 1840-1902 . . . . DLB-123

Zolotow, Charlotte 1915- DLB-52

Zschokke, Heinrich 1771-1848 . . . . . DLB-94

Zubly, John Joachim 1724-1781 . . . . DLB-31

Zu-Bolton II, Ahmos 1936- DLB-41

Zuckmayer, Carl 1896-1977 . . . . DLB-56, 124

Zukofsky, Louis 1904-1978 . . . . . DLB-5, 165

Zupan, Vitomil 1914-1987 . . . . DLB-181

Župančič, Oton 1878-1949 . . . . . . DLB-147

zur Mühlen, Hermynia 1883-1951 . . . . DLB-56

Zweig, Arnold 1887-1968 . . . . DLB-66

Zweig, Stefan 1881-1942 . . . . . . DLB-81, 118

ISBN 0-7876-1931-0